The Seduction of Pessimism in the Novel

The Seduction of Pessimism in the Novel

Eros, Failure, and the Quarrel with Philosophy

Tom Ribitzky

LEXINGTON BOOKS
Lanham • Boulder • New York • London

Published by Lexington Books
An imprint of The Rowman & Littlefield Publishing Group, Inc.
4501 Forbes Boulevard, Suite 200, Lanham, Maryland 20706
www.rowman.com

86-90 Paul Street, London EC2A 4NE

Copyright © 2024 by The Rowman & Littlefield Publishing Group, Inc.

"Cosmic Pessimism in Lady Chatterley's Lover: D.H. Lawrence's Tristan Legend for the Twentieth Century" was previously published as Tom Ribitzky, "Cosmic Pessimism in Lady Chatterley's Lover: D.H. Lawrence's Tristan Legend for the Twentieth Century," *The D.H. Lawrence Review* 41.1-2 (2017): 72–100. It is reproduced here with permission of *The D.H. Lawrence Review*.

All rights reserved. No part of this book may be reproduced in any form or by any electronic or mechanical means, including information storage and retrieval systems, without written permission from the publisher, except by a reviewer who may quote passages in a review.

British Library Cataloguing in Publication Information Available

Library of Congress Cataloging-in-Publication Data

Names: Ribitzky, Tom, 1985- author.
Title: The seduction of pessimism in the novel : Eros, failure, and the quarrel with philosophy / Tom Ribitzky.
Description: Lanham : Lexington Books, 2024. | Includes bibliographical references and index.
Identifiers: LCCN 2024026094 (print) | LCCN 2024026095 (ebook) |
  ISBN 9781666901399 (cloth) | ISBN 9781666901405 (epub)
Subjects: LCSH: Pessimism in literature. | Fiction—History and criticism—Theory, etc. | Literature—Philosophy. | LCGFT: Literary criticism.
Classification: LCC PN56.P4 R53 2024 (print) | LCC PN56.P4 (ebook) |
  DDC 809.3/9353—dc23/eng/20240725
LC record available at https://lccn.loc.gov/2024026094
LC ebook record available at https://lccn.loc.gov/2024026095

∞™ The paper used in this publication meets the minimum requirements of American National Standard for Information Sciences—Permanence of Paper for Printed Library Materials, ANSI/NISO Z39.48-1992.

Contents

Acknowledgments		vii
1	The Genre of Failure	1
2	Kicking and Screaming: Pessimism Between Etiology, Etymology, and Entomology	21
3	Albertine's Absence	59
4	Failed Consolations in Plato's Shadow: Boethius, Medieval Romance, and Goethe	99
5	From a Failed Theory of the Novel to a Novel of Failed Theories: Mann's Response to Boccaccio, Schlegel, and Lukács	123
6	The Criminality and Illegitimacy of the Novel	147
7	Landscapes, Laughter, and Suicide	187
8	Constellations and Consternations	213
9	"A Globed Compacted Thing": Woolf's Cosmogony of Love and the Paradox of Failure in *To the Lighthouse*	243
10	Cosmic Pessimism in *Lady Chatterley's Lover*: D. H. Lawrence's Tristan Legend for the Twentieth Century	273
11	"A Last Mirage of Wonder and Hopelessness": Andersen's "The Little Mermaid" as a Shadow Text of Nabokov's *Lolita*	301
12	Kierkegaard's Kiss: A Contribution to a Theory of the Novel	329

13	In Search of Lost Being: Heidegger's Novelistic Quest	365
14	Seduction Against Production: The Novel as a Tool of Pedagogy in a World Doomed to Neoliberal Optimism	407

Concluding Unscientific Postscript   445

Bibliography   455

Index   479

About the Author   509

Acknowledgments

The secret of every pessimist is that we are all closet sentimentalists (why else are we so disappointed in the world if not for the fact that it fails to live up to a romanticized ideal of what it could be?). The honest ones among us acknowledge our penchant for schmaltz. Within acknowledgment is knowledge itself, and this book is the product of the knowledge—and so much more than knowledge—that I have received from a number of influential people in my life who deserve more praise than can be afforded here.

I would like to dedicate this book to my parents, Ron and Dafna Ribitzky, who were even younger than I am now when they immigrated to a new country, struggling with a new language, and in this new language would read me bedtime stories from Hans Christian Andersen's fairy tales, Charles and Mary Lamb's *Tales from Shakespeare,* and the short stories of Guy de Maupassant, O. Henry, and Oscar Wilde. Even when none of us knew certain words, stumbling our way through comprehension, you carved out the first and perhaps only world that feels familiar to me, a world you would later populate with other stories and books that have shaped and continue to shape who I am. I remember how fiercely my dad defended me against my first-grade teacher, who told me in such anger that I would never be able to learn English. Even as you were also trying to navigate your way through this new language, you encouraged me to think of language itself as something to play with, to have fun with, to explore with joy and humor.

Despite the struggles with language, literature always represented a safe retreat from a world that never made much sense to me. And as I grew up, my mom made sure to nurture this space, populating it with the warm company of Balzac, the Brontës, Jack London, Thomas Mann, and Stefan Zweig, among countless other writers whom I would frequently return to over the years. In the second year of the pandemic, you helped me get through the darkness by revisiting *Ulysses* in honor of what was to be the novel's upcoming centenary, and our weekly discussions about it after listening to each podcast episode of Shakespeare & Company's Bloomcast together breathed new life into me. You taught me that art isn't just central to education, but to life itself. No doctoral education could come close to the education you've been giving me my whole life.

I also wouldn't have been able to write this without my grandparents, Mirjana and Sasha Gross. My introduction to Kafka—before I even knew it was him—was in my grandmother's kitchen when she would tell his stories to me and my brother with a kind of joyful humor and levity. My grandfather also couldn't speak about Nietzsche without laughing. This is how I wish all literature could be encountered. My grandparents lived in a small cottage that they had converted from a shed. Stepping inside felt like entering a fairy-tale world. My memory of their living room, like walking into a past century, feels like a scene from *Fanny and Alexander*, and it always begins with the bookcase to the left of the entrance, an entire shelf lined with several volumes of Shakespeare translated into German by Schlegel. After having lost everything in the Second World War, these few possessions represented for them not only the start of their new lives but also an unbroken connection to the centuries of culture and the highest achievement of human civilization—an achievement that could not be vanquished by the horrors of totalitarianism and its attendant anti-intellectualism.

My sister Romy uncluttered my mind and helped me along the path of this book over the course of our long phone conversations about pessimism and optimism. You were the one to teach me, from an early age, that precision in language is important and beautiful, and is a source of strength and dignity. Thank you for sneaking me into the cinema to see Baz Luhrmann's *Romeo + Juliet* in 1996 when I wasn't allowed to see it.

My sister Laura is my favorite poet, my kin-dread pessimist, my beloved twin. You taught me how to read my first book (*The Prince's Tooth is Loose*), and you've been continuing to teach me ever since. You've let me read entire swathes of this book over the phone to you, and you make me a better thinker, writer, and human.

My brother Roy will never stop giving me grief over the fact that I spent so much time in grad school and my professional career thinking about literally Nothing. And Carolyn patiently listened to my agonizing updates every Friday for years about working on this book.

My aunt Tifrah Warner gave me invaluable guidance, wisdom, and love—not just through this process, but through so much more.

John Brenkman guided me from the earliest stages of this project, giving me crucial insight and advice, along with the space and freedom to explore and develop my own academic voice, to experiment with ideas that I would later discard or reshape into something altogether different. You were patient and generous enough to walk me through the process.

Giancarlo Lombardi has helped me from my first presentation in graduate school as an MA student all the way through my dissertation defense. I am grateful to him for accepting me into the PhD program in Comparative Literature at The Graduate Center (CUNY), and I am grateful to André Aciman for accepting me to the MA program in the first place.

I am also immensely grateful to Richard Kaye, who published the chapter entitled "Cosmic Pessimism in *Lady Chatterley's Lover*: D.H. Lawrence's Tristan Legend for the Twentieth Century" as an article in *The D.H. Lawrence Review* (41.2). I gained valuable feedback from colleagues when I presented early drafts of this chapter at the American Comparative Literature Association conference and the Harvard Institute for World Literature. My research on this chapter started under the guidance of the late Paul Oppenheimer, who, like my grandparents and many from their generation, believed in art and literature as a bulwark against totalitarianism.

I presented my research on Heidegger at the Northeast Modern Language Association conference. It germinated from a term paper I wrote for Simon Critchley, who graciously allowed me to enroll in his courses at The New School for Social Research, and who allowed me to audit a course on mysticism that he co-taught with Eugene Thacker, who, in turn, allowed me to sit in on his pessimism seminar. My understanding of Heidegger, pessimism, mysticism, and tragedy belongs to both of you.

Charles Snyder deepened my understanding of tragedy, of philosophy, and of their correspondences.

I was incredibly lucky to have taken Diana Toman's German translation class early in graduate school. You brought your encyclopedic knowledge to bear on how Mann, Kafka, Schopenhauer, and Nietzsche orchestrated their artistry through rigorous investigations into their use of grammar, diction, and syntax. These close readings of yours were, in themselves, works of art.

I was just as lucky to have Nancy Yousef guide me through the novels of George Eliot. Every seminar session was a tour de force. Thank you for your kindness, encouragement, and brilliance.

Beatrice Hanssen introduced me to Kant, Kleist, Kierkegaard, Benjamin, and Adorno in my freshman year of college. Each extemporaneous lecture of yours was a masterpiece of illumination and precision, by now a nearly lost art form that had always struck me as being a relic from a centuries-old European style of formal teaching, and I would hang on to your every word breathlessly. You deepened my love for Thomas Mann, and you also somehow generously tolerated my juvenile discussions of how German techno music was similar in its structure to *The Arcades Project*.

Jed Rasula's undergraduate lectures on modernism have also stuck with me to this day, and Andrew Cole was deeply inspiring in his magical ability to make a seminar on Hegel the highlight of each week.

I wouldn't be able to do this without the help and generosity of several university administrators and staff who worked so hard to ensure that my material conditions could allow me to do this work. I am immensely grateful to Anne Ellis, Carol Pierce, Jane Tartaro, Matt Schoengood, Junior Borrero, Miguel Perdomo, and everyone who has been there for me over the years.

I am also especially grateful to the helpful librarians at The New York Public Library, The Boston Public Library, and Widener Library.

While discussing Nabokov with Anick Rolland, she suggested that I go back to Kierkegaard (and Feuerbach) just to see if there's anything there for this book, leading me to discover some of the necessary links that I needed to make in this project. Our weekly lunches talking about pessimism, tragedy, and other delights gave me the motivation and clarity of mind to keep writing. Thank you also for making me get around to finally reading *Tess of the D'Urbervilles*, which has clearly left an impression.

Liza Shapiro was literally by my side each Thursday for several months as we both worked on our own research, taking necessary breaks to share pastries and even entire loaves of bread to get through the writing process.

I owe my love for Proust to Katherine Shloznikova, who inspired me to go back and read him again at a time in my life when I was finally ready to fall in love with him. We had a conversation in passing over a decade ago about the connections between Proust, Plato, and Freud, which gave me the inspiration for my analysis in this book.

While I was overwhelmed reading through the entire *Recherche*, Yulia Greyman swooped in to the rescue and helped me wade through the intimidating expanse of Proust scholarship out there. By sending me Martha Nussbaum's article "Fictions of the Soul," you gave me the structure that I needed for this book.

David Bradshaw gave me my love for Virginia Woolf when I was a rudderless student in college, majoring in Pre-Med and International Affairs, neither of which were the right fit for me. Ahead of me was a life like Charles Bovary's, in a field I didn't understand and had no talent in, when I signed up for my first English class as a junior while studying abroad. Professor Bradshaw is the reason why I can write a single word about Woolf. There is a Woolfian mingling of grief and a subdued joy at the memory of spending an hour a week in his medieval office at Worcester College in Oxford University, where I would read my papers out loud to him, and he wouldn't let a stray word pass his forensic scrutiny. I wish I could show this to you now, and listen to what you have to say one last time.

In writing this book, I've been spending a lot of time thinking about the devastating consequences of the World Wars—of Georg Lukács's pessimism, of Virginia Woolf's grief, of D. H. Lawrence's despair, of Erich Auerbach's and Vladimir Nabokov's exile, of Walter Benjamin's melancholia, of Martin Heidegger's abhorrent politics—and of the few stories that have passed down to me from my own family, especially in light of the rise of violent, anti-democratic, and mob-driven movements in this country right now. My grandmother's uncle, Armie von Meixner, wanted to carry on the family's tradition of artistry, having descended from the composer Johann Nepomuk Hummel—the disciple of Mozart, Haydn, and Salieri, as well as a friend of Beethoven, whom he had protected by championing copyright laws for artists after seeing how Mozart was left penniless in the wake of an illustrious career. Armie wanted to be an artist instead of a soldier when World War I broke out, a war he vehemently denounced. He was conscripted to the Eastern Front, where he died from a stomach wound. His brother Egon, who later spoke out against the Nazis in Vienna, was subsequently arrested, tortured, and put into an insane asylum for his subversive politics, where he was killed.

Their mother Juliana had kept a diary in verse documenting these horrors, as though the rigid verse form could provide some structure in the midst of chaos. The only other books we have of hers are a biography of Hummel and an illustrated copy of Andersen's fairy tales in German, passed down through the generations. Juliana's daughter Edith, the younger sister of Armie and Egon, went to art school in Paris, where she met Picasso, Miró, and Matisse, and then married Antonije Georgijević, a Yugoslav lawyer and economist, who also spoke out against both fascism and communism in his country and was later imprisoned and murdered for his opposition. Edith, having come from Austrian nobility, was left an impoverished widow with two young daughters in Communist Yugoslavia, one of them my grandmother, Mirjana Gross. After surviving both wars, Edith worked as a translator of German, French, and English in a quiet effort to piece the fragments of European culture back together. And even as her eyesight rapidly failed her, she painted until she could see no longer, and in her paintings, like Lily Briscoe in *To the Lighthouse*, she had had her vision.

Chapter 1

The Genre of Failure

"I HEREBY RETRACT THIS BOOK"

All academic scholarship falls under the genre of the defense, that intersection between argument and counter-argument, which is why this is the term that is used to formalize the ritual that scholars must go through before attaining their doctoral degrees—a ritual that, if they are lucky enough to join the coveted and increasingly rare ranks of tenured and tenure-track faculty, they will get to repeat over and over again in some form, satisfying either their intellectual curiosity or their masochism, or both.

But how does one *defend* pessimism? In pessimism—what Eugene Thacker calls "the most indefensible of philosophies"—I would imagine, one can only hope to *offend*, if one can even hope at all.[1] But maybe pessimism is not quite so aspirational. Maybe, instead of seeking to offend, it would just rather *fend off*. It preempts and fends off criticism by hurling incendiary claims that may not even be substantiated, that may not necessarily rise to the level of an argument to be argued against, because what's the point? Swatting away gadflies, all those Socrateses who are always so eager for a debate, pessimism instead disengages, withdraws, retreats into a hermetic space fueled by its own curmudgeonly disappointment—in the world, in itself. It fends off; it would prefer not to. "I know you . . . and I want nothing to say to you," the voice of pessimism addresses its would-be interlocutor the way Bartleby addresses—and dismisses—the narrator of his own story at the end, when he is locked away in The Tombs.[2] And instead of engaging, he just persists in staring out into the void, into the abyss, swallowed by silence.

Where the scholarly work aims at animating and enlivening a rich academic discussion, pessimism understands its destination to be the Office of Dead Letters. The scholarly work seeks to explain, but pessimism would much rather complain. The scholarly work makes a gesture toward the exhaustive, but pessimism wallows in the exhausting. The scholarly work aims at a logical, systematic treatment of a well-researched subject, but pessimism sneers at such systematicity, suspicious even of logic itself. "Let it be the ambition of learned doctoral candidates," Søren Kierkegaard taunts in *The Seducer's Diary*, "to avoid every contradiction."[3]

So if there is any ambition in writing a book on pessimism, not to be trolled by Kierkegaard, it would be the ambition to seek out and embrace the contradiction, the lacuna, the dead end. Its subject and its telos is failure. It is a literal *Aufgabe*—the German word for "task," but a word that can also be literally translated as an act of giving up.[4] It is a rejection of the maudlin, but unfortunately ubiquitous, interpretation of Samuel Beckett's injunction to "Fail better," often invoked—out of context—as motivational inspiration for the kinds of people who like that sort of thing. Rather than making progress and getting better *despite* a series of setbacks or failures, I read Beckett's advice more literally: to get better at failure itself. Failure is not a means, but the goal. There is an art to it that, ironically, can be perfected. Perhaps this is the only aspiration that pessimism can allow itself. There is a "point at which writing *about* pessimism must become pessimistic writing," and perhaps this is why the study of pessimism never sat comfortably in academia.[5] The academic is critical, but the pessimist is hypercritical—to the point of being hypocritical.

One of Beckett's friends happened to be E. M. Cioran, the arch-pessimist of the twentieth century, who wrote such lyrically bleak reflections in works with titles such as *A Short History of Decay*, *The Temptation to Exist*, and *The Trouble with Being Born* at a time when postwar optimism was at an all-time high. He had enrolled in a doctoral program at the Sorbonne when he was twenty-six just to use their cafeteria, waiting for them to catch on to the fact that he had never planned on writing, let alone finishing, an actual dissertation (they finally deactivated his student ID when he was forty). He hated university as much as he hated church, but would make his rounds to the Romanian Orthodox Church for their free dinners as well, never missing a chance to insult anyone who had the stupidity to actually believe in God while he was there.[6] His practice of biting the hand that fed him turned that cliché into an art—perhaps this is the emblem of the spite at the core of pessimism itself, and maybe it's not even nearly as obnoxious as the smarmy, disingenuous rhetoric of gratitude peddled by optimists.

Over a century earlier, Arthur Schopenhauer—who labeled optimism "not only a false but also a pernicious doctrine"—took an especially gleeful tone when he wrote, "Your University professors are bound to preach optimism; and it is an easy and agreeable task to upset their theories."[7] Not the soundest advice, and maybe not even the most accurate of characterizations, but

Schopenhauer lived by his word. He applied to teach at the University of Berlin so he could insult Hegel, that "clumsy charlatan," to his face.[8] The fifty-year-old Hegel, who was not only the most famous philosopher in Europe by that time, but also happened to be on Schopenhauer's search committee as Chair of the Philosophy Department, was so unfazed that he couldn't even be bothered to pay much attention to this ranting thirty-two-year-old pessimist. He hired him, and Schopenhauer made sure to schedule his classes at the same time as Hegel's, knowing full well that hardly anyone, if at all, would sign up for his own classes when they could attend the lectures of the celebrity thinker.[9] Schopenhauer's furious rampage failed to get a response in kind. Instead of the legendary showdown he had hoped for, he got a job offer instead, and Hegel neither avoided nor paid much notice to him, ultimately demonstrating the futility, the utter inconsequentiality, of pessimism at work.

Obviously, not everyone gets rewarded for such chutzpah with a professorship. Ludwig Feuerbach, one student of Hegel's who did show up to most of his lectures—all of them in a two-year period except for the lectures on aesthetics, even though he sat through the lectures on logic twice—couldn't find a senior teaching post after the publication of his first book, *Thoughts on Death and Immortality*.[10] On top of this, he also wrote a letter explaining where Hegel had gone wrong and sent it to Hegel himself. (No one is claiming that pessimists have the best tact.) Maybe Feuerbach should have attended the lectures of his fellow atheist Schopenhauer instead.

Schopenhauer's most avid reader, Friedrich Nietzsche, had already been the Chair of the Philology Department at The University of Basel for three years when, at twenty-eight years old, he published his first book, *The Birth of Tragedy*—the subtitle of which is *Hellenism and Pessimism*. But the embarrassment he later felt for it must have been the equivalent of an adult coming across their own teenage diary—an extended love letter to Wagner's art, and now it was available for the world to see. He wanted to distance himself from his own work, but he indulged in a far greater frenetic energy when it came to his self-excoriation. It wasn't enough for him to write, in a later edition, an "Attempt at a Self-Criticism" to dilute the fawning preface that he had written in 1871. He had to follow it up with *The Case of Wagner*, in which he dismissed the composer as a disease, as a neurosis—"*une névrose*," using a Gallicism for this German who despised the French.[11] *The Case of Wagner* is hardly long enough to be called a book, and yet it is composed of a Preface, a Postscript, a Second Postscript, and then an Epilogue, as if to say, I am not done insulting you, I will never be done, and I can't believe I wrote that awful, cringeworthy thing back when I was trying to make a career for myself in academia.

Kierkegaard, decades earlier, also fled from academia, having described his own dissertation as a "pursuit that does not interest me in the least."[12] His public dissertation defense lasted seven and a half hours, and it marked his debut into official academic life as well as his decisive departure from it.[13] He passed the defense just barely, and not without some censure over his "self-indulgent" style and "simple tastelessness," as one of his committee members put it.[14] Kierkegaard quickly turned back to his own pursuits and churned out the more creative *Seducer's Diary* four months later, including it in *Either/Or*, to be published a year after that. He drafted a postscript to *Either/Or* that read, "I hereby retract this book.... Yet I do not need to retract it, for I have never claimed to be its author."[15] He never published that postscript, but Kierkegaard's impulse to retract his writing can be traced to his first publication, a lengthy book review of Hans Christian Andersen. The review begins with, "*Postscript* for the readers who possibly could be harmed by reading the preface: they could skip over it, and if they skipped far enough so that they skipped over the essay as well, it is of no consequence."[16] Maybe this is the exhortation of all pessimistic writers: skip the introduction, skip the entire work if you'd like, skip the whole thing while you're at it—it doesn't matter.

Kierkegaard and Nietzsche belong to a tradition of intellectuals who famously failed at, or retracted, their early scholarly works. To this tradition we can add Theodor Adorno, who also ended up distancing himself from his own book on Kierkegaard, a dissertation that he had used as a way of processing his own pessimism, and which happened to appear in bookstores on the same day that Hitler suspended democratic powers.[17] Mikhail Bakhtin, one of the early novel theorists, went through a much more contentious dissertation defense process than Kierkegaard, which also lasted seven hours, and even ended up with government intervention to officially deny his doctorate for his research on the novel.[18] A decade before this, he had submitted a book-length study on the eighteenth-century German novel, which had been accepted for publication before getting lost in the War. He used the only other copy for paper to roll cigarettes as the Germans invaded the Soviet Union.[19] He had abandoned other unpublished manuscripts in a rat-infested woodshed, and would only agree to publish them decades later after being persuaded by his friends during heated arguments.[20]

Walter Benjamin, too, suffered a humiliating failure in his dissertation defense, which was rejected by his committee for being too weird, too much of a collage. It was too close to the baroque style that it ostensibly failed in its study of the Baroque period. It had too many quotes, and the analysis wasn't clear—the refrain of every advisor, editor, and publisher the world over when it comes to an analysis absorbed in its own pessimism. But then, almost as a punchline to a joke, his response to being rejected for this bizarre method of scholarship was to work on the monstrously unwieldy and virtually unreadable *Arcades Project*. If *The Origin of German Tragic Drama* was a failure, then failure was an art that he would only continue to master, to perfect, and to expand in the form of something that defies form itself, that erodes any sense of structure, amounting to a rubble of details that pile on each other, like the gaze of his "angel of history" that pessimistically views the past not as "a chain of events," but as "one single catastrophe which keeps piling wreckage upon wreckage and hurls it in front of his feet."[21]

There is a sense in which pessimistic writing, in seeing this pile of wreckage climb higher, can only replicate that pile, crowding details and fragments together without unity. Its style is failure. Maybe this is the way to make sense of a work like Stendhal's *Love*, which Denis de Rougemont, in his own survey of the history of love literature in the Western tradition, calls "completely pessimistic."[22] And maybe that pessimism has more to do with the form of this strange book than its message that "love is a disease of the soul," a characterization that is hardly original, since it comes from Andreas Capellanus's medieval *Art of Courtly Love,* yet another work that its own author rejected.[23]

Stendhal pre-dates Nietzsche's neurotic maneuver of providing not just one preface, but four—if we are to include the "attempts" at a preface along with the actual prefaces—each one emphasizing how much of a failure it is. In the "First Attempt at a Preface," Stendhal acknowledges, "This book has met with no success; it has been found unintelligible, and not without cause."[24] He aspires to present an "exact and scientific description" of love and codify all of its different manifestations, an endeavor that can only ever fail spectacularly.[25] His method is obscure, his observations haphazard, anecdotal, and often derived from novels—even as he, a novelist, goes out of his way to disparage those same novels and the genre of the novel at large. He even includes footnotes to his footnotes before narrating his own doubt of the project, admitting, "I have just re-read a hundred pages of this essay. I seem to have given a remarkably poor idea of true love. . . . I am at a loss to express what I can see so clearly; I have never been so painfully aware of my lack of talent."[26] Whatever irony Stendhal is capable of, there is no false modesty here. But, committed to this failure, he goes on for another 220 pages.

For a number of reasons, then, pessimism has not found a hospitable home in academia. Not only is it overwhelming in its negativity, but it's just too messy, too bizarre, too unhinged to deal with. Whiny and even juvenile, maybe it belongs to the "self-incurred immaturity" that academia, following Kant's definition of Enlightenment, sees as its fundamental mission to emancipate itself from.[27] Even today, most successful scholars in academia who are famous for critiquing optimism and toxic positivity are careful to draw the line at pessimism. Often, for whatever reason, they turn around and give the same kind of stern treatment to pessimists, too, as if the pessimist and the optimist were two rowdy children in need of a time out.

Jack Halberstam, for instance, qualifies his groundbreaking and deeply inspiring *Queer Art of Failure*, an exciting embrace of the radical potential of failure itself, by rejecting the dichotomy of "cynical resignation on the one hand and naïve optimism on the other," generating "a new kind of optimism," not one that

> relies on positive thinking as an explanatory engine for social order, nor one that insists upon the bright side at all costs; rather this is a little ray of sunshine that produces shade and light in equal measure and knows that the meaning of one always depends upon the meaning of the other.[28]

If this theory depends "in equal measure" as much on "shade and light," why throw this equality out of balance in favor of optimism, then? What is this resistance to standing on the side of pessimism in a theory of failure, in a theory that emerges out of a rejection of optimistic, capitalistic, patriarchal, and heteronormative standards of success?

Terry Eagleton, in his book *Hope Without Optimism*, is also quick to point out that "pessimism involves much the same kind of spiritual kink" as optimism, and that both involve the same kind of knee-jerk reactions and thoughtlessness.[29] He condescends specifically to the American form of pessimism, which "is thought to be vaguely subversive," a facile and smug comment to make for someone protected by the NHS and a sizeable salary, who never had to deal with the uniquely American problem of exorbitant student loan debt, who doesn't have to worry about deciding between paying the rent or the groceries each month in a way that countless American scholars and contingent faculty have to.[30]

In her book *Bright-Sided: How Positive Thinking Is Undermining America*, Barbara Ehrenreich noted how former president George W. Bush used the word "optimistic" more than any other adjective, and, according to Bob Woodward, Condoleezza Rice "failed to express some of her worries because, she said, 'the president almost demanded optimism. He didn't like pessimism, hand-wringing, or doubt.'"[31] To Eagleton,

> the "faith-based" rather than "reality-based" politics of the George W. Bush White House pressed a familiar American attitude to the point of lunacy. Reality is a pessimist to whose treasonable talk one must shut one's ears. . . . It is a vein of optimism not easy to distinguish from mental illness. Cheerfulness of this kind is a form of psychological disavowal. For all its square-jawed vigor, it is really a moral evasion.[32]

9/11 and the dot-com bust under Bush's tenure "was later attributed to a 'failure of imagination.' But actually there was plenty of imagination at work—imagining an invulnerable nation and an ever-booming economy—there was simply no ability or inclination to imagine the worst."[33]

The next Republican President is often singled out as an aberration in conservative politics, when in fact he represents the fulfillment of this optimistic legacy. His unshakable confidence in himself went several steps beyond Bush in dismissing any kind of criticism as "fake news," and in issuing dog whistles to crush opposition, by violence if necessary. In response to the increasing anxiety around the climate crisis, for example, Trump said, "This is not a time for pessimism. Fear and doubt is not a good thought process."[34] Perhaps more devastatingly, the *Politico* reporter Dan Diamond told Terry Gross that COVID had grown out of control in the early days in this country in part because Trump had

> created an environment where his aides have been afraid to tell him bad news, and that has skewed what the Trump administration ends up pursuing. If the president is only willing to look at the most optimistic scenario, it makes it very hard to do worst-case planning.[35]

There is no greater ringing endorsement for pessimism than the fact that Trump is such a devout optimist. And perhaps there is no greater cause for pessimism than the fact that, even as a convicted criminal, this wannabe tyrant is still the Republican Party's choice for another presidential term, even after he disbanded a government pandemic task force two years in advance of the crisis and separated families at the border. But the strain of optimism that he espouses is by no means limited to him. It is a "familiar American attitude" that was "pressed to the point of lunacy" under Bush, but that has always been dominant in American culture.

The continuation of this legacy under Democratic leadership doesn't give much confidence that things will get better any time soon. In the middle of a pandemic that Biden insisted was over—all the while taking every precaution for himself, while the rest of us have to fend for ourselves—he refused to support Medicare for All. It is difficult to be optimistic about a president whose history in public office has a consistent conservative trajectory, from fighting against school desegregation alongside the openly racist Strom Thurmond, whom he referred to not just as a colleague, but as a "friend," to aggressively orchestrating the 1994 crime bill that increased mass incarceration and fueled the police brutality crisis, as well as the 2005 legislation that made it nearly impossible to discharge student loans in bankruptcy.[36] When capital is the guiding principle of governance, it is no surprise that Democrats and Republicans perform their theatrical narcissism of small differences. It's not even worth cursing them with a plague on both their houses, because they have the safety measures to protect themselves against this plague while denying that accessibility to the rest of us.

And yet, somehow, a pessimistic outlook is dismissed with more of a derisive and condescending response than holding on to any kind of optimism. Ehrenreich is also quick to characterize pessimism as a "romantic attachment to suffering as a source of insight or virtue," making it clear that her book was not written "in a spirit of sourness or personal disappointment of any kind," as if that would somehow be inexcusable or something worth apologizing for.[37] Maybe this age does call for sourness and personal disappointment because the effects of toxic positivity and optimism—life-threatening that they are— are indeed personal.

Eagleton, for his part, goes out of his way to avoiding pessimism at all costs that he engages in a kind of bizarre nominalist maneuvering through terms, such as distinguishing between Leibnizian "optimalism" and "optimism" so that he can make apologies for optimism: "Optimism is not as optimistic as optimalism. For the optimalist, we already enjoy the best of all possible cosmic arrangements; the optimist, by contrast, may acknowledge the shortcomings of the present while looking to a more lustrous future."[38] Okay, I guess. But when Voltaire attacked Leibniz in *Candide*, his subtitle was "*L'optimisme*," not "*L'optimalisme*." Eagleton does a similar maneuver again, more crucially, in his discussion of Walter Benjamin, who "built his revolutionary vision on a distrust of historical progress, as well as on a profound melancholia. Benjamin himself calls this outlook 'pessimism,' but one might equally see it as realism, that most difficult of moral conditions to attain."[39]

This kind of rhetorical dodging and projection is a tired trope, as if somehow pessimists are incapable of discerning reality, and if they do manage to discern and articulate it, then they aren't actually pessimists to begin with, but "realists." Ehrenreich also calls for "realism" instead of "defensive pessimism," which seems to be a defensive move in itself.[40] Eagleton himself displays a knee-jerk and rather patronizing reaction to edit Benjamin, as if Benjamin didn't quite choose his own words properly, because surely he couldn't have meant "pessimism," right? But what if pessimism *is* realism? The word "realism" itself, as the history of the novel shows, is so fraught and problematic as to be thoroughly unhelpful. Anyone will invoke it to defend their ideology.

Maybe we ought to take Benjamin at his word and trust that he is in control of his own language when he writes about his philosophy as a pessimistic one. Benjamin writes of a need for "pessimism all along the line. Absolutely. Mistrust of the fate of literature, mistrust of the fate of freedom, mistrust of the fate of European humanity, but three times mistrust of all reconciliation between classes, between nations, between individuals."[41] Why is this somehow not pessimism, and why does Eagleton feel the need to water it down as "realism," and then later as "skepticism"?[42] This is pessimism through and through, even—and especially—as it works "in the service of human welfare. It is an attempt to remain coldly unmystified for the sake of constructive action."[43] Does pessimism stop being pessimism when it works in the "service of human welfare"?

Not at all, Georg Lukács would argue. It was precisely an "ethically-tinged pessimism" that he had set out to explore and codify in a work that he drafted in the summer of 1914, as World War I broke out. Amid widespread patriotism and jubilation of all the European countries involved, with the optimistic hope that the War would be over by Christmas of that year, Lukács was an early dissenter. He was also one of the earliest champions of Kierkegaard and channeled his contrarian politics and Kierkegaardian outlook to write what turned out to be the first systematic theory of the novel ever written.[44] His title, *The Theory of the Novel: A Historico-Philosophical Essay on the Forms of Great Epic Literature*, is significant because the genre of the novel had largely been ignored by philosophy up to that point. To Lukács, an investigation into the novel was the most insightful and necessary way to process his "mood of permanent despair over the state of the world," since it is a genre that, since the publication of *Don Quixote*, arises out of—and most accurately reflects—the modern world, a world "beyond hope."[45] He identifies the "artistic task" of the novelist as "revealing the point at which such a character's *being-there* and *being-thus* coincides with his inevitable failure."[46]

But that same sense of failure to Lukács ended up overwhelming not just the genre of the novel but his own analysis of it. Reflecting on this work nearly half a century after its publication, Lukács, like Kierkegaard retracting his own work, rejected it as an "attempt which failed both in design and in execution."[47] The systematicity fell apart, particularly in his "'Kierkegaardisation' of the Hegelian dialectic of history" in order to make sense of the catastrophe of modernity.[48]

What is it that made Kierkegaard and Lukács, Nietzsche and Adorno, Capellanus and Stendhal reject their own work? What is it that makes any author reject their own work? Why would Chaucer lead us through the unfinished *Canterbury Tales*, in all its raucous, bawdy humor, only to abruptly end the manuscript after the dull, humorless "Parson's Tale" with a note that he recants everything he had written there? Why did Fakhraddin Gorgani do the same thing at the end of *Vis and Ramin*, the precursor to the European Tristan legend? Or, more famously, Kafka on his deathbed, insisting that Max Brod burn his remaining manuscripts, which would have deprived the twentieth century of some of its most pivotal articulations of the modern experience? Why did Nabokov, on at least two occasions that are known to us, take the only manuscript of *Lolita* that he had and start feeding its pages to the garden incinerator before his wife Véra grabbed the charred remains with her bare hands and stomped on them to put out the flames?[49] Are these just theatrical and ironic performances of self-rejection rather than rejection itself?

This gesture of self-rejection and self-contradiction—to take up Kierkegaard's challenge of facing the contradiction head-on—can be traced back, ironically, to the foundation of Western academia itself: to Socrates, especially in Plato's *Phaedrus*. Socrates is at his most self-contradictory here. This is the only time we see him outside of the city walls of Athens: "landscapes and trees have nothing to teach me—only the people in the city can do that."[50] He is both outside and out of his element, literally in a state of ecstasy, but he still finds a comfortable place to philosophize under the shade of a "tall and very broad" plane tree—in Greek, a *platonos*.[51] Framed and enveloped by this *platonos*, by Plato himself, he reluctantly gives a speech, even though he is more comfortable with the short interrogatory dialogue, the elenchus. But Socrates reads his audience well: Phaedrus is someone who likes speeches, so Socrates gives him what he wants. He delivers a speech about the evils of eros, about how it makes you go mad and do things you otherwise would not do.

He hardly even makes his way to the end of the speech when an astonishing thing happens, which is rare for Socrates: he steps back, admits his mistake, takes back everything he had previously said, and begins again—this time more eloquently, more lyrically, praising eros to the heavens, where our souls once had wings, and these wings allowed us to stare down cosmic distances so that we could see the spectacle of Truth and Beauty (all we know on earth—to Keats, at least—and apparently all we need to know). This spectacle was populated by the ideal Forms from which we derive all our understanding of the universe and our connection to it. It is only when we lose our wings that we fall down to earth, forgetting our cosmic past, but glimpses of beauty down here stimulate our memory, and we recollect that vision again through love.

Socrates's conclusion is that eros is divine; to speak ill of the deity or of the deity's effects on us would be sacrilege. It is precisely this charge of sacrilege, along with corrupting the youth of Athens (which may or may not apply to what he is doing here with Phaedrus), that would ultimately lead to his fatal sentencing. Alexander Nehamas, for one, implicitly refutes this charge because he doesn't interpret this dialogue as a case of Socrates as the older lover seducing Phaedrus as the younger beloved, but rather as a situation in which Socrates is essentially providing Phaedrus with a manual on how to be an older lover in pursuit of the beloved.[52] This is the original seducer's diary, and it is no coincidence that Kierkegaard chose Socrates as the focal point for his dissertation on irony as he was also working on his own *Seducer's Diary*.

Socrates, the champion of reason, abandons the formal strategies of deduction and induction from his other dialogues and resorts to *seduction* as his ultimate strategy. He seduces us into philosophy. Philosophy is an understanding of who we are, where we came from, and maybe even where we're headed. So what Socrates is doing is essentially seducing us not only to ourselves but to the narrative of ourselves as we develop across time. Through philosophy, we fall in love with ourselves and our cosmic origins, just as the younger beloved, in the presence of the older lover, hardly realizes that "he is seeing himself in the lover as in a mirror," which explains his concept of "backlove."[53] Or, to use a more sinister phrase from *Lolita*, seduction is the process by which we become "safely solipsized."[54]

PLATO THE NOVELIST: PESSIMISM AND EROS

The more detailed Platonic account of the origins of eros and the nature of seduction is *Symposium*, a work that appears jovial on the surface but which Martha Nussbaum situates historically in "the midst of Athenian anxiety and pessimism," ushering in the end of the Golden Age of Greece as it falls prey to tyranny and plague.[55] The discrepancy between the joy of this gathering and the impending doom outside the walls of Agathon's house party dramatizes the irony that develops through each of the set speeches. Socrates here is also in a curious state of withdrawal, withholding his own speech about eros in order to ventriloquize Diotima's narrative account of it as a contradictory being, the love-child born from poverty and resource. Eros is the motor of irony; it pushes us outside of ourselves in order to rediscover ourselves. But this point is most memorably illustrated earlier on in the conversation by Aristophanes, the famous comedian who ironically delivers the most earnest speech in the text, a pessimistic myth about our fallen nature—about how we were once globular beings who resembled our ancestors, the sun, the moon, and the stars, and we were punished for not obeying the Olympian gods, which is why Zeus split us in half.[56]

That first generation of severed beings sought desperately to reunite with their other respective halves; some succeeded in finding each other while others resigned themselves to dying alone or uniting with halves that didn't belong to them. Eros is that weak consolation for having been torn asunder and is just as much an expression of grief as it is of fleeting joy. What makes this story pessimistic is that every succeeding generation functions as though they have another missing half to pursue, but that was only a possibility for the originally separated generation. We have inherited the trauma of this split, but are occluded from any true reconciliation. "Eventually there are no true other halves," Allan Bloom explains. "The result is that [humans] continue the quest, but it is hopeless."[57] And yet we are seduced anyways—to ourselves, or to a false image of ourselves, or maybe even just to the contrived narrative of it all, to this pessimistic myth itself.

Is it possible to read *Symposium*, a work that explores through stories how eros and civilization simultaneously clash and shape each other, as a novel? Plato's works are classified as "dialogues," for lack of a better word, even when they involve more than two speakers. It has become something of a cliché to note how similar these dialogues are to the genre of tragedy, which Socrates reviles at the end of *The Republic*. Even as Socrates fantasizes about exiling the tragic poets from his ideal republic, Plato himself inscribes Socrates into a tragedy that also relies on dialogue, in which this historical figure reaches a mythological status as a tragic hero, punished by the state as Antigone is, in pursuit of a higher, divine truth. Plato's irony winks at us from the structure of these so-called dialogues, as when *Phaedrus* ends with a myth about the dangers of writing in a text that, obviously, is written.[58] His Socrates hates drama but takes the leading role in the dramatic dialogues.

But maybe this misses the point. Plato's dialogues, even in structure, have little to do with drama except for when they disparage it. Nothing terribly dramatic or even theatrical happens here. In *Symposium*, we don't actually get the immediacy of a dialogue but a narrated account, from hearsay, of what Aristodemus had told Apollodorus. The text is not even a secondhand account but a thirdhand one—what we're getting is not what Aristodemus tells Apollodorus, but what Apollodorus tells an anonymous friend, of a party he hadn't even been to. The emphasis, then, is on fictional embellishment rather than on the kind of truth one would expect from a transcript—or a script of any kind. And in this narrated account, we just get a series of other narrated stories. And in all of these dialogues, we don't get the stately verse of tragedy but the ordinary prose of everyday speech.

Ordinariness, it turns out, is what Socrates hates most about mimesis, other than the fact that it leads us away from the truth. "Therefore, imitation, an ordinary thing," he tells Glaucon in *The Republic*, "having intercourse with what is ordinary, produces ordinary offspring."[59] And in Plato's typical irony, what he seems to be writing is a genre that looks much less like a dialogue, or a tragedy, or any work of drama, than it does the genre that thematizes ordinariness itself: the novel. Both Friedrich Schlegel and Mikhail Bakhtin suggest that Plato provides the foundation of the Western novel. Schlegel writes that, "Novels are the Socratic dialogues of our time," and Bakhtin comes close to adding: vice versa.[60] In "Epic and Novel," Bakhtin writes, "We possess a remarkable document that reflects the simultaneous birth of scientific thinking and of a new artistic-prose model for the novel. These are the Socratic dialogues."[61] By the time we get to Julia Kristeva, the connection is hardly even worth pointing out: "The resemblance between

Socratic dialogue," Kristeva writes, "and the ambivalent word of the novel is obvious."[62]

We can certainly read *The Republic* as a novel in ten chapters that ends in failure, written in ordinary prose rather than dramatic verse, its hero not a king as one would expect from tragedy, but someone more ordinary, if eccentric. Far from a king, this is a hero who never even becomes a philosopher-king, but just an old, barefoot man who rails at storytelling even as he ends with a story of his own, narrating the myth of Er in the absence of arriving at a single, stable definition of justice. *The Republic* is also a novel just as much about eros as *Phaedrus* and *Symposium* are, narrating the story of the bitter breakup between philosophy and the mimetic arts, two disciplines that used to regard each other as lovers. Socrates warns Glaucon:

> Just like the men who have once fallen in love with someone, and don't believe the love is beneficial, keep away from it even if they have to do violence to themselves; so we too—due to the inborn love of such poetry we owe to our rearing in these fine regimes—we'll be glad if it turns out that it is best and truest. But as long as it's not able to make its apology, when we listen to it, we'll chant this argument we are making to ourselves as a countercharm, taking care against falling back again into this love, which is childish and belongs to the many. We are, at all events, aware that such poetry mustn't be taken seriously as a serious thing laying hold of truth.[63]

Socrates will be "glad" if the breakup between these volatile lovers turns out to be "best and truest"—but what if it doesn't? In his fantasy of demanding an apology from the tragic poets, he is indulging in a fictional reversal of his own fate, in which he was forced to issue an apology to the state, itself a supporter of tragedy with its Theoric fund to subsidize farmers and the poor so that they could go to the theater, siding with tragedy against philosophy.

Doesn't something in Socrates secretly want these lovers to get back together? He can hardly contain his own admiration of Homer and is looking for as many excuses as possible to admit the poets back into the Republic the way any jilted lover would—with apologies and praise: "Isn't it just for it to come back in this way—when it has made an apology in lyrics or some other meter?"[64] Or how about no meter at all? Maybe it doesn't matter. The separation already happened, and the breakup was too bitter. Philosophy would move on through the centuries, and the novel would remain its long-lost and long-forgotten lover. Perhaps this is why it goes by the name of *Roman* in German and French, and *romanzo* in Italian, as a reminder of its romantic past, of its broken engagement with philosophy, even as it struggles to find its way into new territory, into something novel. By forgetting this lover, philosophy also forgets the meaning of Being. Martin Heidegger's answer to recovering the meaning of Being from its forgotten state is to analyze it in its average everydayness—which has been the same project of the novel for centuries.

Eros is at the heart of the novel; it is also at the heart of philosophy. As Georges Bataille argues, "In human consciousness eroticism is that within man which calls his being in question."[65] And Rachel Barney points out that the use of the term "compel" in leading us from the darkness to the light in the allegory of the cave, from Book Seven of *The Republic*, is an erotic force.[66] We are driven to philosophy through eros, as Plato sketches in *Phaedrus* and *Symposium*. Our ascent from the cave mirrors Diotima's "Ladder of Love."[67] In the *Apology*, Socrates famously says that all he knows is that he knows nothing.[68] But in *Symposium*, he says, "I claim to have expert knowledge in nothing but erotics."[69] Eros is precisely that nothing, the negativity at the core of philosophy, the lack that compels it to reach for what it has lost.

Because love is central to philosophy, we are constantly reminded of its lost lover, and Plato can't seem to get over the breakup, reinscribing it—and the failed hope of the lovers' reunion—in the image of eros itself, as that thing which reminds us of our separation from our original nature in *Phaedrus*, and again as the violent rift in our selves that we see in *Symposium*. Maybe his entire project is like Hephaestus approaching the two fragmented lovers in *Symposium* desperately clinging to each other, trying to weld philosophy and the novel together in his own art. Maybe this is the expression of his own failure, sublimating his impulse to become a poet. Or maybe he is articulating precisely that poetic apology his teacher never got.

Despite the inner turmoil and longing for each other, philosophy and the novel have kept up their appearances of mutual animosity. Nabokov, for example, returns the favor. "I am afraid to get mixed up with Plato, whom I do not care for," he said once in an interview, even though he couldn't help describing his own process of writing a novel as first seeing it already written, as though existing as a Platonic Ideal, "ready ideally in some other, now transparent, now dimming, dimension, and my job is to take down as much of it as I can make out and as precisely as I am humanly able to."[70] But still, the "greatest happiness" for him is not the happiness of the philosopher who strives for understanding, but "when I feel I cannot understand, or rather catch myself not understanding."[71] In another interview, his distance from Plato takes on a more derisive tone: "I would say that imagination is a form of memory. Down, Plato, down, good dog."[72]

D. H. Lawrence, however, is mournful of the breakup, saying,

> It seems to me it was the greatest pity in the world, when philosophy and fiction got split. They used to be one, right from the dark days of myth. Then they went and parted, like a nagging married couple, with Aristotle and Thomas Aquinas

and that beastly Kant. So the novel went sloppy, and philosophy went abstract-dry. The two should come together again, in the novel.[73]

The novel, then, is the site to explore both the tensions and the possibilities of reconciliation between philosophy and literature, a claim that has been contested by scholars like Erich Heller, who, in his study of Thomas Mann, warns that "there is no universally valid way of saying what the relationship is between 'philosophy' and 'literature,'" and if there were such a way,

> it is more relevant to the comprehension of poetry than to the appreciation of a work in prose. Yet in neither case can the difference be satisfactorily defined in the abstract. It can only be adumbrated in relation to definite works.[74]

And maybe this is why any foray into such an exercise can only end up as a failure. Even so, when Heller cites love as a focal point that belongs to both philosophy and literature, he cannot resist scaling out from his analysis of *Buddenbrooks* to say that, "Perhaps there are, after all, only two themes which are new in modern literature, distinguishing the nineteenth and twentieth centuries from any previous literary epochs." These two themes are "the tedium of the frustrated spirit" and a "pessimistic ecstasy of love."[75]

These two themes are hardly new, though. Boethius, in his *Consolation of Philosophy*, expresses "the tedium of the frustrated spirit." The Tristan legend popularized the "pessimistic ecstasy of love" in the Middle Ages, but this pessimistic ecstasy—in the literal sense of standing outside of one's self—goes back even further to the *Symposium* myth. In her article "Fictions of the Soul," Martha Nussbaum focuses on the role of eros in the quarrel between philosophy and literature, a quarrel that she analyzes in terms of the fundamental differences in style. To illustrate these differences, she foregrounds the novel, comparing Plato with Marcel Proust as a way of showing that

> the knowing of love [is] . . . very different from a grasping of some independent fact about the world; as something that is in part constituted by the experience of responding to a loss with need and pain. Love is grasped *in* the experience of loving and suffering. That pain is not some separate thing that instrumentally gives us access to the love; it is constitutive of loving itself. Love is not a thing in the heart to be observed . . . ; it is embodied in, constituted by, experiences of loving, which prominently include experiences of suffering.[76]

The novel provides a vision of eros that is altogether different from the one provided by philosophy. Whatever truth-claims the novel makes about eros inhere in the contingency of individual experience, not universal categories, which is perhaps why Plato seems to depart from the Socratic method when the conversations turn to love, resorting to narrative instead. This raises the question, then, of whether these narratives still fall under the domain of philosophy, or whether they sever their ties in order to open up a new genre.

To Nussbaum, a work like *Symposium* falls short of being a novel precisely because it only treats love as an external concept rather than narrating it from inside the experience. This is also what makes it funny to her, as she explains in her article, "The Speech of Alcibiades":

> The story is comic because, while it is about us and our deepest concerns, it at the same time distances itself from the inner pain of those concerns, asking us to watch ourselves as we watch a species remote from us and our needs.[77]

Proust, on the other hand, plunges us into the depths of eros, in all of its suffering, and perhaps more importantly, in the sheer amount of contingent details that distinguish the novel from philosophy. Within the space of the novel, unlike philosophy, the attempt of the narrator, Marcel, "to grasp his soul by a scientific kind of knowing, to treat his experiences as somehow extrinsic or external to himself, is a form of self-avoidance."[78]

This scientific strategy that may work in philosophy does not access the kind of psychological truth that only the novel can. Nussbaum argues that neither method of conveying truth, philosophical or novelistic, is superior, though—they are just different: "To try to grasp love by the Platonic kind of knowing is a way of avoiding loving. To try to *see* suffering is a way of *not* suffering."[79] Like Psyche's intercourse with Eros, the truth that the novel reveals is one that is experienced; it is felt rather than seen. Philosophy, in its pursuit of enlightenment, is Psyche casting her light on Eros only to see him vanish. Our psyche is also divided among different ways of reaching different kinds of truths, and those pathways, while adjacent, do not intersect.

By comparing philosophical and novelistic styles, Nussbaum ends her article by reflecting on her own style, and what style would be appropriate to fairly assess "two such radically different styles and views."[80] She then proposes the question: "'Is a philosophical criticism of literature possible?' Or rather—to help myself to a familiar style of philosophical optimism—'*How* is a philosophical criticism of literature possible?'"[81]

At the risk of indulging this "optimism," maybe we could also pose this question in reverse, and ask how a literary criticism of philosophy is possible, if only because literature has been subjected to the Cyclopean scrutiny of philosophy ever since Socrates demanded the apology and justification for the mimetic arts before entertaining the idea of allowing them back into his utopian republic—a humiliating demand that scholars have been complying with for over 2,500 years. It is not until Friedrich Schlegel's "Letter About the Novel" that we get the suggestion that maybe this demand can be reversed, and instead of accepting literature—and the novel, specifically—on philosophical grounds, we can read philosophy itself as a novel, with Plato being our first novelist, or at least proto-novelist, Nussbaum's convincing arguments notwithstanding.

Instead of beginning with a definition of the novel—of which there are too many and also arguably none—I want to start instead by reading Aristophanes's pessimistic myth of eros from *Symposium* as what Michael Riffaterre would call a "hypogram," or what Paul de Man would call an "infra-text," a text to which other texts respond, as all texts in literature invariably respond to prior texts.[82] I want to explore how these intertextual correspondences contribute to a possible understanding of the novel as a genre that engages with pessimism and eros. *Symposium* is a work that, at its core, gives us an account of who we are—so too does literature at large. If, as Nussbaum says, the "old quarrel between philosophy and literature is, as Plato clearly saw, not just a quarrel about ornamentation, but a quarrel about who we are and what we aspire to become," then the first question to ask is: Who are we?[83]

NOTES

1. Eugene Thacker, *Infinite Resignation* (London: Repeater, 2018), 38.

2. Herman Melville, Bartleby, *The Scrivener: A Story of Wall-Street*, in *Melville's Short Novels*, ed. Dan McCall (New York: W. W. Norton, 2002), 32.

3. Søren Kierkegaard, *The Seducer's Diary*, Foreword by John Updike, ed. and trans. Howard V. Hong and Edna H. Hong (Princeton, NJ: Princeton University Press, 1989), 112.

4. Nietzsche identifies his own "courageous pessimism" as "the way to 'myself,' to *my* task [*Aufgabe*]" (Friedrich Nietzsche, *Human, All Too Human*, trans. R. J. Hollingdale [Cambridge: Cambridge University Press, 2009], 210).

5. Thacker, *Infinite Resignation*, 38.

6. Costica Bradatan, "The Philosopher of Failure: Emil Cioran's Heights of Despair," *Los Angeles Review of Books*, November 28, 2016, https://lareviewofbooks.org/article/philosopher-failure-emil-ciorans-heights-despair/.

7. Arthur Schopenhauer, *The World as Will and Representation* II, trans. E. F. J. Payne (New York: Dover, 1969), II: 584; Arthur Schopenhauer, "On the Sufferings of the World," in *Suffering, Suicide, and Immortality*, trans. T. Bailey Saunders (Mineola, NY: Dover, 2006), 4–5.

8. Schopenhauer, "On the Fourfold Root of the Principle of Sufficient Reason," in *Two Essays*, trans. Mme. Karl Hillebrand, Revised Edition (Oxford: Benediction Classics, 2010), xviii; David E. Cartwright, *Schopenhauer: A Biography* (Cambridge: Cambridge University Press, 2013), 363. Cioran also blames Hegel for being "chiefly responsible for modern optimism" (*A Short History of Decay*, trans. Richard Howard [New York: Arcade, 2012], 146).

9. Cartwright, *Schopenhauer*, 363.

10. Derek Michaud, "Ludwig Feuerbach (1804-1872)," in *Boston Collaborative Encyclopedia of Western Theology,* http://people.bu.edu/wwildman/bce/feuerbach.htm.

11. Friedrich Nietzsche, "The Case of Wagner," in *The Birth of Tragedy / The Case of Wagner,* trans. Walter Kaufmann (New York: Vintage Books, 1967), §5: 166.

12. Kierkegaard, *The Concept of Irony, with Continual Reference to Socrates,* ed. and trans. Howard V. Hong and Edna H. Hong (Princeton, NJ: Princeton University Press, 1989), 424.

13. Kierkegaard, *Concept of Irony,* xi.

14. Qtd. in George Pattison, "The Bonfire of the Genres: Kierkegaard's Literary Kaleidoscope," in *Kierkegaard, Literature, and the Arts,* ed. Eric Ziolkowski (Evanston, IL: Northwestern University Press, 2018), 46.

15. Kierkegaard, *Seducer's Diary,* viii.

16. Kierkegaard, *Early Polemical Writings,* ed. and trans. Howard V. Hong and Edna V. Hong (Princeton, NJ: Princeton University Press, 1990), 59.

17. Robert Hullot-Kentor, *Introduction to Kierkegaard: Construction of the Aesthetic* by Theodor W. Adorno, ed. and trans. Robert Hullot-Kentor (Minneapolis, MN: University of Minnesota Press, 1989), xi.

18. Michael Holquist, Introduction to *The Dialogic Imagination: Four Essays* by M. M. Bakhtin, ed. Michael Holquist, trans. Caryl Emerson and Michael Holquist (Austin, TX: University of Texas Press, 1981), xxv.

19. Holquist, Introduction to *Dialogic Imagination* by Bakhtin, xxiv.

20. Holquist, Introduction to *Dialogic Imagination* by Bakhtin, xxv.

21. Walter Benjamin, "Theses on the Philosophy of History," in *Illuminations,* trans. Harry Zohn (New York: Schocken, 1968), 257–258.

22. Denis de Rougemont, *Love in the Western World,* trans. Montgomery Belgion (New York: Doubleday, 1956), 232.

23. Stendhal, *Love,* trans. Gilbert and Suzanne Sale (London: Penguin Books, 1975), 26.

24. Stendhal, *Love,* 25.

25. Stendhal, *Love,* 25.

26. Stendhal, *Love,* 96.

27. Immanuel Kant "An Answer to the Question: What is Enlightenment?," in *"Toward Perpetual Peace" and Other Writings on Politics, Peace, and History,* ed. Pauline Kleingold, trans. David L. Colclasure (New Haven, CT: Yale University Press, 2006), 17.

28. Jack Halberstam, *The Queer Art of Failure* (Durham, NC: Duke University Press, 2011), 1–5.

29. Terry Eagleton, *Hope Without Optimism* (New Haven, CT: Yale University Press, 2017), 2.

30. Eagleton, *Hope Without Optimism,* 10.

31. Barbara Ehrenreich, *Bright-Sided: How Positive Thinking is Undermining America* (New York: Picador Books, 2009), 10.

32. Eagleton, *Hope Without Optimism,* 11.

33. Ehrenreich, *Bright-Sided,* 10.

34. Mark Landler and Somini Sengupta, "Trump and the Teenager: A Climate Showdown at Davos," *The New York Times*, January 21, 2020, https://www.nytimes.com/2020/01/21/climate/greta-thunberg-trump-davos.html.

35. Gross, "Reporter: White House Knew of Coronavirus' 'Major Threat,' but Response Fell Short," Fresh Air, *National Public Radio*, March 12, 2020, https://www.npr.org/2020/03/12/814881355/white-house-knew-coronavirus-would-be-a-major-threat-but-response-fell-short.

36. Edward-Isaac Dovere, "Joe Biden's Endless Search for the Middle on Race," *The Atlantic*, June 21, 2019, https://www.theatlantic.com/politics/archive/2019/06/bidens-anachronistic-comments-race-and-civil-rights/592252/.

37. Ehrenreich, *Bright-Sided*, 12.

38. Eagleton, *Hope Without Optimism*, 4.

39. Eagleton, *Hope Without Optimism*, 5–6.

40. Ehrenreich, *Bright-Sided*, 200.

41. Qtd. in Eagleton, *Hope Without Optimism*, 6.

42. Eagleton, *Hope Without Optimism*, 6.

43. Eagleton, *Hope Without Optimism*, 6.

44. Georg Lukács, *Theory of the Novel*, trans. Anna Bostock (Cambridge, MA: Massachusetts Institute of Technology Press, 1971), 18.

45. Lukács, *Theory of the Novel*, 12; 38.

46. Lukács, *Theory of the Novel*, 116.

47. Lukács, *Theory of the Novel*, 17.

48. Lukács, *Theory of the Novel*, 18.

49. Vladimir Nabokov, *Strong Opinions* (New York: Vintage Books, 1990), 105. Robert Roper points out that, "Véra came to the rescue because she was nearby; he did not start fires when his wife was out of the house" (*Nabokov in America: On the Road to* Lolita [New York: Bloomsbury, 2015], 149). Nabokov was most likely just being dramatic.

50. Plato, *Phaedrus*, trans. Alexander Nehamas and Paul Woodruff (Indianapolis, IN: Hackett Publishing, 1995), 230D: 6.

51. Plato, *Phaedrus,* 230B: 6.

52. Plato, *Phaedrus,* xiv.

53. Plato, *Phaedrus,* 255D-E: 46.

54. Nabokov, *Lolita,* annotated and ed. Alfred Appel, Jr. (New York: Vintage Books, 1991), 60.

55. Martha Nussbaum, "The Speech of Alcibiades: A Reading of Plato's *Symposium*," Philosophy and Literature 3, no. 2 (Fall 1979): 136. doi:10.1353/phl.1979.0024.

56. Allan Bloom notes that,

> Unlike the cosmic gods, Olympian gods demand worship. Socrates found it much less difficult to believe in the cosmic deities than in these Olympian ones. In the *Apology* he does not even attempt to prove that he believes in the Olympian gods, but he does say that he has never denied that the sun and moon are gods. (Allan Bloom, "The Ladder of Love," in *Plato's Symposium*, trans. Seth Benardete [Chicago, IL: University of Chicago Press, 2001], 106)

57. Bloom, "Ladder of Love," 108.

58. Cf. Jacques Derrida, "Plato's Pharmacy," in *Dissemination,* trans. Barbara Johnson (Chicago, IL: University of Chicago Press, 1981), 61–171.

59. Plato, *The Republic of Plato*, trans. Allan Bloom (New York: Basic Books, 2016), 602B: 285.

60. Friedrich von Schlegel, "Aphorisms from the Lyceum," in *Friedrich Schlegel's Lucinde and the Fragments*, trans. Peter Firchow (Minneapolis, MN: University of Minnesota Press, 1971), §26: 112.

61. Bakhtin, *Dialogic Imagination*, 24.

62. Julia Kristeva, *Desire in Language: A Semiotic Approach to Literature and Art*, ed. Leon S. Roudiez and trans. Thomas Gora, Alice Jardine, and Leon S. Roudiez (New York: Columbia University Press, 1980), 81.

63. Plato, *Republic*, 608A-B: 291.

64. Plato, *Republic*, 607D: 291.

65. Georges Bataille, *Erotism: Death and Sensuality*, trans. Mary Dalwood (San Francisco, CA: City Lights Books, 1986), 29.

66. Rachel Barney, "*Eros* and Necessity in the Ascent from the Cave," *Ancient Philosophy* 28 (2008): 1, http://individual.utoronto.ca/rbarney/Eros.pdf.

67. Barney, "*Eros* and Necessity," 2.

68. Plato, *Apology* in *Five Dialogues*, trans. G. M. A. Grube, revised by John M. Cooper (Indianapolis, IN: Hackett Publishing, 2002), 21D: 26.

69. Plato, *Plato's Symposium*, trans. Seth Benardete (Chicago, IL: University of Chicago Press, 2001), 177D-E: 6–7.

70. Nabokov, *Strong Opinions,* 69.

71. Nabokov, *Strong Opinions,* 69.

72. Nabokov, *Strong Opinions,* 78.

73. Qtd. in Joseph Epstein, *The Novel, Who Needs It?* (New York: Encounter Books, 2023), 60.

74. Erich Heller, *Thomas Mann: The Ironic German* (Cleveland, OH: Meridian, 1961), 55–56.

75. Heller, *Thomas Mann*, 63–64.

76. Nussbaum, "Fictions of the Soul," *Philosophy and Literature* 7, no. 2 (October 1983): 156, doi:10.1353/phl.1983.0040.

77. Nussbaum, "The Speech of Alcibiades," 140.

78. Nussbaum, "Fictions of the Soul," 156.

79. Nussbaum, "Fictions of the Soul," 156–167.

80. Nussbaum, "Fictions of the Soul," 160.

81. Nussbaum, "Fictions of the Soul," 160.

82. Paul de Man, "Hypogram and Inscription: Michael Riffaterre's Poetics of Reading," *Diacritics* 11, no. 4 (Winter 1981): 24.

83. Nussbaum, "Fictions of the Soul," 160.

Chapter 2

Kicking and Screaming

Pessimism Between Etiology, Etymology, and Entomology

PRIMAL SCREAM

To frame this question from the lens of Aristophanes's myth in *Symposium*, what kinds of creatures are we, divided from the beings that we once were, carrying the incision of that division in our own bodies? We are, strictly speaking, "insects"—beings whose bodies are cut up, the *-sect* of our dissection leaving its scars *in* us, and pessimism is the insistent reminder that we can never heal from that original amputation. Maybe this is the *"in"* that the novel narrates in a way that philosophy does not—the *"in"* of Nussbaum's claim: "Love is grasped *in* the experience of loving and suffering."[1] Philosophers like Ludwig Wittgenstein invite us to consider pain as something we give the name "beetle" to, and then imagine that "beetle" in a box, each one of us going through life with our own "beetle" in a box that cannot be seen by anyone else, not knowing if my "beetle" is different or similar to yours.[2] The novel, though, narrates what this "beetle" goes through inside the box itself.

Maybe our souls have always been the souls of insects. Socrates, the gadfly, would know. We certainly looked like enlarged versions of them in our prelapsarian state, our eight limbs outstretched from globular bodies. And maybe this insect nature of ours is why, before our split, we used to give "birth not in one another but in the earth, like cicadas."[3] The "cicadas' chorus" also provides the soundtrack to Plato's *Phaedrus*, humming to the tune of that other dialogue in which eros is what allows us to remember our cosmic nature.[4] Plato's cicadas, like our former selves, "used to be human beings who lived before the birth of the Muses," but when the Muses were born and invented song, these creatures "were so overwhelmed with the pleasure of singing that they forgot to eat or drink; so they died without even realizing it."[5] Their singing is an obsession that destroys them, allowing them to enjoy nothing else.

In Ancient Greek, the word for singer, transliterated as *aoidos*, carries in its first syllable the cry that Hélène Cixous identifies as the primal cry of literature—the "Ay yay!" embedded in the Greek name of Ajax (*Aïas*), and announced in the opening lines of Medea and Hecuba in their respective tragedies, shouting "*AÏAÏAÏ*."[6] Maybe this is that first cry from the pain of that original split, repeated over and over again as a traumatic memory, which is then transformed with the artistic inspiration from the Muses, an inspiration that nonetheless ushers these cicada-singers to their deaths.

The cry is the limit of language, punctuating where it begins and ends. We cry as we enter the world, the medieval pessimist Hildegard von Bingen explains, because we already perceive how terrible it is.[7] It is a vale of tears that accompanies our exit from it with more cries. In William Faulkner's *As I Lay Dying*, Addie Bundren, on her way out of life—unless she is speaking from her coffin in transit—thinks of words as insects, as "spiders dangling by their mouths from a beam, swinging and twisting and never touching."[8] Trying to twist herself out of the web of words, she remembers her father telling her that "the reason for living was to get ready to stay dead a long time," which perhaps explains the urgency of the shrieking cicadas, who, to Plato, die without realizing it, in the same way that Addie thinks of her husband Anse as someone who "did not know that he was dead."[9] She resents him, and she resents when he uses the word "Love" as she resents all words: "I knew that that word was like the others: just a shape to fill a lack."[10] Words for her are "no good; . . . words dont [sic] ever fit even what they are trying to say at."[11]

These thoughts are not, strictly speaking, cries, but they seem to stifle a cry that lies behind and beyond all the words that she is resentful and suspicious of. As Cixous points out, there is no *écrire* without the *cri*, no *schreiben* without the *Schrei*, no writing without this primal cry, which the novel—unlike the performed tragedy or the spoken poem—transmits in muted language. This is perhaps why, in Clarice Lispector's *The Passion According to G.H.*, a novel in which a woman identifies her inner nature as that of an insect as she mystically merges her being with a dead cockroach, she withholds this "first scream":

> Everything could be fiercely summed up in never emitting a first scream—a first scream unleashes all the others, the first scream at birth unleashes a life, if I screamed I would awaken thousands of screaming beings who would loose upon the rooftops a chorus of screams and horror. If I screamed I would unleash the existence—the existence of what? the existence of the world. With reverence I feared the existence of the world for me.[12]

Maybe Plato's cicadas are these "thousands of screaming beings" unleashed by that primal and primordial scream, screaming the world itself into existence. And since, according to Cixous, literature proliferates by "the genie of metamorphosis" in this world governed by insects, we hear it reverberating throughout the canon, from the ancient cries of mourning in Greek tragedy to the "Screaming" that "comes across the sky" at the beginning of Thomas Pynchon's postmodernist novel *Gravity's Rainbow*. It is a cry that lasts for three days in *The Death of Ivan Ilyich* and for a lifetime in *The Sound and the Fury*, with Benjy's haunting, inarticulate cries—the only expression he is capable of—described as both "hopeless and prolonged."[13] It echoes from Smerdyakov's epileptic fits in *The Brothers Karamazov* to Oskar Mazerath's "sing-shattering" in *The Tin Drum*, from Faust's pessimistic "ach!" of despair in the opening line of Goethe's play to Adrian Leverkühn's final gesture in Thomas Mann's *Doctor Faustus*, striking a dissonant chord on the piano as "he opened his mouth as if to sing, but from between his lips there emerged only a wail that still rings in my ears."[14]

And behind Mann and Goethe in the development of the Faust legend is Christopher Marlowe, whose last name is evoked in the protagonist of Joseph Conrad's *Heart of Darkness*, where Marlow is haunted by "a cry, a very loud cry as of infinite desolation," carrying "such a tremulous and prolonged wail of mournful fear and utter despair as may be imagined to follow the flight of the last hope from the earth."[15] This pessimistic cry seems to emerge from the landscape itself, monstrously indistinguishable from humans as the "bush began to howl," and he moves from the metaphor of animals to the metaphor of insects to describe what he can see in the direction of this cry: a "tangled gloom, naked breasts, arms, legs, glaring eyes—the bush was swarming with human limbs."[16]

PROUST'S INSECTARIUM

Cicadas, once humans themselves, according to Plato, also merge into the landscape, burrowing themselves into the ground for an extended period of lost time, and are awoken by a panicked instinct to take flight before they die. To Plato, the cicada is the emblem of artistic inspiration and self-destruction, of eros and pessimism, a vision of our cosmic origins and also of our annihilation. Taking Nussbaum's cue of bringing Plato into conversation with Proust as illustrating the broader tensions between philosophy and literature, Plato's cicadas function similarly to the insect imagery in what is probably the lengthiest response to *Symposium* ever written, *In Search of Lost Time*.[17] To Beckett, Marcel's "imagination weaves its cocoon about this frail and almost abstract chrysalis" of eros when he first sees Albertine in Balbec.[18]

Enduring for roughly the length of a cicada lifecycle, Marcel plunges into the depths of pessimistic despair, obsession, and jealousy over Albertine, but this despair metamorphoses into the literary work that he has devoted his entire life to. The process of artistic inspiration seems to be modeled on the cicadas, largely subterranean and slow-moving, hidden from view, until brief and ecstatic bursts send Marcel's mind soaring in flight as a fight against time.

In Search of Lost Time burrows into the shifting geological strata of consciousness, in which "incessant upheavals raise to the surface ancient deposits."[19] Marcel thinks of his mind as "a basin of rock rich in minerals, in which lay vast and varied ores of great price. But should I have time to exploit them?"[20] The contingency of time traps him to earth, where his attention mines the layers underground, but in those ecstatic bursts of inspiration, he is reminded to look up at the sky, like the moment he "felt once again a longing for my lost freedom on hearing a noise that I did not at first recognize. . . . It was like the buzz of a wasp. 'Look,' said Albertine, 'there is an airplane, high up in the sky, so high.'"[21] Even when he "had at last been able to attach the buzzing to its cause," he still refers to it as "that little insect throbbing up there in the sky."[22]

William C. Carter points out how the airplane is a symbol of artistic liberation and inspiration for Marcel.[23] And as the airplanes keep on flying in and out of the *Recherche*, Marcel continues to associate them with insects. By the final volume, *Time Regained*, these "insects" acquire additional layers of associations, specifically as both a cipher of our cosmic origins and a harbinger of global doom. As the First World War is raging, Marcel's friend Robert de Saint-Loup marvels at how the airplanes "fly off in *constellation*, in obedience to laws as precise as those that govern the constellations of the stars."[24] These airplanes offer a vision of Plato's insects returning back to their stellar homes. And in the same breath that Saint-Loup evokes our starry origins, he asks Marcel,

> But don't you prefer the moment, when, just as you have got used to thinking of them as stars, they break away to pursue an enemy or to return to the ground after the all-clear, the moment of *apocalypse*, when even the stars are hurled from their courses?[25]

What these airplane-insects accomplish in space, Marcel seems to do in time, thinking to himself, "And like an airman who hitherto has progressed laboriously along the ground, abruptly 'taking off' I soared slowly towards the silent heights of memory."[26] This is not a memory that can be willed, but rather the "involuntary memory" unlocked in our mind when we encounter objects or situations that remind us of the past. Dreams also transport us not only to the past that we had lived, but to a prehistory that connects us all. In dreams,

> remote periods . . . come rushing upon us with almost the speed of light as though they were giant aeroplanes [sic] instead of the pale stars which we had supposed them to be, blinding us with their brilliance and bringing back to our vision all that they had once contained for us.[27]

To Saint-Loup, these airplanes represent Hegel's concept of "perpetual becoming."[28] Perhaps a more modest analogy, which Marcel suggests in his association between airplanes and insects, would simply be the metamorphosis—the principle that governs the entire *Recherche*. On vacation in Balbec, he enters the art studio of Elstir, in whose paintings Marcel "was able to discern . . . a sort of metamorphosis of the things represented."[29] More than just an aesthetic principle, though, metamorphosis is both an ontological and epistemological metaphor for Marcel, providing a way for him to make sense of a world that defies sense-making. The entire work is a process of tracing the discarded layers that one sheds in the transformation of individual and social identity, thinking of the transformation of Charlus, for instance—the "man-insect" whom he compares to a "bumblebee"—from the paragon of virile masculinity to a woman emerging from her chrysalis.[30] When Marcel finally sees Charlus in old age, having gone through another transformation in his resemblance to King Lear, Marcel reflects on how "it must be possible for human personality to undergo metamorphoses as total as those of certain insects."[31]

In Proust's world, the cultivation of eros requires as much attention as Mme. de Guermantes pays to her orchid, carefully tending to this "captive flower" so that it may attract a "very rare insect."[32] Marcel even describes himself as a "bee" flying in the shadow of young girls in flower, among them Albertine, whom he would later keep as his "captive."[33] And the orchid of Mme. de Guermantes recalls the cattleya, also an orchid, which becomes so erotically charged with meaning that Charles Swann and Odette de Crécy use the phrase "make cattleya" when "they wanted to signify the act of physical possession—in which, in fact, one possesses nothing."[34] As though replicating the movement of eros in *Symposium*, Swann "had so completely divided himself in two" upon listening to a phrase from Vinteuil's Sonata, which he associates with his own obsessive desire for Odette, and thinks of this Sonata itself as having undergone a "metamorphosis," transforming into a "protective goddess, a confidante of his love."[35]

Gilles Deleuze reads Proust as "a Platonist, but not in the vague sense, not because he invokes essences or Ideas apropos of Vinteuil's little phrase."[36] By this, Deleuze means that Proust is closer to the Plato of *Phaedrus*,

Symposium, and *Phaedo*—the "great Platonic trilogy . . . of madness, love, and death"—than the Plato of *The Republic*.[37] But what disturbs Deleuze is the narrator, not quite convinced that he is a person we can call "Marcel"— a name only suggested once, and provisionally.[38] To Deleuze, the narrator doesn't even seem to possess human organs and exists solely as an entity to weave together a mass of different associations, narrating events, situations, and even states of mind from other characters he couldn't possibly have access to in the amount of detail that he reports.

> But what is a body without organs? The spider too sees nothing, perceives nothing, remembers nothing. She receives only the slightest vibration at the edge of her web, which propagates itself in her body as an intensive wave and sends her leaping to the necessary place.[39]

This is less of a novel, then, than it is a "web," or even a "machine" that keeps on generating new filaments, shooting out threads to each of the characters as "so many profiles of his own madness."[40]

Deleuze wasn't the first one to make this observation. Aside from Lucien Daudet, one of Proust's lovers who had once confided in Jean Cocteau that Proust was "an atrocious insect," Walter Benjamin notes how

> Proust's most accurate, most convincing insights fasten on their objects as insects fasten on leaves, blossoms, branches, betraying nothing of their existence until a leap, a beating of wings, a vault, show the startled observer that some incalculable life has imperceptibly crept into an alien world.[41]

Proust seems to announce this method in the opening pages of the *Recherche*, in his description of Marcel lying in bed as a child, entranced by his magic lantern projecting the moving image of a villain from Arthurian Romance who "accommodated every obstacle, every hindersome object that he encountered by taking it as his skeleton and absorbing it into himself . . . revealing no disturbance at his transvertebration."[42]

Proust has to invent the term "transvertebration" to name not just this optical illusion, but the literary method of exploring how Marcel, over the course of his life, absorbs the external world into his own consciousness. It is a seemingly magical process, like an enchanted insect that, by virtue of lacking a vertebral column, can take someone else's instead and experience who they are from the inside. It is a parasitism he is quick to notice in others, like his sadistic maid Françoise, whom he compares to "the burrowing wasp" that, with "cruelty," captures its prey and "proceeds with a marvelous knowledge and skill to pierce them in the nerve center."[43] The insect in Proust, in addition to a literary method and a principle of eros, ontology, and epistemology, is also just a metaphor of spite.

As much as Proust owes to Plato in his use of insects, he also may have taken this inspiration equally from Balzac, who imagines everyone as belonging to a "swarming beehive."[44] The ambitious Lucien Chardon, who metamorphoses into Lucien de Rubempré, is compared to "beautiful insects ostentatiously designed by some great natural poet and adorned for veritable feasts of love—but . . . meet their death while still in their virginity, crushed underfoot of some passerby."[45] In his quest for poetry, fame, and love, he suffers one abject humiliation after another. In *Lost Illusions*, after reading his poems in public for the first time, his lover Mme. de Bargeton—who later cruelly betrays him—tries calming him down at this point, referring to the people who don't appreciate his poetry as "insects" who "flew to suck the blood from the little stings they inflicted!"[46]

Lucien can't seem to shake off these insects, though. His friend Blondet tells him that, "Poetry is like the sun, making the eternal forests thrive and grow—but it also breeds gnats, flies, and mosquitoes."[47] But it's not just poetry. When Lucien compromises his morals to work in journalism, Lousteau gives him a book to review, warning that "a million mites" will "come crawling out of it."[48] If illusions in this novel were once living and breathing entities, then the lost illusions are those that, having expired, decay and attract insects, which is perhaps why Lucien's friend—and then later brother-in-law—David Séchard, after having abandoned his own illusions of running a successful paper-printing business, takes up an interest in "entomology and is currently studying the metamorphoses of insects, hitherto known to science only in their final guises."[49] This is how the novel ends, suggesting in retrospect that the entire work is a kind of entomology that examines the ugly metamorphoses and molting of illusions.

The genealogy and taxonomy of insects traced from *Symposium* through the history of Western literature reveal patterns of pessimistic thought that are not exclusive to, but ultimately find their home in, the novel. Maybe the pessimist affirms this insect nature against the human, as the Renaissance poet Giovanni Pontano says in his meditation on happiness: "And in the end, human happiness will be spoiled by mosquitoes, flies, and fleas."[50] What's the point of existence, then?—a question posed more eloquently by Hamlet, who is stuck in a play of lapwings, beetles, glowworms, "maggots in a dead dog," and a "convocation of politic worms"—all the things that live off of rot.[51] "As flies to wanton boys," Gloucester identifies us in *King Lear*, "are we to the gods. / They kill us for their sport."[52]

Evolution, as an account of our origins, has given us a narrative of progress from the non-human to the human. The pessimist, though, thinks through how this narrative will end, unwind, and ultimately terminate—or be exterminated. Is the next step in our evolution the Nietzschean Last Man, or the *Übermensch*, or the opposite—something like Dostoevsky's Underground

Man, who thinks of himself as "a foul, obscene fly—more intelligent, more developed, more noble than everyone else—that went without saying—but a fly, ceaselessly giving way to everyone, humiliated by everyone, insulted by everyone"?[53] Or will it be something like Frankenstein's Creature, whose creator exiles him with the insult, "Begone, vile insect!"[54] Will the human race disperse, like the patients in the sanatorium at the end of *The Magic Mountain*, seen from afar as an "anthill in panic"?[55]

Or will our descent be slower, subtler, our lives compartmentalized and determined by repetitive tasks of labor and bureaucracy that we have no choice but to participate in? In one of the most pessimistic American novels, *Revolutionary Road*, Richard Yates visualizes this futility as a "great silent insectarium" of society when Frank Wheeler sees the New York skyline as glass casings that display "hundreds of tiny pink men in white shirts, forever shifting papers and frowning into telephones, acting out their passionate little dumb show under the supreme indifference of the rolling spring clouds."[56] It is no wonder, then, that in *The Metamorphosis*, Gregor Samsa's first reaction upon waking up after his transformation into an unnamed species of vermin, is not to the horror of the transformation, but the horror at the prospect of being late to work.

In *Crime and Punishment*, Raskolnikov is preoccupied with the question about the next step in our evolution, worried that the very act that would prove his greatness—the arbiter, to him, of a more advanced kind of human being—only demonstrates the fact that he is a "louse" or a "spider" who will spend the rest of his life "sucking the life-blood out of" anyone who gets entangled in his web.[57] Svidrigaylov torments him with an image of the afterlife as consisting of one small room "with spiders in every corner, and . . . that is the whole of eternity."[58] Maybe the whole novel is already set in that one little room, with Raskolnikov returning in his mind over and over again to that moment when he killed Alëna Ivanovna and her sister Lizaveta, while he "lurked in a corner like a spider."[59] The claustrophobia of his own apartment seems to carry over into every space where Raskolnikov lurks, whether it is Alëna Ivanovna's apartment or even the open streets and bridges of St. Petersburg. Hemmed in, he is not only cornered, but he corners others. He is not just a victim of eternity's spiders, but is one of those spiders himself.

There is an apocalyptic resonance to the image of the insect as a synonym for humanity emptied even of itself. Richard III is called a "bottled spider."[60] Renfield, the insane asylum inmate in *Dracula*, unmetaphors the images both of Richard III and Raskolnikov sucking the life-blood of whatever gets caught in their web. He literally bottles—or rather, boxes—up his spiders, studying their behavior so that he can act like them.[61] He catches flies in order to eat some and feed the rest to his spiders, which he then devours, as well. Dr. Seward tries to identify "a method in his madness," alluding to *Hamlet* perhaps as the foundation of modern English culture at the same time that Dracula poses an apocalyptic threat to it.[62]

In *Lolita*, Humbert refers to himself as "Humbert the Spider" as he vampirically preys on the young Dolores Haze, not allowing her to metamorphose into anything with autonomy. He uses his prose instead to pin her down the way Nabokov would pin down and study his butterflies.[63] This butterfly motif also recurs throughout *Doctor Faustus* as an apocalyptic symbol of destruction, as when Adrian Leverkühn willingly contracts a venereal disease with a sex worker whom he calls "Hetaera Esmeralda" after a butterfly in his father's collection of insects, with the knowledge that this disease will improve his art.[64]

In these novels, insects indicate the pessimistic aspects of eros. In *The Brothers Karamazov*, Mitya, citing Schiller's line of poetry, "To insects—sensuality!" tells his brother Alyosha, "I am that very insect, brother, and those words are precisely about me."[65] Describing his womanizing tendencies that now torment him with guilt, he confesses, "I loved depravity, I also loved the shame of depravity. I loved cruelty: am I not a bedbug, an evil insect—in short, a Karamazov?"[66] In *Great Expectations*, insects fill the void of time lost to an absent love. In Miss Havisham's room, where the clock stands still, "speckled-legged spiders with blotched bodies" run quickly into and out of the abandoned wedding feast laid out decades before, while "black-beetles took no notice of the agitation, and groped about the hearth."[67] Miss Havisham represents a warning to anyone with great expectations, false hope, and misplaced optimism, seeing her own expectations themselves rot away into fodder for insects, which are all that remain of the eros that keeps her trapped in this misery that erodes time itself.

If the pattern of these insect motifs points to a sense of doom, of endings, of apocalypse, the narrator of *The Passion According to G.H.* keeps that same tone while exploring a vision of our prehistorical origins, tracing the trajectory back to *Symposium* in its treatment of eros. The novel, in recounting the mystical dissolution of the barriers between subject and object, narrates G.H.'s experience of merging her being with a cockroach, whose "existence was existing me."[68] When she sees that the roach is "split in two," she simultaneously sees a vision that "predated humanity," prompting her meditation on love—of how "love is something before love."[69] The word "love" itself is inadequate in describing this primordial revelation of eros, as she tries hunting for some other word that captures its hopelessness, its pessimism: "Maybe I'll find another name, much crueler initially, and much more it-self. Or maybe I won't. Is love when you don't give a name to the identity of things? . . . I, who called love my hope for love."[70]

The pessimistic act of writing itself is to put a language to something like love, which one would prefer not to, especially if love is "when you don't give a name to the identity of things." Love here becomes something "crueler," something experienced in the absence of hope, something not quite human, but which "predated humanity," and is the condition for humanity's existence, something that belongs to the domain of insects.

THE PODIATRY OF PESSIMISM: A FOOTNOTE TO THE QUARREL BETWEEN PHILOSOPHY AND LITERATURE

After G.H. comes out of that mystical union with the roach, she goes

> back to having something I never had: just two legs. I know I can only walk with two legs. But I feel the useless absence of that third leg and it scares me, it was the leg that made me something findable by myself, and without even having to look for myself.[71]

This attention to the leg also seems to evoke an often overlooked detail in the *Symposium* myth, in which we were molded, after that first and only incision, by Apollo, who rearranged some body parts like a plastic surgeon and smoothed out the wrinkles "with somewhat the same kind of tool as shoemakers use in smoothing the wrinkles in leather."[72] The beings that we are today, pessimistic creatures who have inherited the trauma of being torn from ourselves without the option of ever finding our other halves, are creatures shaped by a tool that is compared to one used by shoemakers. And some of us still feel the pain. "I am an amputee," Roland Barthes writes metaphorically of eros as absence, as waiting, as loss, "who still feels pain in his missing leg."[73]

As Zeus orders the human race to be split in two, with Apollo at the ready with his shoemaker's tool, he issues the following threat: "But if they are thought to behave licentiously still, and are unwilling to keep quiet, then I shall cut them again in two . . . so that they will go hopping on one leg."[74] Is this the kind of hubris that Herman Melville sketches in the figure of Captain Ahab in *Moby-Dick*, his amputated leg a vision of what Zeus's second punishment looks like—a vision of our humanity one step closer to annihilation? But even as Ahab lost his leg, his soul seems to acquire several more, as Ishmael says, reflecting on his insect-like nature: "Ahab's soul's a centipede, that moves upon a hundred legs."[75] No wonder Ahab is the voice of pessimism in this novel, saying, "This lovely light, it lights not me; all loveliness is anguish to me, since I can ne'er enjoy. Gifted with the high perception, I lack the low, enjoying power; damned, most subtly and most malignantly!"[76]

Pessimism emerges in the ambiguous space that opens up between Ahab's remaining leg and his missing one, a space indicated by the "indefiniteness" of where Moby Dick resides, the whale that "had actually been encountered in opposite latitudes at one and the same instant of time."[77] Slipping beyond comprehension in all his slippery slippage, Moby Dick is a cipher of both pessimism and of the "indefiniteness" and irreducibility of ambiguity itself.[78] Maybe this is why the Germans call "ambiguity" *Zweideutigkeit*—literally "two-meaning-ness." Philosophy aims to define, to specify, to pin down meaning to a single definition. But ambiguity by nature cannot be defined. It is what escapes the definite and gestures to the infinite, back to our cosmic origins, where we once roamed freely before Zeus's punishment.

Ambiguity, this two-meaning-ness, is not on the side of philosophy, but of pessimism. Refusing to be defined, identified, and named, it flies into a rage, preferring to destroy itself instead—like Rumpelstiltskin, who "stamped his right foot so hard that it went into the ground right up to his waist" when he's named at the end of the fairy tale. "Then in his fury he seized his left foot with both hands and tore himself in two."[79] And maybe this is why Hegel, in *The Phenomenology of Spirit*, tries to lead Spirit through and out of despair, or *Verzweiflung*, another term rooted in the *zwei*, or the "two."[80] The "Unhappy Consciousness" is "the consciousness of self as a dual-natured, merely contradictory being."[81] Hegel moves out of this *Verzweiflung*, this dual-natured Unhappy Consciousness, but pessimists hold on to it—to their despair, to their phantom two-ness in the midst of their loneliness, cynically doubting (in German, *bezweifeln*) everything else as they cling to the festering wound in their feet like Philoctetes.

The root of the word "pessimism," *pessum*, means "downward, to the ground," and comes from the root *ped-* —"foot," but also "to walk, stumble, impair."[82] Both the etymology and etiology of pessimism come down to the foot; pessimism is the grievance against Apollo's shoemaker tool that sculpted us into the miserable creatures we are today. To Thomas Ligotti, pessimism is the realization of this disconnect at the core of our being, the realization that, "we are not what we are: unreality on legs."[83] The etymology of "pessimism" traces the movement that Sylvia Plath captures in *The Bell Jar*, when Esther Greenwood, forcing herself to think "This is what it is to be happy" while ignoring the "disconsolate mosquito" of her "interior voice" that insists on suicide, rushes down the slope on her skis and ends up breaking her leg in two places.[84]

Even in the absence of the word "pessimism," it was clear from the moment of publication that *Candide* opened up the space to think through an alternative to optimism, and that alternative begins with the *pas*, the step forward that always ends up being a step back, illustrated in Schopenhauer's definition of life as "a ceaseless struggle for existence itself, while at every *step* it is threatened with destruction."[85] The pessimistic journey—not only in *Candide*, but perhaps the journey that every novel embarks on—is quite literally a passage as a *pas-sage*. It is a step toward wisdom that also denies wisdom—a step toward philosophy that ultimately rejects philosophy. Maybe this is the meaning that Cervantes ascribes to the name "Quixote," which is the word for leg armor, arming its eponymous hero against reality in his journey into the world. Much good this armor does in *Le Morte Darthur*, arguably the first novel in English, when King Arthur loses his entire kingdom over a random snake bite to an unnamed knight's foot. When this knight draws his sword to kill the snake, Mordred's forces interpret it as a sign for battle, which ultimately ends in the fall of Camelot.

While pessimism is not limited to any specific genre, the history of pessimistic writing and the history of the novel are largely intertwined. Both of them engage with philosophy in an effort to undermine it in some way, or to do something that philosophy is incapable of doing, as Nussbaum asserts. To Kundera, if the novel "is to go on discovering the undiscovered, to go on 'progressing' as a novel, it can do so only against the progress of the world."[86] Progress as literal steps forward—and if the novel wants to make any steps forward, it paradoxically needs to step back from the world. A transgression in reverse. It's not for nothing that, in *The Brothers Karamazov*, as Mitya is accused of murdering his father, his mind instead latches onto the fact that, "above all, he did not like his own feet. . . . This unbearable shame suddenly made him, deliberately now, even more rude."[87] It's his feet themselves that cause him "unbearable shame," rather than anything he had thought or said about his father.

Pessimism is thought drained down to the feet—unlike philosophy, which exists in the hands. Socrates didn't care about his feet; this is why he walked around Athens barefoot. He performed thought with his hands, which is reflected in the most iconic image of him in Raphael's painting *The School of Athens*. Philosophy attempts to *grasp*, to reach, to take hold of, emphasizing the *greifen* in *begreifen*, from which we get the noun *Begriff*, the concept. In *The Republic*, Socrates distinguishes philosophers from non-philosophers by saying that "philosophers are those who are able to grasp what is always the same in all respects, while those who are not able to do so . . . wander among what is many and varies in all ways."[88] It's a differentiation between those who wonder and those who wander, those who grasp and those who walk away in dejection and error, those who use their hands and those who stray off by foot, those who seek philosophical universals and those who dwell in novelistic detail.

Aristotle writes in *Metaphysics* that "all men by their very nature reach out to know," and it is this reaching that he captures in his work.[89] Philosophy gestures, it points, it indexes, from the marginal glosses of hand and finger icons in medieval manuscripts all the way to Heidegger's Dasein, who is always handed and handy; being-in-the-world is the experience of approaching things that are either ready-to-hand or present-at-hand. In *Parmenides*,

Heidegger writes, "Every motion of the hand in every one of its works carries itself through the element of thinking, every bearing of the hand bears itself in that element. All the work of the hand is rooted in thinking."[90] Byung-Chul Han, glossing this statement, says that, "Thinking is handi-craft."[91] Maybe this is also why Socrates is so fond of metaphors from craftsmanship. Philosophy from Plato to Heidegger is as much an activity of the hands as it is of the mind. It is a rhetorical weighing of values ("on the one hand . . . on the other hand") and of perspectives (firsthand account versus secondhand account). In liberal economic theory, the hand is invisible, but it manipulates everything like a puppet-master.

Pessimism parodies the role of the hand in philosophy, as exemplified in Thomas Mann's novels. Thomas Buddenbrook feels a rare moment of intense consolation after haphazardly coming across a copy of Schopenhauer's *World and Will as Representation*, a book that finally articulates his own bleak vision of life as "cruel, mocking, powerful."[92] He is so overcome with emotion that he weeps out of an "intoxicating joy" that "was incomparably sweeter than the world's sweetest pain."[93] He finally feels understood, even vindicated in his pessimistic views. But pessimism can be too frightening, too untenable, to sustain. The next day, he keeps this Schopenhauerian insight at arm's length: "And so Thomas Buddenbrook, who had *stretched his hands out* imploringly for high and final truths, sank back now into the ideas, images, and customary beliefs in which he had been drilled as a child."[94]

In *Doctor Faustus*, the narrator, Dr. Serenus Zeitblom, frequently apologizes for the messy handwriting of the manuscript and for his unsteady hand because of the bombs that are dropping all around him in the midst of the Second World War.[95] Mann frequently draws attention to the uncomfortable positions of his characters' hands. Professor Schlepfuss, whose name ironically draws attention to the way he drags his foot, contorts his body in such a way that, while "half-sitting, half-leaning against a railing," he strikes the posture of a kind of menacingly clownish figure with his "fingers lying interlaced in his lap with thumbs spread wide."[96] The novel ends with Mann, speaking through Zeitblom, articulating his own pessimism: "Today, in the embrace of demons, a hand over one eye, the other staring into the horror, [Germany] plummets from despair to despair."[97]

In *Death in Venice*, the uptight snob Gustav von Aschenbach remembers the painful sting of overhearing someone say in public, "'Here is how Aschenbach has always lived'—and he made a tight fist of his left hand—'not like this'—and he let his open hand dangle freely from the arm of his chair."[98] The irony, of course, is that, once in Venice, Aschenbach

> raised his head and with both arms, which had been hanging limply over the back of his chair, made a slow, rising, circular motion that brought the hands

forward in such a way as to indicate an opening and spreading of the arms. It was a gesture of willingness, welcome, of calm acceptance.[99]

What he welcomes with these open arms, or what he wants to welcome, is the elusive noumenon of beauty and truth, of the highest philosophical endeavor, but these values are embodied in the image of the young boy Tadzio, that Narcissus who "stretched out his arms to the reflection of his own beauty," which turns Aschenbach's intellectual pursuit into one of a stalking predator bordering on criminality.[100] Tadzio, the "charming psychagogue," uses his own hand to lead Aschenbach to his death, "beckoning to him, as if, releasing his hand from his hip, he were pointing outward, floating onward into the promising immensity of it all."[101] That promising immensity is one that, the novel demonstrates, can never be grasped. And in the original German, the word for "immensity" is *Ungeheure*, which could also be translated as "monstrosity," the same term that Kafka uses to introduce Gregor Samsa at the beginning of *The Metamorphosis*.[102]

Pessimism, unlike philosophy, is too exhausted, too tired to reach, unable or unwilling to grasp. Philosophers make mis-takes; pessimists make missteps. The gesture of pessimism is one of withdrawal rather than of reaching. "In vain do I resist," Kierkegaard writes in *Either/Or*. "My foot slips. My life nevertheless remains a poet-existence. Can anything worse be imagined?"[103] Worn out and tired of looking ahead, the head itself hangs heavily, chin folding on neck, and the gaze rests on the feet and on the ground beneath one's feet, where we'll all inevitably end up. Standing like this, one strikes the physical image of despair itself. Lying down in this position, one looks like a corpse. Pessimism has cold feet—not only an expression of non-commitment but also a description of a corpse's feet. In pessimism, as in autopsy tags, we are identified by our feet.

The first hero of Western literature, Achilles, whose epithet is "swift of foot," dies because of an arrow to his heel. His fellow soldier Odysseus is identified by the scar on his thigh in a moment when he displays a vile heartlessness to Eurykleia, the woman who not only welcomes him with warmth but who had essentially raised him and who is the first to recognize him after his return from Troy. Oedipus's identity is revealed in the limp that is also inscribed in his name; Balzac's criminal Jacques Collin and Dickens's criminal Magwitch are also identified by their limps. And Ethan Frome's limp is a cruel and constant reminder of the failed suicide pact that pulls him back to the same moment for twenty-four years, continuing to suffer in the same house with his wife and the woman he wanted to leave her for.

And then, of course, in the world of fairy tales, Cinderella is identified by her foot after her evil stepsisters, at the order of their mother, brutally mutilate their own feet—one cuts off a toe and the other hacks away at her heel—and all to no avail.[104] As if this physical torture isn't enough, they must endure Cinderella's wedding, where the same two doves who magically gave Cinderella her golden slippers and ballgown proceed to pluck out her stepsisters' eyes.[105] Cinderella's wedding can be seen, then, as a day not only of reckoning, but of wrath—and the bleak, violent, and apocalyptic vision sung by the *Dies Irae* Requiem is even inscribed in her own name: "*Dies irae, dies illa / Solvet saeclum in favilla*," meaning, "Day of wrath, that day / will dissolve the world into cinders."[106] A happily ever after, even for a pessimist.

In "The Little Mermaid," the most pessimistic fairy tale, the nameless girl trades her voice and fishtail for a pair of legs. Without a voice, all that's left of her identity is in her feet, which she uses to dance, even though it feels as though every step is taken on sharp knives, ultimately leading nowhere except to her suicide. And in Snow White's wedding, the evil queen ends up being forced into iron slippers that had been set over coal flames, and dances until she dies.[107] Hans Christian Andersen mirrors this final scene in *The Red Shoes*, but the girl with the shoes is no longer the villain. The villains are the shoes themselves, forcing the girl's feet to carry out a will that is not her own, even if she set that will into motion by first wanting to put the shoes on.

Elena Ferrante seems to re-write this dark fairy tale in her own Neapolitan Tetralogy, beginning in *My Brilliant Friend* with Lila's dreamy pastime of sketching shoe designs as a child, which sets into motion a cycle of pain and violence, beginning with her father and brother fighting over who would make these shoes and who they would sell them to, leading to a string of suitors who offer to buy these shoes in order to force her hand into marriage at sixteen. These seemingly magical shoes eventually lead to the first major betrayal of several betrayals in a life full of excruciating disappointment when Marcello, the one man whom she explicitly forbids to attend her wedding, the terror of Naples and the rapist of her friend Ada, storms into her wedding wearing the same shoes of her original design.

Cioran records a moment when he randomly ran into Beckett in Paris while, as a true pessimist, he refused to look "at the faces of passers-by," and looked instead "at their feet, and they all became for me only their footsteps, which went in every direction, making a disorderly dance not worth lingering on. While thinking of this, I looked up and saw Beckett."[108] In *A Short History of Decay*, he attributes the pessimistic condition of humans to their legs:

> Man was born with the vocation of fatigue: when he adopted the vertical posture and thereby diminished his possibilities of *support*, he was doomed to weaknesses unknown to the animal he was. To carry on two legs so much substance and all the disgusts related to it![109]

Likewise, to Dostoevsky's Underground Man, "the best definition of man is: a being that goes on two legs and is ungrateful."[110]

Philosophy aims to under*stand*; pessimism provides a catalog of irritating items that it *can't stand*. From the standpoint of philosophy, pessimism just needs to get a grip. It doesn't have a leg to stand on. Its feet fail. The ground falls beneath the pessimist, as it does for that most pessimistic articulation of what humans are capable of: Kurtz in *Heart of Darkness*, who "can't walk—he is crawling on all fours."[111] This is a man who "had kicked himself loose of the earth," who "had kicked the very earth to pieces."[112] "He was alone," Marlow tells us, "and I before him did not know whether I stood on the ground or floated in the air."[113]

Instead of a *Grund*, that Kantian grounding of philosophy, pessimism dwells in the abyss: the Nietzschean *Abgrund*—or the *Ungrund* of the German mystics of nothingness, Meister Eckhart and Jakob Boehme. Nothing to hold onto and nothing to stand on. Maybe this is why, in Faulkner's pessimistic vision in *The Sound and the Fury*, Benjy cries his inarticulate cry because "the ground wasn't still."[114] And maybe this is also why Thomas Hardy organizes his novels according to a principle of antifoundationalism.[115] Heidegger breaks down the word "existence" into "ek-sistence" to draw attention to its etymology of literally meaning to "stand out."[116] To him, "Ek-sistence so understood is not only the ground of the possibility of reason, *ratio*, but is also that in which the essence of man preserves the source that determines him."[117]

Existence may be outstanding to the philosopher, but to the pessimist it is disappointing. What's the point in standing out, or standing at all, when we can't even trust the ground beneath our feet? To Cioran, "At first we think we advance toward the light; then, wearied by an aimless march, we lose our way: the earth, less and less secure, no longer supports us; it opens under our feet."[118] At the end of *Heart of Darkness*, Marlow sees how Kurtz "had stepped over the edge" while he himself "had been permitted to draw back my hesitating foot" as he comes to the following conclusion:

> Droll thing life is—that mysterious arrangement of merciless logic for a futile purpose. The most you can hope from it is some knowledge of yourself—that comes too late—a crop of unextinguishable regrets. I have wrestled with death. It is the most unexciting contest you can imagine. It takes place in an impalpable greyness with nothing underfoot.[119]

One can't stand out, one can't even stand, even exist, if there is nothing to stand on, if there is "nothing underfoot."

In his *Grounding for the Metaphysics of Morals,* Kant recounts the biblical parable of finding one's talents; in the original parable in the Gospel of

Matthew, the servant who buries his one talent in the ground gets punished by his master. Pessimists bury their talents in the ground and watch the ground give way into a sinkhole beneath their feet, the source of their pain, which is why they can't think like philosophers. As Clov cries out in *Endgame*, "The pains in my legs! It's unbelievable! Soon I won't be able to think anymore."[120] And with this pain, we are still advised to pull ourselves up by our bootstraps—a cliché of optimism and a mainstay of conservative rhetoric that bullishly advises self-reliance.

But this phrase was originally coined in 1834 to denote something ludicrous, an absurdity, an impossibility.[121] Pulling yourself up by your bootstraps was never supposed to get you anywhere—just the opposite. All it does is aggravate you as you reach down to your feet. A pessimistic saying robbed even of its pessimism. If there is anyone who pulled themselves up by their bootstraps, it is Heathcliff, the wild pessimist whose arch-nemesis is the bookish, proper Edgar. "I would not strike him with my fist," Heathcliff claims, "but I'd kick him with my foot, and experience considerable satisfaction."[122] Whatever satisfaction he would get, though, Heathcliff knows that there is no one really to kick except for himself, since Edgar is the one who ends up marrying Catherine in this story that begins with the dramatization of the word "pessimism" in the form of Catherine literally stumbling barefoot near Thrushcross Grange before she is wounded by the dog bite to her ankle. This stumbling eventually tears her away from Wuthering Heights, from Heathcliff, and ultimately from herself.

WUTHERING LOWS

In pessimism, the body becomes inert, the world becomes just the earth, the human disintegrates into the non-human, ceremony dissolves into cerements, and the creations of civilization get reclaimed by the landscape—no longer that stable, passive background of idylls, but that dynamic, gloomy, encroaching force that leaves nothing in its wake but the ruin and the rune. This is the world of Emily Brontë, who, when she was twenty-four, followed her sister Charlotte to Belgium in order to practice her French so that she could teach it back home in England. Homesick and miserable, and annoyed at the rigid pedantry of her instructor Constantin Héger, her mind would wander to the pessimistic realm of insects, and she wrote as one of her academic exercises a brief essay in French called "The Butterfly," which begins with the following sprawling sentence:

In one of those moods that everyone falls into sometimes, when the world of the imagination suffers a winter that blights its vegetation; when the light of life

> seems to go out and existence becomes a barren desert where we wander, exposed to all the tempests that blow under heaven, without hope of rest or shelter—in one of those black humors, I was walking one evening at the edge of a forest.[123]

In this mood that makes her feel that, "All appeared happy, but for me," she describes how she came across an ugly caterpillar, using it as the pretext to pose her pessimistic theodicy, asking, "Why was it created, and why was man created? He torments, he kills, he devours; he suffers, dies, is devoured—there you have his whole story." The universe appears to her as a "vast machine constructed only to produce evil," and she "almost doubted the goodness of God, in not annihilating man on the day he first sinned." She wishes that the "world should have been destroyed" in the same way that she crushes the caterpillar.[124]

The essay takes a turn, though, when she notices a beautiful butterfly, which she interprets as an optimistic "symbol of the world to come," restoring her vision of God as presiding over "an eternal empire of happiness and glory." Pessimism, it would seem, is just a bad mood and a matter of time—in the long run, happiness, justice, and mercy will win out. Janis McLarren Caldwell seems to dismiss the first part of this essay as "hyperbolic, plunging into the depths of pessimism," while noting that these depths "are matched by the heights of an apocalyptic prophecy of the justice to come."[125]

Are they quite "matched" though? Does the end of this essay ring as equally true, or at least as equally convincing, as the insights that had preceded it? Does it even match the tone of anything else she had ever written? Or was this just a conventional, Victorian way to wrap up this academic exercise? Either way, it impressed her stern teacher, who believed that she ought to become a philosopher, writing that she has "a head for logic, and a capability of argument, unusual in a man, and rare indeed in a woman."[126] Her intellectual sights, however, were set far beyond logic and philosophy, though, stretching to the heights of what only a pessimistic genre could allow her to work out.

Two months after writing this essay, she returned home to England, never to travel again in her life. It seems as though the solution to the problem she had posed in her essay was too facile and needed to be discarded. She sat instead with the "inexplicable problem" of nature, which

> exists on a principle of destruction. Every being must be the tireless instrument of death to others, or itself must cease to live, yet nonetheless we celebrate the day of our birth, and we praise God for having entered such a world.[127]

What if she were to envision a world in which we do not celebrate the day of our birth, and we do not praise God for having entered such a world? In this vision, the ominous, hazy contours of *Wuthering Heights* begin to take shape, a world in which the characters curse God and reject even the idea of heaven, a world in which young Cathy cannot properly celebrate her birthday because it also marks the day her mother died, and in which Heathcliff does not even have a known birthday to celebrate.

In this world, everything exists on the same principle of destruction as it does in "The Butterfly," but with no hope for redemption or even relief, or much of anything at all. Every being is the "tireless instrument of death to others," and yet the essence of their being is called into question. Are they humans? Ghosts? Vampires? To Virginia Woolf, these characters are less individuated beings as primal forces. Woolf argues that Brontë "could tear up all that we know human beings by, and fill these unrecognizable transparences with such a gust of life that they transcend reality."[128] Could these characters just be extensions of nature itself working out its "inexplicable problem" of eternal destruction? Maybe this is why half of the characters have names that belong to the landscape and the natural world, like Hindley, Hareton, and of course, Heathcliff—names that function as reminders that we will all be reclaimed by the earth.

Even "Earnshaw" belongs to this category, its etymology reminiscent of the scene that Brontë sketches in her first sentence of "The Butterfly," where she identifies the confluence of her bad mood with her location at the edge of a forest. "Shaw" comes from the Old English *sceaga*, a dweller by a forest, and the prefix "Earn" ominously foreshadows the cruel circulation of capital, debt, and primogeniture that drives much of the conflict in the novel. It is by the edge of the forest in "The Butterfly" where Brontë contemplates "the barren desert" of existence, "where we wander, exposed to all the tempests that blow under heaven, without hope of rest or shelter." This is the landscape of the moors, populated by figures like Heathcliff, who is described as less of a human than he is, in Catherine's own words, "an arid wilderness of furze and whinstone."[129]

The haze and the contours of this novel never quite settle. Everything is violently thrown into motion, buffeted by the winds of the "tempests that blow under heaven," a heaven that the characters reject. Even their names and identities aren't stable, as though they cannot be contained in a book. It is only when Lockwood opens the books belonging to Catherine, who had inscribed her name in three different ways on the ledge—Catherine Earnshaw, Catherine Linton, Catherine Heathcliff—that her apparition appears at the window, as though having escaped from the books themselves. These books were not so much objects of passive reading to her as they were of active writing. She kept a diary in the blank spaces between the printed lines of text, filling "every morsel of blank that the printer had left" so that each page paradoxically gets erased under the excess of her own pen's ink.[130]

40   *Chapter 2*

Catherine's identity exceeds legibility, gesturing to what lies both outside the text and outside Lockwood's window, where her apparition calls to be let in.

Terrified of the ghost, Lockwood piles up the books against the window to prevent her from coming in, suggesting an antagonism between Catherine and books themselves. Throughout her life, she vowed that she "hated a good book," and Nelly says that "she never endeavored to divert herself with reading."[131] She views books with contempt, as objects that are worthy only of being vandalized, and she has no respect for those who hide behind them. On her deathbed, she tells her husband, "I don't want you, Edgar; I'm past wanting you. Return to your books. I'm glad you possess a consolation, for all you had in me is gone."[132] The feckless consolation of books from the Boethian tradition is devoid of meaning in Catherine's pessimistic universe, a universe in which Heathcliff, too, rages against any association with books. Disgusted with how Isabella pictured "in me a hero of romance, and expecting unlimited indulgences from my chivalrous devotion," Heathcliff carries out his most sadistic cruelty and violent abuse against her.[133] Both Heathcliff and Catherine defy description, and almost even being named or located altogether. By the end of the novel, are they buried underground, or do they still roam the moors? What names do they even go by, especially since Catherine exclaims at the climax, "Nelly, I *am* Heathcliff"?[134]

Maybe it is out of cruelty in return that Nelly, who prides herself on being an avid reader of books, tells their story as though it were a novel, to be locked in by Lockwood's frame narrative. And maybe when Catherine's ghost begs to be let in, she is also simultaneously struggling to be let out of the narrative that traps her. This nightmarish disorientation is reflected in the vertigo she recounts of a dream in which she had once inhabited heaven, but

> heaven did not seem to be my home; and I broke my heart with weeping to come back to earth; and the angels were so angry that they flung me out, into the middle of the heath on the top of Wuthering Heights; where I was sobbing for joy.[135]

She sobs for joy even as she is plunged into the depths of despair, imagining the hellish landscape of Wuthering Heights as occupying a space higher than heaven itself.

In the dream logic of this novel, Catherine does not inhabit spaces; rather, spaces seem to inhabit her. "Heath" is just shorthand for "Heathcliff," mapping out the topology of her intense desire that only seems to be fulfilled in death, buried in a "corner of the kirkyard, where the wall is so low that heath . . . [has] climbed over it from the moor," reclaiming her body in an erotic embrace.[136] Sandra M. Gilbert and Susan Gubar point out how readers often miss the fact that Catherine does not technically "*go* to the Grange when she is twelve years old. On the contrary, the Grange seizes her and 'holds [her] fast,' a metaphoric action which emphasizes the turbulent and inexorable nature of the psychosexual *rites de passage Wuthering Heights* describes."[137] Her experience in the interior of the Linton household, with all of its books and culture, tears her away from the outdoor space of Wuthering Heights, not so much a wilderness as a wildness that defines Catherine's own being. Removed from both heath and Heathcliff, she is torn away from herself.

In the same way that Brontë herself seemed to force an optimistic and uncharacteristically clichéd ending to "The Butterfly," Catherine seems to awkwardly recite prescribed, bookish answers as to why she is going to marry Edgar Linton—he is "handsome and pleasant to be with," he is "young and cheerful," "he will be rich"—but she cannot help the "unusual gloom" at resigning herself to this fate.[138] Edgar may have all of these qualities, but she admits that Heathcliff is "more myself than I am. Whatever our souls are made of, his and mine are the same, and Linton's is as different as a moonbeam from lightning, or frost from fire."[139]

If there is any ghost that haunts this novel, it is Plato's. *Wuthering Heights* can be read as a palimpsest of *Symposium*, scrawled in the empty space between the lines of text in order to draw out the pessimism inherent in its vision of eros as an ontological split. Here, though, eros is no consolation—it is pure torment. And if Linton is compared with a moonbeam, then Catherine associates Heathcliff with lightning, presumably Zeus's weapon that had split us apart and turned us into the creatures that we are now. Lightning is just a cruel reminder of that trauma, which is perhaps why one of Heathcliff's most frequent dialogue tags is "thundered."[140] As it so happens, the name "Brontë" also means "thunder" in Greek, and the thunder and lightning so thoroughly reverberate throughout the work that the other Brontë—Charlotte—wrote in the preface of the second edition of *Wuthering Heights* that, "in its storm-heated and electrical atmosphere, we seem at times to breathe lightning."[141]

Heathcliff overhears the first part of Catherine's conversation with Nelly, in which she explains why she will marry Edgar, and that marrying Heathcliff instead would "degrade" her, but most likely leaves before she confesses how deeply, how ferociously, how even frighteningly in love she is with Heathcliff to the point that she can only identify herself in and through him.[142] He vanishes into the night, where "the clouds appeared inclined to thunder," as though he dissolves into the atmosphere and becomes it, re-creating the primordial scene from Plato's *Symposium*.[143] As though it were too painful to admit that he is the victim of the thunderbolt, he becomes the masochistic weapon itself, like the weapon Catherine had requested from her father before he had set out to Liverpool. She wanted a whip, and her father returned with Heathcliff instead.

In the various reversals of this novel, the masochism ends up expressing itself as sadism. Heathcliff returns to Wuthering Heights a gentleman, with all the riches and good looks that were once ascribed to Edgar, and he rubs it in her face now that she's locked into her loveless marriage. Each of them hurts the other by inflicting psychological and physical abuse on Isabella as a proxy for their jealous love. And after both Catherine and Isabella die, Heathcliff takes out his revenge on the next generation of young Cathy, Hareton, and Linton, who all haunt him in the ways that they remind him of Catherine. Both Cathy and Hareton have the same eyes as Catherine, so when they eventually fall in love at the end of the novel, it is as though two halves of one self are peering into a mirror, and what they see is not just the self that they identify with, but the ghost of the previous generation. Maybe this is one possible way to interpret what Cathy's mother meant when she said that Heathcliff was not just her self, but "more" than herself. Identity is something that is always more than itself, something that cannot be contained, that carries the ghosts of what had preceded it.

There is the suggestion of a closed loop of misery that heightens with every cycle, with every passing generation, the pain of that traumatic split inherited in the blood of the progenitors who are descended from these original lovers. Everyone is just a fragment torn off from an original whole, including even Lockwood, who interrupts his own narrative to say, "No, I'm running on too fast—I bestow my own attributes over-liberally on [Heathcliff]."[144] Like Catherine, he identifies with Heathcliff, and even thinks that, "Mr. Heathcliff and I are such a suitable pair to divide the desolation between us."[145] Are they really such a "suitable pair"? Hardly, it seems, as Heathcliff rebuffs him with a short temper. Lockwood may be the writer of Heathcliff's tale, as told to him by Nelly (in a comparable way to Socrates telling Diotima's story, as well as the larger frame narrative, in *Symposium*), but it doesn't mean that he is a good reader. Caldwell argues that, "Lockwood has it exactly backwards: it is Lockwood who wishes to bestow Heathcliff's attributes on himself."[146] Martha Nussbaum interprets Lockwood as more of a double of Catherine than of Heathcliff, since both of them could not bring themselves to articulate their love directly to their lovers before their lovers had abandoned them.[147]

This is exactly why Lockwood finds himself in Wuthering Heights. Quoting Viola from *Twelfth Night* as a way of figuratively hiding behind books before he literally hides behind them at the sight of Catherine's ghost, Lockwood says that he

> "never told my love" vocally; still, if looks have language, the merest idiot might have guessed I was over head and ears: she understood me at last, and looked a return—the sweetest of all imaginable looks. And what did I do? I confess it with shame—shrunk icily into myself, like a snail; at every glance retired

colder and farther; till, finally, the poor innocent was led to doubt her own senses, and, overwhelmed with confusion at her supposed mistake, persuaded her mamma to decamp.[148]

As a result of this missed opportunity to fulfill his erotic desire, he decides to flee to the countryside to console himself, where he ends up in the "perfect misanthropist's heaven" of Wuthering Heights.[149]

It is certainly not a heaven for everyone, but for anyone like Catherine—someone so deeply committed to her pessimism that she would choose the misery of Wuthering Heights over anything that any other conception of heaven could offer—it is perfect. Is it perfect for Lockwood, though, or is he just trying to convince himself? Is he really as much of a misanthropist as someone like Catherine or Heathcliff? When he first meets Heathcliff, he blurts out, "many could not imagine the existence of a happiness in a life of such complete exile from the world as you spend, Mr. Heathcliff." Heathcliff acknowledges this comment only "with an almost diabolical sneer."[150] This is a heaven of hell, a heaven that excludes happiness, that instead thrives in a sadomasochistic way on a misery that festers on itself through the generations.

Despite Heathcliff's aloofness, he still seems to have a hold of Lockwood. In the instability of names and their meanings, Heathcliff is actually the one who locks people, binding them to him. Lockwood cannot lock anything or anyone down. And he is not as rigid and wooden as his name suggests. Under Heathcliff's spell, so it seems, his identity is fluid, malleable, and shape-shifting. When he looks out the window and sees Catherine's ghost in anguish, maybe the window functions as more of a mirror because it is really his own anguish that he encounters. As if he were trapped in a nightmare, the more he tries to escape from his pain, the more he ends up confronting it, until he finally gives in to an obsession that hardly even seems to be his own, but rather an external force that takes over him, a force belonging to the "atmospheric tumult" that he provides as a definition of "wuthering."[151]

Lockwood gives in to the obsession, to the masochistic indulgence, finding his own story reiterated in Catherine's, and this identification underscores the erotic bond he feels for her, attracted to the "brilliant eyes" in her portrait hanging in Thrushcross Grange.[152] In this concatenation of desire, perhaps he is erotically attracted to Heathcliff, as well, since both Heathcliff and Catherine are two halves of the same self, and he fantasizes about absorbing Heathcliff's identity into his own. And through his desire for—and identification with—both Catherine and Heathcliff, he ultimately finds himself longing for young Cathy, who has the same eyes that had originally sparked his erotic desire for her mother.

Like Heathcliff, Lockwood leaves Wuthering Heights and Thrushcross Grange for a while, only to return in the clichéd hope that his absence would have made Cathy's heart grow fonder. But this endeavor fails. He describes himself in terms that he had once described her mother, as an "unwelcome apparition."[153] Like the night that Heathcliff vanishes from Wuthering Heights after hearing of Catherine's engagement to Edgar, Lockwood too "vanished"—now for the last time—in a "dark evening threatening thunder."[154] The infernal cycle ostensibly goes on for eternity, dissolving characters into each other, into the atmosphere, into the landscape, dragging them to the vertiginous depths of the Heights.

BETWEEN THE NOVEL AND THE SIGH

How does one classify *Wuthering Heights*? It is rooted in what can otherwise be called the Platonic novel, using as its blueprint Plato's *Symposium*. Despite the mythologization of Emily Brontë, largely in part due to her sister Charlotte's assertion that neither of her sisters were "learned" and "had no thought of filling their pitchers at the well-spring of other minds," writing instead "from the impulse of nature, the dictates of intuition," it is clear, as Nussbaum demonstrates, that she was an "extremely learned classical scholar" who would have encountered this Platonic story in some way.[155] There are also overwhelming traces of medieval Romance here, like the apocalyptic love between Tristan and Isolde—a love that rejects heaven, a love that instead creates its own heaven that looks more like a hell, destroying everything in its path. Even the doubling of Isolde's name in Isolde the Fair and Isolde of the White Hands seems to be transcribed to almost every name in *Wuthering Heights*.

It can also be read as a fairy tale of sorts. Lockwood even refers to Cathy as a "beneficent fairy" when he first sees her.[156] She, for her part, claims to have "progressed in the Black Art" of witchcraft instead.[157] When she first meets Hareton, she tells him, "I want to see where the goblin hunter rises in the marsh, and to hear about the *fairishes*, as you call them."[158] The basis of their relationship seems to be a fairy tale, albeit a dark one, and this fairy tale is one that Lockwood resents because he is excluded from it. "What a realization of something more romantic than a fairy tale it would have been," he says to himself, "for Mrs. Linton Heathcliff, had she and I struck up an attachment, as her good nurse desired, and migrated together into the stirring atmosphere of the town!"[159]

To Lockwood, this is a failed fairy tale. Perhaps it is no coincidence why he cites *King Lear*, that other fairy tale of failure, at the opening of the narrative, when he fends off the Cerberus-like dogs at what seems like the gates of hell in Wuthering Heights, vowing vengeance against them that "smacked of King Lear."[160] Lear vows that he "will do such things— / What they are, yet I know not, but they shall be / The terrors of the earth."[161] If there is any protagonist in *Wuthering Heights*, it would be these "terrors of the earth," summoned not only by Lockwood but also by Heathcliff and Catherine. Gilbert and Gubar identify *Wuthering Heights* as a fairy tale to the extent that *King Lear* is one, too. The events of the plot are set into motion when the patriarch, "half-consciously beginning to prepare for death," asks "his ritual questions" to his children, whose answers "reveal their true selves."[162] Following the rule of threes in fairy tales, Earnshaw returns with the "gypsy brat" he had found on his travels to join his two other children, giving him the name of his dead son, "Heathcliff." Perhaps, Gilbert and Gubar suggest, this new Heathcliff is "even the true oldest son, as if he were a reincarnation of the lost child."[163] Indeed, almost every character here seems to be a spectral double of someone dead, occupying an uncanny, liminal space between death and life. Maybe he is an undead changeling who exists to wreak havoc on the Earnshaw household before eventually destroying the Linton household as well, challenging the rights of primogeniture and abusing his way to tyrannical power.

Wuthering Heights serves as a microcosm of the history of the novel, moving from the Platonic dialogue (or Platonic novel) to the medieval Romance and the fairy tale, absorbing and surpassing these genres in order to create something new. Even the earliest critics, most of whom panned the novel as demonic and even disgusting, could not avoid admitting how stunningly original it is, even as it draws so heavily from literary tradition. In an unsigned review from *Britannia* in 1848, the critic marvels at how this novel is "so new, so wildly grotesque, so entirely without art," and another critic advised, "We strongly recommend all our readers who love novelty to get this story, for we can promise that they will never have read anything like it before."[164]

Is this work of novelty actually a novel, though? If Lukács defines the genre of the novel as "the epic of a world that has been abandoned by God," then surely this seems to qualify as a novel.[165] But is it accurate to say that the world in *Wuthering Heights* has been abandoned by God, or that God and his heaven have been abandoned by the world, or at least by Catherine and Heathcliff, who constitute the entirety of each other's worlds? Would that be a novel in reverse, then? What if the abandonment is mutual? Northrop Frye is adamant that it is "a different form of prose fiction from the novel, a form which we shall here call the romance." One of the key differences between novel and romance for him is that, in romance, "something nihilistic and untamable is likely to keep breaking out of [the author's] pages."[166] Gilbert and Gubar agree that it is "maybe not a novel at all, but instead an extended exemplum, or a 'prosified' verse drama."[167] Citing Leo Bersani's concept of "ontological slipperiness," in which everyone is not only related but, "in a sense, repeated in everyone else," as if the novel were about "the danger of being haunted by alien versions of the self," they identify it as a "metaphysical romance."[168]

These are convincing arguments, although they seem to ignore Heathcliff himself, who so explicitly and violently opposes being characterized as a "hero of romance."[169] It is a fairy tale, but a failed one. It carries the traces of the Platonic dialogues, but it adamantly rejects the rational in favor of the irrational, Platonic equanimity in favor of fervid passion. Whatever genre it seems to fall under, it ultimately rejects, and anyone who claims to identify it seems to fall into the same trap as Lockwood, whose identification ends up being a misidentification. It is as though the characters, if not the entire work itself, express an anxiety of being categorized, hemmed in, even named. Lockwood's withdrawal from language, unable to articulate his love for the woman he was pursuing, is perhaps symptomatic of the paradoxical condition of the work at large, using language to simultaneously withdraw from it, echoed also in Catherine failing to tell Heathcliff directly how much she loves him before marrying Edgar. She is reduced to sighs that become more prominent on her deathbed and that finally linger around her grave when Heathcliff exhumes her: "it seemed that I heard a sigh from some one above, close at the edge of the grave, and bending down," he recalls. As he continues digging, "There was another sigh, close at my ear. . . . I felt that Cathy was there, not under me, but on the earth."[170] Upon hearing of Catherine's death, even her nemesis Isabella "sighed, for it seemed as if all joy had vanished from the world, never to be restored."[171]

These sighs left a strong impression on the early critics of this work. In one review from 1851, the anonymous critic wrote, "We hear sighs and groans, look up on faded forms and weeping eyes, and turn from the spectacle with a painful conviction that sorrow, in some form or other, is the heritage of man."[172] In one sentence, this is a summary not only of *Wuthering Heights*, but of pessimism at large. Is it possible to conceive of the sigh itself as its own genre, as the genre of pessimism? Thacker defines pessimism itself as "the wavering, the hovering" between "the axiom and the sigh."[173] The definition of the human being: "the animal that sighs," dreaming of sighs "that eclipse living entirely."[174]

Maybe the sigh is pessimism's only axiom, revealing the abyss, the *Abgrund*, behind every *Grund*, or "foundation," in systematic thinking. It is an embodied rejection, an expulsion—but of nothing, of air. If inspiration is optimistic, then pessimism unmetaphors and reverses that process with the sigh—it *expires* in every sense of the term: it exhales, it turns sour, it marks death. Literature may be born with the cry, according to Cixous, but it ends with the sigh, and it is in this space of endings, of expirations and exhalations, that pessimism, in its resignation to the worst of lived experience, dwells. The expression of futility, the sigh is all that remains of the cry after it had run its course. Even Tolstoy's Ivan Ilyich, who screams continuously for three days, when all is said and done, dies in the "midst of a sigh."[175]

If pessimism is a preoccupation with the worst, Edgar in *King Lear* reminds us that, "The worst is not / So long as I can say 'This is the worst.'"[176] "The worst," then, lies beyond what can be said—in the nothingness that both defies and defines language. It is the asymptote that language can only gesture to, infinitely—perhaps even in infinite jest, occupying the space where language fails, where language frays, right before dissolving into silence. Stendhal invokes the sigh as a sign of his own pessimism, his own failure both at language and at silence, devoting an entire chapter of *Love* to these three sentences:

> I am trying extremely hard to be *dry*. My heart thinks it has so much to say, but I try to keep it quiet. I am continually beset by the fear that I may have expressed only a sigh when I thought I was stating a truth.[177]

In Nabokov's nightmarish vision of the worst, Lolita is silenced to the point that all she can express is a "hopeless sigh."[178] In the book Humbert gives her, Andersen's "The Little Mermaid," the mermaid herself, existing on the other side of language, "sighed deeply, for she did not know how to shed tears" when she realizes she will not wed the prince.[179] Disillusioned with her hopes in the world and in a future worth living for, with this sigh as her only expression, the mermaid ends up killing herself.

To the pessimist, the sigh does not just punctuate the end of existence but its primordial beginnings. It is the hollow echo at the core of our being that reminds us of our cosmic origins. Cioran speculates, "Pursuing the antecedents of a sigh can lead us to the moment before—as to the sixth day of Creation."[180] In this sigh, one hears the collapse of the absolute end with the absolute beginning, of the individual with the universal, of destruction with creation. In this way, one can make sense of how Barthes, in *A Lover's Discourse*, thinks of the disjointed lovers from Plato's *Symposium* in terms of their sighs: "the two halves of the androgyne sigh for each other, as if each breath, being incomplete, sought to mingle with the other."[181] This is the sigh that reverberates throughout Brontë's landscape, and Thomas Hardy's, too, in "the occasional heave of the wind" in *Tess of the D'Urbervilles*, which "became the sigh of some immense sad soul, coterminous with the universe in space, and with history in time."[182]

It was between sighing and whistling that Coleridge first coined the term "pessimism" in 1794, complaining to Robert Southey about his poetry and about a pretentious dinner conversation he had had to endure the night before with self-fashioned intellectuals. "I pronounce this a very sensible, apostrophical, metaphorical Rant," he writes.[183] He opens the letter in a way that seems almost like a translation of anything Nietzsche would write nearly a century later: "When I am unhappy, a sigh or a groan does not feel sufficient to relieve the oppression of my Heart—I give a long *whistle*—/ This by way of a detached Truth.—"[184] This is the same whistle of the protagonist in Kafka's "The Country Doctor," who "could not help a low whistle of surprise" upon seeing his patient, who tells him, "I have very little confidence in you."[185] This doctor runs away, "naked, exposed to the frost of this most unhappy of ages," unable to escape unhappiness itself.[186]

Despite its –ism, pessimism is much less a form of organized thought than it is a raw exposure to unhappiness, coming out as a sigh, a whistle, a rant, a "detached Truth," a Truth that endeavors to "connect nothing with nothing," as T. S. Eliot writes in *The Waste Land*.[187] But "Nothing will come of nothing," Lear reminds us. "Speak again."[188] And here, with just one axiom, pessimism already dwells in the space of "paradox, [which] is (paradoxically) a foundation. Pessimism—the philosophy that demonstrates that all philosophy is destined to fail (its first and final proof)."[189] Pessimism ultimately fails even at its own sigh, choosing instead to speak again and again, generating an insistent, repetitive quest for an authentic language to communicate our disappointment and disenchantment with this world, with each other, and with ourselves. This authentic discourse, according to Heidegger, resides in silence, opposed to the idle chatter that Coleridge ranted against, but even Heidegger cannot resist a baroque style to communicate this silence. The sigh just generates more sighs, and between them, language emerges, stutters, rambles, and ultimately fails.

Maybe the sigh is not stable enough to constitute its own genre, and neither is pessimism itself. Between the aphorism and the multivolume work, pessimism defies genre, and even though Coleridge may have coined the term in English, its existence arguably coincides with the earliest modes of expression itself in the form of the sigh, drawing attention to our inevitable shortcomings. Before the term was coined, we can look back to Leibniz, who first used the word *optimum* in his 1710 tract *Theodicy*, claiming that this is the best of all possible worlds. French writers then referred to his philosophy as *optimisme*, a word that Voltaire not only lampooned but even included in the subtitle of his novel *Candide, ou l'Optimisme* in 1759. But as Joshua Foa Dienstag notes, the word "*optimisme*" was admitted by the French Academy three years after the publication of *Candide*, while "*pessimisme*" was only admitted in 1878.[190]

It is worth noting that it was a novel that popularized ways of thinking against optimism, a pattern that, through the centuries, ultimately culminated in what Lukács published as the first theory of the novel, an explicitly pessimistic tract. But it was just six years after the publication of *Candide* that Diderot commissioned an entry in his *Encyclopedia* for "the novel." This entry was written out of spite for the popular French attitude against Samuel Richardson's novels.[191] The entry praises Richardson and identifies him as a model novelist. In 1762, Diderot had already written that, "history is often a bad novel, and . . . the novel, as you [Richardson] have made it, is a good history."[192] Diderot here transvalues the values of "good" and "bad," so that "good" is the designation of the art that most faithfully captures how "bad" people can be in history (that is, reality). The less optimistic this novelistic vision is, the more qualified it is as a "good" novel. And whatever it is he is doing, Richardson was conscious of creating a new "species" of writing just as much as Fielding claimed to be creating a new "kind" or "province."[193] It is arguably at this cultural moment in the eighteenth century that the word "novel" began to crystallize in the recognizable way we use it today.

After writing *Pamela*, Richardson despised the idea of a novel having a happy ending, thinking that it wasn't true to life. Railing against the idea of a happy ending, he wrote:

> It has been said in behalf of many modern fictitious pieces, in which authors have given success (and *happiness*, as it is called) to their heroes of vicious, if not of profligate, characters, that they have exhibited Human Nature as it *is*. Its corruption may, indeed, be exhibited in the faulty character; but need pictures of this be held out in books? Is not vice crowned with success, triumphant, and rewarded, and perhaps set off with wit and spirit, a dangerous representation? And is it not made even *more* dangerous by the hasty reformation, introduced, in contradiction to all probability, for the sake of patching up what is called a happy ending?[194]

This is the ultimate refutation to Socrates's anxiety with tragedy, which "shows us that just people may end up unhappy and unjust people happy."[195] This is not to make the absurd claim that all novels must avoid the happy ending. Jane Austen is the perfect example of how a novelist could pull that off without patronizing her readers. But what the novel does provide is a possible space to explore, with the most heightened specificity, an encyclopedic account of disappointment.

In *Sense and Sensibility*, Edward Ferrars wishes, "as well as everybody else, to be perfectly happy; but, like everybody else, it must be in my own way."[196] We can juxtapose this with the first sentence of *Anna Karenina*, which Tolstoy famously opens with, "All happy families are alike; each unhappy family is unhappy in its own way."[197] Both Austen and Tolstoy treat the issue of happiness—however seemingly different at first glance—with the same sensibility. Unhappiness is particular in a way that happiness is not. *Sense and Sensibility* ends with Edward's happiness; there is nothing more to say about it once the narrative has arrived at that point. The narrative builds up to marriage rather than focusing on the experience of married life. *Anna*

Karenina, on the contrary, begins with both marriage and a statement about happiness—or at least a single clause—and then recounts the journey into unhappiness for seven hundred pages.

Balzac arrives at the same conclusion in *Lost Souls* ("*Splendeurs et misères de courtisanes*"), where the narrator writes, "Happiness carries no story with it, and the storytellers of all lands have understood this so well that the phrase 'they were happy' is the conclusion to every love story."[198] This idea of happiness is so tedious to Balzac that he includes it in a chapter that glosses over four years of the relationship between Lucien and Esther in four pages—hardly anything in the grand scheme of his lengthy novel—but still entitles this chapter, "A Tedious Chapter, Explaining Four Years of Happiness." In this sense, the novel and pessimism share a family resemblance. Only unhappiness can make its particular demands on such a versatile form as the novel, a genre that is necessarily composed of particulars, of contingent details, articulating pain and suffering in a way that can stretch from the compactness of *The Sorrows of Young Werther* to the considerably longer *Anna Karenina* and even the multivolume *In Search of Lost Time*.

Unhappiness festers on details; the literature of happiness, however, perniciously ignores contingency and dwells in empty universal statements of advice, of truths that are supposedly universally acknowledged, but on closer inspection may not even be truths at all. Since the novel is that articulation of the "contingent world and the problematic individual . . . which mutually determine one another," according to Lukács, the novel is, even on the level of its form, fundamentally opposed to the literature of happiness, which inevitably falls flat with its dull, cringeworthy clichés that are marketed as wisdom to undiscerning readers.[199] Glossing Schopenhauer's comment that "Human life must be some kind of a mistake," Dienstag explains that, "The mistake consists in the poor fit between the aims that human beings share and the world in which they are settled to pursue those aims," which effectively just reiterates Lukács's definition of the novel.[200]

Eros is supposedly the consolation for this "mistake" of human life, at least according to Plato, but in this novelistic view of the world, eros just makes matters worse. "It is not an accident," writes Herbert Marcuse in *Eros and Civilization*, "that the great literature of Western civilization celebrates only the 'unhappy love,' that the Tristan myth has become its representative expression."[201] Eros "in a world of alienation . . . necessarily operate[s] as a destructive, fatal force—as the total negation of the principle which governs the repressive reality."[202] The contrast between the reality principle and the pleasure principle is the "fundamental antagonism between sex and social utility."[203] The modern novel, emerging out of capitalist forces as a commodity itself, is the expression that negotiates between these two incommensurable demands of modern life. Eros and civilization do not add up; they are at odds with each other. The narrative that takes this into account is a bleak one, one that undermines any notion of progress in civilization.

D. H. Lawrence had arrived at this conclusion decades earlier, at the same time that Lukács was writing his manifesto of pessimism in *The Theory of the Novel*. In his study of Thomas Hardy's pessimism, Lawrence wrote,

> It seems as if the history of humanity were divided into two epochs: the Epoch of the Law and the Epoch of Love. It seems as though humanity, during the time of its activity on earth, has made two great efforts: the effort to appreciate the Law and the effort to overcome the Law in Love. . . . What remains is to reconcile the two.[204]

His answer to this reconciliation is the novel. And when he addresses how "the real stuff of tragedy" in Hardy is "the Heath," and "the primitive, primal earth, where the instinctive life heaves up," he may as well also be writing about Brontë.[205] To this extent, then, *Wuthering Heights* is not an anomalous work of fiction that falls outside of the category of the novel. On the contrary, it most clearly exemplifies and encapsulates the history of the novel as a genre that developed in response to the Platonic dialogue, the medieval Romance, and the fairy tale, a pattern that the history of the novel largely repeats.

NOTES

1. Nussbaum, "Fictions of the Soul," 156.
2. Ludwig Wittgenstein, *Philosophical Investigations*, trans. G. E. M. Anscombe, P. M. S. Hacker, and Joachim Schulte (London: Wiley-Blackwell, 2009), 106.
3. Plato, *Symposium*, 191C: 20.
4. Plato, *Phaedrus*, 230C: 6.
5. Plato, *Phaedrus*, 259B-C: 52.
6. Héléne Cixous, "Ay Yay! The Shout of Literature" (Keynote Address: Re-Thinking World Literature Conference, New York University, New York, September 20, 2013).
7. Hildegard of Bingen, *Holistic Healing*, trans. Manfred Pawlik, Patrick Madigan, and John Kulas, ed. Mary Palmquist and John Kulas (Collegeville, PA: Liturgical Press, 1994), 60.
8. William Faulkner, *As I Lay Dying* (New York: Vintage Books, 1985), 172.
9. Faulkner, *As I Lay Dying*, 175; 173.
10. Faulkner, *As I Lay Dying*, 172.
11. Faulkner, *As I Lay Dying*, 171.
12. Clarice Lispector, *The Passion According to G.H*, trans. Idra Novey (New York: New Directions, 2012), 58.
13. Cixous, "Ay Yay! The Cry of Literature," in *Ways of Re-Thinking Literature*, ed. Tom Bishop and Donatien Grau (London: Routledge, 2018), 201; Thomas

Pynchon, *Gravity's Rainbow* (New York: Penguin Books, 2006), 3; William Faulkner, *The Sound and the Fury*, 2nd ed. (New York: W. W. Norton, 1994), 179.

14. Thomas Mann, *Doctor Faustus: The Life of the German Composer Adrian Leverkühn as Told by a Friend*, trans. John E. Woods (New York: Vintage Books, 1999), 527; Johann Wolfgang von Goethe, *Faust*, original German and a translation by Walter Kaufmann (New York: Anchor Books, 1963), I.354: 92).

15. Joseph Conrad, *Heart of Darkness* (New York: W. W. Norton, 1988), 41; 47.

16. Conrad, *Heart of Darkness*, 46.

17. For shorthand, I will follow the custom of referring to the work as the *Recherche* (from the French title *À la recherche du temps perdu*), following the standard practice of Proust scholars.

18. Samuel Beckett, *Proust* (New York: Grove Press, 1961), 31.

19. Marcel Proust, *The Fugitive*, in *The Captive and the Fugitive*, ed. William C. Carter, trans. C. K. Scott Moncrieff (New Haven, CT: Yale University Press, 2023), 590.

20. Proust, *Time Regained*, trans. Andreas Mayor and Terence Kilmartin, revised by D. J. Enright (New York: Modern Library, 2003), 514.

21. Proust, *The Captive*, in *The Captive and the Fugitive*, ed. William C. Carter, trans. C. K. Scott Moncrieff (New Haven, CT: Yale University Press, 2023), 440.

22. Proust, *The Captive*, 441.

23. William C. Carter, *The Proustian Quest* (New York: New York University Press, 1992), 191.

24. Proust, *Time Regained*, 99.

25. Proust, *Time Regained*, 99.

26. Proust, *Time Regained*, 243.

27. Proust, *Time Regained*, 323.

28. Proust, *Time Regained*, 90.

29. Proust, *In the Shadow of Young Girls in Flower*, ed. William C. Carter, trans. C. K. Scott Moncrieff (New Haven, CT: Yale University Press, 2015), 450.

30. Proust, *Sodom and Gomorrah*, ed. William C. Carter, trans. C. K. Scott Moncrieff (New Haven, CT: Yale University Press, 2021), 8–9.

31. Proust, *Time Regained*, 339–340.

32. Proust, *Sodom and Gomorrah*, 9.

33. Proust, *In the Shadow of Young Girls in Flower*, 430.

34. Proust, *Swann's Way*, trans. Lydia Davis (New York: Viking Press, 2002), 243.

35. Proust, *Swann's Way*, 365; 361.

36. Gilles Deleuze, *Proust and Signs: The Complete Text*, trans. Richard Howard (Minneapolis, MN: University of Minnesota Press, 2000), 100.

37. Deleuze, *Proust and Signs*, 111.

38. Proust, *The Captive,* 74–75.

39. Deleuze, *Proust and Signs*, 181–182.

40. Deleuze, *Proust and Signs*, 182.

41. Edmund White, *Marcel Proust* (New York: Viking Press, 1999), 3–4; Walter Benjamin, "The Image of Proust," in *Illuminations*, trans. Harry Zohn, ed. Hannah Arendt (New York: Schocken, 1968), 208.

42. Proust, *Swann's Way*, 10.
43. Proust, *Swann's Way*, 126.
44. Honoré de Balzac, *Père Goriot*, translated Burton Raffel, ed. Peter Brooks (New York: W. W. Norton, 1994), 217.
45. Balzac, *Lost Souls*, trans. Raymond N. MacKenzie (Minneapolis, MN: University of Minnesota Press, 2020), 44.
46. Balzac, *Lost Illusions*, trans. Raymond N. MacKenzie (Minneapolis, MN: University of Minnesota Press, 2020), 97.
47. Balzac, *Lost Illusions*, 222.
48. Balzac, *Lost Illusions*, 206.
49. Balzac, *Lost Illusions*, 554.
50. Giovanni Pontano, *Lapham's Quarterly* XII, no. 3 (Summer 2019): 51.
51. Shakespeare, *Hamlet* (New York: Folger, 1992), 2.2.197, 4.3.23.
52. Shakespeare, *King Lear* (New York: Penguin Books, 1998), 4.1.36–37.
53. Fyodor Dostoevsky, *Notes from Underground*, trans. Richard Pevear and Larissa Volokhonsky (New York: Vintage Books, 1993), 52.
54. Mary Shelley, *Frankenstein* (New York: W. W. Norton, 1996), 65.
55. Mann, *The Magic Mountain*, trans. John E. Woods (New York: Vintage Books, 1996), 702.
56. Richard Yates, *Revolutionary Road* (New York: Vintage Books, 2008), 126.
57. Dostoevsky, *Crime and Punishment*, trans. Jessie Coulson (Oxford: Oxford University Press, 1981), 399; 402.
58. Dostoevsky, *Crime and Punishment*, 277.
59. Dostoevsky, *Crime and Punishment*, 400.
60. Shakespeare, *Richard III* (New York: Folger, 1996), 1.3.256.
61. Bram Stoker, *Dracula* (New York: W. W. Norton, 1997), 69.
62. Stoker, *Dracula*, 69.
63. Nabokov, *Lolita*, 67.
64. Mann, *Doctor Faustus*, 151.
65. Fyodor Dostoevsky, *Brothers Karamazov*, trans. Richard Pevear and Larissa Volokhonsky (New York: Farrar, Straus & Giroux, 2002), 108.
66. Dostoevsky, *Brothers Karamazov*, 109.
67. Charles Dickens, *Great Expectations* (London: Penguin Books, 1996), 84.
68. Clarice Lispector, *The Passion According to G.H.*, trans. Idra Novey (New York: New Directions, 2012), 73.
69. Lispector, *Passion According to G.H*, 83; 91.
70. Lispector, *Passion According to G.H*, 85.
71. Lispector, *Passion According to G.H*, 4.
72. Plato, *Symposium*, 191A: 20.
73. Roland Barthes, *A Lover's Discourse: Fragments*, trans. Richard Howard (New York: Hill and Wang, 1979), 39.
74. Plato, *Symposium*, 190D: 19–20.
75. Herman Melville, *Moby-Dick, or, the Whale* (New York: Modern Library, 2000), 804.
76. Melville, *Moby-Dick,* 242.

77. Melville, *Moby-Dick,* 282, 263.

78. In describing the sublime, indefinite ambiguity of the White Whale, which amounts to a sketch of pessimism, Ishmael asks,

> Is it that by its indefiniteness it shadows forth the heartless voids and immensities of the universe, and thus stabs us from behind with the thought of annihilation, when beholding the white depths of the milky way? Or is it, that as in essence whiteness is not so much a color as the visible absence of color, and at the same time the concrete of all colors; is it for these reasons that there is such a dumb blankness, full of meaning, in a wide landscape of snows—a colorless, all-color of atheism from which we shrink? (Melville, *Moby-Dick,* 282)

79. The Brothers Grimm, "Rumpelstiltskin," in *The Annotated Brothers Grimm*, ed. and trans. Maria Tatar (New York: W. W. Norton, 2004), 262.

80. Robyn Marasco, *The Highway of Despair: Critical Theory after Hegel* (New York: Columbia University Press, 2015), 28.

81. G. W. F. Hegel, *Phenomenology of Spirit*, trans. A. V. Miller (Oxford: Oxford University Press, 1977), 126.

82. "Pessimism," https://www.etymonline.com/word/pessimism.

83. Thomas Ligotti, *Conspiracy Against the Human Race: A Contrivance of Horror* (New York: Penguin Books, 2018), 25.

84. Sylvia Plath, *The Bell Jar* (New York: Harper Perennial, 2006), 97.

85. Schopenhauer, *World as Will and Representation,* II: 584 (emphasis added). Maurice Blanchot also sees in this etymology a fundamental pessimism:

> Passivity, passion, past, *pas* (both negation and step—the trace or movement of an advance): this semantic play provides us with a slippage of meaning, but not with anything to which we could entrust ourselves, not with anything like an answer that would satisfy us. (*The Writing of the Disaster*, trans. Ann Smock [Lincoln, NE: University of Nebraska Press, 1995], 16–17)

86. Milan Kundera, *Art of the Novel*, trans. Linda Asher (New York: Harper & Row, 1988), 19.

87. Dostoevsky, *Brothers Karamazov*, 484.

88. Plato, *Republic*, 484B: 163.

89. Aristotle, *Metaphysics*, in *The Basic Works of Aristotle*, ed. Richard McKeon, trans. W. D. Ross (New York: Modern Library, 2001), A1.980a21: 689.

90. Martin Heidegger, *Parmenides*, trans. André Schuwer and Richard Rojcewicz (Bloomington, IN: Indiana University Press, 1998), 84.

91. Byung-Chul Han, *In the Swarm: Digital Prospects*, trans. Erik Butler (Cambridge, MA: Massachusetts Institute of Technology Press, 2017), 38.

92. Mann, *Buddenbrooks: The Decline of a Family,* trans. John E. Woods (New York: Vintage Books, 1993), 631.

93. Mann, *Buddenbrooks,* 725.

94. Mann, *Buddenbrooks,* 727 (emphasis added). Mazzoni argues persuasively that this episode in the novel illustrates Heidegger's process of attaining a brief moment of *Eigentlichkeit* [authenticity] before slipping back into the world of *das Man* [the 'they'] (*Theory of the Novel,* 372). In another part of the novel, Thomas,

now speaking from the point of view of *das Man*, tells his brother Christian, "You do not belong just to yourself alone" (Mann, *Buddenbrooks,* 314). Their father also has a similar message for their sister Tony, writing to her in a letter:

> We are not born, my dear daughter, to pursue our own small personal happiness, for we are not separate, independent, self-subsisting individuals, but links in a chain; and it is inconceivable that we would be what we are without those who have preceded us and shown us the path that they themselves have scrupulously trod, looking neither to the left nor to the right, but, rather, following a venerable and trustworthy tradition. (144)

While I fully agree with this analysis, it is important to note that Mann himself would have been furious with the comparison of his literature to Heidegger's philosophy.

95. Mann, *Doctor Faustus,* 30.
96. Mann, *Doctor Faustus,* 109.
97. Mann, *Doctor Faustus,* 534.
98. Mann, *Death in Venice,* trans. Michael Henry Heim (New York: Ecco, 2004), 13.
99. Mann, *Death in Venice,* 74.
100. Mann, *Death in Venice,* 95.
101. Mann, *Death in Venice,* 141–142.
102. Mann, *Der Tod in Venedig und andere Erzählungen* (Frankfurt: Fischer Taschenbuch Verlag, 1986), 68.
103. Kierkegaard, *Either/Or,* ed. and trans. Howard V. Hong and Edna V. Hong (Princeton, NJ: Princeton University Press, 1987), I: 36.
104. Brothers Grimm, "Cinderella," in *The Annotated Brothers Grimm,* trans. and ed. Maria Tatar (New York: W. W. Norton, 2004), 126.
105. Grimm, "Cinderella," 127.
106. Cyrus Hamlin, in an explanatory note to Goethe's *Faust: A Tragedy,* trans. Walter Arndt., ed. Cyrus Hamlin (New York: W. W. Norton, 2001), 108 n.1.
107. Grimm, "Snow White," in *The Annotated Brothers Grimm,* trans. and ed. Maria Tatar (New York: W. W. Norton, 2004), 255.
108. Qtd. in "E. M. Cioran on Beckett, trans. Thomas Cousineau," *The Beckett Circle: The Newsletter of the Samuel Beckett Society* 28, no. 1 (Spring 2005): 5, http://citeseerx.ist.psu.edu/viewdoc/download?doi=10.1.1.732.4610&rep=rep1&type=pdf
109. Cioran, *A Short History of Decay,* 178.
110. Dostoevsky, *Notes from Underground,* 29.
111. Conrad, *Heart of Darkness,* 64.
112. Conrad, *Heart of Darkness,* 65.
113. Conrad, *Heart of Darkness,* 65.
114. Faulkner, *The Sound and the Fury,* 13.
115. Daniel Wright, "Thomas Hardy's Groundwork," *PMLA* 134, no. 5 (October 2019): 1032.
116. Heidegger, "Letter on Humanism," in *Basic Writings,* ed. David Farrell Krell (London: HarperPerennial, 2008), 228.
117. Heidegger, "Letter on Humanism," 228.
118. Cioran, *A Short History of Decay,* 51–52.

119. Conrad, *Heart of Darkness*, 69.
120. Samuel Beckett, *Endgame* (New York: Grove Press, 2009), 46.
121. Caroline Bologna, "Why the Phrase 'Pull Yourself up by Your Bootstraps' is Nonsense," *The Huffington Post,* September 8, 2018, https://www.huffpost.com/entry/pull-yourself-up-by-your-bootstraps-nonsense_n_5b1ed024e4b0bbb7a0e037d4?guccounter=1.
122. Emily Brontë, *Wuthering Heights,* ed. Alexandra Lewis (New York: W. W. Norton, 2019), 90.
123. Brontë, "The Butterfly," in *Wuthering Heights*, ed. Alexandra Lewis (New York: W. W. Norton, 2019), 265.
124. Brontë, "The Butterfly," 265–266.
125. Janis McLarren Caldwell, "*Wuthering Heights* and Domestic Medicine: The Child's Body and the Book," in *Wuthering Heights*, ed. Alexandra Lewis (New York: W. W. Norton, 2019), 431.
126. Qtd. in Martha C. Nussbaum, "The Romantic Ascent: Emily Brontë," in *Wuthering Heights,* ed. Alexandra Lewis (New York: W. W. Norton, 2019), 381.
127. Brontë, "The Butterfly," 265.
128. Virginia Woolf, *The Common Reader I Annotated*, ed. Andrew McNeillie (San Diego, CA: Harcourt Brace Jovanovich, 1984), 161.
129. Brontë, *Wuthering Heights,* 265.
130. Brontë, *Wuthering Heights*, 16.
131. Brontë, *Wuthering Heights,* 18, 122.
132. Brontë, *Wuthering Heights,* 99.
133. Brontë, *Wuthering Heights,* 117.
134. Brontë, *Wuthering Heights,* 64.
135. Brontë, *Wuthering Heights,* 63.
136. Brontë, *Wuthering Heights,* 131.
137. Sandra M. Gilbert and Susan Gubar, "Looking Oppositely: Emily Brontë's Bible of Hell," in *Wuthering Heights,* ed. Alexandra Lewis (New York: W. W. Norton, 2019), 364.
138. Brontë, *Wuthering Heights,* 61, 63.
139. Brontë, *Wuthering Heights,* 63.
140. Brontë, *Wuthering Heights,* 23, 90, 130, 137.
141. Brontë, *Wuthering Heights,* 308.
142. Brontë, *Wuthering Heights,* 63.
143. Brontë, *Wuthering Heights,* 66.
144. Brontë, *Wuthering Heights,* 5.
145. Brontë, *Wuthering Heights,* 3.
146. Caldwell, "*Wuthering Heights* and Domestic Medicine," 439.
147. Nussbaum, "The Romantic Ascent," 383.
148. Brontë, *Wuthering Heights,* 7.
149. Brontë, *Wuthering Heights,* 3.
150. Brontë, *Wuthering Heights,* 11.
151. Brontë, *Wuthering Heights,* 4.
152. Brontë, *Wuthering Heights,* 120.

153. Brontë, *Wuthering Heights,* 231.
154. Brontë, *Wuthering Heights,* 254–255.
155. Qtd. in Brontë, *Wuthering Heights,* 305–306; Nussbaum, "The Romantic Ascent," 381.
156. Brontë, *Wuthering Heights,* 11.
157. Brontë, *Wuthering Heights,* 13.
158. Brontë, *Wuthering Heights,* 150.
159. Brontë, *Wuthering Heights,* 230.
160. Brontë, *Wuthering Heights,* 15.
161. Shakespeare, *King Lear,* 2.4.280–283.
162. Gilbert and Gubar, "Looking Oppositely," 361.
163. Gilbert and Gubar, "Looking Oppositely," 362.
164. Qtd. in Brontë, *Wuthering Heights,* 279, 276.
165. Lukács, *Theory of the Novel,* 88.
166. Northrop Frye, *Anatomy of Criticism: Four Essays* (Princeton, NJ: Princeton University Press, 1957), 304–305.
167. Gilbert and Gubar, "Looking Oppositely," 356.
168. Qtd. in Gilbert and Gubar, "Looking Oppositely," 356.
169. Brontë, *Wuthering Heights,* 117.
170. Brontë, *Wuthering Heights,* 219.
171. Brontë, *Wuthering Heights,* 135.
172. Qtd. in Brontë, *Wuthering Heights,* 347.
173. Thacker, *Infinite Resignation,* 3.
174. Thacker, *Infinite Resignation,* 183, 177.
175. Leo Tolstoy, "The Death of Ivan Ilyich," in *Tolstoy's Short Fiction,* trans. Louise and Aylmer Maude, ed. Michael R. Katz (New York: W. W. Norton, 2008), 128.
176. Shakespeare, *King Lear,* 4.1.31–32.
177. Stendhal, *Love,* 57.
178. Nabokov, *Lolita,* 128.
179. Hans Christian Andersen, "The Little Mermaid," in *The Annotated Hans Christian Andersen,* trans. Maria Tatar and ed. Maria Tatar and Julie K. Allen (New York: W. W. Norton, 2008), 148.
180. Cioran, *All Gall is Divided,* trans. Richard Howard (New York: Arcade, 2019), 92.
181. Barthes, *A Lover's Discourse,* 15.
182. Thomas Hardy, *Tess of the D'Urbervilles,* (New York: W. W. Norton, 1991), 21–22.
183. Samuel Taylor Coleridge, *Collected Letters of Samuel Taylor Coleridge,* Vol. I: 1785-1800, ed. Earl Leslie Griggs (Oxford: Clarendon Press, 1966), I: 138.
184. Coleridge, *Collected Letters of Samuel Taylor Coleridge,* I: 138.
185. Kafka, "A Country Doctor," in *The Complete Stories,* trans. Willa and Edwin Muir, ed. Nahum N. Glatzer (New York: Schocken, 1983), 223.
186. Kafka, "A Country Doctor," 225.
187. T. S. Eliot, *The Waste Land* (New York: W. W. Norton, 2001), l.301–2: 15.

188. Shakespeare, *King Lear,* 1.1.90.
189. Thacker, *Infinite Resignation*, 45.
190. Joshua Foa Dienstag, *Pessimism: Philosophy, Ethic, Spirit* (Princeton, NJ: Princeton University Press, 2006), 9.
191. Guido Mazzoni, *Theory of the Novel*, trans. Zakiya Hanafi (Cambridge: Harvard University Press, 2017), 167.
192. Qtd. in Mazzoni, *Theory of the Novel*, 209.
193. Michael McKeon, *Origins of the English Novel: 1600-1740,* 15th Anniversary Edi. (Baltimore, MD: Johns Hopkins University Press, 2002), 415–416. 410.
194. Qtd. in McKeon, *Origins of the English Novel*, 415–416.
195. Mazzoni, *Theory of the Novel*, 28; Plato, *Republic,* X.612C: 296.
196. Jane Austen, *Sense and Sensibility* (New York: Modern Library, 1995), 65.
197. Tolstoy, *Anna Karenina*, trans. Richard Pevear and Larissa Volokhonsky (New York: Penguin Books, 2002), 1.
198. Balzac, *Lost Souls*, 58.
199. More recently, Brian Price has come up with a theory of regret through a kind of Lukácsian understanding of contingency, stating that, "Regret . . . brings us into attunement with the contingency of things" (Brian Price, *A Theory of Regret* [Durham, NC: Duke University Press, 2017], 60).
200. Dienstag, *Pessimism*, 33; Arthur Schopenhauer, *Essays and Aphorisms*, trans. R. J. Hollingdale (London: Penguin Press, 1970), 53. Camus also reiterates this point, but uses it as a definition of the absurd: "The absurd is born of this confrontation between the human need and the unreasonable silence of the world" (Albert Camus, *The Myth of Sisyphus and Other Essays*, trans. Justin O'Brien [New York: Vintage, 1983], 28).
201. Herbert Marcuse, *Eros and Civilization: A Philosophical Inquiry into Freud* (Boston, MA: Beacon Press, 1974), 95.
202. Marcuse, *Eros and Civilization,* 95.
203. Marcuse, *Eros and Civilization,* 94.
204. D. H. Lawrence, "Study of Thomas Hardy," in *Selected Literary Criticism*, ed. Anthony Beal (New York: Viking Press, 1966), 222.
205. Lawrence, *Study of Thomas Hardy*, 172.

Chapter 3

Albertine's Absence

CORRESPONDENCES AND OBSESSIONS

Complicating the distinction between happiness and unhappiness, *In Search of Lost Time* can be read as a sigh that is so drawn out that it turns into a wheeze instead. This is how Walter Benjamin reads this multivolume novel, with its winding and winded sentences embodying a "physiology of style" that is symptomatic of Proust's own debilitating asthma attacks, his "syntax rhythmically and step by step reproduc[ing] his fear of suffocating," as though trying to pack everything he has to say into one impossible breath, uninterrupted in writing as he would have been in speech by his ailment.[1] Proust referred to the increasing severity of his asthma as a *"réalité nouvelle,"* a "new reality" that largely confined him to his bed in his cork-lined room. This "new reality" coincided with Proust's invention of a new genre of writing that absorbs countless genres within it—and not just genres from literature and literary criticism, but philosophy, history, entomology, and botany, among others, weaving them all together in a style that evokes breathlessness.[2]

In a 1913 letter to the impresario, art collector, and journalist René Blum (brother of Léon Blum, who would later become the three-time prime minister of France), Proust acknowledged that what he was writing was "an important work," and in a parenthesis added, "let's call it a novel, for it is a kind of novel."[3] That same year, he published *Swann's Way*, the first volume of his *À la recherche du temps perdu*. To Benjamin, "The conditions under which it was created were extremely unhealthy: an unusual malady, extraordinary wealth, and an abnormal disposition. This is not a model life in every respect."[4] It is a life, instead, that is devoted as obsessively to art as the characters are devoted obsessively to their lovers, or at least to the delusions about their lovers, each sinuous sentence symptomatic of obsession itself with its torrent of seemingly never-ending clauses that carry in their wake the traces of as much destruction as creation.

As if testing the limits of how pessimistic eros can be, going further than Tolstoy's distinction between happy and unhappy families at the beginning of *Anna Karenina*, Proust's narrator Marcel arrives at the "discovery that almost every house sheltered some unhappy person," and that "half of the human race was in tears."[5] The cause of this unhappiness is eros, which in Proust is defined by its "permanent strain of suffering," echoing the literary history of love from Capellanus to Stendhal.[6] This suffering can be temporarily "displaced" and "postpone[d]," but at any moment it threatens to dissolve the mirage of happiness in love with "sheer agony."[7]

Until Marcel's revelation at the end of *Time Regained*, it seems to him that only "children in their optimism," imagining that they have "no share" in "the mysteries of life, of love, of death," get to be happy.[8] Growing up is the process by which one loses that optimism, an optimism that Marcel himself never even had as a child, fascinated as he was with the world of adults and their devastating misfortunes in love, not to mention his own debilitating neuroses. By the time he is an adolescent, lovesick for Gilberte, he comes to the conclusion that life itself is ultimately an experience of failure and unhappiness:

> Having failed in every domain of life and action, it is a final impossibility, the psychological impossibility of happiness, that nature creates in us. The phenomenon of happiness either fails to appear or at once gives way to the bitterest reactions.[9]

Marcel's kvetching over his failed relationship with Gilberte occurs only in the second volume of this seven-volume encyclopedia of eros in all its pessimism. At this point, he hasn't yet skimmed the surface of the agonizing torments of eros yet to come. What appealed most to Beckett when he published one of the first major studies of Proust in 1930, at the age of twenty-four, was precisely "Proust's pessimism," which constitutes the "central catastrophe" of Marcel's subsequent relationship with Albertine, a "tragedy" doomed from the start by jealousy, distrust, infidelity, and controlling behavior.[10] "Surely in the whole of literature," Beckett writes in awe of Proust's treatment of this bizarre relationship, "there is no study of that desert of loneliness and recrimination that men call love posed and developed with such diabolical unscrupulousness."[11]

Beckett later admitted, though, that he had somewhat overstated Proust's pessimism.[12] Since Marcel himself acquires a dialectical understanding of the world, coming to realize that "there is no idea that does not carry in itself its possible refutation, no word that does not imply its opposite," then the tragedy that Beckett identifies could also be interpreted—in a very proto-Beckettian twist—as a comedy.[13] In the absurd logic of Marcel's obsession, he pushes Albertine away in an effort to inflame her eros for him, proposing that they part ways only because he wants to stay together with her. But then he thinks to himself, "What if this comedy of parting should lead to a parting!"[14] This is exactly what happens, and Marcel debates with himself about whether to come clean with his sincere desire for her or not, stalling and losing time until it is too late and she dies. The title *In Search of Lost Time* can, in this way, be interpreted not so much as a recovery or a remembrance of time past, but as a commitment to the lost and wasted time itself, to all the decisions that hadn't been made, to all the regret of not making them, to all that sound and fury signifying nothing in the end.

This toxic relationship between Marcel and Albertine is prefigured in *Swann's Way*, when Charles Swann is so entirely consumed with his destructive obsession for Odette de Crécy that he stalks her out of jealousy of her affairs, especially with women, which is also Marcel's fixation in his jealous control of Albertine. At the fever pitch of his obsession, though, Swann casually notes that Odette is not even his type.[15] Of course, as a result, they then get married now that the passion and desire have died out, leaving Swann a shell of himself—as absurd an outcome as Marcel's breakup with Albertine.

It is as though Proust follows up Plato's *Symposium* with the longest sequel to it, checking in with the scions of that first generation of humans who were split in half, observing how we haven't yet shaken off that inherited trauma of the split, but ridiculously behave as if that other half is still available to us, concocting ontological fictions to justify otherwise unjustifiable behaviors, only to realize that every relationship can only ever be a mismatch. Rather than looking for traces of ourselves in eros, desire pushes us "always in the direction of what is most opposite to ourselves," therefore "forc[ing] us to love what will make us suffer."[16] In Proust, erotic relationships inevitably fail, so the suffering therefore doubles: eros tears us away from ourselves and from the people we desire. Jean-François Revel, analyzing how Proust's pessimism answers and even surpasses Plato's, explains that Proust's characters—and indeed all humans—". . . inspire the desire for much more than themselves and reveal their inability to satisfy the need which they arouse. That is why love is identified with suffering. . . . It emerges that man is tortured by a desire for objects which do not exist. It is like that, and that is all there is to it."[17] Lovely.

But even so, happiness and unhappiness are not absolutes in this scheme, as Swann admits to himself, loosely quoting La Rochefoucauld, "You don't know it when you're happy. You're never as unhappy as you think."[18] Proust, who had emerged onto the literary scene with a group of friends who established a monthly literary review that they ended up calling *Le Banquet*, the French title of Plato's *Symposium*, seems to be reminding us that it was a comedian who told this pessimistic origin story, and he even obliquely refers to it in his amoral depiction of homosexual encounters.[19] Marcel ambiguously withholds judgment, since homosexuals are just abiding by their own nature.[20] In a scene that combines humor with horror, Marcel conveniently finds himself, allegedly without realizing it, in a gay S&M brothel in Paris as the whole city is in a blackout during an air raid toward the end of World War I, and he peeps through a small oval window into a room where he recognizes an old acquaintance:

> Chained to a bed like Prometheus to his rock, receiving the blows that Maurice rained upon him with a whip which was in fact studded with nails, I saw, with blood already flowing from him and covered with bruises which proved that the chastisement was not taking place for the first time—I saw before me M. de Charlus.[21]

Charlus complains that the flagellation isn't hard enough, that the sex isn't rough enough. Like today's masc4masc queens on Grindr, he whines about the men not being as masculine, rugged, and brutal as he would prefer. Both the gigolos and Jupien, the ex-tailor whom Charlus pays to run the entire brothel in order to recruit the kinkiest dom tops of his fantasies, try making up stories about how these men are hardened brutes with lurid criminal records, but Charlus can't be turned on by something he doesn't believe in.

Like every character in this novel, the only reality Charlus can accept and be satisfied with is one that doesn't exist—one that conforms to his fantasy, not a cheap simulation of it. This is why all of these characters suffer from excruciating heartache in their failed pursuits of eros. Reality can only ever be disappointing, except for brief moments. Charlus moves from hook-up to hook-up in pursuit of finding a strictly heterosexual man "who is a lover of women and incapable of loving him," incapable of recognizing and having sex with the woman trapped in his own body.[22] The closest Charlus ever gets to love is in his affair with the violinist Charlie Morel, who ends up cheating on him with Charlus's own nephew, Robert de Saint-Loup. Saint-Loup, for his part, at one point obsessed over a female sex worker who went by the name of "Rachel," and Marcel can't figure out why she had such a stranglehold over him, which is the same reaction that Saint-Loup has for Marcel's obsession with Albertine.

From a distance, the individual tragedies that constitute these characters' lives, including Marcel's, dissolve into a comic vision of futility and absurdity. This vision, taken as a whole, dissolves even the humor into a grander sense of comedy, like the comedy of Balzac's *Human Comedy* and Dante's *Divine Comedy*. Ultimately, it is a vision of wholeness, extending from the infernal hellscapes of brothels and the insufferable dinner parties of the high society at the Faubourg Saint-Germain, as well as the psychological landscapes of grief, despair, and even possibly psychosis, to the heavenly moments of ecstatic elation, even in moments like beholding the twin church steeples at Martinville, the row of trees at Hudimesnil, dipping a madeleine in tea, and getting the mother's goodnight kiss after anxiously wondering whether it will come or not.

These individual moments are bursts of joy and even happiness, and there is something about them that taps into Marcel's instinct to write, even from a young age. In *Swann's Way*, as he passes the Martinville steeples in Dr. Percepied's fast-moving carriage, he thinks of them as hiding "something analogous to a pretty sentence," so he promptly asks the doctor for a pencil and paper so that he could try, using his own language, to discover what this "pretty sentence" is, "despite the jolts of the carriage."[23] What he ends up writing in transit is not just a sentence, though, but a full page—a gesture of elongation and prolongation that, in miniature, captures the movement of the entire *Recherche*, and of Stendhal's definition of a novel as a "mirror moving along a highway."[24] Writing is a way of holding on to the moment even as it moves away.

There is a comparable moment in the following volume, *In the Shadow of Young Girls in Flower*, when, while also riding in a carriage, Marcel sees three trees that seem to beckon to him with a special message, and he is suddenly "overwhelmed with a profound happiness that I had not often felt since Combray; a happiness analogous to that which had been given me by—among other things—the steeples of Martinville."[25] But this happiness is quickly drowned out by the anxiety of not being able to capture this special and secret message. Like Charlus in his masochistic, submissive sexual position, Marcel also describes himself as, "Chained to my jump seat like Prometheus on his rock."[26] And in this position, he too is searching for a pleasure that is not readily accessible to him. He is a Prometheus who has failed in stealing any fire, who has chained himself and who proceeds to flagellate himself out of punishment for this failure. As the carriage rides away from the three trees, it seems to carry Marcel "away from what alone I believed to be true, what would have made me truly happy; it was like my life."[27]

The psychological self-flagellation haunts him in a decades-long writer's block as he questions whether he is even up to the task of his vocation, whether he can write anything that is worthwhile, whether he can penetrate into the heart of things and capture their mystery through language. The lasting image he has of these trees is of them waving their despairing arms, seeming to say to me: "What you fail to learn from us today, you will never know. If you allow us to drop back into the hollow of this road from which we sought to raise ourselves up to you, a whole part of yourself that we were bringing to you will fall forever into nothingness."[28]

In his essay "Reading (Proust)," Paul de Man notes how, "Guilt is always centered on reading and on writing, which the novel so often evokes in somber tones."[29] Marcel's impulse to write is, at its core, an impulse to read—and his writer's block stems from the fact that he is unable to first read what he wants to write. He cannot discern the message that these trees have to give him; he has nothing to transcribe from them, except for their warning that he will "fall forever into nothingness." In an oblique way, it may not be so much de Man's essay on Proust, but rather his essay on Charles Baudelaire, the poet whom Proust "most admired," that sheds more insight into Marcel's guilt and anxiety.[30] It was Benjamin who claimed that, "Familiarity with Baudelaire must include Proust's experience with him," so even though de Man doesn't even mention Proust in his Baudelaire essay, there are still enticing correspondences that could be discerned.[31] In *Les fleurs du mal*, Baudelaire opens his poem "*Correspondances*" with the following stanza:

La Nature est un temple où de vivants piliers
Laissent parfois sortir de confuses paroles;
L'homme y passe à travers des forêts de symboles
Qui l'observent avec des regards familiers.
(The pillars of Nature's temple are alive
and sometimes yield perplexing messages;
forests of symbols between us and the shrine
remark our passage with accustomed eyes.)[32]

This is a poem brimming with multiple levels of suggestive ambiguity. In this stanza, the "pillars of Nature's temple" could refer either to trees or to humans—or, if Marcel were interpreting this, the continuum that exists between them, allowing them to traffic in speech that he, due to his own particular inadequacy, cannot understand. He would be able to see himself as the man named in the third line, "*L'homme y passe*"—the one man who passes through and fails to receive the "perplexing messages" that were meant only for him, unless "*L'homme*" were to be translated as "man" in general or, as Richard Howard translates it above, as "us."

Marcel's anxiety at failing to understand what the trees have to tell him is indicative of a broader breakdown in communication that he later endures with Albertine. While these trees may represent the "perplexing messages" in the "forests of symbols," it is important to note that Baudelaire writes "*forêts de symboles*," not "*forêts des symboles*"—it is not so much forests of symbols, but symbol-forests. While the trees and the forests may be populated with symbols, the image here is of a dense network of symbols that themselves can be thought of as a metaphorical forest. It is this symbol-forest that constitutes language, which we all travel through. The travel motif, announced in the verb *"passer,"* which is left untranslated in the English version, connects to the word *"transport"* in the last line of the poem, after a long series of similes and lists of examples: *"Qui chantent les transports de l'esprit et des sens"* ("to praise the senses' raptures and the mind's").[33]

To de Man, Baudelaire is mapping out not just individual metaphors in this poem, but metaphor itself—the Greek *metaphorein*, which is literally a "transfer," an exchange or a bridge that carries items across different spaces. De Man alludes to this original meaning of the word "transports" as "the spatial displacement implied by the verbal ending of meta-*phorein*. One is reminded that, in the French-speaking cities of our century, '*correspondance*' meant, on the trolley-cars, the equivalence of what is called in English a 'transfer.'"[34] But "the problem is not so much centered on *phorein* as on *meta* (trans . . .), for does 'beyond' here mean a movement beyond some particular place or does it mean a state that is beyond movement entirely?"[35]

To Marcel, it would be both. Metaphorically chained as he is to his carriage seat, he is physically carried away beyond the particular place of the trees, but he is psychologically riveted to them. In a correspondence, there need to be at least two reciprocal elements, so what happens when the reciprocation fails? To Baudelaire and Proust, the answer is obsession, which is precisely the tension between motion and fixation. Mentally stuck on an object, the psyche performs repetitive and circular movements around it, expending unfathomable amounts of energy in an effort to reach its heart, but accomplishing nothing but a spiral away from it. In obsession, responding takes the place of corresponding—but it is an incessant and one-sided responding to a being that does not return the *"regards familiers,"* the familiar looks or "accustomed eyes" from *"Correspondances."*

De Man interprets Baudelaire's poem *"Obsession"* as a repetition of sorts of *"Correspondances."* As an "infra-text," it is a poem that

> more than alludes to '*Correspondances*'; it can be called a *reading* of the earlier text. . . . The relationship between the two poems can indeed be seen as the construction and the undoing of the mirrorlike, specular structure that is always involved in a reading.[36]

Here is how the poem begins:

Grand bois, vous m'effrayez comme des cathédrales;
Vous hurlez comme l'orgue; et dans nos cœurs maudits,

Chambres d'éternel deuil où vibrent de vieux râles,
Répondent les échos de vos De profundis.
(Forest, I fear you! in my ruined heart
your roaring wakens the same agony
as in cathedrals when the organ moans
and from the depths I hear that I am damned.)[37]

Baudelaire is not the first writer to link forests to cathedrals; he is drawing here from a literary tradition that stretches from the Tristan legend to Chateaubriand, but in Proust, the link seems to emerge spontaneously, and the meaning of each image changes by virtue of their association. While Marcel first associates the steeples with happiness, he subsequently associates them with the trees, which leave his heart "ruined," cursed to an eternity of nothingness.

What would it take to escape this curse? An affirmation of the nothingness, it would seem. Baudelaire's speaker proclaims, "*Car je cherche le vide, et le noir, et le nu!*" ("I long for darkness, silence, *nothing there . . .*").[38] The "*cherche*" in this line is repeated in the *Recherche* of Proust's title for his entire project, not so much a search for lost time as a literal re-search of it, in the sense of rediscovery and also in the academic sense of researching an encyclopedic amount of source material, including Baudelaire, that is referenced throughout the work. And the search for lost time is both a way of reliving the past and a way of putting it to rest, of relegating it to oblivion, which is what helps him cope with the grief of Albertine's loss. It is in this way that his obsessions are reduced to shadows of what they once were, as Baudelaire's "*Obsession*" also ends:

Mais les ténèbres sont elles-mêmes des toiles
Où vivent, jaillissant de mon œil par milliers,
Des êtres disparus aux regards familiers.
(Yet even shadows have their shapes which live
where I imagine them to be, the hordes
of vanished souls whose eyes acknowledge mine.)[39]

In the Shadow of Young Girls in Flower is a book in which Marcel chases the shadows of young girls who seemingly spring from *The Flowers of Evil*, and among these shadows, one of the "vanished souls" or "*êtres disparus*" that it introduces at the end is Albertine herself, whose disappearance is narrated in a later volume called *Albertine disparue*, translated as *The Fugitive*.

In *Time Regained*, decades after his obsession with Albertine had died down, Marcel reflects on this moment at Hudimesnil in connection to his broader sense of failure and his "lack of talent for literature," ventriloquizing not only Baudelaire but Socrates from *Phaedrus*, when he thinks to himself,

"Trees . . . you no longer have anything to say to me."[40] He even fails in his efforts at self-consolation: "I knew that I was merely seeking to console myself, I knew that I knew myself to be worthless."[41] His pessimism leads him to list his many disappointments in life, but this process paradoxically leads to an observation about truth and art that precedes an unexpected moment of happiness, ultimately leading him to affirm his vocation as a writer. Like Socrates's recantation of his initial diatribe against eros in *Phaedrus*, Marcel rediscovers his own eros for his lifelong project. He begins to notice patterns in his disappointments, like the fact that "the disappointment of travel and the disappointment of love were not different disappointments at all."[42] Travel becomes a metaphor of love, as Marcel regards Albertine in a similar way as he regards the Hudimesnil trees, both carrying secrets he cannot access, and both inspiring the Baudelairean *"transports de l'esprit et des sens"* ("the senses' raptures and the mind's").[43]

With this understanding of Baudelaire's treatment of the word *"transports"* as a metaphor of metaphor itself, Marcel discovers the method he had been searching for his whole life, the only method that can create a sense of wholeness out of the disparate moments of his past: "truth—and life too—can be attained by us only when, by comparing a quality common to two sensations, we succeed in extracting their common essence and in reuniting them to each other, liberated from the contingencies of time, within a metaphor."[44] And once he can establish this metaphorical connection between two sensations, he can continue linking more and more sensations to each other, as in fact he does in the thousands of pages that could easily be classified as the longest prose poem ever written.

This is why Beckett notes that, "The rhetorical equivalent of the Proustian real is the chain-figure of the metaphor."[45] Since there is no transcendent reality to appeal to in Proust as there is in Plato, his image of wholeness can only be gestured to in a chain of metaphors that reach out as far as they can before looping back to previous moments in a circular structure, which is the closest to eternity that we can aspire to. To Revel, this is Proust's way of "not yield[ing] to the temptation" of imagining that eros somehow grants us access to a transcendental reality, because such a reality does not exist. Instead, "passion consists of feeling in the finite an infinite which is simply non-existent."[46] Eros, then, is literally a fantasy in every sense of the word—it is an act of *poiesis*, of creation, of poetry, of fiction, inhering in the metaphor that invents the illusions of eternity and infinity in their absence.

This interpretation is suggested in de Man's reading of the word *"infinies"* or "infinite" in the final stanza of *"Correspondances"* as possibly belonging to "a metaphor aspiring to transcendental totality [but] remaining stuck in an enumeration that never goes anywhere."[47] The Proustian metaphor functions in a similar way, replacing the Platonic ideal with Baudelaire's ideal, especially in light of these two poems that belong to the section of *Les fleurs du mal* called "*Spleen et Idéal.*" To Baudelaire, both are constitutive of each other, the spleen anchored in a melancholy that binds us to our bodies, and the ideal representing the insights revealed through the interconnectedness of things, accomplished through art and specifically through metaphor.

In the closed circuit of infinity and eternity that Proust articulates through metaphor, his sense of time, then, is not eternal time, but what Benjamin calls "convoluted time, not boundless time."[48] The world that Proust recreates in this "space-bound" time is, for Benjamin, "the world in a state of resemblances, the domain of the *correspondances*; the Romanticists were the first to comprehend them and Baudelaire embraced them most fervently, but Proust was the only one who managed to reveal them in our lived life."[49] And the pessimistic insight that Proust reveals in the way time passes through the world of correspondences, of metaphors, is "that none of us has time to live the true dramas of the life that we are destined for. This is what ages us—this and nothing else."[50] This is what raises the stakes for Marcel's vocation, knowing that there is only so much time he can lose, he can waste, before he sits down to start writing. It is time defined by its finitude, what Heidegger would later call Being-toward-death.

Growing up, Marcel admired the novelist Bergotte, whose final thoughts before death dispel the notion of any eternity in art, "for if, among future generations, the works of men are to shine, there must first of all be men."[51] On his deathbed, Bergotte seems to come up with a manifesto of failure, thinking to himself:

> We do not succeed in being happy, but we observe the reasons that prevent us from being happy and that would have remained invisible to us but for these sudden loopholes opened by disappointment. And dreams, of course, cannot be converted into reality, that we know; we would not form any, perhaps, were it not for desire, and it is useful to us to form them in order to see them fail and to be instructed by their failure.[52]

In short, we are instructed by our disappointments to fail better. Bergotte then reverts "to his natural optimism" before dying, and Marcel asks, "Dead forever?"[53] This question seems to point in two directions, like the forked paths of the Méséglise Way and the Guermantes Way, one pointing to the end of the *Recherche*, when Marcel arrives at this same question in *Time Regained*, and the other to the beginning, to *Swann's Way*, when Marcel notes the differences between "voluntary" and "involuntary" memory, and how Combray was—outside of involuntary memory—otherwise "really quite dead for me." But then he asks, "Dead forever?"[54]

It is this first utterance of "Dead forever?" that seems to set the entire *Recherche* into motion, when he describes "involuntary memory" as something that resides in objects, specifically the madeleine dipped in tea, which he likens to a Japanese game of dipping small pieces of paper into a porcelain bowl and watching them unfold and take the shape of various recognizable objects. So too do all the details of Combray suddenly and unexpectedly unfold in his consciousness, and he can only reveal this unfolding through a chain of metaphors and similes.[55] If eros governs the entire *Recherche*, its most fundamental unit is the metaphor, which is why Marcel reflects that, "My uneasy and dissatisfied efforts [at writing] were themselves a sign of love, a love without pleasure but profound."[56]

In *The Captive*, Marcel defines love as "the demand for the whole. It is born, it survives only if some part remains for it to conquer. We love only what we do not wholly possess."[57] It projects the fantasy of wholeness from Plato's *Symposium* onto a reality of absence and fragmentation. Doomed to fail, the closest that one can approach wholeness is through art, through the metaphorical concatenation of fragments. In this way, the Proustian metaphor can be interpreted as the performance of this erotic union, not so much of aligning the halves of the primordial beings that were split in two, but of arranging the residual fragments embodied in their descendants, which is why there are so many different metaphorical connections to be made in a seemingly simultaneous way. The metaphor, like a lover, reaches out beyond itself in order to bind to the Other, dialectically forging a connection of identity out of difference. And in Proust's universe, the metaphors are constantly shifting, the lovers constantly moving between partners, so that the effect is a kaleidoscopic vision of eros in motion, like the moving images from the magic lantern in Marcel's childhood bedroom. Marcel's difficult lesson is that eros can never hold still and be held captive; it is as fast as the carriage that pulls him away from the Hudimesnil trees and as fugitive as Albertine on her bicycle, in the car, and ultimately—and fatally—on her horse.

Like the generations of lovers after that original split in *Symposium*, the matching up of both sides of the metaphor—the connection "between two objects which may well bear little or no essential kinship"—has a necessary element of arbitrariness to it, as Joshua Landy points out. "Yet it is precisely because of this objective arbitrariness that the yoking together of two distinct ideas can convey so exactly a *subjective* truth, namely the way in which an individual mind arranges experience."[58] Metaphor, then, bears the traces of an aesthetically mediated ontology. It conveys one's subjective truth as aesthetic style. At the end of *Time Regained*, Marcel comes to the realization that style

> is a question not of technique, but of vision: it is the revelation . . . of . . . the uniqueness of the fashion in which the world appears to each one of us, a

difference which, if there were no art, would remain for ever the secret of every individual.[59]

To Landy, then, style in Proust is "the unifying or synthesizing faculty within the Self."[60] The project of the *Recherche* is not quite a search for lost time as it is a search for the multiplicity of selves that had metamorphosed over time, each fragmentary self pulling in opposite directions, held together only by the tenuous, arbitrary, and shifting movements of metaphor that spontaneously organize into a unified style.

The pedant will be quick to note that what falls under the broad understanding of "metaphor" in Proust and in Proust scholarship is not always strictly metaphor, but rather the wide range of figures of speech that establish various connections between seemingly unrelated phenomena in the *Recherche*. As with "*Correspondances*," which uses more similes than metaphors while nevertheless highlighting the role of metaphor as a way of understanding the world, Proust is also more partial to similes even as he names the metaphor as his method of arriving at truth. Perhaps, instead of "metaphor," it would be more accurate to simply refer to "correspondences." And if correspondences assimilate those figures of speech that construct the vast web of associations, of attachments between various images, then obsessions can be thought of as dissociations, as attachments to the "*nothing there*" named by Baudelaire's "Obsession."

Obsessions are failed correspondences; they are sites of absence or of rupture. In Proust, they are not merely psychological states, but phenomena so granular that they inhere in rhetorical devices, from figures of speech to neurotically sprawling syntax. More radically disconnected from the apostrophe, obsession does not address an absent object as much as it addresses the absence itself. In *The Fugitive*, Marcel reflects on the cognitive process by which a correspondence breaks down into an obsession, by which a metaphor fails in its transfer, as he reiterates to himself over and over again the news that Albertine had left him: "In order to form a picture of an unknown situation, our imagination borrows elements that are already familiar and, for that reason, cannot accurately picture it." The metaphorical ability to establish a correspondence between the familiar and the unfamiliar here is overwhelmed and incapacitated. But in the next sentence, he resorts to perhaps the most familiar and most primordial terms to process this breakup, borrowing the implied image from that original split, that original loss, from *Symposium*: "But our sensibility, even in its most physical form, receives, as it were, the wake of the thunderbolt, the original and for long indelible imprint of the novel event."[61]

Repeating that he is "thunderstruck," Marcel comes to the realization that Albertine had always been absent from him, noting how "her charm [had] acquired a gradual ascendancy over things that, in course of time, were entirely detached from her, but were nevertheless electrified by the same emotion that she gave me."[62] The metaphor of electricity is just a cipher of this detachment, this charged absence that had always characterized Albertine's role in her relationship with him. Even in *Sodom and Gomorrah*, two volumes before Albertine's disappearance in *The Fugitive*, Marcel imagines the power that Albertine—and every woman he had loved—had to arouse his eros, "raising it to a paroxysm," as a "quasi-electric power" that "had no connection" to her.[63] In this "paroxysm," he experiences rupture as a kind of rapture; eros for him, as it is in Aristophanes's myth in *Symposium*, can only ever be an expression of grief. In *The Captive*, he notes that, "Grief penetrates into us and forces us, out of painful curiosity, to penetrate other people."[64]

To Martha Nussbaum, this primordial grief that continues to propel us to "penetrate other people" is actually central to the comedy of Aristophanes's myth, of our ancestors who had once wanted "to be gods—and here they are, running around anxiously trying to thrust a piece of themselves inside a hole; or, perhaps more comical still, waiting in the hope that some hole of theirs will have something thrust into it."[65] If eros is introduced as the consolation for this grief, then it hardly consoles Marcel, who is more preoccupied with metaphysical, rather than physical, penetration. He cannot access or penetrate Albertine's interiority, so his "painful curiosity" intensifies into an all-consuming, obsessive jealousy, which is as absurdly ridiculous as it is exasperating.

WINGED LOVERS

Proust explores how the eros theorized in *Symposium* operates not just as a form of ontology, but of epistemology as well. "Love helps us to discern things, to discriminate," Marcel reflects in *In the Shadow of Young Girls in Flower*.[66] The problem, though—which Marcel acknowledges in *The Fugitive*—is that love is ultimately a will to knowledge, and "as soon as we have the desire to know, which the jealous man feels, then it becomes a dizzy kaleidoscope in which we can no longer distinguish anything."[67] Jealous love collapses the distinctions even between truth, fantasy, and fear, disintegrating correspondences into obsessions. Jealousy then reveals "the extent to which the reality of external facts and the sentiments of the heart are an unknown element that lends itself to endless suppositions."[68]

It is the pessimistic exploration of possibility, and the element of the unknown—of what will always remain absent and out of reach—that propels the eros behind jealousy. In coming up with as many different scenarios as neurotically possible, Marcel's jealousy is ultimately an expression of his literary creativity, of what will eventually culminate in his project of writing a work that fights against time, "since for jealousy there can be neither past nor future, and what it imagines is invariably the present."[69] As a machine that obsessively churns out story after story, "jealousy . . . prolongs the course of love," extending this present moment, but it "is not capable of containing many more ingredients than are the other forms of imagination."[70] There is a masochistic fear and desire of the jealous lover to be proven right, to paradoxically concoct any number of fictional scenarios that happen to coincide, if not collide, with the truth that the loved one has been cheating and lying. So it is that "jealousy . . . in love is equivalent to the loss of all happiness," leaving Marcel restlessly "toss[ing] to and fro . . . between the desire to know and the fear of suffering."[71]

This fear and desire are part of the same eros that drives philosophy as well, propelling us to make use of what is known in order to chart out territory in the realm of the unknown. And "it is only while we are suffering that we see certain things which at other times are hidden from us."[72] What is known resides in the past, so as much as Marcel fixates on the fantasy of jealousy as inhering "invariably" in the present, his jealousy does maintain a parallax view of the past, into which the present invariably slips with each moment. He obsesses over Albertine's whereabouts by virtue of his previous suppositions, both confirmed and unconfirmed, of her past love affairs. In both *Symposium* and *Phaedrus*, as in the *Recherche*, the unknown can only be accessed through memory—a memory that, by metaphorical chains, stretches back to deep time, stored in our blood and suddenly released whenever we want to penetrate and be penetrated, or when we see a beautiful person who reminds us of the visions of cosmic beauty we had beheld when our souls had wings.

In philosophy, then, as in the novel, erotic desire is articulated as works of fiction that narrate the fundamental void at the heart of eros, seducing us into its abyss that serves as a screen onto which we project our own imagination. In this gesture of projecting our own imagination into the void, eros reveals itself not just through the particular works of fiction, but precisely as a fiction-making project. It is the absence, more than the presence, of the object of desire that fuels the desire. "We fall in love for a smile, a glance, a shoulder," Marcel observes. "That is enough; then, in the long hours of hope or sorrow, we fabricate a person, we compose a character."[73] It makes sense, then, why he would arrive at the conclusion that

> a large proportion of the thoughts that form what we call our love come to us during the hours when she is not by our side. Thus we acquire the habit of having as the object of our reverie an absent person, and one who, even if she remains absent for a few hours only, during those hours is no more than a memory.[74]

Since Albertine can only ever be absent to him, he seems to be most in love with her when she is asleep by his side, as he obsessively stares at her the way only a stalker or an artist could, registering as many details of her appearance, her breathing patterns, as he can. His fixed gaze carries the same fascination and heartbreak that he had experienced at the sight of the trees of Hudimesnil, describing her sleep as "animated now only by the unconscious life of plants, of trees, a life more different from my own, more alien, and yet one that belonged to me."[75] He even likens the occasional "slight, unaccountable tremor" that "ran through her body" as "the leaves of a tree . . . shaken for a few moments by a sudden breath of wind."[76] He still cannot penetrate her interiority, the hidden message of her subjectivity, but during these moments of rest he fulfills his fantasy of arresting what is otherwise in motion, what is fleeing away from him. "In this way her sleep did to a certain extent make her love possible; alone, I was able to think of her, but I missed her, I did not possess her."[77]

In this predatory stance, like Cupid to Psyche, he creeps into bed with her and touches "every part of her body" as she sleeps, while placing his "lips on her cheek and heart."[78] Instead of true intercourse, another way of imagining the term "correspondence" or "transfer," he is locked into a masturbatory obsession, which is the only intimacy he can hope for, noting how "the sound of her breathing as it grew louder might give the illusion of the breathless ecstasy of pleasure, and, when mine was at its climax, I could kiss her without having interrupted her sleep."[79] Sophia Papaioannou interprets the myth of Psyche's journey as a "transition into the unknown," and it is precisely this unknown territory that Marcel is denied entry from.[80]

In *The Golden Ass*, Apuleius tells the story of Psyche as someone whose only experience of the world is marred by torment. Even her extreme beauty is a burden, as it is punished by the jealous wrath of Venus. She is cursed by a prophecy that is at once personal and universally apocalyptic, to wed a monster "born for the destruction of the whole world."[81] Choosing to end her life early, she has her marriage and funeral rites performed simultaneously, and even though she is saved by Zephyr's west wind from her untimely death, she is spirited away to a paradise that quickly reveals itself to be a prison. In this paradise, where she first notices a "grove planted with towering, spreading trees," she goes to bed every night with Venus's son Cupid, who shrouds himself in darkness and anonymity, forbidding her to even look at him.[82] When she succumbs to her curiosity and disobeys, he flees from her at the moment her desire for him is the most aroused, having accidentally pierced herself with one of the arrows in his quiver. She endures agonizing trials at the hands of Venus to get Cupid back, one of them involving the retrieval of a bottle of make-up from Proserpina in the underworld, but—in yet another act of disobedience—her curiosity leads her to open this bottle up, whereby the cloud of death finally claims her. At this moment, Cupid resuscitates and marries her in front of all the gods in a scene of cosmic reconciliation.

If Marcel is the Cupid figure, he is a Cupid who is more curious about Psyche than Psyche is about him. But is he really the Cupid figure, or is he rather the tormented Psyche suffering from the flight of the fugitive lover, obsessed with what he cannot see and cannot know about Albertine's life? Perhaps he is both, and the object of desire is not so much the Psyche figure in this relationship as it is his own psyche itself. He can only love Albertine to the extent that he imagines her as absorbed in the space of his own consciousness, "lodged . . . in our own body."[83] This fantasy is one of the first masturbatory desires Marcel expresses in the *Recherche*, lying in bed as a child in the opening pages of *Swann's Way* and dreaming up a desirous woman born from his own body "as Eve was born from one of Adam's ribs."[84]

The genesis of desire emerges from himself and is ultimately aimed at himself. But it expresses itself as a neediness for others, like the goodnight kiss from his mother, whose kiss he then repeatedly compares with Albertine's, itself a vague but suggestive shadow of the queasy relationship that Cupid has with his own mother in *The Golden Ass* when, before she sends him to punish Psyche, she "kissed her son long and hungrily with parted lips."[85] In love with his own psyche, Marcel realizes that "my love was not so much a love for her as a love in me."[86] And in the image of her sleeping, what he ultimately desires is to climb into his own "chariot of sleep," carrying him outside of linear time to a realm populated by "androgynous" beings who remind him of "our first human ancestors."[87]

Sleep and dreams carry Marcel not only to the origins of desire, but to the historical origins of the novel. As one of the earliest novels, *The Golden Ass* is itself a response to Plato's own novels about love. While the fantasy of an erotic reunion between lovers who were once torn apart comes from *Symposium*, Psyche's specific "separation from, and ultimate reunion with, Cupid is an allegory for the soul's restless aspiration to attain the divine, as Plato depicts it in his *Phaedrus*."[88] In this story is the birth of what would later develop as the medieval Romance and the fairy tale, which would then later be absorbed into the modern novel. The story of Psyche, as the youngest and most beautiful of three daughters, persecuted for her beauty and unjustly suffering for love only to be magically rewarded in the end, is the warp and woof from which countless fairy tales are spun. Cupid keeps her trapped in an enchanted tower in a way that Marcel fantasizes about keeping Albertine as his own captive sleeping beauty until both Psyche and Albertine break the spell.

Cupid's story, framed by a larger narrative, is told by an old woman in response to the captive Charite after she wakes up from a bad dream, so that Charite moves from sleep to stories about sleep in a metaphorical somnambulism that Marcel seems to mirror in the movement of his own thoughts. Charite is held captive alongside the narrator Lucius, newly turned into an ass, who was captured while searching for roses, which would turn him back into a human. Instead, he only finds poisoned laurel-roses, similar in appearance only, which is when he is kidnapped by the same thieves who kidnap Charite. The dreamer's search for the rose, and the violent obstacles he must overcome in his pursuit, is the template for the medieval *Romance of the Rose*.

Marcel also thinks of Albertine as a rose, and as an extension of himself, in the same way that the Lover in *Romance of the Rose* catches a glimpse of his beloved Rose in the Spring of Narcissus. But when Albertine

> was no longer swaying in my imagination . . . but sitting still beside me, she seemed to me often a very poor specimen of a rose, so poor, indeed, that I would gladly have shut my eyes in order not to observe this or that blemish of its petals.[89]

Albertine is neither the rose from *The Romance of the Rose* nor *The Golden Ass*, but more like the poisonous laurel-rose, evoking the Platonic distinction between the ideal form and its poor imitation. Or perhaps she is closer in nature to Baudelaire's "red ideal" / "*rouge idéal,*" which the speaker of his poem "*L'Idéal*" / "The Ideal" contrasts with the artistic beauty of women in paintings, symbolized as "*pâles roses*" (loosely translated by Richard Howard as "sallow blossoms," but which really mean "pale roses").[90] This "red ideal" corresponds to the speaker's "cavernous" heart ("*profond comme un abîme*"), which is hollowed out and sculpted by a personified image of Night.[91]

By the time the Romance evolves into the modern novel, especially in Proust, the hero becomes an anti-hero, and the adventurous quest turns into a withdrawal from action, paradoxically extracting passivity as the essence of passion. Every quest here is simultaneously more modest and more challenging than the ones in Romance, and framed in pessimistic terms from the outset. "Reality," for instance, "is never more than a first step toward an unknown element in quest of which we can never progress very far."[92] But there are still traces of Romance in the novel. Marcel's parallel with Cupid is not just in his relationship with Psyche, but in the fact that they both waste time. Even Venus laments Cupid as a ne'er-do-well, noting that "nothing that he does is worthwhile."[93] In this way, both Cupid and Marcel are like the narrator Lucius, the ass whose long ears allow him to overhear stories about infidelity and betrayal. Marcel, too, has an impossibly superhuman ability to relate details about other people's lives that he wouldn't possibly be able to know. And he is so consumed with details, real and imagined, that he cannot take action, paralyzed with doubt about his ability to do anything of literary merit with these details. In this sense, he is not like that other famous human turned into an ass in *A Midsummer Night's Dream*, but rather Hamlet, beating himself up with cries of, "Why, what an ass am I! . . . / That I . . . Must, like a whore, unpack my heart with words."[94] In what is now known as the famous "Proust Questionnaire," the second time Proust filled it out, he answered the question "Your hero in fiction?" with "Hamlet."[95]

Just as much as the laurel-rose is a poor substitute for an actual rose, so too is an ass a poor substitute for a horse, even though, when Lucius mistakes the laurel-rose for the rose, he runs to it with a "burst of speed [that] made me feel like a racehorse rather than an ass."[96] The juxtaposition between the horse and the ass, like Don Quixote on Rocinante and Sancho Panza on his donkey, seems to travel through the history of the novel to Proust. And behind the recurring image of the horse, from Marcel's metaphorical "horses of sleep" to the literal horse that causes Albertine's death, is Plato's understanding of the soul as "the natural union of a team of winged horses and their charioteer," which he explains in *Phaedrus*.[97] Somewhat prefiguring the Freudian tripartite division of consciousness into the ego, the id, and the superego, Plato sees the rational element of the soul as the charioteer in charge of one horse that obeys its commands and another horse that does not. "This means that chariot-driving in our case is inevitably a painfully difficult business," Socrates tells Phaedrus.[98]

Marcel feels guilty for Albertine's death because he had paid for her horse-riding lessons, lamenting that she had killed "herself on a horse that but for me she would not have owned."[99] But perhaps the guilt runs more deeply than that. If he thinks of Albertine as an extension of his own psyche, then maybe it is the unwieldy horse of his own soul that kills her. Giving in to his baser, obsessive desires, he pursued her with a force that ultimately trampled her. His obsession then gives way not just to guilt but to nihilistic despair, as if paralleling the sequence of poems in *Les fleurs du mal*, whereby Baudelaire follows up "*Obsession*" with "*Le gout du néant*"—literally "The Taste for Nothingness," but which Richard Howard translates as "Craving for Oblivion." It opens with the image of a horse associated with despair:

Morne esprit, autrefois amoureux de la lutte,
L'Espoir, dont l'éperon attisait ton ardeur,
Ne veut plus t'enfourcher! Couche-toi sans pudeur,
Vieux cheval dont le pied à chaque obstacle butte.
(Once you were hot for battle, weary mind!
Now Hope, whose spur awakened all your zeal,
no longer even mounts. No shame in that—
lie down, old horse! You stumble at each step.)[100]

This is the nothingness (*"le vide, le noir, et le nu"*) that the speaker of *"Obsession"* longs for. And Marcel longs for it too, as though fantasizing that he could put that unwieldy horse of his consciousness to rest. Toward the end of the poem, Baudelaire writes:

Et le Temps m'engloutit minute par minute,
Comme la neige immense un corps pris de roideur;
Je contemple d'en haut le globe en sa rondeur,
Et je n'y cherche plus l'abri d'une cahute.
(Moment by moment, Time envelops me
like a stiffening body buried in the snow...
I contemplate the infinitesimal globe,
and I no longer seek asylum there.)[101]

In his grief, Marcel seems to borrow this image of the snow, imagining Albertine "like a stone around which snow has gathered, the generating center of an immense structure that rose above the plane of my heart."[102] That immense structure is both enveloped and undone by time, by *"le Temps"*—which can also be translated as "weather." Proust often arranges the different volumes of the *Recherche* by a change in season, that cyclical measure of time, which is what it takes to melt this snow. While suffering is rendered inert and immured in this poem, Baudelaire subjects it to the natural laws of mutability in the next poem, *"Alchimie de la doleur,"* translated as "Alchemy of Suffering," in which *"L'un t'éclaire avec son ardeur, / L'autre en toi met son deuil, Nature!"* ("Nature glows with this man's joy, / dims with another's grief").[103]

It was this alchemy of suffering that Proust was working out in the *Recherche* after his own lover, Alfred Agostinelli, died in a plane crash. In the same way that Marcel felt intense guilt and responsibility for Albertine's death, Proust was the one who had paid for Agostinelli's flying lessons.[104] By changing the cause of death, though, Proust doesn't swap out the airplane with the horse as much as he superimposes one on top of the other, as though revealing in this composite image the winged horse of the soul described in *Phaedrus*, that ancient work about eros as a function of memory, as a search for lost time.

Even in *Sodom and Gomorrah*, Marcel associates the horse with the airplane in terms of Greek mythology when he describes seeing an airplane for the first time:

Suddenly, my horse reared; he had heard a strange sound; it was all I could do to hold him and remain in the saddle, then I raised, in the direction from which the sound seemed to come, my eyes filled with tears and saw . . . between two great wings of flashing metal that were carrying him on, a creature whose barely visible face appeared to me to resemble that of a man. I was deeply moved as a

Greek on seeing for the first time a demigod. I wept also, for I was ready to weep the moment I realized that the sound came from above my head—airplanes were still rare in those days—at the thought that what I was going to see for the first time was an airplane.[105]

The tears of joy here prefigure the tears of grief that this same superimposed image evokes later. But it is as though Marcel unconsciously returns to this prior image after Albertine's death as a way of eventually finding himself on the other side of grief.

GRIEF AND OBLIVION

To William C. Carter, the "image of the artist as aviator . . . defines artistic genius."[106] Carter sees Proust arranging vertical images like the aviator, the Martinville steeples, and the Hudimesnil trees as emblems of artistic freedom, as opposed to the images of Aunt Léonie lying down horizontally on her bed—or, more vividly, Charlus chained to his—which represent artistic stagnation. Marcel seems to regard Charlus as the embodiment of his own fear of failure, thinking to himself,

> I believe that if M. de Charlus had tried his hand at prose, starting with those artistic subjects that he knew so well, the sparks would have caught, lightning would have struck, and the man of wisdom would have become a master of the pen.[107]

Both of them fall into that same simile of being chained like Prometheus, but Marcel longs for the ecstatic heights of the aviator, who makes him feel "that there lay open before him—before me, had not habit made me a prisoner—all the routes in space, in life itself."[108]

Habit is his lifelong enemy, the barrier between him and his artistic vocation. Obsession and self-flagellation take on the characteristics of habit, circling through the same intense routines that sap him of any energy to write. In *The Golden Ass*, as Psyche is desperately searching for Cupid after he had left her, "a member of Venus's household called Habit confronted her" and "laid a presumptuous hand on Psyche's hair, and dragged the girl in unresisting."[109] Venus, with a sadistic "cackle typical of people in a furious rage," calls in her maids Melancholy and Sorrow, who "laid into poor Psyche with whips and tortured her with implements."[110] This is also the habit of Marcel's own psyche, of the obsessions that torment, grind, and flatten him into a prostrate, horizontal position, preventing him from reaching those aerial heights. Compounded with the grief of Albertine's death, his pain is unbearable.

It is ironically the insight from Schopenhauer, from the depths of his pessimism, that seems to carry Marcel through his grief: "if happiness or at least the absence of suffering can be found, it is not the satisfaction, but the gradual reduction, the eventual extinction of our desire that we must seek."[111] It is ultimately "oblivion alone [that] brings about an ultimate extinction of desire."[112] But in the ontology of desire, whereby our existence is defined as desirous beings, how does one relinquish desire? How does one will oblivion? In short, one doesn't—since "being cured of passion is as much an accident as its birth."[113] Involuntary memory works both ways; it brings the past of its own accord and it also buries it, independently from the individual doing the remembering and forgetting. In Schopenhauer's scheme of the world, Will is not an individual agency, but a series of external forces that move through all things blindly and indiscriminately. In Proust's world, both obsession and grief are similarly imagined as external forces that are intense and all-consuming, but they eventually die out with death itself.

With Marcel, these moments happen to coincide with acts of writing. As soon as Marcel brings himself to write to his friends about his "great sorrow" after the shock of Albertine's death, he "cease[d] to feel it."[114] In *Phaedrus*, Socrates warns against writing because it will erode our faculty of memory, making us increasingly dependent on physical texts rather than our immaterial registry of thought. But this seems to be exactly the cure for Marcel's grief. If he wants to relegate Albertine to oblivion in order to move on, writing can provide him with that consolation. It is therefore a paradoxical gesture of both oblivion and of commemoration, evoking the memories of the past on the page as a way of dispelling them. And the style itself, even on the sentence level, seems to perform this gesture, stacking one vivid detail on top of another in an ascent to increasingly abstract heights, so that the reader cannot possibly retain all the information that each of the intricately constructed sentences conveys after they successively follow each other for thousands of pages. The reading experience of Proust is also a play of memory and oblivion, of discerning the correspondences and obsessions that both constitute and undo each other.

In order to write about the experience of his desire for Albertine, Marcel first learns how to read it. As she begins to lose her specific contours in his memory, she holds a place in his mind "comparable with the insubstantial images, with the memories left us by the characters in a novel that we have been reading."[115] Their relationship was first kindled as adolescents with a written text, in the slightly ambiguous message she had written to him: "*Je vous aime bien*"—which can be translated either as "I love you," "I really do like you," or "I am fond of you," resorting to the formal and distanced "*vous*" rather than the intimate "*tu*."[116] It is the act of reading, interpreting, and deciphering the nuances of this affectionate note that inspires Marcel to think to himself "that it was with her that I would have my romance."[117] The word that he uses for "romance" in French, though, is "*roman*," which can be alternatively translated as "novel" or "medieval Romance."[118] To Marcel, there is most likely no difference between these meanings. He fashions himself, like a medieval knight, on the quest for romantic love, but he is also on the quest for his vocation, to become the author of this love—both the inventor and amanuensis of his desire. It is a love born from the written word in Albertine's message, and it embarks on a journey measured more in time than in space, as it returns back to the written word of Marcel's own pen at the end of the entire *Recherche* as he documents this journey through lost time.

There is a heart-stopping moment when, as soon as Marcel has reconciled himself to the reality that Albertine is dead and that he is ready to move on, he receives a telegram saying, "MY DEAR, YOU THINK ME DEAD, FORGIVE ME, I AM QUITE ALIVE, WHEN DO YOU RETURN? LOVE, ALBERTINE."[119] In this telegram is the call of Psyche to Cupid, of Eurydice to Orpheus, tapping into that primal desire of the surviving lover to bargain with the underworld in order to win back what they had lost. This was once the only thing he had ever wanted, and that intense desire suddenly, and in a seemingly magical way, turned true. But now "that Albertine was no longer alive for me in my mind, the news that she was alive did not cause me the joy that I might have expected."[120] He is not the Cupid who rescues and reconciles her with a happily ever after. He is the Orpheus who deliberately looks back in order to send her to oblivion, once and for all.

In both the Cupid and Orpheus myths, the gaze severs the lovers; the act of looking doesn't so much receive a vision as it projects one—and with a force that pushes the beloved out of sight and effectively into the opposite realm of darkness, of blindness—like the speaker at the end of Baudelaire's "*Obsession*," who beholds a vision of thousands of vanished souls ("*êtres disparus*") that are gushing out of his own eyes ("*jaillisant de mon œil par milliers*").[121] This is an image that falls outside of time, as John Brenkman points out, noting how it evokes "endless vanishing. Loss never ceases. The image is more kinesthetic or proprioceptive than visual: the bodily feeling in the unseeing eye of a tearless outpouring of memory and grief, a grief beyond consolation or catharsis and memories too numerous to hold."[122]

At this point, though, Marcel had already come back from the point at which his grief seemed to be beyond consolation. Time has altered his Being; where once he would have pounced at the idea of returning to Albertine, of forgetting his period of intense grief as though it were a nightmare he had just woken up from, he is now detached and somewhat indifferent. The tumultuous emotions that had run their course left in their wake a philosophical calm. In the same year that *The Fugitive* was posthumously published, Martin Heidegger named this philosophical calm *Angst*, or anxiety, in *Being and Time*.

Not to be confused with psychological anxiety, Heidegger's *Angst* is what he would later describe in "What is Metaphysics?" as "being held out into the nothing."[123] In this "entranced calm" of anxiety, one is attuned to "the nothing" that serves as a "parting gesture toward beings that are . . . slipping away as a whole."[124] Marcel's Orphic gaze, staring into the void of death, creates an image of Albertine in order to watch her slip away, leaving himself with the nothing of his own existence.

Brenkman, by interpreting de Man's reading of Baudelaire as a way of giving "methodological consistency to the Heideggerian problematic of language's deconcealing/concealing oscillation," identifies in Baudelaire's image of the gushing eye an affective correlation with *Angst*, even though there isn't the same sense of calm in Baudelaire as there is with Marcel at this moment.[125] But both Marcel and Baudelaire's speaker share what Brenkman sees here as a "sensation of memory *as* uninterrupted loss, rather than the recollection, memorialization, or preservation of the lost beings."[126] And more importantly, perhaps, is the fact that this attunement to the nothing reveals "one's own finitude, which Heidegger called being-toward-death."[127] It is precisely this sense of mortality that spurs Marcel on in his quest to achieve his vocation, to write before it's too late. As Maurice Blanchot puts it, "Writing begins with Orpheus's gaze."[128]

But writing is contingent on reading. So Marcel reads and re-reads—each re-reading corresponding to the *Re-cherche*, the re-search that must go into this project. A few days later, Marcel reads Albertine's telegram again. It turns out that it is a mistaken transcription from the hotel staff due to the inscrutably florid handwriting of Gilberte, whose love also remains interred in the depths of Marcel's past. His Orphic gaze did, in fact, re-create Albertine's image, gushing out of his eye only to recede into the void opened up by this telegram that wasn't even hers. But just as much as his gaze pushed her back into death, her imagined glance in return seems to restore him to life, as it does for Baudelaire's speaker in *À une passante* ("In Passing"), a poem Marcel explicitly associates with Albertine. In the penultimate stanza, as though conflating the scene of mythical loss in *Symposium* with a passing glance from a woman in an urban crowd, Baudelaire writes:

Un éclair . . . puis la nuit!—Fugitive beauté
Dont le regard m'a fait soudainement renaître,
Ne te verrai-je plus que dans l'éternité?
(Lightning . . . then darkness! Lovely fugitive
whose glance has brought me back to life! But where
is life—not this side of eternity?)[129]

Read alongside "*Obsession*," the passing glance of Albertine, the "*Fugitive beauté*" ("Lovely fugitive") among the crowd of "*êtres disparus*" ("vanished beings") is precisely what is named in the title *Albertine disparu*, which Proust had originally intended to publish as *La fugitive*. Since there is no such thing as eternity in Proust, what there is instead is oblivion, which helps him stay on this side of life. What Benjamin identifies in this poem is the significance of love "not at first sight, but at last sight. It is a farewell forever which coincides in the poem with the moment of enchantment."[130]

Despite the "farewell forever" into the realm of oblivion, Albertine's afterimage occasionally flashes back into Marcel's consciousness. As she was in life, hiding and then suddenly appearing out of the blue, lying and then partially coming clean by turns, Albertine's turns operate by the turns of Heidegger's concept of truth—the revolving door of concealment and unconcealment, of what the gaze fails to capture in its entirety. This is why, for de Man, every insight is a blindness and every blindness is an insight. Truth, like eros, flees from sight as soon as it is spied, but it returns in the darkness, coupling with one's psyche in ways that are not so much seen as felt. What connects blindness and insight is language, which, to de Man, is marked by "its bottomless capacity to deceive, to dissemble, lie, mislead, occlude."[131] Or, as Marcel puts it when he realizes who had actually written the telegram, "We guess as we read, we create; everything starts from an initial error."[132]

Reading, therefore, is not just always misreading, as both de Man and Harold Bloom contend, but it is also writing. It is an act of creating. By reading Bergotte's novels as a child, Marcel experiences the joy of discovering "a deeper, vaster, more unified region of myself, from which all obstacles and partitions seemed to have been removed."[133] Reading allows Marcel to compose himself as he seems to compose other people in his life as though they were his fictional characters, which is why he associates Albertine so heavily with the painter Elstir, who first introduced Marcel to her in his art studio at Balbec. And before her, he fell in love with Gilberte because she happened to be an acquaintance of Bergotte, and his infatuation for Mme. de Guermantes stemmed from his admiration of the beautiful images of her ancestors in the stained-glass windows and tapestries hanging in the medieval church at Combray.

He subsequently regards each object of desire as an empty canvas for him, as a blank page to inscribe his own psyche, like the shadowy canvases (*"toiles"*) on which Baudelaire's speaker in *"Obsession"* projects the "vanished beings" (*"êtres disparus"*) from his eye. Reality disappoints Marcel in a way that tending to his fantasies does not. And, like Romeo going through so many Rosalines without ever finding his Juliet, expending more psychological intensity and erotic desire with each subsequent woman, Marcel seems to ascend the ladder of love until the spell of his obsession breaks and he reaches the state of Heideggerian anxiety, of philosophical calm. "At the start of a new love as at its ending," he observes, "we are not exclusively attached to the object of that love, but rather to the desire to love."[134]

Albertine and Gilberte are therefore interchangeable, as the misreading of the telegram suggests. They blur into each other, dissolving into the space of metaphor, which is essentially a relation established by substitution. He even imagines Albertine as a placeholder for the elusive Mlle. de Stermaria, whom he only admires from a distance. It is not something about Albertine herself, but rather the contingency with which she happens to be woven into Marcel's life that allows her to occupy the space of his erotic fascination. Or, as he explains in Kantian terms: "The idea of her uniqueness was no longer a metaphysical *a priori* based upon what was individual in Albertine . . . but an *a posteriori* created by the contingent and indissoluble overlapping of my memories."[135]

Marcel's way of processing his grief is to transform her into literature, writing her into his own version of the *Symposium* myth. It is a process that begins with repeating to himself the shock of Françoise's news that "Mademoiselle Albertine has gone," and in this repetition he identifies "an allegory of countless other separations. For very often in order that we may discover that we are in love, perhaps indeed in order that we may fall in love, the day of our separation must first have to come."[136] That separation, like the original separation, is experienced both as the loss of the loved one and of oneself. Even as the wound heals, as Marcel feels like his past belongs to a different person, and his

> inner self was now somehow split in two, and while its upper extremity was already hard and cold, it still burned at its base whenever a spark made the old current pass through it, even after my mind had long ceased to conceive of Albertine.[137]

But by sticking to the realm of allegory, of universalizing his experience, he comes to think of Albertine, like all the women he had ever desired, as less of a woman than as a "type of woman."[138]

"THE PROMISE OF HAPPINESS"

It is in this way that Marcel comes to affirm his loss, in the service of art, of establishing correspondences between particularities and universals. Art is what unites the fragments of this separation into a vision of wholeness. Invoking the image of the "flash of lightning," he proclaims,

> let us submit to the disintegration of our body, since each new fragment which breaks away from it returns in a luminous and significant form to add itself to our work, to complete it at the price of sufferings of which others more richly

endowed have no need, to make our work at least more solid as our life crumbles away beneath the corrosive action of our emotions.[139]

The template of *Symposium*, then, provides Proust not just with an allegory of pessimistic fragmentation, but with a way of finding meaning in it through art. By working his way from the particulars of his experience to the realm of generalities, he discovers that the teleology of his desire inhered not in the women he loved, or even the types of women, but rather the conditions for desire itself. In the same way, he had spent his entire life thinking that he needed to find the right subject to write about, when what he really was searching for all this time were rather the conditions for being able to write. The germination of this thought had originated in *Swann's Way*, when, after dipping the madeleine in the cup of tea, he realizes that "clearly, the truth I am seeking is not in the drink, but in me. The drink has awoken it in me."[140] Maybe the gaze of Orpheus had really been the gaze of Narcissus all along.

It is art, though, that breaks this narcissistic gaze. The "feeling for generality" allows him, through art, to "give this love, the understanding of this love, to all, to the universal spirit, and not merely first to one woman and then to another."[141] Just as Heideggerian anxiety does not involve a confrontation with any single being but is the experience of Being in itself, held out into the nothing, so too is Marcel's revelation of eros as a general force rather than something directed at any specific object of desire. Marcel *is* eros; he is Cupid. His eros for Psyche ultimately reveals an eros for the general psyche, for the psychology at work in each of us, enabling love to exist in the first place. Eros is the nothingness that binds us to and separates us from the world of other beings. And it is the intersection of eros and art that demarcates the other intersections of ontology and epistemology, and of ethics and aesthetics: "Through art alone are we able to emerge from ourselves," he realizes, "to know what another person sees of a universe which is not the same as our own."[142]

To Emmanuel Levinas, this is what Albertine's death reveals to Marcel: "Albertine's nothingness uncovers her total alterity."[143] Critiquing Heidegger's view that the experience of death can only be one's own, and that it is one's own death and sense of finitude in the world that confers meaning on one's existence, Levinas argues in his interpretation of Albertine that, "Death is the death of other people, contrary to the tendency of contemporary philosophy."[144] Death, though, doesn't always have to be so literal, and it does not necessarily lead to isolation:

> The daily death—and the death of every instant—of other persons, as they withdraw into themselves, does not plunge beings into an incommunicable solitude: that is precisely what nurtures love. That is Eros in all its ontological purity,

which does not require participation in a third term (tastes, common interests, a connaturality of souls)—but direct relationship with what gives itself in withholding itself, with the other *qua* other, with mystery.[145]

Eros "in all its ontological purity," then, is predicated on withdrawal, on absence, on a relationship with mystery, with holding space for alterity. The cliché of eros as a kind of fusion of beings is here reversed—it is the acceptance of individuation, residing in the empty space between lovers.

Marcel even surprises himself, admitting that he "was a little reluctant to accept" the idea that "general truths . . . [are] for the writer a wholesome and necessary function the fulfillment of which makes him happy."[146] With this surprising conclusion, he is finally able not only to overcome his writer's block, but seemingly the millennia of obstacles between the historically antagonistic traditions of philosophy and the novel, reconciling them at their origins, where they were both first united and broken up—in this palimpsest of *Symposium*. The excruciating pessimism that traveled across seven volumes is now framed in a vision of:

> the work [as] a promise of happiness, because it shows us that in every love the particular and the general lie side by side and it teaches us to pass from one to the other by a species of gymnastic which fortifies us against unhappiness by making us neglect its particular cause in order to gain a more profound understanding of its essence.[147]

That seems like a much-welcomed reward not just for Marcel but for the reader, after having endured the longest epic of pessimism in modernist literature. But what exactly is this "essence" that we are supposed to have a "profound understanding of"? And who is this "we"? Is it the "we" at face value, enticing the reader to identify with Marcel, or is it the multiple selves that he has assimilated in service of his vocation? Instead of clarifying this "essence," he praises the diligence of this specific labor, which, "recommencing the ruined work of amorous illusion, will give a sort of second life to sentiments which have ceased to exist," forcing us to "re-live our individual suffering" as a way of inoculating us from it.[148] Merging the particular with the general will then "turn all mankind into sharers in our pain . . . which is even able to yield us a certain joy."[149]

Very quickly, the "promise of happiness" is qualified more soberly as something that is just "able to yield a certain joy," one that can only be achieved by reliving a lifetime of pain, like a Nietzschean Eternal Return, conveyed with a similarly uncomfortable Nietzschean exuberance. And there is still no strict "essence" to speak of. As far as the reconciliation between the history of the novel and the history of philosophy in this work, Nussbaum is not convinced. "We are invited to find the truths of the text applicable to our human lives," she observes in Proust. "But these are at most contextual truths, true for human beings and at certain times in their lives; that would hardly be enough generality for Plato. Furthermore, the general truths vigorously assert the importance and uniqueness of contingent particulars."[150]

The only generalities that we can extract from the *Recherche* involve the reader's application of their own particular, contingent experiences onto the experiences recorded in the novel, substituting Albertine in our imagination with the lovers—and those unreachable people whom we could only ever hope to have as lovers—from our own past. We are then implicated in the contingent chain of metaphors that Proust constructs, seduced by this chain and linking it up with our own. But there is no "hierarchical deductive system of the sort Plato would have wanted; we do not even have a more modest and open-ended framework."[151] Instead of the strategy of philosophical deduction, Proust operates by the strategy of novelistic seduction. Instead of metaphysics, he supplies metaphor. He invokes Plato only to strip him of his essences, his forms, his ideals, interested only in the literary qualities of his allegories, reconstructing them toward a different kind of generality.

Because there is no escape from contingency in this work, the truths that Proust illuminates are obviously—and thankfully—by no means universal. Each statement that gestures toward a universal truth in the novel, usually beginning with "We" instead of "I," is more of a tenuous conjecture that can only be made within a specific set of circumstances, and can easily be contradicted. And luckily, not everyone is as neurotic, jealous, and off the rails when it comes to love as Marcel, and even other characters like Swann and Saint-Loup. And not every reader is seduced by their peregrinations into eros. For every reader who is transformed by Proust, who has both cried and laughed out loud at his prose, who finds in it the closest to a religious experience that art can afford, who ranks him alongside Shakespeare in the history of literature, Proust has also become the byword for the epitome of snobbery and of a particularly unbearable kind of boredom. It is commonplace for readers to see in the intricate construction of his sentences only the curlicues of an excessively precious and pretentious style that is both unforgivable and unforgiving, especially to the undergraduate student who is forced to read him against their will, without the attention span, the life experience, or just simply the interest to find any entry point into his work. And there are yet those who find themselves oscillating between these two poles, perhaps moved by Marcel's affection for his grandmother, but zoning out during the tedious dinner-party conversations that last for hundreds of pages.

In an effort to reach those readers who have been perennially turned off by Proust, there has been a fad in the self-help industry over the past few decades to publish books like Alain de Botton's *How Proust Can Change Your Life*, which attempt to neatly package his insights into easily digestible personal lessons and even life goals. But this attempt only proves that Nussbaum is correct in her assessment that any kind of impulse to discern any universal or philosophically systematic truths in Proust is misguided. And nowhere is that more clearly demonstrated in the attempt to force the pessimism at work in Proust firstly into something positive, and secondly into something practical that we can learn from and apply to our own lives. This would reverse Nussbaum's insight that it is us as readers who apply the details of our lives to Proust, not the other way around.

Each chapter of *How Proust Can Change Your Life* begins with the words "How to . . . " ("How to Love Life Today," "How to Suffer Successfully," "How to Be Happy in Love," etc.). Five out of the nine chapters end with "The lesson?" or "The moral?" followed by a sentence or two to sum up the ready-made wisdom.[152] The chapter entitled "How to Express Your Emotions" ends with: "The moral? That life can be a stranger substance than clichéd life."[153] Okay, then! It's certainly an interesting choice, though, to write a cliché about a cliché in the context of a literary giant who despised clichés. Even so, the book is filled with some entertaining biographical trivia, and it should be acknowledged that any effort to dust off Proust from the shelves of academic libraries in order to accommodate a wider audience is an effort worth commending. There is also certainly something to be said for brevity (although when it comes to Proust, that inevitably becomes a contentious matter), but what passes for insights here—insights that are simultaneously condensed and watered down—sometimes seems to belong to the Monty Python sketch of the "All-England Summarize Proust Competition," in which contestants are challenged to summarize the entire *Recherche* in fifteen seconds.

De Botton even quotes the first contestant on the comedy sketch, whose answer is

> Proust's novel ostensibly tells of the irrevocability of time lost, of innocence and experience, the reinstatement of extratemporal values and time regained. Ultimately the novel is both optimistic and set within the context of human religious experience. In the first volume, Swann visits—.[154]

The gag is obviously that the contestant runs out of time. But the joke is also that this start of an answer sounds like it could be competent—it certainly has the Proustian lingo and the air of academic authority—but ultimately it doesn't say much at all, and perhaps reveals more about the contestant's own desire to see a redemptive optimism in Proust than what may actually be in the text.

By the end of the *Recherche*, Proust has already primed the reader to accept that there are no stable categories in experience, and that happiness, if anything, is an aberration, and that its nature is ambiguous at best. This is not the kind of happiness that is understood out of context and memed in a daily affirmation quote posted to a self-help guru's Instagram account. Even in Marcel's epiphany and inspiration to finally sit down and write his masterpiece, he acknowledges that "truth, which is not compatible with happiness or with physical health, is not always compatible even with life."[155] And "as for happiness, that is really useful to us in one way only, by making unhappiness possible."[156] It would be easy for anyone too insistent on projecting their optimism onto this work to misread this sentence and unconsciously switch the order of the words "happiness" and "unhappiness" here. Happiness is not the reward for a life of unhappiness, but rather a means to the end of unhappiness—an unhappiness that can be affirmed only through art, but it remains unhappiness nonetheless, one that moreover demands the sacrifices of one's own life in order to achieve the artwork.

"It is necessary for us to form in happiness ties of confidence and attachment that are both sweet and strong," Marcel continues, "in order that their rupture may cause us the heart-rending but so valuable agony which is called unhappiness."[157] As a novelist committed to the cult of eros, he seeks out that original "rupture" from *Symposium*, finding value not so much in happiness, but in "agony," in explicit and abject unhappiness. It is grief that functions "as an incitement to work," that "sets . . . in motion" the imagination needed to write such a work.[158] And he even channels Schopenhauer at this point when he realizes that, "once one understands that suffering is the best thing that one can hope to encounter in life, one thinks without terror, and almost as of a deliverance, of death."[159]

Pessimism, though, doesn't necessarily have the last word, either. In this cyclical structure, in which the end throws the reader back to the beginning, there is no last word or final verdict. While the majority of the novel deals with the pessimism of eros, the word "pessimism" is used sparingly. When it is, Marcel is critical of it, especially from other people. Exhausted with Charlus's pessimism, he thinks to himself,

> It was, indeed, exasperating to hear the whole world accused, and often without any semblance of proof, by someone who omitted himself from the special category to which one knew perfectly well that he belonged and in which he so readily included others.[160]

Of this tendency, he notes that, "we deliver on life a pessimistic judgment that we supposed to be fair" in the absence of novelty.[161] It is habit, Marcel's enemy, that breeds pessimism. Any kind of novelty, like a change in location or a sudden surprise, can overthrow this pessimism, which is perhaps why the epiphany in *Time Regained* that surprises and inspires him to fulfill his vocation as a writer is full of such joy, even as he dwells on the nature of unhappiness.

The mingling of happiness with unhappiness, joy with pain, pessimism with optimism, may trace back to Chateaubriand, who writes in *René* that, "in every land the natural song of man is sad, even when it renders happiness. Our heart is a defective instrument, a lyre with several chords missing, which forces us to express our joyful moods in notes meant for lamentation."[162] Chateaubriand is, in fact, one of the first writers whom Marcel thinks of as he waits in the Guermantes's library in *Time Regained*, as he savors the happiness of his epiphany that he will become a writer. To Benjamin, who notes how the "paralyzing, explosive will to happiness which pervades Proust's writing is so seldom comprehended by his readers," its presence can be explained as "a dual will to happiness, a dialectics of happiness: a hymnic and an elegiac form."[163]

After mentioning Chateaubriand, Marcel returns to Baudelaire, towering above the rest of his literary inspirations, in whose "noble . . . line of descent" Marcel hopes "to establish my place . . . and thus to give myself the assurance that the work which I no longer had any hesitation in undertaking was worthy of the pains."[164] To Benjamin, "These words are a confessional motto for Proust's work."[165] Beckett, too, sees in this moment a climactic realization of "the meaning of Baudelaire's definition of reality as 'the adequate union of subject and object.'"[166] Marcel here discovers the metaphorical method that will organize his work, that will establish the relationship between subject and object. If Baudelaire's poem "*Obsession*" is an interpretation or a "reading" of "*Correspondances*" as de Man contends, then Marcel's metaphorical correspondences will in turn be a way of writing his obsessions, of controlling them with aesthetic form.

The work, though, has a dialectical relationship with control. As much as Marcel exerts control over his style, he is guided by spontaneity, by those flashes of involuntary memory that do not obey any rational order. Like Albertine, the work both submits to and eludes his control. And so, sleeping by day and working by night, Marcel stays up to trace the contours of that part of his psyche that is mysterious, unconscious, sleeping as though beside him, external to him. And in his portrait of this fugitive who is temporarily at rest, his own sentences take on a fugue-like structure of repetition and variation, a structure that is as centrifugal as it is centripetal, accumulating as many details as possible.

And, as if by magic, the hypnotic and soporific style slips into this realm of dreams, where he is no longer individuated but rather absorbed into a realm without subjects and objects, and then wakes up only to discover that "I did not even understand in the first moment who I was," discerning "in a momentary glimmer of consciousness the sleep into which were plunged the furniture, the room, that whole of which I was only a small part and whose insensibility I would soon return to share."[167] He is a child again, the end of the *Recherche* throwing him back to the beginning, to *Swann's Way*, in the opening pages that bear the traces of the influence of books so that, before going to sleep, "it seemed to me that I myself was what the book was talking about."[168]

After reading the entire *Recherche*, this image cannot be untethered from the image of Marcel waiting in the Guermantes's library at the end of *Time Regained*, as he feels the rush of excitement to write, surrounded by all of those books. And, like the multiple memories that seem to unfold from his cup of tea after dipping his madeleine in it, it is as though all of the genres of literature that have charted the history of the novel—from the Platonic dialogue to the Romance and the fairy tale, absorbing even lyric and epic poetry along the way—emerge from that cup of tea and from that library as well, culminating in the pinnacle of the novel's history with this work. And, eschewing the linearity of time, what comes tumbling out of the *Recherche* are not just the prior works of literature that have led up to this one, but the future works that will be written under its influence, in its shadow, as well as the philosophical breakthroughs that emerged shortly after Proust's death.

In the concealing and unconcealing of eros, of truth, of memory, of the images of Albertine and of Marcel's grandmother, all riding the tides in and out of consciousness, or of what Proust calls "the intermittencies of the heart," Proust anticipates Heidegger's conception of truth as something that operates by a similar movement.[169] It is a movement that Freud, too, famously describes in *Beyond the Pleasure Principle* as a way of making sense of his own one-year-old grandson who would periodically and spontaneously entertain himself with the game of *fort-da* ("gone-here"), of pushing an object out of view only to find pleasure in seeing it reappear.[170] Carter invokes this link between Proust and Freud, who never knew or read each other, especially in light of Terry Eagleton's insight that this game of loss and recovery is the origin of all narration.[171] "*Fort-da* is perhaps the shortest story we can imagine: an object is lost, and then recovered," Eagleton explains. "But even the most complex narratives can be read as variants on this model: the pattern of classical narrative is that an original settlement is disrupted and ultimately restored. From this viewpoint, narrative is a source of consolation."[172]

In this way, Proust's intricately structured masterpiece is, in essence, simultaneously the most rudimentary one. And in the chain that links Proust to Heidegger to Freud, and the chain that goes back in time from adulthood to childhood, from sophisticated narrative to the simplest game of *fort-da*, one can follow this chain even further back in time, thousands of years, to that foundational work of consolation in Plato's *Symposium*. Even Freud ends *Beyond the Pleasure Principle* by saying that myth offers greater insight than science in explaining our behavior and the role of eros in our lives, and he explicitly cites Plato:

> What I have in mind is, of course, the theory which Plato put into the mouth of Aristophanes in the *Symposium*, and which deals not only with the *origin* of the sexual instinct but also with the most important of its variations in relation to its object.[173]

By tracing "the origin of an instinct to a need to restore an earlier state of things," maybe the *fort-da* game repeats the memory, inscribed in our inner being, of the first lovers of whom we are the descendants, and of that part of our self that was severed, and the joy we experienced—or fantasized about experiencing—at recovering that missing half.[174] Maybe all of narration is a kind of re-telling of this mythical story of consolation that explains to us who we are. And maybe philosophy, in recognizing that it cannot explain everything even as it gestures toward systematic totalities, in recognizing that it cannot lay a claim to wholeness, itself instinctively dreams up a fiction as we all do when confronted with absence, with loss, relying on fiction not just as consolation, but as revealing a kind of truth that philosophy or scientific reality on their own cannot access.

How adequate is this consolation, though, in assuaging loss, pain, loneliness? The word "consolation" comes from the Latin *consolor*, "to find solace together."[175] Marcel can only see himself not as one single consciousness, but as many divided selves, maybe replicating the split from *Symposium* out of a masochistic pleasure, but also perhaps so that he won't be alone when he is by himself. When Albertine first leaves him, he notes how "at every moment there was one more of these innumerable and humble 'selves' that compose our personality which was still unaware of Albertine's departure and must be informed of it."[176] And to

> each of them I had to relate my grief, the grief that is in no way a pessimistic conclusion freely drawn from an accumulation of lamentable circumstances, but is the intermittent and involuntary revival of a specific impression, come to us from without and not chosen by us.[177]

And just as he thinks of himself as a multiplicity of different selves, so too does he think of Albertine, so that to "find consolation, it was not one, it was innumerable Albertines that I must first forget. When I had reached the stage of enduring the grief of losing this Albertine, I must begin with another, with a hundred others."[178]

There is a curious way in which consolation here doesn't just multiply the self but multiplies the suffering. The *fort-da* game here seems to be played in reverse. While the fiction of *fort-da* inheres in the hiding of the object, in pretending that the object isn't there but then taking pleasure in finding it again, the game of pretend in Marcel's mind is in the imaginary contact with the multiple selves of Albertine, in bringing her "here" ("*da*"), when she is gone. He tries to convince himself that this is the only way she has ever truly been "here," been present in his consciousness, but the argument rings hollow. She is gone, only to return in memory, and the paradox of consolation that Marcel experiences is that it arrives when he no longer wants her back.

In *Time Regained*, Marcel ambiguously says that this "work in which our unhappiness has collaborated may be interpreted both as an ominous sign of suffering and as an auspicious sign of consolation."[179] In the way that eros is the consolation itself in *Symposium*, Proust's own meditations on eros draw on a rich history of consolation and anti-consolation literature that gives rise to the novel as a way of addressing—even if not necessarily settling on—pessimism. "Could life console me for the loss of art?" Marcel wonders in *The Captive*, when he feels like a failure.[180] When he is resolute in fulfilling his vocation, though, the question seems to pose itself in reverse: Could art console us for the loss of life?

NOTES

1. Benjamin, "The Image of Proust," 214.
2. Benjamin, "The Image of Proust," 214.
3. Proust, *Letters of Marcel Proust*, trans. Mina Curtiss (New York: Turtle Point Press, 2006), 286.
4. Benjamin, "The Image of Proust," 201.
5. Proust, *The Guermantes Way*, ed. William C. Carter, trans. C. K. Scott Moncrieff (New Haven, CT: Yale University Press, 2018), 410.
6. Proust, *In the Shadow of Young Girls in Flower*, 171.
7. Proust, *In the Shadow of Young Girls in Flower*, 171.
8. Proust, *The Fugitive*, 588.
9. Proust, *In the Shadow of Young Girls in Flower*, 219.
10. Beckett, *Proust*, 7.
11. Beckett, *Proust*, 38.
12. Ann Banfield, "'Proust's Pessimism' as Beckett's Counter-Poison," *The Romantic Review* 100, no. 1–2 (January 2009): 194, doi:10.1215/26885220-100.1-2.187.
13. Proust, *The Fugitive*, 653–654.
14. Proust, *The Captive*, 385.
15. Proust, *Swann's Way*, 396.
16. Proust, *The Fugitive*, 663.
17. Jean-François Revel, *On Proust*, trans. Martin Turnell (New York: The Library Press, 1972), 99–100.
18. Proust, *Swann's Way*, 367.

19. William C. Carter, *Marcel Proust: A Life* (New Haven, CT: Yale University Press, 2000), 126.

20. In *The Fugitive*, Marcel says, "Personally I found it absolutely irrelevant from a moral point of view whether one took one's pleasure with a man or with a woman, only too natural and too human that one should take it where one could find it" (748). However, he does express disappointment at finding out that his friend Robert de Saint-Loup is a homosexual. Proust found the newly coined word "homosexual" inaccurate, so he preferred the term "invert," conflating gender and sexuality so that gay men, to him were actually closer to trans women (Proust, *Sodom and Gomorrah*, 9).

21. Proust, *Time Regained*, trans. Andreas Mayor and Terence Kilmartin, revised by D. J. Enright (New York: Modern Library, 2003), 181–182.

22. Proust, *Sodom and Gomorrah*, 36.

23. Proust, *Swann's Way*, 185.

24. Stendhal, *The Red and the Black*, trans. Robert M. Adams (New York: W. W. Norton, 2008), 297.

25. Proust, *In the Shadow of Young Girls in Flower*, 322.

26. Proust, *In the Shadow of Young Girls in Flower*, 323.

27. Proust, *In the Shadow of Young Girls in Flower*, 325.

28. Proust, *In the Shadow of Young Girls in Flower*, 325.

29. Paul de Man, "Reading (Proust)," in *Modern Critical Interpretations: Marcel Proust's Remembrance of Things Past*, ed. Harold Bloom (New York: Chelsea House Publishers, 1987), 123.

30. Carter, *Marcel Proust: A Life*, 140.

31. Walter Benjamin, "On Some Motifs in Baudelaire," in *Illuminations*, trans. Harry Zohn and ed. Hannah Arendt (New York: Schocken, 1968), 180–181.

32. Charles Baudelaire, *Les Fleurs du Mal*, trans. Richard Howard (Boston, MA: David R. Godine, 1983), 15; 193.

33. Baudelaire, *Les Fleurs du Mal*, 15; 193.

34. de Man, "Anthropomorphism in the Lyric," in *The Rhetoric of Romanticism*, ed. Paul de Man (New York: Columbia University Press, 1984), 251.

35. de Man, "Anthropomorphism in the Lyric," 251.

36. de Man, "Anthropomorphism in the Lyric," 262; 252.

37. Baudelaire, *Les Fleurs du Mal*, 77; 254.

38. Baudelaire, *Les Fleurs du Mal*, 77; 254.

39. Baudelaire, *Les Fleurs du Mal*, 77; 254.

40. Proust, *Time Regained*, 238. Baudelaire wrote, "I have always thought that there is something impudent and deplorable about rejuvenated and flourishing Nature. . . . In the depths of the woods, confined beneath arches similar to those of sacristies and cathedrals, I think of our astonishing cities" (qtd. in John Brenkman, *Mood and Trope: The Rhetoric and Poetics of Affect* [Chicago, IL: The University of Chicago Press, 2020], 63).

41. Proust, *Time Regained*, 239.

42. Proust, *Time Regained*, 271.

43. Baudelaire, *Les Fleurs du Mal*, 15; 193.

44. Proust, *Time Regained*, 290.

45. Beckett, *Proust*, 68.
46. Revel, *On Proust*, 110.
47. de Man, "Anthropomorphism in the Lyric," 250.
48. Benjamin, "The Image of Proust," 211.
49. Benjamin, "The Image of Proust," 211.
50. Benjamin, "The Image of Proust," 211.
51. Proust, *The Captive*, 195.
52. Proust, *The Captive*, 194.
53. Proust, *The Captive*, 199.
54. Proust, *Swann's Way*, 44.
55. Proust, *Swann's Way*, 48.
56. Proust, *Swann's Way*, 98.
57. Proust, *The Captive*, 109.
58. Joshua Landy, "'*Les Moi en Moi*': The Proustian Self in Philosophical Perspective," *New Literary Review* 32, no. 1 (Winter 2001): 111.
59. Proust, *Time Regained*, 299.
60. Landy, "'*Les Moi en Moi*,'" 111.
61. Proust, *The Fugitive*, 459.
62. Proust, *The Fugitive*, 504–505.
63. Proust, *Sodom and Gomorrah*, 578.
64. Proust, *The Captive*, 153.
65. Nussbaum, "The Speech of Alcibiades," 140.
66. Proust, *In the Shadow of Young Girls in Flower*, 529.
67. Proust, *The Fugitive*, 563.
68. Proust, *The Fugitive*, 562–563.
69. Proust, *The Fugitive*, 532.
70. Proust, *The Guermantes Way*, 384.
71. Proust, *The Fugitive*, 499; 565.
72. Proust, *Time Regained*, 301.
73. Proust, *The Fugitive*, 575.
74. Proust, *The Fugitive*, 568.
75. Proust, *The Captive*, 70.
76. Proust, *The Captive*, 71.
77. Proust, *The Captive*, 69.
78. Proust, *The Captive*, 72.
79. Proust, *The Captive*, 72.
80. Sophia Papaioannou, "Charite's Rape, Psyche on the Rock and the Parallel Function of Marriage in Apuleuius' 'Metamorphoses,'" *Mnemosyne* 51, no. 3 (June 1998): 319, https://www.jstor.org/stable/4432843.
81. P. G. Walsh Apuleius, *The Golden Ass*, trans. P. G. Walsh (Oxford: Oxford University Press, 1999), 79.
82. Apuleius, *The Golden Ass*, 80.
83. Proust, *The Fugitive*, 539.
84. Proust, *Swann's Way*, 4.
85. Apuleius, *The Golden Ass*, 77.

86. Proust, *The Fugitive*, 604.
87. Proust, *Sodom and Gomorrah*, 418.
88. Apuleius, *The Golden Ass*, xli.
89. Proust, *The Guermantes Way*, 388.
90. Baudelaire, *Les Fleurs du Mal*, 25; 203.
91. Baudelaire, *Les Fleurs du Mal*, 25; 203.
92. Proust, *The Captive*, 20.
93. Apuleius, *The Golden Ass*, 76.
94. Shakespeare, *Hamlet*, 2.2.611-14: 119.
95. Proust, *The Guermantes Way*, 587 n.332.
96. Apuleius, *The Golden Ass*, 59.
97. Plato, *Phaedrus*, 246A: 31.
98. Plato, *Phaedrus*, 246A: 31.
99. Proust, *The Fugitive*, 542.
100. Baudelaire, *Les Fleurs du Mal*, 255; 77–78.
101. Baudelaire, *Les Fleurs du Mal*, 255; 78.
102. Proust, *The Fugitive*, 474.
103. Baudelaire, *Les Fleurs du Mal*, 255; 78.
104. Proust, *The Fugitive*, 542 n.51.
105. Proust, *Sodom and Gomorrah*, 470–471.
106. William C. Carter, *The Proustian Quest* (New York: New York University Press, 1992), 187.
107. Proust, *The Captive*, 222.
108. Proust, *Sodom and Gomorrah*, 471.
109. Apuleius, *The Golden Ass*, 104.
110. Apuleius, *The Golden Ass*, 104.
111. Proust, *The Fugitive*, 488.
112. Proust, *The Fugitive*, 488.
113. Revel, *On Proust*, 92.
114. Proust, *The Fugitive*, 640.
115. Proust, *The Fugitive*, 552–553.
116. Proust, *In the Shadow of Young Girls in Flower*, 532; 532 n.381.
117. Proust, *In the Shadow of Young Girls in Flower*, 537.
118. Proust, *In the Shadow of Young Girls in Flower*, 537 n.394.
119. Proust, *The Fugitive*, 697.
120. Proust, *The Fugitive*, 697.
121. Baudelaire, *Les Fleurs du Mal*, 254.
122. Brenkman, *Mood and Trope*, 67.
123. Martin Heidegger, "What is Metaphysics?," in *Pathmarks*, ed. William McNeill, trans. David Farrell Krell (Cambridge: Cambridge University Press, 1998), 91.
124. Heidegger, "What is Metaphysics?," 90.
125. Brenkman, *Mood and Trope*, 71.
126. Brenkman, *Mood and Trope*, 71.
127. Brenkman, *Mood and Trope*, 72.

128. Maurice Blanchot, *The Space of Literature*, trans. Ann Smock (Lincoln, NE: University of Nebraska Press, 1989), 175.
129. Baudelaire, *Les Fleurs du Mal*, 276; 98.
130. Benjamin, "On Some Motifs in Baudelaire," 169.
131. Brenkman, *Mood and Trope*, 57.
132. Proust, *The Fugitive*, 713.
133. Proust, *Swann's Way*, 96.
134. Proust, *In the Shadow of Young Girls in Flower*, 537.
135. Proust, *The Fugitive*, 603.
136. Proust, *The Fugitive*, 549.
137. Proust, *The Fugitive*, 578.
138. Proust, *The Fugitive*, 546.
139. Proust, *Time Regained*, 315.
140. Proust, *Swann's Way*, 45.
141. Proust, *Time Regained*, 306; 301.
142. Proust, *Time Regained*, 299.
143. Emmanuel Levinas, "The Other in Proust," in *Proper Names*, trans. Michael B. Smith (Stanford, CA: Stanford University Press, 1996), 103.
144. Levinas, "The Other in Proust," 103.
145. Levinas, "The Other in Proust," 103.
146. Proust, *Time Regained*, 308–309.
147. Proust, *Time Regained*, 312.
148. Proust, *Time Regained*, 313.
149. Proust, *Time Regained*, 313.
150. Nussbaum, "Fictions of the Soul," 158.
151. Nussbaum, "Fictions of the Soul," 158.
152. Alain de Botton, *How Proust Can Change Your Life* (London: Picador, 1997), 51, 92, 113, 171, 215.
153. de Botton, *How Proust Can Change Your Life*, 113.
154. de Botton, *How Proust Can Change Your Life*, 36.
155. Proust, *Time Regained*, 314.
156. Proust, *Time Regained*, 316.
157. Proust, *Time Regained*, 316.
158. Proust, *Time Regained*, 318.
159. Proust, *Time Regained*, 319.
160. Proust, *Time Regained*, 143.
161. Proust, *In the Shadow of Young Girls in Flower*, 254.
162. François-René de Chateaubriand, "René," in *Atala / René*, trans. Irving Putter (Berkeley, CA: University of California Press, 1980), 97. Flaubert also has a variation of this image in *Madame Bovary*.
163. Benjamin, "The Image of Proust," 203–204.
164. Proust, *Time Regained*, 335.
165. Benjamin, "On Some Motifs in Baudelaire," 183.
166. Beckett, *Proust*, 57.
167. Proust, *Swann's Way*, 5; 4.

168. Proust, *Swann's Way*, 3.
169. Proust, *Sodom and Gomorrah*, 167.
170. Sigmund Freud, *Beyond the Pleasure Principle*, 14.
171. Carter, *The Proustian Quest*, 19.
172. Eagleton, *Literary Theory: An Introduction* (Minneapolis, MN: University of Minnesota Press, 2003), 160–161.
173. Freud, *Beyond the Pleasure Principle*, 69.
174. Freud, *Beyond the Pleasure Principle*, 69.
175. Michael Ignatieff, *On Consolation: Finding Solace in Dark Times* (New York: Metropolitan Books, 2021), 1.
176. Proust, *The Fugitive*, 465.
177. Proust, *The Fugitive*, 466.
178. Proust, *The Fugitive*, 519.
179. Proust, *Time Regained*, 311.
180. Proust, *The Captive*, 166–167.

Chapter 4

Failed Consolations in Plato's Shadow
Boethius, Medieval Romance, and Goethe

FROM BOETHIUS TO MEDIEVAL ROMANCE

In 2021, a year into the COVID-19 pandemic, Michael Ignatieff published his book *On Consolation: Finding Solace in Dark Times*, documenting the literary and philosophical history of the consolation genre in the Western tradition. The book begins on a personal note, recounting his visit to a friend who had lost his wife six months earlier. His friend is

> truly inconsolable. He refuses to believe that he can live without her. Trying to console him takes us both to the limits of language, and so words trail off into silence. His grief is a deep solitude that cannot be shared. In its depths, there is no place for hope.[1]

Consolation is that exercise in failure we do when there is no place for hope. It is, in some ways, an impossible genre—an application of language to what can only lie beyond the limits of language, a gesture of hope that can only be snuffed out by hopelessness.

Maybe this is why true consolation can only exist outside of language, in the infant's pre-linguistic game of *fort-da*, where whatever is gone will come back again. Every subsequent narrative aims to re-create that moment, to bring back the lost object in some transformed but inevitably lesser state, like the boy in Heinrich von Kleist's "On the Theater of Marionettes," who tries and fails to re-create that moment when he looked just like the Greek statue of Spinario, a moment that is compared with a prelapsarian state of grace. What would a narrative—literary, psychological, or political—look like if it would abandon this infantile messianism, if it would just narrate the *fort* (gone) instead of the *da* (here), without any expectation or even the hope of a return, especially the return of something that never existed? Would such a narrative even be possible, replacing infantile regression with infinite resignation?

In his own narrative of brushing up against the limits of language, the consolation that Marcel yearns for in the Guermantes's library—fantasizing about the union between philosophical generalities and novelistic particulars—comes from a long tradition of attempts at reconciliation in the millennia-long lover's quarrel between philosophy and the novel, most famously exemplified by Boethius in his response to Plato. Before his execution in 524 CE by the same government that he had served as a senior statesman, Boethius left behind the first work of prison literature, *The Consolation of Philosophy*. As both a criminal autobiography and a Menippean satire in its alternation of verse and prose, Boethius anchors his flights of imagination in his immediate, actual circumstances. It was his lifelong dream to translate all of Plato and Aristotle into Latin, and demonstrate how they are both in "harmony" with each other and with Christian theology.[2] And while he couldn't get to all of their works, his translations and commentary helped keep their philosophy central to church teachings through the Middle Ages and the Renaissance. In his final moments, aware that he will not be able to fulfill his mission in its entirety, he does still seem to fulfill Socrates's wish of inventing a poetry that would be welcomed by philosophy.

The Consolation of Philosophy begins on a pessimistic note of despair:

> I used to write cheerful poems, happy and life-affirming, / but my eyes are wet with tears and the poems are those / that only grieving Muses would prompt me to compose, / heartbreaking verse from a suffering, heartbroken man, / but those woeful songs turn out to be my consoling companions.[3]

In his loneliness, like Marcel, he seems to divide himself into separate selves for the sake of consolation, addressing this externalized self as Lady Philosophy, an allegorical figure who breaks into his prison cell, armed with a scepter in one hand and a pile of books in the other.[4] Her first reaction is to take offense at these Muses of poetry crowding around him: "Who let these chorus girls in here to approach a sick man's bedside?" she cries out. "They have no cures for what ails him. Indeed, what they offer will only make his condition worse! What we want is the fruits of reason."[5] She then disperses them, taking their place in consoling him, in a way that Socrates would approve of.

But what kind of a consolation does she actually offer? She admonishes him for complaining about his situation, and—like today's devotees to the cult of Cognitive Behavioral Therapy—she says, "Almost nothing is inherently miserable, unless you think it is."[6] There's nothing quite like gaslighting veiled as consolation. Even Hamlet, in all his cruelty, never went so far as to say that misery is a state of mind—to him, "there is / nothing either good or bad but thinking makes it / so."[7] But deciphering between what is good or bad is still not the same thing as denying the experience of misery altogether.

Lady Philosophy knows that Boethius is wrongfully imprisoned, and yet she insists that he is better off because evil people who get away with their crimes are more unhappy than everyone else. Boethius seems to follow along, or at least pretends to, but something about this argument doesn't add up because it doesn't appeal to common sense. He tells her, "if you were to go out into the streets and talk with ordinary people, I'm not sure you could get them to agree with you, or even listen with a straight face."[8] This appeal to ordinary people is one of the first birth pangs of the modern novel, which Lady Philosophy is quick to dismiss, telling him,

> Think of it this way: you can look up at the blue sky and then down at the dirt; everything else in sight disappears and you feel yourself to be now down in the dirt and now up in the stars. Ordinary people don't look up at the stars. But does that mean we have to join them?[9]

The modern novel can be interpreted as a reaction against Lady Philosophy's position, in both its snobbery and optimism, siding instead with ordinary people who turn their attention away from the stars to dwell on the dirt. By 1740, Richardson formulated an idea of the novel, in opposition to Socratic and Boethian optimism, as a genre that must categorically reject the blind faith that wicked people have to end up unhappy. Nearly a century later, Stendhal defined the novel as though it were a direct clapback against Lady Philosophy, using her own imagery:

> Look here, sir, a novel is a mirror moving along a highway. One minute you see it reflect the azure skies, next minute the mud and puddles of the road. And the man who carries the mirror in his pack will be accused by you of immorality! His mirror shows the mud and you accuse the mirror! Rather you should accuse the road in which the puddle lies, or, even better, the inspector of roads who lets the water collect and the puddle form.[10]

The prosaic mud of life—what other genre of literature would hold up a moving mirror to this in all its detail, all its squalor, in a form that ranges in scope from a narrative that could be consumed in a single sitting to one that could be serialized over several years?

The novel, to Stendhal, resides in that familiar paradox of truth-telling in the form of a deception, a con—what Socrates had tried to warn us about. Like Eugene Thacker's characterization of the pessimist who is "usually understood to be the complainer, forever pointing out what is wrong with the world without ever offering a solution," the novelist just absurdly tries to hold up this shaking, unwieldy mirror to the world while in transit, reflecting its mud.[11] But this pessimist-novelist is not to blame as much as the "inspector of roads," that person whose responsibility it is to rectify such a bleak situation—the kind of person who, coincidentally, so often gets offended by truth-telling, and uses the word "pessimism" in as insulting, as pejorative a way as the term "novel" has been used historically.

Over the centuries, the burden seems to have fallen to novelists to address the charges of pessimism, as Thomas Hardy did in 1912, when he penned the general preface to the Wessex editions of his novels:

> That these impressions have been condemned as "pessimistic"—as if that were a very wicked adjective—shows a curious muddle-mindedness. It must be obvious that there is a higher characteristic of philosophy than pessimism, or than meliorism, or even than the optimism of these critics—which is truth.[12]

There is a perfunctory gesture here of dismissing pessimism, perhaps to avoid alienating any more readers—but he pans optimism along with it, and even calls into question whether the term "pessimistic" is "a very wicked adjective" at all. He writes in service of the truth, a truth that represents a "higher characteristic of philosophy." Maybe it is even higher than philosophy itself, which is why the kind of truth he articulates can only reside in the novel.

Whether *The Consolation of Philosophy* actually endorses Lady Philosophy's position or ironically satirizes it is not as straightforward a matter as it might seem. After doing her best to convince Boethius, Lady Philosophy eventually says, "But this has gone on for a long while, and I see that you are tired. What you need is some relief in the charms of poetry."[13] Is this an admission of defeat? Not quite, since the poem she inspires affirms the order of the universe. And she also gets the last word in the book, telling Boethius, "It is required of you that you do good and that you remember that you live in the constant sight of a judge who sees all things."[14] This parting message sounds like more of a threat than a consolation. And what does it accomplish in the end? Armed with her scepter and her pile of books, what does she do with them except for trying to distract Boethius from his earthly reality? And if Boethius does fall for it, then he is no different from Don Quixote or Emma Bovary in their own quest to distract themselves from the world with the imaginary worlds inscribed in their own piles of books.

Jean de Meun, the thirteenth-century French translator of Boethius, makes Lady Philosophy work a bit harder in trying to convince the forlorn prisoner in the continuation of *The Romance of the Rose*, which Guillaume de Lorris had begun nearly forty years earlier. Lady Philosophy, here named "Reason," comes to the captive Lover, like Boethius, at his lowest point of despair. In the first 4,000 lines of the Romance that de Lorris had written, the Lover is lured to the Spring of Narcissus in a walled garden, where Narcissus had met his fate, wasting away in erotic desire for his own reflection. De Lorris makes the Lover regret the "evil hour when I looked at my reflection" and saw the enticing Rose there, wishing he had never given in to the temptation, because he is summarily assaulted and captured by the God of Love, who had been stalking him the entire time.[15]

The God of Love is described as a pessimist's nightmare. Brimming with toxic positivity, he commands the Lover to "prepare yourself for joy and pleasure, for Love cares nothing for gloomy men," while at the same time informing him that, "The lover will never have what he seeks: something is always lacking and he will never be at peace, and this war will never end until I choose to bring about peace."[16] The God of Love is a tyrant and leaves his prisoner with a few paltry gifts, among them Hope. But the Lover quickly realizes that Hope "is dangerous, for many true lovers sustain and will sustain themselves in their love by Hope, but will never achieve their goal."[17] This is where de Meun picks up the poem. In the absence of Hope, Reason comes and tries to console the Lover, but unlike Boethius' Lady Philosophy, de Meun's Reason relies on an eros of her own in an effort to liberate the Lover from the shackles of his erotic disease.

This allegorical figure of Reason is hostile to love, defining it as a "mental illness" that emerges from "a burning desire, born of disordered perception, to embrace and to kiss and to seek carnal gratification."[18] And yet she still tries to seduce him, saying, "Nevertheless, I have no wish for you to remain without a sweetheart. If it please you, fix your thoughts on me. Am I not a beautiful and noble lady, fit to serve any worthy man, were he emperor of Rome?"[19] She insists that he look at her and see himself reflected in her face, as though re-creating the moment he had gazed into the Spring of Narcissus in order to undo and replace that moment. Or, as a representative of Plato, perhaps she is alluding less to the Narcissus myth than the *Symposium* myth and offers him the impossible promise of uniting with his divided self, especially since he is afflicted by the "mental illness" of love that divides him from his reason. Unlike the God of Love, who dooms him to a desire that is "always lacking," Reason promises that the love she can provide him is so abundant that "you will never lack anything you need, whatever misfortune may befall you."[20]

This is seductive enough, so the Lover responds, "Now tell me, not in Latin but in French, what you want me to do for you."[21] Here is a key shift in the movement from the academic Latin of Boethius to the Romantic underpinnings of what would later emerge as the modern novel, written in a clear vernacular for ordinary readers. But Reason, like Boethius' Lady Philosophy, is disappointing to ordinary ears. What she wants is for him to live like Socrates, "who was so firm and strong that he was neither happy in prosperity nor sad in adversity."[22] The disconsolate Lover, unpersuaded by Socratic and Boethian stoicism, snaps back, "I would not give three chickpeas for Socrates . . . and I have no wish to hear any more about him."[23] Reason stalls him in conversation, but ultimately she fails. It is only with the intervention of Venus that the Lover can win the war against the God of Love and consummate his union with the Rose. Reason's exhortation for him to "love generally rather than in particular" is summarily rejected.[24] The Lover is not interested in philosophical generalities, but in novelistic particularities.

The Romance of the Rose can be read as an encyclopedia that summarizes the history of consolation literature, exposing the failure inherent to this genre, which, after Boethius, had acquired a focus on eros. De Lorris introduces this work as one "in which the whole art of love is contained. The matter is fair and new."[25] This is a striking statement, not least because it is aware of its own newness, something that later becomes a key feature of the modern novel. The irony, though, is that de Lorris is aware that this is a deeply referential text, undermining its novelty by echoing the same ambition of Andreas Capellanus's widely popular seducer's manual, *The Art of Courtly Love*, written around 1174, about half a century before de Lorris started writing the first part of *The Romance of the Rose*.

The new movement of literature that took eros as a serious theme for the first time since Plato's dialogues and Ovid's erotic poems occurred "quite suddenly," according to C. S. Lewis, at the end of the eleventh century in Languedoc, with the appearance of the Provençal troubadour poets.[26] These male poets would sing about themselves as helpless vassals of love and of the married women they pursued, lamenting love's torments. Lewis advises current readers, if they are to understand this articulation of eros at all, to "conceive a world emptied of that ideal of 'happiness'—a happiness grounded on successful love—which still supplies the motive of our popular fiction."[27] This erotic experience is fundamentally pessimistic. And this pessimism was so popular and influential that even Nietzsche credits the "Provençal knight-poets, those magnificent and inventive human beings," as the artists "to whom Europe owes so many things and almost owes itself."[28]

The first documented troubadour was Duke William of Aquitaine, whose connections with Muslim Spain may have been, at least in part, responsible for the transmission of the Tristan legend as it made its way from Persia across North Africa and into Europe. This story about cosmically doomed lovers who drink a fateful love potion and are tormented to their deaths by an all-consuming passion for each other is one that also falls under the genre of consolation. Even Gottfried von Strassburg introduces his version by announcing his attention to "solace noble hearts" who are suffering from the particularly heightened pain of love that the troubadours sing about.[29] Thomas of Britain's version was inspired by—and maybe even written for—William of Aquitaine's granddaughter, Eleanor of Aquitaine, who married Prince Louis of France before divorcing him for Prince Henry of England.[30]

It is allegedly Eleanor of Aquitaine's court that also inspired Capellanus's treatise, which crystallizes the notion that "Love is a certain inborn suffering."[31] Capellanus begins this work of consolation by addressing his friend Walter in terms that evoke both Ovid and Plato's *Phaedrus*: "You tell me that you are a new recruit of Love, and, having recently been wounded by an arrow of his, you do not know how to manage your horse's reins properly and you cannot find any cure for yourself."[32] And, like *Phaedrus*, after codifying the different kinds of love through a series of dialogues, Capellanus retracts his work, urging Walter to choose God over erotic love.

This tension between religious love and erotic love is what the genre of the Romance fleshes out, especially in the Tristan legend, but it has its origins in another series of texts that fall into the genre of consolation, and which Jean de Meun had also translated from Latin into French and then cited in *The Romance of the Rose*: the letters of Abelard and Heloise. In the twelfth century, Peter Abelard, one of the most famous and charismatic French intellectuals of his time, despite frequent charges of heresy, turned to Boethius as a model to articulate his own misery when he wrote his *Historia Calamitum*, or "The Story of his Misfortunes." This work details how he brushed up against the law and the church when he took Heloise, a private student of his, as his lover and got her pregnant. Once her uncle found out, Abelard was assaulted and castrated, prompting him to flee and live for a while as a fugitive, which didn't stop Heloise from trying to follow him.

As a letter to an anonymous friend, the *Historia Calamitum* begins with,

> There are times when example is better than precept for stirring or soothing human feelings; and so I propose to follow up the words of consolation I gave you in person with the history of my own misfortunes, hoping thereby to give you comfort in absence.[33]

In this sentence is the intersection of Abelard's entire philosophical career with his own lived experience. The raging theological debate that dominated academia at the time was between the Nominalists, who rejected universal categories, and the so-called Realists, who defended Plato's theory of ideal forms. Abelard's philosophy, which he called "Conceptualism," was one that mediated between both factions, anchoring abstract universals in the immanent details of material and contingent reality. This position is deeply informed by Aristotle, whom Abelard read exclusively through Boethius' translations. But by focusing on the "example" rather than the "precept" in his letter, as a way of "stirring or soothing human emotions," he helps lay one of the foundations of the modern novel.

Heloise, having gotten ahold of this letter that was not addressed to her, fired a missive at him, saying,

> I was not a little surprised and troubled by your forgetfulness, when neither reverence for God nor our mutual love nor the example of the holy Fathers made you think of trying to comfort me, wavering and exhausted as I was by prolonged grief."[34]

His so-called consolation fails to console the right person, and she takes him to task for it. It is humiliating for the most educated female philosopher of her time to be chasing after this man after having birthed his son, trying to rekindle their legendary passion, which is what leaves the most lasting impression across centuries of readers.

By all accounts, Abelard was known not just for his intellect but for how hot he was. People all over France would follow this itinerant philosopher around the country, and it's hard to believe that it was simply for his philosophy, although he did certainly make his lessons livelier than the standard medieval pedagogy of merely lecturing on a text and glossing its contents. He revived the Socratic method and brought a charismatic charm to the immediacy of his interactions with his students. By the time he met Heloise, he was already famous and still "had youth and exceptional good looks as well as my great reputation to recommend me, and feared no rebuff from any woman I might choose to honor with my love."[35] His tutoring sessions with her quickly turned steamy, and—in an image that emerges again nearly two centuries later with Dante's most famous lovers in *Inferno*, Paolo and Francesca—he describes the scene with "our books open before us," but "more words of love than of our reading passed between us, and more kissing than teaching."[36]

Being hot for teacher has never been anything new. Socrates ignites a sense of eros in both Phaedrus and Alcibiades, but directs that eros toward philosophy rather than his own body. He introduces the idea that the pursuit of philosophy is fundamentally an erotic one, and that eros is a source of truth, but it needs to transcend the base appetites of the body to reach the heights of philosophy. At a time when it was customary for older teachers to have sexual relations with their younger students, Socrates stopped short at gentle flirting because that was never his interest anyway—much to the comical frustration of Alcibiades in *Symposium*, who tries and fails to do everything he can to get in Socrates's tunic.

But to Abelard and Heloise, their intense physical passion also becomes a form of experiential knowledge and discovery that, if it doesn't enhance philosophy, seems to replace it with something else, something new. Abelard says, "our desires left no stage of lovemaking untried, and if love could devise something new, we welcomed it."[37] Abelard notes how even the form of his writing shifted during this affair, so that, "when inspiration did come to me, it was for writing love songs, not the secrets of philosophy."[38] And after the inspiration for love songs dissipated, he found himself writing this lengthy epistle, bristling with novelistic detail, as though he himself embodies the erotic tension between philosophy and the novel.

As for Heloise, her intellectual prowess soared far above any living philosopher; if there was any match for her, it would be Abelard. But the value she placed on her eros for him exceeded any philosophical pursuit she could engage in. She fell so deeply in love with him that she even disguised herself as a nun while pregnant so that she could visit him in exile and have sex in a cloister. She eventually became a nun, but only to be closer to him, saying, "When you hurried towards God I followed you, indeed, I went first to take the veil. . . . I would have had no hesitation, God knows, in following you or going ahead at your bidding to the flames of Hell."[39]

In her letters, she makes it abundantly clear that she cares neither for secular nor religious law and doesn't need God if she had him, an expression that would dominate the mood and tone of the Tristan legend that was just making its way into Europe from Persia at this time, a legend that celebrates love as a criminal and heretical act. One of the places that Abelard fled to after his castration was Troyes, where Chrétien de Troyes—a friend of Capellanus—wrote one of the first versions of the Tristan story just a few decades after Abelard's death.

In Heloise, legend and reality merge so that she sounds like Isolde when she tells Abelard, "We shall both be destroyed. All that is left us is suffering as great as our love has been."[40] She claims that she doesn't need to be his wife, but just his lover, and even if the "Emperor of the whole world" would want to marry her and offer the world as her possession, "it would be dearer and more honorable to me to be called not his Empress but your whore," a line that clearly haunted Jean de Meun enough that he inserted a revised version of it into Reason's speech when she is trying to seduce the Lover in *The Romance of the Rose*.[41]

In response to such impassioned pleas and reminders of their torrid love affair that is rivaled only by the stuff of legend, Abelard is cold and distant. Insisting on calling her his "dearly beloved sister in Christ," he offers little more than thoughts and prayers.[42] His tone is infuriatingly pedantic, and he speaks more about universals than the particulars of their relationship, citing more from scripture than addressing any of the details she had brought up. In response to Heloise telling him, "you are the sole cause of my sorrow, and you alone can grant me the grace of consolation," he stalls, deflects, distracts.[43] But she continues writing, continues to press him, to solicit some kind of emotionally engaged response in kind. As a result, he writes, "I have decided to answer you on each point in turn, not so much in self-justification as for your own enlightenment and encouragement."[44] Charming. After fornicating in a church, this isn't exactly the sexiest follow-up. His consolation is a failure.

Ultimately, Abelard cannot reconcile the tension between philosophical and theological universals with the contingent details of his racy affair with Heloise. The answer that de Lorris and de Meun offer in reconciling this categorical tension between philosophical universals with novelistic details is the allegory, which C. S. Lewis defines as both "a struggle between personified abstractions" and "simile seen from the other end."[45] Allegoresis is an indirect kind of sight that offers a glimpse into what otherwise cannot be seen, in the same way that Perseus was able to behead Medusa by looking at her reflection in his shield, because looking at her directly would turn him into stone. It relies on the Platonic notion that the world we call reality is just a shadow of the ideal world of Forms, so allegory opens up the space to consider how these Forms would behave if they acquired human characteristics, like Reason in her attempts to seduce the Lover. But, in line with Plato's thought, the shadow world is never an exact copy of the ideal world, so any reflection is necessarily a deception.

Nowhere is this dramatized more clearly than the Lover gazing into the Spring of Narcissus, seeing the Rose that inspires his desire where he would expect to see his own face mirrored back to him. This is the crisis at the intersection between identity and difference, repeating not only the crisis of Narcissus himself but of the divided lovers in *Symposium*. It is a trap that locks the Lover into bondage with a self that is out of reach. This is why, in surrendering to the God of Love—he has no other choice—the Lover tells him, anticipating Freudian psychoanalysis by over six hundred years, "My heart is yours and not my own."[46] The God of Love represents the force external to him that seizes his entire identity, spinning him into a vertigo of madness so that he cannot distinguish between the inner turn to the self and the external gesture to the Rose, since both are constitutive of each other.

There is something inherent to the way love functions that makes it particularly conducive to allegory. Even by the nineteenth century, long after allegory had fallen out of fashion, Stendhal writes, "From the moment he falls in love even the wisest man no longer sees anything *as it really is* . . . [J]udging by its effects on his happiness, whatever he imagines becomes reality."[47] And Nietzsche echoes this sentiment in *The Anti-Christ*, saying,

> Love is the state in which man sees things most of all as they are *not*. The illusion-creating force is there at its height, likewise the sweetening and *transforming* force. One endures more when in love than one otherwise would, one tolerates everything.[48]

This "illusion-creating force" is the same force behind art itself, as Proust later demonstrates, generating a new way of seeing the world. In art, as in love, one is able to endure more than one otherwise would, which is why the stakes in allegory are so high, involving a full-scale war even with the God of Love himself.

In the deceptive reflection of love, then, conflating self and other, is the organizing principle of the artwork, of the text itself. Even the God of Love at one point seems to stand both inside and outside of the text at the same time, saying that, "all those who are yet to live should call this book the *Mirror of Lovers*, since they will see great benefits in it for them, provided they do not believe Reason, the miserable wretch."[49] The mirror is not just a feature of allegory, but its own genre, imparting didactic wisdom, advice, or consolation. This is the same genre that gave rise to the "Mirror for Princes" tradition that would eventually spawn Machiavelli's *The Prince* in the sixteenth century, as well as the work by Jean de Meun's contemporary, Marguerite Porete, who imagined a mystical union of both God and Love in one's self—or at least the space opened up in the evacuation of selfhood—in the heretical work that bears the magnificently convoluted title, "The Mirror of Simple Souls who are Annihilated and Remain Only in Will and Desire of Love." Even the title performs how obscure this kind of mirror is.

Whatever the mirror is, though, it demands a certain kind of participation, involvement, and identification of the reader with the text. The reader, like the Lover in *The Romance of the Rose*, is supposed to identify something of themselves in a work that takes them outside of themselves. Reading, in this way, mimics the act of love, the erotic encounter of the self as Other. As Barthes writes in *The Pleasure of the Text,* "The text is a fetish object, and *this fetish desires me.*"[50] In the text that is a mirror, this desire is reciprocated.

THE MONSTROUS CONSOLATIONS OF YOUNG WERTHER

Nearly half a millennium after *The Romance of the Rose* was written, the twenty-three-year-old Goethe published the novel that would make him an overnight celebrity, *The Sorrows of Young Werther*. His fame was attributed to the fact that, in Werther, he created a character who so "perfectly expressed the mood of the time while at the same time commenting on it, as it were, from within," that it seemed as though he "actually *was* his (reading) audience, mirroring back to them what they themselves (however inchoately) were claiming to be."[51] And in Werther's first interaction with Lotte—the woman he falls in love with, and on whose account he eventually kills himself—they bond over novels.

Lotte tells him that when she was younger, novels were her favorite genre, but she still likes reading them, specifying that she likes "best those authors in whom I rediscover my own world, in whose books things happen as they do in my environment."[52] Novels function as a mirror for Lotte, which Werther understands as an erotic cue. In response, he seems to transform himself—and the world around him—into such a mirror so that she can recognize herself in it and fall in love with the image of herself through him. It is as though he writes these letters to Wilhelm, whose letters back to him aren't printed, with the awareness that they will be collected as an epistolary novel, a genre already made popular by the mid-eighteenth century by Richardson and Rousseau. Does Wilhelm even exist in Werther's actual life, or is he a fictional character whom Werther has made up as an excuse to construct this novelistic world to catch Lotte's reflection in it? "I see everything in the world around me only as it relates to her," he claims.[53] Seeing himself as the eighteenth-century reincarnation of Dante's Paolo, or perhaps even Abelard, he sneers at Albert, Lotte's fiancé, whose "heart doesn't beat in sympathy at—oh!—at the passage in a beloved book at which Lotte's heart and mine come together in a single point."[54]

The reality that Werther quickly comes to contend with is the fact that he does not belong in Lotte's world and that he is actually trapped in his own reflection in a modernized version of the Spring of Narcissus. The novel opens with him describing a garden and surrounding natural landscape in great detail, which he wishes he could reproduce through language "so that it might become the mirror of your soul."[55] He is particularly drawn to a fountain that makes him think of bygone times—perhaps specifically the medieval era of Romance that he seems to be more familiar and comfortable with. Sitting by this fountain, he thinks to himself, "I withdraw into myself, and I discover a world!"[56] This is the world he resides in for most of the novel, and as he pines for Lotte, it is from this world that he suffers the blindness of Narcissus, saying that, "the whole world around me is lost to my sight."[57] Also similar to Narcissus is the brief moment of misguided hope, where he seems to be encouraged in his erotic pursuit, leading him to declare ecstatically, "how I worship myself now that she loves me!"[58]

The Sorrows of Young Werther seems to pick up where the genre of Romance had left off, resurrecting those old tropes only to wallow in the dust they've collected. *The Romance of the Rose* can hardly qualify as a pessimistic work—not nearly as pessimistic as any of the Tristan poems—but its ending is ambiguous. The Lover wins the war and finally consummates his love with the Rose, but he then wakes up. It was all a dream. And anyhow, the Rose in the Garden of Pleasure is trapped by an enclosed wall that bears images on the outside of Hate, Cruelty, Baseness, Covetousness, Avarice, Envy, Sorrow, Old Age, Religious Hypocrisy, and

Poverty.[59] While de Meun ends the poem on a note of ambiguous triumph, there is no telling what de Lorris had originally planned, especially since he has the Lover, in retrospect, regret having ever looked into the Spring of Narcissus and seeing the Rose there in the first place. If he took as his template Capellanus's *The Art of Courtly Love*, was he going to dramatize the retraction, as well?

Either way, Goethe seems to answer the question of what happens to the Lover when he wakes up from this dream. The reality is an awful comedown. Werther complains about waking up from dreams and finding his arms outstretched for Lotte, only to realize that he's alone in bed, which makes him "weep inconsolably as I face a gloomy future."[60] Whatever fantasy world that Werther tries to create through art can only ever be an illusion, a dream from which he must inevitably wake up, but the world he wakes up to is inhospitable and incompatible with his identity. It is as though he had been raised in the medieval era of Romance, fell asleep for five hundred years, and then suddenly wakes up to a disorienting, modern world that is devoid of transcendental meaning, like Don Quixote and Emma Bovary. This disorientation is the space that the modern novel inhabits.

At times, the discrepancy between Werther's melodramatic medievalism and the modern world is quixotically—if inadvertently—funny in a work that is otherwise notably humorless, as when he describes Lotte in terms of the Tristan legend, the only kind of referential framework that makes sense to him: "She doesn't see, she doesn't feel that she's mixing a poison that will destroy her and me both; and with the deepest pleasure I drain the goblet she hands me for my undoing."[61] Feeling "bored" and "out of place" while visiting a prince's hunting lodge, he has no patience for this prince, firmly rooted in the era of Enlightenment, who "has a feeling for art, and his feeling would be deeper if he weren't limited by that repulsive scientific approach and the usual jargon."[62]

In his repudiation of the Enlightenment values that dominated the end of the eighteenth century, Werther bears a striking resemblance to Goethe himself, who also seemed like a transplant from the age of Romance. Like a Provençal troubadour, he had affairs almost exclusively with married women. And the inspiration for Lotte, a woman named Charlotte Buff, was the daughter of the local representative of the Teutonic Order, a "medieval order of knighthood that . . . still had many commercial interests to protect."[63] In a letter to her, as he was getting ready for the novel's publication, he referred to it as a "prayer book," that distinctly medieval genre, even though this novel is as anti-Christian as the Tristan legend, which replaced Christianity with the religion of love.[64] It is religious only in the sense that his passions replace the Passion of the Christ. Werther even kills himself on Christmas Day. As Terry Pinkard points out, the *Leiden* in the title *Die Leiden des jungen Werther* is the theological term used for Christ's Passion, and has "misleadingly" been translated into English as "Sorrows" or "Sufferings."[65]

Werther, as a passionate, suffering, time-traveling pilgrim from Romance, is so ill-equipped for the necessities of modern life that he can't even hold down a job, a fact that distressed one of the novel's most avid readers, none other than Napoleon himself, who was so obsessed with this novel that he read it seven times. In 1808, when Napoleon met Goethe in person, he complained that it was too much to bear for him to see Werther suffer in both love and work; one or the other would have sufficed, but this kind of double pessimism was overwhelming for Napoleon. Goethe diplomatically informed him that he was the first reader to identify this "error."[66]

This "error" is one of the first literary depictions of dissatisfaction in the modern workplace, articulating what it is like to be micromanaged by a mid-level boss. "I like to work briskly, not worrying over tiny details," Werther says defensively, like any daydreaming Romantic who is detail-oriented only when it comes to the world of nature, of thought, of feeling, rather than bureaucracy.[67] He is disgusted by the modern Protestant work ethic, by the rise of capitalism, complaining to Wilhelm, "And you and your crowd are to blame for this; you talked me into bearing this yoke by continually preaching 'activity' to me. Activity!"[68]

In this world of activity, of busy-ness and business, of tedious tasks and meaningless work, there is hardly any room for contemplation, for simply being. A life dominated by that odious word, "activity," by busywork, doesn't allow for the leisurely space to seek out one's reflection in Homer or Ossian, whom Werther regards as the lifeblood of his imagination. It would be humiliating to expect Tristan to sit behind a desk, swarmed with paperwork, fumbling through his mistakes, when he knows he is capable of slaying dragons, winning wars, and having legendary adventures of love—a particularly intense love that defines both his life and his death. This is the humiliation of Werther, and indeed of every office worker who has ever felt that acute pang of anxiety that their unlived life is being wasted away, siphoned off to bureaucratic procedure, to utter meaninglessness.

In Werther are the embryonic traces not only of Kafka's bureaucrats—including his gods reduced to bureaucrats, like Poseidon, who had "hardly seen the oceans" because he is so overwhelmed with processing paperwork at the bottom of the sea—but of Bartleby.[69] Bartleby is someone who could have been a Byron—as even his own boss notes—but whose passions had been extirpated and dried up by the drudgery of work.[70] And Werther, like Bartleby after him, becomes so disenchanted with the modern world that he is eventually sapped of any strength or interest or will to pursue anything he had once enjoyed. He was once a skilled draftsman, but he abandons his drawings. He loses his "feeling for nature, and books disgust me. When we lack ourselves, we lack everything."[71] As someone whose entire identity consists of books, who seems to self-consciously construct his life as a book, Werther—or rather, Goethe—seems to inaugurate a modern aesthetic of erasure, writing a novel that cancels itself, even kills itself. Things that once held such dear value to Werther transform before his eyes, emptying themselves of value altogether.

The psychological force of the novel seems to be mapped along a seismograph of intensifying and diminishing values, which are constantly in flux, subject to that Romantic principle of mutability. "Can you say 'This is,'" Werther writes to Wilhelm, "when everything is transitory, when everything rolls by with the speed of a storm, and the full strength of its existence so seldom endures?"[72] This process of shifting values, what Nietzsche would later term "the transvaluation of values"—in German, *Umwertung aller Werte*—is inscribed in Werther's name. To this extent, we can read this novel as an allegory, even if the transcendental side of allegory at this point has been eroded by modernity. At one point, he finds himself returning back to his beloved fountain, that relic of the Spring of Narcissus from *The Romance of the Rose*, "which is so dear to me, and now a thousand times dearer"—in German, *„der mir so wert und nun tausendmal werter ist."*[73] The fountain is *werter* to Werther; the feelings that he associates with Romance are so intense that they overwhelm him, eventually exhausting him of feeling altogether. Avital Ronell notes how his name doesn't just mean "value," but "surplus value."[74] But this inflation of Romantic value carries no currency in modern life.

The thing is that Werther understands this. He may not have lucked out at love, and he may have fucked up at work, but he's not stupid and he's not delusional. What is so deeply unsettling about his resolve to kill himself is that it's not a rash decision fueled by passion, but the result of a sobering, measured realization. If his passions defined his life, he is dispassionate in his pursuit of death. "I'm not dreaming, I'm not having delusions!" he proclaims. "Close to the grave, I see things more clearly."[75] There is no convincing reason why he should be doubted here. The inner fantasy world that he creates for himself is the same one that everyone creates for themselves, whether they care to admit it or not. But he understands that it will not translate to reality, and he understands that reality will never give him what he needs in order to live a life full of meaning, full of value, full of *Wert*. In what kind of allegory does a character named "Surplus of Value" find himself, his life, and his world, deprived of value altogether? By the end of the novel, both he and the world seem to be deprived not only of value, but of illusion. Werther here is reduced to that other homonym of his name, to *Wörter*: just words, words, words.

Like Hamlet—or rather, Nietzsche's interpretation of Hamlet—Werther has "looked truly into the essence of things."[76] For Nietzsche, the knowledge derived from looking truly into the essence of things is what "kills action," since "action requires the veils of illusion."[77] Both Hamlet and Werther strip themselves of illusion in the face of deciding whether to be or not to be. But for Hamlet, he can't be bothered to kill himself, however preoccupied he is with the question of suicide, because his suicide wouldn't "change anything in the eternal nature of things."[78] Werther seems to raise the question from a more disturbing angle, though. If his suicide can't change anything in the eternal nature of things, neither could a decision to go on living.

So both Hamlet and Werther peer over the brink of the abyss and see the same thing, but arrive at contradictory insights. What do they see, though? Werther describes the "consuming force concealed in all of nature" in the same way that Emily Brontë does over half a century later, as fundamentally self-destructive, as annihilating everything it has created. When he catches a glimpse of it, he says, "I see nothing but a monster eternally swallowing, eternally chewing its cud."[79] Nature is a monster that both generates and operates by a principle of suicide, a suicide that is trapped in the paradox of eternity, which is why it eternally swallows and destroys everything that it creates, everything that it is. Nature creates itself precisely in order to kill itself; everything in nature is caught in a process of inevitable decay that nature itself inflicts. This is the sickness unto death that Werther comes to understand in all things, and he arrives at this vision of monstrosity by contemplating the landscape around him, noting how "huge mountains surrounded me, abysses opened before me, and torrents plunged down."[80] It seems that it is in response to this imagery and this insight that Nietzsche, in *Beyond Good and Evil*, writes his most famous and cryptic aphorism: "Whoever fights monsters should see to it that in the process he does not become a monster. And when you look long into an abyss, the abyss also looks into you."[81]

Does Werther, by choosing suicide, become the monster that he sees in this abysmal vision of nature? By gazing into this vision, is he catching his own reflection? Or is it nature moving through him and catching its own self-destructive reflection? Is there actually only one character in this novel, and is that character the monster of nature, taking on ever so slightly different modulations that reflect each other, because they are all rooted in the same infinite substance? In light of Goethe's Spinozism, Werther's story seems to be refracted across the background stories of minor characters: the fired clerk who was also in love with Lotte and then loses his mind on the heath, the peasant whose love for his mistress is thwarted by her brother, and the Ophelia-like girl who kills herself over love. And finally there is Albert himself: the fantasy projection of what it would look like to be engaged and ultimately married to Lotte. The edges around these characters seem to blur. Lotte's character was never in focus to begin with; there are hardly any distinguishing details about her, and she comes off as dull, bland, and thoroughly indistinguishable from any other placeholder love interest. She is just the screen onto which Werther projects his own surplus of desire. Everyone blurs into each other, following the same principle of dis-individuation that dissolves Brontë's characters in *Wuthering Heights*, until they all just dissolve into this monster of nature gazing into its own eternal, self-effacing reflection.

If his suicide can be interpreted as an act of uniting with eternal nature, is Werther achieving a kind of eternity that goes on to replicate the suicidal act long after he is gone, carried out by those impressionable readers who, inspired by him, followed his fate? Is this the surplus inscribed in his name, a surplus of suicide that seems to bleed out of the text, as though demanding more blood, more suicide? What kind of a failed "consolation," then, does this novel provide those readers? Goethe insists that we approach this novel as a "friend" who consoles us: "And you, good soul, you that feel the same pressures he did, derive consolation from his suffering, and let this little book be your friend, if you cannot find any closer one, thanks to fate or your own fault!"[82]

But there is something uncanny, perhaps even monstrous, about regarding a book as a person, let alone a friend—a being stitched together by letters that include no answers, as well as the ominous and anonymous editorial voice that steps in to narrate Werther's final days with a spectral kind of omniscience. This novel and this suicide—both become interchangeable in this context—acquire a life of their own, calling to the reader from the grave, in the form of an epitaph that Goethe included in later editions of the novel: "You bemoan him, you love him, dear soul, / You salvage his memory from disgrace; / Behold, his spirit signals to you from his cave: / *Be a man and do not follow after me.*"[83] This is why Hans Rudolf Vaget refers both to Werther and *Werther* as "the undead."[84] Even Goethe himself referred to the novel as something that he "fed with the blood of my own heart."[85] But the novel's thirst for blood doesn't seem to be quenched.

Had Werther been undead for five hundred years? Having fed on Goethe's blood, did he rise from the coffin of *The Romance of the Rose* on the hunt for new blood, seducing his readers despite the numerous protests from his author? Goethe, distancing himself from the horror of his creation almost immediately upon publication, seems to be reflected half a century later in Mary Shelley's *Frankenstein*, where the doctor who had sewn limbs together and galvanized them into life also came to reject his creation in horror. And maybe this is why Frankenstein's Creature finds consolation in reading *The Sorrows of Young Werther*. Not only has he been outcast by his creator, but he also arrives at a similar understanding of identity as Werther. He is not so much a monstrous amalgamation of different limbs as he is a collection, like Werther, of different books. And these books "produced in me an infinity of new images and feelings, that sometimes raised me to ecstasy, but more frequently sunk me into the lowest dejection."[86] In this dejection, Werther represents for him "a more divine being than I had ever beheld or imagined." He even weeps for Werther's death and "applied much personally to my own feelings and condition."[87]

But the Creature realizes that his own situation is far more pessimistic than Werther's because for him, there would be

> none to lament my annihilation. My person was hideous, and my stature gigantic: what did this mean? Who was I? What was I? Whence did I come? What was my destination? These questions continually recurred, but I was unable to solve them.[88]

These are the universal questions of interiority, which are at odds with the contingent world around him, inflicting its violence on him and eliciting violence from him in return. The debris that is left in the wake of the violent collision between the outer world and the inner life is what both *Werther* and *Frankenstein*—and arguably every novel—consist of. It is as though Werther and the Creature can only exist as novels and construct their identities out of novels. And in both cases, the novels hold up a mirror to something deeply monstrous.

In what seems like a cruel parody of the Spring of Narcissus, the Creature stumbles across a pond and recoils at his own reflection:

> But how I was terrified, when I viewed myself in a transparent pool! At first I started back, unable to believe that it was indeed I who was reflected in the mirror; and when I became fully convinced that I was in reality the monster that I am, I was filled with the bitterest sensations of despondence and mortification.[89]

Perhaps the monstrosity that the Creature identifies here is not only the visual traces of the artifice at work in his own creation but also the opposite of artifice—maybe it is the same monster of nature that Werther himself had gazed at and identified his own reflection in. In his reflection, he identifies the monstrosity that belies everything, that connects everything in its horror. In Shelley's pessimistic vision, this is the only connection that the Creature can hope for.

In the Creature's disgust at his own reflection, Stefani Engelstein identifies him as the "Anti-Narcissus."[90] With *Werther* and *Frankenstein*, and even *Wuthering Heights*, the novel has anatomized the Romance, turning it inside out. Whereas the mirror of Romance is a site of seductive illusion, in the novel it becomes the site of disillusionment and even horror. The only seduction at work here is the seduction of pessimism, and it is this pessimism that moves the genre of consolation from Boethius's attempt to bridge the divide between philosophy and the novel to a genre that seems to declare war on philosophy, after having been belittled and dismissed for centuries. Heloise finds no consolation in Abelard's letters or in philosophy. Capellanus seems to model his consolation on Plato, but then gives up and retracts his advice. In *The Romance of the Rose*, the Lover comes out adamantly against Socrates, and *Werther* and *Frankenstein* both seem to dispel with the dreamy illusions of Romance while holding on to the disdain for Socrates's rationalist legacy. The Creature refuses to be reduced to the mere scientific and positivistic attributes of his existence. What gives him a sense of meaning or lack of meaning in the world cannot be addressed by reason.

Werther, too, picks a fight when Albert dismisses people who are too passionate. Albert argues that passionate people run the risk of losing their sense of judgment, to which Werther, in a proto-Nietzschean moment of defiant exuberance, proudly declares:

> Oh, you rational people! . . . Passion! Intoxication! Insanity! You stand there so calmly, so devoid of empathy, you moral people! . . . I've been drunk more than once, my passions have always been close to madness, and I'm not repentant on either count: because, in my measure, I have learned to understand why people have always needed to decry as drunkards and madmen every extraordinary person who accomplished anything great or seemingly impossible.[91]

Is this just Werther railing at Albert, or is it the voice of the novel genre shouting in rebellion against the sober, cold, mechanical representatives of philosophy? Albert himself—perhaps not so much a character as a principle of *Albernheit* ("stupidity")—seems to be drowned out in this tirade, as Werther uses him as an excuse to hurl his insults at philosophers in general, shouting, "Shame on you, you sober folk! Shame on you, you sages!"[92] *The Sorrows of Young Werther*, then, can be read as a novelistic manifesto of passion against Socratic rationalism.

Is the novel, like Werther, just jealous of philosophy? Is it motivated by a petty but energetic hatred that, at its core, is a matter of eros? It is this eros that, despite all of the repudiation of philosophy, still seems to bring the novel back to it, or at least to that moment when philosophy and the novel were united. Before *Wuthering Heights* and *In Search of Lost Time* used the same image for the same purpose, *The Sorrows of Young Werther* seems to trace the same implied lightning bolts that separated humans from their cosmic nature in *Symposium*. Werther seems to occupy a paradise-like state when he first meets Lotte, but as soon as he discovers who Albert is—and the fact that Lotte is engaged to him—a storm breaks out with thunder and lightning, symbolically separating him from Lotte. He dwells on this image of lightning as he contemplates his own mortality in relation to his love for Lotte, writing,

> And why should I be ashamed, at that awful moment when my entire being trembles between existence and nonexistence, when the past flashes like

lightning over the dark abyss of the future, and everything around me subsides and the world perishes along with me?[93]

When Albert hands over the pistols that Werther requests, it "affected [Lotte] like a thunderclap," because on some level she knows what he plans on doing with them.[94] And it is Werther's lethal shot to the head that seems to echo this thunderclap. He cannot unite with his missing half, with the original nature that he once felt he had before that first lightning strike, so he seems to replicate that same wound in his own hands in order to unite him with the only nature that is left to him—the monstrous nature of a disenchanted world, killing itself in perpetuity.

In *Frankenstein*, the lightning motif is modernized to an electric current that can be commanded by science. Instead of separating bodies into separate limbs, it animates a mass of limbs sewn together. But in doing so, it still separates these limbs from their original nature and original contexts, which is where the monstrosity lies. The Creature laments not only his own creation but also the fact that he does not have a partner to share his misery with in eros. That longing for the other half, which does not exist and was never available to him, is the pessimistic eros at the core of our own being. The only commiseration that the Creature can hope for is the one provided by *Werther* and other books. In *Wuthering Heights*, though, Brontë seems to take this pessimism further when Catherine restlessly and scornfully dismisses books as providing no consolation whatsoever. *Wuthering Heights* seems to dance on the grave of Boethian philosophy.

All three of these novels castigate philosophy and its attendant rationalism, but simultaneously open up a space for reconciliation by reminding it of their shared origins. In the same way that Socrates considers accepting poetry that would be apologetic to philosophy, the modern novel considers a philosophy that would have to answer to the novel's terms. Ronell writes,

> I would love to see someone armed by *Werther* and by Goethe address Kant, the Enlightenment, the complex and still latent itineraries of rationalism, and call all this into question, cause it some more trouble. There's something here that has not found an echo in our works of philosophy.[95]

In the next chapter, I hope to cause it some more trouble.

NOTES

1. Ignatieff, *On Consolation*, 2.
2. Boethius, *The Consolation of Philosophy*, trans. David R. Slavitt (Cambridge, MA: Harvard University Press, 2008), xiii.

3. Boethius, *Consolation of Philosophy*, 1.
4. Ignatieff, *On Consolation*, 78.
5. Boethius, *Consolation of Philosophy*, 4.
6. Boethius, *Consolation of Philosophy*, 40.
7. Shakespeare, *Hamlet*, 2.2.268-70.
8. Boethius, *Consolation of Philosophy*, 124.
9. Boethius, *Consolation of Philosophy*, 125.
10. Stendhal, *The Red and the Black*, 297.
11. Thacker, *Infinite Resignation*, 5.
12. Hardy, *Tess of the D'Urbervilles*, xv.
13. Boethius, *Consolation of Philosophy*, 139.
14. Boethius, *Consolation of Philosophy*, 175.
15. *The Romance of the Rose*, trans. Frances Horgan (Oxford: Oxford University Press, 2008), 25.
16. *Romance of the Rose*, 33; 37.
17. *Romance of the Rose*, 62.
18. *Romance of the Rose*, 67.
19. *Romance of the Rose*, 89.
20. *Romance of the Rose*, 89.
21. *Romance of the Rose*, 90.
22. *Romance of the Rose*, 90.
23. *Romance of the Rose*, 105.
24. *Romance of the Rose*, 83.
25. *Romance of the Rose*, 3.
26. C. S. Lewis, *The Allegory of Love* (Cambridge: Cambridge University Press, 2013), 2.
27. Lewis, *Allegory of Love*, 5.
28. Friedrich Nietzsche, *Beyond Good and Evil: Prelude to a Philosophy of the Future*, trans. Walter Kaufmann (New York: Vintage Books, 1966), §260: 208.
29. Gottfried von Strassburg, *Tristan*, trans. A. T. Hatto (London: Penguin Books, 1976), 42.
30. John Jay Parry, "Introduction," in *The Art of Courtly Love* by Andreas Capellanus, trans. John Jay Parry (New York: Columbia University Press, 1960), 13.
31. Andreas Capellanus, *The Art of Courtly Love*, trans. John Jay Parry (New York: Columbia University Press, 1960), 28.
32. Capellanus, *Art of Courtly Love*, 27.
33. *The Letters of Abelard and Heloise*, trans. Betty Radice (London: Penguin Books, 2003), 3.
34. *Letters of Abelard and Heloise*, 50.
35. *Letters of Abelard and Heloise*, 10.
36. *Letters of Abelard and Heloise*, 11.
37. *Letters of Abelard and Heloise*, 11.
38. *Letters of Abelard and Heloise*, 11.
39. *Letters of Abelard and Heloise*, 54.
40. *Letters of Abelard and Heloise*, 16.

41. *Letters of Abelard and Heloise*, 51.
42. *Letters of Abelard and Heloise*, 56.
43. *Letters of Abelard and Heloise*, 51.
44. *Letters of Abelard and Heloise*, 72.
45. Lewis, *Allegory of Love,* 1; 156.
46. *Romance of the Rose*, 31.
47. Stendhal, *Love*, 60.
48. Nietzsche, "The Anti-Christ," in *Twilight of the Idols / The Anti-Christ*, trans. R. J. Hollingdale (New York: Penguin Books, 1990), 145.
49. *Romance of the Rose*, 163.
50. Roland Barthes, *Pleasure of the Text*, trans. Richard Miller (New York: Hill and Wang, 1975), 27.
51. Terry Pinkard, *German Philosophy 1760-1860: The Legacy of Idealism* (Cambridge: Cambridge University Press, 2010), 13.
52. Johann Wolfgang von Goethe, *The Sorrows of Young Werther / Die Leiden des jungen Werther*, trans. Stanley Appelbaum (Mineola, NY: Dover, 2004), 29.
53. Goethe, *Sorrows of Young Werther*, 83.
54. Goethe, *Sorrows of Young Werther*, 119.
55. Goethe, *Sorrows of Young Werther*, 7.
56. Goethe, *Sorrows of Young Werther*, 7; 13.
57. Goethe, *Sorrows of Young Werther*, 39.
58. Goethe, *Sorrows of Young Werther*, 57.
59. *Romance of the Rose*, 5–9.
60. Goethe, *Sorrows of Young Werther*, 81.
61. Goethe, *Sorrows of Young Werther*, 139.
62. Goethe, *Sorrows of Young Werther*, 117.
63. Goethe, *Sorrows of Young Werther*, vi.
64. Goethe, *Sorrows of Young Werther*, viii.
65. Pinkard, *German Philosophy*, 12.
66. Goethe, *Sorrows of Young Werther*, x.
67. Goethe, *Sorrows of Young Werther*, 95.
68. Goethe, *Sorrows of Young Werther*, 97.
69. Kafka, "Poseidon," in *The Complete Stories*, trans. Tania & James Stern (New York: Schocken, 1983), 435.
70. Melville, "Bartleby," 10.
71. Goethe, *Sorrows of Young Werther*, 81.
72. Goethe, *Sorrows of Young Werther*, 79.
73. Goethe, *Sorrows of Young Werther*, 51; 50.
74. Avital Ronell and Anne Dufourmantelle, *Fighting Theory,* trans. Catherine Porter (Champaign, IL: University of Illinois Press, 2010), 20.
75. Goethe, *Sorrows of Young Werther*, 191.
76. Friedrich Nietzsche, *The Birth of Tragedy / The Case of Wagner*, trans. Walter Kaufmann (New York: Vintage Books, 1967), 60.
77. Nietzsche, *Birth of Tragedy*, 60.
78. Nietzsche, *Birth of Tragedy*, 60.

79. Goethe, *Sorrows of Young Werther*, 81.
80. Goethe, *Sorrows of Young Werther*, 79.
81. Nietzsche, *Beyond Good and Evil*, 89 (§146).
82. Goethe, *Sorrows of Young Werther*, 3.
83. Qtd. in Hans Rudolf Vaget, "Werther, the Undead," in *The Sufferings of Young Werther*, trans. and ed. Stanley Corngold (New York: W. W. Norton, 2013), 190.
84. Vaget, "Werther, the Undead," 187.
85. Goethe, *The Sorrows of Young Werther and Selected Writings*, trans. Catherine Hutter (New York: Signet Classics, 1962), 21.
86. Mary Shelley, *Frankenstein* (New York: W. W. Norton, 1996), 86.
87. Shelley, *Frankenstein,* 86.
88. Shelley, *Frankenstein,* 86.
89. Shelley, *Frankenstein*, 76.
90. Stefani Engelstein, *Anxious Anatomy: The Conception of the Human Form in Literary and Naturalist Discourse* (Albany, NY: State University of New York Press, 2008), 215.
91. Goethe, *Sorrows of Young Werther*, trans. Appelbaum, 71.
92. Goethe, *Sorrows of Young Werther*, trans. Appelbaum, 71.
93. Goethe, *Sorrows of Young Werther*, trans. Appelbaum, 139.
94. Goethe, *Sorrows of Young Werther*, trans. Appelbaum, 195.
95. Ronell and Dufourmantelle, *Fighting Theory*, 22.

Chapter 5

From a Failed Theory of the Novel to a Novel of Failed Theories
Mann's Response to Boccaccio, Schlegel, and Lukács

ORIGINAL SEPARATION

Just as much as *Werther* reinscribes *Symposium* in its pessimistic treatment of eros, all of Western philosophy after Plato also seems to re-enact the same movement of the split, the romantic breakup, the original separation, with each new cataclysmic intervention. The "original separation" is the literal definition of the German word *Urteil*, or "judgment." We exercise our judgment to compensate for this rift between subject and object, a rift that Kant had cast in cosmic terms with his Copernican turn, posing a crisis for future generations of thinkers to respond to, articulating their utopian fantasies of unification—or reunification—between subject and object, entailing detailed Absolute Systems and visions of totalities in lieu of an unsystematic, chaotic, and fragmented world.[1] But like the lovers in *Symposium*, Kant sees elements of the object in the subject, allowing the categories of the mind to correspond to the world in a way that gives us a glimpse of the truth into the order of things, even if we may not be able to access things-in-themselves. As Dr. Brichot, Proust's caricature of a Sorbonne professor, says in *The Captive*, Kant's philosophy "is still *The Symposium*, but held this time at Königsberg, in the local style, indigestible and reeking of sauerkraut, and without gigolos."[2]

The history of German Idealism is the history of answers to Kant's subject-object rift (also a literal definition of the word "crisis") and how it could possibly be bridged. Hegel's response was the dialectic, a constant movement that shuttles back and forth between the subject and object. But when he was still in his late twenties, he wrote that love is what "cancels separation," and that "in love, life is present as a duplicate of itself and as a single and unified self."[3] By the time he got to *The Phenomenology of Spirit*, he had de-eroticized the dialectic, which had always been such an erotically choreographed dance between subject and object since Plato. Philosophers ever since have been caught up in the same project, awkwardly speaking of love without the messiness of eros, like Nietzsche's *amor fati* and Arendt's *amor mundi*. Kierkegaard, though, breaks away from this tendency, and he does so in *The Seducer's Diary*, which returns philosophy to the novel as a space to revisit the eros of our original separation.

Before Kierkegaard, Schopenhauer attempted to address the subject-object crisis by re-naming Kant's noumenon as "Will" and his phenomenon as "Representation," but his *World as Will and Representation*, while starting off with Kantian systematicity in the first volume, sputters out into something messier and inconclusive by the end of the second volume. Nietzsche's response to the crisis was art, specifically tragedy, as the answer that would overcome this division, turning Plato on his head. It is not until Heidegger, under the heavy influence of Kierkegaard, that philosophy is dramatically reconstructed—or deconstructed—as fundamental ontology, as a way of thinking through existence not as a confrontation of subjects and objects, but of Being-in-the-world, which closes the chapter on the Kantian subject-object split. To Milan Kundera, though,

> all the great existential themes Heidegger analyzes in *Being and Time*—considering them to have been neglected by all earlier European philosophy—had been unveiled, displayed, illuminated by four centuries of the novel. . . . In its own way, through its own logic, the novel discovered the various dimensions of existence one by one.[4]

Heidegger's project in *Being and Time* is to raise the "forgotten" question of Being. But this question had not been forgotten by novelists. For instance, Terry Pinkard explains the enormous and sudden popularity of *The Sorrows of Young Werther* to its first readers because it "raised in a shocking and thoroughly gripping way the central issue of the time for them: what was it to live one's 'own' life?"[5] This is precisely the question that Heidegger raises in *Being and Time*, and it's astonishing to see what lengths Heidegger will go to in order to avoid directly confronting how the modern novel had already worked through the ontological questions that he is laying claim to. The novel is a way to dis-cover or un-cover, in the play of truth as *alethea*, the meaning of Being, which is why Nabokov sees this question itself as what distinguishes us from animals: "Being aware of being aware of being. In other words, if I not only know that I *am* but also know that I know it, then I belong to the human species."[6] The novel is the space for him to explore, in detail, what constitutes this Being, and the "gap between ape and man," which he sketches in the ape-like qualities of Humbert Humbert in *Lolita*.[7]

Heidegger draws on a long history of ignoring and dismissing the novel. Although it was a novel that made Kant break from his regularly scheduled walks (the only other time was the eruption of the French Revolution),[8] he wrote that "it is important for morality to warn emphatically against such empty and fantastic desires, which are quite frequently nourished by novels . . . of superhuman perfections and fantastical bliss."[9] In his treatment of aesthetics, he had more to say about mountains and storms than about the novel, which is a curious way of actively ignoring *The Sorrows of Young Werther*, the bestseller of his day, which also had quite a lot to say about mountains and storms.

Hegel, whose own *Phenomenology of Spirit* can be read as a Bildungsroman, ends his hefty, two-volume *Lectures on Aesthetics* with lyric and epic poetry, culminating in drama. Novel theorists like Mazzoni are eager to read his treatment of prose as an analysis of the novel in Volume I, but his "prose of thought" largely skips over the novel and enters philosophy itself: "Yet, precisely, at this highest stage, art now transcends itself, in that it forsakes the element of a reconciled embodiment of the spirit in sensuous form and passes over from the poetry of the imagination to the prose of thought."[10] When he asks, "What is poetry and what is prose in art?" the contrast he gives is between lyric poetry and painting rather than the novel.[11] Prose for Hegel is too nebulous to be material as a literary form outside of philosophical prose, which is evident when he uses phrases such as "prose of spiritual existence" or "the common prose of life."[12] His section on "Romantic Fiction" covers barely two pages on chivalric romance before charting the "Dissolution of the Romantic Form of Art," citing *Hamlet* and *Romeo and Juliet* before returning back to his enamored Dutch paintings.[13]

There is a peculiar daftness to his ignorance of the novel in this seemingly comprehensive, encyclopedic account of the arts. The closest he gets to the novel in *Aesthetics*, aside from a few nods to Goethe, Jacobi, Tieck, and Jean Paul, is how "wearisome . . . prose's prolixity" is.[14] It's easy to see how frustrated Schopenhauer was with this man who couldn't even take a cue from himself. The novel seems to occur to Hegel as an afterthought that he clumsily sweeps away when, after 1,100 pages of painstaking analysis of the other arts, he writes:

> In the other spheres of our present national and social life there is opened up in the domain of epic an unlimited field for romances, tales, and novels; yet I am unable here to pursue any further, even in the most general outline, the vast history of their development from their origin up to the present day.[15]

Nietzsche, for his part, is energetic in his contempt for Victor Hugo, the Goncourt Brothers, George Sand, George Eliot, and Émile Zola, writing *Thus Spoke Zarathustra* as an anti-novel instead.[16] Instead of the average everydayness of ordinary language, Nietzsche opts for an artificially biblical tone. Instead of a united narrative, there seems to be nothing but fragments of cryptic fables and aphoristic wisdom. He even goes so far as to replace the domesticated pets of bourgeois novels with an eagle and a snake. He goes to great pains in training his reader to approach his works as the opposite of novels, since they depict nothing of the familiar world, and should not even be read in long, stationary stretches. In *Daybreak,* he writes,

> A book such as this is not for reading straight through or reading aloud but for dipping into, especially when out walking or on a journey; you must be able to stick your head into it and out of it again and again and discover nothing familiar around you.[17]

SCHLEGEL/LUKÁCS AND BOCCACCIO/MANN

There was, however, one German Idealist who did acknowledge the centrality of the novel as the answer to philosophy, as its long-lost lover, and maybe even as the specific answer to the Kantian predicament of the subject-object split. In the late eighteenth century, Friedrich Schlegel used Plato's *Symposium* as a model for his own "Dialogue on Poetry." He abruptly interrupts the piece with a "Letter About the Novel," which begins with a retraction: "I must retract, my dear lady, what I seemed to say yesterday in your defense, and say that you are almost completely wrong."[18] What this lady, Amalia, is apparently wrong about, is her assertion that Friedrich Richter's novels "are not novels but a colorful hodgepodge of sickly wit," and that they amounted to nothing more than a personal "confession."[19] Schlegel, through the figure of Antonio, defends this "sickly wit" and "emphatically maintain[s] that such grotesques and confessions are the only romantic productions of our unromantic age"—a statement that seems to prefigure D. H. Lawrence's opening to *Lady Chatterley's Lover*: "Ours is essentially a tragic age; so we refuse to take it tragically."[20] Both statements, one about a novel and one in a novel, are refutations of the age in which they're written. Schlegel laments "our so unfantastic age, in the actual estate of prose," and detests "the novel as far as it claims to be a separate genre."[21] Like the fantasy of a united self in *Symposium*, Schlegel imagines the novel as an essentially unifying and binding force that removes the distinctions between the other fragments of literary genres, ultimately encompassing all of them.

Schlegel admits that he doesn't "have the courage for a *theory of the novel*"—we would have to wait until Lukács in the twentieth century for that—but he imagines that such "a theory of the novel would have to be itself a novel that would reflect imaginatively every eternal tone of the imagination and would again confound the chaos of the world of knights."[22] This is a utopian vision that inevitably sets up every future novel and theory of the novel for failure, since no single one could possibly "reflect imaginatively every eternal tone of the imagination."

Maybe this is also why Lukács sensed that his own theory was a failure too. He had originally planned a novel of sorts that would, by Schlegel's prescription, also be a theory of the novel, and he modeled it on Boccaccio's *Decameron*, which itself is also modeled on Plato's *Symposium*. As he saw the recognizable world around him collapse in a catastrophe of unprecedented carnage, tearing apart social bonds, Lukács viewed the political situation of 1914 as analogous to the Black Death that swept through Florence in 1348. He envisioned a group of young people who go into lockdown and spend their time exchanging stories that would flesh out a theory of the novel.[23] Boccaccio's escapist fantasy of a quarantine regime governed entirely by the eros of storytelling, where each of the ten citizens gets to be king or queen for a day, was deeply seductive to him.

As one of the first European writers of prose to take its craft seriously rather than treat it as an inferior form of literature, Boccaccio represented for Lukács the perfect inspiration, since he too was the first theorist to take the novel seriously from a philosophical perspective. In *The Decameron* is a new kind of writing that, like the ruptured social bonds he was responding to, departed from the past, engaging ancient and medieval genres only to reinvent them and breathe new life into them. Among these genres are the farcical *fabliau*, the fairy tale, and the Socratic dialogue, especially the kind found in *Symposium*, where the topic of eros is the uniting principle that stitches all of these different genres together.

One of the new techniques Boccaccio uses is the appeal to veracity as a way of anchoring the frame narrative in a recognizable reality, even as he is fabricating a fiction. He claims to be relying on the authority of a "trustworthy person" who told him about seven of the ten storytellers who "found themselves in the venerable Church of Santa Maria Novella."[24] This is a real church that his Florentine readers would have immediately recognized, and it is in this church that these young women gather to commiserate about their daily devastation, about how their lives had been turned upside down by the plague. It is here that they decide to flee to the countryside, taking three young men along with them, and pass the time in an idyllic lockdown, telling each other erotic stories.

In the Church of Santa Maria Novella is arguably the name for the new genre that Boccaccio helped to develop, or at least update, referring to his own stories as *novelle*.[25] This is a word that can mean "stories," "novels," or even "news," like the news that these storytellers get from people they know back in Florence.[26] But the spatial connotation suggested by the association with the place where these storytellers first meet also deserves equal attention, as though the novel can simply refer to the space that occasions the site for both commiseration and erotic exchange, at once sacred and also secular. It is perhaps this spatial definition that percolates into the twentieth century, when D. H. Lawrence uses his sacred-secular novel, *Lady Chatterley's Lover,* to articulate his own theory of the novel in both spatial and sacred terms, writing that "the novel, properly handled, can reveal the most secret places of life: for it is in the *passional* secret places of life, above all, that the tide of sensitive awareness needs to ebb and flow."[27] These *"passional* secret places of life," what Plato's erotic storytellers had outlined in *Symposium,* are illuminated in ever greater detail by the genealogy of novel aesthetics that develop from Boccaccio to Lawrence.

Unlike Dante, whose attention is fixed on the stars and on the grander cosmic unity of the universe, Boccaccio's focus is grounded on earth, where he, like Lawrence six centuries later, takes particular delight in exploring the pleasures of the body.[28] In Wayne A. Rebhorn's interpretation, it is almost as though Boccaccio rescues his ten storytellers from Dante's *Inferno,* trapped "in a deadly vicious circle" of seeing nothing but death and illness around them day after day, and he sends them off to the countryside, where they organize into a different kind of circle: "As they tell their stories, the group sits in a symbolic circle: they turn their backs to the outside world and face one another, reinforcing their connectedness by looking at and listening to the other members of the group."[29]

Lukács, in drafting *The Theory of the Novel,* eventually scrapped the plan of a series of erotic dialogues based on Boccaccio, and wrote the monological text that we now have, but not before confiding in his friend Thomas Mann what that failed plan was supposed to be. Less than a decade after Lukács published *The Theory of the Novel,* his abandoned aspirations seemed to have come to fruition in the publication of Mann's *The Magic Mountain* in 1924, a novel that also follows a series of characters who symbolically turn their backs on the world in order to seek out connection on a higher level, both in terms of intellect and literal altitude. Mann even satirizes Lukács himself in the character of the intellectually pugnacious Naphta, a tenant whose landlord is named Lukaček, as though he temporarily occupies the space of something close enough to Lukács's name.[30]

Mann took the title of his novel from a phrase that appears in *The Birth of Tragedy,* where Nietzsche writes of the "Olympian magic mountain" that allowed the Greeks to endure "the terror and horror of existence."[31] But perhaps it was equally Boccaccio whom Mann had had in mind for his title and his setting. At the beginning of *The Decameron,* Boccaccio directly addresses the reader, saying, "You will be affected by this horrific beginning no differently than travelers are by a steep and rugged mountain, for beyond it there lies a most beautiful and delightful plain."[32] Mann instead seems to hold up a mirror to this statement and say it back in reverse, beginning with a beautiful and delightful mountain setting; the horror lies in the "flatlands," where the First World War erupts at the end of the novel.

This capacious novel takes up Schlegel's challenge in a way that Lukács's *Theory of the Novel* could not, seeming to encompass the entire history of the Western intellectual tradition from Plato to Nietzsche, and—like Proust—nodding to various genres along the way, from the Socratic dialogue to the Romance, the fairy tale, and the Bildungsroman. Through this journey into the void, where nothing really happens except for an exchange and ultimate evisceration of ideas, Mann's answer to Schlegel's fantasy of a novel that would "reflect imaginatively every eternal tone of the imagination" ends up being a meditation on pessimism and eros.

The novel follows Hans Castorp, an aspiring naval engineer whom the narrator stresses is "perfectly ordinary."[33] He withdraws from his familiar social setting in Hamburg to visit his ailing cousin at a sanatorium in the Swiss Alps, where patients impatiently circulate a booklet among themselves called *The Art of Seduction*, and find other erotic ways to pass their time.[34] In this sanatorium, where patients are supposed to heal, Castorp's health deteriorates, but in a way that he relishes, because it allows him to prolong his stay to what ends up being seven years full of lively *Symposium*-like conversations about philosophy, politics, and art. Like Phaedrus, he is not the brightest of the bunch, but he is curious to hear what others have to say and lets their erudition wash over him. He attends a lecture series from one of the resident doctors on "Love as a Force Conducive to Illness," all the while associating a fellow patient, Clavdia Chauchat, with a former schoolboy crush, Hippe Pribislav, merging their identities together in his fantasies through the phallic image of a pencil that he lends to them, evoking the Platonic intersection between logos and eros in *Phaedrus*.[35] In this leisurely environment, he has the time to reflect on the big questions, like what life is, and the answer he arrives at is "the quintessence of sensuality and desire . . . not derived from the spirit," but rather from "reeking flesh."[36]

Among the other acquaintances whom Hans Castorp makes is the garrulous and pedantic Settembrini, a humanist hard at work on his entry for a multivolume encyclopedia commissioned by the "International League for the Organization of Progress" called *The Sociology of Suffering*. His task, on the impossible and futile scale of Casaubon's from *Middlemarch*, is to provide a synopsis and brief analysis of every masterpiece in world literature dealing with suffering, which collectively was meant to serve as "solace and advice for those who suffer."[37] It is only in the exact middle of the novel—its structural summit, as it were—that Settembrini is challenged by a new character, Lukács's fictionalized self in the form of the Jewish-born Jesuit Naphta, who cynically dismisses Settembrini's liberalism and utopian hope for "universal happiness."[38]

Settembrini welcomes the challenge, especially in front of Hans Castorp, modeling to him how any disagreement can be reasoned through and talked out with decorum and politeness, even if that decorum is largely one-sided. Hans Castorp, in turn, comes up with a term from the *Decameron* to describe how he internalizes and treats each of the contradictory thoughts articulated in these debates: "playing king," allowing each idea to hold reign over his mind before passing off the throne to the next one, like Nietzsche's perspectival transvaluation of values.[39] Settembrini, though, is careful to warn Hans Castorp of Naphta's anti-democratic pessimism as "the great seduction," outlining the dangers of following this political position to its logical end.[40] At a certain point, the debates between Settembrini and Naphta get vicious, the attacks become barbed and personal, and perhaps more disturbingly, they each get so caught up in their fights that they end up arguing the opposing points, contradicting not only each other, but their own original positions. The only thing that keeps them going is the will to fight—about what, it eventually doesn't seem to matter anymore.

The end result, confusing for both Hans Castorp and the reader, is Mann pulling back the mask on any European claims to "civilization" and "civilized" behavior, revealing a dissolution of ideas into ideology, of sober-minded discourse into frenetic rage and destruction. Their failed debates also seem to be contagious, as though spreading to the other patients in the sanatorium, until there is a "universal penchant for nasty verbal exchanges and outbursts of rage, even for fisticuffs," and the patients "abandoned themselves emotionally to the frenzy."[41] The mountain consequently loses its magic. "Thus this magnificent 'novel of ideas,'" Kundera explains, "is at the same time . . . a dreadful requestioning of ideas as such, a great farewell to the era that believed in ideas and in their power to run the world."[42]

Mann uses the novel form to articulate a pessimism of ideas themselves, as though the novel functions as a stage for philosophy to unravel, to undo itself, even to die by suicide, emptied of its meaning. By the end of the novel, Settembrini, "the old affirmer of life[,] had turned gloomy," and Naphta shoots himself.[43] The project of consolation that Settembrini had devoted so much energy to ends up as a failure, like so many attempts at this genre from Boethius on. Hans Castorp, disoriented intellectually, also finds himself at one point disoriented in a whiteout, where he hallucinates what seems to be an allegorical triptych of history moving into the future, from an idyllic Greek landscape where he seems to witness the birth of Western civilization to the site of the Virgin Mary giving birth to Jesus. But the vision ends in horror, with a witches' sabbath and the dismemberment of a baby. He comes to the epiphany that, "Love stands opposed to death—it alone, and not reason, is stronger than death. Only love, and not reason, yields kind thoughts."[44] But by the time he safely reaches the Berghof, he forgets this thought.

In the same way that Hans Castorp's thoughts blur and dissolve into each other, so too do all the people around him, abiding by the same principle of dis-individuation that Goethe, Brontë, and Proust had used to illustrate their own visions of pessimism. Before leaving the sanatorium for good in 1914, Hans Castorp is even more disoriented when Settembrini "gave him a Mediterranean—or perhaps a Russian—kiss, a cause of no little embarrassment for our wild traveler, despite his own surge of emotion."[45] This "Russian" kiss links him with the kiss Hans Castorp had exchanged with the Russian Clavdia Chauchat, who is inseparable in his mind from his childhood memory of Hippe Pribislav.

The association of the pencil is what blurs Clavdia's and Hippe's identities for Hans Castorp, but it was Settembrini who had been scribbling away the entire time, in service of humanist ideas that have now been rendered impotent. And in the wake of Naphta's death, it is Settembrini who paradoxically seems to ventriloquize his former interlocutor's Nietzschean embrace of war, telling Hans Castorp, "Fight bravely out there where blood joins men together."[46] The irony here is that Hans Castorp doesn't need spilled blood to join men together; everyone he knows seems to lose the contours of their identities so that they blur and join into one amorphous identity in his mind. Perhaps we can call this humanity, but it is a humanity that is ultimately disappointing. Perhaps it is even an incarnation of that monster of nature in *Werther* who equalizes all beings and all things in their destruction.

As a parody of Zarathustra, Castorp is finally healthy enough to descend the mountain at age thirty, but as intellectually enriched as he is, he is still the modern Everyman rather than the Overman. There is no pomp or grandiosity in his descent; he is still the embodiment of average everydayness, a concept that Heidegger would try to flesh out in the figure of Dasein three years after the publication of *The Magic Mountain*. And instead of Zarathustrian triumph, he comes down to a world that will most likely kill him in a meaningless world war, which Mann's narrator describes as a "thunderstorm and a great cleansing wind that would break the spell cast over the world."[47]

The final chapter is called "Thunderbolt," and perhaps it is less a reference to Nietzsche's aggressive flashes of brilliance than it is—like in *Werther* and *Wuthering Heights*—a reference to Zeus's thunderbolt, the implied weapon in Plato's *Symposium* that was used to divide us from our former selves. Unlike *Werther*, *Wuthering Heights*, and *In Search of Lost Time*, though, the thunderbolt here is not a melodramatic signifier of a single individual's overwhelming passions, but a signifier of a world-historical event that would fundamentally transform identity and modernity. The thunderbolt is foreshadowed in erotic terms when Hans Castorp takes his first X-ray, and is instructed by Director Behrens to "Hug the panel. Imagine it's something else if you like. And press your chest up tight, as if it meant sweet bliss."[48] As he erotically hugs this panel, which reveals a snapshot of a part of himself that is otherwise hidden from view, the process of taking this X-ray is described as a "thunderstorm" that "burst behind him, hissing, crackling, popping—and fell quiet again. The lens had peered inside him."[49] The thunderbolt at the end of the novel also seems to peer inside—not just Hans Castorp, but the entire world on its way to destruction. The novel itself can be thought of as an X-ray of the world in its decay. And in the same way that Aristophanes identifies eros as the consolation for this violent collective trauma, Mann's narrator ends the novel by asking, "And out of this worldwide festival of death, this ugly rutting fever that inflames the rainy evening sky all round—will love someday rise up out of this, too?"[50]

In Mann's irony, pessimism and eros are constitutive. In this account of eros, Mann provides a Schlegelian theory of the novel that is itself a novel but exposes Schlegel's utopian fantasy for such a theory that encompasses all other theories as a nightmare. Schlegel writes that he means "theory in the original sense of the word: a spiritual viewing of the subject with calm and serene feeling," and Mann provides this encyclopedic theory, multiplying it into so many perspectives, "spiritual viewings" from the aerial, rarefied air of the mountain-tops, that this perspectival shifting unravels any theoretical cohesion whatsoever.[51] The irony is that the narrator maintains a sense of Schlegelian "calm" even as the characters get increasingly belligerent. Mann climbs the summits of ideas in order to reduce them to rubble—a seemingly Nietzschean maneuver, but in the genre that Nietzsche despised. While Mann takes his time with over seven hundred pages in the novel, Nietzsche impatiently aspired to "say in ten sentences what everyone else says in a book—what everyone else *does not* say in a book."[52]

The ultimate theory of the novel that Mann provides is similar to T. S. Eliot's characterization of *Ulysses*:

> If it is not a novel, that is simply because the novel is a form which will no longer serve; it is because the novel, instead of being a form, was simply the expression of an age which had not sufficiently lost all form to feel the need of something stricter.[53]

While Harry Levin is famous for saying that *Ulysses* was "the novel to end all novels," he wrote in the same article, "This is no less true of *The Magic Mountain*."[54] *The Magic Mountain* seems to put a punctuation mark not only on the history of ideas, but on the novel itself—what is there left to say when every idea has been hashed out, defeated, and rendered futile? The answer lies precisely in Mann's irony itself, which ends—like *Ulysses*—on a note of eros, perhaps not as affirmative, but as open to its possibility.

Erich Heller, writing a critique of *The Magic Mountain* in dialogue form in order "to provoke memories of Plato or Dryden or even Friedrich Schlegel," insists that, "Thomas Mann's irony brings into question the very possibility of art."[55] To David Halperin, irony is also "the very condition of love, its mode of being."[56] Halperin explains that "love is an ironic condition insofar as it produces a necessary doubling of perspective," like the doubling of perspective that emerges out of our cosmic division—a doubling that acts as a gesture of reunification, a gesture that can never be completed.[57] Because of the fundamentally ironic, if not pessimistic, nature of love, Halperin says that only a "unique literary form" that presses against the limit of what could possibly be rendered into language would be necessary to accommodate the articulation of love, and the way he describes this form seems to be an outline of *The Magic Mountain* without ever naming it:

> Like all great literary forms, the ironic story of love teases us with the contradictions built into its design. What distinguishes it is the way it holds opposed perspectives in unstable and dynamic equipoise. It thereby pushes to an extreme limit what all good writing aims to do—to impress on us a lively consciousness of what it does not, or what it cannot, say.[58]

Halperin never gives a name to this form but marvels at the fact that *Symposium* belongs to it, along with *Lolita*, claiming that *Symposium* particularly cannot be classified into any genre, since it "belongs to a category for which not even Aristotle had a word."[59]

That word, though, could very well be "novel." And even as every novelist seems to reinvent the genre with each new novel and then kill off that genre with the same stroke, the word has stuck, probably due to its irony, which allows it enough elasticity to reshape itself, as T. S. Eliot says, to become "simply the expression of an age." To Schlegel, "Philosophy is the true home of irony," especially when the philosophical dialogues "are not entirely systematical," but Mann demonstrates the opposite: that the true home of irony is in the novel.[60] Kundera would agree, writing that "the novel is, by definition, the ironic art."[61] Lukács also sees irony as the "normative mentality of the novel."[62] As an "epic in an age abandoned by God," and an articulation of our "transcendental homelessness," the novel employs irony to "see where God is to be found in a world abandoned by God; irony sees the lost, utopian home of the idea that has become an ideal."[63] Bakhtin, too, identifies the novel as fundamentally ironic in its function of parody. And, to Lukács's point of transcendental homelessness, Bakhtin notes how "in ancient times the parodic-travestying word was (generically speaking) homeless."[64]

The novel's "spirit," to Kundera, is one of "complexity" and "continuity": "each work is an answer to preceding ones, each work contains all the previous experience of the novel."[65] To this extent, every novel is itself a theory of the novel—another perspective, another take, another guest offering something else to say at the symposium. Kundera sees the novel's only imperative as one of human discovery, but this imperative is by nature pessimistic, at odds with the world, undermining any illusion of progress. If the novel "is to go on discovering the undiscovered, to go on 'progressing' as a novel, it can do so only against the progress of the world."[66] What Kundera, Mann, Lukács, and Schlegel (as well as Boccaccio and Lawrence, in addition to Goethe, Brontë, and Proust) all have in common is that they envision the novel as a paradoxical site of withdrawal from the world in order to encompass it more entirely.

FAILING AT A DEFINITION OF THE NOVEL: SOME FALSE STARTS

What, then, is a novel? And what makes it so pessimistic? To take Schlegel as a starting point, a novel for him is a "novelistic book" ("*Ein Roman ist ein romantisches Buch*").[67] Cute, but not terribly helpful. And yet there is a precise rigor here appropriate to the genre of the novel in its embrace of tautology, the bane of logical systematicity that resides on the other side of the philosophy-art faultline, and what, to Kierkegaard, "is and remains the highest principle, the highest maxim of thought."[68] Ernst Behler and Roman Struc avoid the coyness of Schlegel's definition in their translation: "A novel is a romantic book," which takes away from the impact of his following sentence: "You will pass that off as a meaningless tautology."[69]

But there is merit, however, in translating this word as "romantic," not even necessarily in the sense of the Romantic movement as a reaction to Enlightenment thinking, but "romantic" in its erotic sense. Mme. de Staël identifies the *Roman* as "the only form that has allowed us to depict the passions."[70] And Pierre-Daniel Huet, in one of the first reflections on the development of the novel as a genre, "Letter on the Origin of Novels," written as a preface to Madame de La Fayette's *Zayde* in 1670, contends that "we esteem nothing to be properly Romance but Fictions of Love Adventures, disposed into an Elegant Style in Prose; for the delight and instruction of the Reader."[71] Like *Symposium*, the novel delights and instructs; there is a propaedeutic element to it, teaching us the ways of love and performing this love on the rhetorical level of seducing us with its "Elegant Style in Prose." Schlegel's own "Letter

About the Novel," exemplifying this concept of romance, is an erotically charged work of fiction, a letter sent from Antonio to Alma, in which Antonio instructs Alma to read certain novels for her own edification.

This is also the pretext for *The Decameron*, which Boccaccio says he wrote for sexually frustrated women who

> will be able to derive not only pleasure from the entertaining material they contain, but useful advice as well, for the stories will teach them how to recognize what they should avoid, and likewise, what they should pursue. And I believe that as they read them, their suffering would come to an end.[72]

Boccaccio's purpose in writing his *novelle*, then, is no different from Settembrini's in amassing summaries of all the masterpieces of world literature that have to do with suffering, a great deal of that suffering caused by eros.

Huet's definition reverberates throughout the history of the novel, as when Samuel Richardson writes in his Preface to *Pamela* that this novel aims "to Divert and Entertain, and at the same time to Instruct, and Improve the Minds of the Youth of both Sexes."[73] In Diderot's *Encyclopedia* entry for "The Novel," written just over a century after Huet's treatise, Louis Jaucourt refers to Richardson and Fielding when he writes, "Novels written in good taste are perhaps the last kind of instruction remaining to be offered to a nation so corrupt that any other is useless."[74] And D. H. Lawrence writes of his own *Lady Chatterley's Lover*: "It is better to give all young girls this book, at the age of seventeen," for their own delight and instruction.[75] With overtones of *Symposium*, Lawrence also links his novelistic vision of eros with "completeness" after years "of honest thought of sex, and years of struggling action in sex," which "will bring us at last where we want to get, to our real and accomplished chastity, our completeness, when our sexual act and our sexual thought are in harmony, and the one does not interfere with the other."[76] This echoes the position taken by the Marquis de Sade, who writes, "Wheresoever on earth he dwells, man feels the need *to pray*, and *to love*: and herein lies the basis for all novels."[77] *Lady Chatterley's Lover*, if not all of D. H. Lawrence's novels, can be read as a pessimistic prayer to love itself.

Huet adds to his definition: "I call them Fictions, to discriminate them from True Histories; and I add, of Love Adventures, because Love ought to be the Principal Subject of *Romance*."[78] Translating "*Roman*" from French and German into English poses its own mess of problems, especially since, even as writers like Huet try to distinguish this term from "History," for example, most seventeenth- and eighteenth-century writers used the terms "romance," "history," and "novel" interchangeably.[79] But both Huet and Schlegel clearly identify eros at the core of the *Roman*, which Schlegel sees in Platonic terms as a "hint of something higher, the infinite, a hieroglyph of one eternal love and the sacred fullness of a life of creative nature."[80] The novel functions as eros does itself in the *Symposium* myth—as a gesture to the primordial unity of eternal love, which is how a tautology functions: the repetition dissolves the two sides of the statement into one. The fragment finds its missing but identical half, recognizing itself in the other, calling the other by its own name. *Ein Roman ist ein romantisches Buch.* The novel can only ever be itself.

The novel for Schlegel is the apotheosis of all Romantic poetry. In an aphorism from *The Athenäum*, he writes,

> Romantic [or "Novelistic"] poetry is a progressive universal poetry.[81] Its mission is not merely to reunite all separate genres of poetry and to put poetry in touch with philosophy and rhetorics. It will, and should, now mingle and now amalgamate poetry and prose, genius and criticism, the poetry of art and the poetry of nature, render poetry living and social, and life and society poetic, poetize wit, fill and saturate the forms of art with solid cultural material of every kind, and inspire them with vibrations of humor. . . . The romantic type of poetry is still becoming; indeed, its peculiar essence is that it is always becoming and that it can never be completed. It cannot be exhausted by any theory, and only a divinatory criticism might dare to characterize its ideal. It alone is infinite, as it alone is free; and as its first law it recognizes that the arbitrariness of the poet endures no law above him.[82]

The novel therefore is our key to freedom, replacing the Bible as the book of the world in a world "abandoned by God," as Lukács would say over a century later.[83] Through the novel, the "poet"—or novelist—is elevated to a divine status, enduring "no law above him," returning us back to our cosmic origins of unity, the reunification of our fragmented selves reflected in the novel's reunification of "all the separate genres of poetry," and of poetry and "rhetorics" back with philosophy. Standing at the summit of literature and philosophy, every novel is a wuthering height.

This all sounds lovely, if not embarrassingly naïve—and rather overstated in its *optimism*. But maybe its naïveté is precisely what sets it up for failure. And the joy expressed in Schlegel's accurate observation that "the novel cannot be exhausted by any theory" has been the source of frustration for every theorist—or attempted theorist—of the novel, and their readers, ever since. For one thing, no one can actually agree on a year, or even an era, that marks the birth of the novel. Lukács identifies *Don Quixote* as

> the first great novel of world literature [that] stands at the beginning of the time when the Christian God began to forsake the world; when man became lonely and could find meaning and substance only in his own soul, whose home was nowhere; when the world, released from its paradoxical anchorage in a

beyond that is truly present, was abandoned to its immanent meaninglessness; when the power of what is—reinforced by the utopian links, now degraded to mere existence—had grown to incredible magnitude and was waging a furious, apparently aimless struggle against the new forces which were as yet weak and incapable of revealing themselves or penetrating the world.[84]

The novel for Lukács arises at this pessimistic moment in history—a moment that has stretched four hundred years to echo the historical moment in which he is writing this work, as World War I had just broken out. Both the novel and *The Theory of the Novel* articulate our existential loneliness and "immanent meaninglessness." What he is doing is essentially restating the Kantian problematic of the subject-object split, but in gloomier terms, of "forces which were as yet weak and incapable of revealing themselves or penetrating the world."

Kundera echoes Lukács when he writes, in *The Art of the Novel*:

As God slowly departed from the seat whence he had directed the universe and its order of values, distinguished good from evil, and endowed each thing with meaning, Don Quixote set forth from his house into a world he could no longer recognize.[85]

Don Quixote's homelessness mirrors the Lukácsian "transcendental homelessness" of all his readers at this point in history. To Dienstag, this Quixotic homelessness doubles as a definition of pessimism: "To go on a quest, as has often been observed, one must cut one's ties to home. Pessimism is a kind of freedom from home."[86]

But the Marquis de Sade would object to this origin of the novel and its break from the divine, writing, "Let there be no doubt about it: it was in the countries which first recognized gods that the novel originated; and, to be more specific, in Egypt, the cradle of all divine worship."[87] For Ian Watt, the novel is born in England in the eighteenth century. Michael McKeon, in his deceptively titled *The Origins of the English Novel: 1600-1740*, responds to Watt by addressing the origins not only of the English novel but of the novel at large—and from the title at least, he pushes the date back from the earliest publications of *Don Quixote* (its first volume) by six years. What he actually ends up doing is tracing a dialectic of literary genres and political movements from the Greek Enlightenment and the twelfth-century Renaissance (which one could argue also overlaps with the Middle Ages) to a semantic instability between "novel," "romance," and "history" at around 1600 that then settles down to a more or less common usage of the English word "novel" in the sense that it is used today, which arises at around 1740.

Guido Mazzoni, however, focuses on the year 1550 instead, explaining that the word "novel" around that time had begun to refer to "the genre in which one can tell absolutely any story in any way whatsoever."[88] He then identifies 1800 as the year in which this word "referred to what it is today—a polymorphic space providing a home for stories of a certain length that do not fall within the confines of more rigidly codified narrative genres (epic poems, works of history, and the *chanson de geste*)."[89]

Looking through these different theories, we see that the novel is both transcendentally homeless for Lukács and a "home" for Mazzoni. We can trace its origins either to 1800, or 1740, or 1616, or 1606, or 1600, or the twelfth century, or the Greek Enlightenment, or Ancient Egypt. Schlegel, Bakhtin, and Kristeva all settle on the Socratic dialogues as the origin of the novel. Schlegel envisions the novel as a space in which the "things of the past would live in it in new forms; Dante's sacred shadow would arise from the lower world, Laura would hover heavenly before us, Shakespeare would converse intimately with Cervantes, and there Sancho would jest with Don Quixote again."[90] This kind of necromancy seems to be realized in Jorge Luis Borges's "Pierre Menard, Author of the Quixote," and in *Ulysses*, where James Joyce models his "Circe" chapter on Dante's *Inferno* and Goethe's *Faust*.

But, unlike Joyce's novel, Borges's text is a short story, a form which Boris Eikhenbaum claims is "not only different in kind but also inherently at odds" with the novel.[91] Walter Benjamin emphasized this distinction, going so far as to attribute the decline of storytelling to the "rise of the novel at the beginning of modern times."[92] Coming back full circle to Plato, Benjamin seems to reiterate the complaint leveled against writing at the end of *Phaedrus*, where written texts seem to threaten the status of orality. Stories are rooted in an oral tradition that brings author and listener together; novels are borne of isolated authors who in turn foster a new kind of reader, one who is "isolated more so than any other reader."[93] His pessimism about the novel is more accusatory than Lukács's, but Lukács too points out the difference between the short story as an "abstract" genre and the novel as a genre of particularity. Mazzoni, however, maintains that a "rigid criterion is impossible to establish" between the two, and Kundera insists that there "is no ontological difference between story and novel," that the short story is just the "small form of the novel."[94]

If we're alerted to some degree of pedantic caution in distinguishing the novel from the short story, a task that seems simple enough from afar but frustrating (if not a bit comical) up close, then surely we can set aside the novel from drama with more ease. Not so fast, according to Schlegel, who insists that "there is otherwise so little contrast between the drama and the novel that it is rather the drama, treated thoroughly and historically, as for instance by Shakespeare, which is the true foundation of the novel."[95] Bakhtin takes this further: "In an era when the novel reigns supreme, almost all the remaining genres are to a greater or lesser extent 'novelized,'" citing Ibsen,

Hauptmann, and all of naturalist drama as examples of a novelistic rather than a dramatic project.[96]

At this point, the novel as Schlegel's emblem of freedom begins to look more like a free-for-all. Marthe Robert says that the "novel is free, free to the point of arbitrariness or total anarchy."[97] Collating the different and opposing definitions of the novel feels like Hans Castorp in the presence of a vertiginous debate between Settembrini and Naphta, both of them arguing back and forth, negating each other in a scholarly exchange that seems to threaten aggression at any moment, most likely from a sense of exhaustion and futility. Nabokov gleefully said in an interview that, "One of the functions of all my novels is to prove that the novel in general does not exist."[98] Maybe Schlegel was wiser than any other novel theorist for saying that he doesn't have the "courage for a theory of the novel."[99] It's easy to see why Henry James, in the preface to one of his own novels, was so exasperated in trying to pinpoint what

> such large loose baggy monsters, with their queer elements of the accidental and the arbitrary, artistically *mean*? We have heard it maintained, we will remember, that such things are "superior to art"; but we understand least of all what *that* may mean, and we look in vain for the artist, the divine explanatory genius, who will come to our aid and tell us.[100]

Here, James derisively shreds to pieces Schlegel's effusions over the "divinatory criticism" and the novelist who "endures no law above him" with the withering epithet of "divine explanatory genius," who is nowhere to be found when hard-pressed for an explanation of the art.

To use the intrinsically novelistic metaphor—or, as Bakhtin would call it, "chronotope"—of the road, we've arrived at a dead end. Guy de Maupassant begins his only novel, *Pierre and Jean* (unless we are now to take his short stories as novels, too), by writing that

> the critic who . . . still dares to write, "This is a novel, that is not" seems to me to be endowed with a perspicacity remarkably like incompetence. . . . Is there a set of rules for writing a novel, any deviation from which would require a story to bear a different name?[101]

Maybe we should take his advice and just give up on trying to define something so protean, so slippery, as the novel.

This is precisely Bakhtin's starting point in "Epic and Novel." He points out that the "utter inadequacy of literary theory is exposed when it is forced to deal with the novel."[102] It's not just novel theory, then, but all of literary theory that gets thrown into crisis when it has to confront this loose, baggy monster. Other literary genres, to Bakhtin, are easier to theorize because they've already been formed and by now are "sclerotic."[103] It's not so difficult when you have "a finished and already formed object, definite and clear" to deal with, especially when, right "up to the present day, in fact, theory dealing with these already completed genres can add almost nothing to Aristotle's formulations."[104] Has Bakhtin gone a bit too far, though? Are other literary genres as "completed" as he maintains, especially when, later, he blurs the distinctions between them almost to the point of interchangeability? Has every literary theorist in these other genres really added "almost nothing to Aristotle's formulations"? Michael Holquist comes to Bakhtin's defense, arguing that other novel theorists "seek to elevate *one kind* of novel into a definition of the novel," when Bakhtin is reworking literary theory itself from the ground up, arguing that the novel for him signifies "whatever force is at work within a given literary system to reveal the limits, the artificial constraints of that system."[105]

Where Bakhtin's theory runs the risk of being too fluid to demarcate the porous boundaries of the novel, Lukács risks being too brittle. Lukács drops the bombshell statement that "Dostoevsky did not write novels" at the end of his *Theory of the Novel*, while Bakhtin maintains, in his essay "Discourse on the Novel," that the works of Dostoevsky "occupy an extraordinary and unique place" in the history of the novel.[106] Lukács is also quick to dismiss anything that sinks "to the level of mere entertainment literature."[107] Bakhtin, however, reminds us that novels, by definition, "are mass produced as pure and frivolous entertainment like no other genre."[108] Kundera sides with this statement, but with a modification on its frivolity: "The great European novel started out as entertainment, and all real novelists are nostalgic for it! And besides, entertainment doesn't preclude seriousness."[109] Furthermore, Bakhtin claims that one of the defining features of the novel is its polyphony, what he calls "heteroglossia"—but this is precisely the point that Franco Moretti disputes, arguing that, "rather than nourishing polyphony," the novel "impose[s] a drastic *reduction* of it."[110]

Trying to discern a theoretical framework for the novel is like looking into a funhouse mirror, where every element you want to focus on becomes distorted beyond all proportion. This theoretical mirror struggles to reflect the novel, which, according to Stendhal, is a mirror itself, "moving along a highway."[111] A mirror of a mirror, neither of which is fixed in place. We can no longer even count on our own sight to judge what counts as a novel, barred from that lazy defense of the United States Supreme Court Justice Potter Stewart when asked how to define pornography: "I know it when I see it."[112] To some readers—enough of them, at least, to warrant trials—*Ulysses* and *Lady Chatterley's Lover* counted as pornography. The original readers of Prosper Merimée's *Carmen* and *La Guzla* didn't recognize those works as novels either when they saw them, reading them as horrifying travelogues instead.[113] And if we would like to think of those readers as gullible children of their time from a bygone era, we shouldn't forget the indignant rage that Oprah Winfrey expressed in 2006 when she found out that James Frey had "conned," "duped," and "betrayed" her—and her lucrative book club—into reading his book *A Million Little Pieces* as a memoir when it was later revealed to be a novel.[114]

NOTES

1. Simon Critchley, *Very Little . . . Almost Nothing: Death, Philosophy, Literature*, 2nd ed. (London: Routledge, 2004), 99.

2. Proust, *The Captive*, 304–305.

3. G. W. F. Hegel, "Love," trans. T. M. Knox (1970), https://www.marxists.org/reference/archive/hegel/works/love/index.htm.

4. Milan Kundera, *The Art of the Novel*, trans. Linda Asher (New York: Harper & Row, 1988), 5.

5. Pinkard, *German Philosophy*, 14.

6. Nabokov, *Strong Opinions,* 142.

7. Nabokov, *Strong Opinions,* 142.

8. Granted, the novel was written by the most eminent philosopher of his time, Rousseau.

9. Immanuel Kant, *Critique of Judgment*, trans. Werner S. Pluhar (Indianapolis, IN: Hackett, 1987), 32.

10. Hegel, *Hegel's Aesthetics: Lectures on Fine Art*, Vols. I–II, trans. T. M. Knox (Oxford: Clarendon Press, 1988), I: 89. There is certainly a correspondence between Hegel and Lukács on the concept of a "problematic individual" pessimistically confronting a "contingent world" (*Theory of the Novel,* 78). In his Preface to *Theory of the Novel*, Lukács writes that he was "in process of turning from Kant to Hegel" in this work, and maybe it was specifically this passage from Hegel that he had in mind:

> The individual as he appears in this world of prose and everyday is not active out of the entirety of his own self and his resources, and he is intelligible not from himself, but from something else. For the individual man stands in dependence on external influences, laws, political institutions, civil relationships, which he just finds confronting him, and he must bow to them whether he has them as his own inner being or not. Furthermore, the individual subject is not in the eyes of others such an entirety in himself, but comes before them only according to the nearest isolated interest which they take in his actions, wishes, and opinions. Men's primary interest is simply what is related to their own intentions and aims. . . . This is the prose of the world, as it appears to the consciousness both of the individual himself and of others:—a world of finitude and mutability, of entanglement in the relative, of the pressure of necessity from which the individual is in no position to withdraw. For every isolated living thing remains caught in the contradiction of being itself in its own eyes this shut-in unit and yet of being nevertheless dependent on something else, and the struggle to resolve this contradiction does not get beyond an attempt and the continuation of this eternal war. (*Theory of the Novel,* 12; *Aesthetics,* I: 149–150)

While "the world of prose and everyday" certainly thematizes the novel, it is Lukács who makes this connection explicit, not Hegel.

11. Hegel, *Aesthetics*, I: 161–162.
12. Hegel, *Aesthetics*, I: 190, 245.
13. Hegel, *Aesthetics*, I: 592–598.
14. Hegel, *Aesthetics*, I: 218.
15. Hegel, *Aesthetics*, II: 1110.
16. Nietzsche, "Twilight of the Idols," in *Twilight of the Idols / The Anti-Christ*, trans. R. J. Hollingdale (New York: Penguin Books, 1990), 78–80.
17. Nietzsche, *Daybreak*, ed. Maudemarie Clark and Brian Leiter, trans. R. J. Hollingdale (Cambridge: Cambridge University Press, 2005), 457.
18. Schlegel, "Dialogue on Poetry," in *German Romantic Criticism*, ed. A. Leslie Willson, trans. Ernst Behler and Roman Struc (London: Continuum, 1982), 102.
19. Schlegel, "Dialogue on Poetry," 113.
20. Schlegel, "Dialogue on Poetry," 103; D. H. Lawrence, *Lady Chatterley's Lover and "À Propos of Lady Chatterley's Lover,"* ed. Michael Squires (Cambridge: Cambridge University Press, 1993), 5.
21. Schlegel, "Dialogue on Poetry," 108.
22. Schlegel, "Dialogue on Poetry," 109.
23. Lukács, *Theory of the Novel*, 11–12.
24. Giovanni Boccaccio, *The Decameron*, trans. Wayne A. Rebhorn (New York: W. W. Norton, 2013), 13.
25. Boccaccio, *Decameron*, xxxiv.
26. Boccaccio, *Decameron*, xlvi.
27. Lawrence, *Lady Chatterley's Lover*, 101 (emphasis in original).
28. Boccaccio, *Decameron*, xxix.
29. Boccaccio, *Decameron*, xxxviii; xl.
30. Jonathan Arac, "What Kind of a History Does a Theory of the Novel Require?" *NOVEL: A Forum on Fiction* 42, no. 2, "Theories of the Novel Now, Part I" (Summer 2009): 191.
31. Nietzsche, *Birth of Tragedy*, §3: 42.
32. Boccaccio, *Decameron*, 4.
33. Thomas Mann, *The Magic Mountain*, trans. John E. Woods (New York: Vintage Books, 1996), 3
34. Mann, *Magic Mountain*, 268.
35. Mann, *Magic Mountain*, 114.
36. Mann, *Magic Mountain*, 271–272.
37. Mann, *Magic Mountain*, 241–243.
38. Mann, *Magic Mountain*, 375.
39. Mann, *Magic Mountain*, 383.
40. Mann, *Magic Mountain*, 404.
41. Mann, *Magic Mountain*, 673.
42. Milan Kundera, *Testaments Betrayed: An Essay in Nine Parts*, trans. Linda Asher (New York: HarperCollins, 1993), 163.
43. Mann, *Magic Mountain*, 673.

44. Mann, *Magic Mountain*, 487.
45. Mann, *Magic Mountain*, 702. Anthony Heilbut notes that "Settembrini" is "Venetian dialect for the 'September men,' the pederasts who arrive once the season is over and buy the local boys at half-price" (Anthony Heilbut, *Thomas Mann: Eros and Literature* [Berkeley, CA: University of California Press, 1997]). Settembrini seems to be a reincarnation of sorts of Aschenbach from *Death in Venice*.
46. Mann, *Magic Mountain*, 702.
47. Mann, *Magic Mountain*, 625.
48. Mann, *Magic Mountain*, 213.
49. Mann, *Magic Mountain*, 213.
50. Mann, *Magic Mountain*, 706.
51. Schlegel, "Dialogue on Poetry," 109.
52. Nietzsche, "Twilight of the Idols," 115; Heller, *Thomas Mann*, 168.
53. T. S. Eliot, "*Ulysses,* Order, and Myth," in *Modernism: An Anthology*, ed. Lawrence Rainey (Oxford: Blackwell, 2005), 166.
54. Qtd. in Heller, *Thomas Mann: The Ironic German*, 170.
55. Heller, *Thomas Mann: The Ironic German*, 166–169.
56. David M. Halperin, "Love's Irony: Six Remarks on Platonic Eros," in *Erotikon: Essays on Eros, Ancient and Modern*, ed. Shadi Bartsch and Thomas Bartscherer (Chicago, IL: University of Chicago Press, 2005), 52.
57. Halperin, "Love's Irony," 53.
58. Halperin, "Love's Irony," 58.
59. Halperin, "Love's Irony," 58.
60. Schlegel, "Aphorisms from the Lyceum," §42: 115.
61. Kundera, *Art of the Novel*, 134.
62. Lukács, *Theory of the Novel*, 84.
63. Lukács, *Theory of the Novel*, 92.
64. Bakhtin, *Dialogic Imagination,* 59. Bakhtin also writes, "The novel begins by presuming a verbal and semantic decentering of the ideological world, a certain linguistic homelessness of literary consciousness, which no longer possesses a sacrosanct and unitary linguistic medium for containing ideological thought" (*Dialogic Imagination,* 367).
65. Kundera, *Art of the Novel*, 18.
66. Kundera, *Art of the Novel*, 19.
67. Schlegel, "Brief über den Roman," http://www.zeno.org/Literatur/M/Schlegel,+Friedrich/Ästhetische+und+politische+Schriften/Gespräch+über+die+Poesie/Brief+über+den+Roman.
68. Kierkegaard, *Either/Or*, Vols. I–II, ed. and trans. Howard V. Hong and Edna V. Hong (Princeton, NJ: Princeton University Press, 1987), I: 38.
69. Schlegel, "Dialogue on Poetry," 108.
70. Mazzoni, *Theory of the Novel*, 92–93.
71. Qtd. in Mazzoni, *Theory of the Novel*, 98.
72. Boccaccio, *Decameron,* 3.
73. Samuel Richardson, *Pamela: Or, Virtue Rewarded* (Oxford: Oxford University Press, 2001), 3.

74. Louis Jaucourt, "The Novel," in *The Encyclopedia of Diderot & D'Alembert: Collaborative Translation Project* (University of Michigan, 2005), http://hdl.handle.net/2027/spo.did2222.0000.108.

75. Lawrence, *"Lady Chatterley's Lover,"* 309.

76. Lawrence, *"Lady Chatterley's Lover,"* 308.

77. Marquis de Sade, "Reflections on the Novel," in *The 120 Days of Sodom and Other Writings*, trans. Austryn Wainhouse and Richard Seaver (New York: Grove Press, 1966), 99.

78. Qtd. in McKeon, *The Origins of the English Novel*, 54.

79. McKeon, *Origins of the English Novel*, 25.

80. Schlegel, "Dialogue on Poetry," 106–107.

81. We must keep in mind that this word *romantisch* can also be translated as "novelistic," especially in the way Schlegel is using it.

82. Schlegel, "Athenaeum Fragments," in *Friedrich Schlegel's Lucinde and the Fragments*, trans. Peter Firchow (Minneapolis, MN: University of Minnesota Press, 1971), 126–127.

83. Lukács, *Theory of the Novel*, 88.

84. Lukács, *Theory of the Novel*, 103–104.

85. Kundera, *Art of the Novel*, 6.

86. Dienstag, *Pessimism*, 258.

87. Sade, "Reflections on the Novel," 98.

88. Mazzoni, *Theory of the Novel*, 66, 16.

89. Mazzoni, *Theory of the Novel*, 66.

90. Schlegel, "Dialogue on Poetry," 109.

91. Qtd. in Holquist, introduction to *Dialogic Imagination* by Bakhtin, xxx.

92. Walter Benjamin, "The Storyteller," in *Illuminations*, trans. Harry Zohn (New York: Schocken, 1968), 87.

93. Benjamin, "The Storyteller," 100.

94. Lukács, *Theory of the Novel*, 51; Mazzoni, *Theory of the Novel*, 17; Kundera, *Testaments Betrayed*, 168.

95. Schlegel, "Dialogue on Poetry," 108.

96. Bakhtin, *Dialogic Imagination*, 5–6.

97. Marthe Robert, "From *Origins of the Novel*," in *Theory of the Novel: A Historical Approach*, ed. Michael McKeon (Baltimore, MD: Johns Hopkins University Press, 2000), 58.

98. Nabokov, *Strong Opinions*, 115.

99. Schlegel, "Dialogue on Poetry," 109.

100. Henry James, *The Art of the Novel* (New York: Charles Scribner's Sons, 1962), 84.

101. Guy de Maupassant, *Pierre et Jean*, trans. Julie Mead (Oxford: Oxford University Press, 2001), 3–4.

102. Bakhtin, *Dialogic Imagination*, 8. Yi-Ping Ong also comes to the conclusion that "virtually any plausible theory of the novel begins with the impossibility of giving an account of the novel in terms of its formal essence" (Yi-Ping Ong, *The Art of*

Being: Poetics of the Novel and Existentialist Philosophy [Cambridge, MA: Harvard University Press, 2018], 37).

103. Bakhtin, *Dialogic Imagination*, 8, 292.

104. Bakhtin, *Dialogic Imagination*, 8.

105. Holquist, introduction to *Dialogic Imagination* by Bakhtin, xxvii, xxxi.

106. Lukács, *Theory of the Novel*, 152; Bakhtin, *Dialogic Imagination*, 349. Stefan Zweig, writing five years after Lukács's *Theory of the Novel*, also agrees that Dostoevsky's works "are not novels in the true sense; rather are they heroic masses, no longer related to literature; they seem to be prophetic preludes to the saga of a new humanity" (Stefan Zweig, *Balzac, Dickens, Dostoevsky: Master Builders of the Spirit*, ed. Laurence Mintz [New Brunswick, NJ: Transaction Publishers, 2010], 200). In comparison, Sartre, in his essay on *The Sound and the Fury*, insists that Faulkner's work is not a novel (Jean-Paul Sartre, "On *The Sound and the Fury*: Time in the Work of Faulkner," in *The Sound and the Fury*, 2nd ed. [New York: W. W. Norton, 1994], 271).

107. Lukács, *Theory of the Novel*, 71.

108. Bakhtin, *Dialogic Imagination*, 234, 9.

109. Kundera, *Art of the Novel*, 95.

110. Franco Moretti, *Modern Epic: The World-System from Goethe to García-Márquez*, trans. Quintin Hoare (New York: Verso Books, 1996), 56.

111. Stendhal, *The Red and the Black*, 297.

112. "Movie Day at the Supreme Court or 'I Know it When I See it': A History of the Definition of Obscenity," https://corporate.findlaw.com/litigation-disputes/movie-day-at-the-supreme-court-or-i-know-it-when-i-see-it-a.html.

113. Prosper Merimée, *Carmen and Other Stories*, trans. Nicholas Jotcham (Oxford: Oxford University Press, 1998), ix.

114. Elizabeth Flock, "James Frey Returning to Oprah Five Years Later," *The Washington Post*, May 17, 2011, https://www.washingtonpost.com/blogs/blogpost/post/james-frey-returning-to-oprah-five-years-later/2011/05/17/AF9A3j5G_blog.html; Edward Wyatt, "Author is Kicked Out of Oprah Winfrey's Book Club," *The New York Times*, January 27, 2006, https://www.nytimes.com/2006/01/27/books/27oprah.html.

Chapter 6

The Criminality and Illegitimacy of the Novel

"THE COURAGE OF MY PESSIMISM"

James Frey, Oprah's accidental novelist, may actually prove to be more of the rule than the exception. The novelist as con-artist, as dupe, as prankster, trafficking in tall tales and lengthy stories that are half-lie and half-truth hybrids, is one of the most ubiquitous characterizations of the novelist and the novelistic art that we have. Mazzoni points out that "the hostility that accompanied the new genre for nearly three centuries is one of the most significant and symptomatic traits of its early modern history."[1] If there is any single aspect of the novel that is irrefutable, that every novel theorist can agree on, it is the fact that, despite its popularity and appeal to the mass market, its continued history as the receiving end of a hostile reception singles it out from any other literary genre.

Maybe this is the only accurate starting point in arriving at a definition—if not a theory—of the novel. While individual plays, poems, or other works may have garnered their fair share of notoriety, no genre as a whole has encountered as much of a sustained backlash over the centuries, continuing to this day. The American Library Association regularly compiles lists of books that are facing censorship challenges across the nation. Their "Top 100" lists of most banned and challenged books, decade after decade, almost exclusively consist of novels.[2] This is just the most extreme form of hostility before getting into actual Nazi book burnings. But mild forms of hostility are even more ubiquitous, often taking the form of either critically or casually dismissing, ignoring, or emphatically rejecting those novels that count as "romance"—its roots nevertheless firmly planted in the history of the *Roman* at large—and other novels that fall under "genre fiction."

Sure, Socrates may have fantasized about exiling the tragic poets and other mimetic artists from an imaginary republic, but a generation after Plato wrote down this fiction, his student Aristotle didn't even bother to address that ethical dispute in his *Poetics*, because it was immaterial. The poets were here to stay, and there was nothing immoral about them. The vitriol leveled against novels, however, has lasted for centuries. Socrates was dreaming up a revenge fantasy against the state that, in reality, forced *him* to choose between exile and death, not the tragedians. The tragedians were never the criminals, the enemies of the state, that Socrates painted them out to be. But the early novelists, as well as their heroes and anti-heroes, frequently were.

Gottfried von Strassburg may have endangered his life for threatening religion and the state with his unfinished *Tristan*, a work which "lies half-way between romance and novel."[3] Boccaccio conveniently fled Florence after a failed coup. Cervantes was also forced into exile, and John Bunyan wrote *The Pilgrim's Progress* while serving twelve years in prison for non-conformist religious preaching. Rabelais was forced into hiding under the threat of being officially condemned for heresy over *Gargantua and Pantagruel*. A warrant was written for Aphra Behn's arrest over unpaid debts, and Daniel Defoe served time for the same crime. Samuel Richardson's novels were placed on the Catholic Church's *Index Librorum Prohibitorum*, as were Voltaire's, and the Marquis de Sade spent his adult life in and out of prison.

This pattern even continues well into the modern era, defining the history of the novel in terms of its offense to the state. In 1857, Flaubert was put on trial for *Madame Bovary* on charges of obscenity. These same charges would be brought against *Ulysses*, *Lady Chatterley's Lover*, and *The Tropic of Cancer* in the twentieth century. Dostoevsky was pardoned at the last minute in front of a firing squad while imprisoned in Siberia, and Solzhenitsyn endured a similar fate, charting his experiences and those of other imprisoned novelists and dissidents in *The Gulag Archipelago*.

The novel can be understood as what pits authorship against authority. Authority can be understood as the "ambiguous conflation of divine and positive law, so that the unarguable will of God is burdened with the weight of what in other contexts might well be recognized as its antithesis, its deforming secularization."[4] Here is the site of the *Deus absconditus* that Lukács identifies as the pretext for the rise of the novel. Authority then moves away from God or any magistrate to the author. God is dead, and we have killed him—which lets us identify with the criminal on their fugitive journey that begins after they had left the scene of that crime, a journey that would be told by the novel. In this context, Anthony Cascardi defines the novel as "a genre whose form was determined by a crisis in the belief in any single, extraworldly source of authority."[5]

Every century seems to return to the novel as a space to address this crisis of authority, calling into question what is real, what counts as truth, how we can verify it, and how it runs up against the law. And the novels that raise these questions seem to explicitly engage in dialogue with the novels that had previously asked those same questions. In Balzac's *Lost Illusions*, the cynical critic Émile Blondet praises the novel as "the greatest modern achievement," saying that it is "superior to the cold, mathematical, dry analyses of the eighteenth century. . . . The eighteenth century called everything into question, and the nineteenth century is charged with coming up with the answers."[6] If that is the case, though, then the twentieth century seems to reject those answers. In Ian McEwan's *Atonement*, Briony Tallis contemplates this rejection during the Second World War, thinking to herself, "The age of clear answers was over."[7] She comes to wrestle with the guilt of having falsely reported a rape she thought she had witnessed five years earlier when she jumped to conclusions based on a series of misunderstandings, insufficient evidence, and an overactive imagination. This false accusation, destroying the lives of her sister Cecilia and Cecilia's boyfriend Robbie, then makes her the actual criminal, and Briony seems to turn to the history of the novel in order to work through her guilt.

As a novelist herself, she writes a version of the story in which Cecilia and Robbie seem to fall in love with each other through novels. Cecilia is in the middle of reading Richardson's *Clarissa* when she starts to develop feelings for Robbie, and one of their first conversations in the novel is about whether Richardson or Fielding is the better novelist. When they write letters to each other while he is in prison, they resort to the code of referring to "Tristan and Isolde, the Duke of Orsino and Olivia (and Malvolio too), Troilus and Criseyde, Mr. Knightley and Emma, Venus and Adonis" in order to pass the censors.[8] And when he accidentally breaks the vase in the fountain and she strips down to her underwear in order to retrieve it, the scene echoes *The Golden Bowl* or the broken pickle dish in *Ethan Frome*.

Briony witnesses this moment at a time when she, herself, "had written her way through a whole history of literature, beginning with stories derived from the European tradition of folk-tales, through drama with simple moral intent, to arrive at an impartial psychological realism."[9] She owes this psychological realism to Woolf, having read *The Waves* three times, which leads her to the conclusion that "a great transformation was being worked in human nature itself, and that only fiction, a new kind of fiction, could capture the essence of the change."[10] But as much as she is enamored with *The Waves*, her own narrative seems to be structured more along the lines of *To the Lighthouse*. Woolf's tripartite narrative that breaks between the sections of what happens before, during, and after World War I is here transposed onto the narrative that coincides with World War II, leaving only the final postscript to erase the optimism of the preceding section, where Briony imagines her reconciliation with Cecilia and Robbie, who had since resumed their relationship after his release from prison.

In this postscript, written in 1999, when Briony suffers from vascular dementia, she admits that the reconciliation with her sister and the reunion of the lovers was a novelistic fabrication, since Robbie had died at Dunkirk and Cecilia was killed by the Blitz. Still haunted by her guilt, she asks the question that connects Lukács to Cascardi in their view of the novel as a work that replaces the authority of God: "How can a novelist achieve atonement when, with her absolute power of deciding outcomes, she is also God?"[11] There is no one outside of her who can absolve her of her guilt; what she cannot do in life she tries to do in the novel, which she recognizes is a failure, an "impossible task, and that was precisely the point."[12] This failure largely resides in the fact that she admits, "I no longer possess the courage of my pessimism."[13]

She may no longer possess the courage of her pessimism, but the novelist behind her—Ian McEwan—certainly does. In a novel entitled *Atonement*, but which forecloses even the possibility of atonement altogether, he shatters the illusion that there ever was (or perhaps could ever be) an ending that had any kind of resolution, any kind of reprieve from the chain of loss and devastation that destroyed the lives around Briony. And yet there is never any authorial intrusion outside of her first-person narration, so the fact of her dementia could also call into question the category of reality that she invokes at the end, especially since she had been embellishing reality since the novel had begun. "What are novelists for?" she asks. "Go just so far as is necessary, set up camp inches beyond the reach, the fingertips of the law."[14] If every novel is itself a theory of the novel, according to Schlegel, then the theory proposed by *Atonement* is one that exposes the history of the novel as one that is, at its core, irreconcilable with the law.

ANNA DELVEY, MACHIAVELLI, AND OTHER CRIMINAL ENTERTAINMENTS

To Albert Camus, "The novel is born at the same time as the spirit of rebellion and expresses, on the aesthetic plane, the same ambition."[15] Yi-Ping Ong underscores this definition, contending that, "the problem of existence involves a crisis of authority that can be explored and exploded only from within the form of the novel."[16] Added to this rebellious and criminalized history of the novel is the influence of the criminal biography itself on the novel's development, rising in popularity in the sixteenth and seventeenth centuries.[17] This genre coincided with the new narrative mode of telling stories about *pícaros* like Lazarillo de Tormes in the eponymously titled book that can be traced back to 1554 (although copies of it are likely to have circulated well before then). In this picaresque tradition, which greatly influenced works like *Don Quixote*, amiable thieves and rogues would deceive others in their quest for upward mobility. The criminal biography mirrored this narrative structure, which in turn looped back into enriching the picaresque, and both eventually paved the way for the modern novel.

The protagonist of such a novelistic narrative, in both genres of the picaresque and the criminal biography, is often characterized as "both a noble hero and a villain."[18] The novel arises out of ambiguity and irony, exposing all power structures as contrived fictions, as well—which is the source of the novel's power and also of its threat to the social order. The case of Mary Carleton and her husband John Mandeville, for example—both criminals who turned on each other when they got caught—yielded twenty-five pamphlet publications in the decade leading up to Carleton's execution in 1673.[19] She was accused of defrauding men and landlords while posing under various disguises, including that of a German princess, which allowed her to mix in social circles that cut across class lines. As McKeon notes of her narratives, her "power derives not from state authority but from personal authenticity, and as long as she is telling her own story she resembles a self-constructed heroine more than an official example of the unregenerate."[20] But her husband dismissed her "personal history" as "a pretty Romance," and as "innumerable cursed fictions."[21] Her biographer Francis Kirkman writes, "if I should promise to give you a true account of her whole life I should deceive you, for how can truth be discovered of her who was wholly composed of falsehood?"[22]

The criminal biography, the picaresque, and the budding novel emerge from this crisis of truth against "Romance" and "fiction," because the narrative strategies of documenting truth are parodied in the novel, and even in the biography. The novel blurs the distinctions between these categories, so that a general proverb of the seventeenth century was "that Travellers [sic] may tell Romances or untruths by authority."[23] It is under these circumstances that we get the stories of Don Quixote, Robinson Crusoe, and Lemuel Gulliver—each adventurer in pursuit of his own authority, his own authorship—in the form of the novel, a genre that increasingly demanded the constraints of what Ian Watt calls "formal realism," a narrative style grounded in its legal history of the courtroom, where the truth or untruth of a crime could be discerned:

> The novel's mode of imitating reality may . . . be equally well summarized in terms of the procedures of another group of specialists in epistemology, the jury in a court of law. Their expectations, and those of the novel reader coincide in many ways: both want to know "all the particulars" of a given case—the time and place of the occurrence; both must be satisfied as to the identities of the parties concerned, and will refuse to accept evidence about anyone called Sir

Toby Belch or Mr. Badman—still less about a Chloe who has no surname and is "common as the air"; and they also expect the witnesses to tell the story "in his own words." The jury, in fact, takes the "circumstantial view of life," which T.H. Green found to be the characteristic outlook of the novel.[24]

The novel becomes the genre of particularity, heaping details upon details in a meticulous appeal to veracity.[25]

In a novel overwhelmed by details like *The Brothers Karmazov*, Dostoevsky draws the reader's attention to the ambiguous space in which the novel and the court of law overlap. The trial of Fyodor Pavlovich's murder begins with the prosecutor saying that "psychology prompts novels even from the most serious people, and quite unintentionally. I am speaking of excessive psychology, gentlemen of the jury, of a certain abuse of it."[26] The term "novels" is here used as an insult, one which is bandied back and forth between the prosecutor and the defense attorney, who retorts: "The prosecution liked its own novel."[27] He goes further: "And with such novels we are prepared to ruin a human life!"[28] He ends his final speech on this note, asking, "Is this not also a novel?"[29] And the charge is thrown back in the prosecutor's rebuttal: "We are reproached with having invented all sorts of novels. But what has the defense attorney offered if not novel upon novel?"[30] What Dostoevsky ultimately gives us is a novel that uses "novel upon novel" as a way to access truth, but the truth is irreducible to mere fact, and doesn't coincide with justice. His novel is a pessimistic account of truth and justice themselves. In order to argue the truth, Dostoevsky seems to show us, "novels"—those things that always necessarily exceed and fall short of the truth they are trying to portray—are all we have, and they are hardly adequate as a defense.

By the time we get to the twentieth century, the question is no longer a matter of who did the crime or whether or not we sympathize with the criminal, but what the crime actually was in the first place. They are already guilty, but for what? Josef K. in Kafka's *The Trial* has no idea why he's being arrested. And we learn, only at the end of Nabokov's modern picaresque *Lolita*, that Humbert Humbert is not imprisoned for raping and kidnapping Dolores Haze, but for killing her other predator, Clare Quilty. Humbert himself taunts his readers as "Ladies and gentlemen of the jury," drawing attention to the history of this epistemological crisis dramatized by the court of law in pursuing the truth.[31] Humbert plays this game of veracity and falsehood from the other side, as well. When his wife Charlotte Haze discovers his diary, which exposes his sexual desires for her twelve-year-old daughter, he gaslights her and says, "The notes you found were fragments of a novel."[32] This statement is clearly a lie, except for the fact that they are inscribed into a novel itself, so the lie is actually a perverse and paradoxical truth.

We are still working through this epistemic and legal crisis well into the twenty-first century. Avatars of Mary Carleton continue to appear in news stories of people like Anna Delvey, who—like Carleton—claimed to be a wealthy German heiress, convincing a bank employee to give her $100,000 that she never intended to pay back, while managing to stay in luxury Manhattan hotels for free and duping other banks and a private jet company out of an additional $100,000, not to mention the $62,000 she had stolen from her friend on a lavish trip to Marrakesh and wasn't convicted for. On top of this, she has admitted to writing bad checks in the amount of $160,000.[33]

What makes this news story relevant to the history of the novel is not just the similarity of her crimes with Carleton's, and not even the deception at work that fundamentally lends itself to a fiction that tricked others into mistaking it for truth, but her careful attention to how the narrative of her story is told. She is rumored to be working on a memoir, as well as a second book about her experience at Riker's Island. As Kirkman notes about Carleton's biography, the genre of the memoir authored by the same person who was guilty of passing off fiction for truth could easily slip into the territory of the novel. Even as Netflix was casting the biopic about her escapades, she expressed that she was more fixated on who would get to play her than her actual trial.[34] Her concern has always been about the fiction, about the deception and the glamor, about the semi-fabricated narrative that will be told about her life of crime in an entertainment medium like Netflix rather than the facts of the crime itself.

This story also arrives in the midst of a cultural moment when news reporting itself is called into question. But the epistemic crisis of "fake news" and "alternative facts," consisting of malicious lies, technological manipulation, and falsified documentation to simulate veracity, is anchored in a history that tells the same story as the rise of the novel. The rise of the printing press helped begin the gradual process of untethering the word "romance" from "novel" so that "romance"—referring predominantly to those prose stories in circulation before the printing press—was now periodized as a medieval genre.[35] The dichotomy between "romance" and "history," as evidenced in Mandeville's repudiation of his wife's account, began to be replaced with the dichotomy of "news" and "novels."

Before the advent of the printing press, news in Europe would be officially disseminated by sermons.[36] But in the growing secular culture, printed news started replacing the sermon, and its authority relied on verification by witnesses. These techniques of authentication, though, could easily be replicated to brand fictional stories as real news, since any testimony could be fabricated. For Richard Brathwaite in the 1630s, the "newness" of the "newsmongers argues not truth but false invention, and he called their works 'novels' in order to disparage them in this spirit."[37] To Brathwaite, my Contemporaries the Novelists have, for the better spinning out Paragraphs, and working down to the End of their Columns, a most happy Art in saying and unsaying, giving Hints of Intelligence, and Interpretations of indifferent Actions, to the great Disturbance of the Brains of ordinary Readers.[38]

The "novelist" in this sense is that pernicious charlatan who poses as a reporter of current events, who betrays the trust of the people in order to peddle sensationalist fictions and appeal to the lowest common denominator, the vulgar masses, the "ordinary Readers." These "ordinary" readers in the sixteenth and seventeenth centuries were essentially *new* readers—literally *novel* readers. Many of them had just learned to read, as scribal culture was being replaced with print culture, a shift that coincided with the rise of the middle class.[39]

One of the first books written for these new readers was Baldesar Castiglione's *The Book of the Courtier*, a work that modernizes the genre of the seducer's manual from Plato to Capellanus. Rushing to publish this popular work officially in 1528 after discovering that a prior draft had been leaked to the public four years earlier, Castiglione comments on how "men are always eager for something new," and how he is eager to meet this demand.[40] This "something new" inheres not so much in the content—which essentially covers the same material as *Symposium* and *The Art of Courtly Love*—but in the language and style, which he claims is a refreshing departure from Boccaccio, whose style had already become antiquated by this point. Castiglione essentially lays down the aesthetic of novelistic realism by saying that "it is always wrong to employ words which are not current," and that the text he is composing is "acceptable in upper-class speech and yet understood without any trouble by ordinary people."[41] In revisiting Plato's Ladder of Love, then, he is also offering his ordinary readers a way to climb up the ladder of social mobility, saying explicitly that "ordinary people" can learn the "certain air and grace" that ostensibly distinguishes those of "noble birth."[42]

There is, then, a threat to the political order if ordinary people can simulate how noble people behave. The goal that Castiglione advises is to hide the traces of this simulation, so that the end result is dissimulation, or *sprezzatura*—the famously untranslatable word that is often rendered as "grace" or "nonchalance." One must

> steer away from affectation at all costs . . . and (to use perhaps a novel word for it) to practice in all things a certain nonchalance which conceals all artistry and makes whatever one says or does seem uncontrived and effortless.[43]

This practice of dissimulation, of the art that hides its traces of artifice, is a tool that proves useful in matters of love, of politics, of social station, and of a new kind of aesthetic that lays the groundwork for the modern novel. For Castiglione, "true art is what does not seem to be art; and the most important thing is to conceal it, because if it is revealed this discredits a man completely and ruins his reputation."[44]

This dissimulation, especially in matters of eros, becomes a trademark of the modern novel, from *La Princesse de Clèves* to *In Search of Lost Time*. It is as though the dissembling artistry at work in the operations of love generates a new form, a new style, that gravitates to the novel in its portrait of ordinary life. Castiglione takes this cue from Capellanus, who advises anyone who has a love affair to "be careful not to let it be known to any outsider."[45] This secrecy draws attention to the space of interiority, which the novel can accommodate in ways that drama or poetry cannot, navigating between a network of external actions and the narration of internal thoughts, some of which may not be fully or consciously acknowledged by the characters themselves.

Cervantes ends up citing *The Book of the Courtier* in both *Don Quixote* and *Galatea*, and Pierre-Daniel Huet, who in 1670 was one of the first writers to reflect on the development of the genre of the novel, owned a copy of it, as did Daniel Defoe.[46] Peter Burke also documents how the popularity of this book shaped the history of publication, moving from the 1528 folio version, which was "impressive to look at but difficult to handle," to the "smaller and more manageable octavos, or even tiny duodecimos like the Giolito editions of 1549 and 1551, true 'pocket-books.'"[47] This history coincides with the same kind of dissemination and mass market appeal that helped foster the rise of the modern novel.

Something else that also carries over into the modern novel from this blockbuster hit is a sense of pessimism about modernity. As Castiglione discusses eros as a way of working through his theory of a new kind of art form that can also pass as general life advice, he seems to be struggling against a pessimistic frame of mind that interrupts the otherwise jovial atmosphere. The conversations take place in the house at the Court of Urbino, which "could truly be called the very inn of happiness," and he begins the second of four books that comprise the volume by saying, "if the world were always growing worse and if fathers were generally better than their sons, we would long since have become so rotten that no further deterioration would be possible."[48] But by the time he reaches the beginning of the fourth and last book, he reflects,

> As I prepare to record the discussions held on the fourth evening, following those described in the preceding books, there is one bitter thought among my reflections that assails me with its reminder of human wretchedness and hopelessness and of how when we are midway in our course, or even nearing the end,

Fortune frustrates our weak and feeble plans, sometimes wrecking them even before we sight harbor.[49]

He is here reminiscing about three of the interlocutors from that fourth evening in 1507 who had since died. One of them, Cesare Gonzaga, remarks in the final pages of *The Book of the Courtier* that, "The road that leads to happiness seems to me so steep that I hardly think anyone can travel it."[50]

So, is *The Book of the Courtier* even a manual after all? What's the point in dispensing advice if the road that leads to happiness is too steep to climb in the first place? Maybe happiness itself was never the goal. Maybe all we have are tactics of manipulation to get the most strategic advantages out of life as possible. This is the position of Castiglione's contemporary, Niccolò Machiavelli, who was also writing for a broad readership of ordinary people in *The Prince*, written in 1513 but published in 1532. Even though he addresses it to Lorenzo di Medici, Machiavelli—like Castiglione—writes in ordinary Italian rather than Latin, which makes this a text aimed more at a commoner than a Medici. In *The Prince*, the elegiac pessimism of Castiglione is replaced with pragmatic cynicism.

The self-conscious awareness of a "new" class with "new" interests fuels this iconoclastic work, where Machiavelli codifies how a "newly-risen man" would "introduce new laws and measures," ushering in a modern world that would definitively break from its medieval past.[51] In his chapter entitled "Of New Dominions Acquired by the Power of Others or by Fortune," Machiavelli writes of these new men who "rise from private citizens to be princes."[52] Practices that may otherwise be deemed criminal for the former private citizen would serve to protect and benefit the newly minted prince.

Crime, both in the Machiavellian scheme and in the novel, becomes an axiological pivot, soliciting a transvaluation of values based on who is committing the crime and for what purposes. In his chapter on "Those Who Have Attained the Position of Prince by Villainy," Machiavelli makes no moral judgments about "the merits of this method, as I judge them to be sufficient for any one obliged to imitate them."[53] He then proceeds to provide examples of how this "villainy" is accomplished. As if fulfilling Socrates's worst nightmare, he offers an imitation, in prose, of destructive political behavior that is specifically aimed at ordinary readers who, in turn, would "imitate" this behavior in life. From a Platonic point of view, this would spell out anarchy.

The idea that long-standing regimes could potentially be toppled by these new, ordinary readers of the vulgar masses reading in the vulgate of their own spoken languages piqued an interest in the new genres of the novel and the news about ordinary people just like them. The novel is a receptacle of that anarchic vision, evident even in its unwieldy structure and nebulous formal properties, leveraging its authorship against authority, and thereby taking aim at the power structures in place. In response to this text written for "newly-risen men," the term "Machiavellian" became just as much of an insult at the same time that the word "novel" did.

NEW MAN, WHO DIS?:
BALZAC, DOSTOEVSKY, STOKER

It is from this Machiavellian groundwork, then, that the novel emerges as an articulation of the "newly-risen man." Even by the nineteenth century, Machiavellianism was still associated with innovation in the novel. Reviewing *The Charterhouse of Parma*, Balzac praised Stendhal for having "written the modern *Il Principe* . . . the novel that Machiavelli would have written had he been exiled to nineteenth-century Italy."[54] And in his own novels, Balzac's characters profess an affinity for Machiavelli when they want to reinvent themselves, to enter the world anew. In *Lost Illusions*, the aspiring poet Lucien Chardon wants to reinvent himself as Lucien de Rubempré, trying to reclaim a lost family title, and moves from the countryside to Paris in order to break into the literary scene. But as the pessimistic title of the novel suggests, his ambitions are frustrated by the harsh reality of trying to make a living. He becomes involved in a group of other starving artists, collectively known as the Cénacle, and suggests that he take up journalism on the side in order to make some quick cash, just to the extent that he can sell his poems and his novels, and then quit. To the Cénacle, there is no greater contrast between pure art and the drivel that they identify in journalism, demonstrating Balzac's own struggle to drive a wedge between the novel and other forms of print media. It is tantamount to a choice between good and evil. A member of this group, Léon Giraud, tells him, "Machiavelli could manage to do that, but not Lucien de Rubempré," to which Lucien responds, "I'll just have to show you that I'm as good as Machiavelli!"[55]

Lucien makes a Faustian bargain and sells his soul to journalism, descending into the lowest circles of the capitalist hellscape, where he takes part in tearing down other people's talent while rewarding mediocrity, all through the transaction of the written word, and for the profits of greedy, talentless stakeholders. He eventually sees his own reputation go up in flames that are public and humiliating, and, on the verge of suicidal despair, he meets his Mephistopheles, who delays Lucien's death for the duration of the novel's sequel in *Lost Souls*. This Mephistopheles character is Balzac's true Machiavellian creation, a man who reinvents himself so many times that he goes by three different names and makes pivotal appearances in three of Balzac's novels.

In *Père Goriot*, he goes by Vautrin; in *Lost Illusions*, he dons the disguise of the Abbé Carlos Herrera; in *Lost Souls*, he is revealed as Jacques Collin. Described as the "Machiavelli of the Penal Colony," Vautrin is an escaped convict "armed with the most Machiavellian powers of dissimulation."[56] In *Père Goriot*, at times it sounds as though Machiavelli himself is speaking through him, like when he proudly proclaims to his fellow tenants at the Maison Vauquer that, "there are no principles, just things that happen; there are no laws, either, just circumstances, and the superior man espouses both events and circumstances, so he can guide them."[57]

This is arguably not just Machiavellian philosophy, but the aesthetic mandate of any novelist. A novel is a set of interrelated circumstances, and the novelist guides characters through them. One of the aesthetic principles observed by the modern novelist is, in accordance with Vautrin's statement, to avoid moralizing. To this extent, Vautrin's "Machiavellian powers of dissimulation" allow him not only to continue engaging in crime, but to serve as a kind of novelistic writer of the world within Balzac's universe, treating other people in his orbit as his own characters whom he has control over. In *Père Goriot*, Rastignac gets the uncanny feeling that Vautrin could "cut right through his passions and read his very soul."[58] Vautrin even tells him, "I know you as well as if I'd made you."[59]

If, to Lukács, the novel is an "epic in an age abandoned by God," this Machiavellian character who constantly reinvents himself, ultimately pitching himself to the God's eye view of the novelist, seems to usurp the role that God had abandoned. One of the nicknames he goes by is "Death-Dodger," because he seems to have tempted fate so many times that he eventually declares, "I play the role of Fate," itself.[60] This statement is more aspirational than accurate, though. While he wields considerable power over the people around him, he is not infallible. Rastignac manages to escape his orbit by the end of *Père Goriot*, which is how Vautrin eventually sets his sights on Lucien at the end of *Lost Illusions*, thinking about what to do with him in *Lost Souls* "as an author combing over his manuscript to root out any remaining faults."[61] After openly declaring to Lucien that he is his "author," he then informs him that, "We're making prose now, not poetry."[62]

This "prose" may seem like a metaphor of his schemes, but Balzac stresses its literal meaning, anchored in the rhetoric that constitutes Vautrin's identity and approach to life. In the last part of *Lost Souls*, called "Vautrin's Last Incarnation," Balzac explores his criminal past as a way of highlighting how slang originates in the prison and in the criminal underworld, following "right behind civilization, right on its heels, enriching it with new expressions constantly."[63] It is the novel's duty to faithfully record these new expressions, to keep up with the vernacular, a legacy that can be traced to Castiglione, but which Balzac traces back even further to Rabelais: "At least one hundred argot words come from the language of Panurge, who, in Rabelais' work, symbolizes the people, for his name is made up of two Greek words, meaning 'the one who does everything.'"[64] Vautrin is precisely that carnivalesque reincarnation of Panurge; he is "the one who does everything," who seems like he is behind and beyond all the action, speaking in a language that may not be acceptable to the Académie Française, but which is readily recognizable and up to date with Balzac's first readers.

In *Père Goriot*, the narrator notes how

> this sort of jargon is always changing. . . . The new invention, the Diorama, which carries an optical illusion to an even higher level than did the Panorama, has led a number of painters' studios to coin the jesting word "rama".[65]

Vautrin, in a sense, uses this novelistic jargon, this slang, as part of an illusion that allows him to slip into and out of different and newly created identities across the panoramic display of these three novels. The new rhetorical expressions, emerging from both prisons and painters' studios, are literally what keep the genre *new*, truly novel; they don't just enable language to reinvent itself, but people, too. Crime, slang, and Machiavellianism are all central to the advent of the modern novel in that they all challenge and undermine authority, allowing ordinary people to refashion themselves as extraordinary beings.

Dostoevsky's characters function in similar ways. *Crime and Punishment* opens with Raskolnikov already contemplating the murder of the moneylender Alëna Ivanovna as he thinks to himself, "I wonder what men are most afraid of. . . . Any departure, and especially a *new word*—that is what they fear most of all."[66] New words, in both Raskolnikov's and Vautrin's minds, are rooted in crime, in transgression, because they function in service of dismantling the existing social order to create a new reality, the process of which the novel as a genre documents and bears witness to. The term "new people" was used to describe the young Russian radicals of the 1860s who threatened to upend the status quo; it is precisely the "newness" of their philosophy and rhetoric that characterizes Raskolnikov.[67] Even when Raskolnikov clarifies his proto-Nietzschean philosophy, he still does so in terms of rhetoric, distinguishing extraordinary people from ordinary people by virtue of "the gift or talent of saying *something new* in their sphere."[68] To Raskolnikov, these extraordinary people "move the world and guide it to its goal," which is precisely Vautrin's aspiration in Balzac's novels.[69]

And just as much as Vautrin appears as both a Machiavellian and Mephistophelean character to replace God, so too does the Devil who appears in Ivan Karamazov's fever dream. He seems to borrow Raskolnikov's philosophy to sketch out the portrait of who this "new" extraordinary man would be:

Since God and immortality do not exist in any case, even if this period should never come, the new man is allowed to become a man-god, though it be he alone in the whole world, and of course, in this new rank, to jump lightheartedly over any moral obstacle of the former slave-man, if need be.[70]

Both Balzac and Dostoevsky imagine this new Machiavellian man in a world without God as somewhat supernatural and demonic, veering far away from the realistic and even emancipatory portrait of this figure in *The Prince*, the template of the first bourgeois. But since, by the time of the nineteenth century, the bourgeoisie had consolidated its power so that they now represented the ancien régime that ought to face resistance, Balzac and Dostoevsky untethered their vision of this "newly risen man" from that context and made him a hero of the oppressed, but still along nightmarish lines. Since Marx even defines capital itself as "dead labour, that, vampire-like, only lives by sucking living labour, and lives the more, the more labour it sucks," it would seem to require seemingly greater supernatural forces to overcome it, especially from disadvantaged circumstances.[71] Only an extraordinary being with this kind of power, to Raskolnikov, could defeat those who, like Alëna Ivanovna, "sucked the life-blood of the poor."[72]

By the late Victorian era, this supernatural hero and supernatural opponent are conflated into the same figure—another demonic creature who emerges in the absence of God as a way of channeling both fear and desire. The Machiavellian trajectory of the "newly risen man" across the centuries seems to come to a dead end—or rather an undead end—in the figure of a character who has existed for just as long: Dracula. But as Franco Moretti notes, "Count Dracula is an aristocrat only in manner of speaking."[73] He doesn't actually seem to come from an old culture, but functions instead on the other side of Marx's simile of capital. In Jonathan Harker's trip to Transylvania, to discuss matters of real estate, he finds only gold heaped up in Dracula's castle: "The money that had been buried comes back to life, becomes capital and embarks on the conquest of the world: this and none other is the story of Dracula the vampire."[74]

This story of vampires and capital has been told before, and not just by Marx. In *Wuthering Heights*, Heathcliff is the foreigner who seems to emerge as the ghost of the Earnshaws' dead son who went by the same name. He is simultaneously external to the Earnshaw household while reincarnating their ghosts—maybe not just of the dead son, but of the entire Earnshaw lineage that stretches back to the year 1500, the year that is carved into the entrance of the estate at Wuthering Heights.[75] It was at the start of that century that Machiavelli laid out the blueprint for the newly risen man, which the upstart Heathcliff emblemizes. His seemingly magical transformation from an impoverished outsider, referred to as a "gipsy brat," to a gentleman of extraordinary and even predatory wealth, is never explained.[76] He leaves for a time and comes back with riches and with vengeance. Lockwood wonders whether he had escaped to America, the newly established country that was synonymous with capital, to "earn honours by drawing blood from his foster country."[77] Whatever blood he may have drawn empowers him to turn his former foes into debtors. His vengeance may be fueled by eros, but it expresses itself in usurping capital. There may be more meanings, then, in Lockwood's first impression of Heathcliff, his landlord, as "a capital fellow."[78]

Heathcliff, like Dracula after him, fixates on matters of real estate and possessions as a way of exerting control beyond the grave through a bloodline, saying that he wants "the triumph of seeing *my* descendent fairly lord" of the Lintons' "estates; my child hiring their children to till their fathers' lands for wages."[79] He relishes in calling Linton "*mine*," which he repeats, "with particular gusto," when he says to Hareton, after Hareton's father Hindley dies, "Now, my bonny lad, you are *mine!*"[80] From the mouth of a capitalist, this italicized "*mine*" reduces people to exploited resources, such as those that can be found in a mine, which is why Heathcliff refers to both Linton and Hareton by saying that, "one is gold put to the use of paving stones, and the other is tin polished to ape a service of silver."[81] When Lockwood returns to Wuthering Heights under the pretext of being invited "to devastate the moors," perhaps he aspires to this same kind of control, especially if, in his fantasy of marrying Cathy, he would inherit the estate.[82]

There is, of course, the suggestion of a more literal vampirism at work here, such as Heathcliff's wish to drink Edgar's blood, the way he terrifies Isabella with his "sharp cannibal teeth, revealed by cold and wrath, gleam[ing] through the dark," and the way that "Time had little altered his person" after eighteen years.[83] And if Catherine *is* Heathcliff, as she famously confesses to Nelly, then it makes sense for her to also exhibit these features. Catherine's teeth are so sharp that she tears an entire pillow with them, and neither her face nor her body decays in her grave.[84] When Heathcliff leaves her upon hearing of her engagement to Edgar, she is in so much distress that Kenneth comes to bleed her, but it seems rather that she bleeds everyone else around her instead. Convalescing at Thrushcross Grange, where Edgar's parents take care of her, she only gets better after they die—maybe even because they die, and she comes back to life "saucier and more passionate, and naughtier than ever."[85]

Catherine and Heathcliff, taken together as one single entity, constitute the androgyne. So too does Dracula, who epitomizes not only the "newly risen man"—even if he's just newly risen out of his coffin—but actually the late Victorian category of the New Woman. He is an androgynous figure who, embodying the Victorian fear of the vagina dentata, strikes more or less once a month, and sails along the schooner *Demeter*—named after the goddess of fertility—to engender discord and chaos.[86] Dracula is the personification of hysteria itself, a wandering womb that allows his victims like Lucy Westenra to indulge in a new, voracious, and highly sexualized appetite, as well as an atavistic lack of moral restraint. Vampirism abides by the principle of mimesis; the victim of the vampire becomes the new vampire—and Lucy's vampish behavior embodies the political anxieties surrounding the New Woman and the fear that this modern figure would replicate and spread beyond control, undermining the patriarchal foundations of civilization. Dracula is therefore feared on the grounds that he is a Machiavellian and even protofascist "father or furtherer of a new order of beings," whose power would overwhelm the law, whose criminality could itself become a law in its own right and alter the course of civilization toward apocalypse.[87]

Despite the countless reproductions of *Dracula* across various media, it is only the 1897 novel itself that stresses the role of novelty, structurally shifting across various technological advances to narrate the story, from the phonograph to the typewriter and probably the first reference in literature to the Kodak camera, carefully calibrating the new experiences of average everydayness.[88] Like Balzac, who goes to great lengths in *Lost Illusions* to foreground the material production and technological advances in paper production that allow such a novel to be written, published, and disseminated in the first place, Stoker treats the genre of the novel as something that makes use of the most recent innovations of its day. In addition to newspaper clippings and even a ship log, the novel absorbs phonograph transcriptions, telegrams, journal entries, and letters from a number of different characters into an unnervingly cohesive narrative, essentially erasing the distinctions in tone and voice between them, so that they all seem to be narrated by the same voice, in the same way that the baby born at the end of the novel claims an impossible lineage of five simultaneous fathers who all somehow merge into one.

In this way, *Dracula* is emblematic of Marthe Robert's definition of the novel as "a newcomer onto the literary scene" that is marked by its "encroachments on the neighboring territories it surreptitiously infiltrated, gradually colonizing almost all of literature." Its "parasitic, protean nature doubtless reflects the rebellious, go-ahead upstart who apes it in the lower ranges of ambition."[89] If there is any vampirism here, it is more of a formal characteristic of the novel at large than any scenes of lurid bloodsucking that Stoker inserted into this potboiler. And in this collection of largely firstperson accounts, the glaring omission is the account of Dracula himself, in his own voice. His perspective is the absent center of the novel, even as this nihilistic absence threatens to swallow the whole. The narrative attention is never focused on him so much as it is on the narrators themselves—all of whom question their own sanity in their quest to destroy him, as Carol A.

Senf argues.[90] Perhaps they are trapped and deluded by their own fantastic projections.

The horror of this novel begins when Jonathan Harker looks into a mirror and cannot see Dracula's reflection. But the mirror certainly shows Harker's reflection, and neither he nor any of the other narrators are willing to take a good look into this mirror and recognize how they, themselves, exhibit traits of vampirism even as they are the ones who claim to be eradicating it. Lucy, after all, exhibits her vampiric traits only after a blood transfusion from the American capitalist Quincy P. Morris, who first introduces the word "vampire" in the novel, and whose unexplained voyages around the world rival only those, maybe, of Dracula himself.[91] Lucy's vampiric traits, moreover, are hardly anything more than an open expression of sexuality that violates the Victorian code of decorum. As a result, she ends up being punished in a scene that Senf describes as "the combined group rape and murder of an unconscious woman; and this kind of violent attack on a helpless victim is precisely the kind of behavior which condemns Dracula in the narrators' eyes."[92]

Perhaps Dracula cannot be reflected in a mirror because he is that mirror itself. His threat inheres in the possibility that those who catch their reflection will recognize the horror in themselves, a horror at the understanding that they are already drones of a greater power that has inculcated them into doing its bidding in the name of patriarchy, empire, and capital. In this way, they represent the very real agents of historical atrocities, which is why they feel the need to deflect with a fabricated myth of victimhood, deviating so far from reality that they require superstition. "Dracula's behavior confirms that he is an internal, not an external threat," which is why "he usually employs seduction, relying on others' desires to emulate his freedom from external constraints."[93] Maybe this is the erotic seduction of the novel genre at large, a seduction that carries with it the threat of annihilation.

MIRROR, MIRROR, ON THE PAGE: THE FAILURE OF REALISM AND THE DISENCHANTMENT OF THE FAIRY TALE

If Balzac holds up a mirror to society, stripped of its illusions, then Stoker holds up a mirror to the absence of illusions as such, an absence that still haunts and distracts the spectator from their own reflection. As Oscar Wilde writes in his Preface to *The Picture of Dorian Gray*, "It is the spectator, and not life, that art really mirrors."[94] This may explain why Victorian readers were so offended when they read his own novel of vampirism, *The Picture of Dorian Gray*: they were horrified at their own reflection. In *Dracula*, published seven years after Wilde's only novel—and largely in response to it—Stoker at least gave them the fantasy of not focusing on themselves in the mirror, so that they could instead fixate on the empty space and fabricate a separate entity that embodied their own dissociated anxieties and insecurities.

As for Wilde, he found in Balzac's novels a construct of reality that felt more realistic to him than reality itself. "The nineteenth century as we know it," he said, "is largely the invention of Balzac.... We are merely carrying out, with footnotes and unnecessary additions, the whim or fancy or creative vision of a great novelist."[95] In typical Wildean fashion, the mirrored relationship is reversed so that reality reflects art. But the appeal to reality is still something that defines Balzac's aesthetic. To Lukács, reality can only ever be understood in its opposition to illusion, which is why he traces the history of the novel along a path of winnowing out illusions altogether, from *Don Quixote* to *Lost Illusions*.[96] What is left after the illusions have been shorn is the pessimistic understanding that reality is unbearably bleak—a bleakness which, after 1915, Lukács fought against with the hope of Marxism.

Erich Auerbach, too, identifies Balzac as "the creator of modern realism."[97] But Auerbach, even in the landmark study that he entitled *Mimesis: The Representation of Reality in Western Literature*, is careful not to define "realism," waiting for the Epilogue to say, in a parenthesis, that, "Not even the term 'realistic' is unambiguous."[98] Whatever the term means, though, it is inextricable from the development of the novel. In this study that spans the history of literature from Homer to Woolf, he still tracks the development of "the representations of reality" across the ages from a number of different genres until he sees it crystallizing in the form of the modern novel to which he devotes half of the book.

There is something irreconcilable, though, between the history of the novel understood as the aspiration to a realist aesthetic and the crucial ways in which this verisimilitude breaks down—even in Balzac, the quintessential realist. The unifying thread of *Père Goriot*, *Lost Illusions*, and *Lost Souls*—Vautrin himself—is a character who at once refers to a recognizable and immediate reality with his use of slang, but also challenges any semblance of reality with his seemingly supernatural powers of peering into people's souls with a glance and of dodging death so many times that he earns the nickname "Death-Dodger." To Lukács, "Vautrin stands in truth in the graveyard of all illusions developed during several centuries, on his face the satanic grin of the bitter Balzacian wisdom that all men are either fools or knaves."[99] By standing in the "graveyard of illusions," doesn't he resurrect some supernatural illusions of his own, the "satanic grin" on his face characterizing him as a Mephistophelean character, the master illusionist from folklore rather than the real world, who tricks everyone else into confusing his machinations with reality? And isn't this role, in some ways, the role of the novelist? Does

Vautrin represent the principle by which realism—if not reality—must fail in the novel at large?

By what measure can this failure be assessed? Maybe the novel emphasizes not just the ways that illusions fail in translating to reality, but the ways that reality fails to live up to illusions. It is reality that fails. It inevitably exposes itself, as it does to Lucien at the end of *Lost Illusions*, in his suicidal despair before chancing upon Vautrin, to be something not even worth the bother— what's the point of it, after all? There is no point; reality just disappoints. But maybe the point of Balzac's novel is that Lucien—and maybe all of us—are actually quite incapable of losing all of our illusions. As Nietzsche reminds us, "Truths are illusions which we have forgotten are illusions."[100] Any pursuit of "truth" or "reality" can only ever end up being a pursuit of illusion— Socrates's nightmare. We are just doomed to swapping out old illusions for new ones, as Lucien indeed does in his pact with Vautrin, prolonging both the fantasy and the misery of his life, which, perhaps, is the only way to confront reality at all.

If reality inevitably fails, and the only truths about it are revealed to be nothing more than a perspectival shifting of various sets of illusions, then each one of these paradoxical illusion-truths can only be conveyed and understood through art, through Nietzsche's definition of truth as a "movable host of metaphors, metonymies, and anthropomorphisms: in short, a sum of human relations which have been poetically and rhetorically intensified, transferred, and embellished."[101] To this extent, any aspiration to a realist aesthetic must also necessarily fail. But paradoxically, the closest we can get to understanding what passes for the experience of reality, in all the richness of its referential detail, is through literature—and especially the novel, which organizes these literary tropes that Nietzsche lists into a reflection of lived experience. In this way, the novel discards the truth-illusion binary and instead engages in the tension between what Heidegger would later call authentic and inauthentic modes of existence, where inauthenticity is the mode by which the individual, like a novelistic character, is tangled in a dense network of other people's lives and circumstances. Authenticity is the brief flash of disentanglement, of existential isolation—like Werther peering into the abyss and discerning the monster of nature, or of Marcel reading the telegram he initially thinks is from Albertine— by which we get to know ourselves on a level that is otherwise inaccessible, before falling back into inauthenticity.

This is ultimately the crisis at the core of *Crime and Punishment*, as well. Raskolnikov is arguably not so much tormented by his guilt as by the accusation of his friend Razumikhin: "you aren't original, but steal from other authors. There isn't a sign of independent existence in you!"[102] In this charge, Razumikhin—whose name means "reason"—ventriloquizes the same accusation of Reason in *The Romance of the Rose* and Lady Philosophy in *The*

Consolation of Philosophy. Raskolnikov, to him, is inauthentic precisely in his desire to untether himself from the rest of the world, pathetically trying to distinguish himself as superior. He is too attached to his illusions, even at the end of the novel when he serves his time in Siberia, haunted by an apocalyptic dream that similarly separates superior beings from everyone else who dies in a pandemic. Dostoevsky's tormented characters may capture something that can be called psychological realism, but their states of mind deviate from any semblance of reality. While Ivan Karamazov hallucinates the Devil in what may or may not be a fever dream, Raskolnikov's vision of the apocalypse is orchestrated by intelligent microbes that infect and wipe out the human race. The coincidences are also too many and too uncanny to resemble any kind of reality, either—like the random student Raskolnikov overhears, who somehow articulates his own inner thoughts about Alëna Ivanovna.

Like Dostoevsky and Balzac, Stoker and Wilde also set up their novels with painstaking details that paint a picture of a recognizable reality before warping that reality. Stoker's preoccupation with technology seems to invoke a scientific appeal to veracity, and the mimicry in tone and style of various kinds of reporting makes the novel read like a collection of documentary evidence in a case that seems to force an epistemological crisis, calling the category of reality itself into question. And Wilde sketches a London that is recognizable on all strata—from the interiors of aesthetes to the carnivalesque world of the theater and even the criminal underworld of the opium dens. The element of the supernatural appears not in opposition to reality but as a slight modulation of it, which is what makes the horror so uncanny. Even as the surfaces become less recognizable, there is still an underlying element that reveals the truth behind reality so that, like Nietzsche, Wilde presents a vision of the world where truth can only be accessed through illusion.

"Reality," then, is not the most helpful or even accurate category that the novel seems to replicate. Whatever passes for "reality" ends up in frustration and disappointment, trapped only in the list of figurative devices that Nietzsche cites in his definition of truth. Maybe realism has less to do with reality than it does to do with possibility, as Swann discovers in *Swann's Way*, when he interrogates Odette about her past: "Swann had envisaged all the possibilities. Reality is therefore something that has no relation to possibilities, any more than the stab of a knife in our body has any relation to the gradual motions of the clouds overhead."[103] It is the realm of possibility that opens up the range between idealism and pessimism.

In his analysis of the first French modern novel, Madame de Lafayette's *La Princesse de Clèves*—which lays the foundation for Proust—Laurence A. Gregorio identifies the organizing principle as "the paradox of idealism and pessimism," which can be extrapolated to the organizing principle of the entire genre.[104] Gregorio identifies the discrepancy between the perfection of the "fairy-tale setting" and the imperfections of "human nature" that render such a setting incompatible and ultimately uninhabitable for these characters who hide behind so many layers of dissimulation that any direct speech is practically impossible. This is why the Princess of Clèves's direct confession to her husband of her desire for the Duc de Nemours is what ends up as the least believable moment in the novel.[105] While de Lafayette grounds the novel in the historical reality of life at the Dauphin's court in the sixteenth century, this history is so idealized as to belong to another realm altogether, a realm that even the characters don't quite seem to belong to.

To Gregorio, this discrepancy is the "fatalistic basis of pessimism" in the novel, which ultimately drives the Princess of Clèves to "renounce the illusory ideal of happiness in this life."[106] Instead of consummating her affair with the Duc de Nemours, she frequently runs away from Paris, and ultimately ends up in a convent, where even the "habitually omniscient" narrator refuses to follow her, the narrative omniscience here failing at accessing her interior thoughts once she is behind the convent's doors.[107] It is as though the modern novel, the genre that cannot possibly take seriously any established authority—let alone the authority of the church—must insist on drawing the line here.

In the development of the history of the novel, one can read Flaubert's *Madame Bovary* as *La Princesse de Clèves* in reverse. Instead of ending with the church, Flaubert begins with it in charting Emma Bovary's adolescence—this is where she cultivates her fairy-tale fantasies of what a fulfilled life would look like. Unlike the Princess of Clèves, who longs to run away from Paris, Emma desperately wants to flock to it. And while the Princess of Clèves holds on to the chastity of her desire for the Duc de Nemours, Emma takes the opportunity to cheat on her husband with two men, both of whom are ultimately disappointing. As much as these two novels seem to gesture in diametrically opposed directions, they both ultimately just offer two different models of pessimism vis-à-vis a fairy-tale world that the characters can never attain.

What does the genre of the novel owe to the fairy tale? Is it merely the overcoming of the fairy tale with a bleak snapshot of "reality"? But if the "truth" of this reality is an illusion which we have forgotten is an illusion, then is the novel a fairy tale which we have forgotten is a fairy tale? Certainly, *Dracula* and *The Picture of Dorian Gray* are closer to the fairy tale than to the realistic novel, but this question seems to haunt the entire history of the novel, especially in the tradition that links *La Princesse de Clèves* to *Madame Bovary* and beyond. "Great novels," Nabokov said in his introductory remarks to his lectures on literature at Cornell University, "are above all great fairy tales."[108] It is in this light that he even refers to works like Proust's *In Search of Lost Time* as a fairy tale.[109] This expansive understanding and connection between the novel and the fairy tale offers considerable insight into his own *Lolita* as a pessimistic fairy tale—one that articulates the voracious violence of a monstrous predator who even calls himself a "pentapod monster," preying on a girl whom he kidnaps and drugs with "capsules loaded with Beauty's Sleep" so that she becomes Sleeping Beauty.[110] Nabokov's novel reads like an encyclopedic compendium of literary history, its intricate web of extratextual references ultimately organized along the fairy-tale simplicity of the barebones plot: two evil sorcerers, Humbert Humbert and Clare Quilty, are in competition with each other to trap a lost girl described as a "nymphet."

There is no happy ending, but of course, not all fairy tales have happy endings. In Hans Christian Andersen's "The Little Mermaid," a story that Humbert gives to Lolita, the nameless creature sacrifices the world of merfolk for the world of humans but is ultimately disappointed in both, so she kills herself. Fairy tales are not just stories of enchantment. Sometimes the enchantment itself carries in its wake a devastating disenchantment, like "The Little Match Girl" and "The Red Shoes." In this way, "The Little Mermaid" is also a story of lost illusions, except for the ambiguous ending—the mermaid's one last remaining hope for an eternal soul, which perhaps even Andersen himself didn't have the heart to discard entirely.

Bruno Bettelheim, however, is so insistent in his claim that "the myth is pessimistic, while the fairy story is optimistic, no matter how terrifyingly serious some features of the story may be," that, in his comprehensive study of the fairy tale genre, *The Uses of Enchantment: The Meaning and Importance of Fairy Tales*, he never mentions "The Little Mermaid" at all.[111] It is too problematic to fit into his reductive view of the optimism that is supposedly inherent in the genre. He begrudgingly brings up Andersen only to say that stories like "The Little Match Girl" and "The Steadfast Tin Soldier" are too sad to properly be called fairy tales, even though he notes that they are some of the most popular stories of this genre and are widely anthologized in fairy-tale collections.[112]

If we were to accept Bettelheim's claim and ignore Andersen, the novel still seems to return to the fairy tale as a way of underscoring a recurring pessimism. This is not just true of a novel like *Wuthering Heights*. Even Dickens, perhaps the most optimistic of novelists, cannot help the impulse to invoke a fairy-tale sensibility in novels like *Great Expectations*, a sensibility that arguably undermines the optimism promised by the title. Satis House provides nothing but the cruel hope of a delayed satisfaction that never comes, and Pip enters it as though stepping into another world in which time itself no longer exists, although it has clearly plundered its way through the decaying interior. Pip describes Miss Havisham as "the Witch of the place" before she becomes his "fairy godmother."[113] As an adult, he is convinced that she is his benefactor, allowing him to rise up the ranks in society, when the benefactor is really that other witch, Magwitch, the escaped convict he had helped as a child. But for most of the novel, he is under the spell of Miss Havisham, who eggs him on in his desire for Estella while simultaneously encouraging Estella to remain cold and aloof to Pip. She nevertheless urges Pip to "do all the shining deeds of the young Knight of romance, and marry the Princess."[114]

Pip certainly tries to marry the "Princess," but lives out his life in an "ecstasy of unhappiness," pining away for her as she manipulates him long into their adulthood. The fairy tale dissolves, swallowed up by the novelistic and pessimistic frame as he comes to the realization that, "Miss Havisham's intentions towards me [were] all a mere dream; Estella not designed for me; I only suffered in Satis House as a convenience, a sting for the greedy relations."[115] He occasionally reverts back to thinking "how happy I should be if I lived there with her," but catches himself in the midsentence of this thought: "and knowing that I never was happy with her, but always miserable."[116] Pip's maturity stems from the realization that he has failed in his great expectations, acknowledging to himself, "It was an unhappy life that I lived."[117]

The novel doesn't end there, though. In the original draft that Dickens had intended to publish, Pip insists that his "poor dream, as I once used to call it, has all gone by."[118] He then happens to run into Estella, who had also led an "unhappy life," widowed from a cruel and brutal husband, with a child in tow. She introduces Pip to her child, and Pip walks away, "glad afterwards to have had the interview" because she gave him the "assurance that suffering had been stronger than Miss Havisham's teaching, and had given her a heart to understand what my heart used to be."[119] His torments over Estella have so hardened him that he has become just as cynical and cruel as she was to him, indulging in this vengeful moment of schadenfreude. While this ending was already in proofs, ready to be published, he made the mistake of showing it to his friend and fellow novelist, Edward Bulwer-Lytton, who reacted so adamantly against it that Dickens changed it to a happy—and thoroughly unconvincing—reconciliation between Pip and Estella. Bulwer-Lytton was worried that the ending was too dark, and the Victorian readership (at least judging by some of the scathing reviews of *Wuthering Heights*) would be too disappointed.[120]

As the Victorian period waned, though, novelists like Thomas Hardy and Joseph Conrad turned back to Brontë's sensibility rather than Dickens's, refusing to shy away from pessimism in their novels, and explicitly drawing on a fairy-tale register in order to do so. In *Tess of the D'Urbervilles*, Hardy presents a vision of the world that only has moments of enchantment, when we are seduced, like Angel Clare, into seeing the world "like a fairy place suddenly created by the stroke of a wand," a place that seduces us even into happiness. But Tess reminds us, before she gets caught and eventually executed, that, "This happiness could not have lasted—it was too much."[121]

Ours is a world that is fundamentally incompatible with a happiness that can last, especially for people like Tess, victims of cruelty and circumstances beyond their control.

But a more prominent fairy-tale element in Hardy that serves as an emblem of both enchantment and disenchantment is the night, which the narrator personifies as a being that "swallow[s]" characters up.[122] After Angel discovers the truth about Tess's past, the narrator's attention shifts again to "the night which had already swallowed up his happiness, and was now digesting it listlessly; and was ready to swallow up the happiness of a thousand other people with as little disturbance or change of mien."[123] The night here functions both as a fairy-tale villain and an impersonal force like Schopenhauer's Will or Werther's view of nature, indiscriminately moving through, dismantling, swallowing, and digesting people's happiness, like the Arctic winds that blast "with dumb impassivity" as they "dismissed experiences which they did not value . . . suggesting an achromatic chaos of things."[124]

In *Heart of Darkness,* Conrad seems to take Hardy's particular description of the night as a threatening force with an insatiable appetite and ascribe it to Kurtz, who withdraws into the darkness of the night as though that were his only natural element. Marlow describes Kurtz as an ogre who swallows everyone and everything in his path, saying that he saw him "open his mouth wide—it gave him a weirdly voracious aspect as though he had wanted to swallow all the air, all the earth, all the men before him."[125] This image appears again when Marlow "had a vision of him on the stretcher opening his mouth voraciously as if to devour all the earth with all its mankind."[126]

It is as though Marlow exists only in this space, like Jonah inside the mouth of the leviathan, on his way to warn the world about God's impending doom. His memory itself is "like a passage through some inconceivable world that had no hope in it and no desire."[127] This is a world that is so bleak that there is no room even for any recantation, which Marlow never gives. Instead, he only speaks of Kurtz as a "remarkable man," despite his genocidal brutality.[128] The horror of the novel resides partly in the fact that Marlow paints him as something like a passive victim, "as though he had been an enchanted princess sleeping in a fabulous castle."[129] He is both the hideous ogre guarding the castle and the sleeping beauty trapped inside. He wants to possess all the ivory he can hoard, but it is as though the ivory, like a fetish, magically possesses him instead. He looks "as though an animated image of death carved out of old ivory had been shaking its hand with menaces at a motionless crowd of men made of dark and glittering bronze."[130]

From ivory to bronze, people in this novelistic fairy tale are not so much human as they are just animated features of the landscape, and Marlow, sailing on the "fierce river-demon beating the water with its terrible tail and breathing black smoke into the air," tries "to break the spell, the heavy mute spell of the wilderness that seemed to draw [Kurtz] to its pitiless breast by the awakening of forgotten and brutal instincts, by the memory of gratified and monstrous passions."[131] But this pessimistic fairy tale is one in which the spell is never broken, in which imperialism inexorably eats into the heart of darkness, swallowing everything in its path until there is nothing left in its wake but the ghostly silence that Conrad manages to put a language to, a silence that persists long after its last pages are closed, accompanying the real violence of empire and conquest.

What is so uncanny about *Heart of Darkness* is the continuum between the fairy tale and historical reality rather than their opposition, especially when it comes to the language that is available in the face of mass atrocities. Mann draws on this same continuum in describing the First World War in *The Magic Mountain*, which the narrator even introduces as a "fairy tale" in the Foreword.[132] The word "Magic" in the title certainly invites such a reading, especially since "the magic mountain," in addition to the Nietzsche reference, is also the term used to describe the Brocken mountain that provides the setting for the witches' sabbath on Walpurgis Night in German folklore.[133]

Mann plays with the invocation of the number seven, a magical number that links Hans Castorp to "Hans in Luck" by the Brothers Grimm, who serves his master for seven years. Hans Castorp also spends what Mann called in his Princeton lecture "seven fairy-tale years" on the mountain, beginning his journey in the seventh month of 1907, and finds himself stalling in front of room number seven, where his love interest Clavdia Chauchat resides. He keeps the thermometer in his mouth for seven minutes, the dining hall has seven tables, the Italian word for seven is inscribed in Settembrini's name, and the novel itself is divided into seven chapters.[134]

But even outside of the enchanted symbolism of this number, Mann ironically seems to heighten the fairy-tale sensibility at the novel's denouement, in its disenchantment. The cataclysm of the First World War is described as a "thunderclap that shook the foundations of the earth; but for us it is the thunderbolt that bursts open the magic mountain and rudely sets its entranced sleeper outside the gates."[135] Everyone else around him, meanwhile, "were tumbling head over heels all five thousand feet down to the flatlands."[136] The final image of the novel, before Hans Castorp "disappears from sight," is of a shell that explodes "like the Devil himself . . . with ghastly superstrength," carrying with it "dismembered humanity."[137] It is as though the only way to capture disenchantment is through the language of enchantment itself.

All of these examples seem to illustrate a recurring observation that the novel is simultaneously a work that lays claim to some kind of recognizable reality in its average everydayness and also to a fairy-tale realm, and the most striking thing about this seemingly double gesture in opposite movements is that they are not mutually opposed. "We describe the everyday," Mann once said about the task of the novelist, "but the everyday becomes strange if it is cultivated on strange foundations."[138] The novel seems to document the ways in which the only fairy tale that is simultaneously a reality—and which not only persists to this day but fundamentally structures our human relations and lived experience—is the fairy tale of capital. Marx documents how capital is nothing more than a fetish that has been assigned a magical, mystical, and ultimately arbitrary assignation of value, and it ends up taking ownership over those who had assigned this value in the first place while wreaking havoc on a planetary scale. There is nothing real about capital except the extent to which it is enforced by violence and power structures. Without this enforcement, it is as real as pixie dust.

This is the pessimistic fairy tale that the modern novel tells over and over again. Capital is what transforms both Heathcliff's and Pip's trajectories in life and ultimately prolongs their misery; the lack of capital is what puts Tess in danger, setting off a chain of events that leads to her execution. Marcel's obscene amount of wealth frees up his time to mope around all day and cultivate his obsessions, along with a taste for art. The same can be said of Werther, who doesn't even last five months at a sinecure before being offered the opportunity to spend the entire spring season with a prince who lavishes money on him to do nothing. Capital is what allows all the guests in Mann's sanatorium to stay for as long as they do before they come tumbling down into an absurd world war that is also fought on the basis of nothing but capital, empire, and a meaningless display of national pride.

Capital is also what, in part, allows monsters like Dorian Gray and Humbert Humbert to get away with all of their crimes, since they belong to a social class that, for the most part, continues to be untouchable precisely because it is protected by wealth. And Raskolnikov, trying to take revenge against this monstrous intrusion of capital's fairy-tale narrative into a reality that has terrorized the entire world, ends up supplanting this narrative in his mind with another fairy-tale narrative of superheroes. Dracula is a fairy tale about a dragon who hoards his pile of gold and breathes pestilence on anyone who is trying to increase their piles, as well. But more monstrous than Dracula is Kurtz, the ogre who pillages his way through Africa in pursuit of capital, a pursuit that can only strip him of any humanity. Three years after Conrad first published *Heart of Darkness* in 1899, he re-released it in a collection published as *Youth: A Narrative and Two Other Stories*, with the title page bearing a quote from Grimms' fairy tales: "But the Dwarf answered: 'No; something human is dearer to me than the wealth of all the world.'"[139] *Heart of Darkness*—if not every novel that invokes the fairy-tale genre to articulate its pessimism—seems to respond to this epigram as if it were a question, struggling to mine what remains of the human in a story about how wealth operates.

BALZAC'S PESSIMISTIC FAIRY TALE

There is nothing closer to capturing the reality of capital—closer than any economic analysis that already accepts capital as axiomatic—than exposing it as a fairy tale, albeit a terrifying one. Capital is the illusion at the source of modern disillusionment. It is what gets in the way of Lucien de Rubempré's illusions of creating art for art's sake; capital cannot allow art unless it turns a profit for the artless cynic. It is in this sense, then, that Balzac—as the most exemplary representative of realism—can only describe capital in fairy-tale terms while documenting how it shapes our reality. The narrator of *Père Goriot* is quick to introduce the novel by writing, "This drama is not fictional; it's not a novel. *All is true*—so true you'll be able to recognize everything that goes into it in your own life, perhaps even in your own heart."[140]

And in this "true" fairy tale, Rastignac understands the magical value of connections in high society, which is why he implores Madame de Beauséant to "play the role of the good fairy" in introducing him to Goriot's daughter Anastasie, certainly a strategic move that has the effect of the "waving of a magic wand" and the "chanting of a magic spell," since Madame de Beauséant's social rank is impressive to Anastasie.[141] Rastignac, fully absorbed in the seductions of the Parisian high life, builds "all sorts of fairy castles in his head" as he moves "from one enchantment to another," quickly discarding Anastasie for Goriot's other daughter, Delphine.[142]

Goriot, for his part, seems to belong to a distorted version of the Rumpelstiltskin story, spending all night "rolling out silver" instead of gold, seemingly out of nothing, in order to provide his daughters with a lavish lifestyle for nothing in return, as he wastes away, deprived of even the most modest of possessions.[143] He sustains himself by the alchemical illusion of his daughters' love, saying that they "throw me a little laugh that splashes gold over everything."[144] Except that they don't, and the only gold in this world is the elusive and literal gold of capital. His daughters, in fact, drain his finances so thoroughly that he isn't even left with enough money to cover his own funeral costs. But he still insists on spending the last of his money on an apartment for Delphine and Rastignac, where he says, "I'll come and I'll go like some good fairy who's everywhere, someone you know is always around even if you don't see him."[145]

Goriot as a good fairy balances Vautrin's role as the bad fairy; both of them compete with each other for a kind of authorship of Rastignac's destiny. Vautrin ultimately loses out to Goriot, while Goriot desperately tries to convince both Rastignac and Delphine, "I'm the author of your happiness."[146] Goriot even asks Rastignac if he would be his "dear child, too," and Rastignac thinks to himself that he would take care of him as if he were his own father, making sure "he experiences a thousand sorts of happiness."[147] The pessimism of this novel hinges on the use of this word, "happiness." When Goriot hears compliments about how beautiful his daughters are, he is filled with joy, saying, "I have my own kind of happiness."[148] But where does this happiness lead him? All he wants is his daughters' love in order to "die happy," but even on his deathbed, Delphine is too busy getting ready for a party, and Anastasie makes several excuses not to arrive earlier.[149]

In his final moments, Goriot suffers an unbearable clarity, advising Rastignac not to get married or have children, since, "You give them life, and they give you death."[150] Before this flash of disillusionment fades back into his former delusions that he will see his daughters again, blessing instead of cursing them, he says, "Human society—the whole world—it all turns on fatherhood, and everything will collapse if children stop loving their fathers."[151] This is precisely the apocalyptic vision that Balzac portrays in this novel. If the novel at large is the Lukácsian epic in a world abandoned by God, Goriot seems eager to replace the absence that God had left behind. He says that he would "sell the Father, the Son, and the Holy Ghost" to keep either of his daughters "from shedding a single tear," saying that he loves them "better than God loves the world, because the world isn't as lovely as God is and my daughters are lovelier than I am."[152] He also tells Rastignac, "I'll be even more than a father to you. I'll be your whole family. I'll be God, I'll throw the entire universe down at your feet."[153] Rastignac's friend, the medical student Bianchon, examines Goriot's head along phrenological principles and concludes that one bump is "the one for paternity, so that makes him an *Eternal* Father."[154] But in what kind of universe does an "Eternal Father" die?

Perhaps the ending of happy fairy tales, "And they lived happily ever after," is cruelly suggested at the end of this fairy tale of modernity, since most of the characters who are alive by the end—aside from Madame Vauquer, who pinches every penny out of Goriot on his deathbed—do live happily ever, and certainly not in the squalor of Goriot's final days, devoid of dignity and love. If, like *Wuthering Heights*, it is a re-telling of *King Lear*, one of Shakespeare's most pessimistic plays—which itself seems like a fairy tale gone awry—then it is a re-telling that outdoes even Shakespeare in its pessimism. At least in *King Lear*, there is a misunderstood Cordelia figure who is stalwart in the defense of her cantankerous father, even going so far as to lead an entire army in his defense, ultimately dying out of an unconditional love for him. It may be all too easy to associate Anastasie and Delphine with Regan and Goneril, leaving Rastignac in the position of Cordelia as Goriot's third child of sorts. Rastignac, like Cordelia, does end up being the only one to express any sort of affection, let alone urgency, for Goriot and his precipitous decline. When he makes the situation of Goriot's impending death clear to Delphine and she dismisses him in annoyance because of her party plans, Rastignac "saw the world as an ocean of mud into which a man would fall right up to the neck, if he ever stepped in at all."[155] But that is precisely the pessimism at work in the novel—how can one choose not to step into the world, into the mud?

The novel's haunting final image seems to illustrate that fantastical choice. After the pauper's funeral of Goriot, with neither of his daughters in attendance, Rastignac is seen looking down on Paris from the height of Père-Lachaise Cemetery, as though removed from the world and deciding what his role will be in it. He then exclaims, "Now it's just the two of us!—I'm ready!" before making plans to have dinner with Delphine that evening.[156] If he is fulfilling Goriot's wish of looking after his daughter, he does so in such a way that seems to dishonor whatever dignity was left behind in Goriot's memory. This is a *King Lear* where Cordelia survives only to join Regan and Goneril in celebration the night of their father's disgraced funeral.

PROUST'S BALZAC

"I know that Balzac is all the rage this year," Dr. Brichot says dismissively at a pretentious dinner party in Proust's *Sodom and Gomorrah*, "as pessimism was last."[157] The stupidity of this statement, of course, fails to acknowledge that there is essentially no distinction between Balzac and pessimism. But he goes on to complain of Balzac's departure from realism, saying, "I like a book to give an impression of sincerity and real life."[158] Charlus, Proust's most pessimistic character, is offended by Brichot's philistine lack of taste, telling him, "You say that because you know nothing of life."[159] As yet another reincarnation of Vautrin, from the "piercing hardness" of his gaze to his Mephistophelean propositioning of young men, failing in this endeavor with Marcel as Vautrin had failed with Rastignac, Charlus is also described as a would-be novelist, but all he ends up doing in his literary endeavors is to defend Balzac as a novelist instead.[160] And even as he is described in his old age with the "Shakespearean majesty of King Lear," he is a Lear who has passed through Balzac's imagination.[161]

Proust himself "never claimed to be particularly fond of the great nineteenth-century novelist," but "his notes contain a revealing statement about Balzac: he singles out the novelist's audacious treatment of sexual deviations," which gave literary license for him to mold Charlus with a candor that came out of Balzac's world.[162] While Proust, in writing such a character, risked drawing undue public attention to his own homosexuality at a time when it was still criminalized, he could invoke the literary reputation of Balzac as a shield to hide behind. When Marcel peeps through the "small oval window" in the gay brothel to see Charlus flogged with the nail-studded whip in *Time Regained*, this image recalls the way he had described Charlus's experience of gender identity and sexuality in *Sodom and Gomorrah*.[163] As a woman trapped inside a man's body, this captive woman must "make use of the narrowest apertures in her prison wall to find what was necessary to her existence."[164] Maybe this captive is Marcel all along, and maybe Charlus is the hidden focal point of the *Recherche* as the externalized image of Marcel's own pessimism and his fear of failure in pursuing his vocation of being a writer.

Marcel's voyeurism looks just as much from the inside out as the outside in, and carries the same intensity as the penetrative stare of Charlus, that King Lear who is also the king of leering. And there is a cruelty to this gaze, especially when fixed on those who do not reciprocate it. Photographs in the *Recherche* function as receptacles and reminders of the cruelty of those who gaze upon them. In *Swann's Way*, Marcel's voyeuristic gaze at one point lingers on Mlle. Vinteuil's open window, and he can make out that she is having sex with her unseen lesbian lover, whom he later suspects is Albertine. As a postcoital kink, this lover dares Mlle. Vinteuil to spit on the framed photograph of her dead father.[165]

There is also the photograph that Marcel had taken with his beloved grandmother during their vacation in Balbec, which she was so excited to take with him. As much as Marcel adores his grandmother, he was in a foul mood that day, uncharacteristically acting like a little shit to her as she was getting herself ready for the camera session, which he later regrets:

> I added a few stinging words of sarcasm, intended to neutralize the pleasure that she seemed to find in being photographed, so that if I was obliged to see my grandmother's magnificent hat, I succeeded at least in driving from her face that joyful expression that ought to have made me happy and that, as too often happens, while the people we love best are still alive, appear to us as the exasperating manifestation of some petty flaw rather than as the precious form of the happiness that we would dearly like to procure for them.[166]

Years later, he finds out that his grandmother wanted to take this photograph with him because she knew she was dying at that point, and she wanted him to have it as a final memento of her love and warmth for him. He breaks down in tears of grief and guilt, two volumes and over a thousand pages after this sentence (probably the most devastating sentence in the entire *Recherche*), feeling as though her spirit had come back to him. It is at this moment that he

> now recaptured . . . the living reality. That reality has no existence for us, so long as it has not been recreated by our mind. . . . At whatever moment we estimate it, the total value of our spiritual nature is more or less fictitious, in spite of the long inventory of its treasures.[167]

This revelation of "reality" rejects the realist imperative of verisimilitude. Reality is not the surface-level snapshots that can be captured by a camera but, paradoxically, the "fictitious" nature that constitutes the "total value of our spiritual nature." In addition to the theme of family cruelty inflicted on the older generations by the younger ones, Proust takes this insight from Balzac as well. And perhaps this is what Brichot objects to in his complaint that Balzac doesn't show him an image of "real life," and why Charlus tells him that he knows nothing of life itself to be able to make that assessment. It is life—lived experience—not surface-level "reality" that Balzac's and Proust's novels capture. The novel supplements the surface-level image of reality with the experience of responding to it, of modifying it with one's gaze, of contextualizing it within a web of associations that by turns stain, tarnish, obscure, and then illuminate it in surprising ways that ultimately give it meaning. It is rather an "underlying reality" that Balzac and Proust are after—like the "old, damp walls at the entrance" of the public lavatory where Marcel waits for Françoise at the Champs-Élysées, emitting "a chill and fusty smell" that "invited me . . . to descend into the underlying reality that it had not yet disclosed to me."[168] This is perhaps why Beckett begins his essay on Proust with an epigraph from the nineteenth-century pessimist Giacomo Leopardi: "*E fango è il mondo*," which can be translated as "the world is filth" or "the world is mud," echoing Rastignac's conclusion at the end of *Père Goriot* that "the world is an ocean of mud."[169]

MIRROR, MIRROR, ON THE MUD

This "ocean of mud" that defines the world for Rastignac—a world he ultimately decides to join with zealous cynicism—is, for Stendhal, also central to the definition of the novel as a mirror moving along a highway that reflects the mud. There is something about Stendhal's mirror that gestures toward the possibility of undermining the function of the mirror altogether. If the image it reflects is too shaky, moving along the highway, it may end up threatening to produce optical illusions, or otherwise fragment the reality it ostensibly claims to capture across the duration of its movement, distorting it into something beyond recognition. Does this mirror just reflect the mud, or does some of the mud end up splattering on it, partially obfuscating the ever-changing view that it claims to reflect? Are some of these stains even intentionally placed there? Isn't that one of the many gags of Cervantes, who has Don Quixote hail from "La Mancha," a town that literally means "the stain"? Does the novel really aspire to mimesis, or does its artistry lie just as much in what it obscures as what it shows, in what it refracts as much as it reflects?

It is Hamlet, the self-proclaimed "muddy-mettled rascal," who lays down the ethos of modern realism when he talks to the Players—in prose rather than verse—and instructs them to hold "the mirror up to nature."[170] This may seem straightforward enough, except for the fact that the play he is directing is supposed to reflect his father's "unnatural" murder.[171] And the lines of *The Murder of Gonzago* are so rigid and stilted in their rhymed couplets that they resemble anything but natural speech. In the end, Hamlet gets what he wants—a reaction from Claudius that reveals his guilt, as though Hamlet were avenging not just his father's death, but the entire genre of tragedy that had been maligned since Plato. Reversing Socrates's understanding that tragedy strays entirely from the truth, Hamlet uses tragedy specifically as an epistemological device to confirm the truth. But there's still little that can be called "natural" in *The Murder of Gonzago*, especially when productions use this opportunity for humor, letting the Players discard Hamlet's advice and go rogue, overacting in a way that makes sense for the melodramatic lines that were given to them.

Does Hamlet actually hold a mirror up to nature, or does he hold it up to Shakespeare himself? This is the theory that Stephen Dedalus expounds in *Ulysses* before he and Bloom, in the "Circe" chapter, find themselves in one of a seemingly infinite number of uncanny situations: "Stephen and Bloom gaze in the mirror. The face of William Shakespeare, beardless, appears there, rigid in facial paralysis, crowned by the reflection of the reindeer antlered hat-rack in the hall."[172] This is the image of literary cuckoldry, of Joyce overpowering Shakespeare, of the novel overpowering drama. In *Ulysses* alone, Joyce uses about 30,000 different words, as many different words as Shakespeare used in his whole career. In the reflection that stares back at Stephen and Bloom, Shakespeare isn't reduced to mere words, words, words, but something that doesn't even rise to the level of words at all. With "paralytic rage," Shakespeare says through the mirror, "Weda seca whokilla farst."[173]

Joyce builds up to this moment from the opening image of the novel, with Buck Mulligan carrying his "bowl of lather on which a mirror and a razor lay crossed."[174] Both the mirror and the razor seem to serve as symbolic weapons that Joyce uses to cut through the history of literature and reassemble its fragments into this novel. Laughing at Stephen, Buck takes the mirror from him while saying, "The rage of Caliban at not seeing his face in a mirror. . . . If Wilde were only alive to see you."[175] In the Preface to *The Picture of Dorian Gray*, Wilde writes that this rage of Caliban at not seeing his face in a mirror is "the nineteenth century dislike of Romanticism," while Caliban's rage at actually seeing his face in a mirror is "the nineteenth century dislike of Realism."[176] The nineteenth-century dislike of both realism and romanticism opens the space for twentieth-century modernism, where the mirror is not expected to reflect nature at all. Even scientifically, a reflection can only ever be an image of reality in reverse.

But long before the advent of the modernist novel, it was the fairy tale that held this insight, understanding that the mirror is always in excess of verisimilitude, always running ahead of itself along a highway, always at a remove from the reality that it purports to reflect. The mirror is something that cracks and curses the Lady of Shalott when she turns her attention away from it to look directly at Lancelot rather than his reflection. Lewis Carroll's Alice uses the mirror as a form of transport. Snow White's wicked stepmother doesn't so much look into her mirror as listen to it, and what she hears has less to do with herself than it does with Snow White.

If the mirror in this literary history inevitably fails in reflecting nature, what kind of category is "nature" to begin with, and what is the impulse behind the aesthetic imperative to hold a mirror up to it? Hamlet's credo was hardly new. In *The Republic*, Plato imagines the world as a poor copy of the transcendental realm of ideal forms. In *Symposium*, Aristophanes offers a vision of humans permanently divorced from their cosmic nature, and the consolation of eros turns into a torment whereby we are doomed to search for our missing half, a reflection that no longer exists. This doom, in turn, becomes our second nature—the nature that grounds us on earth and turns our attention away from our cosmic origins. In the twelfth century, Alain de Lille lamented in his pessimistic tract, *The Complaint of Nature*, how humans are doomed precisely because they do not mirror nature. As a result, he says, "The world grows worse, and now its golden age departs."[177] And to illustrate this divide between humans and nature, he also turns to eros, which he describes as an exhausting litany of oxymorons: "Love is peace joined with hatred, faith with fraud, hope with fear, and fury mixed with reason, pleasant shipwreck, light heaviness."[178]

This paradoxical formulation of love echoes down the ages and becomes a central feature of Romance. Jean de Meun transcribes this list almost verbatim in *The Romance of the Rose*, and Gottfried von Strassburg articulates love as a "sorrow . . . so full of joy" in *Tristan*, where Tristan and Isolde, after having drunk the love-potion, look at each other as though staring into "a mirror. They shared a single heart. Her anguish was his pain: his pain her anguish."[179] By the time this trope makes its way to Shakespeare, it is already stale to the point of being comical, as when Romeo introduces himself by indulging in his own list of clichéd oxymorons: "O brawling love, O loving hate, / O anything of nothing first create, / O heavy lightness, serious vanity." And he goes on until he gets self-conscious at Benvolio's—and maybe even the audience's—reaction of laughter.[180] Hamlet's own giddy reaction to *The Murder of Gonzago*—and more so to Claudius's reaction to the play—is also a "heavy lightness." The play for him is a thing of nothing, but a nothing that creates.

For de Lille, love is a mirror that reflects opposites. But the paradox that frames this list of paradoxes is both ontological and normative: he laments the fact that humans do not reflect nature, but in natural love, he maintains that a mirror *cannot* ever reflect the identity in front of it, and it *should* not reflect it. The other side of the mirror has to be the opposite; this is the "nature" that humans *should* follow. In a roundabout way, he is condemning homosexuality, most likely in an effort to sanitize Plato for the Christian Middle Ages. Homosexuality is not just the love that dares not speak its name, but dares not even show its face in the mirror, which is probably why Jonathan Harker doesn't see Dracula in the mirror, since he's afraid of recognizing his own homoerotic desires.

And if homosexuality is a deviation from what is "natural," according to de Lille, both Stoker and Wilde would have to resort to the supernatural in order to show it. In *The Picture of Dorian Gray*, the mirror is not even a mirror, but a painting that is hidden away in shame, shrouded in darkness. As Talia Schaffer notes, Stoker modeled Dracula on the sensationalized and monstrous version of Wilde as he was portrayed by the conservative press during his humiliating trials. In the association between homosexuality and anality, which in turn "led many writers to connect homosexuality with defecation, dirt, and decay," the evidence summoned at court against Wilde included a bedsheet with small fecal stains.[181] Stoker captured the Victorian hysteria over the lurid coverage of Wilde's trial and exaggerated those small stains into an entire bed of dirt that Dracula lies in nightly.

Is this the same mud that lies at the bottom of Narcissus's reflecting pool, behind the image of his own desirous face—an image that traps him to his doom because of the curse of a queer youth whose love Narcissus had spurned? And when the Lover in *The Romance of the Rose* peers into this same body of water, is it really the Rose he sees or himself? And is that desire fundamentally homoerotic? When he is captured, restrained, and erotically bound in submission to the God of Love, the Lover feels more enthralled in his desire for him than for the Rose, saying, "I was very proud when his mouth kissed mine: it was this that gave me the greatest joy."[182] The God of Love, dominant top that he is, then "touched my side and locked my heart so gently that I could scarcely feel the key."[183] Andreas Capellanus also writes his *Art of Courtly Love* out of a "continual urging of my love for you, my revered friend Walter."[184] Is he protesting too much when he insists on the necessity of heterosexual relationships, and does this insistence lead him to retract his work in frustration?

There are many different kinds of "mud" that are reflected in Stendhal's definition of the novel. If Balzac presents an image of the world as nothing but an "ocean of mud," then the novel can be understood as a geological survey of what the various layers of mud can show us about what it means to inhabit this world. Lockwood notes that the only way to embark on a journey to Wuthering Heights is to wade "through heath and mud."[185] Maybe it is the only way to embark on the journey to the novel *Wuthering Heights*, as well (which one early critic panned as a "Pandemonium . . . of mud rather than fire")—if not the entire genre of the novel.[186] If Lady Philosophy urges Boethius to turn his attention away from the mud on account that only ordinary people have their sights set so low, then the novel draws the attention right back to it, pulling away from philosophy. It makes sense, then, for Mann to end *The Magic Mountain*, with its quintessentially ordinary protagonist, with the image of "dusk, rain, and mud," as the narrator scours the battlefield to locate Hans Castorp, who "limps and stumbles forward on mud-laden feet" before disappearing from view.[187] If the mud of the novel at large is associated with criminality, transgression, and destruction, then it is a criminality that by turns invites sympathy and horror—pity and fear, but with the opposite of Aristotelian purification. The novel doesn't purify; it soils.

NOTES

1. Mazzoni, *Theory of the Novel*, 100.

2. "Top 100 Most Banned and Challenged Books: 2010-2019," American Library Association, https://www.ala.org/advocacy/bbooks/frequentlychallengedbooks/decade2019.

3. A. T. Hatto, introduction to *Tristan* by Gottfried von Strassburg, trans. A. T. Hatto (London: Penguin Books, 1976), 21.

4. McKeon, *Origins of the English Novel*, 98.

5. Anthony J. Cascardi, "The Novel," in *The Oxford Handbook of Philosophy and Literature,* ed. Richard Eldridge (Oxford: Oxford University Press, 2013), 173.

6. Balzac, *Lost Illusions*, 303.

7. Ian McEwan, *Atonement* (New York: Anchor Books, 2003), 265.

8. McEwan, *Atonement*, 192.

9. McEwan, *Atonement*, 38.

10. McEwan, *Atonement*, 265.

11. McEwan, *Atonement*, 350.

12. McEwan, *Atonement*, 351.

13. McEwan, *Atonement*, 350.

14. McEwan, *Atonement*, 349.

15. Albert Camus, *The Rebel: An Essay on Man in Revolt*, trans. Anthony Bower (New York: Knopf, 1960), 259.

16. Ong, *Art of Being*, 239.

17. McKeon, *Origins of the English Novel*, 96–128.

18. McKeon, *Origins of the English Novel*, 99.

19. McKeon, *Origins of the English Novel*, 99.

20. McKeon, *Origins of the English Novel*, 100.

21. Qtd. in McKeon, *Origins of the English Novel*, 100.
22. Qtd. in McKeon, *Origins of the English Novel*, 100.
23. Qtd. in McKeon, *Origins of the English Novel*, 100.
24. Ian Watt, *The Rise of the Novel: Studies in Defoe, Richardson, and Fielding* (Berkeley, CA: University of California Press, 1957), 31.
25. Ong, *Art of Being*, 45.
26. Fyodor Dostoevsky, *The Brothers Karamazov*, trans. Richard Pevear and Larissa Volokhonsky (New York: Farrar, Straus & Giroux, 2002), 728.
27. Dostoevsky, *Brothers Karamazov*, 731.
28. Dostoevsky, *Brothers Karamazov*, 731.
29. Dostoevsky, *Brothers Karamazov*, 734.
30. Dostoevsky, *Brothers Karamazov*, 748.
31. Nabokov, *Lolita*, 9.
32. Nabokov, *Lolita*, 96.
33. Emily Palmer, "A Fake Heiress Called Anna Delvey Conned the City's Wealthy. 'I'm Not Sorry,' She Says," *The New York Times*, May 10, 2019, https://www.nytimes.com/2019/05/10/nyregion/anna-delvey-sorokin.html?auth=login-email&login=email; Anna Quintana, "Fake NYC Heiress Anna Delvey's Scams Landed her a Netflix Show," *Distractify.com*, May 2019, https://www.distractify.com/p/what-did-anna-delvey-do.
34. Michael Love, "Meet Neff Davis, Anna Delvey's Only Friend in New York," *Paper*, June 13, 2018, https://www.papermag.com/neff-davis-2577568832.html.
35. McKeon, *Origins of the English Novel*, 45.
36. McKeon, *Origins of the English Novel*, 46.
37. McKeon, *Origins of the English Novel*, 47.
38. Qtd. in McKeon, *Origins of the English Novel*, 50.
39. Watt, *Rise of the Novel*, 35–59.
40. Baldesar Castiglione, *The Book of the Courtier*, trans. George Bull (London: Penguin Books, 2003), 31.
41. Castiglione, *Book of the Courtier*, 33–34.
42. Castiglione, *Book of the Courtier*, 54–55.
43. Castiglione, *Book of the Courtier*, 67.
44. Castiglione, *Book of the Courtier*, 67.
45. Capellanus, *Art of Courtly Love*, 151.
46. Peter Burke, *The Fortunes of the Courtier: The European Reception of Castiglione's Cortegiano* (University Park, PA: Penn State University Press, 1995), 63; 128; 132.
47. Burke, *The Fortunes of the Courtier*, 41.
48. Castiglione, *Book of the Courtier*, 43; 107.
49. Castiglione, *Book of the Courtier*, 281.
50. Castiglione, *Book of the Courtier*, 343.
51. Niccolo Machiavelli, *The Prince*, in *The Prince* and *The Discourses*, trans. Luigi Ricci. Modern Library College Edition (New York: Random House, 1950), 96.
52. Machiavelli, *The Prince*, 23.
53. Machiavelli, *The Prince*, 31.

54. Qtd. in Georg Lukács, *Studies in European Realism* (New York: Grosset & Dunlap, 1964), 69.
55. Balzac, *Lost Illusions*, trans. Raymond N. MacKenzie (Minneapolis, MN: University of Minnesota Press, 2020), 185.
56. Balzac, *Lost Souls*, 248; 292.
57. Balzac, *Père Goriot*, trans. Burton Raffel (New York: W. W. Norton, 1994), 89.
58. Balzac, *Père Goriot*, 79.
59. Balzac, *Père Goriot*, 81.
60. Balzac, *Père Goriot*, 88.
61. Balzac, *Lost Souls*, 83.
62. Balzac, *Lost Souls*, 70; 50.
63. Balzac, *Lost Souls*, 363.
64. Balzac, *Lost Souls*, 364.
65. Balzac, *Père Goriot*, 40.
66. Dostoevsky, *Crime and Punishment*, 2 (emphasis in original).
67. Dostoevsky, *Crime and Punishment*, 533.
68. Dostoevsky, *Crime and Punishment*, 250.
69. Dostoevsky, *Crime and Punishment*, 251.
70. Dostoevsky, *Brothers Karamazov*, 649.
71. Karl Marx, *Capital: Volume One*, in *The Marx-Engels Reader*, ed. Robert C. Tucker, 2nd ed. (New York: W. W. Norton, 1978), 362–363.
72. Dostoevsky, *Crime and Punishment*, 498.
73. Franco Moretti, "A Capital *Dracula*," in Bram Stoker, *Dracula*, ed. Nina Auerbach and David J. Skal (New York: W. W. Norton, 1997), 431.
74. Moretti, "A Capital *Dracula*," 432.
75. Brontë, *Wuthering Heights*, 4.
76. Brontë, *Wuthering Heights*, 30.
77. Brontë, *Wuthering Heights*, 72.
78. Brontë, *Wuthering Heights*, 3.
79. Brontë, *Wuthering Heights*, 160.
80. Brontë, *Wuthering Heights*, 160.
81. Brontë, *Wuthering Heights*, 168.
82. Brontë, *Wuthering Heights*, 230.
83. Brontë, *Wuthering Heights*, 116, 136, 216.
84. Brontë, *Wuthering Heights*, 95.
85. Brontë, *Wuthering Heights*, 70.
86. Stoker, *Dracula*, 79.
87. Stoker, *Dracula,* 265.
88. Stoker, *Dracula,* 29.
89. Robert, "From *Origins of the Novel*," 58.
90. Carol A. Senf, "*Dracula*: The Unseen Face in the Mirror," in Bram Stoker, *Dracula*, ed. Nina Auerbach and David J. Skal (New York: W. W. Norton, 1997), 424.
91. Moretti, "A Capital *Dracula*," 435.
92. Senf, "*Dracula*: The Unseen Face in the Mirror," 429.

93. Senf, "*Dracula*: The Unseen Face in the Mirror," 427.
94. Oscar Wilde, *The Picture of Dorian Gray* (New York: W. W. Norton, 1988), 3.
95. Qtd. in Balzac, *Lost Illusions*, "Translator's Introduction," vii.
96. Lukács, *Studies in European Realism*, 47.
97. Erich Auerbach, *Mimesis: The Representation of Reality in Western Literature*, trans. Willard R. Trask (Princeton, NJ: Princeton University Press, 2003), 468.
98. Auerbach, *Mimesis*, 556.
99. Lukács, *Studies in European Realism*, 62.
100. Nietzsche, *Philosophy and Truth*, ed. and trans. Daniel Breazeale (Amherst, MA: Humanity Books, 1999), 84.
101. Nietzsche, *Philosophy and Truth*, 84.
102. Dostoevsky, *Crime and Punishment*, 161.
103. Proust, *Swann's Way*, 376.
104. Laurence A. Gregorio, "The Gaze of History," in *The Princess of Clèves,* ed. Madame de Lafayette (New York: W. W. Norton, 1994), 269.
105. Gregorio, "The Gaze of History," 274.
106. Gregorio, "The Gaze of History," 277.
107. Gregorio, "The Gaze of History," 278.
108. Qtd. by Alfred Appel, Jr. in an explanatory note to *Lolita* by Nabokov, 347.
109. Nabokov, *Strong Opinions,* 57.
110. Nabokov, *Lolita,* 284, 122.
111. Bruno Bettelheim, *The Uses of Enchantment: The Meaning and Importance of Fairy Tales* (New York: Knopf, 1976), 37.
112. Bettelheim, *The Uses of Enchantment,* 37.
113. Charles Dickens, *Great Expectations* (London: Penguin Books, 1996), 85; 157.
114. Dickens, *Great Expectations,* 231.
115. Dickens, *Great Expectations,* 323.
116. Dickens, *Great Expectations,* 271.
117. Dickens, *Great Expectations,* 382.
118. Dickens, *Great Expectations,* 508.
119. Dickens, *Great Expectations,* 508–509.
120. Dickens, *Great Expectations,* 508.
121. Thomas Hardy, *Tess of the D'Urbervilles* (New York: W. W. Norton, 1991), 312.
122. Hardy, *Tess of the D'Urbervilles*, 15.
123. Hardy, *Tess of the D'Urbervilles*, 184–185.
124. Hardy, *Tess of the D'Urbervilles*, 226–227.
125. Conrad, *Heart of Darkness*, 59.
126. Conrad, *Heart of Darkness*, 72.
127. Conrad, *Heart of Darkness*, 70.
128. Conrad, *Heart of Darkness*, 69.
129. Conrad, *Heart of Darkness*, 44.
130. Conrad, *Heart of Darkness*, 59.

131. Conrad, *Heart of Darkness*, 65–66.
132. Mann, *Magic Mountain*, xii.
133. Ignace Feuerlicht, *Thomas Mann* (Boston, MA: Twayne Publishers, 1968), 29.
134. Feuerlicht, *Thomas Mann*, 29–30.
135. Mann, *Magic Mountain*, 699.
136. Mann, *Magic Mountain*, 702.
137. Mann, *Magic Mountain*, 705–706.
138. Qtd. in Georg Lukács, *Essays on Thomas Mann*, trans. Stanley Mitchell (London: Merlin Press, 1979), 35.
139. Conrad, *Heart of Darkness*, 2.
140. Balzac, *Père Goriot*, 6.
141. Balzac, *Père Goriot*, 56; 47.
142. Balzac, *Père Goriot*, 100; 96.
143. Balzac, *Père Goriot*, 62.
144. Balzac, *Père Goriot*, 92.
145. Balzac, *Père Goriot*, 162.
146. Balzac, *Père Goriot*, 162.
147. Balzac, *Père Goriot*, 116; 151.
148. Balzac, *Père Goriot*, 93.
149. Balzac, *Père Goriot*, 207.
150. Balzac, *Père Goriot*, 202.
151. Balzac, *Père Goriot*, 204.
152. Balzac, *Père Goriot*, 117; 103.
153. Balzac, *Père Goriot*, 183.
154. Balzac, *Père Goriot*, 65.
155. Balzac, *Père Goriot*, 192.
156. Balzac, *Père Goriot*, 217.
157. Proust, *Sodom and Gomorrah*, 494.
158. Proust, *Sodom and Gomorrah*, 495.
159. Proust, *Sodom and Gomorrah*, 494.
160. Proust, *The Guermantes Way*, 312.
161. Proust, *Time Regained*, 245.
162. Anka Muhlstein, *Monsieur Proust's Library* (New York: Other Press, 2012), 71–73.
163. Proust, *Time Regained*, 181.
164. Proust, *Sodom and Gomorrah*, 25.
165. Proust, *Swann's Way*, 167.
166. Proust, *In the Shadow of Young Girls in Flower*, 399.
167. Proust, *Sodom and Gomorrah*, 173.
168. Proust, *In the Shadow of Young Girls in Flower*, 71–72.
169. Beckett, *Proust*, I; Balzac, *Père Goriot*, 192.
170. Shakespeare, *Hamlet* (New York: Folger, 1992), 2.2.594; 3.2.23–24.
171. Shakespeare, *Hamlet*, 1.5.34.
172. James Joyce, *Ulysses* (New York: Vintage Books, 1990), 567.
173. Joyce, *Ulysses*, 568.

174. Joyce, *Ulysses*, 2–3.
175. Joyce, *Ulysses*, 6.
176. Oscar Wilde, *Dorian Gray* (New York: W. W. Norton, 1988), 3.
177. Alain of Lille, *The Complaint of Nature*, trans. Douglas M. Moffat (New York: Henry Holt & Company, 1908), 110.
178. Alain of Lille, *Complaint of Nature*, 89.
179. Gottfried von Strassburg, *Tristan*, trans. A. T. Hatto (London: Penguin Books, 1976), 42; 195.
180. Shakespeare, *Romeo and Juliet* (New York: Bantam, 1988), 1.1.176–77.
181. Talia Schaffer, "The Homoerotic History of *Dracula*," in Bram Stoker, *Dracula*, ed. Nina Auerbach and David J. Skal (New York: W. W. Norton, 1997), 473; 480.
182. *Romance of the Rose*, 30.
183. *Romance of the Rose*, 31.
184. Capellanus, *Art of Courtly Love*, 27.
185. Brontë, *Wuthering Heights*, 7.
186. Qtd. in Brontë, *Wuthering Heights*, 291.
187. Mann, *Magic Mountain*, 703–705.

Chapter 7

Landscapes, Laughter, and Suicide

PESSIMISTIC LANDSCAPES

What kinds of landscapes open up in this inhospitable "ocean of mud," and where is the human located in these landscapes? In *Tess of the D'Urbervilles*, like *Wuthering Heights*, characters vanish into the landscape, as though swallowed up by it. When Tess Durbeyfield first sees Angel Clare, the "rays of the sun had absorbed the young stranger's retreating figure on the hill," and as Tess marches deeper into her own tragedy, the narrator observes, "Thus Tess walks on; a figure which is part of the landscape."[1] Her face is "as white as the scene without" during the spell of dry frost, blurring her out of sight, and just as much as Hardy describes her face in terms of the landscape, he also describes the landscape in terms of a face:[2]

> Every leaf of the vegetable having already been consumed the whole field was in colour a desolate drab; it was a complexion without features, as if a face from chin to brow should be only an expanse of skin. The sky wore, in another colour, the same likeness; a white vacuity of countenance with the lineaments gone. So these two upper and nether visages confronted each other, all day long the white face looking down on the brown face, and the brown face looking up at the white face.[3]

It is as though the only faces worth describing in any detail are the metaphorical faces that the landscape assumes, the abyss that stares into the people who inhabit it until they, too, dissolve into the abyss themselves.

It is this scale denoted by the landscape that underscores how Thomas Hardy's characters aren't even given the dignity of tragedy, but of a far bleaker pessimism. In tragedy, one is at least seen and recognized—even if only on the tragic stage, and even if the recognition is delayed. But Tess understands that "the thought of the world's concern at her situation—was founded on an illusion. She was not an existence, an experience, a passion, a structure of sensations, to anybody but herself. To all humankind besides Tess was only a passing thought."[4] At least Richard III can shout at the top of his lungs about how he had lost his "kingdom for a horse!"[5] Tess had no kingdom to lose, except for the quasi-mythical lineage that connected the destitute Durbeyfields to the aristocratic D'Urbervilles. But it was still the death of the family horse that plunged the Durbeyfields into ruin, precipitating the events that would lead to her rape, followed by the stalking of her rapist, the abandonment by her husband, and every subsequent episode of misery that encircles her, like the landscape of Stonehenge, where she is eventually caught for Alec's murder, and like the noose that eventually kills her. But she is no Richard III, and she knows it. Angel even calls her "Mistress Teresa d'Urberville," as though nodding to George Eliot's treatment of the unknown Saint Theresas in *Middlemarch*, "who had found for themselves no epic life wherein there was a constant unfolding of far-resonant action," who "sank unwept into oblivion."[6]

Joseph Conrad takes up this same vision in his novels, evoking a horror that denies its victims the dignity of tragedy, relegating them to the silence of the landscape instead. *Heart of Darkness* seems to walk us through the history of the novel, its opening paragraphs highly reminiscent of the way the Ancient Greek novelist Heliodorus begins his *Aethiopica*, with its image of a ship anchored in the river, an ominous stillness preceding Marlow's story, a story that mirrors what Heliodorus describes as a scene "strewn with fresh carnage; some of the victims were dead, of others the limbs were still quivering."[7] Both Heliodorus and Conrad take us to the mouth of the river not just as the symbolic origin—and perhaps even apocalyptic end—of civilization, but of the novel itself.

Even its title, *Heart of Darkness*—like Heliodorus's opening image of carnage—dissolves bodies into landscape, a landscape that takes on a cosmic scope and is charged with a sense of gloom that stretches across the globe. The novel begins with the "dark" air in London, "above Gravesend, and farther back still seemed condensed into a mournful gloom brooding motionless over the biggest, and the greatest, town on earth."[8] The sun then sets, as if "stricken to death by the touch of that gloom brooding over a crowd of men."[9]

Maybe the horror of the novel is that, for all the international distance covered by the ship's journey—and by Marlow's tale of another international journey—the landscape doesn't actually seem to change at all. The gloom of the Congo River is the same gloom along the Thames. The horror appears in both places; maybe this is why it has to be repeated twice at the end in "The horror! The horror!"[10] As in a nightmare, the vertiginous description of both places seems to blur them into one claustrophobic space, allowing for no escape, no matter how far one seems to move away from it.

The reader belongs to this darkness, aligned with the frame narrator who is one of Marlow's listeners, interrupting Marlow's hellish narrative by noting: "It had become so pitch dark that we listeners could hardly see one another. For a long time already he, sitting apart, had been no more to us than a voice."[11] This, of course, is exactly how Marlow first approaches Kurtz, who only "presented himself as a voice."[12] Just as the landscapes of two different countries dissolve into each other, so too do the characters in their disembodied voices. By the time we get to the end of the novel, when Marlow meets Kurtz's fiancée, the "glitter of her eyes full of tears" does not distance him from the horrors he had witnessed in the Congo, but mentally pulls him back to the "glitter of the infernal stream, the stream of darkness."[13]

Despite the disembodied voices, the dominant voice of the novel is the voice of the landscape itself, in its harrowing silence, which, "driven away by the stamping of our feet flowed back again from the recesses of the land."[14] This is the Schopenhauerian "stillness of an implacable force brooding over an inscrutable intention."[15] Marlow describes how the "great wall of vegetation, an exuberant and entangled mass of trunks, branches, leaves, boughs, festoons motionless in the moonlight, was like a rioting invasion of soundless life."[16] To him, this is the sound of "travelling back to the earliest beginnings of the world," in the same way that Hardy, at the end of *Tess of the D'Urbervilles*, returns to the origins of English civilization in the landscape of Stonehenge, where there "was no joy in the brilliance of sunshine. The long stretches of the waterway ran on, deserted, into the gloom of overshadowed distances."[17] And just as Tess feels like she is impossibly far away from anyone who could possibly reach her, separated by stellar distances, Marlow too observes that, "The earth seemed unearthly," and that it "wore the aspect of an unknown planet."[18] "The rest of the world was nowhere as far as our eyes and ears were concerned," he continues. "Gone, disappeared, swept off without leaving a whisper or a shadow behind."[19]

History moves backward in *Heart of Darkness*, stretching back to deep time, but it also moves to various starting points in the history of the novel, not just in the parallel with Heliodorus, but in the time when the modern novel began to emerge in the Renaissance, coinciding with the first wave of European imperialism and the age of exploration. The discourse around European conquests in the "New World" raised philosophical questions about possible worlds and whether this was the best or worst of possible worlds. In the following centuries, Leibniz used philosophy to demonstrate that this is the best of all possible worlds; Voltaire used the novel to demonstrate that this is the worst. And the novel, from Voltaire to Hardy and Conrad, is the genre that explores, in the greatest detail, just how much of the worst of all possible worlds this one is. The result of that optimistic exploration for the New World, for other possible worlds, is bound up in the violence and bloodshed waged in the name of empire.

Even today, it is no coincidence that the richest people on earth are thinking about other possible worlds in terms of colonization, spending billions on travels to Mars while driving structural violence and inhumane living conditions on the one world we have. In the midst of the COVID pandemic, a space shuttle was launched to Mars while funds that could have gone toward social programs went, instead, to a rover model named OPTIMISM (Operational Perseverance Twin for Integration of Mechanism and Instruments Sent to Mars).[20] Empire always adorns itself in the rhetoric of optimism. And what Conrad shows is that the violence of empire is carried out not just in the brutal slaughter of its victims, but in the silence that takes away their narratives. This is the palpable silence that roars through Conrad's landscape, interrupted only by brief and chilling cries, as though people here are merely extensions of the landscape as they suffer in their voyage toward death.

The absorption of humans into the landscape seems to evoke the pessimism of Thomas Browne, who viewed bodies as mere entities waiting to inevitably become part of the landscape, subsumed and overpowered by it—a running theme through Schopenhauer and then Freud, who defined the "universal endeavor of all living substance" in *Beyond the Pleasure Principle* as "to return to the quiescence of the inorganic world."[21] Browne was most likely sneering at the insufferable optimism of thinkers from the generation before his, like Francis Bacon, who pioneered a method of what he called "true induction," which would "let humans recover that right over nature which belongs to it by divine bequest, and let power be given it."[22]

Bacon's optimism recalls the image of Odysseus strapped to the mast of his ship, his ears stopped up with wax to avoid the fatal but alluring song of the Sirens. This becomes the central image for Adorno and Horkheimer in their *Dialectic of Enlightenment*, the pessimistic excoriation of what gets labeled as "progress" in a world that had just come out of the Holocaust.[23] Odysseus's innovation for them is the first example of technology used to conquer nature, as well as the "atomistic interest" that foreshadows the rise of capitalism and, ultimately, totalitarianism.[24] Freud, too, ends his *Civilization and Its Discontents* on a similar note, saying that

> men have gained control over the forces of nature to such an extent that with their help they would have no difficulty in exterminating one another to the last man. They know this, and hence comes a large part of their current unrest, their unhappiness and their mood of anxiety.[25]

The seemingly optimistic image of the Sirens being overpowered by Odysseus, then, becomes the image of our own eventual doom.

Kafka, though, wonders whether we've got the whole story wrong, whether Homer himself got the story wrong. In his short story, "The Silence of the Sirens," he points to the futility of the rope, of the wax, to protect Odysseus and his sailors from the Sirens:

> The song of the Sirens could pierce through everything, and the longing of those they seduced would have broken far stronger bonds than chains and masts. But Ulysses did not think of that. . . . He trusted absolutely to his handful of wax and his fathom of chain, and in innocent elation over his little stratagem sailed out to meet the Sirens.[26]

The Sirens "have a still more fatal weapon than their song, namely their silence."[27] Their whole interaction is a misunderstanding. They refrain from singing, and Odysseus succumbs to the pretentious self-satisfaction of having outwitted those who did not even feel like annihilating him at the moment: "Against the feeling of having triumphed over them by one's own strength, and the consequent exaltation that bears down everything before it, no earthly powers can resist."[28]

Kafka here both reads and writes Odysseus not as an accomplished epic hero but as a small, ridiculous, unremarkable man who belongs in a novel, like Charles Bovary, similar to how Adorno and Horkheimer think of him as "a prototype of the bourgeois individual, a notion originating in . . . consistent self-affirmation."[29] In this same essay, "Odysseus, or Myth and Enlightenment," they speak of the "translation of myths into the novel, as in the adventure story," which "does not so much falsify the myths as sweep myth into time, concealing the abyss that separates it from homeland and expiation."[30] Time is what ultimately moves through us, disintegrating us, seducing us into reuniting with nature, with landscape. Here Adorno and Horkheimer explicitly invoke Novalis with his definition of philosophy as "homesickness," which Lukács takes to articulate his own theory of the novel.[31]

The Sirens operate by seduction ("those they seduced" are *die Verführten*), by a sophistic *psychagogia*, a soul-conducting orchestrated by an enchantment without chant. Their silence doesn't echo through the void of nature so much as it echoes the void itself, waiting to engulf Odysseus, but not just yet. Odysseus himself is like the angry Socrates in *The Republic*, who vows to "chant this argument we are making to ourselves as a countercharm, taking care against falling back again into this love."[32] He's the one doing the chanting, trying to seduce himself into reason rather than the enticements of the imagination. As opposed to Bacon's "true induction" and the formal logic of deduction, what emerges as an alternative to these modes of cognition is seduction itself—an embodied cognition, gesturing to the world while withdrawing from it in an erotic reacquaintance with and reimagining of ourselves as finite beings in the process of fading into our landscape, like Plato fading into the *platonos*, the shade of the broad plane tree that, on a hot summer's day, seduces Socrates to philosophize about seduction itself.

And maybe this is what Socrates is always doing, in every dialogue. Maybe this is why Alcibiades, frustrated with Socrates for not giving in to his erotic advances, says, "I stopped my ears and took off in flight, as if from the Sirens, in order that I might not sit here in idleness and grow old beside him."[33] It's not Socrates's chanting or even pontificating that brings Alcibiades back, though—it is, like Kafka's Sirens, Socrates's silence, his restraint, his gesture of negation, that is what is most seductive about him. Seduction has always been at the heart of philosophy.

LATE BANQUET GUESTS

Socrates, though, is rarely found in any landscape beyond the city walls of Athens. Far away from the typical landscapes of the novel, its high seas and muddy roads, philosophy is shut indoors, enjoying its symposium among like-minded folk. Marx's critique of philosophers, that they "have only *interpreted* the world, in various ways," when the "point, however, is to *change* it," goes unheeded.[34] If the road inspectors that Stendhal calls out in his definition of the novel are not going to do their job, then something needs to, in Marx's italicized words, "*change*"—and drastically. Marx's response was to write something that could arguably be read as a gothic novel of sorts: *Das Kapital*, a work that not only explicitly draws on *Robinson Crusoe*, but that is structured like a dilapidated, gothic cathedral, haunted by the vampire of capital itself.

The hellish edifice that enshrines capital is sustained only by the depletion of nature, of the world outside its walls. From de Lille's *Complaint of Nature* to *The Sorrows of Young Werther*, *Tess of the D'Urbervilles*, and *Heart of Darkness*, the history of the novel traces the incompatible relationship between humans and nature. Marx documents how natural resources are killed, and how their spectral afterlives are exchanged in a dark sorcery that he calls commodity fetishism. But, like Schlegel before him, he envisions a future that could unify the outer world with the inner life of mind. His seminovelistic work, no less than anything by Balzac, Dickens, or even Stoker, details what those material obstacles are and how they operate behind closed doors.

It is also behind closed doors that Socrates focuses his ire on the tragic poets, banning them from his ideal republic. But for what it's worth, at least they're named as a worthy opponent of philosophy, of anyone who claims to be on the side of truth. Eugene Thacker defines pessimism as "that gloomy late-comer to the banquet of philosophy," but this could also double as a definition for the novel, as well—a genre denoted by its new arrival.[35] Marthe Robert defines the novel as "a newcomer to the literary scene, a commoner made good who will always stand out as something of an upstart, even a bit of a swindler, among the established genres it is gradually supplanting."[36] Pessimism and the novel—these two late, unkempt, and uninvited arrivals at this banquet, this symposium—either ignored or condescendingly dismissed by the other philosopher-guests, definitely seem to notice each other, though. Maybe they exchange a sly smirk in solidarity out of the corner of their mouths; maybe also an eyeroll at everyone else in attendance, from Socrates to Kant, Hegel, and Heidegger.

"For whatever reason," writes Joshua Foa Dienstag, "the idea of a pessimistic novelist has never been as illegitimate as the idea of a pessimistic philosopher."[37] Maybe this is so because, from the standpoint of philosophy, the novel is already illegitimate in and of itself. And it's precisely this illegitimacy inscribed into the novel that binds it to pessimism. The novelist questions legitimacy and authority to begin with—that is the starting point. So too is the pessimist's, who mocks the "notion that there *must be* an answer to our fundamental questions, even if we have not found it yet, and that this answer will deliver us from suffering."[38] Leopardi dismisses philosophy as "useless," writing that, "Philosophy in short, hoping and promising at the beginning to cure our ills, is in the end reduced to a longing in vain to heal itself."[39] Philosophy cannot escape its own absurd and inadvertently destructive commitment to pragmatism. Pessimism is the up-ending of philosophy, its futile pragmatism, and all its elaborate systems:

> Pessimism abjures all pretenses towards system—towards the purity of analysis and the dignity of critique. We didn't really think we could figure it out, did we? It was just passing time, something to do, a bold gesture put forth in all its fragility, according to rules that we have agreed to forget that we made up in the first place.[40]

The novel, too, shares that challenge to the authority of philosophical systematicity. It's that thing that Emma Bovary herself turns to in her boredom, to pass the time, something to do—only to realize that it inevitably becomes a site of disappointment.[41] "Maybe disappointment is the fear of no longer belonging to a system," G.H. tells us in Clarice Lispector's novel *The Passion According to G.H.*[42] The novel itself is the site to explore this disappointment, this turn away from systematicity.

It is no wonder that pessimism and the novel gravitate to each other. This explains why Kierkegaard chooses the form that he does when he writes *The Seducer's Diary*, and why Schopenhauer has been such a consistent inspiration for novelists who have advanced the craft. Erich Heller even writes of Schopenhauer's philosophy as abiding by a "plot":

> The plot of Schopenhauer's philosophy, like the plot of all good stories, turns upon a contrast and an opposition: the conflict between the world—a world the true nature of which is the *Will* to be what it is, a will willing *itself* without sense or reason—and the mind of man.[43]

In Mann's own personal opinion of Schopenhauer, he writes,

> Never probably in the history of the mind has there been so wonderful an example of the artist, the dark and driven human being, finding spiritual support, self-justification, and enlightenment in another's thought, as in this case of . . . Schopenhauer.[44]

After writing *War and Peace*, Tolstoy too indulged in what he called "Constant raptures over Schopenhauer and a whole series of spiritual delights which I've never experienced before."[45] These "raptures" may well have left their influence on the pessimism that Tolstoy explores in *Anna Karenina*. Bryan Magee also traces Schopenhauer's profound influence on Zola, Maupassant, and Proust, not to mention Hardy and Conrad.[46] But is the affinity that the novel feels like it shares with pessimism reciprocated in the same way? What do other pessimists have to say about the novel?

"RIDICULUS SUM": QUIXOTISM, CHARLES BOVARY, AND THE QUESTION OF SUICIDE

In E.M. Cioran's essay "Beyond the Novel," he says, "I shall never forgive myself for being inwardly nearer the first novelist I meet at a party than the idlest sage of antiquity."[47] The essay is fervid in its vitriolic attack against the novel, defining the novel itself as "the rubbish of Western civilization."[48] And yet, like Socrates—and perhaps even more honest than Socrates—Cioran admits his deep affinity for this nemesis, despite himself: "Let me make myself clear: the most disturbing books I have ever read, if not the greatest, have been novels. Which does not keep me from loathing the vision responsible for them: a loathing without hope."[49] What appears to be yet another diatribe against the novel betrays a somewhat ambivalent attitude to it, recognizing in the novel something he cannot ignore, perhaps even the articulation of his own pessimism. What else is the definition of pessimism if not "a

Landscapes, Laughter, and Suicide 195

loathing without hope'"? He catches himself being too harsh, uncharacteristically mustering a tone that borders on apology, when he writes,

> Right or wrong, I have come to blame the whole genre for this state of affairs, fastening my fury upon it, seeing in the novel an obstacle to myself, the agent of disintegration—my own and other people's, too—a stratagem of Time to infiltrate our substance, the final proof that eternity will never be anything more for us than a word and a regret. 'Like everyone else, you're a child of the novel'—that is my refrain, and my defeat.[50]

Maybe the novel is *too* pessimistic for this most pessimistic of thinkers, who admits in this essay that, "Attack is merely the desire to free oneself from infatuation or to punish oneself for it."[51] If the novel is a mirror of sorts, then what he is responding so vehemently to in reaction is himself. He can't help heaping insult upon insult onto the novel, resorting to misogyny when he calls the novel "the streetwalker of literature" that "forages in ashcans and consciences with equal ease."[52]

But he uses this same trope in *A Short History of Decay* to describe the "philosopher, disappointed with systems and superstitions but still persevering in the ways of the world."[53] This figure of the disillusioned philosopher, no longer a proponent of systems, is a description of the pessimist, of Cioran himself. And he says that such a philosopher ought to "imitate the Pyrrhonism exhibited by the least dogmatic of creatures: the prostitute."[54] Ultimately, Cioran ends his essay on the novel by calming himself down, perhaps even in an effort at reconciliation, by saying, "Let us not be needlessly bitter: certain failures are sometimes fruitful. Such as the novel's. Let us salute it, then, even celebrate it: our solitude will be reinforced, affirmed."[55]

Thacker places more of a distance between the philosopher and the pessimist, writing that the "very term 'pessimism' suggests a school of thought, a movement, even a community. But pessimism always has a membership of one—maybe two (one of them imaginary)."[56] Is the novel that unacknowledged, imaginary double of this "membership of one"? Thacker makes a point of calling Dostoevsky's *Notes from Underground* as "one of the great anti-novels," perhaps in keeping with Lukács's claim that Dostoevsky did not write novels, and later "think[s] of the great non-novels of the past century," including Kafka's *The Castle*, as if somehow the novel cannot attain greatness in the eyes of the pessimist in the way a "non-novel" can.[57]

Pessimism, to Thacker, clings to the short form—the fragment, the aphorism, the maxim, the joke, the insult: as far away in scope as possible from the novel.[58] In Nietzsche, someone who mostly hated novels, this is most apparent. Schopenhauer's *World as Will and Representation* deceptively seems like a systematic work of Kantian philosophy, at least at first glance. But it gradually fails at this system, and crumbles away, so that it can be read not just as a work of continuous prose, but as a series of barbed, short fragments that are closer in genre to his separately published aphorisms.

Thacker clarifies the "two strategies" of writing pessimism, one literary and one philosophical: "For literary pessimism, there is the diary, the confession, the parable, the monologue."[59] As examples, he cites Goethe's *The Sorrows of Young Werther*, Hamsun's *Hunger*, Lagerkvist's *The Dwarf*, Hrabal's *Too Loud a Solitude*, and other novels without ever naming the novel as a genre.[60] What is left out from this list is a novel like *Lolita*, which is not an example of just simply the diary, the confession, the parable, or the monologue, but a work that makes use of all of these forms for a bleak vision of the world at its worst. The list of works he provides ostensibly demonstrates this literary strategy whereby "thought expands, cataloguing and accounting for a horizonless panoply of events, experiences, ideas, and affects, whereas in the philosophical strategy, thought contracts, condensed into epiphanies, maxims, and glimpses into the horizon of thought itself."[61] Doesn't the expansive "cataloguing and accounting for a horizonless panoply of events, experiences, ideas, and affects" count not just as any general literary strategy, but as a specifically *novelistic* strategy? This distinction between the novel and the anti-novel made no sense to Nabokov, either, who said in one interview that, "This 'anti-novel' does not really exist," or in another, "I just don't know what an 'anti-novel' is specifically. Every original novel is 'anti-' because it does not resemble the genre or kind of its predecessor."[62]

Thacker positions the novel at a remove from pessimism, but Sartre makes the opposite gesture, dismissing a work like *The Sound and the Fury* as "unnovelistic" precisely *because* of its pessimism.[63] "Faulkner's despair seems to me to precede his metaphysics," Sartre complains. "For him, as for all of us, the future is closed."[64] And Sartre then resorts to quoting Heidegger to justify his position: "The loss of all hope, for example, does not deprive human reality of its possibilities; it is simply a way of *being* toward these same possibilities."[65] But Sartre here, in his invocation of Heidegger, is assuming that the range of possibilities in human reality is something worth celebrating. Faulkner does away with this assumption and, in fact, does the exact opposite of what Sartre accuses him of doing. He stretches the realm of possibilities both inside and outside of time itself, so that Benjy knows neither past nor future, and Quentin, in killing himself after smashing the watch his father gave him, liberates himself from the burden of any experience of temporality. Maybe it is this treatment of time, of hopelessness, of pessimism, that is—against Sartre's claim—the novel's most novelistic quality.

This symptom of dismissing the novel appears again when Thacker chooses to write about how "farcical" Proust's and Knausgaard's works are— but he only refers to them as autobiographies, not the novels that they are.[66]

He returns to the question of literary pessimism in his introduction to "The Patron Saints of Pessimism," where he catalogs another list of writers, many of whom are novelists. And without acknowledging the novel as a distinct genre yet again, he writes, "The list quickly expands, soon encompassing the entirety of literature itself. In the end it's overwhelming; all of literature becomes a candidate."[67]

For a work that so thoroughly refuses to acknowledge the novel as a genre of pessimism, it is striking to see *Infinite Resignation* end on the following note, with a reference to *Don Quixote*, which Miguel de Unamuno also cites at the end of his own pessimistic work, *The Tragic Sense of Life*:

> To ridicule. To be ridiculous. These are, for Unamuno, the only responses to the "tragic sense of life." The philosophy of ridicule, and also a ridiculous philosophy. "Don Quixote," Unamuno writes, "made himself ridiculous—but was he aware of the most tragic ridicule of all, the ridicule reflected in oneself, the ridiculousness of the human being in his own eyes?" A Quixotic philosophy.[68]

Don Quixote fights "out of despair," but "it is despair and despair alone that begets hope, absurd hope, mad hope."[69] For this reason, Unamuno tells us, Don Quixote "is not a pessimist."[70] But he repeats that he isn't a pessimist four times on the same page, maybe protesting a bit too much. True, Don Quixote himself may be no pessimist, but the "absurd hope, mad hope" that he clings to offers the reader of Cervantes—and of Unamuno—little consolation. It is, as Unamuno admits, "ridiculous."[71] For Dienstag, "*Don Quixote* represents what I am terming a 'practice of pessimism,' a mode of conduct and action founded on an absence of expectation and hope."[72]

Quixote "fights against this Modern Age that began with Machiavelli and that will end comically."[73] The irony is that this protagonist who desperately clings to a world of medieval chivalry becomes the cipher of everything he fights against—modernity, newness, novelty, the novel. What he "bequeathed to *Kultur*" is "Quixotism," a "whole method, a whole epistemology, a whole esthetic [sic], a whole logic, a whole ethic—above all, a whole religion—that is to say, a whole economy of things eternal and things divine, a whole hope in what is rationally absurd."[74] Quixotism, then, is what supplants philosophy itself in all its rationality and systematicity; the alternative vision that pessimism embraces is one that is sketched out by the novel, in all its ridiculousness.

"*Ridiculus sum*" is the phrase that the young Charles Bovary, humiliated by his classmates at elementary school for stuttering and not being able to say his own name, is forced to write on the chalkboard twenty times.[75] Maybe all pessimistic writing is a way of repeating this refrain, adding new layers of meaning—or unraveling the meaning—with each repetition, struggling and failing to balance the cruelty of the world with a reciprocal response before we can hardly even name ourselves. *Ridiculus sum, ergo sum*. But, written by a pessimist, this phrase also means to say: as ridiculous as I am, at least I'm not as ridiculous as an optimist, as Leibniz, as Pangloss.

The pessimist Jean Améry, in his novel-essay *Charles Bovary, Country Doctor: Portrait of a Simple Man*, writes from Charles's point of view after the death of his wife, hurling insults at his creator like the Creature to Doctor Frankenstein, not forgiving him for the simple, reductive, ridiculous caricature of a man stuck in a "comedy of rage and pain" he is forced into.[76] In the chapter called "*Ridiculus Sum*," he positions Flaubert himself in that traumatic classroom scene, as one of the boys who had laughed at him: "Gustave Flaubert, I was nothing to you," he writes.[77] To Améry/Bovary, Flaubert's "irony is hard, maybe even wicked, in any case profoundly unfair."[78] A former Resistance fighter in the Second World War, and a survivor of Auschwitz, Buchenwald, and Bergen-Belsen, Améry found life worth living in the novel, and in becoming a novelist. In response to a scathing review of his foray into literature by Germany's leading critic Marcel Reich-Ranicki entitled "Terrible is the Temptation to the Novel," he attempted suicide in 1974, and survived it only to write a defense of suicide and then this final work on Charles Bovary in the same year that he did end up killing himself, in 1978.[79]

There is a point at which ridicule and rejection are too much to bear, and pessimism becomes the means through which one can think through, and perhaps even justify suicide—or justify the opposite of suicide, whatever that would be.[80] In 1910, three days after defending *Persuasion and Rhetoric*, a dissertation that aimed to prove the futility of human life, the twenty-three-year-old Carlo Michelstaedter shot himself dead.[81] Philip Mainländer, obsessed with Schopenhauer, turned the philosopher's concept of the "Will-to-Live" into a "Will-to-Die" in his 1876 book *Philosophy of Redemption*, where he wrote that "God is dead" years before Nietzsche plagiarized him.[82] The day it was published, Mainländer took the hefty manuscript, stacked it up on the ground, and used it as a pedestal that he eventually kicked away once the noose was firmly tightened around his neck.

"Hang yourself, and you will regret it," Kierkegaard writes in *Either/Or*. But he continues: "Do not hang yourself, and you will also regret it. Hang yourself or do not hang yourself, you will regret it either way. . . . This, gentlemen, is the quintessence of all the wisdom of life."[83] The metronomic repetition of "hang yourself" and "do not hang yourself" and "you will regret it either way" seems to empty these phrases of all meaning the way repetition of any phrase would—including "*Ridiculus sum*" several times on the chalkboard.[84] It is as if the meaninglessness and ridiculousness performed by the repetition itself becomes the "quintessence of all the wisdom of life." In

Voltaire's *Candide*, the Old Woman who had been told to "cheer up" after she was enslaved and had one buttock sliced off, says,

> This ridiculous weakness for living is perhaps one of our most fatal tendencies. For can anything be sillier than to insist on carrying a burden one would continually much rather throw to the ground? Sillier than to feel disgust at one's own existence and yet cling to it?[85]

Other thinkers like Cioran offer this unexpectedly—and even uncomfortably—hilarious advice for not killing oneself: "It is not worth the bother of killing yourself, since you will always kill yourself too late," echoed by Thacker, who writes, "One commits suicide not because one wants to die, but because one is already dead ... in which case suicide is not worth the trouble."[86] Cioran also uses his characteristically aggressive sophistry when he argues that, "Only optimists commit suicide, optimists who no longer succeed at being optimists. The others, having no reason to live, why would they have any to die?"[87]

Is someone like Werther, then, an optimist? Does he choose suicide not as an act of despair but as an act of hope—a hope of transcending his own life in order to affirm it, to give it meaning? Is he still too tethered to a Christian metaphysics, especially in the Christological imagery that surrounds his death, suggesting that he transforms his erotic passion into a religious Passion? Does this transformation offer some kind of promise of messianic wisdom to his readers? Does he then fail at his own pessimism? This is what Maurice Blanchot would seem to argue when, in *The Space of Literature*, he says, "The weakness of suicide lies in the fact that whoever commits it is still too strong.... Whoever kills himself is linked to hope, the hope of finishing it all."[88] For Blanchot, suicide is not an option because it is not pessimistic *enough*. It is still too affirmative:

> He who kills himself is the great affirmer of the *present*. I want to kill myself in an 'absolute' instant, the only one which will not pass and will not be surpassed.... Surely because of this, suicide retains the power of an exceptional affirmation.[89]

In *The Trouble with Being Born*, Cioran writes, "The fact that life has no meaning is a reason to live—moreover, the only one."[90] And in *On the Heights of Despair*, he takes a more candid tone, echoing Schopenhauer and Freud: "If I were to be totally sincere, I would say that I do not know why I live and why I do not stop living. The answer probably lies in the irrational character of life which maintains itself without reason."[91] It is paradoxically the "irrational character of life," the absurdity, the meaninglessness of it, that the pessimist embraces *in order* to live. The optimistic spirit of philosophy is what becomes suicidally depressing. There is a kind of consolation in avoiding the optimistic delusions that mask reality. Nietzsche takes this a step further, finding comfort in the thought of suicide itself: "The thought of suicide is a powerful comfort: it helps one through many a dreadful night."[92] It's not suicide per se that comforts Nietzsche, but the thought of it—and then the ability to contain it in words, in language, like Hamlet, who talks non-stop in order to talk himself through suicide so as to postpone the act, while Ophelia, who is hardly given any lines at all, who isn't even given a chance to put language to her own crisis, ends up being the one who kills herself.

And maybe this is where pessimistic reflections on suicide converge with the novel—coming out on the other side in the form of either writing or reading a book that engages the topic while staving it off. Maybe this is what Kafka is after when he writes in *The Blue Octavo Notebooks* that, "One of the most important quixotic acts . . . is: suicide."[93] But this quixotic act, in a novel, can be therapeutic, which is why he also noted in a letter that "we need the books that affect us like a disaster, that grieve us deeply, like the death of someone we loved more than ourselves, like being banished into forests far from everyone, like a suicide."[94]

In *Time Regained*, Marcel reflects on how "I had twenty times wanted to kill myself" for Albertine, but the "history and the circumstances of Werther, the noble Werther, had not alas! been mine." It was writing that pulled him through it, his commitment to the vocation that, in his mind, has a higher value than life itself: "For when it is a question of writing, one is scrupulous, one examines things meticulously, one rejects all that is not truth. But when it is merely a question of life, one ruins oneself, makes oneself ill, kills oneself all for lies."[95] One of Proust's most avid readers, Virginia Woolf, articulated this same experience in her diary, "writing to test my theory that there is consolation in expression," feeling a sense of "invigoration" and clarity as she was drafting *To the Lighthouse*, but as soon as she finished it, she fell back into a suicidal despair.[96] To Cioran, "A book is a postponed suicide," and according to some accounts, Unamuno, too, began *The Tragic Sense of Life* as a way of avoiding suicide.[97]

Pessimists are undoubtedly enticed by the Siren song of suicide and spend an inordinate amount of time—exhausted, spent, and still traveling on a journey without being sure that they'll ever get back home, or that there is even a home to return to—thinking about it. They have the energy neither to stop up their ears with wax and strap themselves to the mast nor to take the wax out and unstrap themselves. They feel that they are faced with an absurd, ridiculous choice: to be or not to be. Didn't Gorgias prove that being *was* non-being anyway?[98] Or was his mathematical proof more of a performance of logic itself dying by suicide, demonstrating its inadequacy in grasping the world to begin with? Or was it all a joke? Maybe that's what we'll all end up as anyway—just punchlines to bad jokes by the Gravediggers (Shakespeare originally called them "Clowns" instead), and the remains of Yorick will make their way from the tragedy of *Hamlet* to the comic novel of *Tristram Shandy*.

Maybe the pessimist lies somewhere between suicide and non-suicide, like Nicolas Chamfort, who was one of the first people to have stormed the Bastille in 1789 but then mocked the Revolution with as much cynicism as his opposition to the monarchy it overthrew. To avoid arrest in 1793, he fired a pistol at his temple, but misfired so that the bullet made its way through his right eye and blew off his nose instead.[99] Disappointed at his own failed suicide, he took an ivory-handled razor to slit his throat, and when it slipped on the first try, he pressed it harder against his throat until his larynx was exposed. Still not enough. He then took another razor to make over twenty deep incisions in his chest, his thighs, and his calves. His housekeeper had to break into his locked room after seeing the blood pooling outside the door and called for a doctor who was able to resuscitate him. In the days that followed, the new head librarian, Lefebvre de Villebrunne, paid him a visit to say, "But M. de Chamfort hasn't read my article against suicide! It has had enormous success. In it, I prove *primo* . . . and *secondo*, I prove."[100] He left Chamfort as abruptly as he had entered, without asking how he was doing or what the prognosis was. Sitting up in bed, Chamfort said about himself, "This is what it means to be clumsy—you don't succeed at anything, not even killing yourself."[101] He died a year later.

It is perhaps the subject of suicide itself that distinguishes the pessimist from the existentialist, or even the nihilist, even though these categories do overlap considerably:

> Above all, the pessimist is incapable of suicide, that solution of solutions that constitutes a horizon for even the most dyed-in-the-wool existentialist. Ironically, it is the pessimist's deep-seated misanthropy that keeps them alive. Weary of the all-too-human drama of life and the living, the pessimist is also aware that suicide solves nothing—that suicide is *insoluble*.[102]

Maybe this is putting it a bit too strongly. Maybe, knowing that nothing is solved in life either, that suicide is just as "insoluble" as staying on this side of life, either choice becomes somewhat interchangeable and equally meaningless. Camus's existentialism is a bit too gimmicky, forcing us to see in suicidal thought an opportunity for energetic action to embrace life instead. "Happiness and the absurd are two sons of the same earth. They are inseparable," he wants to convince us.[103] The pessimist wouldn't go that far. "One must imagine Sisyphus happy"—?[104] No, thanks. As for the nihilist, maybe they're not pessimistic enough either. Maybe it's not so much a matter of identifying no meaning in the world, in life, in existence, but in identifying this meaning as a meaning of the worst, the *pessimus*. We are in the worst of all possible worlds, as Schopenhauer tells us.[105]

However unconvincing Camus can be, at least he acknowledges the role of the novel in existentialism to an extent that pessimists do not, perhaps because he was one himself. But he recasts even the characters of philosophy as novelists, and novelists as philosophers:

> The philosopher, even if he is Kant, is a creator. He has his characters, his symbols, and his secret action. He has his plot endings. On the contrary, the lead taken by the novel over poetry and the essay merely represents, despite appearances, a greater intellectualization of the art. . . . The novel has its logic, its reasonings, its intuition, and its postulate. . . . The great novelists are philosophical novelists.[106]

Here again the dream of Schlegel is rearticulated, but to say that the "great novelists are philosophical novelists" also seems to sidestep the point that the novel challenges philosophy, engaging it on one level only to reject it on another, in the way that Mann illustrates by the end of *The Magic Mountain*.

This is also part of the humor of Stendhal, who makes up quotes and falsely attributes them to philosophers—like the anecdote that opens the second chapter of the second book of *The Red and the Black*, an unhinged quote that drips in sentimentality about the glance of a woman and first stepping into a drawing room at the age of eighteen, which he attributes to Kant, who would never be caught dead writing such drivel.[107] The novel responds to the ridicule and laughter of the world with irony, with parody, and with ridicule and laughter of its own. The pessimistic laughter of the schoolboys taunting Charles Bovary at the beginning of Flaubert's novel comes back at the end of the novel in the form of Emma Bovary's death rattle as she dies by suicide, but here the laugh is aimed back at the world: "Emma burst into laughter, horrible, frantic, despairing laughter" as she confronts the "looming . . . terror itself in the darkness of eternity."[108]

RIDICULOUS LAUGHTER

This is the sound of pessimistic laughter, the laughter at the realization of *ridiculus sum*, the hard truth Charles had to live with since he was a child, but which Emma only confronts in her death, in all its horror and ridiculousness. As Dienstag notes, "laughing at our existence is not an overcoming of pessimism. It is in fact the embrace of it."[109] Pessimism "is no more than a satire on earlier philosophies—a kind of cackling at their misfortunes."[110]

This is perhaps why Kierkegaard writes, "I choose one thing—that I may always have the laughter on my side."[111] Nietzsche instructs us in this "art of *this-worldly* comfort . . . ; you ought to learn to laugh, my young friends, if you are hell-bent on remaining pessimists."[112]

It shouldn't be forgotten that Aristophanes, in whose mouth Plato places the most beautiful prose in *Symposium*, in actuality used his comedy to poke fun at Socrates, and was also one of his first accusers, ultimately leading to Socrates's death. And the only reason, for instance, that Medea gives for killing her children is because she doesn't want to be laughed at: "Why should I, just to cause their father pain," she deliberates, "feel twice the pain myself by harming them? / I will not do it. Farewell to my plans. / But wait—what's wrong with me? What do I want? / To allow my enemies to laugh at me?"[113]

The laughter of pessimism is the motor of chaos, of anarchy. It "surrenders itself," as Adorno and Horkheimer put it, "to the power of destruction."[114] It is this laughter that frequently heightens, rather than breaks, the tension in *Crime and Punishment*, especially when Raskolnikov returns to the scene of the crime in one of his nightmares but is unable to repeat the murder because Alëna Ivanovna is essentially castrating him with her laughter, which "grew stronger and louder" with every blow of the axe.[115] This nightmare occurs only as an interruption from the agonizingly tense cat-and-mouse game he is playing with Porfiry Petrovich, the magistrate on his case, who rarely interacts with him without laughing. In *The Brothers Karamazov*, Doctor Herzenstube says that a "Russian laughs when he ought to weep," a statement personified by Ivan's brother Mitya, who often looks as though he has "something pensive and gloomy in his eyes," but one "would suddenly be struck by his unexpected laughter, betraying gay and playful thoughts precisely at the moment when he looked so gloomy."[116]

For Mikhail Bakhtin, the history of the novel can be told as a history of laughter. Apuleius stages the "Festival of Laughter" to essentially make an ass out of Lucius before he is mistakenly turned into an actual ass, despite his pleas to be turned into Cupid. In a way that anticipates Dostoevsky and Kafka, Lucius in *The Golden Ass* is on trial for murder in a theater full of people who can't stop laughing. It is only explained to him later that this humiliation is a prank, part of an annual "Festival of Laughter," which "always owes its success to some novel subterfuge."[117] Max Brod famously reported how Kafka would read passages out loud from one of his unfinished novels, *The Trial*, and despite the horrors recounted there, "his listeners laughed through their tears, and Kafka too had to laugh so hard that his reading was interrupted."[118] But Kafka himself wrote a letter confessing that "the laughter was not pleasant; it had no apparent reason, was painful, shameful."[119]

Maybe this is the same laughter as Ivan Karamazov's when he tells his brother Alyosha the story of the Grand Inquisitor: "Observe that I'm speaking seriously, though I may be laughing."[120] This anxiety around laughter is echoed later by the young boy Kolya, who confides to Alyosha how "profoundly unhappy" he is: "Sometimes I imagine God knows what, that everyone is laughing at me, the whole world, and then I . . . then I'm quite ready to destroy the whole order of things."[121]

Pessimism pivots around laughing disdainfully at the world and fearing that this act is reciprocated. This is the dynamic that Walter Benjamin identifies in Proust's style, which "is comedy, not humor; his laughter does not toss the world up but flings it down—at the risk that it will be smashed to pieces, which will then make him burst into tears."[122] In his work, as in his life, the "pretensions of the bourgeois are shattered by laughter," perhaps most memorably depicted in the self-important Mme. Verdurin, who dislocates her own jaw with affected laughing.[123] Proust would often be invited by aristocrats "for country weekends not because of his art but because he [was one of] . . . the funniest people in Paris."[124] But he would occasionally be "doubled up with a crazy bout of laughter" which "could go on so long it struck strangers as weird, even slightly mad."[125] Conspiring with his friend Lucien Daudet in a juvenile game well into their adulthood, they would both compile a running list of pretentious expressions that they would hear at dinner parties. Any time they would catch someone saying one of those expressions on their list, they would make eye contact in a silent challenge to maintain their composure, although Daudet would see "gleaming the diabolical light of uncontrollable laughter" in Proust's eyes, and then they would both erupt into hysterics, much to the chagrin of the dinner party hosts.[126]

Bakhtin characterizes laughter as "ambivalent," but also "at the same time cheerful and annihilating."[127] In one of his favorite passages from *Gargantua and Pantagruel*, where Rabelais describes in great detail how the giant Gargantua gets so annoyed with the smaller humans living in the vicinity of Notre-Dame that he urinates all over them, leaving the survivors (his piss ends up drowning 260,418 men alone, not counting women and children), "sweating, coughing, spitting, and out of breath, they began to swear and curse, some in a fury and others in sport (*par ris*)."[128] The Paris of Rabelais, baptized in Gargantua's piss, is literally the landscape of laughter, "*par ris*," a landscape that encompasses both fury and fun, both spite and mirth, the disgusting and the beautiful, the physiological and the contemplative, all of which dissolve into the kind of laughter that is the wellspring of the novel because it collapses hierarchical distances to bring everything up close in all its detail.

"Everything that makes us laugh is close at hand," Bakhtin says, sounding like Heidegger if the German philosopher had a sense of humor, as though the novel functions like the concept of *Ent-fernung*, as a vehicle of de-distancing, of bringing objects close to us so that we can inspect them and ultimately make fun of them.[129] Laughter to Bakhtin "demolishes fear and piety before an object, before a world, making of it an object of familiar contact and thus clearing the ground for an absolutely free investigation of it."[130] The novel, for him, is that method of free investigation, liberated from any narrowly defined poetics that have restricted genres established before it.

Laughter as the demolition of "fear and piety before an object, before a world," is itself the subject of Umberto Eco's *The Name of the Rose*, a novel that seems to sketch out Bakhtin's theory of novels as jovial agents of irreverence and anarchy. In this novel, the only extant copy of the second book of Aristotle's *Poetics*, which discusses comedy and laughter, is so threatening that the blind monk Jorge of Burgos ends up eating it and setting the monastery library on fire so that no one would ever be able to access it. To Burgos, laughter is incommensurate with the Christian philosophical tradition that owes much of its intellectual weight to Aristotle's influence on Aquinas. It only makes sense, then, that laughter—in its opposition to philosophy, to religion, and to political hierarchies—finds its natural home in the novel, in *The Name of the Rose* itself.

Whereas Lukács identifies the novel as a site of withdrawal, spoken of in abstract and transcendental terms, Bakhtin sees the novel as the opposite: as a close-up of the world and of ourselves in all its detail. Both theorists, however, agree that the novel is an expression of incongruity with the world, which is rooted in Schopenhauer's theory of laughter: "laughter itself is just the expression of this incongruity."[131] And Bakhtin refers to this incongruity in anatomical terms, viewing laughter as a "comical operation of dismemberment" that reveals the "innards, not normally accessible for viewing" of the object of ridicule.[132]

This *sparagmos*, the dismemberment of the body, is a parody of Eucharist symbolism, as well as the more ancient myths of Orpheus and the tragic stories of Hippolytus and Pentheus, which is perhaps what Adrian Leverkühn embodies in his fits of demonic laughter in *Doctor Faustus*.[133] Ultimately, though, Northrop Frye defines *sparagmos* as "the sense that heroism and effective action are absent, disorganized or foredoomed to defeat, and that confusion and anarchy reign over the world."[134] While this definition may seem pessimistic enough, he is emphatic in categorizing it under the "archetypal theme of irony and satire."[135]

No one exemplifies this ironic, satiric *sparagmos* through laughter better than Rabelais. "But Rabelaisian laughter not only destroys traditional connections and abolishes idealized strata," Bakhtin argues, "it also brings out the crude, unmediated connections between things that people otherwise seek to keep separate."[136] In *Gargantua and Pantagruel*, Rabelais paints anatomically detailed and fantastically grotesque descriptions, such as the one of Friar John punishing his enemies who had broken into the monastery vineyard. In one sentence alone, we get a cascading catalog of physical violence:

> He beat out the brains of some, broke the arms and legs of others, disjointed the neck-bones, demolished the kidneys, slit the noses, blackened the eyes, smashed the jaws, knocked the teeth down the throats, shattered the shoulder-blades, crushed the shins, dislocated the thigh-bones, and cracked the fore-arms of yet others.[137]

Bakhtin is also particularly tickled by how Friar John slices a man's head in two, providing details about the skull fractures and lobe incision.[138] In another episode in the novel, Panurge—after quarrelling with a ship merchant—throws the merchant's bellwether into the sea, leading the other sheep to run overboard to chase it, and the merchant and his herdsmen follow suit to save them:

> Panurge stood beside the galley with an oar in his hand, not to help the drovers but to prevent them from clambering aboard and escaping their death. . . . With rhetorical flourishes, he pointed out to them the miseries of this world, and the blessings and felicities of the other life, affirming that the dead were luckier than those who lived on in this vale of tears.[139]

This is the same kind of humor that we see centuries later in Voltaire's *Candide, or: Optimism*, who, amid graphic portrayals of mutilated bodies—from brains that "lay scattered on the ground beside severed arms and legs" to the Old Woman's story about how her buttock was sliced off—lampoons Leibniz's claim in *Theodicy* that this is the best of all possible worlds.[140]

It is curious why Voltaire, a philosopher in his own right, would turn to the form of the novel to articulate his most scathing attack against Leibnizian optimism. "Deeply suspicious of metaphysical 'systems,'" like any other pessimist after him, Voltaire "was constantly appealing to the facts; fiction, paradoxically, allowed him to show the ways in which the muddle and miseries of life could not be reduced to neat, abstract theories."[141] It wasn't just fiction that he turned to in this work, but that specific Rabelaisian literary tradition that Bakhtin associates with the rise of the modern novel. As much as contemporary pessimists may want to handle the novel at arm's length—or, for whatever reason, refer to them as "non-novels"—it is important to note that Schopenhauer, himself an avid translator of Laurence Sterne's *Tristram Shandy* into German, has this to say about Voltaire's novel: "to return to Leibniz, I cannot assign to the *Théodicée*, that methodical and broad development of optimism, in such a capacity, any other merit than that it later gave rise to the immortal *Candide* of the great Voltaire."[142]

In Voltaire's companion piece to *Candide*, the interstellar adventurer Micromegas—whose name draws the reader's attention to absurdity as a game of scale—travels from his star Sirius to Saturn before stopping by Earth. In contrast to the inhabitants of Saturn, he expects humans, microscopic "animalcules" to him, "being apparently all mind and spirit . . . [to] spend your lives loving and thinking—the true life of the spirit. Nowhere have I seen real happiness, but no doubt it exists here."[143] He's specifically addressing philosophers here who, in a rare moment of candidness, unanimously shake their heads in disagreement. One of them admits that, "except for a small number of inhabitants of little consequence, the rest were a collection of the mad, the malevolent, and the miserable."[144] Philosophers, these supposed experts of the mind and spirit, still cannot figure out how to alleviate misery. But at least pessimistic novelists have learned how to laugh at the misery.

And this is how *Micromegas* ends. When one of the philosophers claims that "everything, their persons, their worlds, their suns, their stars, had been made uniquely for man," Micromegas "fell about, choking with that irrepressible laughter which, according to Homer, is the portion of the gods."[145] Voltaire describes how Micromegas's shoulders and belly "heaved and sank" in "convulsions" of laughter, even as

> he was a trifle vexed to see that beings so infinitesimally small should have a degree of pride that was almost infinitely great. He promised to write them a nice book of philosophy, in very small script just for them, and that in this book they would discover what was what. Sure enough, he gave them this volume before he left. It was taken to Paris to the Academy of Sciences. But when the secretary opened it, he found nothing but blank pages.[146]

A book of blank pages—the ultimate send-up of all those systematic tomes of philosophical scribbling. Eight years after the publication of *Micromegas* (and just one year after the publication of *Candide*), the genre of the novel itself took a page out of this book, so to speak, when, toward the end of *Tristram Shandy*, Sterne includes two chapters consisting entirely of blank pages, perhaps to match the two fully blacked-out pages at the beginning.[147] The novel provides a wisdom that philosophy, being "apparently all mind and spirit," doesn't have the guts for—especially the literal guts populating the pages of Rabelais, Voltaire, and Sterne. It is a Micromegian wisdom that coincides with the stance of pessimism, acknowledging that the cosmos, the stars, the world, are not "for us."[148] This is how we turn our attention away from the stars as ciphers of eternity to the finitude of our bodies, in all their ridiculousness and all their pain, even though they're lined with chemical traces of stardust itself.

NOTES

1. Hardy, *Tess of the D'Urbervilles*, 10, 220.
2. Hardy, *Tess of the D'Urbervilles*, 230.
3. Hardy, *Tess of the D'Urbervilles*, 223-24.
4. Hardy, *Tess of the D'Urbervilles*, 71.
5. Shakespeare, *Richard III*, 5.4.7.
6. Hardy, *Tess of the D'Urbervilles*,149; George Eliot, *Middlemarch* (New York: W. W. Norton, 2000), 3
7. Heliodorus, *Aethiopica: An Ethiopian Romance*, trans. Moses Hadas (Philadelphia, PA: University of Pennsylvania Press, 1957), 1.
8. Conrad, *Heart of Darkness*, 7.
9. Conrad, *Heart of Darkness*, 8.
10. Conrad, *Heart of Darkness*, 75.
11. Conrad, *Heart of Darkness*, 30.
12. Conrad, *Heart of Darkness*, 48.
13. Conrad, *Heart of Darkness*, 74–75. Woolf notes how Conrad's "characters are exposed far more to the forces of sea and forest, storm and shipwreck, than to the influence of other human beings" (*The Essays of Virginia Woolf*, Volume II: 1912-1918, ed. Andrew McNeillie [London: Hogarth, 1987], II: 159).
14. Conrad, *Heart of Darkness*, 32.
15. Conrad, *Heart of Darkness*, 35.
16. Conrad, *Heart of Darkness*, 32.
17. Conrad, *Heart of Darkness*, 35.
18. Conrad, *Heart of Darkness*, 37.
19. Conrad, *Heart of Darkness*, 41.
20. "NASA Readies Perseverance Mars Rover's Earthly Twin," September 4, 2020, https://www.jpl.nasa.gov/news/nasa-readies-perseverance-mars-rovers-earthly-twin.
21. Sigmund Freud, *Beyond the Pleasure Principle*, trans. James Strachey (New York: W. W. Norton, 1961), 76.
22. Francis Bacon, "The New Organon," in *The New Organon and Related Writings*, ed. Fulton H. Anderson (New York: Macmillan, 1960), CXXIX: 119.
23. Max Horkheimer and Theodor W. Adorno, *Dialectic of Enlightenment*, trans. John Cumming (London: Continuum, 2000), 46.
24. Horkheimer and Adorno, *Dialectic of Enlightenment*, 61.
25. Freud, *Civilization and Its Discontents*, ed. and trans. James Strachey (New York: W. W. Norton, 2000), 112.
26. Kafka, "The Silence of the Sirens," in *The Complete Stories*, trans. Willa and Edwin Muir, ed. Nahum N. Glatzer (New York: Schocken, 1971), 431.
27. Kafka, "Silence of the Sirens," 431.
28. Kafka, "Silence of the Sirens," 431.
29. Horkheimer and Adorno, *Dialectic of Enlightenment*, 43.
30. Horkheimer and Adorno, *Dialectic of Enlightenment*, 78.
31. Horkheimer and Adorno, *Dialectic of Enlightenment*, 78.

32. Plato, *Republic*, X.608A: 291.
33. Plato, *Symposium* 216A: 47.
34. Karl Marx, "Theses on Feuerbach," in *The Marx-Engels Reader*, ed. Robert C. Tucker, 2nd. ed. (New York: W. W. Norton, 1978), 145.
35. Thacker, *Infinite Resignation*, 29.
36. Robert, "From *Origins of the Novel*," 57.
37. Jonathan Foa Dienstag, *Pessimism: Philosophy, Ethic, Spirit* (Princeton, NJ: Princeton University Press, 2006), 6.
38. Dienstag, *Pessimism*, 6.
39. Giacomo Leopardi, *The Moral Essays*, trans. Patrick Creagh (New York: Columbia University Press, 1983), 187.
40. Thacker, *Infinite Resignation*, 20.
41. Paradoxically, Heidegger sees boredom as a way of accessing beings as a "whole," which all previous systems of philosophy have aspired to explaining: "Even and precisely when we are not actually busy with things or ourselves, this 'as a whole' comes over us—for example, in authentic boredom. . . . This boredom manifests beings as a whole" (Martin Heidegger, "What is Metaphysics?," in *Pathmarks*, ed. William McNeill, trans. David Farrell Krell [Cambridge: Cambridge University Press, 1998], 87).
42. Lispector, *The Passion According to G.H.*, trans. Idra Novey (New York: New Directions, 2012), 5.
43. Heller, *Thomas Mann: The Ironic German*, 28.
44. Mann, *Essays of Three Decades*, trans. H. T. Lowe-Porter (New York: Knopf, 1947), 331.
45. Qtd. in Bryan Magee, *The Philosophy of Schopenhauer* (Oxford: Oxford University Press, 1983), 331.
46. Magee, *Philosophy of Schopenhauer,* 405–406, 415.
47. E. M. Cioran, *The Temptation to Exist*, trans. Richard Howard (New York: Arcade, 2012), 143.
48. Cioran, *Temptation to Exist*, 143.
49. Cioran, *Temptation to Exist*, 142.
50. Cioran, *Temptation to Exist*, 142–143.
51. Cioran, *Temptation to Exist*, 143.
52. Cioran, *Temptation to Exist*, 143.
53. Cioran, *Short History of Decay*, 77.
54. Cioran, *Short History of Decay*, 77.
55. Cioran, *Temptation to Exist*, 148.
56. Thacker, *Infinite Resignation*, 8.
57. Thacker, *Infinite Resignation*, 23, 139.
58. Thacker, *Infinite Resignation*, 54–55.
59. Thacker, *Infinite Resignation*, 65.
60. Thacker, *Infinite Resignation*, 65.
61. Thacker, *Infinite Resignation*, 65–66.
62. Nabokov, *Strong Opinions,* 4, 173. Nabokov is aware of the "anti-novel" and "*nouveau roman*" movement often associated with Robbe-Grillet but insists on

treating Robbe-Grillet as "one great French writer" rather than an exemplar of any movement (*Strong Opinions,* 4). "The French New Novel does not really exist," he clarifies, "apart from a little heap of dust and fluff in a fouled pigeonhole" (173).

63. Jean-Paul Sartre, "On *The Sound and the Fury*: Time in the Work of Faulkner," in *The Sound and the Fury*, 2nd ed. (New York: W. W. Norton, 1994), 271.

64. Sartre, "On *The Sound and the Fury*," 271.

65. Qtd. in Sartre, "On *The Sound and the Fury*," 271.

66. Thacker, *Infinite Resignation*, 207.

67. Thacker, *Infinite Resignation*, 250.

68. Thacker, *Infinite Resignation*, 386.

69. Miguel de Unamuno, *Tragic Sense of Life*, trans. J. E. Crawford Flitch (New York: Dover, 1954), 324.

70. Unamuno, *Tragic Sense of Life*, 326.

71. Unamuno, *Tragic Sense of Life*, 323.

72. Dienstag, *Pessimism*, 205.

73. Unamuno, *Tragic Sense of Life*, 326.

74. Unamuno, *Tragic Sense of Life*, 325.

75. Gustave Flaubert, *Madame Bovary*, trans. Lydia Davis (New York: Penguin Books, 2010), 5.

76. Jean Améry, *Charles Bovary, Country Doctor*, trans. Adrian Nathan West (New York: New York Review Books, 2018), 76.

77. Améry, *Charles Bovary,* 32.

78. Améry, *Charles Bovary,* 62.

79. Qtd. in Adrian Nathan West, introduction to Améry, *Charles Bovary,* ix.

80. Cioran sees the core of our being as "nothing," and "this nothing, this everything, cannot give life a meaning, but it nonetheless makes life persevere in what it is: *a state of non-suicide*" (*A Short History of Decay,* 19). Thinking of Werther—perhaps the most famous novelistic suicide—while articulating an alternative to his ending, Barthes writes, "*I have no hope, but all the same . . .* Or else: I stubbornly choose not to choose; I choose drifting: *I continue*" (Barthes, *A Lover's Discourse*, 62).

81. Thomas Ligotti, *The Conspiracy Against the Human Race: A Contrivance of Horror* (New York: Penguin Books, 2018), 15–16.

82. Ligotti, *Conspiracy Against the Human Race,* 18

83. Kierkegaard, *Either/Or*, I: 38–39.

84. Repetition, though, is one of the central principles of a meaningful existence to Kierkegaard, and regret "is the quintessence of all the wisdom of life" (*Either/Or*, I: 39).

85. Voltaire, *Candide*, in *Candide and Other Stories*, trans. and with an introduction by Roger Pearson (Oxford: Oxford University Press, 1998), 31.

86. Cioran, *The Trouble with Being Born,* trans. Richard Howard (New York: Arcade, 2013), 32; Thacker, *Infinite Resignation,* 49.

87. Cioran, *All Gall is Divided*, trans. Richard Howard (New York: Arcade, 2019), 87.

88. Maurice Blanchot, *The Space of Literature*, trans. Ann Smock (Lincoln, NE: University of Nebraska Press, 1989), 103.

89. Blanchot, *Space of Literature*, 103.
90. Cioran, *Trouble with Being Born*, 188.
91. Cioran, *On the Heights of Despair*, trans. Ilinca Zarifopol-Johnston (Chicago, IL: University of Chicago Press, 1992), 33.
92. Friedrich Nietzsche, *Beyond Good and Evil: Prelude to a Philosophy of the Future*, trans. Walter Kaufmann (New York: Vintage Books, 1966), §157: 91.
93. Kafka, *The Blue Octavo Notebooks*, ed. Max Brod, trans. Ernst Kaiser and Eithne Wilkins (Cambridge: Exact Change, 1991), 18.
94. Kafka, *Letters to Friends, Family, and Editors*, trans. Richard Winston and Clare Winston (New York: John Calder, 1978), 16.
95. Proust, *Time Regained*, 320.
96. Virginia Woolf, *The Diary of Virginia Woolf*, Volume III: 1925-1930, ed. Anne Olivier Bell, assisted by Andrew McNeillie (New York: Harcourt Brace Jovanovich, 1981), III: 81; 57; 60.
97. Cioran, *The Trouble with Being Born*, 99; Thacker, *Infinite Resignation*, 383.
98. Gorgias, "On Non-Being," in *The Greek Sophists*, ed. and trans. John Dillon and Tania Gergel (New York: Penguin Books, 2003), 67–75.
99. Claude Arnaud, *Chamfort: A Biography*, trans. Deke Dusinberre (Chicago, IL: University of Chicago Press, 1992), 249.
100. Qtd. in Arnaud, *Chamfort*, 251.
101. Arnaud, *Chamfort*, 251.
102. Thacker, *Infinite Resignation*, 49. Dienstag identifies a category of thinkers (Camus, Cioran, and Unamuno) as "existential pessimists," whom he separates from "metaphysical pessimists" (Schopenhauer and Freud) and "cultural pessimists" (Rousseau and Leopardi) (Dienstag, *Pessimism*, 42–43).
103. Camus, *Myth of Sisyphus*, 122.
104. Camus, *Myth of Sisyphus*, 123.
105. Schopenhauer, *World as Will and Representation*, II: 583.
106. Camus, *Myth of Sisyphus*, 100.
107. Stendhal, *The Red and the Black*, 198.
108. Flaubert, *Madame Bovary*, 290.
109. Dienstag, *Pessimism*, 40.
110. Dienstag, *Pessimism*, 256.
111. Kierkegaard, *Either/Or*, I: 43.
112. Nietzsche, *Birth of Tragedy*, 7.
113. Euripides, *Medea*, in *The Norton Anthology of World Literature*, trans. Diane Arnson Svarlien, Volume A, 3rd ed. (New York: W. W. Norton, 2012), 1.1068–1072, 813.
114. Horkheimer and Adorno, *Dialectic of Enlightenment*, 77.
115. Dostoevsky, *Crime and Punishment*, 266–267.
116. Dostoevsky, *Brothers Karamazov*, 675; 68.
117. Apuleius, *The Golden Ass*, 45.
118. Qtd. in Jeffrey Meyers, "Kafka's Dark Laughter," *The Antioch Review* 70, no. 4 (Fall 2012): 767, https://www.jstor.org/stable/10.7723/antiochreview.70.4.0760.
119. Qtd. in Meyers, "Kafka's Dark Laughter," 768.

120. Dostoevsky, *Brothers Karamazov*, 229.
121. Dostoevsky, *Brothers Karamazov*, 557.
122. Benjamin, "The Image of Proust," 207.
123. Benjamin, "The Image of Proust," 207.
124. Edmund White, *Marcel Proust* (New York: Viking Press, 1999), 4–5.
125. White, *Marcel Proust*, 8.
126. Qtd. in Carter, *Marcel Proust: A Life*, 206.
127. Bakhtin, *Dialogic Imagination*, 21.
128. Rabelais, *Gargantua and Pantagruel*, 74.
129. Bakhtin, *Dialogic Imagination*, 23.
130. Bakhtin, *Dialogic Imagination*, 23.
131. Schopenhauer, *World as Will and Representation*, I §13: 59.
132. Bakhtin, *Dialogic Imagination*, 23–24.
133. Northrop Frye, *Anatomy of Criticism: Four Essays* (Princeton, NJ: Princeton University Press, 1957), 192.
134. Frye, *Anatomy of Criticism*, 192.
135. Frye, *Anatomy of Criticism*, 192.
136. Bakhtin, *Dialogic Imagination*, 170.
137. François Rabelais, *The Histories of Gargantua and Pantagruel*, trans. J. M. Cohen (New York: Penguin Books, 1985), 99.
138. Bakhtin, *Dialogic Imagination*, 172.
139. Rabelais, *Gargantua and Pantagruel*, 467.
140. Voltaire, *Candide*, 6, 30. Northrop Frye writes that the "literary ancestry" of "*Candide* runs through Rabelais" (*Anatomy of Criticism*, 308).
141. Roger Pearson, introduction to *Candide* by Voltaire, ix.
142. Schopenhauer, *World as Will and Representation*, II: 582.
143. Voltaire, *Micromegas*, in *Candide and Other Stories*, trans. and with an introduction by Roger Pearson (Oxford: Oxford University Press, 1998), 117.
144. Voltaire, *Micromegas*, 117.
145. Voltaire, *Micromegas*, 121.
146. Voltaire, *Micromegas*, 121.
147. Sterne, Laurence, *The Life and Opinions of Tristram Shandy, Gentleman* (New York: Penguin Books, 1978), 521–522; 29–30.
148. Thacker, *In the Dust of this Planet: Horror of Philosophy*, Volume 1 (Alresford: Zero Books, 2011), 4.

Chapter 8

Constellations and Consternations

NO PITY IN THE STARS

In *Heart of Darkness,* Marlow is haunted by a cry from the landscape that takes on the menacing sound of "a prodigious peal of laughter that would shake the fixed stars in their places."[1] Neither stars nor bodies have any fixed place in this novel—or, for that matter, perhaps any novel. The centrifugal act of laughter and its association with the dismemberment of the body in the novel moves away from the serious, concentrated, centripetal gaze of the cynosure in what Northrop Frye calls the "high mimetic" of Renaissance literature.[2] The cynosure, the center of attention, is a sixteenth-century word that "originally denoted the constellation Ursa Minor, or the Pole Star which it contains, long used by navigators," according to the Oxford English Dictionary.[3] The novel distracts this attention, pulls it apart in different and often disorienting directions, so that by the time we get to *Ulysses* in the twentieth century, the hero of the novel is no longer the protagonist but the reader of the novel itself, as we navigate our own circuitous paths through the text, its impenetrable passages slowly revealing themselves as clearings in the dense, dark void.

It is in this way that Joyce's novel simulates the map not just of Dublin, but of the night sky, and the reader—named by the novel's title—struggles to find one's way back to an unstable home of unstable meaning by reading the work as a series of dizzying constellations in motion, seemingly re-patterning themselves with each reading until we arrive at Leopold Bloom's final thoughts in the novel, contemplating "the futility of triumph" and "the apathy of the stars" before he gets turned on by the sight of his wife's "rump," making sure to kiss each cheek as he gets into bed.[4] Joyce invites us to perform the novel's Copernican turn, moving our attention away from the celestial spheres above us that had once given us transcendental meaning, to the immanence of our body, and of the bodies he populates in the novel, in their Rabelaisian humor.

Sixty-five years before *Ulysses*, Flaubert used the novel form to thematize the constraints, the failure, of his own medium in these cosmic terms. Language for him can only ever be "like a cracked kettle on which we beat out tunes for bears to dance to, when we long to inspire pity in the stars."[5] The stars are what we had once relied on to understand our place in the cosmic order. Odysseus uses them as a map to find his way back home to Ithaca. Dante navigates his own epic journey from hell to paradise, using the stars—the Ptolemaic mediator between the light of God's mind and the fallen humans on earth—as his lodestone. *The Inferno* ends as he "walked out once more beneath the Stars."[6] *The Purgatorio* ends with him "perfect, pure, and ready for the Stars."[7] And *The Paradiso* ends with the "Love that moves the Sun and the other stars."[8]

This stellar canopy over our home was proof of divine protection, an organizing principle of meaning, structure, and comfort. This is the supposed comfort that Lady Philosophy provides for Boethius, repeatedly reminding him to look at the stars as proof of a divine order, and of a happiness that can stave off despair: "How happy is mankind, / if the love that orders the stars above / rules, too, in your hearts."[9] Even melancholia, unlike pessimism, had the privilege of being explained away as a planetary affliction, reflecting the balance of stellar and planetary bodies in the universe with the humors in the body. In Albrecht Dürer's 1514 engraving *Melencolia I*, the saturnine angel heavily, lethargically rests her head on her hand, deep in contemplation, in consideration, with the blazing star in the background. The word "consideration" itself is etymologically rooted in the *sidera*, the stars—to consider, weigh the options (to be or not to be?) is to synchronize the orb of your mind with the orbs and orbits of the stars, following their movements.

But as Copernicus, Kepler, and Galileo dismantled the Ptolemaic system, they demolished with it the sense of cosmic order that undergirded our sense of who we are, where we came from, where we are going, and how we can arrive at meaning and values, ushering an ontological and epistemic crisis of the highest order. Shakespeare stages this contemporary cataclysm in *King Lear*, when Edgar, disguised as Poor Tom, characterizes the quasi-apocalyptic storm as "star-blasting."[10] No one, not even his own father, recognizes him after the storm, echoing the sentiment that governs *Hamlet* and sets that entire play into motion with its inaugural line: "Who's there?"[11] Recognition fails; cognition needs to start anew. Shakespeare drags us through the stellar rubble of outmoded value systems, as when Edgar's brother Edmund cynically observes,

> The excellent foppery of the world, that, when we are sick in fortune, often the surfeits of our own behavior, we make guilty of our disasters the sun, the moon, and stars; as if we were villains on necessity, fools by heavenly compulsion.[12]

Macbeth implores the stars to hide their fires so as to conceal his murderous, "dark and deep desires," but in *Hamlet*, stars are even doubted to be fire at all.[13] They "start from their spheres," falling out of their fixed orbits into a new, unknown, terrifying reality, calling the natural itself into question—not to mention the supernatural.[14]

Romeo, for his part, wants nothing to do with them, shouting, "Then I defy you stars!" after hearing the misinformation of Juliet's death.[15] Juliet for him had already replaced the stars; even the "brightness of her cheek would shame those stars / As daylight doth a lamp."[16] She herself "is" the sun, and their love constitutes a cosmic unity that emerges out of the chaos of their surroundings just as much as, on a purely linguistic level, their first encounter takes the shape of a formal sonnet that isolates them from the insults and vulgar language that opened the play.[17] Instead of a big bang, they do not so much collide as coalesce into the covert and literal space of the "little sound"—the literal definition of a sonnet—while the loudness of the Capulets and Montagues feuding with each other roars on the other side of their silence. But this cosmic—or rather microcosmic—unity is also doomed to failure. Juliet Capulet, even in her initials, replaces Jesus Christ in this new scheme. But in her pessimistic resurrection, she wakes up to a world not even worth the bother of redeeming. She kills herself again instead, and in her suicide, maybe she takes the world with her. To Schopenhauer, the "terrors of death rest for the most part on the false illusion that then the I or ego vanishes, and the world remains. But rather is the opposite true, namely that the world vanishes."[18] Cioran echoes this when he says, "The universe begins and ends with each individual, whether he be Shakespeare or Hodge; for each individual experiences his merit or his nullity *in the absolute*."[19]

"Thus runs the world away," Hamlet sings after staging his play within the play.[20] Nothing, especially not the world we spin on, in the abyss of space, has any kind of stability anymore. Maybe it doesn't even deserve redemption. According to the New Testament, "In the beginning was the Word, and the Word was God, and the Word was with God," but now that that order has been sundered, all we are left with are "words, words, words."[21] A cracked kettle that solicits no pity from the stars—but a kettle we are condemned to use regardless.

It is no wonder, then, why Schlegel sees Shakespeare as laying the ground for "the true foundation of the novel."[22] Adapting to the present moment of his own time, Shakespeare takes a novel view into the dissolving order of the world and the precariousness of how we arrive at meaning and understanding of this world.[23] Perhaps it is no coincidence, as well, that Lukács begins his *Theory of the Novel* with, "Happy are those ages when the starry sky is the map of all possible paths—ages whose paths are illuminated by the light of the stars."[24] Those ages—along with the possibility of happiness—are long past, relegated to an era dominated by the epic form. Lukács writes a pessimistic tract about the novel as a pessimistic genre, beginning his work with the word "Happy" and ending with undermined "hopes which are signs of a world to come, still so weak that it can easily be crushed by the sterile power of the merely existent."[25]

In the time of Homer, by contrast,

> everything in such ages is new and yet familiar, full of adventure and yet their own. The world is wide and yet it is like a home, for the fire that burns in the soul is of the same essential nature as the stars.[26]

This was a time that, to Lukács, pre-dated philosophy—a time when we felt at home in the world, when there was no distinction yet between subject and object, when meaning could be gleaned from the stars. The "happy ages have no philosophy," he insists.[27] And now that we do have philosophy, as that structure of meaning to replace the stars, it does little to guide our path the way the stars had once guided the paths of Odysseus and Dante. "Kant's starry firmament," as he calls it, "no longer lights any solitary wanderer's path."[28] The novel for Lukács is by no means the first genre to articulate this solitary experience, since he identifies it as the "very essence of tragedy, for the soul that has attained itself through its destiny can have brothers among the stars, but never an earthly companion."[29] The loneliness of the novel, however, cannot find any brotherhood among the stars whatsoever.

This is the stellar loneliness that *Tess of the D'Urbervilles* narrates. Hardy's landscape takes on a cosmic scope, so that all the other people around Tess "were at stellar distances from her present world."[30] These stellar distances are first explored by Tess's younger brother Abraham, who

> made observation the stars, whose cold pulses were beating amid the black hollows above, in serene dissociation from these two wisps of human life. He asked how far away those twinkles were, and whether God was on the other side of them.[31]

In his mind, he associates the possibility of Tess being "made rich by marrying a gentleman" with the ability to "draw the stars as near to her as Nettlecombe-Tout" because she would then be rich enough to purchase a "spy-glass."[32] It is in the context of this association that Abraham marvels at the "beautiful diamond ring" Alec D'Urberville wears, as though it were a star itself: "And I seed it! And it did twinkle."[33]

But neither stars nor people ever broach the cosmic distance that separates Tess from everyone around her. Alec only trespasses this distance through violence and rape; Angel assumes a false intimacy but withdraws as soon as he finds out about Tess's past with Alec, as though she were at fault. When

Abraham asks Tess if stars were worlds, she tells him, "I don't know; but I think so. They sometimes seem to be like the apples on our stubbard-tree. Most of them splendid and sound—a few blighted."[34] Abraham then asks whether we live on a splendid or a blighted one, and she responds, "A blighted one."[35]

It is the shift from the Ptolemaic to the Copernican understanding of the universe that reveals the world to be a "blighted" planet. Both Lukács and Bakhtin think of the novel as a kind of Copernican turn, which we can see embedded even in Lukács's metaphor of the "Kantian starry firmament." Bakhtin, in emphasizing the concern with the body and its *sparagmos*, defines the novel as "the expression of a Galilean perception of language, one that denies the absolutism of a single and unitary language . . . as the sole verbal and semantic center of the ideological world."[36] The heteroglossia at work in the novel simulates, on the level of form, the multiplicity and division of bodies. Opposed to the novel is the language of poetry, which Bakhtin characterizes as "a unitary and singular Ptolemaic world outside of which nothing else exists and nothing else is needed."[37] It is a dead, fixed "language"; the novel is open-ended and polyvalent.

From the opposite point of view, Frye articulates his discomfort with using the word "novel" as a "catchall term which can be applied to practically any prose book that is not 'on' something," by saying that, "this novel-centered view on prose fiction is a Ptolemaic perspective which is now too complicated to be any longer workable, and some more relative and Copernican view must take its place."[38] But even as Bakhtin and Frye differ about where exactly the novel falls on the turn between the Ptolemaic and the Copernican, they both identify it as the axis of that turn.

This consistent metaphor for the rise of the novel reflects the anxiety that the novel expresses about the tenuous state—or even loss—of any transcendental meaning we assign to ourselves. Opposed to melodrama, which transports "the anthropocentrism of tragedy and epic—the idea that the struggles internal to a small group of individuals have a collective meaning—to the world inhabited by average or middle-class characters," the novel dissolves this meaning.[39] Kundera observes that, for Emma Bovary, whose private drama has little or no consequence to anyone outside her immediate relations, the "horizon shrinks to the point of seeming a barrier. . . . The lost infinity of the outside world is replaced by the infinity of the soul."[40] But what is that? "The infinity of the soul—if it ever existed—has become a nearly useless appendage."[41] The novel traces the pessimistic trajectory of any life, in which the limitless horizon of the stars that had once inspired us gradually shrinks to something far more disappointing until, as a corpse, we are nothing but one useless appendage after another.

This rift between our bodies and the unreachable stars that no longer constitute our home plays out the same drama told by Aristophanes in

Symposium. We are descended from the stars, and now we are condemned to these fragile, insufficient bodies. Why else would we, like Rodolphe, seek to solicit pity from them if we didn't identify in them some nebulous prehistory to our being, some prelapsarian home to which we can never return? And the means by which we seek this pity, language itself, can never be as articulate as we want it to be. It is, in fact, the opposite. Failing at articulation, language reflects our disarticulated body, the anatomy we are left with after that primordial cosmic incision.

THE NOVELTY OF ANATOMY

Pessimism is an experience fundamentally rooted in the body, in the body's anatomy. Unamuno thinks that, "It is not usually our ideas that make us optimists or pessimists, but it is our optimism or our pessimism, of physiological or perhaps pathological origin, as much the one as the other, that makes our ideas."[42] Cioran echoes this sentiment: "Every metaphysic begins with an anguish of the body, which then becomes universal."[43] Any anatomy of pessimism would inevitably become a pessimism of anatomy, of how our bodies fail us, in which "the philosopher and the physician trade places."[44] There seems to be a certain point at which any philosophy will also inevitably slip into pessimism, especially if, as Nietzsche says, philosophy is just "merely an interpretation of the body and a *misunderstanding of the body*."[45] Pessimism seems to be the destiny of everybody and every body.

Any anatomy of pessimism, then, must begin with anatomy itself. This brings us back to the Renaissance, when the "inner body had a more potent novelty than that conferred by its universally secretive quality."[46] This is because anatomy up to that point had been outlawed as a morbid practice, performed only by criminal body-snatchers who would disinter corpses from the cemetery in the dead of night. Medicine relied on the medieval works of Galen, along with their commentaries, through the centuries. But as people began to lose faith in the stars, they turned to the body for meaning: "Increasingly, a once cosmically meaningful organism is spiritually hollowed and neutralized into an entity which talks only about itself, in the most limited mechanical sense."[47] Through anatomy, Renaissance doctors hoped to locate the physical organ of the eternal soul and thereby explain the mystery of mysteries.[48] For this reason, Henry VIII in 1540 gave these doctors—or, rather, barber-surgeons, whose tools allowed them to supplement their barbershop income with the occasional amputation—official permission for the first time to dissect the bodies of four criminals.[49]

But the more these anatomists tried to locate the organ of the soul, the more they were overcome with a particularly modern sense of anxiety: "Could the scalpel in fact pierce not only a living human body, but the ultimate, supposedly indestructible source of all human existence?"[50] Could dissection "indeed annihilate both body and soul"?[51] And, perhaps even more frightening: what if there is no such thing as a soul to begin with? Or what if it has nothing to do with the body? What if we are all just sacks of limbs sewn together, like puppets or like Frankenstein's Creature, only to be unsewn in order to expose the nothingness at the core of our existence?

Schelling gives the term *Unheimlich* ("uncanny") to "everything that ought to have remained . . . hidden and secret and has become visible," a definition used by Freud at the beginning of his essay on "The Uncanny."[52] Anatomy is then the operation of the uncanny—literally, the "un-home-like." Lukács, who defines the novel as the expression of transcendental homelessness, insists that "crime and madness are objectivations of transcendental homelessness—the homelessness of an action in the human order of social relations, the homelessness of a soul in the ideal order of a supra-personal system of values."[53]

Just a few decades before Henry VIII sanctioned the first legal use of anatomy, Ariosto illustrated the crime and madness that is constitutive of the Lukácsian homelessness of the soul in *Orlando Furioso*, the fantasy in which Orlando, mad with love for Angelica, destroys everything in his path from Europe to Africa in his lunacy. His wits had fled to the moon, and the English knight Astolfo rides his hippogriff there in order to bottle his wits up and return them to Orlando. With the advent of anatomy, and the turn away from the moon and the stars to locate our soul, maybe we're just doomed to destroy everything in our own paths, like Orlando, but without a cure. Thomas Browne said as much a century later, in *Urne-Buriall*: "In vain do individuals hope for Immortality, or any patent from oblivion, in preservations below the Moon."[54] And a century after that, one of the philosophers in Voltaire's story tells Micromegas, "They're doing enough to destroy themselves as it is," about what it's like to inhabit earth. "The fact is that after ten years there's never a hundredth of the wretches left, and even if they never draw a sword, starvation or exhaustion or intemperance carry most of them off."[55]

This self-destruction in pursuit of locating the soul is most vividly depicted in *Wuthering Heights*, in which Heathcliff's homelessness as a child seems to prefigure Catherine's Lukácsian expression of transcendental homelessness. When Nelly asks Catherine what the obstacle is in her engagement with Edgar—a shorthand for essentially asking her what the obstacle is in her life at large—Catherine breaks down. "*Here!* and *here!*" she replies, "striking one hand on her forehead, and the other on her breast. 'In whichever place the soul lives.'" She isn't sure where exactly the soul lives, but she is sure that, "Whatever our souls are made of, [Heathcliff's] and mine are the same."[56] The soul is an ambiguous space that eludes locating; it is "wuthering" in this sense, between the physical and the metaphysical. It is everywhere and nowhere, anchored in the body but also suffused in the atmosphere and the landscape, which is Catherine's substitute for a spiritual heaven, that other location of souls.

But even this landscape seems to function like a body itself, as when Lockwood describes the estate on Wuthering Heights as an "anatomy [that] lay bare to an inquiring eye."[57] And this "anatomy" also seems to invite other kinds of anatomy, as when Heathcliff, regarding young Cathy and Linton, tells Nelly, "Had I been born where laws are less strict, and tastes less dainty, I should treat myself to a slow vivisection of those two, as an evening's amusement."[58] Anatomy, it seems, is never far from criminality, monstrosity, and insanity. And the operation of anatomy just seems to extend beyond the text, in the same way that Catherine's writing gestures out of the texts of the books that she owns, so that, according to Ivan Kreilkamp, "the very experience of reading the novel becomes something like that 'slow vivisection' Heathcliff yearned to perform on his enemies."[59] In showing what ought to have remained hidden and secret, there is something monstrous about this kind of anatomy—from the Latin *monstrare*, to show.

It is in this context that we can read *Frankenstein* as a pessimistic novel about how anatomy can be exploited, in a quasi-criminal way, by Dr. Victor Frankenstein. In *Ruins of Empires*, one of the books that the Creature reads to educate himself about the people who so vehemently exclude him, Constantin François Volney writes,

> Like the world of which he is part, man is governed by *natural laws*, regular in their course, uniform in their effects, immutable in their essence; and those laws, the *common source of good and evil*, are not written among the stars, nor hidden in codes of mystery.[60]

These laws are not written among the stars, but inscribed in the body. Volney was one of the first modern theorists to advocate for self-love and happiness; Shelley demonstrates how this pursuit leads to narcissism. Shelley's vision of society is, needless to say, a bleak one: it is a choice between the Narcissus of Frankenstein or the Anti-Narcissus of the Creature who flees from the sight of his own image in a pool of water.[61] The narcissist in pursuit of happiness is eager to sniff out criminality as somehow legible in the body of someone else, like the anatomically constructed Creature, who is essentially criminalized and demonized for not being happy.

The criminal activity of anatomy then flips around to become a state-sanctioned dissection of the criminal to inspect if any traces of criminality can be located in one's physiognomy. Influenced by the circulation of *Lazarillo de Tormes* in 1554, the criminal biography emerged as a popular genre, which is also an anatomy of sorts in its attempt to dissect the criminal's behavioral traits. The novel, moreover, begins to be defined and attacked on the grounds of its own criminality, transgressions, and false claims to veracity at this time. It is no surprise, then, that the rise of anatomy, along with the circulation of *Lazarillo de Tormes* as a criminal biography, also coincides with the similar narrative of another rogue figure who likes to play pranks: Doctor Faustus, who appears first in an anonymous sixteenth-century German chapbook that spread like wildfire throughout Europe.

Like *Lazarillo*, it is a loosely structured, episodic narrative organized in chapters that apparently tell a "Historia" of this Doctor, "wherein is described specifically and veraciously" the course of his life and death, appealing to our sense of truth from the title page to the last page, which leaves us with a warning of his "quite veritable deeds."[62] Faust is educated as a theological doctor of philosophy, even though "soon he refused to be called a *Theologus*, but waxed a worldly man, called himself a *Doctor Medicinæ*," turning his attention away from the heavens to the body.[63] The pact he signs with the forces of hell is written in his own blood, reflecting the belief in the body's inherent legibility and serving as a parody of Christ's material embodiment of the Word. It is through this somatic pact that he is able to access all the knowledge of the world—except, of course, the nature of the soul, which he has arguably forsaken through the act of anatomy itself.

Anatomy runs through this chapbook as a thread of the grotesque, like when Faustus cuts off his leg knowing that he could magically make it reappear, or when he comes across four sorcerers who chop off each other's heads to send them to the barber for trimming before getting the heads reattached to their bodies.[64] We never end up seeing the damnation of his soul in hell, but what we do see is a graphic account of how he is punished on the level of the body: "The parlor was full of blood. Brain clave unto the walls where the Fiend had dashed him from one to the other. Here lay his eyes, here a few teeth."[65] His students find his body parts "in many places," and when "they came out to the dung heap, here they found his corpse. It was monstrous to behold, for head and limbs were still twitching."[66] The more that the literal anatomy coincides with monstrosity, the more distance the narrator places between their own views and what is being narrated, playing the politically and theologically dangerous game of admonishing Faustus's actions while exploring, in great detail, just how much he undermined religious and secular authority. Anatomy is the genre that articulates as much as it disarticulates.

In 1543, the Flemish anatomist Andreas Vesalius published the *De Humani Corporis Fabrica*, which gave us a newer and more accurate depiction of the body, marking a sharp break from all medieval medical texts that had preceded it, and the novel began to explore the body in the same way.[67] Judith Folkenberg writes that "the new vision of man and woman enshrined in Vesalius" is analogous to "the new vision of the place of the earth in the universe that was slowly gaining adherents."[68] Two years later, Thomas Germinus issued pirated copies of Vesalius's work, publishing it in English in 1553 and again in 1559.[69]

In the decades that followed, the word "anatomy" emerged as a distinctly rhetorical, if not literary, genre. Between 1576 and 1650, over 120 literary texts were published with the word "anatomy" included in their titles, including the famous *Anatomy of Wit* by John Lyly in 1578 and *Anatomy of Melancholy* by Robert Burton in 1621.[70] The word "section," too—from the Latin *sectio*: to cut off or cut up—appeared for the first time in 1559 as "unequivocally dissective, deriving from Germinus's Vesalian epitome: 'neither in man only . . . but in the anatomy or section of any other beast.'"[71] By 1576, it was being used as a metaphor for a "subdivision of a written or printed work," according to the *Oxford English Dictionary*.[72] Whatever meaning these words came to acquire, they are all rooted in the principle of discovering hidden truths about ourselves.

For this reason, perhaps, Stendhal writes in *Love*—a work composed of nothing but digressive sections—that, "One must have the courage to engage in a little anatomy in order to discover an unknown principle."[73] In this vein, Barthes even finds something erotic about literary anatomy, reflecting on the act of writing itself as a kind of "cutting":

> Two edges are created: an obedient, conformist, plagiarizing edge (the language is to be copied in its canonical state, as it has been established by schooling, good usage, literature, culture), and *another edge,* mobile, blank (ready to assume any contours), which is never anything but the site of its effect: the place where the death of language is glimpsed. . . . Neither culture nor its destruction is erotic; it is the seam between them, the fault, the flaw, which becomes so.[74]

Barthes here is writing in reference to Sade, to a particular kind of writing that cuts, that dissects, in order to explore, to surprise, to engage, and to hold and prolong tension. But Sade is by far not the first novelist to write like this. The literary technique of the "section" also has its precedents in strategies of suspense from the medieval and ancient Greek novel, such as Heliodorus's *Aethiopica* from the third century. The opening scene of the remnants of a massacre leaves the reader hanging in suspense until four chapters later.[75] The fragmentation and sectioning off of narrative, developing through the Middle Ages in interwoven techniques of interrupted storytelling, piques interest and curiosity, and extends that curiosity by delaying it.

Mazzoni traces this technique from *Aethiopica* to *Orlando Furioso*, finding that this delay—longer than those found in epic, for instance, in the flashback episode of Odysseus's scar that Auerbach focuses on—"assumes a reader more than a listener."[76] In short, it becomes an elastic organizing principle of the novel and can be manipulated with great effect in works that vary in length and scope. Jacques Amyot published his French translation of *Aethiopica* in 1547, which in turn ushered "the age of the individual reader, the individual purchaser of discrete fictions," and ultimately shaped the Baroque novel in the latter half of the sixteenth century.[77]

But this technique continues to shape the novel long after the latter half of the sixteenth century. To Kundera, the genius of Sterne's novels "lies not in the action but in the *interruption* of the action."[78] This technique places Sterne "on the other side of Leibniz's statement" of "*Nihil est sine ratione—* that there is nothing without its reason," which prompts science to explore "the *why* of everything, such that whatever exists seems explainable, thus predictable, calculable."[79] The novel, in Sterne's hands, resists predictability and calculability. It is the opposite of Leibniz's optimistic faith in explaining away every phenomenon by reason. This is what Emma Bovary, that lover of novels, loves about novels—and what she wishes she could translate into her own life. "I always find disruption interesting," she says, "I like a change of scene."[80]

THE ANATOMY OF THE NOVEL

Madame Bovary, the quintessential novel that exemplifies the operations of pessimism in eros, can be read as an anatomy of a failed anatomist, Charles Bovary, who owns six shelves of the *Dictionary of Medical Science*, but the pages are uncut.[81] In one of the traditions of pessimistic writing, Flaubert organizes his novel around the foot and how it becomes the site of Emma's disappointment. After the novel opens with the humiliating "*Ridiculus sum*" episode, Charles, now an adult, receives an urgent letter begging him immediately to set a broken leg.[82] Luckily for Charles, it's an easy procedure that doesn't require too much work or skill on his part to fix.

The man whose leg Charles sets is M. Rouault, and Charles ends up marrying his daughter Emma, who is never really in love with him and just grows to resent him with every passing day for not giving her the Parisian life she is desperate to have. When he reads an article about a new medical procedure to treat clubfeet, Emma pushes him to purchase the new apparatus so that he can perform the operation on their neighbor Hippolyte. At this prospect, Charles "saw his reputation growing, his prosperity increasing, his wife loving him forever; and she was happy to find herself reinvigorated by a new sentiment, a healthier, better one, a feeling of some affection for this poor man who cherished her so."[83] Charles performs the operation, and it seems to go well until a "black liquid" begins seeping from the leg. Another doctor, M. Canivet de Neufchatel, comes to fix Charles's mistake, complaining that, "These are inventions originating in Paris!"[84] Hippolyte's leg ends up getting amputated as a result of Charles's botched operation, and Charles, distancing himself from any responsibility, claims that, "Fate had had a hand in it."[85]

"Fate" becomes the empty and cruel signifier of stupidity and ridiculousness in Flaubert. No longer are we in the realm of tragedy, where fate is a monolithic force of absolute necessity. In the novel, the appeal to fate is a cop-out. This pessimistic novel is an anatomy of the history of literature that had led to this work. As a parody of tragedy, it deflates any tragic gravitas so that the false promise of happiness is inscribed in the name of Yonville's sleazy merchant Lheureux, the space of the dramatic caesura is instead ironically filled with the empty prattling of Homais (*Ô mais,* "oh but"), Teiresias is reincarnated as "The Blind Man" who howls like a dog and fills Emma with disgust, and Hippolyte—who was mythically dismembered as a result of Phèdre's ominous silence in Racine's tragedy—now just has a leg amputated as a result of Emma goading Charles on in the medical procedure. And his operation haunts her even to the moment of her death, when "a stream of black liquid," like the same black liquid from his gangrenous leg, "ran out of her mouth like a vomit."[86]

As Emma becomes increasingly irritated with her husband, even her affairs become sources of disappointment, Rodolphe flaking out on her by writing, "Is it my fault? Oh, Lord, no! Fate is to blame, only fate!"[87] This same phrase recurs after Emma's death, when Charles actually runs into him—and, knowing about their affair, tells Rodolphe that he doesn't blame him, even adding "a grand phrase, the only one he had ever spoken: 'Fate is to blame!' Rodolphe, who had determined the course of that fate, found him very good-natured for a man in his situation, comical even, and rather low."[88] Charles dies that same day, in the banal horror of ordinariness rather than in the grandeur of tragedy, without being shown any respect or dignity from anyone around him, judged by others as comical, as rather low, as ridiculous.

As for Emma, before her death, she finds herself stuck in a novel called *Madame Bovary,* and is forced to play a part that is not hers but is a type that she must end up fulfilling, as if pulled along by the marionette strings of the novel. The first Madame Bovary the novel introduces is not her, but Charles Bovary's mother, who was fond of stories and was "full of melancholy" and "beguiling chatter," who puts into his head "all her sparse, shattered illusions" from "the isolation of her life."[89] The second Madame Bovary we are introduced to is Charles's first wife, a jealous woman named Heloïse, who runs up several debts and dies after spitting blood.[90] Emma Rouault, our protagonist, now becomes the third Madame Bovary, but her story had already been played out before she could enter the scene. She is literally the *Nouvelle Heloïse,* and when she meets Rodolphe, he tells her, "Madame Bovary! . . .

Oh, everyone calls you that. . . . It's not your name, anyway; it belongs to someone else."[91]

Emma is just as much written by the narrator as she is by the stories of women she reads about in romances and histories. René Girard argues that she "desires through the romantic heroines who fill her imagination," which "triangulates" the role of desire in the novel.[92] When she attends a performance of *Lucie de Lammermoor*, "Lucie's voice seemed the echo of Emma's own consciousness, and the illusion that so charmed her, something from her own life."[93] But what is, as Heidegger might say, her "own" life? It is a series of fictions that she uses against the fictions that have typecast her. Growing up, when "she went to confession, she would invent little sins in order to stay there longer. . . . The metaphors of betrothed, spouse, heavenly lover, and marriage everlasting that recur in sermons stirred unexpectedly sweet sensations in the depths of her soul."[94] She would also write, herself, against the writing that inscribes her in this story of her life that she rejects:

> But as she wrote, she saw a different man, a phantom created out of her most ardent memories, the most beautiful things she had read, her strongest desires; and in the end he became so real, and so accessible, that she would tremble, marveling, and yet be unable to imagine him clearly, so lost was he, like a god, under the abundance of his attributes.[95]

Eventually, she succumbs to what Heidegger calls *das Man*, the world of others, determined by others. Even her death is not her own, as it is for Dasein; it is an imitation of the previous Madame Bovary's death, with the same kind of black liquid from Hippolyte's clubfoot, and maybe even from the ink of Flaubert's own pen that confines her to an existence that is never actually hers. She is dead before she can live, a corpse stalked by insects, like the flies that walk up the used glasses in her first solo encounter with Charles, which later multiply into a "swarm of flies" that buzz in front of her on her first solo walk with Léon, a walk that ends along the water's edge, where "thin-legged insect[s]" climb on water lilies.[96] The novel ends, after her death, with the sound of beetles "buzz[ing] around the lilies in flower," as though this presence of insects is all that remains of our tumultuous struggles, of our puppet-like existence.[97]

Anatomy interrogates the limits of our autonomy, constrained as we are by the bodies we are trapped inside of, with organs that operate independently of us and with competing wills and drives that undermine any fiction of selfhood as something singular and stable. Anatomy is a way of asking that same question from philosophy: Who are we? And in some ways, the answer is no different from the one we get in *Symposium*. We are fragmentary creatures drawn to fictions of wholeness out of a sense of loss, which expresses itself as eros. Always already anatomized, born from an original bisection, we paradoxically perform many more dissections on our bodies and our minds in order to find meaning in our lives. It is no wonder, then, that Freud, the most famous anatomist of the psyche, is also one of the greatest philosophers of eros. And, as he famously said, in the hierarchy of the different fragments that compose us, "the ego is not the master in his own house."[98] Whoever this "we" that we identify as is an entity that is constantly being interrupted, thwarted, and sabotaged by forces that also act in our name.

The novel, then, charts a parallel history to the medical development of our understanding of anatomy, replicating that principle of dissection and interruption from the original barber-surgeons of the sixteenth century through the development of psychoanalysis and the X-ray. In *The Magic Mountain*, Hans Castorp marvels at the sight of his own hand under an X-ray, which Director Behrens refers to as "Illuminated anatomy, the triumph of the age."[99] The novel as a genre functions as a process of what Dr. Krokowski in *The Magic Mountain* calls "psychic dissection," illuminating the inner activity of the mind.[100] It is a process foreshadowed even by one of the earliest novels, *The Golden Ass*, where Psyche is not shot by Cupid's arrow but rather incurs a minor incision from the blade without his knowledge. This cut is still deep enough to fill her with enough erotic desire to see what is otherwise unseen. And what she ends up seeing in Cupid is a vision of eros itself—the substance of her own soul, which is why eros and psyche are ultimately wedded.

All of *In Search of Lost Time* can also be called a "psychic dissection," or what Nussbaum refers to as a "scientific project of self-analysis."[101] And Proust treats "analysis" in the way this word was used in the Renaissance, so that there isn't so much of a cohesive self that can be called "Marcel" or "The Narrator," or even any other character for that matter, but rather a multiplicity of selves that, subject to the trained gaze, are constantly in the process of dissection, of splitting apart. In *Time Regained*, Marcel thinks of himself as a

> surgeon who beneath the smooth surface of a woman's belly sees the internal disease which is devouring it. If I went to a dinner-party I did not see the guests: when I thought I was looking at them, I was in fact examining them with X-rays.[102]

This ultimately drives what Beckett calls Marcel's "Röntgen rays of jealousy," referring to Wilhelm Röntgen, the inventor of the X-ray.[103] Suspecting that Albertine was Mlle. Vinteuil's lover whom he had seen through the window in *Swann's Way*, Marcel says that he "would have wished not to tear off her dress in order to see her body but through her body to see and read that notebook of her memories and her future, passionate engagements."[104]

While Marcel tries to fix his X-ray gaze on what he can see through this window, Hans Castorp describes his own X-ray as a "magic window" to see what he otherwise could not see, eliciting the same wonder about the inner secrets of the human body and the human soul as crude anatomy did in the Renaissance.[105] This is perhaps why Mann also chooses an engraving of Rembrandt's *The Anatomy Lesson* as one of the decorative background items in the room where the patients conduct séances, conflating science and superstition in an attempt to reveal hidden truths about the soul.[106]

Joyce also brings up this Renaissance question in light of the modern invention of the X-ray in his novel that seems to be composed of nothing but digressions and dissections. Toward the end of his long day's journey into night, Bloom asks Stephen whether he believes in the soul. "I believe in that myself," Bloom says, "because it has been explained by competent men as the convolutions of the grey matter. Otherwise we would never have such inventions as X-rays, for instance. Do you?"[107] Woolf seems to respond to this question, but more along the lines of Mann than Joyce, invoking the X-ray as a Mann-like "magic window," but just metaphorically. In *To the Lighthouse*, Lily Briscoe's "X-ray vision" resolves the aesthetic problem that is described anatomically—of uniting two fragmented, or dissected, spaces of a canvas, consisting of "lines cutting across, slicing down."[108] Mrs. Ramsay's window can also be said to be "magic" when she looks out and sees the lighthouse, which "seemed to her like her own eyes meeting her own eyes."[109]

These magic windows, to both Mann and Woolf, seem to connect characters not just to themselves but to each other. In *Mrs. Dalloway*, Clarissa walks to the window at her party after hearing about Septimus Smith's suicide. He had thrown himself out of his window to his death, but his ghost seems to have fallen through her window instead, making her think to herself, "Death was an attempt to communicate, people feeling the impossibility of reaching the center which, mystically, evaded them; closeness drew apart; rapture faded; one was alone. There was an embrace in death."[110] This "center" is exactly where Lily ends up resolving her aesthetic problem in *To the Lighthouse*, using her art also as a way of embracing Mrs. Ramsay in her death.

As Lily concentrates her X-ray vision on the center of the painting, Woolf reiterates the anatomical image of slicing in her struggle to "achieve the razor edge of balance between the two opposite forces; Mrs. Ramsay and the picture."[111] It is as though Lily wields the paintbrush like a scalpel, slicing through the fragile connective tissue that holds the world together—not in order to cut it apart, but to render the invisible visible, to show precisely what these connections are. Each of Woolf's characters seems to move through life with a scalpel of their own, as though they were reflecting her own narrative technique of dissecting the world, in all of its interruptions, in order to suture the fragments back together in unexpected ways.

For instance, Clarissa Dalloway—like Woolf's narrator—"sliced like a knife through everything; at the same time was outside, looking on."[112] She likes "cutting people up" in order to re-create them according to her imagination.[113] When she remembers her "moment of happiness" with Sally Seton decades earlier, she recalls too how it was interrupted by Peter Walsh.[114] It is no surprise, then, that he is constantly fidgeting with his pocket-knife. As though defending herself against the threat of this pocket-knife, and perhaps even against the idea of Peter as an interruption in her own life, Clarissa takes up a pair of scissors when he first sees her in the novel. This is also the one image that paradoxically connects rather than cuts her off from the other characters she doesn't even meet, like Rezia Smith, who puts down her scissors in the moments before her husband Septimus cuts short his own life.[115]

And outside of these characters, but slicing through them, is time itself, as in the image of the Harley Street clocks "shredding and slicing, dividing and subdividing" the day, cutting into the lives of everyone trapped in the "leaden circles" that expand centripetally from Big Ben, with a seemingly infinite reach.[116] To Septimus, time shreds and slices until even the "word 'time' split its husk."[117] All that seems to remain of it are the leaden circles, which, in his mind, may be the same eternal circles from Dante's *Inferno*, which he had been currently reading.[118] This may explain why one of his final, fragmented thoughts is, "do not cut down trees."[119] He is fixated on the idea of trees being alive, perhaps less in the way that Marcel does in response to the Hudimesnil trees, and more in the way that Dante describes the souls of suicides as being forever trapped in trees. In this way, the "leaden circles" of time that connect Septimus with everyone else in London—and indeed everyone at all, both living and dead—are the same circles of hell that trap him in isolation, in despair.

Mann uses the same cutting imagery to describe time in *The Magic Mountain*, as well. When Hans Castorp gets lost in the snowstorm, the cold air that "cut through like a knife," accompanied by a wind that "swung its scythe at him," seems also to cut through time itself, presenting the hallucinatory visions that not only blur the present moment with moments in his recent and distant past, but between temporality and eternity, as well.[120] The German word for "scythe" is embedded in the name of Pribislav Hippe, his childhood crush who had lent him a sharpened pencil that he then, years later, "returns" to Hippe's reincarnation in Clavdia Chauchat.[121] It is through this contemplation of time as something that slices in order to connect that Hans Castorp looks into the eternal "nature of man," coming to the realization that "our interest in death and illness is nothing but a way of expressing an interest in life."[122]

Septimus, also contemplating time as a force that cuts through us, arrives at the opposite conclusion, but in equally grand and absolute terms. He claims that he "knew everything. He knew the meaning of the world."[123] And that meaning is just as empty as the Cenotaph that the soldiers pass by in front of him. The "world itself is without meaning," he thinks to himself, seeing this meaninglessness as the greatest insight passed down to us, from Aeschylus to Dante to Shakespeare.[124] This is what anatomy ultimately reveals. Both time and the anatomist slice through the human body and discover that there is no inherent or transcendent meaning to life. The only meaning in life is fabricated, provided through art—a consolation offered by Nietzsche, but also by Lily Briscoe in her painting, and even, by extension, Proust, Woolf, Mann, and arguably every artist.

Life is a series of interruptions that delay this revelation, as it does for James Ramsay, who is first seen in *To the Lighthouse* "sitting on the floor, cutting out pictures" with his scissors, before the "arid scimitar of his father," who, irritably averse to interruption himself, intrudes on the moment James is sharing with his mother, as an "interruption."[125] At dinner that evening, William Bankes is annoyed at all the interruptions at the table, and Mrs. Ramsay feels "cut off from them all," a feeling echoed by Lily Briscoe, who is "cut off from other people."[126] The entire novel is a sequence of interruptions that delay James from going to the lighthouse. Once he arrives as an adult, having lost his mother, that former childhood excitement gives way to an anti-climactic arrival: "they ought to be so happy, but as a matter of fact James thought, looking at the Lighthouse stood there on its rock, it's like that."[127] As he approaches it, something

> he remembered, stayed and darkened over him; would not move; something flourished up in the air, something arid and sharp descended even there, like a blade, a scimitar, smiting through the leaves and flowers even of that happy world and making them shrivel and fall.[128]

The darkness eventually lifts somewhat, and he "rose and stood in the bow of the boat, very straight and tall, for all the world, James thought, as if he were saying, 'There is no God.'"[129]

It is anatomy itself that leads to this conclusion, secularizing the soul into something that no longer has any correspondence to God, operating in a body that obeys its own laws. The inquiry into these laws increasingly replaces faith, the acceptance of a whole narrative passed down from a distance, with the up-close examination of this narrative, its secular dissection into minutiae, into the fragment, the detail—trademarks of the novel itself.

There are traces of this principle in George Eliot, too, which is perhaps why Northrop Frye categorizes *Middlemarch* as an "anatomy," marking a break from her early fiction, which he designates as "romance."[130] And in this anatomy, we meet a literal anatomist, Dr. Lydgate, whose profession mirrors the operation of the narrator, as he wanted to pierce the obscurity of those minute processes which prepare human misery and joy, those invisible thoroughfares which are the first lurking-places of anguish, mania, and crime, that delicate poise and transition which determine the growth of happy or unhappy consciousness.[131]

In this sense, his project is not much different from Casaubon's in the *Key to all Mythologies*; both endeavors end in failure.

As Lydgate's ambitions begin to deflate under the oppressive provincialism of Middlemarch, he is increasingly and anxiously preoccupied with the thought of Vesalius, the famous doctor "who was about as old as I am three hundred years ago, and had already begun a new era in anatomy."[132] He tells his wife Rosamond about how Vesalius had to criminally "snatch bodies at night, from graveyards and places of execution," and how he had faced fierce opposition from conservative doctors who still abided by Galen, like the "medical fogies in Middlemarch" who object to Lydgate's own pursuit of the latest advances in modern medicine.[133] Nevertheless, "the facts of the human frame were on his side; and so he got the better of them."[134]

Except he didn't quite get the better of them, after all. Vesalius was forced "to burn a good deal of his work. Then he got shipwrecked just as he was coming from Jerusalem to take a great chair at Padua. He died rather miserably."[135] Lydgate's own death is not as dramatic but is just as pessimistic, after living a rather unremarkable life—significantly less remarkable than Vesalius's. The narrator tells us, "We are on a perilous margin when we begin to look passively at our future selves, and see our own figures led with dull consent into insipid misdoing and shabby achievement. Poor Lydgate was inwardly groaning on that margin," until he eventually dies at fifty, having "always regarded himself as a failure: he had not done what he once meant to do."[136] And perhaps even more depressing is that, to all appearances, he "was what was called a successful man."[137]

Eliot's narrator ends *Middlemarch* with a direct appeal to the reader, writing,

> the growing good of the world is partly dependent on unhistoric acts; and that things are not so ill with you and me as they might have been, is half owing to the number who lived faithfully a hidden life, and rest in unvisited tombs.[138]

The role of the novel—not just of *Middlemarch*, but of the novel at large—is precisely to scope out this "hidden life" that belongs to the prosaic world of "unhistoric acts," a life so hidden that it cannot possibly be staged in the theater or condensed in a poem, but can only come to light in the novel. And the novelist, by visiting these unvisited tombs and disinterring and dissecting the vestiges of all that remains of this hidden life, is just as much of an anatomist as Lydgate wishes he could be.[139]

It bears mentioning that the anatomy of the sixteenth and seventeenth centuries did not just follow one historical trajectory that culminated in the somewhat pessimistic explorations of the nineteenth- and twentieth-century novel. It also inspired a new form of optimism that took off with Francis Bacon who, in 1620, wrote the *New Organon*, a "new" philosophy for a new era, outlining the sciences according to new anatomical divisions, new organs. This was a philosophy that he presented as "a very diligent dissection and anatomy of the world," aimed at "the removing of despair and the raising of hope through the dismissal or rectification of the errors of past time."[140] His optimistic method of "true induction" involved "reject[ing] all forms of fiction and imposture."[141] The Ptolemaic system itself was a fiction that demanded a gullibility beyond what could be proven by empirical induction. Better to stay closer to our body than our imaginations—especially now that we are beginning to have a better anatomical understanding of the body—and trust the senses that are our only bonds to the world outside of us.

"There remains but one course for the recovery of a sound and healthy condition," Bacon writes, "namely, that the entire work of the understanding be commenced afresh, and the mind itself be from the very outset not left to take its own course, but guided at every step; and the business be done as if by machinery."[142] This "business" of viewing the "understanding" as operating by "machinery"—as part of the larger optimistic project of "the removing of despair and the raising of hope"—lays the groundwork for Jeremy Bentham, a century and a half later, to outline his mechanistic vision of modern happiness and optimism that has become the dominant neoliberal ideology of Western discourse today. In following Bacon's legacy, Bentham was so firmly on the side of science and machinery that he hoped it would obviate the need for language altogether. He therefore rejected the role of the novel in shaping our understanding of the world and of ourselves.

The irony, though, is that contemporary critics like Henry Stubbe of the Royal Society taunted Bacon and his followers of "new" philosophers by calling them "*Novellists.*"[143] The novel, for all its popularity, has never been widely accepted as laying an equal claim to truth as the sciences. As such, Stubbe dismissed Bacon's aspirational philosophy as novelistic. Anatomy itself then splits into two directions. The first follows the direction of the sciences—verifiable, replicable, and respectable. The second follows the direction of the novel—a pejorative term used to question the veracity it lays claims to.

Frye attempts to bridge the two directions in his aptly titled *Anatomy of Criticism*. He takes Bacon's inductive method to say that "the first thing the literary critic has to do is to read literature, to make an inductive survey of his own field and let his critical principles shape themselves solely out of his knowledge of that field."[144] He goes on to say that the "word 'inductive' suggests some sort of scientific procedure. What if criticism is a science as well as an art? Not a 'pure' or 'exact' science, of course, but these phrases belong to a nineteenth-century cosmology which is no longer with us."[145] It is in this sense that Aristotle, who wrote the first work of literary criticism with *Poetics*, can be seen as just as much of a biologist as a literary critic in this work, approaching "a system of organisms, picking out its genera and species, formulating the broad laws of literary experience."[146]

Frye begins *Anatomy of Criticism* with the dubious category of the novel, noting that the

> Greeks hardly needed to develop a classification of prose forms. We do, but have never done so. We have, as usual, no word for a work of prose fiction, so the word "novel" does duty for everything, and thereby loses its only real meaning as the name of a genre.[147]

His analysis of prose ultimately ends with a look at Burton's *Anatomy of Melancholy*, which has been singled out for centuries as the prime example of the anatomy genre, that genre of failure and impossibility—sprawling, intimidating, almost never-ending, an impossible project that cannot be finished, gesturing to the infinite, like a Borges nightmare of a book, or Casaubon's attempt at a *Key to all Mythologies*, or Settembrini's contributions to *The Sociology of Suffering*. But Frye calls this work "the greatest Menippean satire in English before Swift" for its "creative treatment of exhaustive erudition."[148] In Burton's *Anatomy*, a "symposium of books replaces dialogue, and the result is the most comprehensive survey of human life in one book that English literature had seen since Chaucer, one of Burton's favorite authors."[149]

If we read the *Anatomy of Melancholy* as essentially melancholic, then we miss out on its fundamental irony, which it shares with the novel, itself rooted in the polyvocal symposium, full of laughter and delight. Burton even called himself "Democritus Junior" because he was a "philosopher who laughed at mankind."[150] The definition Frye offers for an anatomy, one that would include both Burton's and his own, is a

> form of prose fiction, traditionally known as the Menippean or Varronian satire and . . . characterized by a great variety of subject-matter and a strong interest in ideas. In shorter forms it often has a *cena* or symposium setting and verse interludes.[151]

As if engaging Schlegel's hope for a theory of the novel to itself be a novel, Frye's archetypal criticism gives us an anatomy about an anatomy. He furthermore defines the symposium, that kernel of literary anatomy, as the extreme limit of social comedy . . . the structure of which is, as we should expect, clearest in Plato, whose Socrates is both teacher and lover, and whose vision moves toward an integration of society in a form like that of the symposium itself, the dialectic festivity which, as is explained in the opening of the *Laws*, is the controlling force that holds society together.[152]

In the absence of God or the gods, the symposium, with its emphasis on nourishment in food, wine, and ideas, is "the controlling force that holds society together."

Kristeva, in response to Bakhtin, arrives at the same conclusion as Frye, seeing the "laughter of the carnival" as "no more comic than tragic," but something that gives rise to a new form: "Situated within the carnivalesque tradition, and constituting the yeast of the European novel, these two genres are *Socratic dialogue* and *Menippean discourse*."[153] Kristeva also points out that the genre of Menippean satire actually pre-dated Menippus of Gadara and was most likely the creation of Antisthenes, a student of Socrates, and someone who had also written Socratic dialogues.[154] And, in a Lukácsian moment, Kristeva writes, "Only modernity—when freed of 'God'—releases the Menippean force of the novel."[155] So here we have a direct lineage from the Socratic dialogue to the Menippean satire, down through anatomy and the novel, linking the genres of Boethius, Burton, and even the modernists back to Socrates.

In this way, it is possible to interpret the symposium or the literal *cena* as a "controlling force" in novels that are not just restricted to "shorter forms." In *Lost Illusions*, the *cena* is even inscribed in the "Cénacle," the name given to the group of writers who meet over supper, representing the only bulwark against the cynical destruction of art.[156] In *The Magic Mountain*, this group is tenuously held among the patients themselves, and in the intellectual balance of power between Settembrini and Naphta, before everything collapses.

And Woolf sketches her own symposium or *cena* in *To the Lighthouse*, especially in the dinner scene that begins in a state of disarray, of interruption and fragmentation, with characters feeling remote from each other. William Bankes pessimistically thinks to himself, "What does one live for? Why, one asked oneself, does one take all the pains for the human race to go on? Is it so very desirable? Are we attractive as a species? Not so very, he thought."[157] But something happens over the course of the meal, as Mrs. Ramsay helps Bankes to another serving of meat, and this something rises up "like a flag [which] floated in an element of joy," or "like a fume rising upwards, holding them safe together."[158] This feeling "partook . . . of eternity," of a "coherence in things, a stability," reflecting the "controlling force" that Frye reads in Plato as "hold[ing] society together."[159]

PROUST'S BROOD

Woolf was working on *To the Lighthouse* under the influence of Proust, that Democritus Junior of the twentieth century. More than just the "philosopher who laughed at mankind," the original Democritus was the philosopher who had first theorized the concept of the atom, and thought of all matter as being essentially composed of minute fragments. Proust, in his endless dissections, atomizes and anatomizes the world so thoroughly, in such minute detail, that, however intimidating he is for readers, he is more so for writers. After finishing *In Search of Lost Time*, the novelist Robert Halloran wrote to a friend about his anxiety: "I don't know what to say—the idea that Joyce ended the novel is so absurd; it's Proust who ended the novel, simply by doing something so complete, so monumental, perfect, that what the fuck can you do afterwards?"[160]

Woolf felt the same thing, if not in so many words. When she started reading him, she told her friend Roger Fry that

> Proust so titillates my own desire for expression that I can hardly set out the sentence. "Oh, if I could write like that!" I cry. And at the moment such is the astonishing vibration and saturation that he procures—there's something sexual in it—that I feel I *can* write like that, and seize my pen, and then I *can't* write like that.[161]

In Woolf's reading and writing process, there is a tension between eros and pessimism that eventually gets grafted onto *To the Lighthouse*, itself about an artist trying to find her own vision. She later told Fry,

> My great adventure is really Proust. Well—what remains to be written after that? . . . How, at last, has someone solidified what has always escaped—and made it too into this beautiful and perfectly enduring substance? One has to put the book down and gasp.[162]

She felt crushed under the weight of this "beautiful and perfectly enduring substance," though. Even after finishing *To the Lighthouse*, she wrote in a diary entry from 1928, "Take up Proust after dinner & put him down. This is the worst time of all. It makes me suicidal. Nothing seems left to do. All seems insipid & worthless."[163] And a year later, a diary entry reads: "I will go upstairs & read Proust I think, since I am fabricating a few remarks on him for that cursed book—that stone that plunges me deeper & deeper in the water."[164]

D. H. Lawrence's reaction was the exact opposite. In order to write after Proust and find something new to say, his answer was to reject Proust completely. But he did so in a way that self-consciously named Proust as the interlocutor, if not the outright enemy, of his art, and he transcribes that imaginary argument in *Lady Chatterley's Lover*, when Connie picks a fight with her sexless husband Clifford:

> "Have you ever read Proust?" he asked her.
> "I've tried—but he bores me."
> "He's really very extraordinary."
> "Possibly! But he bores me: all that sophistication! He doesn't have feelings, he only has streams of words about feeling. I'm tired of self-important mentalities."
> "Would you prefer self-important animalities?"
> "Perhaps! But one might possibly get something that wasn't self-important."
> "Well, I like Proust's subtlety and his well-bred anarchy."
> "It makes you very dead, really."[165]

Under the surface of this argument is really the frustration that Connie isn't having any sex with him, which is also precisely what is lacking in Proust. All those thousands of pages about eros, and the only real glimpses of sex are distanced, voyeuristic, and analyzed as if they were academic subjects, case studies in a course on psychology.

In this fight with Clifford over Proust, Connie notes how, "He seemed to sit there like a skeleton, sending out a skeleton's cold grisly *will* against her. Almost she could feel the skeleton clutching her and pressing her to its cage of ribs."[166] This is the same dead skeleton of Proust that seems to press itself to Lawrence as he tries to break free from its grip. Proust dwells in death; the only thing to fight against that is life—which, to Lawrence, has to be deeply embodied in a way that is muscular, throbbing, heart-pounding. Instead of the neurotic abstractions and cold dissections of eros that preoccupy Marcel, Connie's lover Mellors believes in living life according to one principle, that of "fucking with a warm heart."[167]

Yet for all the obvious differences between Proust's and Lawrence's aesthetics, their works are deeply rooted in the tradition of medieval Romance. Jean-François Revel reads the *Recherche* "as a sort of *Tristan and Iseult*," and the same can be said of *Lady Chatterley's Lover*.[168] What Romance gets right about, well, romance—which is incompatible with the tradition of realism—is that eros is instantaneous. There is no explanation or justification for it. It just happens, and it demands the immediate religious fervor of a zealot. "We fall in love for a smile, a glance, a shoulder," Marcel says in *The Fugitive*.[169] Everything else is fiction, fabrication, and retroactive rationalization.

As much as lovers like Tristan and Isolde, or Romeo and Juliet, are dismissed for not "knowing" each other enough to know that they are in love, this kind of eros acknowledges a truth that has been eroded and de-fanged by centuries of artificial bourgeois courtship rituals that have been rehearsed so many times that we take them to be natural. But eros is a sudden attack. There is a fundamental stupidity to it in that it intoxicates us into a state of stupor, so seductive that even one's intelligence cannot help succumbing to it, bowing to it and acknowledging it as a deity, as indeed even Socrates does—but through narrative rather than philosophical analysis. This is why, in Gottfried von Strassburg's *Tristan*, the love potion is not as necessary as it is in Béroul's version—it's just an externalization of an eros that had already attacked the two lovers. In Romance, the attack of eros is a given, and the sorcery and strangeness of it doesn't have to be defended or explained in order for it to be accepted as true. The same is true even in Proust. His extensive analyses of eros are merely a postmortem of its many attacks, and he acknowledges that eros dwells in the void between the lover and the beloved, that it is contingent on the many fictions we fabricate about it and then pass off as "reality."

Of course, there is still something humorous about this kind of stupidity in love, as when Marcel blames caffeine for exacerbating the palpitations of his heart, and the "anguish" he feels as an adolescent when he contemplates breaking up with Gilberte, a prospect to him as impossible as staying with her, so that he likens the caffeine to "the potion that, long after they have absorbed it, continues to bind Tristan to Isolde."[170] There is a self-deprecating humor and irony in Proust that, along with a touch of levity, are non-existent in Lawrence (or at least in *Lady Chatterley's Lover*, his re-telling of the Tristan story), even though they are both working with the same material, but from different angles.

The other possible solution that can allow one to write after Proust is to resort to parody. This is the route Nabokov takes in *Lolita*, a book that can also be read as an encyclopedic symposium, an anatomy consisting of prior literary works that intersect with each other in order to create something new. Nabokov once referred to the *Recherche* as a fairy tale, and he's right. As rudimentary in plot as it is sophisticated in style, structure, and analytical insight, the entire *Recherche* can be summed up in one moment, when Swann, who senses that the young Marcel knows more about the humiliating lengths he had gone to with Odette before marrying her, out of shame lashes out, and, like a sorcerer, issues a curse:

> A prophetic warning that I had no sense to heed: "The danger of that kind of love . . . is that the woman's subjection calms the man's jealousy for a time but also makes it more exacting. After a little he will force his mistress to live like one of those prisoners whose cells they keep lighted day and night to prevent their escaping. And that generally ends in tragedy."[171]

Marcel, at this point, hadn't even seen Albertine yet, but over the next five volumes, he is ensorcelled by this curse, doomed to repeat the same suffering that Swann had endured, doomed to become this sorcerer himself, trapping his captive sleeping beauty until her disappearance and death, after which the spell is broken. In *Time Regained*, he is able to look back and reflect that "loving is like an evil spell in a fairy-story against which one is powerless until the enchantment has passed."[172]

Nabokov parodies this same fairy tale in *Lolita*, and even includes subtle nods to Proust, like the image of Dolores Haze evoking memories of young girls at the beach, which is how Marcel first encounters Albertine at Balbec. Dolores even makes an attempted escape from her captivity on a bicycle, which Albertine was also particularly fond of. Nabokov also treats the role of memory as a form of artistic creation, a kind of metamorphosis that allows different characters to seemingly morph into each other, like the dead Annabel Leigh, whom he imagines as reincarnated in Dolores, a girl he thinks of as a butterfly.

The butterfly motif is something that Woolf also picks up from Proust, as when she wrote in a diary entry from 1925 that

> the thing about Proust is his combination of the utmost sensibility with the utmost tenacity. He searches out these butterfly shades to the last grain. And he will I suppose both influence me & make me out of temper with every sentence of my own.[173]

And she returns to this motif in *To the Lighthouse* when Lily Briscoe tries solving the "problem of space" on her canvas in her attempt to create a work of art that is "feathery and evanescent, one color melting into another like the colors on a butterfly's wing," essentially translating Proust's aesthetic into painting, and then back into literature, in the frame of Woolf's own art.[174] It is as though the twentieth-century novel largely emerges out of the chrysalis of the *Recherche*, out of the imagination of Proust, cocooned in his hermetically sealed, cork-lined bedroom as he wrote, by night, to the pulse of rhythms less circadian than cicadian, enunciating that primordial cry of Plato's chorus of insects, that mythical prayer to eros and the Muses.

This brooding work in turn spawns a brood of other novels that all echo this same cry but in different notes, in different keys. Every novel bears traces of the entire history of the novel, exemplified most clearly in works like the *Recherche*, *Atonement*, *Madame Bovary*, *Wuthering Heights*, and *Don Quixote*. Proust is just the immediate pretext for considering the triptych of *To the Lighthouse*, *Lady Chatterley's Lover*, and *Lolita*, three novels that would otherwise be somewhat oddly aligned by virtue of their vastly different aesthetic styles. But taken together, the range in this triptych recapitulates the history of the novel in its movement from the Platonic dialogue to the medieval Romance to the fairy tale, in addition to the other genres that have contributed to the novel along the way, like the consolation, the lover's manual, the criminal biography, and the anatomy. These three novels can trace an immediate lineage to Proust, but they also go back further so that, using a kind of X-ray vision, *To the Lighthouse* can be read as an engagement with *Symposium, Lady Chatterley's Lover* as a re-telling of the Tristan legend, and *Lolita* as an answer to "The Little Mermaid."

This history is one that documents the pessimism of eros in the novel. In Nabokov's *Pale Fire*, John Shade imagines paradise as "talks / With Socrates and Proust in cypress walks," like the *platonos* trees that provided shade in *Phaedrus*.[175] The novel emerges between the long shadows of Socrates and Proust, in a paradise that, in *Lolita* (that other interplay of shadows), becomes one "whose skies were the color of hell-flames," emerging out of "the horrible hopelessness of it all."[176]

NOTES

1. Conrad, *Heart of Darkness*, 49.
2. Frye, *Anatomy of Criticism*, 58.
3. "Cynosure." Oxford English Dictionary Online, https://www.lexico.com/en/definition/cynosure.
4. James Joyce, *Ulysses* (New York: Vintage Books, 1990), 734.
5. Flaubert, *Madame Bovary*, 167.
6. Dante Alighieri, *The Divine Comedy: The Inferno, The Purgatorio, and The Paradiso*, trans. John Ciardi (New York: New American Library, 2003), *Inferno* XXXIV.143: 269.
7. Alighieri, *Purgatorio*, XXXIV.143: 577.
8. Alighieri, *Paradiso*, XXXIII.146: 894.
9. Boethius, *Consolation of Philosophy*, 58.
10. Shakespeare, *King Lear* (New York: Penguin Books, 1998), 3.4.58
11. Shakespeare, *Hamlet* (New York: Folger, 1992), 1.1.1.
12. Shakespeare, *King Lear,* 1.2.112–115.
13. Shakespeare, *Macbeth* (New York: Folger, 2013), 1.4.57-58; Shakespeare, *Hamlet,* 2.2.124.
14. Shakespeare, *Hamlet,* 1.5.22.
15. Shakespeare, *Romeo and Juliet*, 5.1.24.
16. Shakespeare, *Romeo and Juliet,* 2.2.19–20.
17. Shakespeare, *Romeo and Juliet,* 2.2.3.
18. Schopenhauer, *World as Will and Representation,* II: 500.
19. Cioran, *Short History of Decay,* 148–149.
20. Shakespeare, *Hamlet,* 3.2.300.
21. "Gospel of John," in *The Bible: Authorized King James Version,* ed. Robert Carroll and Stephen Prickett (Oxford: Oxford University Press, 2008), 1:1; Shakespeare, *Hamlet,* 2.2.210.
22. Schlegel, "Dialogue on Poetry," 108.

23. *"Words, words, words . . .* Hamlet must have been reading a novel," Cioran speculates (*Temptation to Exist,* 144).
24. Lukács, *Theory of the Novel*, 29.
25. Lukács, *Theory of the Novel*, 153.
26. Lukács, *Theory of the Novel*, 29.
27. Lukács, *Theory of the Novel*, 29.
28. Lukács, *Theory of the Novel*, 36.
29. Lukács, *Theory of the Novel*, 45.
30. Hardy, *Tess of the D'Urbervilles*, 167.
31. Hardy, *Tess of the D'Urbervilles*, 21.
32. Hardy, *Tess of the D'Urbervilles*, 21.
33. Hardy, *Tess of the D'Urbervilles*, 33.
34. Hardy, *Tess of the D'Urbervilles*, 21.
35. Hardy, *Tess of the D'Urbervilles*, 21.
36. Bakhtin, *Dialogic Imagination*, 367.
37. Bakhtin, *Dialogic Imagination*, 286.
38. Frye, *Anatomy of Criticism,* 304.
39. Mazzoni, *Theory of the Novel*, 265.
40. Kundera, *Art of the Novel*, 8.
41. Kundera, *Art of the Novel*, 9.
42. Unamuno, *Tragic Sense of Life*, 3.
43. Cioran, *Short History of Decay,* 154.
44. Thacker, *Infinite Resignation*, 44.
45. Nietzsche, *The Gay Science*, trans. Walter Kaufmann (New York: Vintage Books, 1974), 34–35.
46. Richard Sugg, *Murder After Death* (Ithaca, NY: Cornell University Press, 2007), 1.
47. Sugg, *Murder After Death,* 5.
48. Sugg, *Murder After Death,* 206.
49. Sugg, *Murder After Death,* 2.
50. Sugg, *Murder After Death,* 207.
51. Sugg, *Murder After Death,* 207.
52. Freud, "The Uncanny," 3–4, https://web.mit.edu/allanmc/www/freud1.pdf.
53. Lukács, *Theory of the Novel,* 61–62.
54. Thomas Browne, *Religio Medici and Urne-Buriall*, ed. Stephen Greenblatt and Ramie Targoff (New York: New York Review of Books, 2012), 136.
55. Voltaire, *Micromegas*, 118.
56. Brontë, *Wuthering Heights*, 62–63.
57. Brontë, *Wuthering Heights*, 4.
58. Brontë, *Wuthering Heights*, 204.
59. Ivan Kreilkamp, "Petted Things: Cruelty and Sympathy in the Brontës," in *Wuthering Heights,* ed. Alexandra Lewis (New York: W. W. Norton, 2019), 404.
60. Constantin François Volney, *A New Translation of Volney's Ruins; or Meditations on the Revolution of Empires*, trans. Robert D. Richardson, Jr. (New York: Garland, 1979), 42–43.

240   Chapter 8

61. Stefani Engelstein, *Anxious Anatomy: The Conception of the Human Form in Literary and Naturalist Discourse* (Albany, NY: State University of New York Press, 2008), 215.

62. *Historia and Tale of Doctor Johannes Faustus*, Ch. XLIV, http://lettersfromthedustbowl.com/fbk1.html.

63. *Historia and Tale of Doctor Johannes Faustus*, Ch. I.

64. *Historia and Tale of Doctor Johannes Faustus*, Ch. XXVI, Ch. XXI.

65. *Historia and Tale of Doctor Johannes Faustus*, Ch. XLIV.

66. *Historia and Tale of Doctor Johannes Faustus*, Ch. XLIV

67. Sugg, *Murder After Death*, 1.

68. Judith Folkenberg, Benjamin A. Rifkin, and Michael J. Ackerman, *Human Anatomy: A Visual History From the Renaissance to the Digital Age* (New York: Abrams, 2006), 95.

69. Sugg, *Murder After Death*, 2.

70. Sugg, *Murder After Death*, 3.

71. Sugg, *Murder After Death*, 3.

72. Sugg, *Murder After Death*, 3.

73. Stendhal, *Love*, 256.

74. Barthes, *Pleasure of the Text*, 6–7.

75. Mazzoni, *Theory of the Novel*, 143.

76. Mazzoni, *Theory of the Novel*, 144.

77. Qtd. in Mazzoni, *Theory of the Novel*, 143.

78. Kundera, *Art of the Novel*, 161.

79. Kundera, *Art of the Novel*, 161–162.

80. Flaubert, *Madame Bovary*, 70.

81. Flaubert, *Madame Bovary*, 28.

82. Flaubert, *Madame Bovary*, 11.

83. Flaubert, *Madame Bovary*, 155.

84. Flaubert, *Madame Bovary*, 159.

85. Flaubert, *Madame Bovary*, 161.

86. Flaubert, *Madame Bovary*, 293.

87. Flaubert, *Madame Bovary*, 177.

88. Flaubert, *Madame Bovary*, 310.

89. Flaubert, *Madame Bovary*, 7.

90. Flaubert, *Madame Bovary*, 17.

91. Flaubert, *Madame Bovary*, 136.

92. René Girard, *Deceit, Desire, and the Novel: Self and Other in Literary Structure*, trans. Yvonne Freccero (Baltimore, MD: Johns Hopkins University Press, 1961), 5.

93. Flaubert, *Madame Bovary*, 196.

94. Flaubert, *Madame Bovary*, 31.

95. Flaubert, *Madame Bovary*, 258.

96. Flaubert, *Madame Bovary*, 80, 82.

97. Flaubert, *Madame Bovary*, 310.

98. Freud, "A Difficulty in the Path of Psycho-Analysis," in *The Standard Edition of the Complete Psychological Works of Sigmund Freud*, Vol. XVIII, trans. and ed. James Strachey (London: Hogarth Press, 1955), 143.

99. Mann, *Magic Mountain*, 212.
100. Mann, *Magic Mountain*, 127.
101. Nussbaum, "Fictions of the Soul," 159.
102. Proust, *Time Regained*, 40.
103. Beckett, *Proust*, 41.
104. Proust, *The Captive*, 95.
105. Mann, *Magic Mountain*, 127; 216.
106. Mann, *Magic Mountain*, 662.
107. Joyce, *Ulysses*, 633.
108. Woolf, *To the Lighthouse*, ed. David Bradshaw (Oxford: Oxford University Press, 2006), 130.
109. Woolf, *To the Lighthouse*, 56.
110. Woolf, *Mrs. Dalloway*, ed. David Bradshaw (Oxford: Oxford University Press, 2000), 156.
111. Woolf, *To the Lighthouse*, 158.
112. Woolf, *Mrs. Dalloway*, 7.
113. Woolf, *Mrs. Dalloway*, 7.
114. Woolf, *Mrs. Dalloway*, 31.
115. Woolf, *Mrs. Dalloway*, 120.
116. Woolf, *Mrs. Dalloway*, 87, 4.
117. Woolf, *Mrs. Dalloway*, 59.
118. Woolf, *Mrs. Dalloway*, 75.
119. Woolf, *Mrs. Dalloway*, 125.
120. Mann, *Magic Mountain*, 473; 480.
121. Heller, *Thomas Mann: The Ironic German*, 201.
122. Mann, *Magic Mountain*, 483; 489.
123. Woolf, *Mrs. Dalloway*, 57.
124. Woolf, *Mrs. Dalloway*, 75.
125. Woolf, *To the Lighthouse*, 7; 34; 24.
126. Woolf, *To the Lighthouse*, 121.
127. Woolf, *To the Lighthouse*, 166.
128. Woolf, *To the Lighthouse*, 152.
129. Woolf, *To the Lighthouse*, 169.
130. Frye, *Anatomy of Criticism*, 312-3.
131. George Eliot, *Middlemarch* (New York: W. W. Norton, 2000), 106.
132. Eliot, *Middlemarch*, 283.
133. Eliot, *Middlemarch*, 284.
134. Eliot, *Middlemarch*, 284.
135. Eliot, *Middlemarch*, 284.
136. Eliot, *Middlemarch*, 483, 512.
137. Eliot, *Middlemarch*, 512.
138. Eliot, *Middlemarch*, 515.
139. Proust, who read George Eliot voraciously, came to the conclusion that "a book is a huge cemetery in which on the majority of the tombs the names are effaced and can no longer be read" (Proust, *Remembrance of Things Past*, trans. C. K. Scott Moncrieff and Terence Kilmartin [New York: Vintage Books, 1982], III: 940).

140. Bacon, "The New Organon," CXXIV: 113, CVIII: 100.
141. Bacon, "The New Organon," CXXII: 112.
142. Bacon, "The New Organon," 33.
143. Qtd. in McKeon, *Origins of the English Novel,* 71.
144. Frye, *Anatomy of Criticism,* 6–7.
145. Frye, *Anatomy of Criticism,* 7.
146. Frye, *Anatomy of Criticism,* 14.
147. Frye, *Anatomy of Criticism,* 13.
148. Frye, *Anatomy of Criticism,* 311.
149. Frye, *Anatomy of Criticism,* 311.
150. Frye, *Anatomy of Criticism,* 230. Bacon also admires Democritus for his anatomical approach to knowledge: "But to resolve nature into abstractions is less to our purpose than to dissect her into parts; as did the school of Democritus, which went further than the rest" (Bacon, "The New Organon," LI: 53).
151. Frye, *Anatomy of Criticism,* 365.
152. Frye, *Anatomy of Criticism,* 286.
153. Kristeva, *Desire in Language,* 80.
154. Kristeva, *Desire in Language,* 82.
155. Kristeva, *Desire in Language,* 85.
156. Balzac, *Lost Illusions,* 251.
157. Woolf, *To the Lighthouse,* 73.
158. Woolf, *To the Lighthouse,* 85.
159. Woolf, *To the Lighthouse,* 85; Frye, *Anatomy of Criticism,* 286.
160. Qtd. in White, *Marcel Proust,* 2.
161. Qtd. in de Botton, *How Proust Can Change Your Life,* 203.
162. Qtd. in de Botton, *How Proust Can Change Your Life,* 203.
163. Woolf, *Diary III,* 186.
164. Woolf, *Diary III,* 226.
165. Lawrence, *Lady Chatterley's Lover,* 194.
166. Lawrence, *Lady Chatterley's Lover,* 194–195.
167. Lawrence, *Lady Chatterley's Lover,* 206.
168. Revel, *On Proust,* 102.
169. Proust, *The Fugitive,* 575.
170. Proust, *In Search of Young Girls in Flower,* 203.
171. Proust, *In Search of Young Girls in Flower,* 151.
172. Proust, *Time Regained,* 23.
173. Woolf, *Diary III,* 7.
174. Woolf, *To the Lighthouse,* 141.
175. Nabokov, *Pale Fire* (New York: Vintage Books, 1989), 41.
176. Nabokov, *Lolita,* 166.

Chapter 9

"A Globed Compacted Thing"

Woolf's Cosmogony of Love and the Paradox of Failure in To the Lighthouse

"CONSOLATION IN EXPRESSION"

Toward the end of *To the Lighthouse*, Lily Briscoe sits down in front of a blank canvas in order to re-create a painting she had left unfinished a decade earlier. She remembers the particular obstacle to finishing this painting: the question of "how to connect this mass on the right hand with that on the left."[1] As though mirroring this painting split into two halves, Lily "felt curiously divided, as if one part of her were drawn out there— . . . the Lighthouse looked this morning at an immense distance; the other had fixed itself doggedly, solidly, here on the lawn."[2] And behind this divided painter—behind even the narrator—is Woolf herself, reflecting on the origins of the work of art after its completion, writing to Vita Sackville-West in 1928, a year after the novel's publication:

> The main thing in beginning a novel is to feel, not that you can write it, but that it exists on the far side of a gulf, which words can't cross . . . a novel, as I saw, to be good should seem, before one writes it, something unwriteable: but only visible; so that for nine months one lives in despair and only when one has forgotten what one meant, does the book seem tolerable.[3]

Much has been made of Lily standing as a cipher for Woolf, and of the visual structure of Lily's painting replicating the tripartite structure of the novel— "two blocks joined by a corridor," as Woolf describes it in her working notes below a visual sketch of this plan.[4] But Woolf here outlines a paradoxical pessimism that is necessary for any novelist to move through their "despair" and forgetfulness, writing something that is "unwriteable," using words to gesture toward something "on the far side of a gulf, which words can't cross."

The end result is not so much a triumph of having built a narrow bridge of art over this gulf, but of mapping out the attempts and inevitable failures to do so, molding them into something that seems, at best, only "tolerable."

Scholars are quick to note how Woolf moved at an unusually rapid clip through the process of writing the novel, citing *Moments of Being*, where she says that she "wrote the book very quickly; and when it was written, I ceased to be obsessed by my mother."[5] She also writes in her diary that she "might become one of the interesting—I will not say great—but interesting novelists."[6] But over half a year after this diary entry, she writes of her frustration at not making any progress: "Reading & writing go on. Not my novel though. And I can only think of all my faults as a novelist & wonder why I do it."[7] A month later, after T. S. Eliot had sent her a tepid response to her recently published work, *On Being Ill*, she questioned her entire current project, writing that he

> increases my distaste for my own writing, & dejection at the thought of beginning another novel. What theme have I? Shan't I be held up for personal reasons? It will be too like father, or mother: &, oddly, I know so little of my own powers. Here is another rat run to earth.[8]

She wants to "weep away this life," writing only to "test my theory that there is consolation in expression."[9]

This consolation propelled her through another nervous breakdown in July 1926, and she eventually became "encouraged by my own abundance as I write" to the point that she was even "frightfully contented" as she approached the end of the novel.[10] She quickly qualified the "relief" at finishing the novel with "the disappointment, I suppose."[11] And it only took two days for this disappointment to emerge as a "horror—physically like a painful wave swelling about the heart—tossing me up. I'm unhappy, unhappy! Down—God, I wish I were dead. . . . Failure. Yes; I detect that. Failure failure. (The wave rises)."[12] Even after her husband Leonard praised the novel, her "mind dismisses the whole thing, as usual," in her "intense depression."[13]

Although Woolf was plagued with self-doubt and a fear of failure, it is precisely failure itself that her aesthetic paradoxically perfects. In response to a letter from Gerald Brenan, praising her beautiful prose in *Jacob's Room*, she wrote:

> I think I mean that beauty, which you say I sometimes achieve, is only got by the failure to get it; by grinding all the flints together; by facing what must be humiliation—the things one can't do—To aim at beauty deliberately, without this apparently insensate struggle, would result, I think, in little daisies and forget-me-nots—simpering sweetness—true love-knots.[14]

To scholars like Emily Dalgarno, this "planned failure" is central to her modernist innovations.[15] In *The Common Reader*, Woolf herself defines beauty, from the vantage point of "modern skepticism," as "part ugliness"—its other missing half.[16] Like Baudelaire—and like Lily Briscoe—Woolf sees modernity as fundamentally fragmented, as essentially composed of two halves. "Modernity," Baudelaire writes, "is the transitory, the fugitive, the contingent, the half of art of which the other half is the eternal and immutable."[17]

WOOLF'S SYMPOSIUM

Woolf's modernism, as one that disavows any pretense toward a deliberate completeness, identifying instead the recurrent motif of two halves separated by an impassable gulf, has roots that stretch farther back beyond Baudelaire. About half a decade before drafting what would become *To the Lighthouse*, Woolf wrote to the Greek scholar Janet Case, "I am reading the Symposium [Plato]—ah, if I could write like that! . . . We are sitting in a brown vapour, hearing fog signals from time to time, while your moon, I suppose, is stuck among the apple trees."[18] This rearrangement of spatial relations among objects, with *Symposium* clearly on her mind, later becomes an aesthetic technique in *To the Lighthouse*.

The novel is full of characters like Lily Briscoe, "curiously divided" in half, and the frustrated Mr. Ramsay, who similarly imagines himself stuck just a little over halfway along the vast expanse of all knowledge—he thinks that if it were mapped out along the alphabet, his location would be at "Q," without being able to quite reach "R." Although Mr. Ramsay writes books about "subject and object and the nature of reality," it is his wife, Mrs. Ramsay, who reconciles the two sides of the subject-object split, arranging halves into wholes not only through her social practices of matchmaking but of exploring her own expansive self. When she looks out through the window at the Lighthouse and catches its third stroke, like the "dactylic pulse of elegiac meter," it "seemed to her like her own eyes meeting her own eyes."[19]

This discovery of the self, or a missing part of the self, as an object in the distance recalls the account of eros as told by Aristophanes in Plato's *Symposium*, about how eros emerged as a consolation for our first experience of loss, a consolation that is ultimately "hopeless."[20] To Plato, wholeness is hopeless, and yet we still gesture to it in the act of love, even as we are doomed to fail. The pursuit of love coincides with the pursuit of truth—also a project doomed to fail. Socrates never arrives at any definition of Justice in *The Republic*. In *Phaedrus*, he offers an account of eros, but only to take it back and offer yet another account, ending the dialogue with a meditation on the limits of the written word and how this medium of language fails us.

In *Symposium*, rather than offering a definition of eros once and for all, Plato displays multiple and often contradictory explanations for it, ending with the distractions of a drunken mob. Truth stands always at a remove, as elusive as Woolf's Lighthouse. The most we can do is approach it as an asymptote. What Plato leaves behind is the vehicle to approach it—the dialogue itself, literally two halves summoned together in intercourse, pursuing love and truth as interchangeable categories.

The philosophical underpinnings of *To the Lighthouse*, as with Plato's dialogues, are imbued with love and loss. In Woolf's imagination, both love and loss are irrevocably linked, and love for Woolf encompasses more than just eros.[21] Theodore Koulouris, while not focusing on the specific links between *To the Lighthouse* and *Symposium*, traces Woolf's "tendency to link love with death and 'loss'" back to her earliest rigorous study of the *Symposium* as a twenty-six-year-old in her unpublished *Greek Notebook* from 1908.[22] Perhaps in the Greeks, and particularly in this dialogue, she identified a missing half of herself, as Lily and Mrs. Ramsay do when they look at the Lighthouse: "How I wish something would tear away the veil that still separates me from the Greeks—or is it inevitable?" she wrote in her notebook.[23]

By documenting the experience of loss, Woolf re-creates the Platonic cosmogony of love. Love for her is figured in cosmic terms, as a force that both simultaneously binds all things in the universe and bears the mark of their separation from each other. This explains the hesitation of Lily painting a mark down the middle of her canvas—while it could unify the two halves of the painting, it also carries the risk of the precise opposite effect: "By doing that the unity of the whole might be broken."[24]

At one point in the first section of the novel, "The Window," Lily looks up at Mr. and Mrs. Ramsay, and "what she called 'being in love' flooded them. They became part of that unreal but penetrating and exciting universe which is the world seen through the eyes of love. The sky stuck to them; the birds sang through them."[25] The sky "stuck to them" just as much as the moon "stuck" to the apple trees in Woolf's letter to Janet Case about reading and admiring the *Symposium*. But undermining how "stuck" these objects are to each other is the sense of their mobility and their porousness, of being able to dislodge themselves from the empirical distances that keep them apart, fusing and rearranging themselves in endless combinations through love.

THE MOSAIC TECHNIQUE

This cosmic vision of Mr. and Mrs. Ramsay in love makes Lily think of life as minuscule and fragmentary moments that become, for a moment, "curled and whole like a wave," but only to be dashed and dispersed into debris once again on the shore.[26] This process imitates Woolf's own account of attaining beauty through failure, of "grinding the flints together" into something that can only obliquely suggest wholeness before dissolving.[27] This is a love that Lily notices in passing, as it is not so much a private moment between two people as it is a vision of the world that she wants to capture in her own art.[28] It is a "love that never attempted to clutch its object; but, like the love which mathematicians bear their symbols, or poets their phrases, was meant to spread over the world and become part of the human gain."[29] It is through this love "that barbarity was tamed, the reign of chaos subdued"—a dual reference not only to the impending First World War that occupies the middle section of the novel, "Time Passes," but to the primordial chaos of Greek mythology, the original void, the non-existence from which all existence has come from and will return to.[30] Perhaps this chaos is what's denoted in the double exclamation of "Nothing! Nothing!" that occupies the space between Lily and Mrs. Ramsay, even as Lily rests on her knee, wondering,

> Could loving, as people called it, make her and Mrs. Ramsay one? for it was not knowledge but unity that she desired, not inscriptions on tablets, nothing that could be written in any language known to men, but intimacy itself, which is knowledge, she had thought.[31]

This trail of thought begins by rejecting knowledge—presumably the kind of stuffy, academic knowledge that gives Mr. Ramsay and Charles Tansley a sense of self-importance—and pursuing unity instead. However, Lily arrives at the conclusion that this unity, this intimacy, is still knowledge, albeit a knowledge that precedes all language, that underlies all existence. To the first generation of cosmic beings split in half by Zeus's thunderbolts in Plato's myth, eros was the means by which they came to know and understand themselves, each other, and the world, prior to any mode of articulation. Its purpose is both ontological and epistemological; eros reveals not only who we are but the memory of where we had come from, situating us in the cosmic order of things.

Hermione Lee identifies Lily's affinity for Mrs. Ramsay as a lesbian desire.[32] She does, after all, have to resist the urge to declare that she's in love with her, struggling with what words to choose in this declaration. But as soon as the thought passes her mind, she quickly revises it: "No, that was not true. 'I'm in love with this all,' waving her hand at the hedge, at the house, at the children? It was absurd, it was impossible. One could not say what one meant."[33] Lily withdraws from language, as it inevitably fails her, and shifts her attention to her art, trying to forge a unity out of the two halves on her canvas. Even across a ten-year period, she returns to this moment at the end of the novel, where the same thoughts are echoed:

It was some such feeling of completeness perhaps which, ten years ago, standing almost where [Lily] stood now, had made her say that she must be in love with the place. Love had a thousand shapes. There might be lovers whose gift it was to choose out the elements of things and place them together and so, giving them a wholeness not theirs in life, make of some scene, or meeting of people (all now gone and separate), one of those globed compacted things over which thought lingers, and love plays.[34]

There is a suggestion here that love falls under the domain of art and that the artist supplements the fragmentary nature of life with a vision of something that approaches wholeness, making out of it a "globed compacted thing," like the globular cosmic beings that we once were in our prelapsarian state, before we were divided in half.

The lover-artists who "choose out the elements of things and place them together" assemble their material into something like a mosaic in motion, a technique that Woolf translates from the visual arts into literature. Her sister, the painter Vanessa Bell, referred to her own technique as a form of "mosaicing" [sic], considering her paintings as "patches each of which has to be filled by the definite space of colours as one has to do with mosaic or woolwork, not allowing myself to brush the patches into each other."[35] In 1920, the Bloomsbury art critic Roger Fry wrote in his influential *Vision and Design* how "the artist does not distinguish individual objects as 'separate unities' but as 'so many bits in the whole mosaic of vision.'"[36] He even echoes Bell's articulation of her mosaic technique when he writes that "every solid object is subject to the play of light and shade, and becomes a mosaic of visual patches, each of which for the artist is related to other visual patches in the surroundings."[37]

A mosaic is a kind of cutting up of fragments in order to bring them into new spatial relationships with each other. From the very beginning of the novel, we see James "sitting on the floor cutting out pictures from the illustrated catalogue of the Army and Navy Stores," among them a "picture of a pocket knife with six blades," and his act of cutting is at odds with his father, who, standing "lean as a knife, narrow as the blade of one, grinning sarcastically," speaks to him "sharply."[38] The tension between them emerges from the humiliation of feeling cut down by the other. Mr. Ramsay is likened to an "arid scimitar, which smote mercilessly, again and again, demanding sympathy," while James wishes he could kill him with "an axe . . . , a poker, or any weapon that would have gashed a hole in his father's breast."[39] While this drama plays out, Lily walks along the beach with William Bankes, looking at "the swift cutting race of a sailing boat, which, having sliced a curve in the bay, stopped."[40] Perhaps this "sliced curve" is what she imagines transferring onto her painting, which she later remembers as a series of "relations of . . .

lines cutting across, slicing down," and which Mr. Bankes later taps with his penknife in order to ask her questions about it.[41]

The cutting imagery at first distances all the characters from each other, setting them far apart. At one moment in the dinner party, Mrs. Ramsay feels "cut off from them all," hearing the dislodged words of the conversation sounding "as if they were floating like flowers on water out there."[42] Lily, returning back to the Ramsays' summer home after Mrs. Ramsay's death, mirrors Mrs. Ramsay's sentiment by feeling like she

> had no attachment here . . . no relations with it . . . and whatever did happen, a step outside, a voice calling . . . was a question, as if the link that usually bound things together had been cut, and they floated up here, down there, off, anyhow. How aimless it was, how chaotic, how unreal it was, she thought.[43]

The paradox, though, is that this identical imagery does end up binding Lily to Mrs. Ramsay, even in Mrs. Ramsay's absence. The feeling of being cut off from relations becomes the precondition for bonds to be established and renewed. It opens the space for new patterns of the imagination to emerge, as when Cam's "hand cut a trail in the sea" on her way to the Lighthouse, "as her mind made the green swirls and streaks into patterns and, numbed and shrouded, wandered in imagination in that underworld of waters."[44] Similarly, Lily struggles to "achieve that razor edge of balance between two opposite forces; Mrs. Ramsay and the picture."[45]

The entire novel abides by the principle of cutting and splitting. In her diary, Woolf wrote, "I think I might do something in To the Lighthouse, to split up emotions more completely. I think I'm working in that direction."[46] Mrs. Ramsay practices this splitting after the dinner party:

> She felt rather inclined just for a moment to stand still after all that chatter, and pick out one particular thing; the thing that mattered; to detach it; to separate it off; clean it of all the emotions and odds and ends of things, and so hold it before her, and bring it to the tribunal where, ranged about in conclave, sat the judges she had set up to decide these things. Is it good, is it bad, is it right or wrong? Where are we going? and so on. So she righted herself after the shock of the event, and quite unconsciously and incongruously, used the branches of the elm trees outside to help her to stabilize her position. Her world was changing; they were still.[47]

The technique of cutting becomes a technique of approaching a vision of permanence, so that "now one thought of it, cleared of chatter and emotion, it seemed always to have been, only was shown now, and so being shown struck everything into stability."[48] The stability itself is not as emphasized as the fact that it is "shown," much like the permanent line down the middle of

Lily's painting is not as emphasized as much as her "vision" of it is. The elm tree that Mrs. Ramsay stabilizes herself with emerges in Lily's painting—"Move the tree to the middle," she thinks to herself, aligning Mrs. Ramsay not just with the tree, but with the central line that holds her entire vision together.[49] Out of these ephemeral moments, both Mrs. Ramsay and Lily gesture toward a vision of something not just as stable as a tree, but as the Platonic forms. Auerbach himself uses the metaphor of cutting to explain how, in this novel, "an insignificant occurrence releases ideas and chains of ideas which cut loose from the present of the exterior occurrence and range freely through the depths of time," coming as close to eternity as possible.[50] Out of a dinner party in which "nothing seemed to have merged" and "they all sat separate," Mrs. Ramsay is able to arrange these separate guests the way Lily arranges her colors, into a cohesive whole that would transcend the fleeting moment, so that "they would, she thought, going on again, however long they loved, come back to this night; this moon; this wind; this house: and to her too."[51]

Undermining the sense of fragmentation, then, is the unity that holds the fragments together. While "The Window" ends with Mr. Bankes taking Charles Tansley onto the terrace to finish a discussion about politics, "Time Passes" begins with Mr. Bankes "coming in from the terrace" at some point in the intervening decade, as though there are two competing experiences of time, one accelerated and one slowed down, both of which interrupt each other.[52] The entire section of "Time Passes" is an interruption in a novel composed of interruptions—James's trip to the Lighthouse delayed by a decade, Mr. Ramsay having a "child-like resentment of interruption," William Bankes annoyed at all the interruptions at the dinner table, and Mrs. Ramsay interrupting even her own thoughts with reminders to pay the bill for the greenhouse.[53] "Time Passes" abruptly inserts death into the narrative of life, and even the empty spaces between the numbered sections re-create the sense of loss on the level of the form.

The use of square brackets, moreover, "the tool of textual editors for restoring or marking absent matter, takes on a poetry of its own here."[54] They form a "set of connected or entombed utterances that form a narrative, or fragmented narrative, a central line, within the larger work."[55] These utterances are both central and peripheral, bracketed off from a cosmic narrative that shifts its attention from the human world to an uninhabited landscape. These brackets perform a kind of mutilation, which is perhaps why an entire section of "The Lighthouse" is composed of two sentences in square brackets: "[Macalister's boy took one of the fish and cut a square out of its side to bait his hook with. The mutilated body (it was alive still) was thrown back into the sea.]"[56] This section intrudes as an interruption in the narrative of Lily finishing her painting, and Lily herself feels mutilated without Mrs. Ramsay.

In Lily's question, "What does it mean, then, what can it all mean?" there is the echo of Mrs. Ramsay's question to herself at the dinner table: "What did it all mean?"[57] This same question, echoed across the lapse of ten years, illustrates the ontological mutilation at the core of Plato's *Symposium*, in the quest of the self finding its missing half, asking the same questions. Dalgarno argues that these

> questions are like those of the Platonic dialogue in the sense that they ask for definitions as a means to engage the attention of the reader, and to prevent our taking for granted a vocabulary that includes not only *truth* but also *knowledge* and *love*.[58]

In "Time Passes," the

> mystic, the visionary, walked the beach, stirred a puddle, looked at a stone, and asked themselves, "What am I?" "What is this?" and suddenly an answer was vouchsafed them (what it was they could not say): so that they were warm in the frost and had comfort in the desert.[59]

There is a sense in which these questions and their answers transform how one experiences one's spatial surroundings, which is why Lily's concern as a painter is predominantly one of organizing space. The answers lie beyond the threshold of language, and Woolf's aesthetic becomes one that approaches the silence beyond this threshold, the empty gaps in the mosaic that nevertheless hold all the pieces together.

Even as far back as 1919, Woolf wrote a letter to Janet Case, with whom she spoke regularly about the Greeks, saying,

> There's the whole question, which interested me . . . of the things one doesn't say; what effect does that have? and how far do our feelings take their color from the dive underground? I mean, what is the reality of any feeling? . . . And then there's the question of things happening, normally, all the time.[60]

Even though it would be years before she would embark on the project that would end up being *To the Lighthouse*, Woolf here is already beginning to think through her formulation of a language of silence, a language that undoes itself. On the day she ended up publishing the novel, she sent her sometime lover Vita Sackville-West a dummy copy of it, inscribing the book full of nothing but blank pages with the note, "In my opinion the best novel I have ever written."[61] Without hearing a response from Sackville-West for a few days, she was worried that the joke had fallen flat, that her self-deprecating humor would be mistaken for arrogance. "Dearest donkey West," she wrote in a follow-up message, "Did you understand that when

I wrote it was my best book I merely meant because all the pages were empty?"[62]

François Mauriac thinks of this dummy copy as

> not the product of an author who had nothing more to say (those who have nothing to say, go on for ever [sic] saying it) but of one who had too much, and when I say too much, I mean in terms of quality rather than quantity.[63]

Woolf, for him, is one of the writers who "are moving towards silence."[64] It is this charged silence that Lily inhabits toward the end of the novel, struggling to put the finishing touches on her painting just as much as she struggles with language itself. She looks up to address Augustus Carmichael, lying "on his chair . . . like a creature gorged with existence."[65] What does one say to such a "creature"? What does it even mean to be "gorged with existence"? She seems to be looking at him as though from another vantage point, if not vanishing point, of existence altogether, aligned as she is with the "Ghost, air, nothingness" of the dead Mrs. Ramsay.[66] To Mr. Carmichael, Lily

> wanted to say not one thing, but everything. Little words that broke up the thought and dismembered it said nothing. "About life, about death; about Mrs. Ramsay"—no, she thought, one could say nothing to nobody. The urgency of the moment always missed its mark. Words fluttered sideways and struck the object inches too low. Then one gave it up; then the idea sunk back again. . . . For how could one express in words these emotions of the body? express the emptiness there? (She was looking at the drawing-room steps; they looked extraordinarily empty.) It was one's body feeling, not one's mind.[67]

Like D. H. Lawrence in *Lady Chatterley's Lover*, Woolf treats language as an inadequate but necessary medium of linking nothing with everything, of tracing a primordial and unspoken language of the body, of the "emptiness there"—in the subject—that discovers its unity with the "extraordinarily empty" nature of the object it confronts. This is an emptiness that is at once intensely physical but fundamentally abstract. Words inevitably "broke up" and "dismembered" this unity of emptiness, suggesting the kind of failure expressed earlier in the novel by Mr. Ramsay, who writes books about "subject and object and the nature of reality."[68]

We see him pacing to and fro, "so ridiculous and so alarming" in his demeanor, reciting Tennyson's "The Charge of the Light Brigade" out loud in his restless meanderings.[69] The poem commemorates the failure of the cavalry, as a result of miscommunication, during the Battle of Balaclava in the Crimean War. The line he settles on is "Someone had blundered," repeating it incessantly, "as if he were trying over, tentatively seeking, some phrase for a new mood, and having only this at hand, used it, cracked though it was."[70]

Words are "cracked" in the mouths of Woolf's characters, like the "cracked kettle" of language in Flaubert.[71] They are blunders. They miscommunicate more than they communicate. Words obscure meaning rather than reveal it, as when Lily considers asking Mr. Carmichael what the meaning of everything is and how to explain it—an impossible task, since the world itself seemed to her as though it dissolved "into a pool of thought, a deep basin of reality," and if Mr. Carmichael would have spoken, "a little tear would have rent the surface of the pool. And then? Something would emerge. A hand would be shoved up, a blade would be flashed. It was nonsense of course."[72]

The images of the hand and the blade here are also borrowed from Tennyson, who ends his *Idylls of the King* with the dying Arthur ordering Sir Bedivere to throw Excalibur into the lake.[73] The Lady of the Lake emerges before the sword falls into the water, catching and brandishing it three times before descending with it back into the depths. The poetic allusion recalls Mrs. Ramsay (who identifies with the third stroke of the Lighthouse), pessimistically contemplating the future loss and grief her children will experience: "curled up from the floor of her mind, [she] rose from the lake of [her] being," and tells herself, in silence, "brandishing her sword at life, nonsense."[74]

By refraining from speech, dwelling in the kind of silence that is heavily evocative of Mrs. Ramsay, Mr. Carmichael avoids the "little tear [that] would have rent the surface of the pool," keeping it whole. In this extended metaphor, language then functions as a kind of Excalibur, a tool of violence, of divisiveness—something that one uses to strike at one's enemy, even if it "struck the object inches too low."[75] It is, in the last resort, something that one discards in the "pool of thought, a deep basin of reality," threatening to "rent the surface of the pool." Perhaps thought and reality themselves are the enemies. In her art, Lily moves away from the language of thought to the expression of the body, away from reality and verisimilitude to the space of created forms. The "whole world seemed to have dissolved," as it later does with D. H. Lawrence's lovers in *Lady Chatterley's Lover*, and in its place Lily wants to recover her vision of Mr. and Mrs. Ramsay a decade prior to this moment, when they belonged to "that unreal and penetrating and exciting universe which is the world seen through the eyes of love."[76]

An "unreal" universe emerges in the wake of the dissolved world. It is "penetrating," not penetrated. It is a universe in which objects "stuck" and "sang through" subjects, eliminating their separation from each other. This new universe is comprised of solidity as opposed to the realm of reality, of the outer world, which dissolves into fluidity. During the dinner that Mrs. Ramsay hosts, she notices the effect of the panes of glass that distort "any accurate view of the outside world," offering a vision "in which things wavered and vanished, waterily." By contrast, the solidity of the interior space, which seems to be just as fragile, tenuous, and even fleeting in its composition, stands as a bulwark against the threat of the outer world, and this realization ripples through everyone at the dinner table: "Some change at once went through them all, as if this had really happened, and they were all conscious of making a party together in a hollow, on an island; had their common cause against the fluidity out there."[77] The fluidity, the pool of reality, the world outside, a world "in which things wavered and vanished," are what Woolf's characters—but Mrs. Ramsay and Lily especially—battle against, trying to construct some kind of order, stability, and permanence out of the transient chaos.

The result, then, is not just a static mosaic, but something that is more comparable to a shifting kaleidoscope that continuously reinvents itself and the relations among the fragments that compose the whole. Jean O. Love attributes this technique to Woolf's "mythical consciousness," in which spatial

> relationships among objects, for example, are inconstant, a consequence to be expected from the lack of certain spatial dimensions and from the omnipotence of mythical consciousness. The distance of objects from one another changes without the objects being moved, an impossibility in an empirical world.[78]

Lily's memory of this same thought of love ten years prior is thus literally an act of recollection, of re-collecting and reassembling the impressions of her past into a postimpressionist vision of the fleeting moment in the present. Writing about the *Symposium* in her *Greek Notebook*, Woolf explores how "the body is always changing; a new birth; a new birth is no more than the change & continuation of the old body. Knowledge is recollection; rebirth."[79] *Symposium* itself is a shifting mosaic, one in which Aristophanes trades places with Erixymachus because of his hiccupping, another motif of interruption. By trading places in the order of speakers, Aristophanes's story becomes the structural center of the work, the central line down the middle.

T. E. Apter notes how the perceiver in *To the Lighthouse*, whether Mrs. Ramsay, Lily, or the disembodied narrator, "either fixes the external object, or releases its potential mobility from the mass of impressions available to her."[80] Lily, though, seems to want to achieve both at once, to use her painting as a means of fixing what she finds elusive and at the same time to release its potential mobility, to incorporate the moving distances she perceives.[81] Perhaps Woolf's most striking use of this technique is when her narrator shifts from the interior of Lily's mind to the adjacent, external reality of Jasper shooting at a flock of starlings. Without causality, Woolf concatenates these two actions, drawing out a pattern that recurs throughout the novel:

> All of this danced up and down, like a company of gnats, each separate, but all marvelously controlled in an invisible elastic net—danced up and down in

Lily's mind . . . until her thought which had spun quicker and quicker exploded of its own intensity; she felt released; a shot went off close at hand, and there came, flying from its fragments, frightened, effusive, tumultuous, a flock of starlings.[82]

Lily's thoughts, likened to gnats, are all discrete and separate, but "marvelously controlled," dancing according to a pattern she is trying to trace in the same way that starlings, too, fly according to rhythmic murmurations. Her role as an artist is

> not inventing; she was only trying to smooth out something she had been given years ago folded up; something she had seen. . . . One had constantly a sense of repetition—of one thing falling where another had fallen, and so setting up an echo which chimed in the air and made it full of vibrations.[83]

"GIGANTIC CHAOS STREAKED WITH LIGHTNING"

The architecture of the novel enables these echoes to reverberate across the "two blocks joined by a corridor." If Woolf doubles for Lily, then the "globed compacted thing" that the artist forges from a mosaic of fragments, out of love and commemoration, is the entire novel itself. The two blocks on either end of the novel are like the two missing halves of our original being from *Symposium*, mirror images of each other as they reach across the empty corridor of the "Time Passes" section. It is this section where we are first told of Mrs. Ramsay's death: "[Mr. Ramsay stumbling along a passage stretched his arms out one dark morning, but Mrs. Ramsay having died rather suddenly the night before he stretched his arms out. They remained empty]."[84] The jarring news, encased in coffin-like square brackets, interrupts the disembodied narrative of the landscape, as though it were a lightning bolt accompanying the "nights full of wind and destruction" from the previous paragraph.[85] The lightning emerges again, more explicitly, as an image that unites a Schopenhauerian pessimism with the pessimism of *Symposium*:

> Listening (had there been anyone to listen) from the upper rooms of the empty house only gigantic chaos streaked with lightning could have been heard tumbling and tossing . . . until it seemed as if the universe were battling and tumbling, in brute confusion and wanton lust aimlessly by itself.[86]

This lightning is the cosmic division, the expression of the universe in "brute confusion," rending apart not just the chaos—the great void that the world is tumbling into—and not just the beings we once were, but the two adjacent halves of the novel as though this itself were a vision of that original separation.

Commenting on the form of the *Symposium* from her *Greek Notebook*, Woolf writes, "This is a charming opening; in spite of the awkwardness of the form—a repetition after some years of what someone else had told the speaker. But it is very natural & easy."[87] What we get in *To the Lighthouse* is also "a repetition after some years." "The Lighthouse" recollects details from "The Window," reflecting and refracting these details across "Time Passes." In the first part of the novel, Mrs. Ramsay endows the window with the properties of a mirror. As a transparent boundary that lets her look out to the lighthouse, what she ends up seeing is an extension of herself. The mirror gives us a vision of the wholeness we had lost when we had been broken apart into two fragments, but what Woolf explores is what happens when the mirror itself is broken:

> Did Nature supplement what man advanced? Did she complete what he began? With equal complacence she saw his misery, condoned his meanness, and acquiesced in his torture. That dream, then, of sharing, completing, finding in solitude on the beach an answer, was but a reflection in a mirror, and the mirror itself was but the surface glassiness which forms in quiescence when the nobler powers sleep beneath? Impatient, despairing yet loth to go (for beauty offers her lures, her consolations), to pace the beach was impossible; contemplation was unendurable; the mirror was broken.[88]

Across this threshold of the broken mirror, images such as the one of Mr. Ramsay looking at his wife and son in the window—"the way one raises one's eyes from a page in an express train and sees . . . a confirmation of something on the printed page to which one returns, fortified"—are refracted across the three sections.[89] In "Time Passes," the narrator describes solitude "like a pool at evening, far distant, seen from a train window, vanishing so quickly that the pool, pale in the evening, is scarcely robbed of its solitude, though once seen."[90] By the time we reach "The Lighthouse," this analogy is transported to Lily's mind, where she compares herself to "a traveler, even though he is half asleep, knows, looking out of the train window, that he must look now, for he will never see that town, or that mule-cart, or that woman at work in the fields again."[91]

In this triptych of the same image refracted across three fragmented sections, Woolf moves from a vision that can be captured and confirmed on the printed page to something that is more elusive and ephemeral. Implicit in this movement is a critique of Wordsworth's Romantic optimism, according to Dalgarno:

> Wordsworth fosters the "comfortable conclusion" that outward vision serves to confirm inward. His image of the mind as mirror achieves its optimism by reducing the three-dimensional complexity of perception in the cave, where men see only shadows, to a two-dimensional model of reflection.[92]

Woolf shatters this image of the mirror and its accompanying optimism. And yet, the artistry of both Woolf and her character Lily emerges from the paradoxical gesture of committing to the page and the canvas the very nature of reality that, as they acknowledge, cannot be grasped.

It is in this way that Woolf offers a vision of the wholeness that we once were, inscribing it into the form of the novel, writing about it not just as a "globed compacted thing," but as a body itself: "What I feel is that it is a hard muscular book, which at this age proves that I have something in me. It has not run out & gone flabby."[93] But her tone was not as confident just days after she had finished it, feeling an "Intense depression," something that was common to finishing her process of writing novels, which she referred to as a gestation over a period of "nine months . . . in despair."[94] In the same diary entry, she asks herself, "But why am I feeling like this? . . . Children. Failure."[95] In the absence of having any children, she sees this finished novel as a failed surrogate, as a part of herself that is now separated from her, leaving behind something akin to postpartum depression.

THE ACOUSTICS OF GRIEF

As much as this novel can be seen as the progeny of a new generation, its other silent half is comprised of the generations that are no longer alive. As such, it is more of an elegy than a novel. Even in her working notes for *To the Lighthouse*, she writes, "I have an idea that I will invent a new name for my books to supplant 'novel.' A new—by Virginia Woolf. But what? Elegy? . . . ?"[96] An elegy, more than a novel, is heard, and Woolf had to listen in mourning to the ghosts of her past in order to orchestrate this work that would supplant "novel." When she articulates the language of loss in "Time Passes," the lightning image is perceived not by anyone seeing it, but by "Listening (had there been anyone to listen)."[97]

In 1904, still traumatized by the death of her mother, Woolf suffered a mental breakdown when her father died. In this breakdown, she "heard birds singing Greek choruses."[98] Ancient Greek, to her, stood "for the most distant horizon of intelligibility, the point beyond which the sane mind does not reach."[99] The Greek chorus, accompanied by the flute, "constantly threatens to dissolve song into wailing, music into moaning, and the voice into a primordial, disarticulate anti-music," as Eugene Thacker notes in *Cosmic Pessimism*.[100] "The mourning voice delineates all the forms of suffering—tears, weeping, sobbing, wailing, moaning, and the convulsions of thought reduced to an elemental unintelligibility."[101]

She would work through this elemental unintelligibility over the next two decades, writing *To the Lighthouse* as a way of putting the ghosts of her parents to rest, as she recounts in *Moments of Being*: "when it was written, I ceased to be obsessed by my mother. I no longer hear her voice; I do not see her."[102] In her acoustics of grief, Woolf eventually came to mute both the birds singing in Greek and the sound of her mother's voice while amplifying the sound of the waves crashing on the beach: "I am making up 'To the Lighthouse'—the sea is to be heard all through it."[103] In the same year, though, she wrote the essay "On Not Knowing Greek," where she positions herself back in the aural space of Ancient Greece, in that linguistic "horizon of intelligibility," imagining what the Greeks heard and how they interpreted the sounds of nature around them:

> With the sound of the sea in their ears, vines, meadows, rivulets about them, they are even more aware than we are of a ruthless fate. There is a sadness at the back of life which they do not attempt to mitigate. Entirely aware of their own standing in the shadow, and yet alive to every tremor and gleam of existence, there they endure, and it is to the Greeks that we turn when we are sick of the vagueness, of the confusion, of the Christianity and its consolations, of our own age.[104]

Woolf's consolation, then, is a rejection of that genealogy of consolation that can be traced back to Boethius. It is rather an adoption of the legacy of Walter Pater, Oscar Wilde, and the Uranian poets, who turned particularly to Plato's *Symposium* for a narrative of "spiritual procreancy" that would replace the Judeo-Christian creation myth.[105] Like the biblical account of the Fall, *Symposium* provides the myth of a literal fall from the farthest reaches of the cosmos to the earth; it is an account of how we come to know the world, ourselves, and the sense of loss that accompanies the awareness of our bodies, but without any hope for a lasting salvation.

While composing the novel, Woolf wrote in her diary that she wanted to articulate the "mystical side of this solitude; how it is not oneself but something in the universe that one's left with. It is this that is frightening & exciting in the midst of my profound gloom, depression, boredom, whatever it is."[106] Solitude for Woolf, as for Aristophanes in *Symposium*, is a cosmic feeling of "something in the universe that one's left with," a feeling that is rooted in a "profound gloom." Woolf's narrative, like her description of the landscape, "always seemed to be running away into some moon country, uninhabited by men," a similar desire expressed by Mellors in *Lady Chatterley's Lover*.[107] The moon is that reminder in the universe of the shape we had once taken, and the freedom we once had from the earth.[108] The Platonic myth, then, is the original story that narrates the "sadness at the back of life," which she still hears in the sound of the sea—a sadness that paradoxically endows us with the capacity to be alive to "every tremor and gleam of existence."

MRS. RAMSAY'S PESSIMISM

Such is the pessimism of Mrs. Ramsay, a pessimism that moves away from an anthropomorphic focus of the world, shifting its perspective away from the human and toward the inanimate landscape. Mrs. Ramsay feels her being merge with the gleam of the lighthouse, the gleam of her own existence, attuned to the sound of the sea, its waves alternating between a consoling effect that seems to protect her and one that threatens destruction, "like a ghostly roll of drums" that

> remorselessly beat the measure of life, made one think of the destruction of the island and its engulfment in the sea, and warned her whose day had slipped past in one quick doing after another that it was all ephemeral as a rainbow—this sound which had been obscured and concealed under the other sounds suddenly thundered hollow in her ears and made her look up with an impulse of terror.[109]

The sound of the sea to Mrs. Ramsay is, by turns, comforting and terrifying. It is both protective and threatening. There is a sense in which it underlies all other sounds, both intelligible and unintelligible. It is as though she actively listens away from intelligible speech to train her ear on sounds beyond thought, as when she looks out the window during the dinner party, in the direction of the sea that is now invisible behind the black panes, and "the voices came to her very strangely, as if they were voices at a service in a cathedral, for she did not listen to the words."[110]

In "Sketch of the Past," Woolf writes of the memory of her mother "in the very center of that great Cathedral space which was childhood; there she was from the very first."[111] A vast space like a cathedral amplifies and echoes the sounds it contains. An echo itself is a repetition of a sound that had previously occurred—it is the acoustic lingering of a moment already past, and in Mrs. Ramsay, one hears the echo of Julia Stephen herself. Mrs. Ramsay, at the dinner table, "did not know what they meant, but like music, the words seemed to be spoken by her own voice, outside her self, saying quite easily and naturally what had been in her mind the whole evening while she said different things," an analogous passage in the overall auditory mosaic that resonates with the sound of Jasper's gunshot dispersing the flock of starlings concomitantly with the dispersal of the "gnats" of Lily's thoughts.[112] Mrs. Ramsay understands the music behind the words, their musical shape, as though they belong to her, dissolving the boundary between her voice, her being, and the voices of the others at the dinner table. Sound seems to be what unites everyone at the dinner party "with a common cause against the fluidity out there," in which "things wavered and vanished, waterily."[113]

Both she and Lily try to mold out of the transient chaos some kind of order, stability, and permanence. The curious use of the adverb "waterily" recalls the function of the sea to Woolf, as communicating the "sadness at the back of life" that the Greeks understood. And, like the waves themselves, the narrative by turns confronts this sadness and then protectively withdraws from it. Like Socrates joining his interlocutors at an indoor party in *Symposium*, the inner space seems like a temporary protective shield, one in which the guests are invited to contemplate the permanence of forms while everything outside poses a threat of fickle change, of dissolution, of a plague and a war that would end up decimating their civilization.

Still looking out the window, Mrs. Ramsay notes how the words "sounded as if they were floating like flowers on water out there, cut off from them all, as if no one had said them, but they had come into existence of themselves."[114] These words, reduced to meaningless sounds, registering as flowers floating on water, recall Ophelia in her descent into madness and eventual suicide by drowning, her final words also straining intelligibility and dissolving into pure sound. It is only appropriate, then, for Mrs. Ramsay to end her evening with Shakespeare, a "magnet" that gathers "all the odds and ends of the day."[115] She reads his Sonnet 98 as though it were a coda to *Symposium*, a vision of the completeness that emerges out of the fragments of words and sounds flowing across the day, taking on a "rounded" shape like our original rounded selves, a shape she uses to denote every image of completeness in the novel: "And then there it was, suddenly entire shaped in her hands, beautiful and reasonable, clear and complete, the essence sucked out of life and held rounded here—the sonnet."[116] The sonnet itself is one of melancholic longing, in which the beauty of spring reminds the speaker of a lost lover. But the landscape is animated with language, including the "lays of birds" that could not "make me any summer's story tell."[117]

The association of birds with words appears right before she settles on this sonnet, when

> words, like little shaded lights, one red, one blue, one yellow, lit up in the dark of her mind, and seemed leaving their perches up there to fly across and across, or to cry out and to be echoed; so she turned and felt on the table beside her for a book.[118]

When she begins reading,

> here and there at random . . . she felt that she was climbing backwards, upwards, shoving her way up under petals that curved over her, so that she only knew this is white, or this is red. She did not know at first what the words meant at all.[119]

In this aural mosaic, the sounds occur to her first, and then the colors, and she continues to shove her way up under petals that curved over her so that she finally arrives at the surface meaning of the line, "Nor praise the deep vermilion in the rose."[120] The separation between the lover and the absent beloved for a moment seems to echo the gulf between her and her husband, even as he lies in bed right next to her, but she looks up from her book, "echoing his smile dreamily" instead.[121]

She hopes he will "say something . . . wishing only to hear his voice," and as they come closer together in bed, "she could feel his mind like a raised hand shadowing her mind; and he was beginning now that her thoughts took a turn he disliked—towards this 'pessimism' as he called it—to fidget, though he said nothing."[122] Despite this pessimism, however, "she began to smile, for though she had not said a word, he knew, of course he knew, that she loved him."[123] Looking out the window, as she did during dinner, she thinks to herself, "Nothing on earth can equal this happiness."[124] In the space of one brief, wordless, almost telepathic conversation, Mrs. Ramsay emerges as a pessimist who is happy, who articulates neither her pessimism nor her happiness, but sounds the depths of these experiences, following the frequencies on the other side of sound that merge them together.

MR. RAMSAY'S PESSIMISM

Mr. Ramsay, for his part, sees in Shakespeare the anxiety of civilization, unwittingly adopting a pessimistic worldview of his own. "The very stone one kicks with one's boots will outlast Shakespeare," he thinks to himself on a walk earlier that day.[125] He certainly appears to be the initial pessimist in the work, opening the novel by ruining James's hopes of going to the lighthouse the next day, rigidly adhering to his belief that everyone "should be aware from childhood that life is difficult; facts uncompromising."[126] In this sense, he seems like a parody of a Victorian father—like Thomas Gradgrind in Charles Dickens's *Hard Times*—out of step with the Edwardian era when "The Window" takes place. Like Gradgrind, he imagines the totality of thought as something that could be quantified, something that could be divided up in the same way that "the alphabet is ranged in twenty-six letters all in order." Contemplating the vantage point of his "splendid mind" from the letter Q, he stops by a stone urn used as a geranium planter and imagines seeing his wife and son "far far away . . . entirely defenceless against a doom which he perceived, his wife and son, together, in the window. They needed his protection; he gave it them."[127]

What kind of protection exactly he has in mind is just as unclear as the kind of doom he perceives. If anything, it seems as though Mrs. Ramsay and

James—or at least just James—are seeking protection from him rather than by him. However "splendid" he thinks his own mind is, the narrator, even in free indirect discourse, delineates a widening chasm between Mr. Ramsay and his family, "far far away" from each other, a chasm that also traces the distance between the seriousness of his own thought and the satirical portrait he strikes.

His pessimism takes on the metaphors of spatial dimensions; the distance that emerges between him and his family then translates to the daunting crevice between his intellectual achievement—his venerable "Q"—and the next letter, "R," the next summit of knowledge to be attained. Pessimism here seems to realign his spatial relations so that when he sees "R" from this distance, a "flash of darkness" comes over him, and "he heard people saying—he was a failure—that R was beyond him. He would never reach R."[128] The splendidness of his own mind is something that fails him; he is painfully aware of how his smugness is just a veneer that conceals a deeper anxiety that he has not achieved greatness, repeating to his wife "that he was a failure."[129]

He is stuck at Q; he even "dug his heels in at Q. . . . Here he knocked his pipe out, with two or three resonant taps on the ram's horn which made the handle of the urn."[130] Since the root of the word "pessimism" is *ped-*, the foot—the lowest most part of the body, farthest away from the lofty reaches of the mind—we see Mr. Ramsay at his most pessimistic when he digs his heels in, or when he contemplates the "stone one kicks with one's boots" that "will outlast Shakespeare."[131] The stone urn he gravitates to will also outlast the funerary significance ascribed to it; in fact, it already has. It is just a vase of geraniums, reclaimed by the landscape, a constant reminder to everyone of mortality. In a moment that lays bare the influence of Hardy and Conrad on Woolf's treatment of landscape, we see William Bankes and Lily looking at the

> dunes far away, . . . instead of merriment felt come over them some sadness—because the thing was completed partly, and partly because distant views seemed to outlast by a million years (Lily thought) the gazer and to be communing already with a sky which beholds an earth entirely at rest.[132]

Mr. Ramsay is obsessed with "how we know nothing and the sea eats away the ground we stand on—that was his fate, his gift."[133]

The landscape Mr. Ramsay imagines himself inhabiting in his "desolate expedition" is one of "icy solitudes of the Polar region," and he sees himself as "the leader of a forlorn hope," whose "temper, neither sanguine nor despondent, surveys with equanimity what is to be and faces it."[134] But the problem is that he cannot help his melodramatic despondency, still standing beside the urn with the geraniums as he imagines himself on a snowy mountain-top, where "he would die standing," knowing that he would "never reach R."[135] Mr. Ramsay is a kind of self-proclaimed, would-be Zarathustra, looking "from a mountain-top down the long wastes of the ages" into the inevitable dissolution of civilization, seen from the perspective of deep time.[136]

This, perhaps, is why he is drawn to stone, why he "stood very upright by the urn," why he finds "some crag of rock" to hold onto, why he "dwells upon fame, upon search parties, upon cairns raised by grateful followers over his bones," so that he can hold on to whatever it is in this world that lasts.[137] But even in this fantasy of martyrdom into the doomed expedition of the intellect, he imagines a kind of rebirth, one in which life itself stems from the same feet that marked his morbid pessimism, starting from "some pricking in his toes" as a reminder "that he lives, and does not on the whole object to live, but requires sympathy, and whisky, and someone to tell the story of his suffering to at once." He imagines returning home from this "doomed expedition," stopping by the window where he "gazes at his wife and son, who very distant at first, gradually come closer and closer" in a vision that confirms "the beauty of the world" for him.[138]

The distance opened up by his pessimism narrows—if not between Q and R, then at least between him and his family. But this proximity is still undermined by the first sentence of the next chapter: "But his son hated him."[139] The distance doesn't simply vanish because he is now ready to return from the polar expedition of his mind. Nevertheless, this pessimism of the "forlorn hope" is one he cannot maintain. At his core, he is quite happy, but this happiness catches him off-guard; it is something he is even ashamed of, "as if to be caught happy in a world of misery was for an honest man the most despicable of crimes. It was true; he was for the most part happy."[140] From his wife's perspective, he has nothing of the cheerlessness or the "bleached look of withered old age."[141] On the contrary, she contemplates how young he looks for his age "and how untamed and optimistic, and how strange it was that being convinced, as he was, of all sorts of horrors, seemed not to depress him, but to cheer him."[142] Ultimately, then, Mr. Ramsay's own pessimism fails him, leaving him "untamed and optimistic."

Mrs. Ramsay experiences and revels in moments of "intense, exquisite happiness," while happiness makes Mr. Ramsay uncomfortable.[143] He resorts to cheer instead. She withdraws into a sphere of reticence, of a language behind language, while he, like Bernard in *The Waves*, is known for his "phrase-making." She picks up on minute details of daily existence while he is "dumb, to the ordinary things, but to extraordinary things, with an eye like an eagle's."[144] Their perceptions, their outlooks, even their pessimistic attitudes seem at times diametrically opposed—so much so, that she even thinks of him as an optimist, and he bristles at her sense of doom even though she accommodates his. When she tells him how her children will never be "so happy again," lamenting how they will have to grow up "and lose it all," he gets angry with her, asking, "Why take such a gloomy view of life?"[145] She herself does not consider herself a pessimist, but when she thinks about life, her thought either trails off, or she imagines brandishing her sword against it.[146]

A LOVELY PESSIMISM

What Woolf traces in *To the Lighthouse* are different models of pessimism, different inflections and even rejections—but, ultimately, engagements with—a pessimistic worldview. It is in this sense that we can hear William Bankes echoing both Mr. and Mrs. Ramsay: "What does one live for? Why, one asked oneself, does one take all these pains for the human race to go on? Is it so very desirable? Are we attractive as a species? Not so very, he thought."[147] At the dinner table, he "felt rigid and barren," words that recall the barren landscape of Mr. Ramsay's polar expedition, but the simile Woolf pairs this with is "like a pair of boots that has been soaked and gone dry so that you can hardly force your feet into them. Yet he must force his feet into them."[148] The only other time we see boots is when they kick the stone that will outlast Shakespeare, and we do hear Bankes echoing this precise thought later on, when he asks, "Who could tell what was going to last—in literature or indeed in anything else?"[149] In the knowledge that all traces of humanity will vanish before stones do, the one recourse available to us is to force our feet into the boots and keep on kicking away these stones. "Let us enjoy what we do enjoy," he concludes.[150]

To the Lighthouse seems to have sprung just as much from this sense of joy as from Woolf's own grief. Just over a week after her letter to Janet Case about how she wished she could write like Plato in the *Symposium*, she turned to her diary with a fresh burst of energy after not having written during her study of Plato. She was now ready to write again, and in the same entry, she recorded the dinner conversation from the previous evening, in which "Sydney boomed out in the background that he was too unhappy 'of course I'm unhappy—aren't we all unhappy?—isn't it inevitable, seeing that no one of us has any satisfactory things?' . . . I laughed a good deal, & cheered myself at their discontent."[151]

Like Lily contemplating the dependence of all things on distance, Woolf's relationship to pessimism is one that, up close, reveals a vision of unbearable doom—but can also just as well generate humor, laughter, and cheer, reflecting the intersecting genres on display in *Symposium*. One would expect Aristophanes, the most famous comedian of his time, to give a humorous account of eros, even in the context of celebrating Agathon's victory for writing his tragedy. Instead, Plato uses Aristophanes as the mouthpiece for his own melancholic myth. In the shifting mosaic of the novel, and especially in the tension between Mr. and Mrs. Ramsay, Woolf's pessimism adapts to and dispenses with different patterns at every turn of thought. What holds these patterns together, though, is her treatment of love—a love that encompasses more than just the eros of Plato's *Symposium*. Auerbach, ends his chapter on Woolf—and the whole of *Mimesis*—by writing that "there is in all these works a certain atmosphere of universal doom," while still pointing out that *To the Lighthouse* "is one of those books of this type which are filled with good and genuine love," even with its "irony, amorphous sadness, and doubt of life."[152]

Even though love is not sufficient to withstand the sense of loss that pervades the novel, love here nevertheless accompanies every articulation of pessimism to assemble the debris left in its wake into a new arrangement that preserves the traces of what had been lost. Mrs. Ramsay's pessimism is followed by a warm, unarticulated expression of love for her husband. The coda to James's childhood hatred of his father is his sister Cam's adolescent realization that their father is actually "most lovable"—an opinion that James gradually warms up to.[153] Charles Tansley, introduced as a "miserable specimen" who is perpetually "not satisfied," finding fault with everyone around him—"You all of you are wrong," he thinks to himself at the dinner party—ends up "preaching brotherly love."[154] Lily chases the "demons" who "often brought her to the verge of tears and made this passage from conception to work as dreadful as any down a dark passage for a child" with the "love" she feels "with this all."[155]

In the dark passage of "Time Passes," love takes the form of loveliness, standing resolutely in defense against the cosmic destruction wrought on the landscape and on civilization in the intervening decade that spans the First World War. Balancing the violent imagery of lightning,

> loveliness reigned and stillness, and together made the shape of loveliness itself . . . Loveliness and stillness clasped hands in the bedroom . . . and the soft nose of the clammy sea airs, rubbing, snuffling, iterating, and reiterating their questions—"Will you fade? Will you perish?"—scarcely disturbed the peace, the indifference, the air of pure integrity, as if the question they asked scarcely needed that they should answer: we remain.[156]

These are the forces that anchor what remains in the chaotic wreckage, functioning as both consolation and as a painful cipher of loss in the same way that Zeus employs eros in *Symposium*. Lily translates this double gesture of loveliness—and love—into her painting just as much as Woolf translates it into her own writing, referring to writing itself as "the great solace, &

scourge" while working on the novel.[157] Love in this novel, like pessimism, "had a thousand shapes," offering art as a means for the characters to confront life at its most painful and horrific, "giving them a wholeness not theirs in life, making of some scene, or meeting of people (all now gone and separate), one of those globed compacted things."[158]

Woolf rounds out the wholeness of this novel, her own "globed compacted thing," with affirmation. The first sentence of "The Window" begins with "Yes," the word that also begins the last sentence of "The Lighthouse."[159] Jane Goldman argues that "these two bracketing yeses, two blocks joined by the intervening text's corridor, constitute another form of parenthesis, framing its matter."[160] Even within "The Window," the last paragraph begins with "Yes," as well: "'Yes, you were right. It's going to be wet tomorrow.' She had not said it, but he knew it. And she looked at him smiling. For she had triumphed again."[161] This whole section is framed by the word "Yes," but it comes around full circle to have opposite meanings. At first, Mrs. Ramsay tells James, "Yes, of course" he will be able to go to the Lighthouse, but then uses this "Yes" to acknowledge that her husband was right in saying that he would not be able to go.[162] This word becomes a kind of self-effacing affirmation that dissolves into nothingness without being negative—it bears the trace of the shifting alliances in character, at first binding Mrs. Ramsay closer to her son than her husband, and then gradually shifting so that she finds a "triumphant" way of bridging the emotional distance with Mr. Ramsay. But this word

> may also function as a . . . unifying, structuring line or corridor, yet simultaneously a destabilizing and fragmentary force, right through the text; it can no longer be read off as signifying anything permanent, affirmative or otherwise, merely pegging a central line through the narrative patchwork, like the lighthouse, the butterfly's wing, the round and square brackets: "Yes, with all its green and blues, its lines running up and across, its attempt at something."[163]

Just as James, finally reaching the Lighthouse, says that "nothing was simply one thing," this "yes" also cannot be reduced to simply one thing. It is both a framing device and a central line down the middle, like the line that finally ends up running down the middle of Lily's canvas. It is what holds the characters and the structure of both the novel and the painting together while illuminating the gaps in the underlying mosaic that keep this structure fragmented. It is a word that, in its movement from hope to disappointment—and finally to a quiet triumph—manages only to be an "attempt at something," tracing out this attempt as a process that recedes from sight as soon as it appears. It achieves perfection only in the verb tense with which Lily, painting the central line down the middle of her canvas, says to herself, "I have had my vision," in the present perfect.

Lily's triumph is not so much the line itself as having had her vision in the tension between the ephemeral moment that is now fading into the past and the permanent mark of that moment on the painting. The "governing form" of the painting, like the novel itself, "is not the static noun image of the title but its transitive syntax suggesting the elusiveness of the object of knowledge, celebrating open process over finite arrival."[164] Her vision mirrors Mrs. Ramsay's vision in "The Window," after having arranged her guests at the dinner party the way Lily arranges her colors:

> With her foot on the threshold she waited a moment longer in a scene which was vanishing even as she looked, and then, as she moved and took Minta's arm and left the room, it changed, it shaped itself differently; it had become, she knew, giving one last look at it over her shoulder, already the past.[165]

In her diary, Woolf wrote, "I can only note that the past is beautiful because one never realizes an emotion at the time. It expands later, & thus we don't have complete emotions about the present, only about the past."[166] The purpose of the present, then, is to gesture toward the past with the aim of completing it, even if this completion does not reach any permanence. Lily herself is reconciled to the thought that her painting "would be hung in the servants' bedrooms. It would be rolled up and stuffed under a sofa. What was the good of doing it then."[167] The "good" becomes the process itself, of having the vision and seeing it fade into the past. This is precisely where love and pessimism coincide; as with *Symposium*, love is a confrontation with the past, gesturing toward a vision of completeness even as it falls out of reach.

NOTES

1. Woolf, *To the Lighthouse*, 46.
2. Woolf, *To the Lighthouse*, 129.
3. Qtd. in Emily Dalgarno, "Reality and Perception: Philosophical Approaches to *To the Lighthouse*," in *The Cambridge Companion to To the Lighthouse*, ed. Allison Pease (Cambridge: Cambridge University Press, 2015), 1.
4. Qtd. in David Bradshaw's introduction to *To the Lighthouse* by Woolf, xlii.
5. Woolf, *Moments of Being: A Collection of Autobiographical Writing*, 2nd ed., ed. Jeanne Schulkind (New York: Harcourt Brace Jovanovich, 1985), 92–93.
6. Woolf, *Diary III*, 12.
7. Woolf, *Diary III*, 47.
8. Woolf, *Diary III*, 49.
9. Woolf, *Diary III*, 46, 81.
10. Woolf, *Diary III*, 90, 107.
11. Woolf, *Diary III*, 109.

12. Woolf, *Diary III*, 110.
13. Woolf, *Diary III*, 123.
14. Woolf, *Letters II*, 599.
15. Dalgarno, *Virginia Woolf and the Visible World* (Cambridge: Cambridge University Press, 2001), 86.
16. Qtd. in Dalgarno, *Virginia Woolf and the Visible World*, 87.
17. Qtd. in Dalgarno, *Virginia Woolf and the Visible World*, 87.
18. Woolf, *Letters II*: 446. There also seems to be an echo here of Thomas Hardy, when Tess uses the apple tree as a metaphor to describe the stars to Abraham: "They sometimes seem to be like the apples on our stubbard-tree. Most of them splendid and sound—a few blighted" (Hardy, *Tess of the D'Urbervilles*, 21).
19. Jane Goldman, "*To the Lighthouse*'s Use of Language and Form," in *The Cambridge Companion to To the Lighthouse*, ed. Allison Pease (Cambridge: Cambridge University Press, 2015), 35; Woolf, *To the Lighthouse*, 53.
20. Bloom, "Ladder of Love," 108.
21. Theodore Koulouris, *Hellenism and Loss in the Work of Virginia Woolf* (London: Routledge, 2011), 100.
22. Koulouris, *Hellenism and Loss in the Work of Virginia Woolf*, 100. "Judging from her analysis in the *Greek Notebook*, there is a lot of material in the *Symposium* which appealed to her. From the intricate start, to the mythological framing of the narrative by Aristophanes, Plato's *Symposium* contains multiple significances for Woolf" (Koulouris, *Hellenism and Loss in the Work of Virginia Woolf*, 102–103). Emily Dalgarno also mentions the influence of the *Symposium* on Woolf in *To the Lighthouse*, but only in terms of how the conception of beauty had evolved across time:

> To the Lighthouse may be read in part as a study of the changes in the conception of beauty, from its valuation in the *Symposium* as the form that leads to the philosophical ascent of the mind, to its status in Victorian culture, where it is associated with Mrs. Ramsay. (*Virginia Woolf and the Visible World*, 86)

23. Qtd. in Koulouris, *Hellenism and Loss in the Work of Virginia Woolf*, 103.
24. Woolf, *To the Lighthouse*, 46.
25. Woolf, *To the Lighthouse*, 40.
26. Woolf, *To the Lighthouse*, 41.
27. Woolf, *Letters II*, 599.
28. Woolf, *To the Lighthouse*, 41.
29. Woolf, *To the Lighthouse*, 41.
30. Woolf, *To the Lighthouse*, 41.
31. Woolf, *To the Lighthouse*, 44.
32. Hermione Lee, *Virginia Woolf* (New York: Vintage Books, 1999), 474.
33. Woolf, *To the Lighthouse*, 19.
34. Woolf, *To the Lighthouse*, 157.
35. Qtd. in Goldman, "*To the Lighthouse*'s Use of Language and Form," 36.
36. Goldman, "*To the Lighthouse*'s Use of Language and Form," 36.
37. Qtd. in Goldman, "*To the Lighthouse*'s Use of Language and Form," 36.

38. Woolf, *To the Lighthouse,* 7, 26.
39. Woolf, *To the Lighthouse,* 34, 7.
40. Woolf, *To the Lighthouse,* 20.
41. Woolf, *To the Lighthouse,* 130, 45.
42. Woolf, *To the Lighthouse,* 90.
43. Woolf, *To the Lighthouse,* 122.
44. Woolf, *To the Lighthouse,* 150.
45. Woolf, *To the Lighthouse,* 158.
46. Woolf, *Diary III,* 38.
47. Woolf, *To the Lighthouse,* 91.
48. Woolf, *To the Lighthouse,* 92.
49. Woolf, *To the Lighthouse,* 122.
50. Auerbach, *Mimesis,* 477.
51. Woolf, *To the Lighthouse,* 92.
52. Woolf, *To the Lighthouse,* 91, 103.
53. Woolf, *To the Lighthouse,* 24, 73, 81.
54. Goldman, "*To the Lighthouse*'s Use of Language and Form," 40.
55. Goldman, "*To the Lighthouse*'s Use of Language and Form," 41–42.
56. Woolf, *To the Lighthouse,* 148.
57. Woolf, *To the Lighthouse,* 121, 86.
58. Dalgarno, "Reality and Perception," 70, (italics in original).
59. Woolf, *To the Lighthouse,* 107.
60. Woolf, *Letters II,* v.
61. Qtd. in Lee, *Virginia Woolf,* 478.
62. Qtd. in Lee, *Virginia Woolf,* 478.
63. François Mauriac, *Mémoires Interieurs,* trans. Gerard Hopkins (London: Eyre & Spottiswoode, 1960), 101; cf. Lee, *Virginia Woolf,* 478.
64. Mauriac, *Mémoires Interieurs,* 101; cf. Lee, *Virginia Woolf,* 478.
65. Woolf, *To the Lighthouse,* 146.
66. Woolf, *To the Lighthouse,* 146.
67. Woolf, *To the Lighthouse,* 146.
68. Woolf, *To the Lighthouse,* 22.
69. Woolf, *To the Lighthouse,* 18.
70. Woolf, *To the Lighthouse,* 30.
71. Flaubert, *Madame Bovary,* 167.
72. Woolf, *To the Lighthouse,* 147.
73. Alfred Lord Tennyson, *Idylls of the King* (London: Penguin Books, 1989), 297.
74. Woolf, *To the Lighthouse,* 51–54.
75. Woolf, *To the Lighthouse,* 146.
76. Woolf, *To the Lighthouse,* 40.
77. Woolf, *To the Lighthouse,* 79–80.
78. Jean O. Love, *Worlds in Consciousness: Mythopoetic Thought in the Novels of Virginia Woolf* (Berkeley, CA: University of California Press, 1970), 45.
79. Qtd. in Koulouris, *Hellenism and Loss in the Work of Virginia Woolf,* 177.

80. T. E. Apter, *Virginia Woolf: A Study of her Novels* (New York: New York University Press, 1979), 86.

81. "So much depends then, thought Lily Briscoe, looking at the sea . . . upon distance: whether people are near us or far from us; for her feeling for Mr. Ramsay changed as he sailed further and further across the bay" (Woolf, *To the Lighthouse,* 156).

82. Woolf, *To the Lighthouse,* 24.

83. Woolf, *To the Lighthouse,* 162.

84. Woolf, *To the Lighthouse,* 105.

85. Woolf, *To the Lighthouse,* 105.

86. Woolf, *To the Lighthouse,* 110.

87. Theodore Koulouris, "Virginia Woolf's 'Greek Notebook' (VS Greek and Latin Studies): An Annotated Transcription," *Woolf Studies Annual* 25 (2019): 1, 53.

88. Woolf, *To the Lighthouse,* 110.

89. Woolf, *To the Lighthouse,* 30.

90. Woolf, *To the Lighthouse,* 106.

91. Woolf, *To the Lighthouse,* 158.

92. Dalgarno, *Virginia Woolf and the Visible World,* 91–92.

93. Woolf, *Diary III,* 123.

94. Woolf, *Diary III,* 123; qtd. in Dalgarno, *Virginia Woolf and the Visible World,* 1.

95. Woolf, *Diary III,* 110.

96. Woolf, *Diary III,* 34.

97. Woolf, *To the Lighthouse,* 110.

98. Dalgarno, *Virginia Woolf and the Visible World,* 33.

99. Dalgarno, *Virginia Woolf and the Visible World,* 33.

100. Thacker, *Cosmic Pessimism* (Minneapolis, MN: Univocal, 2015), 24.

101. Thacker, *Cosmic Pessimism,* 24.

102. Woolf, *Moments of Being,* 92–93.

103. Woolf, *Diary III,* 34.

104. Woolf, *Common Reader I,* 58–59.

105. Koulouris, *Hellenism and Loss in the Work of Virginia Woolf,* 84. Linda Dowling writes that Greek culture was promoted as a "ground of transcendent value alternative to Christian ideology" in Victorian Oxford (Linda Dowling, *Hellenism and Homosexuality in Victorian Oxford* [Ithaca, NY: Cornell University Press, 1994], xiii).

106. Woolf, *Diary III,* 113.

107. Woolf, *To the Lighthouse,* 14.

108. Woolf also uses the moon as a means to express her frustration in her diary:

> How, at a certain moment, I see through what I'm saying; detest myself; & wish for the other side of the moon; reading alone, that is. How many phases one goes through between the soup & the sweet! I want, partly as a writer, to found my impressions on something firmer. (Woolf, *Diary III,* 63)

109. Woolf, *To the Lighthouse*, 16–17.
110. Woolf, *To the Lighthouse*, 89.
111. Woolf, *Moments of Being*, 81.
112. Woolf, *To the Lighthouse*, 90.
113. Woolf, *To the Lighthouse*, 79–80.
114. Woolf, *To the Lighthouse*, 90.
115. Woolf, *To the Lighthouse*, 98.
116. Woolf, *To the Lighthouse*, 98.
117. Shakespeare, "Sonnet 98," in *Shakespeare's Sonnets and Poems,* ed. Barbara A. Mowat and Paul Werstine (New York: Folger, 2006), 1.5: 215; 1.7: 215.
118. Woolf, *To the Lighthouse*, 96.
119. Woolf, *To the Lighthouse*, 96.
120. Woolf, *To the Lighthouse*, 98; Shakespeare, "Sonnet 98," 1.10: 215.
121. Woolf, *To the Lighthouse*, 98.
122. Woolf, *To the Lighthouse*, 99.
123. Woolf, *To the Lighthouse*, 100.
124. Woolf, *To the Lighthouse*, 100.
125. Woolf, *To the Lighthouse*, 32.
126. Woolf, *To the Lighthouse*, 8.
127. Woolf, *To the Lighthouse*, 30.
128. Woolf, *To the Lighthouse*, 31.
129. Woolf, *To the Lighthouse*, 33.
130. Woolf, *To the Lighthouse*, 31.
131. Woolf, *To the Lighthouse*, 32.
132. Woolf, *To the Lighthouse*, 20.
133. Woolf, *To the Lighthouse*, 38.
134. Woolf, *To the Lighthouse*, 31–32.
135. Woolf, *To the Lighthouse*, 31.
136. Woolf, *To the Lighthouse*, 32.
137. Woolf, *To the Lighthouse*, 32.
138. Woolf, *To the Lighthouse*, 32.
139. Woolf, *To the Lighthouse*, 33.
140. Woolf, *To the Lighthouse*, 39.
141. Woolf, *To the Lighthouse*, 31.
142. Woolf, *To the Lighthouse*, 58.
143. In her diary, though, Woolf makes the distinction between "natural happiness" and "intense happiness," aligning "intense happiness" with an overall bleaker view of life:

> Only I am exiled from this profound natural happiness. That is what I always feel; or often feel now—natural happiness is what I lack, in profusion. I have intense happiness—not that. It is therefore what I most envy; geniality & family love & being on the rails of human life. Indeed, exaggeration apart, this is a very satisfactory form of existence. And it exists for thousands of people all the time. Why have we none of us got it, in that measure? (Woolf, *Diary III,* 73)

144. Woolf, *To the Lighthouse,* 59.
145. Woolf, *To the Lighthouse,* 50.
146. Woolf, *To the Lighthouse,* 50.
147. Woolf, *To the Lighthouse,* 73.
148. Woolf, *To the Lighthouse,* 73–74.
149. Woolf, *To the Lighthouse,* 87.
150. Woolf, *To the Lighthouse,* 87.
151. Woolf, *Diary II,* 74.
152. Auerbach, *Mimesis,* 551.
153. Woolf, *To the Lighthouse,* 155.
154. Woolf, *To the Lighthouse,* 10, 75, 160.
155. Woolf, *To the Lighthouse,* 19.
156. Woolf, *To the Lighthouse,* 106.
157. Woolf, *Diary III,* 40.
158. Woolf, *To the Lighthouse,* 157. The way Woolf treats art as the consolation for bearing life's miseries is analogous to the function of art in Nietzsche's *Birth of Tragedy.*
159. Woolf, *To the Lighthouse,* 7, 170.
160. Goldman, "*To the Lighthouse*'s Use of Language and Form," 43.
161. Woolf, *To the Lighthouse,* 100.
162. Woolf, *To the Lighthouse,* 7.
163. Goldman, "*To the Lighthouse*'s Use of Language and Form," 44; Woolf, *To the Lighthouse,* 170.
164. Goldman, "*To the Lighthouse*'s Use of Language and Form," 32.
165. Woolf, *To the Lighthouse,* 90.
166. Woolf, *Diary III,* 5.
167. Woolf, *To the Lighthouse,* 131.

Chapter 10

Cosmic Pessimism in *Lady Chatterley's Lover*

D. H. Lawrence's Tristan Legend for the Twentieth Century

AGAINST SELF-HELP

When Jessie Chambers—D. H. Lawrence's "most important female companion and friend" in late adolescence and early adulthood, as well as the model for Miriam Leivers in *Sons and Lovers*—was turning nineteen in 1906, her brother Alan turned to Lawrence for advice on what birthday gift to get her.[1] He recommended a slim volume of Schopenhauer's essays, newly translated into English less than a decade before, and he even ended up reading aloud from the book to them at the birthday party. The essay he chose to read was "The Metaphysics of Love," and it was one of the earliest occasions that Lawrence used to identify the philosophical position that he would spend the rest of his writing career fleshing out. "Every kind of love," Schopenhauer writes in the essay, according to the translation Lawrence read out loud, "however ethereal it may seem to be, springs entirely from the instinct of sex."[2] Schopenhauer continues,

> Love is of such high import because it has nothing to do with the weal or woe of the present individual, as every other matter has; it has to secure the existence and special nature of the human race in future times; hence the will of the individual appears in a higher aspect as the will of the species.[3]

To David Ellis, the "advantage of this view is that it allows Schopenhauer to explain the feeling lovers often have of being in the grip of powers quite beyond their control."[4] The "old stable ego" that Lawrence was intent on challenging in his works is obliterated through love, exposing the passivity behind passion, the blind Will behind scopophilic desire, and raw sexuality behind sentimental affection.[5] In sex is a vision of the future, a dissolution of the conscious self by the instinct of the species. Just twenty-one at the time of his initial enthusiasm for Schopenhauer's pessimism, Lawrence's own vision of the future grew bleaker over time, ultimately culminating in *Lady Chatterley's Lover* over two decades later.

Beth Blum situates Lawrence's bleak vision as a response to the self-help industry that took over Europe and the United States in the nineteenth century, only continuing to boom ever since.[6] Even though modernism "has long been defined by its rejection of Victorian moral imperatives," she sees "the concomitant rise of the self-help industry" as highlighting "the stakes and objectives of modernism's own genre of anti-advice."[7] In "Mr. Bennett and Mrs. Brown," for example, Woolf identifies the modernist novel as a space that, to Blum, "exceeds instrumentalism, surpassing the needs of 'happiness, comfort, or income' (precisely the province of self-help)."[8] Lawrence himself traces this self-help genre back to Benjamin Franklin and ended up rewriting and reversing Franklin's maxims, "confessing that they inspired him to develop his moral philosophy," which "forms the backdrop to the sexual reform advocated in *Lady Chatterley's Lover*."[9]

Lawrence belongs to a tradition that includes Baudelaire, who complained of the "stupidity" of "those volumes which treat of the art of making people happy, wise, and rich, in twenty-four hours."[10] Flaubert was an early detractor, too—in his 1842 novella *November*, the narrator sounds almost identical to Schopenhauer, wondering if "happiness too is a metaphor invented on a day of boredom?"[11] Lawrence didn't think much of Flaubert, but he did admire G. K. Chesterton, who noted how, in 1909, "On every bookstall, in every magazine, you may find works telling people how to succeed . . . they are written by men who cannot even succeed in writing books."[12] Nevertheless, bestsellers like Samuel Smiles's 1859 book *Self-Help* and Wallace Wattle's *The Science of Getting Rich* from 1910 ensured that this genre was here to stay.[13]

As this industry took a stronghold of European and American culture, Schopenhauer's writings—balancing a curmudgeonly impatience and disgust with an eloquent lyricism—emerged as an antidote, inspiring artists from music to literature to reject the cheap optimism of these hack self-help writers. After a period of writer's block, Wagner wrote in his autobiography that in 1854, his "poetic impulses" were finally "stimulated. It was no doubt in part the earnest frame of mind produced by Schopenhauer, now demanding some rapturous expression of its fundamental traits, which gave me the idea for a *Tristan und Isolde*."[14] With the opening bars of the unstable Tristan leitmotif, Wagner ushered in a new era of music in 1865. Swinburne, spearheading the British decadent movement less than two decades later, also turned to this medieval love story in his poem *Tristram of Lyonesse*, and Thomas

Mann, influenced by both Schopenhauer and Wagner, reinvented the Tristan story at the turn of the century in his novellas *Tristan* and *Death in Venice*. Even in *Swann's Way*, Proust echoes Schopenhauer's concept of sexuality from "The Metaphysics of Love" when he writes,

> Vinteuil's phrase, like some theme, say, in *Tristan*, which represents to us also a certain emotional accretion, had espoused our moral state, had ended a vesture of humanity that was peculiarly affecting. Its destiny was linked to the future, to the reality of the human soul, of which it was one of the most special and distinctive ornaments.[15]

Proust here uses the Tristan reference to signal a historical shift in consciousness and morality, disrobing the "vesture of humanity that was peculiarly affecting," a vesture of the past, in order to uncover—literally, to discover—the "reality of the human soul" in some future revelation. As avant-garde artists flocked to the pessimism of Schopenhauer (and later, Nietzsche, another one of the "subterranean intellectual influences" on Lawrence), they each seemed to rediscover the medieval Tristan legend as a way to think through the most modernist innovations.[16] Nothing could be further from self-help than a bizarre story about lovers who do nothing but inflict pain on each other and themselves, thinking of their love in terms of apocalyptic destruction.

Despite its variations across the centuries, the rough outline of the legend goes something like this: Tristan and Isolde are enemies, but because Tristan killed a dragon that had threatened Ireland, he is able to bring back Isolde as the bride of his king, Mark of Cornwall. Isolde's mother prepares a love-potion for Isolde to drink so that she will fall in love with Mark on their wedding night, but on the ship, both Tristan and Isolde get thirsty, and Isolde's nurse mistakenly administers the potion to them. The two enemy lovers cannot resist the potion's work on their bodies, even as they continue to hate each other. This triggers a series of events in which they continually risk their lives for pure lust, committing adultery and fleeing into the woods, where they feed on nothing but their passion for each other. They are miserable when they are together and miserable when they are not. Doomed to this intense love, they eventually die because of it.

Tristan and Isolde see themselves not as excited lovers acting on their desire, but as lethargic, passive slaves to a blind, destructive, violent, and incomprehensible Will. This understanding of love fits Schopenhauer's definition in the essay that had left such a deep impression on Lawrence from a young age. It also provides a template to think through human relations in light of global, even apocalyptic, disaster. After World War I, this pessimistic vision of love became more resonant to artists like James Joyce, who uses the structure of this story in his 1918 play *Exiles*, and Virginia Woolf, who inserts an episode of seeing Wagner's *Tristan und Isolde* in her war novel *Jacob's Room*.[17] T. S. Eliot cites Jessie L. Weston, who had translated Gottfried von Strassburg's *Tristan* into English in 1899, as the inspiration for "not only the title, but the plan and a good deal of the incidental symbolism" of *The Waste Land*, which itself has allusions to Wagner's version of the story.[18]

Denis de Rougemont, who researched his landmark study *Love in the Western World* in the aftermath of the First World War and published it on the eve of the Second, in 1939, sees in the Tristan legend the bedrock of modern history. "Happy love has no history," he writes in his introduction. "Romance only comes into existence where love is fatal, frowned upon and doomed by life itself."[19] He systematically works from Dante and Shakespeare to Stendhal and Wagner, viewing their love stories as variants of this legend. Rather than hiding in the delusional comforts of self-help optimism, de Rougemont turns to this story as a trajectory of Western culture in decline even as it inspired some of the greatest artistic achievements.

It is this particular legend that Lawrence re-writes in *Lady Chatterley's Lover*, enabling him to make sense of modernity after the cataclysm of the First World War while informing his pessimistic vision of the future as one in which civilization will "have lovingly wiped each other out."[20] This pessimism is one that mediates between love and apocalypse, between self-help and anti-self-help. Using Blum's recent insights into modernism as a response to the self-help genre, and responding to critics like Stefania Michelucci about Lawrence's treatment of physical and metaphorical space, I want to shed new light on how Lawrence uses the novel to challenge novelistic constraints.

COSMIC SCALE, ANCIENT MELANCHOLY

In the years after World War I, Lawrence wrote several essays as he began drafting what would eventually become *Lady Chatterley's Lover*, a number of which also read as excoriating tracts against the self-help genre. "The 'sweet' novel is more falsified, and therefore more immoral, than the blood-and-thunder novel," he insists in "Morality and the Novel."[21] "A new relation, a new relatedness hurts somewhat in the attaining; and will always hurt. So life will always hurt," he continues.[22] In his essay "The Future of the Novel," he writes that, "Some convulsion or cataclysm will have to get this serious novel out of its self-consciousness. The last great war made it worse."[23] He imagines himself to be the bomb that would explode this genre into something new, so that we can find "a new world outside."[24]

Lady Chatterley's Lover maps out this new world. Lawrence's lovers, like the Tristan lovers, return to the language of cosmic doom even when they are together, as when Mellors launches into the following postcoital monologue after their first tryst:

> When I feel the human world is doomed, has doomed itself by its own mingy beastliness—then I feel the colonies aren't far enough. The moon wouldn't be far enough, because even there you could look back and see the earth, dirty, beastly, unsavoury among all the stars: made foul by men. Then I feel I've swallowed gall, and it's eating my inside out, and nowhere's far enough to get away.[25]

Lawrence uses similar language, even as early as 1915, to articulate the effect of the First World War on him in a letter to Ottoline Morell:

> So it seems our cosmos is burst, burst at last, the stars and moon blown away, the envelope of the sky burst out, and a new cosmos appeared, with a long-ovate, gleaming central luminary, calm and drifting in a glow of light, like a new moon, with its light bursting in flashes on the earth, to burst away the earth also. So it is the end—our world is gone, and we are like dust in the air.[26]

In this letter, Lawrence seems almost to exult in the destruction of "our cosmos" even as he laments it, illustrating the template for a new cosmos organized around something "like a new moon" that would wipe away even the traces of destruction. There is something generative and creative in this "long-ovate, gleaming central luminary." Mellors, however, still sees the old moon in the wake of this destruction—and from the vantage point of that moon, imagines the dismal sight of earth in its rubble. Mellors's pessimism is more intense than Lawrence's from his 1915 letter; Mellors is less willing to adopt a narrative of cosmic redemption. But Mellors's pessimistic language is still a language of love—a language of engagement and connection even in its withdrawal and disavowal.

In the spirit of disavowal, perhaps it is possible to read *Lady Chatterley's Lover* along the same lines as his previous essays. Just like his reversal of Franklin's optimistic maxims, we can see him rejecting and reversing the standard modes of coping with loss in the post–World War I era, including even the methods of psychoanalysis, which he particularly reviled.[27] Blum notes how, despite their differences, "self-help and psychoanalysis both stem from a new interest in the power of the invisible dimension of thought to shape one's present and future actions."[28] Lawrence is not so much interested in this dimension of thought as he is in the grounding of experience in the body. So when Freud distinguishes mourning from melancholia by writing, "In mourning, it is the world which has become poor and empty[; in] melancholia, it is the ego itself," Lawrence's novel seems to trace a melancholia beyond melancholia—something that approaches an act of mourning both for the ego and the world, and whatever lies beyond the world. It is a cosmic pessimism that cannot be pathologized, treated, and cured.[29]

This pessimistic vision is one in which Connie and Mellors carry on a litany of how the world, not the ego, has become apocalyptically poor and empty after the War. No grief-work will enrich it again. Connie wonders in her melancholy, "Couldn't one go right away, to the far ends of the earth, and be free from it all?"[30] When she begins to acknowledge the attraction she feels for Mellors, she "felt herself released, in another world."[31] This world of ecstasy, in which "she walked away from herself," becomes the only world she can inhabit with him.[32] The pessimistic withdrawal from this world, then, paradoxically grounds the affirmative love that emerges between Connie and Mellors. It is a love that initiates what Mellors calls "a new cycle of pain and doom."[33]

Right before consummating their affair, Connie experiences an inner expansion of self, in which her interiority merges with the interiority of the forest. Lawrence writes, "from the old wood came an ancient melancholy, somehow soothing to her, better than the harsh insentience of the outer world."[34] This "ancient melancholy" stretches back to the earliest iterations of the Tristan legend, where the most intense love intersects with the deepest sadness, the most sublime *tristesse*. The melancholy is just as "soothing" as it is destructive, just as stimulating as it is paralyzing, like the love-potion—a kind of *pharmakon*—that the Tristan lovers accidentally drink on the ship back to Cornwall. To the Tristan lovers, neither this world nor the next can provide the necessary space to accommodate the intensity of their passion for each other, so they have to create their own universe, their own world, their own enclosed space, renouncing and replacing all secular and religious law with the law of their love. Like Gottfried von Strassburg's poem and Wagner's opera, Lawrence's novel treats love as its own religion.[35] His aesthetic "[proposes] a Newer Testament to replace the extant one."[36] Mark Kinkead-Weekes writes that this novel is, "at its deepest . . . a religious book. Since 1913 Lawrence had been maintaining in various ways that sex was a religious mystery."[37] Lawrence's religious reverence for erotic passion necessarily demands an iconoclastic view of the world.

The Tristan legend still risks repelling readers on the basis of its preachiness as it once offended its earliest readers on the basis of its sacrilege. Its language of self-indulgence and passionate excess aims to alienate the majority of its readership, picking out the select few who can appreciate this cultivated form of love. It is so exclusive that Gottfried, in his thirteenth-century rendering of the tale, begins his epic poem by choosing only the most finely selected audience worthy enough of listening to it—an audience that constitutes a world in itself:

> Thus I have undertaken a labour to please the polite world and solace noble hearts—those hearts which I hold in affection, that world which lies open to my

heart. I do not mean the world of the many who (as I hear) are unable to endure sorrow and wish only to revel in bliss.... What I have to say does not concern that world and such a way of life; their way and mine diverge sharply. I have another world in mind which together in one heart bears its bitter-sweet, its dear sorrow, its heart's joy, its love's pain, its dear life, its sorrowful death, its dear death, its sorrowful life.[38]

Before the story even begins, Gottfried performs its inner actions, revealing the paradoxes and palindromes that govern every nuance of this most unusual love about to be spelled out. Only the reader sophisticated enough to follow the sinuous paths of these paradoxes is invited to continue reading. Lawrence, too, begins *Lady Chatterley's Lover* in a similarly paradoxical fashion: "Ours is essentially a tragic age, so we refuse to take it tragically."[39] The love that both authors proceed to delineate exists in "another world," but bears drastic consequences on the familiar one. It is a love that is as tender as it is violent, destroying as much as it unites, and upsetting order for disorder. But in this disorder, it teases out a higher harmony that justifies the destruction.

IMPOSSIBLE SPACES

This paradox of an apocalyptic harmony is mapped out in the setting of every Tristan story, which conflates lush gardens and dense forests with barren wastelands and inhospitable climates. In the eleventh-century Persian epic *Vis and Ramin*, one of the earliest versions of this legend, Fakhraddin Gorgani writes, "to the lovers, all this barren waste, / The fierce simoom, the countless trials they faced, / Seemed like a garden filled with sweet delight / So dear to them was one another's sight."[40] The enemy lovers, having renounced any allegiance to their King and faith, indulge in saccharine exclamations of how each other's bodies provide the space for their own idealization of heaven. Like Connie and Mellors, "clinging to each other with uncanny force," a force neither one can resist, Vis and Ramin are unable to let go of each other.[41] They even drink while locked in their mutual embrace, a rather awkward image of obsession, "sucking the sugar of each other's lips" in "greedy sips."[42] These are not just any sips—these are "greedy" sips. This is not just any love—this is the love of addicts. Every time they unite, there is not only a sense of euphoric relief but also a sense of pain and dread. After making love with each other, they think "of the dawn when all the pain / Of separation would be theirs again."[43] It is, however, precisely this separation— this physical distance—that they need in order to feel the same rush, the same high, when they reunite again. Ramin, the male lover, tries to break this cycle of pain and doom by escaping to a nearby kingdom, where he finds another bride. But he comes back to Vis, telling her, "Why should I seek the world? If you're not there / My soul knows only sickness and despair."[44] If he does not seek the world, and he returns to Vis, then the question arises as to what kind of space she occupies, being at odds with the world.

What is striking about the scope of this love—a scope that takes the expanse of the universe without being universal—is how the narrator inscribes himself into it. In one of the rare moments when Gorgani's narrator shifts the attention away from the lovers to himself, he exclaims:

> O world, I will not hear your voice repeat / Its everlasting message of deceit. / And since I've witnessed everything you do / To other men, I'll turn aside from you; / I've scoured my heart now of the scraps of trust / And love I felt for you, like so much rust. . . . The world's not worth our knowing, and its name / Should be unspoken and a source of shame.[45]

If the name of the world should be unspoken, then what kind of utterance is available to the telling of the Tristan story? There is a Wagnerian caterwaul to its exclamatory presence, but there is simultaneously a stark reticence to it, as when Connie contemplates the "unspeakable beauty to the touch" of Mellors's naked body, feeling that she herself is "ocean rolling its dark, dumb mass" when she is with him, a "voiceless song of adoration moving through her."[46] It is the "unspeaking reticence of the old trees" that draws Connie to the woods, where she has sex with Mellors, whose "recoil away from the world was complete. His last refuge was this wood."[47] By speaking of the world as a source of unspeakable shame, and contrasting it with ebullient praise for the lovers, both Gorgani and Lawrence solicit us to imagine this particular experience of love as occupying a parallel space that emerges at the expense of this world, a space they invent through art. Gorgani even invites us to think of his own name as a space to protect these lovers from the rest of the world. Gorgan is a territory where the lovers frequently escape to, and when Vis's husband King Mobad finds out, he shouts, "Damn Vis, and damn Ramin, and damn Gorgan."[48] Both Gorgan and Gorgani provide the space for the love of Vis and Ramin, damned both from this world and the next. Gorgan, then, is not so much a place that exists in this world as it is the fictional space in Gorgani's imagination that opens up in its wake.

In Gottfried's *Tristan*, the narrator similarly draws attention to himself only on the rare occasion when he calls on us to reconsider our notions of space. In the episode when Tristan and Isolde flee from King Mark and run off into the woods, they ultimately come across the Cave of Lovers. Gottfried abruptly interrupts the poem to say, without further elaboration, "I have known that cave since I was eleven, yet I never set foot in Cornwall."[49] It is a cave accessed only through this obsessive, addictive, all-consuming kind of love. He writes that, "No paths or tracks had been laid towards [this cave] of which one might avail oneself," and that it lies in the midst of "wilderness and wasteland."[50] But the Cave here is not so much a feature of the natural landscape as it is a work of art, a hidden cathedral constructed by former giants for the worship of Love. The fugitive lovers lie together on "the bed of crystalline Love," which we are somehow supposed to accept as being comfortable.[51] And, like Vis and Ramin, who subsist on the "greedy sips" of each other's lips, Gottfried's Tristan and Isolde "fed in their grotto on nothing but love and desire."[52]

In this space where this kind of love occurs, the most stylized form of art emerges from the depths of the wasteland and the wilderness. Crystalline beds are more desirable than anything softer. The lovers nourish their bodies on nothing but their bodies alone. A life of crime and addiction are glorified as states of divine ecstasy. And, in this space, the lovers violate not only the laws of the state and of religion, but even the laws of the natural world, especially if Gottfried could set foot here without ever having set foot in Cornwall. The Nurse who facilitates the love between Vis and Ramin tells them that rivers will flow into deserts before their love can ever be realized. The fact that their love *is* realized then suggests that the natural world order has already been disrupted. Ramin, when he is separated from Vis, sighs with longing, which Gorgani compares to a "wind that blows / In April, bringing cold December's snows."[53]

A UTOPIA OF FAILURE

It would seem, by contrast, that Lawrence aligns the love between Connie and Mellors with the natural order against the artificial behemoth of industrialization, but in the hut where Connie and Mellors end up having sex, we see Connie "crying blindly, in all the anguish of her generation's forlornness. His heart melted suddenly, like a drop of fire."[54] In the outside world, tears drop and fires rise, but here fire drops like tears, and the melancholic tears instead rouse and elevate the lovers' desire for each other. In every version of the story, the Tristan love arises only out of paradoxes. It is a love that equates tears with fire, melancholy with happiness, pessimism with affirmation, apocalypse with genesis, poetry of the highest order with reticence and silence. This love erupts in a world without world, in a space that somehow defies spatial dimensions. They literally inhabit a utopia, but it is a utopia of failure, a utopia that cannot be sustained.

It seems like the narrators get too carried away with their sentimentality when they say that the lovers can subsist only on their love. Of course, this cannot be true; they eventually abandon their self-imposed exile in the Cave of Lovers, or the hut, or the wasteland, where everything supposedly is so perfect. De Rougemont argues that these lovers deliberately create obstacles for themselves, where none may exist otherwise.[55] This is a melancholy not of loss, but of its opposite. Perhaps the only thing worse than the melancholy of unrequited love is the terror of a love fulfilled, a love that is reciprocated with an intensity that is aimed at obliterating the world. It is in this space where we see the lovers profess their love not through direct speech, but through a withdrawal from speech altogether. Language itself seems like it must necessarily fail in describing this love, just as much as speech necessarily fails in the act of kissing.

And yet, this failure also paradoxically indicates a remarkable achievement of language. Amid constant wordplay and word-reversals, The Cave of Lovers is where "the name was well suited to the thing."[56] In "À Propos of *Lady Chatterley's Lover*," Lawrence explains that he also wrote the novel as a way to reconcile the Word with the Deed.[57] Connie finds refuge in Mellors's hut, not just as a way to fulfill her sexual desire, but to escape the world in which words no longer hold any value. The mystical space that the lovers inhabit is a space that dissolves the "hypocrisy" of language, a space that allows them to name themselves and their own world anew.[58]

Language and space are mutually constitutive in the Tristan legend. The writers of the Tristan legend use language to carve out a privileged space, one in which language itself is actively reevaluated by both the narrator and the lovers. Even on a formal level, the way language is organized across the page often corresponds to the space that these lovers occupy. Both Gottfried and August Graf von Platen structure their verses in quatrains, and within each one, the final rhyme is always a repetition of a word that had been introduced in the first line. In Platen's "Tristan," the entire last line repeats the first line, sectioning off each stanza from the rest of the poem. If the end and the beginning mirror each other, the enclosed space of the quatrain creates its own cyclical universe, paradoxically opening up this space to infinity and thereby effacing all notions of a beginning or an end. In this structural arrangement, Platen's poem displays a total unity composed of isolated units, each one of these units just as complete in their own symmetries. Wagner similarly orchestrates the doom at the end of the opera in the opening bars of the prelude. But the delay of the tonic key in the Tristan chord, and the onerously repetitive and cyclical structure of the opera that fills the gap of this delay, create a musical space that allows the lovers to escape into the infinity of their own making.

THE SPACE OF THE NOVEL: SUITING THE NAME TO THE THING

Instead of poetry or any other art form, Lawrence chooses the novel to create this unique space for his lovers. And within the novel itself, the narrator reflects on the novelistic form in spatial terms: "the novel, properly handled, can reveal the most secret places of life: for it is in the *passional* secret places of life, above all, that the tide of sensitive awareness needs to ebb and flow."[59] In every Tristan story, the lovers escape to the forest or the garden to explore their "sensitive awareness," and it is an exploration not just on the level of the body, but of language as well. Only the vernacular, for Lawrence, can reveal this *"passional* secret" place, and the vernacular is what has historically distinguished the novel from other literary genres. In Gottfried's *Tristan*, the secret place is The Cave of Lovers, a place just as literal as it is figurative. For Lawrence, this secret place is not just the hut in the woods, but the novel itself.

In yet another paradoxical reversal, Lawrence's meditations on the novel—which he places within a novel, as if fulfilling Schlegel's injunction for a theory of the novel itself—bring him full circle back to the genre of self-help, the genre he adamantly rejected. Looking closely at Woolf's essays, Blum examines how both the genres of self-help and anti-self-help overlap, demonstrating how modernist aesthetics end up replicating some of the rhetoric it attacks.[60] The same can also be said of Lawrence, who never felt quite comfortable with the other modernists because he believed, as Laura Frost writes, "the pursuit of novelty in and of itself produces overly self-conscious, too-deliberate art. The true artist, then, struggles between novelty and cliché."[61] It is as though he enters the self-help genre through the back door, unwilling to relinquish his pessimistic understanding of the world, which to him is a place overwhelmed by death and destruction. In *Cosmic Pessimism*, where Eugene Thacker paradoxically defines the titular term as, among other things, "the last refuge of hope," he writes that he "like[s] to imagine the idea of pessimist self-help."[62] The novel, for Lawrence, weds this idea of pessimism to self-help. It is precisely this last refuge of hope, this space we retreat to, in order to learn how to live. It is "not life" itself, as Lawrence writes in "Why the Novel Matters," but only "tremulations on the ether" that stimulate us into life.[63] In the same essay, he writes, "at its best, the novel, and the novel supremely, can help you. It can help you not to be dead man in life."[64]

Perhaps it is not just the novel as a genre he has in mind, but this specific one, aimed at instructing us in life the way Mellors instructs Connie in sex and the way Tristan tutors Isolde under the disguise of his name in reverse, Tantris. It is this awkwardly didactic—not to mention condescending—quality that Lawrence finds most admirable in the genre of the novel, even though any work that entertains such a pedagogic tone seems to be less of a novel than an instructional manual or a self-help book at such moments of authorial intrusion.[65] Petar Penda argues that Lawrence "follows the same rule in the fictitious world of *Lady Chatterley's Lover*" as he does in his essay "Morality and the Novel," where he "convincingly argues that any imposition of morality on art is immoral."[66] This hardly seems to be the case, though, since Lawrence is imposing—quite heavy-handedly—his own moral code on this novel.

Like Gottfried's Cave of Lovers, where "the name was well suited to the thing," the novel is the space for Lawrence the pedagogue to instruct us on how to use language after all "the great words, it seemed to Connie, were cancelled for her generation: love, joy, happiness, home, mother, father, husband, all these great dynamic words were half-dead now, and dying from day to day."[67] Lawrence demonstrates that the "King's English" is incompatible with the love he sets out to describe.[68] This English is a language associated with the mechanized, industrial England and its ruling classes, all of whom speak, act, and think in equally mechanical, inhuman ways.

Gottfried comes to a similar conclusion when he writes about the first word that Connie feels is canceled for her generation, 'Love':

> All that we have is the bare word, only the name remains to us: and this we have so hackneyed, so abused, and so debased, that the poor, tired thing is ashamed of her own name and is disgusted at the word.[69]

Lawrence's project, like Gottfried's, is to wrest this word away from the shame that had become attached to it in its worldly, vulgar usage. In the wake of the First World War, the rupture between the Word and the Deed had never been greater. To Connie's generation, "the only reality was nothingness, and over it, a hypocrisy of words."[70]

Her husband, Sir Clifford, participates in this hypocrisy. Paralyzed below the waist from the War, he is Connie's husband in name alone. He turns his physical disability into contempt for all things bodily, withdrawing into the world of the cerebral and insisting on a language that has been deprived of its meaning. Chatterley is reduced to idle chatter, stubbornly perpetuating this empty language in his mediocre novels: "It was as if the whole of his being were in his stories."[71] If there is any obscenity in this novel, it is the misappropriation of language in instances when Clifford pronounces false banalities of love to Connie.[72] She resorts to a silent but growing resentment, as if using her silence as resistance to the empty noise of his words. "She was angry with him, turning everything into words. . . . How she hated words, always coming between her and life! They did the ravishing, if anything did: ready-made words and phrases sucking all the life-sap out of living things."[73] By retreating from language, both Connie and Mellors create a clearing for a new kind of utterance to take shape—a discourse eloquent in its mystical silence. And yet neither the characters nor the narrator can ever get outside language; all they can do is gesture to its limits and reimagine its possibilities. "In life and in art," writes Daniel R. Schwartz, Lawrence "believed the best we can do is open up infinite possibilities."[74]

Unlike his modernist contemporaries, Lawrence addresses this twentieth-century catastrophe in language by resisting standard usage without resorting to abstract language experiments. It is not abstraction he is after, but quite the opposite. To Andrew Harrison,

> the full, conscious realisation of sex in the relationship between Connie and Mellors assumes an urgent role in counteracting wider cultural trends towards prurience and hypocrisy, so that language of sex is employed to stem the flow of linguistic abstraction and (if possible) to cleanse the Anglo-Saxon words of their dirty associations.[75]

Lawrence uses language to mine a physical reality largely abandoned after World War I. He uses the term "stream of consciousness" not as a Joycean literary technique, but as an organic, phenomenal substance: "The quiver was going through the man's body, as the stream of consciousness again changed its direction, turning downwards."[76] This "stream" appears again in the fight Clifford and Connie have about Proust, when she tells him, "But he bores me: all that sophistication! He doesn't have feelings, he only has streams of words about feelings. I'm tired of self-important mentalities."[77] To Lawrence, Joyce and Proust use these "streams" as ways to signal how clever they are, concatenating ideas and impressions in ways that are largely abstract and cerebral, even if the technique is used to capture the experience of something intensely physical like Molly Bloom's orgasm.

Instead of re-creating the ubiquitous sense of alienation in the inter-war period through the language of "self-important" sophistication, Lawrence resorts to the vernacular Derbyshire dialect to recuperate the only possible connections available to humans in this seemingly apocalyptic world. If Standard English is the language of civilization, it is also the language of death, destruction, and alienation wrought by this same civilization during and after the War. The language of life, then—of sex, of establishing bonds instead of breaking them—is the language of the colliers, among the only people left after the War who have physical and intimate contact with the earth, with the land, and with each other. Humanity's last hope of endurance depends on this contact, this intercourse, both linguistic and physical. To Charlie May, with whom Connie agrees, "sex is just another form of talk, where you act the words instead of saying them."[78] As Candis Bond notes, Lawrence's treatment of sex, "when viewed as a language *of* the body, becomes generative in a new way."[79] Sex as language and language as sex resist the hierarchy of English culture, threatening the sense of civilization it purports to uphold. To Penda, Mellors's "use of dialect is a purposeful way of opposing civilization, which is often seen in the proper use of language."[80]

Critics such as George Levine, however, have criticized Lawrence for not neatly resolving this impasse in language, and for resorting to the outdated mode of realism when he purports to be dispensing with it.

> In his rejection of the conventions of realism, Lawrence belongs nevertheless to that great struggle of the realists both to use and to reject literature and language, for the sake of a reality beyond language. He is trapped like those before him in language.[81]

This failure of advocating for a new language without inscribing it into his novel places Lawrence not among his contemporary modernists, but among "the last of the great Victorians."[82]

Julian Moynahan similarly questions "the inadequacy of words—any words—to set forth the meaning and drama of intimate physical and emotional experiences in which consciousness, on the narrator's own admission, surges in a dimension of reality inaccessible to language."[83] He compares the efforts of *Lady Chatterley's Lover* to the accomplishments of "Wagner's *Liebestod* sequence in *Tristan und Isolde*, which might be interpreted as orgasmic, [where] such questions do not arise."[84] Wagner is able to dissolve language into music; in his *Gesamtkunstwerk*, all of the arts merge to create a new mode of art. As a novel, *Lady Chatterley's Lover* relies only on language—but it is a language that, despite its controversial diction, is not adventurous enough in dislodging itself from traditional narrative practices to reveal the inner sacred bonds that Lawrence is so intent on portraying.

Lawrence seems to recognize this problem, however. His attempts at distancing himself from self-help, Victorianism, realism, and even modernism all end up in failure. In light of this failure, he ends up nudging language toward a silence that is rich in meaning, an absence that is not empty. "Well, so many words," Mellors writes to Connie at the end of the novel, "because I can't touch you. If I could sleep with my arm around you, the ink could stay in the bottle."[85] Language is not the word made flesh; the flesh will always be holier. While characters like Charles May and Tommy Dukes may view sex as a form of communication, Mellors views it as a form of communion, transcending any linguistic parallels.

RECONFIGURATION OF SPACE

Lawrence's merging of the linguistic and the physical creates a space that dissolves the boundary between interior and exterior. Before her affair with Mellors, the void of Connie's interior world echoes the weariness of the world around her. "The world looked worn out," she thinks to herself.[86] But then this exterior world becomes synonymous with her own: "To Connie, everything in her world and life seemed worn out, and her dissatisfaction was older than the hills."[87] Among the many reversals in the novel is that the characters do not quite inhabit their spaces as much as the spaces inhabit the characters. Connie is drawn to the "*inwardness* of the remnant of forest," because it allows her to escape from Clifford and his exterior world of empty formalities and hollow language.[88] The inwardness of the forest becomes her own, so that when she has sex with Mellors, "[she] was like a forest, like the dark interlacing of the oakwood, humming inaudibly with myriad unfolding buds."[89] In a later episode, during anal intercourse, the metaphorical space of Connie's interiority opens up a foreign territory with a foreign climate: "she came to the very heart of the jungle of herself. She felt, now, she had come to the real bed-rock of her nature, and was essentially shameless. She was her sensual self, naked and unashamed."[90]

In the same way that Gottfried could enter the Cave of Lovers without traveling to Cornwall, Connie's space transports and transforms her from a forest to a jungle. She essentially merges with the alternative space that opens up in the course of consummating her love. By affirming her self against the world, a world that cannot be spoken of without shame, she discovers another space worth inhabiting, a space of shamelessness. The passage from the forest to the jungle is itself the *passus*, the passion, that these lovers endure. It is a passion that denotes as much erotic desire as suffering, and it becomes a religious rite that replaces Christ's *passio*.[91] From the very beginning, they are haunted by a premonition of inevitable doom and destruction, and yet they precipitate this doom by loving each other all the more fiercely. When Connie first sees Mellors, "she [sees] in his blue, impersonal eyes a look of suffering and detachment, yet a certain warmth."[92] The entire course of their relationship is a struggle to affirm both this suffering and this warmth, which are the only values that Mellors believes in.[93] But even with this belief, he "dreaded with a repulsion almost of death, any further close human contact."[94] When Connie asks him, "And were you sorry when I came along?" he replies, "I was sorry—and I was glad."[95]

Mellors's face before copulation is "pale and without expression, like that of a man submitting to fate."[96] Like Tristan, his unbridled passion is tinged with fatalist resignation and dread. "The desire rose again, his penis began to stir like a bird. At the same time an oppression, a dread of exposing himself and her to that outside Thing that sparkled viciously in the electric lights, weighted down his shoulders."[97] Connie, for her part, also dreads sex with him as much as she desires it. She "watched his face, and the passion for him moved in her bowels. She resisted it as far as she could, for it was the loss of herself to herself."[98] Returning repeatedly to her lover, who makes her "half afraid," she "quivered again at the potent inexorable entry inside her, so strange and terrible. It might come with the thrust of a sword in her softly-opened body, and that would be death."[99] Whether she is fearful of the pain or of his anger, sex for her—as for the Tristan lovers—carries with it the dread of death.

In *Space and Place in the Works of D.H. Lawrence*, Stefania Michelucci leaves her only comments on *Lady Chatterley's Lover* at the end, dismissing the novel as a return to "less ambitious objectives, abandoning every hope of rebirth for the entire community and limiting the range of the quest to individual existence."[100] By focusing on individual existence, though, Lawrence illustrates what is at stake not just for any community but the global community, the scope of his novel panning out not just onto the world but the entire space of the cosmos. Michelucci nevertheless goes on to identify Lawrence's treatment of space here as an opposition between

> the line and the circle, or between the open and the closed, that is between *movement* onward towards new, always more distant places versus *staying* within the circularity of a world with fixed, but controllable limits, which is in the end the only effectively habitable space. Whereas the "line" is oriented in the direction of large open spaces (which are never actually fully reached) . . . the "circle" is formed by the circumscribed horizons of places culturally marked by human beings (albeit foreign) . . . [In] *Lady Chatterley's Lover*, the circle is a familiar, circumscribed environment, the woods near her husband's ancestral home, which makes it possible for . . . Connie to find a haven for her existential quest through her rediscovery of her own instincts.[101]

While Michelucci's readings of Lawrence's works are deeply insightful, this particular reading does not address how Lawrence's circular imagery also fulfills the function that Michelucci ascribes to the line. It is precisely in the "familiar, circumscribed environment, the woods," that Connie is able to move "onward towards new, always more distant places" even as they are located inside herself. But if the border between inside and outside blurs, then the distinction between movement and staying is no longer an entirely accurate one.

I would argue that Lawrence is at his most sophisticated in his mystical reconfiguration of space in this novel. Linearity for Lawrence, moreover, paradoxically ends in a cul-de-sac: "I don't want to grow in one direction any more," he writes in "Why the Novel Matters." "A particular direction ends in a cul-de-sac."[102] And circularity for him is anything but fixed or limited. He begins "Morality and the Novel" by writing, "The business of art is to reveal the relation between man and his circumambient universe, at the living moment."[103] This circumambience is predicated on change and flux, not stasis or familiarity. Lawrence illustrates this world in flux with a recurrent image of fluidity, heavily evocative of the fateful episode at sea when the Tristan lovers drink the love-potion and become aware of their mutual love and doom. Unmoored from this world, Connie feels as though she "had been fastened by a rope, and jagging and snaring like a boat at its moorings," but now drifts to the new world she creates with Mellors.[104] With him, "she was like the sea" itself, and "her womb was open and soft and softly clamouring like a sea-anemone under the tides."[105] She dissolves into "one perfect concentric fluid of feeling" rippling across the space they inhabit so that their surroundings reflect themselves: "In the dimness of it all trees glistened naked and dark, as if they had unclothed themselves."[106] Everything around her seems enchanted, buoyed by the tidal currents of her consciousness: "As she ran home in the twilight, the world seemed a dream; the trees in the park seemed bulging and surging at anchor on a tide, and the heave of the slope to the house was alive."[107] Even this prose sentence is propelled by a poetic tide of anapests, mirroring the structure of Swinburne's *Tristram of Lyonesse*.

Sex itself is figured as a kind of baptism, in which Connie would "sink in the new bath of life, in the depths of her womb."[108] The holiness of Mellors's touch replaces any lingering traces of religion, and even this metaphorical bath replaces any literal bath she would have expected to take: "Connie would not take her bath this evening. The sense of his flesh touching her, the very stickiness upon her, was dear to her, and in a sense, holy."[109] As with Gottfried's *Tristan*, the only character seen taking a bath is Tristan himself, and the observer—more of a voyeur—is Isolde,

> who stole glance after glance at his hands and face [and] studied his arms and legs, which so openly proclaimed what he tried to keep secret. She looked him up and down; and whatever a maid may survey in a man all pleased her very well.[110]

When Connie chances upon Mellors taking a bath, "it was a visionary experience: it had hit her in the middle of her body.... Perfect, white solitary nudity of a creature that lives alone, and inwardly alone."[111]

THE ART OF COURTLESS LOVE

Perhaps it is not so much love-sickness as sea-sickness that Connie suffers from when she first sees Mellors, dissolved as she is into "one perfect concentric fluid of feeling" and seeing the trees as though they were "surging at anchor on tide." "I'm not well lately, and I don't know what's the matter with me," she writes to her sister Hilda.[112] Hilda arrives from the Midlands at once and is astonished at Connie's unnamed illness. She takes her to a doctor, who "examined Connie carefully" and yet cannot diagnose her because "there's nothing organically wrong."[113] In the Tristan legend, the presence of some kind of medical figure only serves to indicate that whatever illness is plaguing the lovers is beyond remedy and even beyond proper diagnosis. The illness, like the love itself, is otherworldly and therefore unaffected by any earthly treatment. The only intoxicating *pharmakon* that both relieves and intensifies the illness is the love she must repeatedly consummate with Mellors.

Hilda takes Connie back with her to the Midlands so that she can regain her health, and Clifford hires Ivy Bolton to look after his own disability in Connie's absence. Even though she is Clifford's nurse, Mrs. Bolton "felt more at home with Lady Chatterley" upon Connie's return.[114] Like Brangaene to Isolde and the Nurse to Juliet, Mrs. Bolton serves as Connie's confidante and private messenger, keeping "a cherishing eye on Connie, feeling she must extend to her female and professional protection."[115] She encourages the affair with Mellors, suggesting the path that Connie would eventually take to see him on the first occasion that they have sex.[116] When Connie vacations in Italy, it is Mrs. Bolton she writes to in order to redirect her private missives to Mellors. Mrs. Bolton also underscores Lawrence's scathing treatment of social class in the novel. She panders to Clifford's self-importance and feels drawn to the luxury of Wragby Hall, even though she is simultaneously repelled by his lifestyle: "She liked the colliers, whom she had nursed for so long: but she felt very superior to them. She felt almost upper class. At the same time, a resentment against the owning class smouldered in her."[117] She is fundamentally "a nihilist, and really anarchic," implicating herself in the destructive repercussions of Connie's affair with Mellors.[118] Clifford, for his part, feels that he is a potent ruler of the masses, even though all evidence points to the contrary. "I believe there is a gulf and an absolute one," he says, "between the ruling and the serving classes. The two functions are opposed. And the function determines the individual."[119] When he considers the practical ramifications of bearing an heir, he consents to the idea that Connie would have sex with any other man for the sole purpose of conception, as long as he is of noble pedigree. The thought that she would be carrying a passionate affair with his gamekeeper is inconceivable.

The Tristan romance is fundamentally a tale of courtly love—the lovers must be of noble rank; all appearances to the contrary are disguises to protect them from punishment. Both Gottfried and Béroul narrate episodes in which Tristan disguises himself as a member of the lower class, but it is always made clear to the reader that Tristan is a noble knight. Yet in an age when courtly love is an anachronism, Lawrence treats class itself as anachronistic, as well. Love for him outranks rank itself, instituting its own hierarchy in place of the enfeebled aristocracy. The Tristan lovers are necessarily foreign enemies to each other; now that the First World War is over, there is no greater enemy to British civilization than the lower classes who no longer believe in it.

But Mellors belongs to no class. He had a modest upbringing, although he was well-educated, having attended Sheffield Grammar School on scholarship. As much as he tutors Connie in the vernacular language of sex, he had also tutored Mrs. Bolton, decades earlier, in anatomy.[120] Like Tristan, he distinguished himself as a valiant soldier in the War. Also like Tristan, he faced combat in foreign lands, earning the respect of anyone who had seen him in battle. He "had been an officer, a lieutenant with a very fair chance of being a captain," but returned to England after "his own narrow escape from death: his damaged health: his deep restlessness."[121] When Connie thinks to herself, early in the novel, of the man who would inseminate her to give her husband an heir, she "had an idea that he would have to be a foreigner."[122] In a certain light, Mellors is precisely this foreigner, having returned from foreign countries to find himself even more estranged in his own. All he wanted after the War was "to be alone, and apart from life."[123] The only way to be as alone as possible was to return to the working classes and find work as Clifford's gamekeeper. He is unimpressed with the "toughness, a curious rubber-necked toughness and unlivingness about the middle and upper classes," but he is just as out of place in his own class: "So, he had come back to his own class. To find there, what he had forgotten during his absence of years, a pettiness and a vulgarity of manner extremely distasteful."[124]

To Mrs. Bolton, though, Mellors is "quite the gentleman, really, quite the gentleman!"[125] Even Connie's sister Hilda, who despises and condescends to him as an underling, "could not help realising that he was instinctively much more delicate and well-bred than herself."[126] He knows how to speak the English of the upper classes, but would prefer not to. Like Connie, he recognizes the pretensions of the "King's English," so he decides to speak the Derbyshire dialect instead, but he "spoke the vernacular with a curious calm assurance, as if he were the landlord of the inn."[127] Meanwhile, the more that Clifford insists on the rigidity of the class system, the less he notices that he actually uses "turns of speech that oddly had a twang of Mrs. Bolton."[128]

If class is revealed through language, then Mellors's disguises are not so simple to unravel.[129] By speaking in dialect, Mellors disguises his gentlemanly awareness, but by speaking in Standard English, he disguises his working-class life. His nobility, though, is a nobility that cannot be communicated through language. It is much stronger, much more immediate and impressive than any nobility of class, or even of spirit. His nobility is in his physical prowess, in his virility, his accomplishments of the body. Admiring his penis, Connie exclaims that it is "so lordly!"[130] She then proceeds to knight him as the "Knight of the Burning Pestle," to which he responds that she is "the Lady of the Red-hot Mortar."[131] It is in this way that Lawrence "represents sexual intercourse as the annulment of class segregation."[132]

THE LAST REFUGE OF THE HUMAN

Untethered from the world, Connie and Mellors exist in another realm where their free-floating bodies and their surroundings need to be named and honored as though for the first time. With strongly biblical overtones, their love is as much genesis as it is apocalypse. With the thunder and rain crashing down outside of their hut, "it was like being in a little ark in the Flood."[133] For all they know, civilization has been wiped out—and the thought provides some relief for Mellors, who exclaims:

> Quite nice! To contemplate the extermination of the human species, and the long pause that follows before some other species crops up, it calms you more than anything else.—And if we go on in this way, with everybody, intellectuals, artists, government, industrialists and workers all frantically killing off the last human feeling, the last bit of their intuition, the last healthy instinct—if it goes on in algebraical progression, as it is going now: than ta-tah! to the human species! Good-bye![134]

Mellors's pessimism here takes on a tone of exuberance. "Is that warning, or is that yearning?" Scott R. Sanders wonders.[135] "The gamekeeper seems half to dread the prospect of extermination, half to relish it," as the Tristan lovers do.[136] It is as though, like the sorcery of Isolde, their affair magically conjures up the elements to celebrate their passion at the world's expense. It also provides them a clearing so that they can re-name the new world of their own creation, beginning with the re-naming of their genitals and the flowers they use to decorate each other's pubic hair.[137]

In this vertigo of genesis and apocalypse, their love transcends the finite end of procreation to include all creation itself: "And as his seed sprang in her, his soul sprang towards her too, in the creative act that is far more than procreative."[138] Connie tells Hilda that, "love can be wonderful; when you feel you *live*, and are in the very middle of creation."[139] By renouncing their faith in the outer world, they affirm a higher faith in the world of their *poiesis*. In this transvaluation of values, the lovers postulate a new set of beliefs. After Mellors proclaims his only set of beliefs—that of "fucking with a warm heart"—Connie later reaffirms this belief by telling him what distinguishes him from other men: "It's the courage of your own tenderness, that's what it is."[140] Mellors responds, "Ay! it's tenderness, really; it's cunt-awareness. Sex is really only touch, the closest of all touch. And it's touch we're afraid of. We're only half-conscious, and half alive. We've got to come alive and aware."[141]

Lawrence's working title for *Lady Chatterley's Lover* was *Tenderness*—but, as Mark Spilka points out, "Tenderness implies personal feelings, affections, soft sentiments from the conscious heart; and Lawrence usually speaks for dark impersonal passions from unconscious depths. Tenderness is, moreover, a conventionally romantic feeling, an aspect of romantic love; and Lawrence usually speaks against conventional romance."[142] Lawrence's tenderness is precisely a departure from convention and a wholehearted disavowal of it. This kind of tenderness is a singular achievement of humanity, not a clichéd experience shared by the masses. It is primordial, not derivative; it destroys convention in order to create a new world in its wake. Connie feels it when Mellors "came with a strange slow thrust of peace, the dark thrust of peace and a ponderous, primordial tenderness, such as made the world in the beginning."[143]

The word "tender" does not just correspond to the way that Mellors treats Connie's body, but to the way that he lives on earth, tending to the land as a gamekeeper, protecting it from the threatening world of civilization and industrialization.[144] He exists "to fight that sparkling-electric Thing outside there, to preserve the tenderness of life, the tenderness of women, and the natural riches of desire."[145] In this word are also resonances of Isolde tending to Tristan's wounds long before drinking from the fated love-potion, already establishing their relationship as intensely physical from the very beginning, on the verge of death—but also on the verge of a new kind of living. The only meaning of "tender" that Lawrence actively renounces is the sense of a contractual offer. "So in the world as it is, what have I to offer a woman?" Mellors asks Connie.[146] She responds, "But why offer anything? It's not a bargain. It's just that we love one another."[147] Their tenderness is beyond tendering.

The pursuit of this tenderness is a battle against the world. "I stand for the touch of bodily awareness between human beings," Mellors says to himself, "and the touch of tenderness. And she is my mate. And it is a battle against the money, and the machine, and the insentient ideal monkeyishness of the world."[148] Both tenderness and the external world are mutually exclusive—as, for instance, when Connie "saw the forgetfulness of the world coming over him again, his face taking the soft, pure look of tender passion."[149] Like Tristan, Mellors is among the few sensual men in the world who are courageous enough in their own tenderness. "What a pity that fine, sensual men are so rare!" Connie thinks to herself, before contemplating the extent of this rarity: "Ah God, how rare a thing a man is!"[150]

In her newly charted lexicon of love, a man by definition is a sensual being—and as such, is exceedingly rare. Most of the people who populate the earth, to Connie and Mellors, are neither men nor women, but humanoid automatons, slaves to an industrial annihilation of their own making. They delude themselves into the myths of productivity, substituting happiness for profit while pillaging the earth for their own gain. These are the same sterile people whom Clifford entertains in his parlor room, postulating hopes for a post-sexual world in which "all the love business, for example . . . might as well go. I suppose it would, if we could breed babies in bottles."[151] Tenderness, by contrast, is the last refuge of the human. Connie and Mellors are figured as the last humans, the last ones capable of this tenderness—but they are also the first ones, too. They are the first humans of a future world that will be inherited by their unborn child.

Even so, this future world will be a miserable one. The sense of foreboding at the beginning of the affair persists until the end, wrecking the domestic order that Clifford stands for. Appropriately, Clifford tries reducing his devastation to the level of language, to the level of the word, asking Connie, "I suppose you don't at all mind having gone back on your word?"[152] The affair also makes Mellors endure public humiliation when his legally married wife, Bertha Coutts, attempts to move back in with him.[153] But the prophetic gloom reaches far beyond the domestic spaces of the lovers' legal partnerships, encompassing the entire world. Mellors writes to Connie at the end, "There's a bad time coming. . . . If things go on as they are, there's nothing lies in the future but death and destruction, for these industrial masses."[154]

Even with the extended passages prophesying universal doom and the destruction of civilization, Mellors ends by writing, "John Thomas says good-night to lady Jane, a little droopingly, but with a hopeful heart—"[155] The dash, though, replaces the more conventional period not just to end the letter but the entire novel, providing an end that resists ending. Friedman notes how much

> of Lawrence's major fiction . . . concludes irresolutely, as if impelled by desire toward unreachable solutions, ones impossible of fulfillment or completion this side of death. Lawrence, it seems, lacked faith in the future he craved, one predicated upon affirmation of human relations and mortality.[156]

It is as though Lawrence's final punctuation mark empties out the penultimate word of any optimism, tenuously opening up the expressed hope to the abyss of the future.

NOTES

1. David Ellis, *Love and Sex in D. H. Lawrence* (Clemson, SC: Clemson University Press, 2015), 2.
2. Schopenhauer, "The Metaphysics of Love," in *Essays of Schopenhauer*, trans. Mrs. Rudolf Dircks (London: Scott Library Ltd., 1897), 171.
3. Schopenhauer, "The Metaphysics of Love," 172.
4. Ellis, *Love and Sex in D. H. Lawrence*, 3.
5. Mark Kinkead-Weekes, "D. H. Lawrence: 'A Passionately Religious Man,'" *The Sewanee Review* 109, no. 3 (Summer 2001): 379.
6. The term itself first emerged in its modern usage in 1859, but the industry had already been primed by decades of moralizing writers who found an eager audience raised on the Enlightenment values of progress, improvement, and individualism (Beth Blum, "Modernism's Anti-Advice," *Modernism/Modernity* 24, no. 1 (2017): 117–139, 118, doi:10.1353/mod.2017.0005).
7. Blum, "Modernism's Anti-Advice," 118.
8. Blum, "Modernism's Anti-Advice," 131.
9. Blum, "Modernism's Anti-Advice," 120.
10. Baudelaire, "Let Us Flay the Poor," in *Baudelaire: His Prose and Poetry*, trans. T. R. Smith (New York: Boni and Liveright, 1919), 102–104.
11. Flaubert, "November," in *Memoirs of a Madman* and *November*, trans. Andrew Brown (London: Alma, 2005), 92. In the first volume of *The World as Will and Representation*, Schopenhauer writes, "life swings like a pendulum to and fro between pain and boredom" (I: 312).
12. G. K. Chesterton, "The Fallacy of Success," in *All Things Considered* by G. K. Chesterton (New York: John Lane, 1909), 21; John Worthen, *D. H. Lawrence: The Life of an Outsider* (New York: Penguin Books, 2005), 64.
13. Blum, "Modernism's Anti-Advice," 118.
14. Richard Wagner, *My Life*, trans. Andrew Gray, ed. Mary Whittall (Cambridge: Cambridge University Press, 1983), 510. The enthusiasm Wagner had for Schopenhauer was, hilariously, not reciprocated. "He is a poet but no musician," Schopenhauer quipped (qtd. in Wagner, *My Life*, fn.510/1: 776).
15. Proust, *Swann's Way*, 381.
16. Worthen, *D. H. Lawrence*, 59.
17. Timothy Martin, *Joyce and Wagner: A Study of Influence* (Cambridge: Cambridge University Press, 1991), 55.
18. Eliot, *The Waste Land*, 140.
19. Denis de Rougemont, *Love in the Western World*, trans. Montgomery Belgion (New York: Doubleday, 1956), 1.
20. Lawrence, *Lady Chatterley's Lover*, 218.
21. Lawrence, "Morality and the Novel," in *Study of Thomas Hardy and Other Essays*, ed. Bruce Steele (Cambridge: Cambridge University Press, 1985), 173.
22. Lawrence, "Morality and the Novel," 174.
23. Lawrence, "The Future of the Novel," in *Study of Thomas Hardy and Other Essays*, ed. Bruce Steele (Cambridge: Cambridge University Press, 1985), 152.

24. Lawrence, "The Future of the Novel," 118.
25. Lawrence, *Lady Chatterley's Lover,* 220.
26. Lawrence, *The Letters of D. H. Lawrence*, Vol. II: 1913–1916, ed. George J. Zytaruk and James T. Boulton (Cambridge: Cambridge University Press, 2002), II: 390.
27. Charles Michael Burack, *D. H. Lawrence's Language of Sacred Experience: The Transfiguration of the Reader* (New York: Palgrave Macmillan, 2005), 20. For an opposite reading, in which "D.H. Lawrence was a virtual textbook embodiment of Freud's theories about the pleasure principle and the death instinct" (207), see Alan W. Friedman, "D. H. Lawrence: Pleasure and Death," *Studies in the Novel* 32, no. 2 (Summer 2000): 207–228.
28. Blum, "Modernism's Anti-Advice," 122.
29. Freud, "Mourning and Melancholia," in *The Standard Edition of the Complete Psychological Works of Sigmund Freud*, Vol. XIV, trans. James Strachey (New York: Vintage Books, 1999), 246.
30. Lawrence, *Lady Chatterley's Lover,* 281.
31. Lawrence, *Lady Chatterley's Lover,* 84.
32. Lawrence, *Lady Chatterley's Lover,* 66.
33. Lawrence, *Lady Chatterley's Lover,* 119.
34. Lawrence, *Lady Chatterley's Lover,* 65.
35. "It is widely known that Wagner wrote a religious drama, but not so widely realised which of his works that is. *Tristan und Isolde*, often described as a paean to sensuality, a hymn to romantic love, even an exposé of its impossibility, is the work in question" (Michael Tanner, *Wagner* [Princeton, NJ: Princeton University Press, 1995], 140).
36. Daniel R. Schwartz, *Reading the Modern British and Irish Novel 1890-1930* (Oxford: Blackwell, 2005), 111.
37. Kinkead-Weekes, "D. H. Lawrence: 'A Passionately Religious Man,'" 392.
38. Gottfried von Strassburg, *Tristan*, trans. A. T. Hatto (London: Penguin Books, 1976), 42.
39. Lawrence, *Lady Chatterley's Lover,* 5.
40. Fakhraddin Gorgani, *Vis and Ramin*, ed. and trans. Dick Davis (New York: Penguin Books, 2008), 166.
41. Lawrence, *Lady Chatterley's Lover,* 173.
42. Gorgani, *Vis and Ramin*, 192.
43. Gorgani, *Vis and Ramin*, 193.
44. Gorgani, *Vis and Ramin*, 419.
45. Gorgani, *Vis and Ramin*, 485-86.
46. Lawrence, *Lady Chatterley's Lover,* 174–175, 136.
47. Lawrence, *Lady Chatterley's Lover,* 88.
48. Gorgani, *Vis and Ramin*, 482.
49. Gottfried, *Tristan*, 266.
50. Gottfried, *Tristan*, 262.
51. Gottfried, *Tristan*, 264.
52. Gottfried, *Tristan*, 262.

53. Gorgani, *Vis and Ramin*, 76.

54. Lawrence, *Lady Chatterley's Lover,* 115. It is no coincidence, then, that even Swinburne, in his *Tristram of Lyonesse*, begins by describing desire as leading "these twain to the life of tears and fire." (Charles Algernon Swinburne, *Tristram of Lyonesse* [New York: Elibron, 2006], 6).

55. Rougemont, *Love in the Western World*, 33.

56. Gottfried, *Tristan*, 261.

57. D. H. Lawrence, *D. H. Lady Chatterley's Lover and "À Propos of Lady Chatterley's Lover,"* ed. Michael Squires (Cambridge: Cambridge University Press, 1993), 329.

58. Lawrence, *Lady Chatterley's Lover,* 50, 227.

59. Lawrence, *Lady Chatterley's Lover,* 101 (emphasis in original).

60. Blum, "Modernism's Anti-Advice," 129–134.

61. Laura Frost, *The Problem with Pleasure: Modernism and Its Discontents* (New York: Columbia University Press, 2013), 106.

62. Thacker, *Cosmic Pessimism,* 47, 4.

63. Lawrence, "Why the Novel Matters," in *Study of Thomas Hardy and Other Essays*, ed. Bruce Steele (Cambridge: Cambridge University Press, 1985), 195.

64. Lawrence, "Why the Novel Matters," 197.

65. Laura Frost cites Michael Squires, Ian Gregor, John Worthen, and other critics who "concur that *Lady Chatterley's Lover* became more didactic and polemical as Lawrence revised it" (Frost, *The Problem with Pleasure,* 118). Andrew Harrison writes that the novel "proved to be his most polemical work of fiction on the relations between the sexes" (Andrew Harrison, *The Life of D.H. Lawrence: A Critical Biography* [Oxford: Wiley-Blackwell, 2016], 354).

66. Petar Penda, *Aesthetics and Ideology of D. H. Lawrence, Virginia Woolf, and T. S. Eliot* (Lanham, MD: Lexington Books, 2018), 39.

67. Lawrence, *Lady Chatterley's Lover,* 62.

68. Lawrence, *Lady Chatterley's Lover,* 298.

69. Gottfried, *Tristan*, 203.

70. Lawrence, *Lady Chatterley's Lover,* 50.

71. Lawrence, *Lady Chatterley's Lover,* 16.

72. Lawrence, *Lady Chatterley's Lover,* 112. Aldous Huxley, defending Lawrence, explains this reversal of obscenity:

> It is against this unnatural vice and the life-hating perverts who practice [*sic*] it that Mr. D. H. Lawrence appears to be fighting. A militant, crusading author, he hurls himself on what he calls "the evil thing, the wicked people." But the evil thing is sacred in our modern world and the wicked people are precisely those Good Citizens who wield the powers of the State. (Aldous Huxley, "The Censor," in *The Critical Response to D. H. Lawrence*, ed. Jan Pilditch [Westport, CT: Greenwood Press, 2001], 169).

73. Lawrence, *Lady Chatterley's Lover,* 93.

74. Schwartz, *Reading the Modern British and Irish Novel 1890-1930*, 111.

75. Andrew Harrison, *The Life of D. H. Lawrence: A Critical Biography* (Oxford: Wiley-Blackwell, 2016), 355.

76. Lawrence, *Lady Chatterley's Lover*, 211. Writing to the novelist Compton Mackenzie in 1920, Lawrence complains of Joyce's *Ulysses*, particularly Molly Bloom's final speech: "This *Ulysses* muck is more disgusting than Casanova. . . . I must show it can be done without muck" (qtd. in Derek Britton, *Lady Chatterley: The Making of the Novel* [Sydney: Unwin Hyman, 1988], 8). Mackenzie "later came to wonder whether *Lady Chatterley* might have been conceived in that moment" (8).

77. Lawrence, *Lady Chatterley's Lover*, 194.

78. Lawrence, *Lady Chatterley's Lover*, 34.

79. Candis Bond, "Embodied Love: D. H. Lawrence, Modernity, and Pregnancy," *D. H. Lawrence Review* 41, no. 1 (2016): 23 (italics in original).

80. Penda, *Aesthetics and Ideology*, 33.

81. George Levine, "Lady Chatterley's Lover," in *D. H. Lawrence*, ed. Harold Bloom (New York: Chelsea House Publishers, 1986), 236.

82. George Levine, "Lady Chatterley's Lover," 236.

83. Julian Moynahan, *The Deed of Life: The Novels and Tales of D. H. Lawrence* (Princeton, NJ: Princeton University Press, 1963), 162.

84. Moynahan, *The Deed of Life*, 163.

85. Lawrence, *Lady Chatterley's Lover*, 301.

86. Lawrence, *Lady Chatterley's Lover*, 47.

87. Lawrence, *Lady Chatterley's Lover*, 48.

88. Lawrence, *Lady Chatterley's Lover*, 65 (emphasis in original).

89. Lawrence, *Lady Chatterley's Lover*, 138.

90. Lawrence, *Lady Chatterley's Lover*, 247.

91. Rougemont, *Love in the Western World*, 41.

92. Lawrence, *Lady Chatterley's Lover*, 47.

93. Lawrence, *Lady Chatterley's Lover*, 206.

94. Lawrence, *Lady Chatterley's Lover*, 89.

95. Lawrence, *Lady Chatterley's Lover*, 203–204.

96. Lawrence, *Lady Chatterley's Lover*, 116.

97. Lawrence, *Lady Chatterley's Lover*, 120.

98. Lawrence, *Lady Chatterley's Lover*, 135.

99. Lawrence, *Lady Chatterley's Lover*, 125, 173.

100. Stefania Michelucci, *Space and Place in the Works of D. H. Lawrence*, trans. Jill Franks (London: McFarland, 2002), 107–108.

101. Michelucci, *Space and Place in the Works of D. H. Lawrence*, 108 (emphasis in original).

102. Lawrence, "Why the Novel Matters," 196.

103. Lawrence, "Morality and the Novel," 171.

104. Lawrence, *Lady Chatterley's Lover*, 86.

105. Lawrence, *Lady Chatterley's Lover*, 174, 133. At the same time that Lawrence published *Lady Chatterley's Lover*, Freud was working on *Civilization and its Discontents*, in which he describes the sensation of eternity as "a feeling of something limitless, unbounded—as it were, 'oceanic'" (Freud, *Civilization and its Discontents*, 11).

106. Lawrence, *Lady Chatterley's Lover*, 134, 122.

107. Lawrence, *Lady Chatterley's Lover,* 178.
108. Lawrence, *Lady Chatterley's Lover,* 136.
109. Lawrence, *Lady Chatterley's Lover,* 137.
110. Gottfried, *Tristan,* 173.
111. Lawrence, *Lady Chatterley's Lover,* 66.
112. Lawrence, *Lady Chatterley's Lover,* 76.
113. Lawrence, *Lady Chatterley's Lover,* 78.
114. Lawrence, *Lady Chatterley's Lover,* 82–83.
115. Lawrence, *Lady Chatterley's Lover,* 85.
116. Lawrence, *Lady Chatterley's Lover,* 85.
117. Lawrence, *Lady Chatterley's Lover,* 81.
118. Lawrence, *Lady Chatterley's Lover,* 140.
119. Lawrence, *Lady Chatterley's Lover,* 183.
120. Lawrence, *Lady Chatterley's Lover,* 145.
121. Lawrence, *Lady Chatterley's Lover,* 141.
122. Lawrence, *Lady Chatterley's Lover,* 64.
123. Lawrence, *Lady Chatterley's Lover,* 141.
124. Lawrence, *Lady Chatterley's Lover,* 141–142.
125. Lawrence, *Lady Chatterley's Lover,* 145.
126. Lawrence, *Lady Chatterley's Lover,* 244.
127. Lawrence, *Lady Chatterley's Lover,* 243.
128. Lawrence, *Lady Chatterley's Lover,* 180.

Clifford, while he was better-bred than Connie, and more "society," was in his own way more provincial and more timid. He was at his ease in the narrow "great world"—that is, landed-aristocracy society—but he was shy and nervous of all that other big world which consists of the vast hordes of the middle and lower classes, and foreigners. If the truth must be told, he was just a bit frightened of the vast hordes of middle and lower-class humanity, and of foreigners not of his own class. He was, in some paralysing way, conscious of his own defencelessness: though he had all the defences of privilege. Which is curious, but a phenomenon of our day. (Lawrence, *Lady Chatterley's Lover,* 10)

129. "That Lawrence felt compelled, in writing each successive version of the novel, to reduce the social distance between the lady and the gamekeeper is a measure of how seriously he regarded divisions of class as impediments to love" (Scott R. Sanders, "Lady Chatterley's Loving and the Annihilation Impulse," in *D. H. Lawrence's 'Lady': A New Look at Lady Chatterley's Lover,* ed. Michael Squires and Dennis Jackson [Athens, GA: University of Georgia Press: 1985], 12).

130. Lawrence, *Lady Chatterley's Lover,* 210.

Though it is impossible to take him seriously when he has Connie rhapsodize about phallic worship, Lawrence here creates a couple who know and articulate as well as feel: their becoming open to multiple ways of communicating suggests that Lawrence means them to serve as fully realized exemplars of heterosexual love. (Alan W. Friedman, "D. H. Lawrence: Pleasure and Death," *Studies in the Novel* 32.2 [Summer 2000], 224)

131. Lawrence, *Lady Chatterley's Lover,* 227.
132. Penda, *Aesthetics and Ideology,* 37.

133. Lawrence, *Lady Chatterley's Lover*, 216.
134. Lawrence, *Lady Chatterley's Lover*, 218.
135. Sanders, "Lady Chatterley's Loving and the Annihilation Impulse," 1.
136. Sanders, "Lady Chatterley's Loving and the Annihilation Impulse," 1.
137. Lawrence, *Lady Chatterley's Lover*, 221–224.
138. Lawrence, *Lady Chatterley's Lover*, 279.
139. Lawrence, *Lady Chatterley's Lover*, 241.
140. Lawrence, *Lady Chatterley's Lover*, 206, 277.
141. Lawrence, *Lady Chatterley's Lover*, 277.
142. Mark Spilka, "Lawrence's Quarrel with Tenderness," in *The Critical Response to D. H. Lawrence*, ed. Jan Pilditch (Westport, CT: Greenwood Press, 2001), 171.
143. Lawrence, *Lady Chatterley's Lover*, 174.
144. Mark Spilka, "Lawrence's Quarrel with Tenderness," 179.
145. Lawrence, *Lady Chatterley's Lover*, 120.
146. Lawrence, *Lady Chatterley's Lover*, 275.
147. Lawrence, *Lady Chatterley's Lover*, 275.
148. Lawrence, *Lady Chatterley's Lover*, 279.
149. Lawrence, *Lady Chatterley's Lover*, 278.
150. Lawrence, *Lady Chatterley's Lover*, 247–248.
151. Lawrence, *Lady Chatterley's Lover*, 74.
152. Lawrence, *Lady Chatterley's Lover*, 294.
153. Their daughter is also named Connie, hinting at a parallel with the Tristan legend. Like Tristan's relationships with the two Isoldes, Isolde the Fair and Isolde of the White Hands, the two Connies serve as indicators of vastly different but simultaneous relationships.
154. Lawrence, *Lady Chatterley's Lover*, 300.
155. Lawrence, *Lady Chatterley's Lover*, 302.
156. Friedman, "D. H. Lawrence: Pleasure and Death," 207.

Chapter 11

"A Last Mirage of Wonder and Hopelessness"

Andersen's "The Little Mermaid" as a Shadow Text of Nabokov's Lolita

THE MOST PESSIMISTIC FAIRY TALE

It is no secret that Nabokov despised *Lady Chatterley's Lover*, as he went out of his way to say so: "I must fight a suspicion of conspiracy against my brain when I see blandly accepted as 'great literature' by critics and fellow authors Lady Chatterley's copulations."[1] It is common for scholars to compare both *Lady Chatterley's Lover* and *Lolita* solely for their publication history and the similar legal battles that had ensued in the 1950s and early 1960s, but they are rarely compared for their treatment of pessimistic love.[2] Despite Nabokov's dismissive attitude toward Lawrence, *Lolita*'s narrator, Humbert Humbert, echoes Mellors in the expression of his desire to escape from the world in his pursuit of an apocalyptic vision of eros.[3] It is this sentiment that makes Denis de Rougemont read *Lolita* the way I read *Lady Chatterley's Lover*, as a modern reincarnation of the Tristan legend, with two doomed lovers whose hopelessness and pessimism outscale the world itself. As with *Tristan*, de Rougemont reads this novel as a story of "lovers [who] flee the world, and the world with them."[4]

But they are not "lovers," however much the controlling narrator wants us to believe this, and the reminder of this fact exposes the pessimism that is far bleaker than anything in the Tristan legend. In perhaps the most horrifying act of violence, Humbert takes it upon himself to give Dolores, the young girl he nicknames "Lolita," immortality—"the only immortality you and I may share."[5] She is granted immortality only as long as it is tethered to his own, only as long as it belongs to his narrative and serves his artistry, only as long as he gets to write her, create her, impose on the surface of her identity anything he wishes to, imagining her as his possession, "having no will, no consciousness—indeed, no life of her own."[6] He claims to write this work "to save not my head, of course, but my soul."[7] And what is designated by "my soul" is Dolores herself, whom he refers to as, "My sin, my soul."[8] It is never her soul that is Humbert's concern, even in retrospect, but only his. She exists even after her death only as *his* soul.[9] She is nothing but an extension of him, "safely solipsized"—trapped as a mirror of his desires.[10]

Since it is impossible to violate an aesthetic object in the way that one can violate a human, he transforms her in his mind into something akin to a statue, so that when he holds her, he is "ivory-full of Lolita."[11] And in this transformation, the ivory of her body seems to turn his body into a statue as well, so that he fantasizes about "a mute moan of human tenderness" that "would deepen to shame and despair, and I would lull and rock my lone light Lolita in my marble arms, and . . . mutely ask her blessing."[12] This is a far cry from the tenderness in *Lady Chatterley's Lover*. This is a tenderness that denies the subjectivity of the Other. It is not even clear from this passage whether the tenderness, as well as the shame and despair, belong to him or to her. From Humbert's perspective, he would like us to think that it is shared. To him, both he and Dolores are marble statues to each other, mutely asking for the other's blessing, mutely soliciting the other, in despair, in a bid for their own immortality.

Lolita is a palimpsest that explicitly draws on a vast number of shadow texts, but the one that highlights this marmoreal dynamic and this plea for immortality is the most pessimistic fairy tale ever written, Hans Christian Andersen's "The Little Mermaid." It is the story of a young mermaid who falls in love with a prince by first seeing a marble statue of him, and gives up her voice to the sea-witch in order to trade her fishtail for a pair of human legs so that she can secure the prince's love. Only through holy matrimony can she be granted an immortal soul, but after rescuing the prince from a shipwreck and unable to explain herself without a voice, the prince mistakenly chooses another bride whom he thinks had rescued him instead. The nameless girl who had once been a mermaid then dies by suicide as a result, throwing herself into the sea on their wedding night. It is the only fairy tale where the protagonist dies by suicide and the witch goes unpunished.

Nabokov himself writes about how he had cried over this story as a child with his English governess.[13] The story is indelibly bound up with his own childhood as it is with his relationship to the English language. Jane Grayson identifies his preoccupation with the figure of the mermaid in his transition from writing in Russian to English, seeing in the mermaid a representation of "continuity through change, a way through from one world to the next."[14] Mermaids, like the butterflies that Nabokov was obsessed with, are emblems of metamorphosis. And we can actually trace the metamorphosis of *Lolita*'s mermaid-like story to the last work of fiction he had written in Russian before moving over to English, a posthumously published work translated as *The Enchanter*.

The story is roughly the same as *Lolita*, although its prose is often just as cringeworthy as its subject matter, like when the nameless Humbert figure, as the "Enchanter" of the title, euphemistically passes his "magic wand over her body."[15] Enchantment, of course, invokes a particular use of language, summoning its supernatural power to cast a spell. Enchantment is the chant that, in its enunciation, overwhelms the power of any other kind of language to resist its force, which is why its victim, like the mermaid, is rendered voiceless.

This kind of enchantment is part of the Ur-Humbert's "pact with happiness."[16] It is a pact that dissolves past, present, and future so that his victim is trapped in an enclosed eternity that is entirely governed by him:

> As he imagined the coming years, he continued to envision her as an adolescent—such was the carnal postulate. However, catching himself on this premise, he realized without difficulty that, even if the putative passage of time contradicted, for the moment, a permanent foundation for his feelings, the gradual progression of successive delights would assure natural renewals of his pact with happiness, which took into account, as well, the adaptability of living love. Against the light of that happiness, no matter what age she attained—seventeen, twenty—her present image would always transpire through her metamorphoses.... And this very process would allow him, with no loss or diminishment, to savor each unblemished stage of her transformations. Besides, she herself, delineated and elongated into womanhood, would never be free to dissociate, in her consciousness and her memory, her own development from that of their love, her childhood recollections from her recollections of male tenderness. Consequently, past, present, and future would appear to her as a single radiance whose source had emanated, as she had herself, from him, from her viviparous lover.[17]

By the time Nabokov scraps this project for *Lolita*, Humbert ends by insisting that he loves "*this* Lolita, pale and polluted," just a few years older and now pregnant from another man, but it's difficult not to read this solicitation for the reader's sympathy as yet another trap.[18] Through the "pollution" of Dolores's seventeen years, Humbert still sees the nymphet Lolita of his own imagination and his own control, just as his literary predecessor would see the same image "transpire through her metamorphoses."[19] Pregnant and "elongated into womanhood," she still "would never be free to dissociate" from him.[20]

"Happiness," then, becomes a cipher of horror, of violence, of pessimism. Through this "enchantment," the girl is forever trapped in an eternity of the worst. By the time we get to *Lolita*, the word "happy" is issued as a threat, as an act of violence that hides all the other acts of violence in the novel. When Humbert warns her about what would happen if she would go to the police, he describes a life more miserable than what she has to endure with him, taunting her with the epithet of "you happy, neglected child."[21] That threat persists throughout the novel, even to the end, when he claims to be a changed man but still wishes "we shall live happily ever after."[22] It is that same sinister meaning of "happiness" that still rears its monstrous head, glowing through Humbert's mask. Humbert breaks down Dolores into the "happy, neglected child" precisely in order to envision his complete control over her, ensorcelling her into his fairy-tale ending. The rhetoric of happiness here insidiously hides and ignores the pain and violence that are inflicted in its name.

And this bleak vision of happiness is what binds *Lolita* not only to *The Enchanter*, but to an even earlier novel that Nabokov had written in Russian, translated as *The Gift*, where Boris Ivanovich tells Fyodor:

> Ah, if only I had a tick or two, what a novel I'd whip off! . . . Imagine this kind of thing: an old dog—but still in his prime, fiery, thirsting for happiness—gets to know a widow, and she has a daughter, still quite a little girl—you know what I mean—when nothing is formed yet but already she has a way of walking that drives you out of your mind—A slip of a girl, very fair, pale, with blue under the eyes—and of course she doesn't even look at the old goat. What to do? Well, not long thinking, he ups and marries the widow. Okay. They settle down the three of them. Here you can go on indefinitely—the temptation, the eternal torment, the itch, the mad hopes. . . . Eh? D'you feel here a kind of Dostoevskian tragedy?[23]

Narratologists point out that behind Humbert's narrative is the narrative of John Ray, Jr., and behind that one is the narrative of Nabokov himself. But maybe there's one more narrator even behind Nabokov, who happens to be this minor character from one of his other novels, giving us here the summary of the entire plot of *Lolita* in its earliest iteration, a summary framed by "thirsting for happiness" and "mad hopes."[24] And when Humbert tells us that he "felt a Dostoevskian grin dawning (through the very grimace that twisted my lips)," maybe this is Boris Ivanovich twisting those lips from behind Humbert's mask.[25] Since *The Gift* was written between 1934 and 1937, and Humbert first meets Dolores Haze when she is twelve years old in 1947, then both *Lolita* and Lolita can be said to have been born in *The Gift*, and not, as Nabokov said, when he saw a caged ape—whom he would model Humbert after—at the Jardin des Plantes in 1939.

The gift that Humbert ends up giving Dolores, a year after he first intrudes into her life, is a copy of Andersen's "The Little Mermaid" for her thirteenth birthday.[26] As Emily Collins notes, even though Humbert evokes an eclectic array of fairy tales, this is the only one we know of that he buys her as a gift;

all of his other presents are non-fiction.[27] It could be that, within the universe of this dark fairy tale that traps Dolores to Humbert, "The Little Mermaid" is meant to be taken as non-fiction, accurately reflecting the story of the eponymous but voiceless child. There is never any indication of what Dolores herself thinks of the gift, or whether she had even read it, but two years later, on her fifteenth birthday—the same birthday that Andersen's mermaid gets to experience the land of humans on the surface—Humbert gets rid of all her belongings while shedding "merman tears."[28] He even has to appropriate her sobs from years of sexual abuse and make them his own, as if he himself were the victim, seduced by what he calls her "nymphean evil."[29]

Nabokov's use of mermaids has been well-documented.[30] However, so far only Collins has focused on the role of Andersen's particular mermaid in *Lolita*. But where Collins concludes her perceptive close reading of the novel in light of the fairy tale with the claim that "Lolita's outlook is not as pessimistic . . . as Humbert would like it to be," I think it would be a mistake to downplay the pessimism not just in Dolores's outlook, but in the entire work.[31] Other scholars like Jane Grayson are also just as uncomfortable with settling on a pessimistic reading of *Lolita*, arguing that Nabokov's gradual transition from the use of the mermaid as the vengeful *rusalka* figure from Eastern European lore to Andersen's gentle creature moves "from the negative to the positive variants of the legend—from the loss, despair, guilt, revenge aspects of the tale, to those versions which highlight motifs of intercession, reconciliation and immortality."[32] But Nabokov demonstrates in this novel that any notion of immortality is predicated on loss, despair, and guilt. And as the pessimistic blueprint of these associations, he turns to Andersen's fairy tale.

A FAILED FAIRY TALE

In his first lecture of the Great Novels course at Cornell, Nabokov issued this opening statement:

> Great novels are above all great fairy tales. . . . Literature does not tell the truth but makes it up. It is said that literature was born with the fable of the boy crying, 'Wolf! Wolf!' as he was being chased by the animal. This was *not* the birth of literature; it happened instead the day the lad cried 'Wolf!' and the tricked hunters saw no wolf . . . the magic of art is manifested in the dream about the wolf, in the shadow of the invented wolf.[33]

If *Lolita* is a "great novel," then it is because it aspires to the pre-novelistic genre of the fairy tale.[34] Humbert is at once the boy crying 'Wolf!' as well as the animal itself. He plays every part in the story, even the "tricked hunter"—or, rather, the enchanted hunter—who dreams about the wolf, and whose name, etymologically derived from the Latin *umbra*, suggests its shadow. This is a novel that lays bare its genealogy of genre, tracing back to the origins of storytelling.

But both *Lolita* and "The Little Mermaid" only touch on the fairy tale genre while refusing categorization. In addition to Bruno Bettelheim, folklorists like Sheldon Cashdan refuse to call "The Little Mermaid" a fairy tale precisely because of how bleak it is.[35] If anything, this work subverts the Romantic genre by moving from enchantment to disenchantment and disappointment. The magical creature ends up being disappointed both in her sea realm and in the world of humans. She gives up her mermaid tail and her voice so that she can live in a reality that is far removed from any fantasy land, but finds that this reality is just as unforgiving. The story draws on a composite of genres, from Romance to anti-Romance and Bildungsroman. Andersen's original manuscript even ends on the note of a personal confession. *Lolita*, too, is framed as a confession and a fictional autobiography. In the Foreword, John Ray, Jr. refers to this work as a memoir, a case history, even "a work of art," or just "simply as a novel."[36]

The genre changes, seemingly, based on who is reading it. And Humbert loves to dismiss his readers by naming them. At first, it is "Ladies and gentlemen of the jury," but then he even mocks any reader: "my patient reader, whose temper Lo ought to have copied."[37] "Imagine me," he taunts us, "I shall not exist if you do not imagine me."[38] This is the boy crying wolf, trying to trick the hunter into imagining his story. But once we fall for the ruse, we engage in a dizzying reassignment of roles. We are not the hunter, but rather the hunted, falling into his traps. He has a special disdain for readers who read with the hubris of hunters, sniffing out clues to explain away his story in a reductive manner. Leading the reader on with questions about why a child arouses his sexual desire, he mocks us with a command: "Analyze it."[39]

This is a disdain that Humbert actually shares with Nabokov himself. "In addition to conventional moralists," Thomas R. Frosch writes, "Nabokov detests psychiatrists and literary critics, and it is against these types of readers—or these metaphors for the Reader—that Humbert wages constant war."[40] In short, this is a novel written for someone who either isn't a reader (like Dolores), or for someone who reads too well. The novel becomes a substitute for an impossible love (if it can even be called that)—a "love that is more than love"—narrated by someone like Othello, who thinks of himself as loving not wisely but too well. The novel reads like echoes of Othello's lyrical lament, proclaiming his love for Desdemona after strangling her to death. Both the Little Mermaid and Desdemona—and even Ophelia, who dies a "mermaidlike" death—endure fatal violence inflicted specifically on their throats, at the site of language.[41]

Humbert needs to silence Dolores so that only he can be heard—but by whom? Brian Boyd writes that the "careful reader is precisely Nabokov's ideal audience."[42] But maybe the careful reader is not exactly *Humbert's* ideal audience. For someone who despises allegory and symbolism, Nabokov's "hero-villains are often allegorists like Humbert, who imposes his fantasy of Annabel Leigh on Lolita and turns her into a symbol of monomania," not to mention the original transposition of Edgar Allan Poe's Annabel Lee onto Annabel Leigh.[43] Humbert draws on literature as an allegory for his own experiences in much the same way that Dante's Paolo and Francesca fall in love with each other through the act of reading itself, learning about love by reading the Arthurian romances of Lancelot and Guinevere. The story, of course, is told in the *Inferno*, and Humbert takes on the roles of not only these lovers, but of Dante and Virgil themselves, guiding us through his own allegorical hell.

The intimidation tactics of not only Humbert but also Nabokov, in aggressively dismissing allegorical interpretations of their narratives, are symptomatic of their proprietary claim to allegory and literary criticism in the first place.[44] "Allegory, as Angus Fletcher has shown, is demonic and compulsive; it is a spell, enchanted discourse. Nabokov, on the contrary, tries to create structures that defy interpretation and transcend the reader's allegorism."[45] The hubris, then, is not in the reader's "allegorism," but in Nabokov's—and Humbert's—attempt at creating "structures that defy interpretation." Such a utopian attempt is bound to fail. There is no art and no language that defies interpretation, and any sneer at the literary critic is an expression of contempt at the fact that criticism and interpretation are necessary for the artwork to have any sort of meaning.

Maybe it is for this reason that critics are not likely to read Nabokov as a pessimistic writer, bullied by his dismissive attitude toward pessimists. In an early short story, he wrote that a minor character "was a pessimist and, like all pessimists, a ridiculously unobservant man."[46] At the risk of being "ridiculously unobservant," I think the evidence of pessimism in his work warrants re-evaluation. He seems to invoke Schopenhauer, for example, when he writes in *Speak, Memory*:

> The cradle rocks above an abyss, and common sense tells us that our existence is but a brief crack of light between two eternities of darkness. Although the two are identical twins, man, as a rule, views the prenatal abyss with more calm than the one he is heading for.[47]

Schopenhauer writes that "our existence is but an infinitesimal moment between two eternities," which is his justification for not being afraid of death.[48] Nabokov captures the concept of two eternities on either end of an infinitesimal moment in the image of the hourglass, the name of the lake that separates him from Lolita. Anyone who gets in the way is treated with scorn and ridicule.

To Humbert, especially, the ridiculed "Reader" is just the haze that stands in the way of his ideal and impossible reader: Lolita, who is dead by the time Humbert's manuscript would have been read by anyone, and who was never much of a reader to begin with. It is she whom he directly addresses both at the beginning of the work ("Lolita, light of my life, fire of my loins") and the end ("And this is the only immortality you and I may share, my Lolita").[49] Her name frames the entire narrative, and is even echoed in the first word of John Ray, Jr.'s Foreword, which itself is framed by the title on the cover of the book, so that her name reverberates through the circles of hell that imprison Humbert in its frozen center. As much as he wants to fix her like a pinned butterfly, he ends up being the one frozen in place, tormenting both himself and the memory of those who had suffered because of him.

Any reader who is not Lolita is then positioned as an intruder in the text—an invader, an enchanted hunter who responded to the wrong cry. It is as though the reader interrupts Humbert calling out to her just as much as his first sexual experience with Annabel Leigh was interrupted in his "princedom by the sea"—not so much a place as a time that remains forever unfulfilled.[50] He writes this as a letter with an impossible addressee, a book for no living reader, a modern equivalent to a medieval verse lapidary, the beginning and ending coming full circle with the same word, the same name, uttered in futility.[51] This is the only immortality he can hope to share with her.[52]

Andersen also ended the original manuscript of "The Little Mermaid" with a plea for immortality, one which he hoped to share with the man he loved: "I myself shall strive to win an immortal soul . . . that in the world beyond I may be reunited with him to whom I gave my whole heart."[53] He transforms the dark fairy tale into a private confession, into a letter that would never be read by the man he was deeply in love with, Edvard Collin, who had married a woman the day before Andersen started writing this story.[54] Like the mermaid herself, Andersen ended up removing his own personal voice articulating his own desire, and deleted these lines before publication. Instead, he ends with a sinister warning to the children reading the tale of this girl who had just died by suicide and has now become a "daughter of the air," equipped with absolute surveillance of children's behavior. Her "time of trial" before entering heaven and attaining an immortal soul is set at three hundred years, but if she or any other daughter of the air comes across a child who is "mean or naughty," they would "shed tears of sorrow and each of those tears adds another day to our time of trial."[55] P. M. Pickard calls Andersen's ending "unsuitable for children," and P. L. Travers, the author of

Mary Poppins, says, "Andersen, this is blackmail. And the children know it, and say nothing."[56]

REWRITING ANDERSEN

The reader in both works, then, is singled out as delaying or interrupting both the mermaid and Humbert from attaining immortality with those they love. But while Andersen's vision of immortality is a Christian one, Nabokov empties his articulation of immortality from any religious notions whatsoever. Dolores herself dies on Christmas Day in 1952, giving birth to a stillborn child instead of a figure of hope and salvation who would have shared the same birthdate as Jesus.[57] The Via Dolorosa is hinted at in her given name, Dolores, a name that is erased in the diminutive nickname that Humbert invents for her.[58] He actively chooses to ignore the pain explicitly spelled out in her name.[59] When he marries her mother, the platitudinous Charlotte Haze, she tells him that if she ever found he did not believe in "Our Christian God," she would kill herself, a prospect not entirely unwelcome for the man who plots to get rid of her in order to have sex with her prepubescent daughter.[60]

If there is any Second Coming in the novel, it is Annabel Leigh coming back in the form of Dolores. Humbert is convinced that Dolores is the reincarnation of his childhood crush, whose "seaside limbs and ardent tongue" have haunted his imagination ever since they had to interrupt their copulation. When Annabel would kiss him, her mouth was "distorted by the acridity of some mysterious potion," and her "seaside limbs" became "lovely live legs . . . not too close together."[61] It is as though Annabel, who never says a word in Humbert's narrative, is not just the Annabel of his childhood or even of the Edgar Allan Poe poem, but the voiceless mermaid of Andersen's story, especially with the emphasis on the "mysterious potion" and her "seaside limbs." Humbert casts himself as the mermaid's prince, which is why he changes Poe's "kingdom by the sea" to "princedom by the sea."[62]

When Humbert first sees Dolores by the pool, "a blue sea-wave swelled under my heart" as he seems to recognize his long-lost Annabel.[63] Dolores is a girl whom Humbert imagines to have been, in her fetal state, "a little curved fish," but who has now grown up to engage in "backfisch foolery," a term Nabokov borrows from German to signify a young girl with the "seaside of her schoolgirl thighs."[64] Humbert thinks of her as a "pet," in the same way that the prince in Andersen's story also treats the mermaid as a pet, especially when he insists "that she must never leave him, and she was allowed to sleep outside his door on a velvet cushion."[65]

Dolores is a talented swimmer, being one of only two girls at camp who could swim to Willow Island, perhaps a nod to Andersen's mermaid, who retreats to her underwater garden with a weeping willow.[66] She idolizes a man in a magazine advertisement that she pastes to her wall (above an image of Clare Quilty) in the same way that the mermaid idolizes the statue of the prince that falls to her garden from a shipwreck. The "conquering hero" in this ad, dressed in a robe over pajamas, looks remarkably similar to Humbert, which also parallels the attraction the mermaid has both for the artistic representation of the prince and for the prince, himself.[67] Humbert, for his part, is careful to wear his own pajamas with a "cornflower blue" design around her, echoing the opening of Andersen's fairy tale: "Far out at sea, the water is as blue as the petals of the prettiest cornflowers and as clear as the purest glass."[68] Nabokov also refigures the second simile in Andersen's opening sentence, comparing water to glass in the pun on "Hourglass Lake" as "Our Glass Lake," where Dolores's mother Charlotte disappoints Humbert as "a very mediocre mermaid."[69] Humbert fantasizes about drowning her, leaving her body "in the inky ooze, some thirty feet below the smiling surface of Hourglass Lake."[70] This "inky ooze" could also refer to the ink of his printed words as well—in the doom that hides in the depths "below the smiling surface" of his "gloomy good looks."[71]

After Nabokov's puppet-mastery removes the hindrance of Charlotte by having her die in a car accident, Humbert dives headlong into his fantasy of sharing the rest of his life with Dolores. When he goes to buy clothes for her, he "moved about fish-like," comparing the store to an "aquarium" and the sales associates to sirens.[72] He ends up kidnapping Dolores, who holds the clothes he bought her "between her silent hands" and walks "through dilating space with the lentor of one walking under water."[73] In The Enchanted Hunters hotel, paneled in "seasick murals," he plies her with sleeping pills, which he likens to a "magic potion" so that he can rape her.[74] Violating her, he effectively takes her voice away so that, "Loquacious Lo was silent."[75]

"THE HORRIBLE HOPELESSNESS OF IT ALL"

It is at this point in the narrative that Humbert acknowledges the discrepancy between reality and fantasy, that the real Dolores behind his fairy-tale reincarnation of Annabel is the victim of his "pain and horror."[76] But this doesn't stop him from continuing to inflict this pain and horror on her. Like Andersen's prince, who mistakenly asserts that the girl he is marrying is the same one who had saved him at sea in the past, Humbert conflates the identities of Lolita with Annabel. But even after he disentangles them in his mind, he continues to think of them as contiguous figments of his imagination that he gets to mold along the way, failing to respect and protect the real girl who had been entrusted to his care.

Dolores, for her part, perhaps with some premonition about what is to happen to her on the first night of their hotel stay, turns away from him "with a hopeless sigh."[77] Humbert, in his violence, inserts himself even into this hopelessness, saying that despite "the horrible hopelessness of it all, I still dwelled deep in my elected paradise—a paradise whose skies were the color of hell-flames—but still a paradise."[78] No earthly space can accommodate Humbert's apocalyptic desire for Dolores. It is only through apocalypse that he can imagine freedom, imagining a colossal catastrophe that would shake his bonds from society and tighten Dolores's to him: "A free man, I enjoy her among the ruins."[79]

What frustratingly eludes readers like de Rougemont and Lionel Trilling is the painfully obvious way in which this is not a story of love that is reciprocated, which fundamentally undermines de Rougemont's understanding of this novel as a modernized Tristan legend. He overemphasizes the "mutual attraction" between the older man and the underaged girl, never once addressing the lack of consent between these "lovers," as he calls them.[80] Tristan never rapes Isolde (this would violate the code of chivalry he exemplified), and while neither of them can be said to have any agency or control over their desires or actions, there is never such a disproportionate imbalance of power and violence in the relationship. Humbert, of course, knows this, which is why he goes to great lengths—as any predator would—to make himself out to be the victim, arguing that he is falling under Dolores's spell rather than the other way around.

At stake here is the issue of freedom at work in Humbert's conception of love. The Tristan lovers can only imagine freedom as a postapocalyptic fantasy, as Humbert imagines himself as a "free man" to "enjoy her among the ruins." He may be free, but she never is. It's not entirely necessary to resort to Sartre to make the case that someone in her state is not in a position to reciprocate what passes as "love" for Humbert, but Sartre articulates the concepts of love and freedom, as does Nabokov, with the image of metamorphosis: "Just as wisdom is proposed as a state to be attained by an absolute metamorphosis, so the Other's freedom must be absolutely metamorphosed in order to allow me to attain the state of being loved."[81] Humbert does everything he can to prevent Dolores's metamorphosis, her freedom, so that he can keep her as a child for as long as possible.

Ellen Pifer traces Nabokov's idea of freedom back to the Romantic role of the child in Wordsworth, Blake, and Dickens, where "the child's wonder, innocence, and spontaneity constitute the image and embodiment of human freedom and creativity. In striving to attain his perfect world or paradise, Humbert deprives Lolita of her rightful childhood—and betrays the principles of romantic faith and freedom."[82] Dolores only ever speaks about freedom in clichés: "This is a free country," she fires back at her mother after being told that there will be no picnic the next day.[83] She is denied even the language to speak specifically about her own freedom, which amounts to another form of silencing. Her liberation from Humbert symbolically occurs on the Fourth of July, a holiday to celebrate both American independence and optimism, but this liberation becomes only another kidnapping, another instance of sex trafficking and imprisonment, this time from Quilty.

A closer analog to this expression of freedom and love than the Tristan legend is "The Little Mermaid" itself, which still bears heavy traces of this legend with its potion, prominent sea imagery, the doubling of Isolde figures—and the prince eventually abandoning his first love interest for the second—and the overwhelming, fatal passion. But Andersen's particular story centers on the one-sided experience of a child's desire; *Lolita* mirrors this story, narrating the one-sided desire for the child. "The Little Mermaid" traces a determined girl's struggle for freedom and recognition, traveling across the seascape and the landscape, traveling across genre from the Romance to the Bildungsroman, and even across gender when she dons a page's costume to explore the world of humans on horseback through forests and mountains.[84] The tragedy of *Lolita* is that her own determination and struggle to escape her captor is hardly narrated, and she ends up just as world-weary as Andersen's mermaid.

BETWEEN HUMBERT AND BEARDSLEY: AGAINST OPTIMISM

Early on in the novel, Humbert writes that, in becoming an adult with his appetite for nymphets, his "world was split.... One moment I was ashamed and frightened, another recklessly optimistic."[85] It is paradoxically his reckless optimism that leads him to commit the most horrific acts of violence and violation, which he describes as a state *"beyond happiness."*[86] He ostensibly intends this to mean a joy beyond happiness to match his love that is more than love, but he quickly qualifies this state beyond happiness as one of "horrible hopelessness."[87] It is a paradise for him, but one "whose skies were the color of hell-flames."[88] He is so beyond happiness that he stands on the other side of it, residing in a space of deep gloom, like the "inky ooze" beneath the "smiling surface of Hourglass Lake."[89]

The mask of optimism in this novel slips to reveal either a nightmarish world of sadistic torture, which is then aggressively defended as "love," or just a world of empty, sentimental stupidity. When Humbert enrolls Dolores at Beardsley, headmistress Pratt explains the school's philosophy to him: "we do try to turn our backs to the fog and squarely face the sunshine."[90] Perhaps contemporary and future readers of the novel will soon miss the humor in Humbert's account of this school's philosophy, since its utilitarian curriculum does not include "irrelevant topics"—like Shakespeare—in a frightening parallel to today's data-driven and STEM-heavy evisceration of humanities curricula across the nation's high schools and colleges, and for the same reason as Beardsley: for a "financially remunerative modern touch."[91] Humbert tries to make up for this gap in the humanities by purchasing books for her—among them "The Little Mermaid"—but both Humbert and the Beardsley school attempt to reduce Dolores to their image of what she ought to be, insidiously passing off this confinement as an education. "Jean-Jacques Humbert," as he calls himself at one point, is hardly a Rousseau, and Dolores is hardly his Julie or Émile.[92]

Dolores, in her search for freedom, does not fully align with either Beardsley's or Humbert's models of education but casts her own critical eye on them both, studying just enough to withdraw into a space beyond their reach. Like Andersen's mermaid, she has an uncanny power of perception—enough so that she can eventually make her escape.[93] She picks up on details that even Humbert does not notice until she is gone. Under Humbert's surveillance, it is impossible to truly communicate openly with anyone else. One of the many dangers of being enslaved to him is that she does end up being plunged into a musty old book, into *Lolita* itself. But the "sunshine" that Beardsley promises does not impress her, either. Whereas Beardsley encourages its girls to "turn our backs on the fog," the older that Dolores gets, the more she actually retreats into the fog spelled out in her last name, until she is cosmically unreachable, a distant cloud of pain, Dolores Haze—a gray star residing in Gray Star, past hope and past help.[94]

One of her school reports hints at an opaque interiority, out of reach from anyone else, especially in her use of spoonerisms.[95] Of course, these spoonerisms are indicative of Humbert's own rhetorical patterns, especially from the night when he first rapes her, saying things like, "What's the katter with misses?" and "Show, wight ray."[96] The fact that she seems to ventriloquize Humbert in her own private jokes with herself suggests the degree of control that Humbert wields over her. In the absence of her own voice, all she has is his to control her narrative.

But the use of spoonerisms in this novel identifies moments in which this power is reversed. Despite his fastidious attention to a bookish precision of language, Humbert even admits that his "word-control [is] gone" when he says, "What's the katter with misses?"[97] He is no longer the pursued prince in his own narrative but the mermaid who has lost control of her voice. When he tells her, "Show, wight ray," it is as though John Ray, Jr.—who introduces this narrative—demonstrates his own editorial control over the text. Ray's ray beams through the holes in the mask that Humbert takes great pains to avoid from slipping. Ray warns the reader in his Foreword that this text is a "mask—through which two hypnotic eyes seem to glow."[98] His metaphorical light aims to outshine the hypnotic effect of Humbert's eyes, cutting through the entire narrative.

Dolores, in turn, does not participate in this game of narrative control by shining an even brighter light through the text. She moves in the opposite direction, withdrawing into a dark space that cannot be seen by either of these men and refusing to play by their rules. Through insults, she distinguishes herself from the book that traps her, leaving Humbert behind in that book: "You talk like a book, *Dad.*"[99] Ray notes how there is no obscenity to be found in the entire work, but Dolores carries out her own narrative rebellion, writing four-letter obscenities on pamphlets distributed at school before saying "unprintable things" to Humbert in a fight.[100] From all sides, she is forced into being nothing more than a sex object—even her Beardsley report card expresses disappointment in how she takes no interest in anything having to do with sex.[101] And on top of this objectification, she is punished for naming the sexuality that is expected of her in terms that her abusers find offensive, if only for the fact that it puts an accurate language to their violence. Her linguistic transgressions, through spoonerisms and curse words, afford her the little agency she is able to hold onto in a world of predatory forces.

Dolores performs this reversal of power in the play *The Enchanted Hunters*, where her performance breaks free from the roles of either adoring mermaid or adored statue that Humbert assigns to her in his imagination. She is now a witch who hunts the hunter, but the tragedy is that this power is short-lived. She succumbs to the "spell of a vagabond poet," namely Humbert, himself—even though the poet is performed by Mona Dahl in the play—and the play itself is written by Clare Quilty, her other abuser.[102] Behind this performance is a girl who, like Andersen's mermaid, engages in a rebellious quest for independence, treading through both the realms of fantasy and reality in pain, harmed and disappointed in this impassive world.

ROLE REVERSAL

As Dolores begins to show signs of a fierce and desperate independence, wresting as much power for herself as she can, Humbert manipulates the narrative so that this role reversal works to his advantage. No longer the enchanted hunter, he fashions himself as Andersen's mermaid—the innocent victim of a passionate love. Collins points out that, "Humbert's reading of Andersen justifies his claim that he is a victim as well as an artist, and adds weight to his contention that Lolita herself is merely fictional."[103]

When Dolores is hospitalized for a throat infection, again drawing emphasis to the site of lost speech, Humbert aggressively seeks out the same kind of permission that Andersen's prince grants the mermaid by allowing her to sleep outside his room on a velvet cushion, saying that he tried pleading to sleep on the "'welcome' mat" in the corner of the hospital.[104] His "despair and weariness" reach their own fever pitch as he comes to the conclusion that his "love was as hopeless as ever."[105] But even his pessimism is no match for Dolores's. When he tells her that "there is no point in staying here," she pessimistically responds, "There is no point in staying anywhere."[106] She ultimately ends up escaping, but to a life full of more pain and misery. Frustrated with her escape, Humbert gets rid of all her belongings on her fifteenth birthday, the same birthday that Andersen's mermaid escapes to the world of humans. In this analogy, he is neither the mermaid nor the prince, but the mermaid's father. And as such, Humbert finds himself alone with his "merman tears."[107] Humbert is not the one who had broken her heart, as he comes to realize. The man responsible for that was Quilty. "*You* merely broke my life," he imagines her telling him instead.[108]

In this realization, Humbert recognizes that Dolores/Lolita is just a cipher of emptiness for him. The more he tries to seize her, to fix her, to render her immobile, the more she vanishes and slips away. Nabokov seems to map out this movement across the map of lakes in the novel. Camp Q, where Dolores has her first sexual experience (with the boy Charlie Holmes) and where she makes her first contact with Clare Quilty, is located next to three lakes: Onyx, Eryx, and Climax. Onyx is a kind of stone, and Eryx—according to Greek mythology—was turned to stone by Perseus. The association of water with stone again brings to mind the role of the marble statue in "The Little Mermaid." And the explosion of "more than a hundred rockets" on the prince's birthday at sea, when the mermaid first recognizes him as the model of this stone statue, simulates her own sexually climactic excitement at seeing him.[109] All three names seem interchangeable in their trochaic meter, and they each end with the same letter that suggests the cliché of X marking the spot—the degree zero of a fixed, immovable point on which Humbert aims at pinning Dolores.[110]

Meghan Vicks notes that it is no coincidence that the Russian word for "lake" is *ozero*, and that this wordplay "establishes the possibility that all of Nabokov's lakes are signifiers of nothing, in addition to markers of otherworldly realms."[111] The nothingness that these lakes suggest marks the "limits of human perception" on the one hand, as well as a "transcendent realm," one that is "'more real' than our world."[112] It is this watery, transcendent, and fantastical realm that both Nabokov and Humbert place Dolores in. There is something about her that will always elude the perception of her predator, her novelist, and even her reader, as she constantly slips out of reach. Humbert is flailing in this realm, his murderous plans foiled at Hourglass Lake while Dolores is away at camp near the other three lakes. Altogether, these four lakes seem to mark the four corners of Humbert's prison cell, the nothingness that traps him to his mortality. Hourglass Lake is the only one of these four lakes he swims in, and its name, rather than the longevity of Onyx or Eryx, reduces stone to sand as a measure of time running out, of finitude trapped between two globes.[113] The eighteenth-century thinker Georg Christoph Lichtenberg, one of the earliest people to use the word "*pessimismus*," wrote that, "Hour-glasses remind us, not only of how time flies, but at the same time of the dust into which we shall one day decay."[114]

Humbert situates Dolores in a world beyond time while he is caught in the hourglass of time itself. Comparing Humbert to Andersen's mermaid, Melanie McKay writes that, "Humbert can dimly perceive another level of existence beyond the walls of time just as the mermaid can perceive another existence beyond the sea, and both try desperately to escape their mortal prison."[115] If Humbert is also to be compared to the ape that Nabokov saw in the Jardin des Plantes, drawing the prison bars of his cage, then he "has drawn not the world but what separates him from the world."[116] In *Speak, Memory*, Nabokov writes of "captivity in the zoo of words," and it is precisely this captivity that Humbert is stuck in: "Oh, my Lolita, I have only words to play with!"[117] The difference between the realm of the word and the realm of the world—the world beyond the literal prison and the metaphorical prison of language—is a single letter, Lolita's initial. He wants to move through language to go beyond it and reside wherever it is that Lolita resides, in the voiceless, watery, but magical void. Her name is central to the narrative, and yet she only skirts its periphery, belonging to another world instead.

Michael Wood writes how Nabokov would take issue with Plato and Derrida with their claims that "there is nothing outside the text. . . . There is plenty outside the text, Nabokov would say, but the text is usually what we've got, and pretty much all we've got. Outside the text is silence."[118] In the same way that he does not just want to be an ape in a cage—ape meaning, as Frosch reminds us, not just an animal, but an imitator—Humbert wants to create rather than imitate, and use his artistic creativity to approach the point of the mermaid's silence and of Dolores's silence, sketching an ellipsis in the world he is stuck in: a lake, a zero, a space of nothingness he can dive into and share with Lolita, turning Hourglass Lake into Our Glass Lake, the finitude of the hour metamorphosing into an eternal "immortality that you and I may share, my Lolita."[119]

The significance of the Hourglass Lake episode is also that this is the first time Humbert receives a clue about the identity of Dolores's future abductor. Jean Farlow almost mentions Clare Quilty's name, but she is interrupted. Right before she almost says it, she notices that Humbert had swum with his watch, and Charlotte, the "very mediocre mermaid," responds "softly, making a fish mouth," that it is "Waterproof."[120] Nearly two hundred pages later, when Dolores says Quilty's name "in a kind of muted whistle," Humbert begins the next paragraph of his narrative with: "Waterpoof. Why did a flash from Hourglass Lake cross my consciousness? I, too, had known it, without knowing it, all along."[121] While critics like Alfred Appel, Jr. marvel at the clever way in which the word "waterproof" points to Clare Quilty, the logic of Quilty being Humbert's double suggests that this word actually points at Humbert, himself.[122] He, of course, is also Dolores's predator. He is both the hunter and the hunted, the detective and the fugitive. Like Oedipus—the first two syllables of whose name literally mean "I know," despite all his protestations at saying he does not know what is plaguing Thebes—Humbert admits, "I, too, had known it, without knowing it, all along." What exactly does he know, beyond Quilty's identity, and what is it that is waterproof? Quite literally, the first time the word is mentioned, it refers to his watch. Time itself is waterproof; it does not blur and dissolve under Humbert's spell, despite all his artistic attempts at overpowering it.

The mermaid in folklore is also a figure that is waterproof, moving between sea and land, between human and superhuman, in a way that Humbert wishes he could emulate. To Elena Sommers, the mermaid "carries the most otherworldly characteristics, being the only mythological heroine that is truly situated between this and [the] other world."[123] Water brings Humbert as close as he can possibly be to the world of Dolores, which he suggests even in seemingly throwaway lines such as his oblique reference to the "Sirens" chapter of *Ulysses* with his use of the word "*ormonde*" as the rain around him increases in intensity."[124] Joyce's "Sirens" chapter takes place in the Hotel Ormonde, a name short for *hors-de-ce-monde*, "out of this world."[125]

AN ETHICAL PESSIMISM: HOW TO READ DOLORES HAZE IN *LOLITA*?

However much Humbert glorifies Dolores and the magical realm out of this world that he identifies her with, both he and Nabokov place an ethical burden on the reader of how to interpret Dolores as a cipher of nothingness, as someone whose voice has been subsumed by her predator. Critics like Eric Naiman articulate the dilemma in terms of necessarily having to adopt Humbert's perspective:

> Since readers have no way of knowing what sort of person Humbert prevents from speaking her mind, those who want to imagine Lolita as a real-world girl (or, at least, as a real girl's representation), have to construct the character themselves or attack the construction of others. In the process, they are required

to emulate Humbert, creating Lolita in a way that inevitably makes her reflect their own anxieties and desires.[126]

But David Packman frames the dilemma in terms that would align the reader closer to Lolita's perspective, identifying how the

> breach between the representation and that which is represented, between the language that makes up the novel and the fictive world that it unfolds ... mirrors the reader's desire for the text; this doubling calls the reader's attention to his own activity, resulting in a subversion of the fictive world.[127]

Dolores tries to subvert the fictional fantasy of the text imposed on her, slipping away from the role of a nymphet into a human, just as much as Andersen's mermaid subverts the magical, fictional realm of supernatural creatures in order to inhabit the world of humans as well. Packman's reading strategy of subverting the fictive world within the text itself then functions as a gesture of empathy for Dolores's struggle. Julia Bader sees this "tantalizing part of Lolita which is resistant to the process of artistic abstraction" as something that "transcends and resists even [her] creator, the author himself."[128]

Dolores refuses to be an artistic abstraction and vies to be an artist in her own right. Maybe this is rooted in her own pessimism, her own sense of negativity. Even her mother, filling out questionnaires in *A Guide to Your Child's Development*, underlines adjectives that are rebellious and antagonistic. She even underlines the word "negativistic" twice.[129] Her negativity, her pessimism, and her artistry win her the little autonomy that she has, just as much as the mermaid's artistry does, as well. The mermaid's talent for singing is praised at such a high cost that it is worth the transaction with the Sea-Witch for human legs, allowing her to escape. Dolores, tired of being stuck with the role of playing Humbert's mermaid, shows more of an interest in acting than swimming, and uses her talent at acting—which she learned from Quilty—to escape from Humbert's control through dissimulation.[130]

She is clearly sharper and more intelligent than the vulgar veneer with which Humbert presents her to us, outsmarting him and even reproducing, mocking, and outwitting his own verbal acrobatics. She is the opposite of a passive figure; she literally acts both in the sense that she takes to the stage and takes action against her circumstances. Maybe it is for this reason that Nabokov personally ranked her second, after Pnin, "of all the characters he ever created that he admired as a person."[131] His wife Véra noted in her diary, after reading all the reviews upon its initial publication, "I wish, though, somebody would notice the tender description of the child's helplessness, her pathetic dependence on monstrous HH, and her heartrending courage all along."[132]

The tragedy is that this is hardly any consolation. Even the most sensitive and well-intentioned critics, after generations of outlandishly misogynistic scholarship on the novel, feel the need to reclaim Dolores's unsung narrative through the lens of optimism.[133] Kirsten Rutsala, for example, celebrates her "bravery and optimism," ignoring her when Dolores writes, in her own words, "I have gone through much sadness and hardship."[134] Nomi Tamir-Ghez writes, "While all the efforts of the narrator to win over the reader fail, the author finally wins us over, using as his strongest weapon the protagonist's own realization of his guilt."[135] H. Grabes emphasizes this point, insisting that *Lolita* is

> less pessimistic than the story that suggested it: at the end of the novel Humbert Humbert succeeds in finding another more selfless relationship to Lolita, that is, in escaping from his cage to some extent. He is successful because he had managed to find a different approach to other people, no longer characterized by selfishness, namely in his encounter with Rita whose actions were determined by "compassion" and "comprehension". Quilty's murder . . . appears in this context as the destruction of the personification of the "selfish vice" whose mastery the narrator had just overcome himself.[136]

For too long, critics have insisted that the ending of the novel is some kind of transformative moment, that Humbert—by falling in love with "*this* Lolita, pale and polluted, and big with another's child"—is now "selfless," as Grabes puts it.[137] Humbert's obsession with the girl he had raped, long after the age he had otherwise been attracted to, hardly counts as "selfless," and characterizing her as "polluted" betrays Humbert's persistent misogyny and objectification. Rita is such a minor character that she is hardly given any attention, and Quilty's murder redeems nothing. The end result is that a girl named Dolores Haze, now Mrs. Richard F. Schiller, had her life destroyed by this man, and will never recover from it. And maybe even Nabokov himself rejects such a transformative reading, saying that, "Humbert Humbert is a vain and cruel wretch who manages to appear 'touching.'"[138] Any critic who falls for his ruse—like Douglas Fowler, who insists that Humbert's refusal to kill Charlotte "is a moral achievement," setting a pretty low bar for moral achievements in general—is just fooled by this appearance.[139]

Other scholars take a radically different approach to the ending, arguing that Dolores never became pregnant and that there never actually was a Richard F. Schiller. Because of our unreliable narrator, maybe we can justify the position that "she actually died at the age of fourteen and a half. Her short, tragic adult life is in fact Humbert Humbert's delusion, a projected fantasy in order to create some sort of romanticized ending for the girl he defiled."[140] Sarah Weinman argues, in this version, rather than bearing responsibility for her death, Humbert can indulge in the illusion that—at least for a short time—Dolores found her way to a kind of happiness. By extension, he can mold their rapist-victim power dynamic into real life,

duping generations of readers in the process.[141]

This is the "pact with happiness" that his earliest avatar, in *The Enchanter*, had made, and that stuck with this character, crossing from one novel to the other just as much as Humbert's kidnapping of Dolores crosses state lines.[142] Happiness, in this story, is precisely what is transgressive, criminal, monstrous. For Dolores, there is no happy ending, no matter what interpretation we take. The final declaration of hope that Humbert may share an immortality with her in death is chilling in its horror rather than moving in any kind of semblance of authenticity or sensitivity—this is the last domain of control that Humbert wishes to exert on her, the last act of violence he could inflict. It is the last one and the everlasting one.

Michael Bell insists that it "is not simply the warm humanity of the person, then, that subverts his inhuman view of her," but it is her acting itself that temporarily gives Dolores a reprieve from his abuse.[143] Through acting, she "learns what her unfortunate mother never knew: the difference between an actual and a romanticized or fictitious self."[144] If the reader were to adopt Grabes's interpretation, and fall for that last trap of letting Humbert manipulate us into sympathy for him, then we also need to recognize that this so-called "realization of her humanity . . . occurs within the context of a more radically impersonal contemplation of her, himself and the whole relationship than he has ever been capable of before," as the novel closes and we are invited to regard the novel now in its entirety as "being consciously reified into an aesthetic object."[145]

The novel ends with Dolores positioned back in the place where she tried to escape from, in a magical world of immortality, which she shares with Humbert. Any optimistic interpretation of her story just serves to silence her even more. Her immortality, of course, is contingent on the extent to which she continues to live in the imagination of generations of readers, just as much as Andersen's mermaid does. Where Andersen comes right out and tells his readers that the time before the mermaid can enter heaven and finally acquire a human soul depends on how "good" or how "mean or naughty" his readers are, the implied injunction in Nabokov's ending seems to be similar. In the muted cry of Dolores is an ethical call to recognize and articulate horror and violence, even with the knowledge that however we may respond to such acts will do little to prevent them from being perpetrated on a scale that has always been overwhelmingly unfathomable. The cry emerges from this aesthetic, highly stylized, fairy-tale world, attempting to be heard by the world of reality outside it. But this outside world, this world of reality, is located beyond the walls of Humbert's prison, so—to him—it is the world of nothingness, a world that swallows up these cries and lets them die off in the void.

Before Humbert ends up in prison, he stands still on a high slope overlooking a children's playground, which "evoked a last mirage of wonder and hopelessness."[146] The "hopelessly poignant thing was not Lolita's absence from my side, but the absence of her voice from that concord."[147] If anything, this novel teaches us to listen to—and listen for—absence in concord, if not with wonder, then at least with a poignant hopelessness. "At this or that twist of it I feel my slippery self eluding me, gliding into deeper and darker waters than I care to probe," he continues.[148] Perhaps this "self," this part of him, is the soul he imagines to have created for Dolores, letting it slip back to where it came from, back into the enchanted void.

NOTES

1. Nabokov, *Strong Opinions,* 102.
2. Rachel Bowlby, "*Lolita* and the Poetry of Advertising," in *Vladimir Nabokov's Lolita: A Casebook,* ed. Ellen Pifer (Oxford: Oxford University Press, 2003), 156.
3. Nabokov, *Lolita,* 123.
4. Rougemont, *The Myths of Love,* trans. Richard Howard (London: Faber & Faber, 1964), 53.
5. Nabokov, *Lolita,* 309.
6. Nabokov, *Lolita,* 62.
7. Nabokov, *Lolita,* 308.
8. Nabokov, *Lolita,* 9.
9. Nabokov, *Lolita,* 9. Julia Bader observes that

Lolita is described in minute detail: her smell, her mannerisms, her thigh, and arm measurements are given with meticulous precision. But only too late does Humbert realize that he has given her no soul, that in spite of his painstaking artistry he has failed to appreciate her wonder and mystery, and it shocks him to the border of unconsciousness to think that "I simply did not know a thing about my darling's mind, and that quite possibly, behind the awful juvenile clichés, there was in her a garden and a twilight, and a palace gate." (Julia Bader, *Crystal Land: Artifice in Nabokov's English Novels* [Berkeley, CA: University of California Press, 1972], 77)

10. Nabokov, *Lolita,* 60.
11. Nabokov, *Lolita,* 58, 67.
12. Nabokov, *Lolita,* 285.
13. Nabokov, *Speak, Memory: An Autobiography Revisited* (New York: Vintage Books, 1989), 87. Emily Collins notes Nabokov's association of this governess,

Miss Norcott, with the sea, since her two other appearances in *Speak, Memory* are on beaches (Emily Collins, "Nabokov's *Lolita* and Andersen's 'The Little Mermaid,'" *Nabokov Studies* 9 [2005]: 90).

14. Jane Grayson, "*Rusalka* and the Person from Porlock," in *Symbolism and After: Essays on Russian Poetry in Honour of Georgette Donchin*, ed. Arnold McMillin (Bristol: Bristol Classical Press: 1992), 170.

15. Nabokov, *The Enchanter*, trans. Dmitri Nabokov (New York: Vintage Books, 1991), 73.

16. Nabokov, *Enchanter*, 56.

17. Nabokov, *Enchanter*, 56–57.

18. Nabokov, *Lolita*, 278.

19. Nabokov, *Enchanter*, 56.

20. Nabokov, *Enchanter*, 57.

21. Nabokov, *Lolita*, 150–151.

22. Nabokov, *Lolita*, 278.

23. Nabokov, *The Gift*, trans. Michael Scammell with the collaboration of the author (New York: Vintage Books, 1991), 186.

24. Nabokov, *Gift*, 186. Nabokov, of course, would disagree with such a reading, rejecting the notion "of how a character takes hold of [a writer] and in a sense dictates the course of the action" (Nabokov, *Strong Opinions*, 69). "My characters are galley slaves," he insists (Nabokov, *Strong Opinions*, 95).

25. Nabokov, *Lolita*, 70.

26. Nabokov, *Lolita*, 174.

27. Collins, "Nabokov's *Lolita* and Andersen's 'The Little Mermaid,'" 77.

28. Nabokov, *Lolita*, 255.

29. Nabokov, *Lolita*, 125.

30. See especially Grayson, "*Rusalka* and the Person from Porlock," 162–185; D. Barton Johnson, "'L'inconnue de la Seine' and Nabokov's Naiads," *Comparative Literature* 44, no. 3 (1992): 224–248; Priscilla Meyer, *Find What the Sailor Has Hidden: Vladimir Nabokov's Pale Fire* (Middletown, CT: Wesleyan University Press, 1988); Priscilla Meyer and Jeff Hoffman, "Infinite Reflections in Nabokov's *Pale Fire*: The Danish Connection (Hans Christian Andersen and Isak Dinesen)," *Russian Literature* 41 (1997): 197–222.

31. Collins, "Nabokov's *Lolita* and Andersen's 'The Little Mermaid,'" 95.

32. Grayson, "*Rusalka* and the Person from Porlock," 175.

33. Qtd. by Appel in an explanatory note to *Lolita* by Nabokov, 347.

34. Douglas Fowler, whose work has otherwise not dated well, also refers to *Lolita* as a "great fairytale" (Douglas Fowler, *Reading Nabokov* [Ithaca, NY: Cornell University Press, 1974], 175).

35. Sheldon Cashdan, *The Witch Must Die: The Hidden Meaning of Fairy Tales* (New York: Perseus, 1999), 163.

36. Nabokov, *Lolita*, 3–5.

37. Nabokov, *Lolita*, 9, 139.

38. Nabokov, *Lolita*, 129.

39. Nabokov, *Lolita*, 41.

40. Thomas R. Frosch, "Parody and Authenticity in *Lolita*," in *Vladimir Nabokov's Lolita: A Casebook*, ed. Ellen Pifer (Oxford: Oxford University Press, 2003), 43.

41. Carl Proffer maintains that the "most important literary echo of her real name, Dolores Haze, is from Algernon Swinburne's 'Dolores'" (Carl R. Proffer, *The Keys to Lolita* [Bloomington, IN: Indiana University Press, 1968], 28). In the poem, Swinburne also draws attention to Dolores's throat as the intersection between desire, pain, youth, and violence: "Wert thou pure a maiden, Dolores, / When desire took thee first by the throat?" (qtd. in Proffer, *Keys to Lolita,* 29).

42. Brian Boyd, "Even Homais Nods," in *Vladimir Nabokov's Lolita: A Casebook*, ed. Ellen Pifer (Oxford: Oxford University Press, 2003), 58.

43. Frosch, "Parody and Authenticity in *Lolita*," 44.

44. Nabokov's own literary criticism leaves much to be desired, claiming that "many accepted authors simply do not exist for me" (Herbert Gold, "Interview with Vladimir Nabokov," in *Vladimir Nabokov's Lolita: A Casebook*, ed. Ellen Pifer [Oxford: Oxford University Press, 2003], 202). Among these "complete nonentities" are Brecht, Faulkner, and Camus, as well as "the pretentious nonsense of Mr. Pound, that total fake" (Gold, "Interview with Nabokov," 203). Balzac, Dostoevsky, Stendhal, Conrad, and Henry James are also not worth his attention. He is too eager to dismiss *Death in Venice* as "asinine" (Nabokov, *Strong Opinions,* 57) as well as any influence from James Joyce (Nabokov, *Strong Opinions,* 102). *Don Quixote* is a "cruel and crude old book," and Kafka's "The Metamorphosis" interests him only insofar as he mistakenly reads in the text an invitation to identify the specific kind of bug that Gregor Samsa turns into, demonstrating only that Nabokov could not even begin to understand Kafka (Nabokov, *Strong Opinions,* 203). Nabokov is certainly entertaining, if not entirely persuasive, in his idiosyncratic readings and heavy-handed opinions presented as incontrovertible truths. He relishes in the practice of literary criticism insofar as he can condescend to any other critic as a mediocrity. But for all his "instinct to digs at great reputations," as Edmund Wilson observed, his own reputation should not be exempt from similar treatment (qtd. in Nabokov, *Strong Opinions,* 266).

45. Frosch, "Parody and Authenticity in *Lolita*," 44.

46. Nabokov, "An Affair of Honor," in *The Stories of Vladimir Nabokov,* ed. Dmitri Nabokov (New York: Vintage Books, 2008), 218.

47. Nabokov, *Speak, Memory*, 19.

48. Schopenhauer, *The Wisdom of Life and Counsels and Maxims*, trans. T. Bailey Saunders (Mineola, NY: Dover, 2004), 14. Pascal, however, found this concept terrifying: "The eternal silence of these infinite spaces fills me with dread" (Blaise Pascal, *Pensées*, trans. A. J. Krailsheimer [New York: Penguin Books, 1995], 66).

49. Nabokov, *Lolita,* 9, 309.

50. Nabokov, *Lolita,* 9. Time and space are interchangeable in this novel, as Humbert notes:

> It will be marked that I substitute time terms for spatial ones. In fact, I would have the reader see [the ages of] 'nine' and 'fourteen' as the boundaries—the mirror beaches and rosy rocks—of an enchanted island haunted by those nymphets of mine and surrounded by a vast, misty sea. (Nabokov, *Lolita,* 16)

324   Chapter 11

51. It is worth noting that the sketch for Humbert in *The Enchanter* was a jeweler, so we can read *Lolita* as a kind of jewel in his possession. The crystalline effect of his prose was apparent even to its earliest readers. Walter Minton, the president and publisher of G. P. Putnam's Sons, found an excerpt of the novel in the apartment of his mistress Rosemary Ridgewell, a nightclub showgirl who said, in 1958, "I thought Nabokov had a very interesting way of writing, very, you know—crystalline?" (qtd. in Sarah Weinman, *The Real Lolita: A Lost Girl, an Unthinkable Crime, and a Scandalous Masterpiece* [New York: Ecco, 2018], 212). As a result of Ridgewell introducing *Lolita* to Minton, G. P. Putnam published the novel in the United States after its bowdlerized version was first published in France.

52. The hopelessness suggested by the spherical architecture of the novel is also reiterated in Nabokov's memoir *Speak, Memory*: "I have journeyed back in thought—with thought hopelessly tapering off as I went—to remote regions where I groped for some secret outlet only to discover that the prison of time is spherical and without exits" (Nabokov, *Speak, Memory*, 20).

53. Andersen, "Little Mermaid," 155.

54. Maria Tatar and Julie K. Allen, in an explanatory note to "The Little Mermaid" by Andersen, 123.

55. Andersen, "Little Mermaid," 155.

56. Qtd. in explanatory notes to "The Little Mermaid" by Andersen, 155.

57. Nabokov, *Lolita*, 4. The last time Humbert sees her, she is already pregnant, and letting him pass through the doorway, she "flattened herself as best as she could . . . and was *crucified* for a moment" (Nabokov, *Lolita*, 270, emphasis added).

58. Nabokov chose this name for the "roses and tears" embedded in it: "My little girl's heartrending fate had to be taken into account together with the cuteness and limpidity" (Nabokov, *Strong Opinions*, 25).

59. Brian Boyd points out that Lolita "is not the name she, her mother, her friends, or her teachers ever use" (Boyd, *Vladimir Nabokov: The American Years* [Princeton, NJ: Princeton University Press, 1991], 229). This name, and the fantasy identity of a magical nymphet that Humbert tethers to it, is entirely Humbert's own creation.

60. Nabokov, *Lolita*, 75.

61. Nabokov, *Lolita*, 14–15.

62. Nabokov, *Lolita*, 9.

63. Nabokov, *Lolita*, 15, 39.

64. Nabokov, *Lolita*, 76, 113, 376, 42.

65. Nabokov, *Lolita*, 172; Andersen, "Little Mermaid," 147. Humbert later refers to Dolores as a "pet" (Nabokov, *Lolita*, 49, 120, 146).

66. Nabokov, *Lolita*, 137; Andersen, "Little Mermaid," 125.

67. Nabokov, *Lolita*, 69.

68. Nabokov, *Lolita*, 57; Andersen, "Little Mermaid," 120. Frosch interprets the cornflower blue insignia as a reference to Spenser and Novalis: "Like Spenser's Red Cross Knight, [Humbert] rides forth on his quest adorned by the image of his guiding principle, in his case a blue cornflower on the back of his pajamas—the blue cornflower being Novalis's symbol of infinite desire" (Frosch, "Parody and Authenticity in *Lolita*," 40).

69. Nabokov, *Lolita*, 81, 43, 86.
70. Nabokov, *Lolita*, 87.
71. Nabokov, *Lolita*, 104.
72. Nabokov, *Lolita*, 108.
73. Nabokov, *Lolita*, 120.
74. Nabokov, *Lolita*, 122.
75. Nabokov, *Lolita*, 140.
76. Nabokov, *Lolita*, 124–125.
77. Nabokov, *Lolita*, 128.
78. Nabokov, *Lolita*, 166.
79. Nabokov, *Lolita*, 53. Nabokov here is echoing Proust when, in *The Guermantes Way,* Marcel obsesses over Mme. de Guermantes with apocalyptic fervor, imagining that,

> The greatest happiness that I could have asked of God would have been that He should cast down on her every imaginable calamity, and that ruined, despised, stripped of all the privileges that separated her from me, having no longer any home of her own or people who could condescend to speak to her, she should come to me for refuge. (68)

80. Rougemont, *The Myths of Love,* 49.
81. Jean-Paul Sartre, *Being and Nothingness*, trans. Hazel E. Barnes (New York: Philosophical Library, 1956), 370.
82. Ellen Pifer, "Nabokov's Novel Offspring: Lolita and her Kin," in *Vladimir Nabokov's Lolita: A Casebook*, ed. Ellen Pifer (Oxford: Oxford University Press, 2003), 103.
83. Nabokov, *Lolita*, 46.
84. Andersen, "Little Mermaid," 147.
85. Nabokov, *Lolita*, 18.
86. Nabokov, *Lolita*, 166, (emphasis in original).
87. Nabokov, *Lolita*, 166.
88. Nabokov, *Lolita*, 166.
89. Nabokov, *Lolita*, 87.
90. Nabokov, *Lolita*, 177.
91. Nabokov, *Lolita*, 178.
92. Nabokov, *Lolita*, 124.
93. When the mermaid has human legs, she looks down from the railing of the prince's ship, from where "she thought she could see her father's palace, and there at the top of it was her old grandmother, a silver crown on her head as she stared through the turbulent currents at the keel of the vessel" (Andersen, "Little Mermaid," 149). With her bare eyes, she plumbs a distance that the narrator has established in the beginning as "so deep that even the longest anchor can't touch bottom" (120). Earlier, when she first sees the prince, the narrator adopts her perspective when describing the ship, which "was so brightly illuminated that you could see even the smallest piece of rope" (133). When she rescues the prince from a shipwreck, there is a moment in which "it was so dark that she couldn't see a thing, but then a flash of lightning lit everything up so that she could make out everyone on board" (133).

94. In Sarah Weinman's *The Real Lolita*, a devastating biography of Sally Horner, the eleven-year-old girl who was kidnapped, raped, and taken across the country from 1948–1950 by a man named Frank La Salle as Nabokov was drafting *Lolita* (Nabokov only makes a parenthetical reference to her in the novel), Weinman notes how one of La Salle's "most notorious aliases was that of Frank Fogg" (58). The crime made national headlines, and Nabokov documented its details in his index cards that he had used to draft *Lolita* (177–178). In a draft of the screenplay that Nabokov had written for *Lolita*, he introduces a character named "Dr. Fogg," who turns out to be a disguise for Quilty (246). Since La Salle presented Sally to the public as his own daughter, sometimes even while he was going by his own name, this would make Sally's name coincidentally sound Nabokovian: "Sally La Salle" (with the same ring to it as another *Lolita* character, Vanessa Van Ness). Another alias La Salle gave Sally was "Madeline LaPlante" (89). Nabokov plays on the "madeleine" motif from Proust, and Humbert has sex with a child prostitute "on a gray spring afternoon somewhere near the Madeleine" (21). The actual name of La Salle's ex-wife, Dorothy Dare, also sounds as though she were a Nabokov character. One of the most depressing aspects about this case was that, "The consensus about Sally and her 'father' was that they 'seemed happy and entirely devoted to each other"—the same kind of terrifying vision of "happiness" that is portrayed in *Lolita* (114).

95. Nabokov, *Lolita*, 195.
96. Nabokov, *Lolita*, 120.
97. Nabokov, *Lolita*, 120.
98. Nabokov, *Lolita*, 3.
99. Nabokov, *Lolita*, 114.
100. Nabokov, *Lolita*, 4, 197, 205.
101. Nabokov, *Lolita*, 195.
102. Nabokov, *Lolita*, 200.
103. Collins, "Nabokov's *Lolita* and Andersen's 'The Little Mermaid,'" 81.
104. Nabokov, *Lolita*, 240.
105. Nabokov, *Lolita*, 241, 243.
106. Nabokov, *Lolita*, 244.
107. Nabokov, *Lolita*, 255.
108. Nabokov, *Lolita*, 279.
109. Andersen, "Little Mermaid," 132.
110. James Tweedle sees this novel as occupying "a place on the literary map akin to those cartographic idiosyncrasies where several states converge at a single spot; within the limits of a single page [Nabokov] can wander into different forms, using their often vastly different conventions" (James Tweedle, "Nabokov and the Boundless Novel," *Twentieth Century Literature* 46, no. 2 (Summer 2000): 154).
111. Meghan Vicks, *Narratives of Nothing in Twentieth-Century Literature* (London: Bloomsbury, 2015), 78.
112. Vicks, *Narratives of Nothing*, 79.
113. In *Speak, Memory*, Nabokov refuses to accept the "utter degradation, ridicule and horror of having developed an infinity of sensation and thought within a finite

existence" (Nabokov, *Speak, Memory,* 297). This refusal is at the core of Humbert's artistic struggle as well.

114. Georg Christoph Lichtenberg, *Aphorisms,* trans. R. J. Hollingdale (London: Penguin Books, 1990), 42; cf. Dienstag, *Pessimism,* 9, 14.

115. Melanie McKay, *Spatial Form and Simultaneity in Nabokov's Fiction* (PhD dissertation, Tulane University, New Orleans, LA, 1983), 76.

116. Michael Wood, *The Magician's Doubts: Nabokov and the Risks of Fiction* (Princeton, NJ: Princeton University Press, 1994), 108.

117. Nabokov, *Speak, Memory,* 233; Nabokov, *Lolita,* 32.

118. Wood, *The Magician's Doubts,* 106.

119. Frosch, "Parody and Authenticity in *Lolita,*" 46; Nabokov, *Lolita,* 309. Even in The Enchanted Hunters Hotel, Humbert imagines redecorating the mural to accommodate his fantasy: "There would have been a lake" (Nabokov, *Lolita,* 134).

120. Nabokov, *Lolita,* 86–89.

121. Nabokov, *Lolita,* 272.

122. Appel, "Introduction" to *Lolita* by Nabokov, lxiii–lxiv.

123. Elena Sommers, "Nabokov's Mermaid: 'Spring in Fialta,'" *Nabokov Studies* 12 (2009/2011): 34.

124. Nabokov, *Lolita,* 207.

125. Appel, explanatory note to *Lolita* by Nabokov, fn.207/3: 407.

126. Eric Naiman, *Nabokov, Perversely* (Ithaca, NY: Cornell University Press, 2010), 149.

127. David Packman, *Vladimir Nabokov: The Structure of Literary Desire* (Columbia, MO: University of Missouri Press, 1982), 1.

128. Bader, *Crystal Land,* 69.

129. Nabokov, *Lolita,* 81.

130. Nabokov, *Lolita,* 232.

131. Weinman, *The Real Lolita,* 182.

132. Qtd. in Weinman, *The Real Lolita,* 182.

133. Even in the introduction to the authoritative *Annotated Lolita,* Appel arrogantly dismisses anyone who finds this novel shocking as someone who doesn't even know how to read at all, saying that, "*Lolita* may still be a shocking novel to several aging non-readers" (xxxiii). Kirsten Rutsala compiles a list of some of the most inflammatory remarks critics have made over the years about *Lolita*:

> So convincing is Humbert as a narrator that he has managed to persuade numerous critics to take him at his word. Robertson Davies states that the theme of *Lolita* "is not the corruption of an innocent child by a cunning adult, but the exploitation of a weak adult by a corrupt child" (30); Lionel Trilling claims that Lolita "seems to have very few emotions to be violated" (11); Douglas Fowler calls Lolita "meretricious and far less vulnerable than Humbert" (164) and asserts that "she is quite as indifferent to his love of her" (165).

(Kirsten Rutsala, "A Garden and a Twilight and a Palace Gate: Lolita Outside Humbert's Control," in *Critical Insights: Lolita,* ed. Rachel Stauffer [Amenia, NY: Grey House, 2016], 203). Elizabeth Patnoe "argues that the novel has been misinterpreted because it has been co-opted by a hegemonic paradigm that insists on both the invisibility of child abuse and the evil of female sexuality" (Naiman, *Nabokov, Perversely,* 154).

134. Rutsala, "A Garden and a Twilight and a Palace Gate," 208; Nabokov, *Lolita*, 266.

135. Nomi Tamir-Ghez, "The Art of Persuasion in Nabokov's *Lolita*," in *Vladimir Nabokov's Lolita: A Casebook*, ed. Ellen Pifer (Oxford: Oxford University Press, 2003), 18.

136. H. Grabes, *Fictitious Biographies: Vladimir Nabokov's English Novels* (Berlin: De Gruyter Mouton, 1977), 42.

137. Nabokov, *Lolita*, 278.

138. Nabokov, *Strong Opinions*, 94.

139. Fowler, *Reading Nabokov*, 148.

140. Weinman, *The Real Lolita,* 180.

141. Weinman, *The Real Lolita,* 180.

142. Nabokov, *Enchanter*, 56.

143. Michael Bell, "*Lolita* and Pure Art," in *Vladimir Nabokov's Lolita: Modern Critical Interpretations*, ed. Harold Bloom (New York: Chelsea House, 1987), 78.

144. Bell, "*Lolita* and Pure Art," 78.

145. Bell, "*Lolita* and Pure Art," 79.

146. Nabokov, *Lolita*, 307.

147. Nabokov, *Lolita*, 308.

148. Nabokov, *Lolita*, 308.

Chapter 12

Kierkegaard's Kiss

A Contribution to a Theory of the Novel

MERMAN TEARS

In *Fear and Trembling,* Kierkegaard summarizes the legend of *Agnete and the Merman* in a way that allegorically prefigures the plot of *Lolita*: "The merman is a seducer who rises up from concealment in the depths, and in wild desire grasps and breaks the innocent flower standing in all its charm by the shore, pensively bending its head to the ocean's roar."[1] Kierkegaard then proposes two changes to the legend. In the first, Agnete's innocence and "absolute faith" in the merman overpower and disarm him so that he is unable to take advantage of her. He eventually "turns back alone, and the ocean rages, but more wildly still rages the merman's despair."[2] In the second, which Kierkegaard provides in a footnote, the merman "does not want to seduce Agnete, even though he has seduced many previously."[3] He is no longer even a merman, but just a "pitiable" figure who "sorrowfully" waits to "be saved by an innocent girl's love."[4] He sees her from a distance, and it is only when he blends his pessimistic "sigh with the whispering of the reeds" that "she turns her ear towards it," and he takes her down into the ocean with him in a "wild" fulfillment of his love until "he became tired of Agnete," and "her body was never found; for she became a mermaid, who tempted men with her songs."[5]

In the working notes for *Fear and Trembling*, Kierkegaard writes about how he had thought of adapting this legend "from an angle that has not occurred to any poet," emphasizing that, in order to "belong to her entirely," the merman "must initiate her into his whole tragic existence."[6] The merman is "a monster at certain times," and because "the Church cannot give its blessing" to them, he "despairs and in his despair plunges to the bottom of the sea and remains there, but leads Agnes to believe that he only wanted to deceive her."[7] Just as in Andersen's "The Little Mermaid," the "complication can be resolved only by the religious . . . [If] the merman could believe, his faith perhaps could transform him into a human being."[8]

Kierkegaard insists that this unwritten version of the legend "is poetry, not that wretched, miserable trash in which everything revolves around ridiculousness and nonsense."[9] Perhaps this is a barbed comment aimed at Andersen himself, who had staged an adaptation of *Agnete and the Merman* for the Royal Danish Theater in 1843 (he had also written another version of it as a short story a decade earlier), the same year Kierkegaard wrote and published *Fear and Trembling*. The play was a disastrous failure, both at the box office and among critics. If Kierkegaard was thinking through alternative versions of this fairy tale as "poetry," in contradistinction to the "wretched, miserable trash" of Andersen's play, then his poetic vision also ended in a kind of failure, never materializing beyond the drafted outlines he had inserted in *Fear and Trembling*. He was uncomfortable in the field of aesthetics, which, he writes in a footnote, "is the most faithless of all sciences. Anyone who has truly loved it will in a way become unhappy; while anyone who has never done so is and will remain a *pecus* [ox, or blockhead]."[10] By gesturing toward a withdrawal from aesthetics, from this pessimistic choice between unhappiness and idiocy, he ends up retracting his own suggestions for revising the fairy tale, reaching the conclusion that "it is nonsense and sheer coquetry as well as an insult to the female sex to imagine a seduction where the girl is in no way, in no way at all, to blame."[11]

This disturbing characterization of seduction, as well as his literary techniques of withdrawal, had already been worked out in his other major work published the same year, *Either/Or*. In the second edition of this two-volume tome that spans a number of different genres, Kierkegaard drafted a postscript that he would later decide against publishing:

> I hereby retract this book. It was a necessary deception in order, if possible, to deceive men into the religious, which has continually been my task all along. Maieutically it certainly has had its influence. Yet I do not need to retract it, for I have never claimed to be its author.[12]

In classic Kierkegaardian fashion, he ended up retracting this retraction (one that claims there is no need for a retraction in the first place). And the method is not just one of literary posturing, but of autobiographical seduction itself— a seduction that ultimately ends up in failure. In 1837, when Kierkegaard was a twenty-five-year-old graduate student, he met the fourteen-year-old Regine Olsen at a party of girls her age at the home of another girl he was pursuing, whose father had died. He only begins to mention Regine in his journal two years after that party, and in 1840 proposed to the teenager with an intensity that was both awkward and overwhelming. She initially refused him, but two days later, with her father's consent, she accepted the proposal. And yet Kierkegaard wrote in his journal that he regretted the whole thing and was incapacitated by his melancholy.[13] They kept the engagement going for a year until Kierkegaard sent her back her ring with a note telling her to forget him. Regine rejected the rejection and tried working on mending their relationship for two months, but Kierkegaard eventually ran off to Berlin, where he began *Either/Or*, using the breakup as its inspiration. He was shocked when she accepted an earlier suitor two years later, and then married that suitor in 1847. Until the end of his life, Kierkegaard constantly wrote about her in his journals.

It is no wonder that the first volume of *Either/Or* ends in a section called "The Seducer's Diary," which Kierkegaard later claimed was his effort to come off looking like an asshole to make it easier for her to leave him.[14] This section marks the middle of an unwieldy, two-volume work of multiple genres framed by the literary conceit of a found text, edited by a fictional Victor Eremita into Volume A, written by an anonymous young man, and Volume B, written by Wilhelm, a former judge. The fact that "The Seducer's Diary" is written by a character named Johannes, a young man who is also preoccupied with aesthetic concerns, and this diary ends Volume A, suggests at first glance that Johannes had written everything that had preceded this section. Or it opens up the proto-Nabokovian space of competing authorship in a single work.

The extent of Nabokov's familiarity with Kierkegaard is unclear—he never cites him as an influence the way he cites Andersen. In fact, none of his works reference Kierkegaard by name, and surprisingly no scholarship has demonstrated any kind of influence, even though Nabokov was living in Berlin in the 1920s at a time when Lukács said that Kierkegaard "was present everywhere."[15] Lukács was not exaggerating this point. Even by 1918, Kafka was writing to Max Brod how "Kierkegaard is always in my mind these days," a sentiment that was also shared by Thomas Mann around the same time.[16] But Nabokov scholars find themselves in particularly contentious territory when it comes to the question of influence at all, especially because of the "single-minded Nabokovian belief that art supersedes influence, and so influence must be brushed off."[17] And yet the Russian émigré writer Nina Berberova, who documented the lives of Russians in Parisian exile, noted how she "gradually got used to [Nabokov's] manner of . . . taking something from a great author and then saying he'd never read him."[18]

Even so, Priscilla Meyer and Jeff Hoffman trace motifs of the "Agnete and the Merman" story in *Pale Fire*, but Kierkegaard's reimagining of the fairy tale suggests a much closer connection with *Lolita*.[19] Herner Sæverot links Kierkegaard's form of deception with Nabokov's, following up a chapter on *The Seducer's Diary* in his book *Indirect Pedagogy: Some Lessons in Existential Education* with a chapter on *Lolita*, but without engaging the question of influence.[20] Nabokov's itinerant life in exile, moreover, has made the scholarly task of tracking down his library a notorious nightmare.[21] The Nabokovs also "were not book collectors, and as a rule Vladimir Nabokov did not buy books."[22] Of the books that were purchased in the household, mainly by his wife Véra and his son Dmitry, "no special effort was made to retain them" once they had been read.[23] The catalog of his father's library, published in 1904 and then in 1911, also does not include any works by Kierkegaard, either.[24]

This is not to say that Kierkegaard did not shape, to any extent, Nabokov's writing—nor is this an attempt to force a Kierkegaardian interpretation of Nabokov, either, but a close look at Kierkegaard's experimentation with the novel form, in addition to his treatment of the "Agnete and the Merman" fairy tale, seems to open the space for the literary strategies that Nabokov uses in *Lolita*. It is odd to think of Kierkegaard as a novelist; *The Seducer's Diary*, if anything, seems to be a proto-Nabokovian parody of a novel. Its seemingly random insertion in a kaleidoscopic text that could also just be labeled as a parody of philosophy, occasionally lapsing into philosophical jargon in order to undermine the systematicity of philosophy itself, also draws attention to its generic instability.

The Seducer's Diary seduces us into reading it as a separate work. In its English translation, it even appears as a separate publication, with a foreword by a novelist. In this foreword, John Updike situates it in the context of *Either/Or* not as a work of philosophy, but as a work of fiction.[25] Kierkegaard adopts a number of different perspectives from different characters in order to draw out ideas from his readers, a "maieutic" tradition that he takes from Socrates. So he turns to Socrates specifically as the starting point of his fiction, more so than his philosophy. In this sense, he seems to be bridging the chasm between philosophy and the novel in a work that itself reads like a novel.[26]

While Updike reads *The Seducer's Diary* as part of a broader tradition in the novels of sentimental education, ranging from Jane Austen to Henry James, it is Kierkegaard's maieutic method that is strikingly modern, that comes into full force with Nabokov's *Lolita* a century later.[27] Using the same technique of embodying various perspectives through different characters for the precise purpose of eliciting—in provocative ways—a response from his readers rather than imposing his own outlook, Nabokov's narrative strategies achieve the same effect. And both Kierkegaard and Nabokov employ these narrative strategies in the context of treating a young girl as an aesthetic object of erotic fascination and predatory attention. Johannes writes in *The Seducer's Diary* that he wants to intellectually sculpt the image of his beloved in the same way that painters and sculptors do, but he wants to do so without her knowledge of it.[28] Johannes and Humbert aim at immortalizing the young girl in a work of art designed "to confuse poetry and actuality, truth and fiction, to frolic in infinity."[29] Just as much as Humbert wants to take Lolita and "leave the town, the country, the continent, the hemisphere,—indeed, the globe," Johannes writes, "I am carrying you away, not from some people to others, but out of the world."[30]

Like John Ray, Jr. introducing Humbert's narrative, the anonymous writer "A" warns us that the veracity of this diary is questionable, so we need to read this text with what would later be called a hermeneutics of suspicion.[31] The novelist Nathalie Sarraute famously used the phrase "age of suspicion" in her 1950s essay on the genre of the novel, which she took from Stendhal's 1832 remark that the "spirit of suspicion has entered the world."[32] Paul Ricoeur, in turn, labeled Marx, Nietzsche, and Freud as the "masters of suspicion," prefiguring the hermeneutics laid down by Foucault and Barthes, but behind these masters is, to Gabriel Josipovici, a glaring omission: Kierkegaard himself.[33] Barthes maintains that, "to read with suspicion is . . . to retain our freedom," and Foucault insists that, "Writing unfolds like a game," creating "a space into which the writing subject constantly disappears."[34] Both of these positions on reading and writing echo the fictional worlds created by Nabokov and Kierkegaard, but in these worlds we see a suspicion even of suspicion itself: "Kierkegaard's 'genuine' negative thinker always recognizes how easy it is for suspicion itself to harden into a new conviction, the conviction of the unquestioning value of suspicion. Kierkegaard never does this. In that regard his first major work, *Either/Or*, is exemplary."[35]

In both Kierkegaard and Nabokov, the reader becomes this "'genuine' negative thinker," shifting between positions of suspicion and persuasion. Eros, to Anne Carson, resides in this liminal, in-between space.[36] It is out of this erotic space that a new sense of self emerges: "The self forms at the edge of desire, and a science of self arises in the effort to leave that self behind."[37] Carson here refers to her reading of Neville in Woolf's *The Waves*, who is "contracted" with Bernard into "a single being" out of love for him.[38] Similarly, Humbert wishes to "safely solipsize" Lolita, and Johannes wants to seduce Cordelia just as much to himself as he wants to seduce her to her own self, her newly expanded sense of self that emerges out of their interaction.

WHAT'S IN A NAME?

A informs us, before Johannes gets a chance to speak in his own voice, that this young girl "was very correctly named Cordelia but not, however, Wahl."[39] The German last name *Wahl* (rather than the Danish *Valg*) means "choice." While it seems that Cordelia doesn't have much of a choice here, maybe she does in fact make a choice, the most existential of choices: what she chooses is her self, a self that she discovers in what Heidegger would later call authenticity:

> And because Dasein is in each case essentially its own possibility, it *can*, in its very Being, "choose" itself and win itself; it can also lose itself and never win itself; or only "seem" to do so. But only in so far as it is essentially something which can be *authentic*—that is, something of its own—can it have lost itself and not yet won itself.[40]

It could very well be that Heidegger took this concept straight from Kierkegaard, and from the same work, *Either/Or*, that includes *The Seducer's Diary*. In the second volume, Judge Wilhelm writes,

> The ethical individual knows himself, but this knowing is not simply contemplation, for then the individual comes to be defined according to his necessity. It is a collecting of oneself, which itself is an action, and this is why I have with aforethought used the expression "to choose oneself" instead of "to know oneself."[41]

This is the either/or situation that seems to confront Cordelia. But to what extent is her self a discrete entity if it is manipulated and modulated by a seducer? Is A right, after all? Or is there an erotically charged space of in-between?

In choosing this last name for Cordelia, Kierkegaard also seems to be writing this work as a parody of the popular novel of unrequited love—as though this is *The Sorrows of Young Werther* in reverse. Goethe's novel takes place in the idyllic town of *Wahlheim*—literally a "home of choice," where Werther chooses, or at least discovers, a new sense of self when he falls in love with Lotte. Or, to go back to Heidegger, "only 'seems' to do so."[42] The thinly illustrated basis of this intense infatuation is the source of the novel's sentimental and melodramatic quality. Goethe seems to stage the literal loss of a self in inauthenticity with Werther's suicide. Kierkegaard turns the tables so that he retains the story of unrequited love, but instead of this inauthentic experience of self, we get an authentic gaining of a self—and not of the lover, but of the beloved. Goethe's epistolary novel is written as letters to an unresponsive Wilhelm, but the letters feel more like diary entries, addressed to a self in dissolution rather than a self in formation (that of a Wilhelm Meister, for instance).[43] Kierkegaard gives us the opposite: *The Seducer's Diary* is, by its title, a diary, and yet it is written as letters both sent and unsent, ostensibly to Cordelia. Or, on further reading, maybe these are also letters to Wilhelm, too—Judge Wilhelm, that is, the author of Volume B who responds to the author of Volume A in *Either/Or*.

Nabokov, too, parodies *The Sorrows of Young Werther*, alluding to Lotte both in the name of Charlotte and her daughter's nickname Lo.[44] Charlotte wants to play the part of the beloved until she is killed off by the narrator, and Dolores's emerging sense of self rebels against this role that has been forced on her. Cordelia, too, ends up severing ties with Johannes—in his words, "she herself breaks it in order to soar into a higher sphere," reminiscent of Andersen's mermaid.[45] But even after this break, as though crying with Humbert's "merman tears," Johannes writes of his fantasy to seduce her again "under the sea," where "we shall meet again, for only in the deeps of the sea shall we really belong together."[46]

This is precisely the image of seduction that Kierkegaard sketches in his version of "Agnete and the Mermaid," and which appears also in *Lolita*. The sea he is referring to here is the sea of his mind, as when he says, "My mind roars like a turbulent sea in the storms of passion."[47] After admitting, like Humbert, that he "continually seek[s his] prey among young girls, not among young women," he claims to "have gone under in love-rapture" for Cordelia, whose nymphet-like "glance is so childlike and yet so saucy."[48] In this disturbing characterization, A suggests that Cordelia is the one who seduces Johannes, and Johannes himself declares that his entire goal was to train Cordelia into becoming his seducer.[49]

In this vertigo of seduction, we are taken from the depths of the sea to cosmic heights. Nabokov associates Lolita with Jupiter in her final destination of "Gray Star" in Juneau (the homonym of Juno). Her last name, Haze, alludes both to the gray appearance of this planet and to the elusive self that lies behind this haze, something that can never be captured. In *The Seducer's Diary*, it is Johannes who characterizes himself as Jupiter and as a hazy cloud.[50] He imagines Cordelia as springing from his own head, fully formed, without developing any further, the way Humbert fantasizes about controlling Lolita. And maybe it is the planet Jupiter that Johannes has in mind when he notices that Cordelia perceives him as though he were a "new planet" on "her horizon," without any awareness of this planet's influence.[51]

Johannes imagines himself as belonging to an otherworldly realm, in the same way that Humbert imagines himself residing in "an enchanted island haunted by those nymphets of mine and surrounded by a vast, misty sea."[52] Out of this misty sea, he envisions the hazy Dolores Haze, just as Johannes says, "I see everything as a sea of fog, where feminine creatures resembling you appear and disappear everywhere."[53] To Humbert, this enchanted island is surrounded by "mirror beaches," an image later mirrored itself in Hourglass Lake.[54] When Johannes happens to see Cordelia alone outside, he notices how the "lake was still, smooth as a mirror."[55] In this mirrored universe, Johannes mirrors the characterization of Cordelia as a cloud, so that when she throws her arms around him, she writes that, "everything changed, and I embraced a cloud."[56] Johannes then in turn calls on Cordelia to "dispel your fog," using the same epithets for her that Humbert uses for Lolita: "Enchanting troll woman, fairy, or witch."[57] He falls short of calling her a mermaid, even though he sees her as belonging "to the deeps of the sea."[58]

And this may be where Nabokov's explicit reference to *The Seducer's Diary* is hiding in plain sight. In the earlier iteration of *Lolita*, published as *The Enchanter*, the narrator writes,

> Thus they would live on—laughing, reading books, marveling at gilded fireflies, talking of the flowering walled prison of the world, and he would tell her tales and she would listen, his little Cordelia, and nearby the sea would breathe beneath the moon.[59]

In a flight of imagination, the previous version of Humbert names the previous version of Lolita "Cordelia," a reference that has been lost on critics for decades since its posthumous publication in 1986, especially with Dmitri Nabokov insisting that this must be referring to Shakespeare's Cordelia in the book's Afterword, "On a Book Entitled *The Enchanter*," where he explores how his father had written this as a draft for *Lolita*. But his explanation of this passage is hardly convincing: "The Enchanter . . . [is] a kind of lecherous Lear living in a fairy-tale seclusion by the sea with his 'little Cordelia,' whom, for a flicker of an instant, he imagines as an innocently loved daughter."[60] Lear wasn't lecherous, though, and is more associated with the heath than the sea. It is not an avatar of Lear that we are reading here, but of Johannes, Kierkegaard's Seducer, who imagines living in a fairy-tale seclusion—in his own kingdom by the sea—with Cordelia.[61]

Given her fairy-tale, mermaid-like characteristics, Cordelia's frustration at Johannes's fickle games of seduction and control, and the fact that she hardly speaks in her own voice (the only time she does is, like Dolores, through letters), maybe A is wrong about her name. It's not her last name that seems to be a problem, but her first. Out of all Shakespearean names to exemplify her situation, she seems to be closer to her fellow Dane, Ophelia, than to Cordelia. But in *King Lear*, Cordelia chooses her reticence, acting rather than speaking, challenging not only the assumptions of Lear and her sisters, but of the audience as well. The young girl at the beginning who quietly challenges her father but then passively suffers through his flights of rage hardly seems to be the same character who leads an army at the end. After two asides— "Love, and be silent"—she first announces herself with the word "Nothing."[62] As Nothing, she is pure possibility, and she chooses her self in authenticity as opposed to the Heideggerian "they" exemplified by the obsequiously scheming Regan and Goneril. She loves and is silent, as is Kierkegaard's Cordelia.

But what Shakespeare shows is that the resolute self that Cordelia attains is tragically insufficient; neither her love nor her silence achieves anything.

At the root of Cordelia's name is the core, the *coeur*, the heart (in her name is also inscribed the cord, the rope by which she is hanged). "Unhappy that I am," Cordelia reluctantly responds to her father, "I cannot heave / My heart into my mouth."[63] As Lear slowly begins to realize his mistake, he cries, "I have full cause of weeping; but this heart / Shall break into a hundred thousand flaws."[64] It is as though Lear and Cordelia share the same heart that prevents them from speaking and weeping. Cordelia is the structural heart of the play, the absent center on which the entire chaotic structure collapses into a thousand flaws.

For Kierkegaard, the heart at the core of Cordelia's name may have a different but equally central significance. Johannes establishes this connection between his Cordelia and Shakespeare's precisely with the heart: "Cordelia! That is really a splendid name—indeed, the same name as that of King Lear's third daughter, that remarkable girl whose heart did not dwell on her lips, whose lips were mute when her heart was full."[65] Claire Carlisle also identifies the heart as the organizing metaphor in *Fear and Trembling*, gathering "together the text's key themes: love, suffering, and courage."[66] Could Johannes de Silentio, Kierkegaard's pseudonym in *Fear and Trembling*, be the same Johannes who pens *The Seducer's Diary*? Perhaps. But more "generally, throughout Kierkegaard's work the central concept of appropriation—that process through which the existing individual relates herself to the truth, at once making it her own and becoming herself—is understood as a 'taking to heart' (*Inderliggjørelse*), a passionate 'making-inward.'"[67] Heidegger, too, translates the Greek term for thinking as "taking to heart."[68] Thinking with the heart, for both Kierkegaard and Heidegger, involves an "active trait of undertaking something."[69] The fact that Heidegger, in the same lecture, goes out of his way to say that Kierkegaard "has nothing whatever to say" about the question of being is perhaps a symptom of his own anxiety of influence.[70]

Cordelia Wahl's name, then, suggests an allegory of actively, authentically choosing one's self with the most philosophically rigorous form of thinking, which is thinking with the heart. While Heidegger awkwardly eschews any eroticism in this process—a process that may nevertheless be latently present in his work, despite himself—Kierkegaard views this mode of accessing the truth as purely erotic. But it is an eros tinged with pessimism and hopelessness for both the lover and the beloved. In her third letter to Johannes, Cordelia writes, "Is there no hope at all, then?"[71] Johannes, for his part, aligns himself with the "unhappy mirror" which "assuredly can grasp her image but not her."[72] He is drawn to her precisely because of her pain, the same pain inscribed in Dolores's name: "Her bearing is a harmonious blend of sadness and pain. She is really attractive."[73]

EROS AND IRONY

Cordelia is the daughter of an officer in the Royal Navy, establishing a lineage that is strongly associated with the sea, but both he and her mother are dead.[74] Even though she lives with her aunt, who "almost worships" Johannes as much as Dolores's mother worships Humbert, Cordelia's status as an orphan, like Dolores's, makes her more vulnerable and more alluring for the older man. The absence of her parents and the devotion of her guardian to him allows Johannes access to the girl in a way that is ideal for him, a way in which he can freely imagine her as a work of his own aesthetic creation.[75] He thinks of himself both as a lover and as her surrogate father, in the same way that Humbert thinks of Dolores, both of them imagining that they can invent or reinvent these girls as novelistic creations.

Both Johannes and Humbert are self-conscious narrators in this sense, vying for absolute narrative control—Johannes fashions himself as "[t]he humble narrator who follows your triumphs," while Humbert ironically refers to himself as "Humbert the Humble" while engaging in the same kind of narrative manipulation.[76] The drama emerges from whether—and how—Cordelia and Dolores escape this control. The irony is that both Johannes and Humbert can only imagine Cordelia and Dolores existing within the ontological boundaries that they themselves provide. "In me she is seeking her freedom," Johannes writes, "and the more firmly I encircle her, the better she will find it."[77]

Encircling her and prefiguring Humbert's own name, Johannes lurks in the shadows, where she "will be unable to see me."[78] He imagines himself as an invisible dancer, a shadow in the place of someone with whom Cordelia dances in a dreamlike trance. This is how Anne Carson imagines Eros: "He never looks at you from the place from which you see him. Something moves in the space between. This is Eros."[79] Johannes oversteps his boundary as a potential lover in pursuit of his beloved and tries to play the role of Eros himself, tensing his bow as he takes aim. "I am pulling the bow of love tighter in order to wound all the deeper," he writes.[80] He describes himself as "almost like a mood" that seizes her, completing "her thought, which nevertheless is completed within itself. She moves to the melody in her own soul; I am merely the occasion for her moving."[81] And from this voyeuristic vantage point of seeing her without being seen, Johannes chillingly observes, "she is selected, she will be overtaken."[82] The selection—the choice, the *Wahl*—now resides with him rather than her, and yet the passive voice of his grammar seems to undermine this choice. Or at least this is what he is trying to seduce us into believing. Just as Humbert fashions himself as "Humbert the Spider," Johannes keeps with the passive voice in writing that, "she must be spun into my web."[83]

Also like Humbert, Johannes contemplates how this young girl regards him, from a distance, as "a nice man from quite another world."[84] He schemes how to begin his "attack," plotting his seduction, like Humbert, as a game. Johannes is someone who sees everything as a game, even freedom itself. This game of seduction, however, carries with it the threat of abduction. Unlike *Lolita*, this only remains a threat, though, and is never actualized. "I shall very covertly lead her to this point," Johannes writes, "and let her fall down through this trapdoor."[85] This trap in the game may be like Nabokov's Lieutenant Trapp, or Clare Quilty, the man Dolores escapes with to run away from Humbert. Because Cordelia eventually breaks off the engagement with Johannes, whichever man she will end up with instead lies on the other end of this trapdoor, outside of the boundaries of the game he had played on her. According to the rules of this game, once he has won, "she must, as the philosophers say with a play on words: *zu Grunde gehn* [sic] [fall to the ground]."[86] But Cordelia is the one who wins this game, so she doesn't so much fall down as float up. Johannes imagines her soaring above him in an atmosphere that "must not narcotically entrap her soul"—as Humbert uses narcotics to entrap Dolores—"but continually allow it to soar aloft as she views it all as a game."[87]

Cordelia wins this game by catching on to his irony, which is what Johannes claims he had wanted her to do all along.[88] The question is whether the reader wins the game, too, by identifying the irony in Johannes's claim. Does Johannes really think we buy the conceit that he only seduced Cordelia in order to have her reject him and walk away from the engagement more edified as a result? "To poetize oneself into a girl is an art," he brags. But "to poetize oneself out of her is a masterstroke."[89] And he finally concludes, "But now it is finished, and I never want to see her again."[90] The barely concealed bitterness in this irony is something Proust would later exhibit when, after obsessively chasing Odette, Charles Swann tries to convince himself that she's not even his type.[91]

At times, though, Johannes's mask slips, as when he claims that love can only emerge out of freedom, but he still wishes that in her freedom she would "gravitate toward me," not fall to him "like a heavy body but as mind should gravitate toward mind."[92] Cordelia does not fall, but neither does she gravitate to him in her intellectual ascent. His traps do not promote freedom, and his game does not establish a meaningful connection with her, no matter how many layers of irony he wants to hide behind. He wishes he could "raise an erotic storm" in order to "lift her off the ground."[93] But it is all for naught. She operates by different laws of gravity that ultimately resist his orbit, his cosmic influence over her.

And yet he still deludes himself into thinking he is operating from a position of power over her mind and soul, as does Humbert with Dolores. He is proud of the fact that he controls the books she reads, which consist of "mythology and fairy tales."[94] Humbert also tries to educate Dolores through books, like "The Little Mermaid," and her frustrated response is, "You talk like a book, *Dad.*"[95] As though Johannes takes Humbert's place, he seems to preempt this objection over a century earlier, pedantically explaining, "A person who talks like a book is extremely boring to listen to, but sometimes it is rather expedient to talk that way. That is, a book has the remarkable characteristic that it can be interpreted as one pleases."[96] This freedom of interpretation, to him, carves out a space for the reader's autonomy.

The awkwardness of talking like a book, especially in the context of Socratic irony—which was the subject of Kierkegaard's dissertation that he was writing as he was drafting *The Seducer's Diary* in parallel—brings to mind Plato's *Phaedrus*, in which the differences between oral speech and written text are hashed out in a discussion of love as a discovery of one's self in the tension between memory and forgetfulness. "I have forgotten myself in order to recollect you," Johannes writes before recapitulating Socrates's theory of "backlove," writing, "I am in love with myself. And why? Because I am in love with you."[97] The irony here is that Johannes tries leading Cordelia to an understanding of herself as he forgets and abandons his own self, thinking of his own love as "an expression of most inspired self-annihilation."[98]

"A CONTRIBUTION TO A THEORY OF THE KISS"

Johannes even cites *Phaedrus* as an inspiration for his seduction.[99] Maybe it is for this reason that Lukács calls Kierkegaard "the sentimental Socrates."[100] Johannes also flatters himself with an implicit comparison with the gadfly philosopher, noting his own penchant for asking questions, much to the irritation of others.[101] But when he arrives at the subject of speaking like a book, and of the written word at large, he turns Socrates on his head, insisting that written language has "more influence" than oral speech.[102] While this may carry some truth, the irony arguably is that Cordelia ends up liberated from his influence, in both written and spoken forms. But Johannes's preference for writing draws attention to written text itself as an erotic artifact.

Carson, in tracing the literature of eros, asks, "Is it a matter of coincidence that the poets who invented Eros, making of him a divinity and a literary obsession, were also the first authors in our tradition to leave us their poems in written form?"[103] Writing about love rather than speaking about it "cues us to certain radically new conditions of life and mind within which [these erotic poets] were operating."[104] Just as Plato's *Phaedrus* "electrifies" Johannes's "whole being," Carson observes that there "is something like an electrification" in "the resemblance between the way Eros acts in the mind of a lover and the way knowing acts in the mind of a thinker," which would also explain why Marcel, in *The Fugitive*, uses the metaphor of electricity to make sense of the world around him, imagining that "we live surrounded by electric, seismic signs, which we must interpret in good faith in order to know the truth about the characters of other people."[105] This resemblance between the lover and the thinker, to Carson, is worked out most richly in the genre of the novel:

> Novels institutionalize the ruse of eros. It becomes a narrative texture of sustained incongruence, emotional and cognitive. It permits the reader to stand in triangular relation to the characters in the story and reach into the text after the objects of their desire, sharing their longing but also detached from it, seeing their view of reality but also its mistakenness. It is almost like being in love.[106]

The novel that Johannes—and Kierkegaard—end up writing emerges out of a failed attempt at a work of systematic philosophy. Johannes thinks about writing a book called *A Contribution to a Theory of the Kiss*, and wonders how odd it is "that there is no book on this topic. . . . Can the reason for this deficiency in the literature be that philosophers do not think about such things or that they do not understand them?"[107] It is clear that, from Plato, philosophers do think about such things, but maybe the form of philosophical discourse is inadequately matched with the subject matter.

What would *A Contribution to a Theory of the Kiss* look like, and why must it fail? It is certainly more of a modest proposal than Casaubon's *Key to All Mythologies*. A kiss is something narrower, more specific, more physical, more immediate than the elusive, abstract concept of love—and maybe it is for this reason that philosophers have a hard time with it. Its embodied particularity resists any kind of theoretical framework. Johannes imagines a highly systematic, but ultimately ridiculous, taxonomy of kisses, classified according to duration, to touch, and to sound.[108]

This comical and clumsy understanding of how one can understand the phenomenon of the kiss seems to foreshadow the definition later provided by Freud (who cleverly avoids the trap of ever defining sexuality, the subject of his entire career):

> One of these contacts in particular, the mutual contact of the mucous membrane of the lips, has also achieved high sexual value as a kiss among many peoples (including the highly civilized), although the parts of the body in question are not part of the sexual apparatus, but in fact form the entrance to the alimentary canal.[109]

No definition of a kiss could be more, well, tongue-in-cheek. Cioran echoes this definition in his pessimistic account of love: "so much ardor produces only a variety of mucus."[110] Both Freud and Cioran sound like Plato mocking

Erixymachus, the doctor in *Symposium*, by putting in his speech the most de-eroticized account of eros, reducing it to an absurd narrative of mechanics. It is too bad that Nabokov was so biliously anti-Freudian that he couldn't even pick up on his humor ("including the highly civilized"!). When Humbert wishes he could "apply voracious lips" to Dolores's "nacreous liver," Nabokov seems to be setting a trap for readers on the hunt for a Freudian analysis of his text without realizing that he himself fell into the trap of taking Freud too seriously when even Freud himself possibly wrote this definition as a joke.[111] Any philosophical, physiological, or psychological definition of a kiss inevitably falls flat, leaving the task for literary writers to imbue this phenomenon with meaning.

What Johannes is most interested in is exploring, outside of the classification of kisses he had outlined, is not just the significance of the first kiss and how it is fundamentally different from any subsequent kiss, but how very few people seem to think about this.[112] One person who did think about not just any first kiss, but the first kiss to have ever taken place, was Plato, whose *Symposium* is a philosophical text that slips into literary narrative. John Vignaux Smyth, in thinking of Kierkegaard's "ironist as *eroticist*," says that "the most venerable or well-known precedent might perhaps be found in . . . Plato's *Symposium*."[113] In Aristophanes's myth of our severed cosmic ancestors, after one of these beings is split in half, they find each other again and cling to one another with such steadfastness that Hephaestus offers to weld them together so that they would live one life and die one death, never to be apart ever again after that traumatic incision by the Olympian gods.[114] It is significant that the lovers' response to this offer is never heard, but Aristophanes suggests that any lover "wants nothing else than this."[115]

Maybe the lovers' response is not heard because their lips are locked into each other the way the rest of their bodies are, in this erotic ritual, this reminder of what they once were. The movement of language, like the movement of desire, reaches across a gap, a void, in its attempt to apprehend, to comprehend. In the moment that desire is reached, fulfilled, grasped, and pulled toward me, the need for language dissolves. It has already been apprehended, arrested; it surrenders to the object in the awe of silent communion rather than chatty communication. The kiss is the emblem, the symbol, of this arrest of language. *Symbollein* is the process of bringing two different things together to share one meaning. When two people share one kiss, the mouth, as the site of speech, is now incapable of it; language becomes instead a physical grammar that operates by rules that mute speech. Johannes understands this either/or choice between language and the kiss when he says that Cordelia's "heart does dwell on her lips, not in the form of words but in a more heartfelt way in the form of a kiss."[116]

But a kiss, as any lover knows, can only last so long, and in the desperate clinging to each other of these severed beings in Plato's image, there is a sense that this bodily proximity is not close enough. As with the Tristan lovers, they feel apart even when they are together, which is why Hephaestus offers his services. Carson, though, has her suspicions, suggesting that they don't value their "oneness" as much as Hephaestus might think they do.[117] These beings—that is to say, ourselves—may claim to value oneness, but again, like the Tristan lovers, cling as much to their separation as they do to each other.

Even the avatars of these *Symposium* lovers in *Wuthering Heights* seem to cherish their separation as much as their union. Before Catherine dies, she tells Heathcliff, "I wish I could hold you . . . till we were both dead!"[118] Maybe she can only say that with the knowledge that death is just around the corner, and that this gesture to eternity actually just relishes the finite moment. Heathcliff, for his part, "locked" her "in an embrace from which" Nelly thinks that Catherine "would never be released alive," but the ferocity and tightness of this embrace owes its power to the fact that he had previously escaped from her.[119]

The kiss is an act of locking lips not just to come together, to *symbollein*, but precisely to do its opposite: to disengage, to withdraw. Eros resides in that gap, that in-between space, that dialectic between the systole and diastole of desire. Eros exists between engaging and withdrawing, in the rhythmic tension between thrusting and pulling away. It is for this reason that these lovers locked in entropy could strike one as ridiculous, and even rather comic (it is Aristophanes telling us this story, after all).[120]

The build-up to the kiss and the withdrawal from it—even if only to repeat the kiss again—demands narrative sequence. And, as Carson reminds us, the mouth is not the only site of language. The noun *symbolon* "means, in the ancient world, one half of a knucklebone carried as a token of identity to someone who has the other half."[121] The symbol as that token of our identities resides not in our mouths, but in our hands—symbols in themselves of comprehension, of reaching across the void to the outer world and erotically pulling it toward us only to push it back again in understanding our selves as separate beings, albeit beings that have an involvement with the world, or what Heidegger would call "being-in-the-world."

This is what Shakespeare stages when Romeo and Juliet, withdrawing from what Heidegger calls *das Man*—"the 'they'" or the world of others—of the Capulet's party, gravitate to each other and use their lips to mutely pray: "Let lips do what hands do," Romeo pleads, "purg[ing]" his "sin" through a kiss. When Juliet playfully asks whether he had just given her his sin by kissing her, he kisses her again to take it back. Inscribed in a kiss is the hope of its repetition; we kiss for the moment when we are no longer kissing, so that we may kiss again, summoning the deity Eros in this push and pull. Juliet's response to Romeo is, "You kiss by the book."[122] In line with the rest of the biblical imagery in the sonnet that contains their dialogue which builds up to their kiss, "the book" in question is most likely the Bible, but it could also refer to any number of the seduction manuals in vogue at the time, from Capellanus's *The Art of Courtly Love* to Castiglione's *The Book of the Courtier*, where the kiss is defined as "a joining of souls rather than of bodies."[123] Castiglione here cites "the divinely enamored Plato," who "says that, in kissing, the soul came to his lips in order to escape from his body."[124] Whatever book Juliet is referring to, it is a text that is just as mute as their kiss that imitates hands in prayer.

The language of hands then imitates the muteness of the mouth when occupied by a kiss. Sign language is a language without verbal speech, as is written language. The novel departs from drama and poetry in that it fundamentally inheres in the muteness of written language, which, for Carson, imitates eros itself, siding with the muteness of the kiss. The ancient Greek novels that Mikhail Bakhtin refers to went by the name of "*erotica pathēmata*, or 'erotic sufferings': these are love stories in which it is generically required that love be painful. The stories are told in prose and their apparent aim is to entertain readers" rather than auditors.[125]

Maybe this is why, in *The Magic Mountain*, right as Hans Castorp finally gets to kiss Clavdia Chauchat—who in his mind also stands in for his schoolboy crush Pribislav Hippe—he tells her, as if speaking to Pribislav instead, that, "as a boy I borrowed a pencil from you."[126] His love inheres in an instrument for writing, and the long novel thematizes how the genre of the novel itself performs the erotic delay and gratification of a kiss, demonstrating the failure of Dr. Krokowski's scientific explanations of eros in communicating the experience of it, as the narrator makes sure to point out: "But even as we record this kiss . . . we cannot help finding in it a reminder of Dr. Krokowski's elaborate, if not always unobjectionable way of speaking about love."[127]

The pencil is also associated with the erotic delay and gratification of a kiss in Proust, when Albertine gives Marcel "a little gold pencil" in Balbec, and Marcel "told Albertine that by giving me this pencil she had brought me great pleasure, and yet not so great as I would have felt if, on the night she had spent at the hotel, she had permitted me to kiss her."[128] He doesn't get to kiss her until the next volume, in *The Guermantes Way*, when the kiss "revealed . . . in its whole extent the novel of this little girl."[129] It is the novel that he ends up writing, a novel that is structured around his own anticipation of kisses, from his mother's goodnight kiss that begins *Swann's Way* to the kisses he pursues from Albertine in the central volumes, and finally to what can be thought of as the sublation of the kiss in *Time Regained* when he finally finds the resolve to sit down and write his novel. Writing with the pencil that belongs to the beloved is, in the *Recherche* as in *The Magic Mountain*, both a form of kissing and a way of delaying the kiss.

The thing about pencils, though, is that—unlike pens—they are subject to erasure. As with all of Marcel's excited anticipations in the *Recherche*, the kiss is disappointing. "I believed that there was such a thing as knowledge acquired by lips," he thinks to himself before arriving at the assessment that humans lack "a certain number of essential organs, and notably possess none that will serve for kissing." Lips are the best we have, and produce just "a slightly more satisfying result" than if we "were reduced to caressing the beloved with a horny tusk."[130] He is annoyed that,

> in this matter of kissing our nostrils and eyes are as ill placed as our lips are shaped—suddenly my eyes ceased to see; next, my nose, crushed by the collision, no longer perceived any odor, and, without thereby gaining any clearer idea of the taste of the rose of my desire, I learned, from these detestable signs, that at last I was in the act of kissing.[131]

This is conceivably the complaint of the original lovers from *Symposium*, split apart in ways that don't exactly line up anymore, even though they are awkwardly gesturing toward it.

Novels flesh out the contradictory movement of the kiss, the engagement and disengagement, the push and pull that we see, for example, in Marcel's relationship with Albertine: "The novelists play out as dilemmas of plot and character all those facets of erotic contradiction and difficulty that were first brought to light in lyric poetry."[132] To contradict is, literally, to use one's tongue against another. It engages in order to reject; it both denies and affirms, attacks and defends, resists and yields. The history of the novel is a history of returning to this kiss, this mute contradiction, from the pessimistic image of the clinging lovers in *Symposium*, *Tristan*, and *Wuthering Heights* to the greatest happiness that can exist in Kafka's universe, when Frieda tells K. in *The Castle*:

> I know of no greater happiness than to be with you, constantly, without interruption, without end, but in the dreams I dream there's no tranquil place on earth for our love in the village or anywhere else, so I picture a deep and narrow grave where we embrace each other as if with clamps, I hide my face in you, you hide yours in me, and nobody will ever see us again.[133]

In Frieda's vision of love is a genealogy of lovers traced back to what they always have been, and what they have always wanted—these archetypal lovers from the *Symposium*, whose answer to Hephaestus cannot be heard because they hide their faces in each other as if with clamps, holding on to each other constantly, without interruption, without end. When she says that "there's no tranquil place on earth for our love," she says this with the recollected conviction of her cosmic ancestors, who knew this to be true because they could compare the dismal life on this earth with the happier existence they had held in the far reaches of the universe. And this pessimistic conviction echoes through the ages, through the Tristan lovers who also experienced their love in life as if they were already in the grave, down to the modern lovers, Frieda and K. Frieda's love for K. is triangulated by this ancient memory.[134]

THE NOVEL AS SEDUCER, THE SEDUCER AS NOVEL

"Tactics of triangulation are the main business of the novel," Carson writes.[135] The written text is an artifact that not only triangulates between lovers as a passive medium but as the agent of seduction itself. Carson here cites Paolo and Francesca in Dante's *Inferno*, who fell in love with each other by reading Arthurian legends together and ended up in hell for their act of adultery.[136] It is worth noting that the particular book of Arthurian legends they were reading is *Galeotto*, the Romance about Gallehault, the knight who served as a go-between for Lancelot and Guinevere. Boccaccio referred to *The Decameron* as his own *Galeotto*, mediating between his female readers and their erotic desires.[137] This kind of triangulation is at the core of René Girard's theory of how desire functions in the novel.[138] The erotic tension between Lotte and Werther heightens when they both read Ossian together, leading to nothing but Werther's eventual suicide. Emma Bovary also engages in love affairs with Rodolphe and Léon not so much because she is ever actually seduced by them, but because she is seduced by the image she projects onto them from the romantic novels she had read, which also only leads to disappointment and suicide.

Yi-Ping Ong highlights a similar situation in *Anna Karenina* when, after meeting Vronsky for the first time, Anna reads an English novel on the train back home, "but it was unpleasant for her to read, that is, to follow the reflection of other people's lives," because she wanted to inhabit the roles of the characters, themselves.[139] She, in a sense, wants to abandon her own actuality so that she can exist only as a novelistic creation. Tolstoy tells us that the "hero of the novel" she is reading "was already beginning to achieve his English happiness, a baronetcy and an estate, and Anna wished to go with him."[140] While riding on the train, she is seduced into a false promise of happiness, wanting to follow this hero's path while the train takes her down a different path, and this fictional happiness inevitably sets her up for failure. In a moment of distraction from reading, though, she comes to ask herself, "And what am I? Myself or someone else?"[141] It is as though she gets caught up in what Heidegger would call the *Wirbel*, the turbulence, of the novel—matched in velocity by the speed of the train—so that, in her loss of self, she later dies just as much from the impact of the train as from the impact of the novel. Nabokov himself, in his Cornell lectures, diagrammed the space of Anna's sleeping car on the train when she reads this novel, indicating also the outside blizzard that seems to encompass the train as a threat, and advised his students to copy down the diagram. "*This*, he seems to be saying, *is the reality of the novel.*"[142]

This also simulates the reality of *reading* the novel. As Ong notes, "The experience of novel reading requires prolonged solitude and stillness," citing also Isabel Archer in Henry James's *The Portrait of a Lady*, who takes her novels to an office with a door "fastened by bolts which a particularly slender little girl found it impossible to slide."[143] And in Nabokov's translation of Pushkin's novel in verse, *Eugene Onegin*, Carson draws attention to Tatiana just as absorbed in the novelistic universe:

With what attention she now
reads a delicious novel,
with what vivid enchantment
drinks the seductive fiction! [. . .]
She sighs, and having made her own
another's ecstasy, another's melancholy,
she whispers in a trance, by heart,
a letter to the amiable hero.[144]

Tatiana learns love through a novel, and later projects this love onto Onegin. Here she "whispers in a trance, by heart, / a letter to the amiable hero," but she ends up writing this letter to Onegin, who, in response, writes her off. Once he flees after accidentally killing Lensky in the duel, Tatiana visits his abandoned mansion, poring over the books he had annotated in his library and wondering whether there was no "real Onegin," but a "parody" of the literary heroes he had modeled himself after.[145] The next time they meet, years later, she is married, and now that he falls in love with her, she rejects him.

Nabokov uses this outline in *Lolita*, of a young girl who has a crush on an older, handsome man who seems like a collage of celebrity looks, but then begins to see through his character as someone who talks like a book instead of a real person, and as someone who wants to teach her how to love him through giving her books. Once he starts pursuing her, her fantasy dissolves, and she ends up fleeing from him. This movement between attraction and repulsion is the same movement that Kierkegaard traces in *The Seducer's Diary*, beginning with Johannes's seduction of Cordelia, followed by the books he gives to instruct her as part of this seduction, which is then followed by Cordelia's rejection of him.

Anna Karenina, Isabel Archer, and the adolescent Tatiana (before she gets married) all want to dissolve in the novels they read and lose their sense of self. But both Cordelia and Dolores encounter Johannes and Humbert respectively as though these men themselves were books, were novels—and their encounter with them allows their own consciousness, their own sense of self, to unfold in contradistinction from these walking books. They both seek an autonomy outside of the novels they are trapped in.

Just as Humbert's gift to Dolores is a copy of "The Little Mermaid," thematizing the muteness that he prizes in her, Johannes thinks of erotic love as something that flees away in silence from "chatter."[146] Reading Kierkegaard alongside Heidegger, perhaps the experience of Authenticity, in fleeing from the inauthenticity of idle chatter, is tinged with an eros that Heidegger refuses to acknowledge. The element of muteness that Johannes values in eros is what Carson identifies as the novel's most salient feature. Simone de Beauvoir, too, defines the novel as a "silent whole" that "says nothing but rather shows a whole set of difficulties, ambiguities and contradictions which constitute the lived meaning of an existence."[147]

Inasmuch as Cordelia and Dolores seem to read Johannes and Humbert as novels, Johannes and Humbert attempt to write these girls into their own novels—that is, to write them into silence. But in this silence, they learn to see right through these controlling men in the same way that Tatiana eventually sees through Onegin, identifying these men not so much as artists as artificers—as inauthentic, dissembling manipulators who hide behind layers of irony and let other books speak for themselves. When Cordelia breaks off the engagement, Johannes asks in his Diary, "What does erotic love love?"[148] Carson asks this question in reverse, tracing the answer in the history of lyric poetry moving into its written form and ultimately developing into the novel:

> "What does the lover want from love?" is the question to which the [ancient Greek] lyric evidence led us. But now we should consider the matter from another side, for the nature of the lyric evidence cannot be separated from the fact of its transcription, and that fact remains mysterious. . . . New genres of expression developed to meet its demands. . . . Let us superimpose on the question "What does the lover want from love" the questions "What does the reader want from reading? What is the writer's desire?" Novels are the answer.[149]

It is a novel that Johannes—and behind him, Kierkegaard—ends up writing with *The Seducer's Diary*. And it is eros that seemingly draws its fictional reader, Victor Eremita, who comes across the manuscript locked inside the antique desk: "For a time, I again walked by every day and gazed at the desk with enamored eyes," Eremita tells us.[150] He eventually takes a hatchet to the desk, where a secret compartment opens to reveal a box designed for the storage of a pair of pistols—perhaps another allusion to Werther—but what he finds there instead is the mass of papers that he would later edit under the title of *Either/Or*, including *The Seducer's Diary*.[151] Eros's arrows are replaced with images of a hatchet and pistols—the pistols being interchangeable with the manuscript—and the violence works hand in hand with the seduction. Maybe the novel is the genre that emerges out of the pistol box, in all of its erotic pessimism.

Eremita, as a reader, is ultimately seduced by the novel inside, by *The Seducer's Diary*, however much its novelistic narrator may disparage novels themselves. "To see her was to love her, as the novels say," Johannes tells us, "but what, indeed does one come to know about love from novels? Sheer lies—which helps to shorten the task."[152] However, this could just be part of Johannes's ironic posturing. He openly champions "not the poetic but the prosaic," and finds the "infinite prosiness of an engagement" as the "sounding board for the interesting."[153] If the book he wanted to write was called *A Contribution to a Theory of the Kiss*, then this novel could itself be an attempt at that theory, especially if we recall Schlegel's formulation of a theory of the novel that would itself have to be a novel.[154]

KIERKEGAARD CONTRA SCHLEGEL

Kierkegaard himself would probably object to this point, siding with Hegel when he writes in his dissertation that "Schlegelian irony was . . . on a very dubious wrong road."[155] He then proceeds to criticize *Lucinde*, Schlegel's own novel that could very well stand in for a theory of the novel, because it "is an attempt to suspend all ethics":[156]

> [By] starting from the freedom and the constitutive authority of the *I*, one does not arrive at a still higher spirituality but comes only to sensuousness and consequently to its opposite. In ethics, the relation to spirit is implied, but because the *I* wants a higher freedom, it negates the ethical spirit and thereby falls under the laws of the flesh and of drives.[157]

And it is not so much that the characters in *Lucinde* have questionable ethics, but the fact that the entire work feels too "doctrinaire" that offends Kierkegaard the most.

> If it were possible to imagine *Lucinde* as a whole to be merely . . . a hilarious playfulness that took joy in setting everything on its head, in turning everything

upside down; if it were merely witty irony over all the ethics that is identical with custom and habit,

then anyone, to Kierkegaard, would "have the time of his life relishing it."[158]

It is possible, then, to read *The Seducer's Diary*, which he was writing in parallel to his dissertation—when Schlegel was very much on his mind—as a response to *Lucinde*. Sylvia Walsh interprets Johannes as "modeled after the hero of *Lucinde*, only he is far more calculating and intellectually sensuous than Julius, Schlegel's romantic hero."[159] She even goes so far as to see all of *Either/Or* as a work "that corresponds to what Friedrich Schlegel has dubbed an 'arabesque novel' with its 'mixture of genres—aphorisms, essays, diaries, letters, and a sermon.'"[160] Schlegel did, after all, think of novels as "the Socratic dialogues of our time" that are anchored in "the ideas and rhetorics of irony and parody," so what we see in *The Seducer's Diary* is an attempt to parody the parody, and to split the Socratic dialogue into the monologue of a diarist, as though the text itself were missing its other half that would make it a novel, simulating the division of the primordial lovers.[161]

The Seducer's Diary replaces the earnest, cloying tone of *Lucinde* with the "playfulness" and "witty irony" that he wishes Schlegel would have used. Johannes, like Julius, also represents an ethically dubious "I," but one who does not fall "under the laws of the flesh and of drives." Johannes is more cerebral; he contemplates a contribution to a theory of the kiss instead of performing the act. But the Platonic image of lovers stuck in a kiss is what Kierkegaard highlights in his criticism of *Lucinde*, noting that "one of Julius's great tasks is to picture to himself an eternal embrace, presumably as the one and only true actuality."[162]

Kierkegaard dismisses this actuality and suggests it as a theory instead—and not even that, but a contribution to one. He supplements this image with its opposite: just as much as these Platonic lovers kiss without disengaging, Kierkegaard gives us a disengagement without kissing. The only kiss Cordelia ever gives Johannes is described as "vague" and hardly pleasurable to either him or her.[163] He waits for the moment when the kiss will be more passionate, but this moment never arrives.

What happens instead is that the kiss is what transforms Johannes's relationship with her. When he had once thought of himself as a self-fashioned artist, animating her like Pygmalion animates Galatea, he then becomes a passive, helpless witness, as when he imagines himself as "witness to this farewell scene" when "nature, like a tender and luxuriant mother," releases Cordelia "from the land of illusions" and gives her "a kiss, unlike a human kiss, which subtracts something, but rather a divine kiss, which gives everything, which gives the girl the power of the kiss."[164] *The Seducer's Diary*, then, is the account of a kiss withheld, told from the perspective of a seducer who fails at his own seduction.

Lukács thinks of Johannes as "the Platonic idea of the seducer, who is so deeply a seducer and nothing else that really he is not even that."[165] Johannes even deludes himself into saying, "I am and remain an optimist," but the irony that he had used to instruct Cordelia—and, by extension, the reader—allows us to take away an opposite interpretation, especially when he sneers at another seemingly happy couple walking past him, making fun of their "infallible hope" and the "*harmonia praestabilita* [preestablished harmony]"—a phrase taken from Leibniz—"in all their movements."[166] Johannes understands that he is not "the right one" who will come to receive Cordelia's kiss, except from a distance, where he can only witness her "leap" away from him. And on the other side of this leap, "she throws a kiss over to us who stand on this side."[167] Johannes's contribution to a theory of the kiss fails, as he writes: "it is my opinion that a kiss comes closer to the idea when a man kisses a girl than when a girl kisses a man."[168] But Cordelia here has "the power of the kiss"; it is hers to bestow, and she chooses not to bestow it onto him.

KIERKEGAARD AS NOVEL THEORIST

Just as much as we can read *The Seducer's Diary* as a parody of either *Lucinde*, *The Sorrows of Young Werther*, or the novel form at large, Victor Eremita, Kierkegaard's fictional editor of *Either/Or*, has this to say about it:

> We sometimes come upon novels in which specific characters represent contrasting views of life. They usually end with one persuading the other. The point of view ought to speak for itself, but instead the reader is furnished with the historical result that the other was persuaded. I consider it fortunate that these papers provide no enlightenment in this respect.[169]

Kierkegaard also makes reference to *The Seducer's Diary* in a note to a passage from a draft of *The Concept of Anxiety*, where he says that anyone who "looks at it closely . . . will see that this is something quite different from a novel, that it has completely different categories up its sleeve."[170] These categories, in his mind, have to do with narrative. In his journal, he wrote that *The Seducer's Diary* lacked a narrative, so he was planning a companion piece in narrative that he would call "Unhappy Love" to "form a contrast to the Seducer."[171] What he wanted to write in "Unhappy Love" is more or less the same story, except that the girl "surrendered" to the man and loved him passionately, leading him to fall into a depression. He would then reject her advances, which "made him indescribably happy at the moment; as soon as he thought of time, he despaired."[172]

What distinguishes the purportedly non-narrative *Seducer's Diary* from the unwritten narrative of "Unhappy Love," shelved along with the plans for his unwritten *Agnete and the Merman* (which could have been one and the same project), is only that the latter introduces time as a central thematic concern rather than just a structural principle. This is an idiosyncratic understanding of narrative, since *The Seducer's Diary* does take place across a narrative sequence of events. "A" introduces the work with his own gloss, followed by three of Cordelia's letters to Johannes. Johannes's first entry is dated "April 4th," but without a year. Even so, the question of time in *The Seducer's Diary* catches Eremita's attention enough for him to figure out that the year Johannes begins the diary is 1834.[173] But in subsequent entries, Johannes occasionally drops the month, and then the entire date altogether, the more he contemplates love as a feature of eternity, envisioning Cordelia moving "eternally forward."[174] The Unhappy Lover, by contrast—perhaps an analog to Hegel's "Unhappy Consciousness" in *The Phenomenology of Spirit* and a preview of Heidegger's Dasein—is bound by his finitude, his consciousness of being as time.

If *The Seducer's Diary* is not a novel and not even a narrative, then that point was surely lost on its early reviewers, one of whom compared all of *Either/Or* to the novels of Edward Bulwer-Lytton and Eugène Sue.[175] The earliest articles about Kierkegaard in English also situated him in the context of Flaubert and Dostoevsky.[176] Lukács acknowledges him as the direct influence on his own *Theory of the Novel*, and Adrian Leverkühn's first encounter with Mephistopheles occurs while he is reading Kierkegaard in Thomas Mann's *Doctor Faustus*. Kierkegaard no doubt shaped the history of the novel and of novel theory, but his own relationship to the novel is worth exploring. "What Bakhtin sees occurring in the novel applies fairly directly to Kierkegaard," George Pattison notes, reading *Either/Or* as a kind of Bildungsroman that offers "a set of choices about personal, cultural, and religious values that related to the life situation of its likely readers" in "an exceptionally carnivalesque multiplicity of styles and genres."[177]

Scholars like Edward F. Mooney disagree. "Kierkegaard is not a novelist," he says emphatically, "though 'The Seducer's Diary,' from the first volume of *Either/Or*, reads like a novella."[178] But maybe he overstates the point by insisting that Kierkegaard "has no wish that a *new* genre be inaugurated in his honor, and no wish to found a new philosophical style."[179] Joakim Garff, though, offers more nuance when he writes:

> Kierkegaard never wrote a Bildungsroman; indeed, it is a matter of debate whether any text among the mountains of written paper he left behind can

meaningfully be called a *novel*. It is indisputable, however, that Kierkegaard thinks in character types and populates his work with *textual characters* that he either imports from the rich stock of world literature or single-handedly conjures up from the magical darkness of the ink bottle.[180]

If *The Seducer's Diary* is not a novel (or a novel within a novel), it still engages in dialogue with the genre, "which is sometimes said to hold a mirror to its time, but Kierkegaard held a kaleidoscope to a kaleidoscopic time"— something that could equally be said of Proust, Mann, Musil, Kafka, Joyce, and Woolf.[181]

One thing that cannot be disputed, however, is that Kierkegaard was actively thinking about the novel—its aesthetic form and social function— throughout his career. It's not for nothing that his dissertation, *The Concept of Irony, with Continual Reference to Socrates*, veers away from Socrates into a sustained criticism of Schlegel, not so much as a philosopher but as a novelist. Smyth sees in Schlegel's "prescription for a novelistic theory of the novel . . . an instance of that perennial but deceptive fruit: an ironical theory of irony."[182] So for Kierkegaard to think through the concept of irony, it was necessary for him to think through Schlegel and the novel. And while Kierkegaard was still a graduate student procrastinating on his dissertation, he published his first major work, oddly titled: *From the Papers of One Still Living, Published Against His Will*—a work that he actually fought very hard to get published, with all his will.[183] This cryptically titled work is a review of Hans Christian Andersen's novel, *Only a Fiddler*, published in the same year as "The Little Mermaid." At twenty-five years old and already eight years into his graduate program, Kierkegaard was antsy about getting anything published at this point. While hard at work on this review, his journal entries were ebullient, describing "an indescribable joy" and inspiration, even going so far as to say, "I would like to write a novella with my own mottoes."[184]

It must have been an awkward situation when, as Andersen describes it, Kierkegaard ran into him on the street in Copenhagen, assuring him that he would write a positive review of the novel, and saying that most critics misunderstood Andersen.[185] Either Kierkegaard was lying, or he had changed his mind, because the review was scathing.[186] It may have been as a result of this interaction that Kierkegaard wrote a puzzling preface to the book-length review, signed by "The Publisher" as opposed to the author of the review, as though another person were critiquing the critic, even alluding to the "quarrel I have had for quite a long time with the actual author of this essay."[187] And then, quoting a verse from a popular song, he writes:

Although I love him "with tongue and mouth and from the bottom of my heart" and truly regard him as my sincere friend, my *alter ego* [other self], I am still far from being able to describe our relationship by substituting another expression that might perhaps seem identical: *alter idem* [another of the same kind].[188]

The image of two sides of the same self, or two selves coming together both in erotic union and in quarrelsome contradiction, "perpetually in conflict with each other, although under it all we are united by the deepest, most sacred, indissoluble ties," is this same image from *Symposium* that would later haunt *The Seducer's Diary*. He describes this erotic dialectic in terms of "magnetic repulsion," yet "we are still, in the strongest sense of the word, inseparable."[189] It is not so much "as if one soul resided in two bodies," but "that with respect to us it must rather seem as if two souls resided in one body."[190] Maybe this is what he sees in the tragic condition of the two lovers clinging to each other in front of Hephaestus—not that they share one soul, but that, as a result of the incision, they now have two souls and try—but fail—to re-create what it was like to have one body. This *alter idem* "is actually close to casting a gloom over me"—and it is precisely this gloomy, pessimistic image of two lovers clinging to each other that becomes the guiding emblem for Kierkegaard's reflections on the novel, from this review to *The Seducer's Diary*.[191]

The fact that the review was so harsh ended up being of little consequence, because hardly anyone read it anyway, due to its inordinate length for a review and its heavy, plodding, Hegelian style, even though Kierkegaard tries hiding this insecurity by disparaging "graduate-student prose" in this work.[192] But it is Kierkegaard's first articulation of what it means to be an "authentic individual who does not depend on external events in order to survive."[193] *Only a Fiddler* is about a man by the name of Christian (Andersen's middle name), a genius who dies in poverty after failing to find any funding from a patron that would allow him to pursue his art. Kierkegaard's problem with Andersen is that the novel is too saturated with his own autobiography—a general point that Schlegel defends in his "Letter about the Novel," which may in part be why Kierkegaard argues against Schlegel in his dissertation.[194] For Kierkegaard, the "authentic novel must express an authentic view of life and not be a projection of personal problems and a revelation of other deficiencies."[195]

Kierkegaard begins his review in a way that both echoes "Hegel's great attempt to begin with nothing" and rehearses Heidegger's later procedure for outlining the problem of the forgetting of Being:[196]

> Far from remembering with thankfulness the struggles and hardships the world has endured in order to become what it is, the whole newer development—in order to begin again from the beginning—has a great tendency even to forget, if possible, the results this development has gained in the sweat of its brow.[197]

He then proceeds to disparage the "gaping mob" against the authentic individual, the same way that Heidegger would distinguish *das Man* ["the 'they'"] from authentic Dasein.[198]

This rant turns into an ad hominem attack against Andersen, who "early in life was wrapped up in himself," and subsequently "felt thrown back on himself like a superfluous cornflower amid the useful grain."[199] This detail of the useless cornflower could also be a barb against his recently published "The Little Mermaid"—which also must have struck Kierkegaard as too autobiographical in its own way—in which the nameless mermaid lives far out at sea, where "the water is as blue as the petals of the prettiest cornflowers."[200] This mermaid, too, is artistic, but she gives up her musical talents by giving away her voice, and then passively waits to be accepted and loved by the prince. This must have struck Kierkegaard as a narrative of absolute inauthenticity. And he continues to attack Andersen:

> And because he was thus continually thrust down in the funnel of his own personality, inasmuch as his original elegiac mood modified itself through such reflection to a certain gloom and bitterness against the world, his poetic powers, productive in their self-consuming activity, must manifest themselves to a low flame that again and again flares up rather than, as would be the case with a more significant personality, as an underground fire that by its eruption terrifies the world.[201]

This excoriation seems as much an appraisal of Kierkegaard's own "gloom and bitterness against the world" as it is of Andersen's. It is as though in Andersen he sees his own *alter idem* that he identifies in the preface, the one who "is actually close to casting a gloom over me," but whom he clings to nonetheless, as a part of his own being.[202] Smyth notes how Kierkegaard

> reserves his most . . . sarcastic and dismissive . . . assaults for those positions most dangerously close to his own. This indeed is essentially characteristic of irony and the ironist *per se*, and Kierkegaard himself is fully aware of this tendency.[203]

Maybe this was also an exercise at articulating his own anxiety over not being "a more significant personality" that "terrifies the world" with its erupting flames of genius. Kierkegaard returns to this image of flames in an artistic setting when he later writes in *Either/Or*:

> A fire broke out backstage in a theater. The clown came out to warn the public; they thought it was a joke and applauded. He repeated it; the acclaim was even greater. I think that's just how the world will come to an end: to general applause from wits who believe it's a joke.[204]

In both cases, the flames make no difference, which is the little consolation that could end up redeeming the "gloom and bitterness against the world."

What Andersen lacks most is a "life-view," which is "more than a quintessence or a sum of propositions maintained in abstract neutrality."[205] It is, instead, "an unshakable certainty in oneself won from all experience."[206] A life-view is more than just a perspective, but something closer to what Lukács would call "form" in the novel: "A life-view is really providence in the novel; it is its deeper unity, which makes the novel have the center of gravity in itself. A life-view frees it from being arbitrary or purposeless."[207] When a life-view is lacking, the novel disintegrates into either dogma or thinly veiled autobiography. If the author is speaking in their own voice, then there would be no space for irony, the driving motor of the novel—and also the method of Kierkegaard's indirect communication. The reality of the outer world would then violate the fictional reality created in the space of the novel. As Ong interprets it, "the reader's failure to be convinced by the reality of the novel registers in a growing awareness either of herself or of an authorial presence, who awkwardly intervenes within the unfolding of the work itself and thereby falsifies it."[208]

Kierkegaard took his concept of "life-view" from Friedrich Schleiermacher's own critique of *Lucinde,* so even through his critique of Andersen, he is still engaging Schlegel's take on the novel, and the life-view that Kierkegaard identified as the crux of the novel is what he ended up cultivating throughout the rest of his writings.[209] In his posthumously published *Point of View for my Activity as an Author*, he explains that the pseudonyms he wrote under were meant to avoid any situation where the reader would confuse those points of view with Kierkegaard's own.[210] What he wanted to foster was an autonomous structure that would both hold a novel together and invite the reader to explore their own autonomy.

Bakhtin takes Kierkegaard's concept of the life-view when he analyzes the role of character in Dostoevsky's novels:

> the hero interests Dostoevsky not as some manifestation of reality that possesses fixed and specific socially typical or individual characteristic traits, nor as a specific profile assembled out of unambiguous and objective features . . . [but] as *a particular point of view on the world and on oneself*, as the position enabling a person to interpret and evaluate his own self and his surrounding reality.[211]

Bakhtin, like Lukács, was not only open about the influence of Kierkegaard on his work as a novel theorist, but proud of the fact that he seemed to have discovered Kierkegaard before he came into vogue throughout Europe in the 1920s. In an interview with the literary journal *Tjelovek*, Bakhtin even boasted about how he was the first Russian to study Kierkegaard and to note the parallels between Kierkegaard and Dostoevsky.

While Bakhtin and Lukács were explicitly working through Kierkegaard to make sense of the novel at a time when Kierkegaard, to them at least, seemed to be everywhere, one of their contemporaries, aside from Nabokov, was conspicuously silent about acknowledging the debt he owed to Kierkegaard, and specifically to Kierkegaard's work on the novel: Martin Heidegger.

NOTES

1. Kierkegaard, *Fear and Trembling*, trans. Alastair Hannay (London: Penguin Books, 2003), 120.
2. Kierkegaard, *Fear and Trembling*, 121.
3. Kierkegaard, *Fear and Trembling*, 121.
4. Kierkegaard, *Fear and Trembling*, 121.
5. Kierkegaard, *Fear and Trembling*, 121.
6. Kierkegaard, "Supplement," in *Fear and Trembling / Repetition*, ed. trans. Howard V. Hong and Edna V. Hong (Princeton, NJ: Princeton University Press, 1983), 242.
7. Kierkegaard, "Supplement," 242.
8. Kierkegaard, "Supplement," 243.
9. Kierkegaard, "Supplement," 242.
10. Kierkegaard, *Fear and Trembling*, 121.
11. Kierkegaard, *Fear and Trembling*, 121.
12. Kierkegaard, *Seducer's Diary*, viii.
13. Qtd. in John Updike's introduction to *Seducer's Diary* by Kierkegaard, ix.
14. Updike, introduction to *Seducer's Diary* by Kierkegaard, xii.
15. Lukács, *Theory of the Novel*, 19. Hullot-Kentor also refers to the 1920s in Germany as a time that could be referred to as a "Kierkegaard renaissance" (Hullot-Kentor's introduction to *Kierkegaard* by Adorno, xii).
16. Kafka, *Letters to Friends*, 199.
17. Weinman, *Real Lolita*, 224. With his trademark hubris, Nabokov says, "As for influence, well, I've never been influenced by anyone in particular, dead or quick" (Nabokov, *Strong Opinions*, 116). In another interview, he says, "Alas, I am not one to provide much sport for influence hunters" (Nabokov, *Strong Opinions*, 152).
18. Qtd. in Priscilla Meyer and Rachel Trousdale, "Vladimir Nabokov and Virginia Woolf," *Comparative Literature Studies* 50, no. 3 (2013): 490. To this point, Priscilla Meyer and Rachel Trousdale have researched the extensive ways in which Nabokov mined material from Woolf's novels (Meyer and Trousdale, "Vladimir Nabokov and Virginia Woolf," 490–522).
19. Priscilla Meyer and Jeff Hoffmann, "Infinite Reflections in *Pale Fire*: The Danish Connection (Hans Andersen and Isak Dinesen)," *Russian Literature* 41 (1997): 206.

20. Herner Sæverot, *Indirect Pedagogy: Some Lessons in Existential Education*, ed. Michael A. Peters (Rotterdam: Sense, 2012), 33.

21. Stephen Jay Parker, "Library," in *The Garland Companion to Vladimir Nabokov*, ed. Vladimir E. Alexandrov (New York: Garland, 1995), 283–290.

22. Parker, "Library," 285.

23. Parker, "Library," 285.

24. Vladimir Dmitrievich Nabokov, "1904 Library Catalogue," The Nabokovian, https://thenabokovian.org/sites/default/files/2018-06/VDNabokov%20Library%20Catalog%201904.pdf; Vladimir Dmitrievich Nabokov, "1911 Library Catalogue," The Nabokovian, https://thenabokovian.org/sites/default/files/2018-06/VDNabokov%20Library%20Catalog%201904.pdf.

25. Updike, introduction to *Seducer's Diary* by Kierkegaard, vii.

26. Updike, introduction to *Seducer's Diary* by Kierkegaard, vii.

27. Updike, introduction to *Seducer's Diary* by Kierkegaard, xiv.

28. Kierkegaard, *Seducer's Diary*, 122.

29. Kierkegaard, *Seducer's Diary*, 127.

30. Nabokov, *Lolita*, 123; Kierkegaard, *Seducer's Diary*, 132.

31. Kierkegaard, *Seducer's Diary*, 5.

32. Qtd. in Gabriel Josipovici, *On Trust: Art and the Temptations of Suspicion* (New Haven, CT: Yale University Press, 1999), 7.

33. Josipovici, *On Trust*, 10.

34. Qtd. in Josipovici, *On Trust*, 15–16.

35. Josipovici, *On Trust*, 17.

36. Anne Carson, *Eros the Bittersweet* (Princeton, NJ: Princeton University Press, 2015), 109, 167.

37. Carson, *Eros the Bittersweet*, 39.

38. Carson, *Eros the Bittersweet*, 38.

39. Kierkegaard, *Seducer's Diary*, 6.

40. Martin Heidegger, *Being and Time*, trans. John Macquarrie and Edward Robinson (New York: HarperPerennial, 2008), 68.

41. Kierkegaard, *Either/Or*, II: 258.

42. Heidegger, *Being and Time*, 68.

43. Louis Mackey reads all of *Either/Or* as modeled on *Wilhelm Meister*, even though it is essentially "a *Bildungsroman*, but without *Bildung*" (Louis Mackey, *Kierkegaard: A Kind of Poet* [Philadelphia, PA: University of Pennsylvania Press, 1972], 273–274).

44. There is also a brief moment in *The Seducer's Diary* when Johannes is drawn to a woman named "Charlotte Hahn" (Kierkegaard, *Seducer's Diary*, 117).

45. Kierkegaard, *Seducer's Diary*, 190.

46. Kierkegaard, *Seducer's Diary*, 193–194.

47. Kierkegaard, *Seducer's Diary*, 33.

48. Kierkegaard, *Seducer's Diary*, 33, 40.

49. Kierkegaard, *Seducer's Diary*, 172.

50. Kierkegaard, *Seducer's Diary*, 43.

51. Kierkegaard, *Seducer's Diary*, 57.

52. Nabokov, *Lolita*, 16.
53. Kierkegaard, *Seducer's Diary*, 136.
54. Nabokov, *Lolita*, 16.
55. Kierkegaard, *Seducer's Diary*, 42.
56. Kierkegaard, *Seducer's Diary*, 12.
57. Kierkegaard, *Seducer's Diary*, 27.
58. Kierkegaard, *Seducer's Diary*, 194.
59. Nabokov, *Enchanter*, 57.
60. Dmitri Nabokov's afterword to Vladimir Nabokov's *Enchanter*, 98.
61. The working title for *Lolita* was *The Kingdom by the Sea*, clearly a reference to Poe's "Annabel Lee," but also an illustration of Johannes' fantasies in *The Seducer's Diary* (Weinman, *Real Lolita*, 54).
62. Shakespeare, *King Lear*, 1.1.61, 1.1.86.
63. Shakespeare, *King Lear*, 1.1.90–91.
64. Shakespeare, *King Lear*, 2.4.281–82.
65. Kierkegaard, *Seducer's Diary*, 49–50.
66. Claire Carlisle, "Kierkegaard and Heidegger," in *The Oxford Handbook of Kierkegaard*, ed. John Lippitt and George Pattison (Oxford: Oxford University Press, 2013), 436.
67. Carlisle, "Kierkegaard and Heidegger," 436.
68. Carlisle, "Kierkegaard and Heidegger," 437.
69. Carlisle, "Kierkegaard and Heidegger," 437.
70. Carlisle, "Kierkegaard and Heidegger," 437.
71. Kierkegaard, *Seducer's Diary*, 16.
72. Kierkegaard, *Seducer's Diary*, 20.
73. Kierkegaard, *Seducer's Diary*, 30.
74. Kierkegaard, *Seducer's Diary*, 51.
75. Kierkegaard, *Seducer's Diary*, 55.
76. Kierkegaard, *Seducer's Diary*, 146.
77. Kierkegaard, *Seducer's Diary*, 154.
78. Kierkegaard, *Seducer's Diary*, 18.
79. Carson, *Eros the Bittersweet*, 167.
80. Kierkegaard, *Seducer's Diary*, 67–68.
81. Kierkegaard, *Seducer's Diary*, 111.
82. Kierkegaard, *Seducer's Diary*, 22.
83. Kierkegaard, *Seducer's Diary*, 67.
84. Kierkegaard, *Seducer's Diary*, 25.
85. Kierkegaard, *Seducer's Diary*, 60.
86. Kierkegaard, *Seducer's Diary*, 72.
87. Kierkegaard, *Seducer's Diary*, 192.
88. Kierkegaard, *Seducer's Diary*, 74.
89. Kierkegaard, *Seducer's Diary*, 93.
90. Kierkegaard, *Seducer's Diary*, 199.
91. Proust, *Swann's Way*, 396.
92. Kierkegaard, *Seducer's Diary*, 83.

93. Kierkegaard, *Seducer's Diary,* 91.
94. Kierkegaard, *Seducer's Diary,* 154.
95. Nabokov, *Lolita,* 114.
96. Kierkegaard, *Seducer's Diary,* 102.
97. Kierkegaard, *Seducer's Diary,* 142–143.
98. Kierkegaard, *Seducer's Diary,* 144.
99. Kierkegaard, *Seducer's Diary,* 162.
100. Lukács, *Soul and Form,* ed. John T. Sanders and Katie Terezakis (New York: Columbia University Press, 2010), 50.
101. Kierkegaard, *Seducer's Diary,* 161.
102. Kierkegaard, *Seducer's Diary,* 158.
103. Carson, *Eros the Bittersweet,* 41.
104. Carson, *Eros the Bittersweet,* 42.
105. Carson, *Eros the Bittersweet,* 70; Proust, *The Fugitive,* 662.
106. Carson, *Eros the Bittersweet,* 85.
107. Kierkegaard, *Seducer's Diary,* 159–160.
108. Kierkegaard, *Seducer's Diary,* 161.
109. Freud, *The Psychology of Love,* trans. Shaun Whiteside (London: Penguin Books, 2007), 128. In the introduction to Sartre's *Nausea,* Hayden Carruth writes, "Long before Freud, Kierkegaard was aware of the hidden forces within the self, forces that, simply by existing, destroyed all rational, positivistic, and optimistic delusions" (Hayden Carruth, introduction to *Nausea* by Sartre, trans. Lloyd Alexander [New York: New Directions: 1964], viii). There is more fascinating research to be done in connecting Freud with Kierkegaard vis-à-vis their pessimism.
110. Cioran, *Short History of Decay,* 157.
111. Nabokov, *Lolita,* 114.
112. Kierkegaard, *Seducer's Diary,* 161.
113. John Vignaux Smyth, *A Question of Eros: Irony in Sterne, Kierkegaard, and Barthes* (Gainesville, FL: Florida State University Press, 1986), 6–7.
114. Plato, *Symposium,* 192D-E: 21–22.
115. Plato, *Symposium,* 192E: 22; cf. Carson, *Eros the Bittersweet,* 68.
116. Kierkegaard, *Seducer's Diary,* 161.
117. Carson, *Eros the Bittersweet,* 68.
118. Brontë, *Wuthering Heights,* 123.
119. Brontë, *Wuthering Heights,* 125.
120. Cf. Nussbaum, "The Speech of Alcibiades," 140.
121. Carson, *Eros the Bittersweet,* 74.
122. Shakespeare, *Romeo and Juliet,* 1.5.106, 1.5.108, 1.5.111.
123. Castiglione, *The Book of the Courtier,* ed. Daniel Javitch (New York: W. W. Norton, 2002), 253.
124. Castiglione, *Book of the Courtier,* 253.
125. Carson, *Eros the Bittersweet,* 78.
126. Mann, *Magic Mountain,* 587.
127. Mann, *Magic Mountain,* 590.
128. Proust, *In the Shadow of Young Girls in Flower,* 565.

129. Proust, *The Guermantes Way*, 399.
130. Proust, *The Guermantes Way*, 402.
131. Proust, *The Guermantes Way*, 403.
132. Carson, *Eros the Bittersweet*, 79.
133. Kafka, *The Castle,* trans. Mark Harman (New York: Schocken, 1998), 138.
134. In the critical reception that links Kierkegaard with Kafka, Judith Butler notes how "the very notion of the gesture that Lukács begins to elaborate in the context of reading Kierkegaard is later taken up by Benjamin and Adorno to retrieve the social and historic significance of Kafka" (Judith Butler, introduction to *Soul and Form* by Lukács, 9).
135. Carson, *Eros the Bittersweet*, 79.
136. Carson, *Eros the Bittersweet*, 79.
137. Boccaccio, *Decameron,* trans. Rebhorn, lvii.
138. René Girard, *Deceit, Desire, and the Novel: Self and Other in Literary Structure*, trans. Yvonne Freccero (Baltimore, MD: Johns Hopkins University Press, 1961), 5.
139. Tolstoy, *Anna Karenina*, trans. Richard Pevear and Larissa Volokhonsky (New York: Penguin Books, 2002), 99–100; cf. Ong, *Art of Being*, 5–11.
140. Tolstoy, *Anna Karenina*, 100.
141. Tolstoy, *Anna Karenina*, 101.
142. Ong, *Art of Being*, 1.
143. Ong, *Art of Being*, 8; Henry James, *The Portrait of a Lady*, in *Novels, 1881-1886*, ed. William T. Stafford, Vol. 2 (New York: Library of America, 1985), 214.
144. Aleksandr Pushkin, *Eugene Onegin: A Novel in Verse*, trans. Nabokov (Princeton, NJ: Princeton University Press, 2018), 153–154; cf. Carson, *Eros the Bittersweet*, 106.
145. Pushkin, *Eugene Onegin*, 262.
146. Kierkegaard, *Seducer's Diary,* 163.
147. Simone de Beauvoir, "My Experience as a Writer," in *"The Useless Mouths" and Other Literary Writings*, ed. Margaret A. Simons and Marybeth Timmerman, trans. Marybeth Timmerman (Champaign, IL: University of Illinois Press, 2011), 287; Ong, *Art of Being*, 88–89.
148. Kierkegaard, *Seducer's Diary,* 195.
149. Carson, *Eros the Bittersweet*, 77–78.
150. Kierkegaard, *Either/Or*, I: 5.
151. Kierkegaard, *Either/Or*, I: 6.
152. Kierkegaard, *Seducer's Diary,* 61.
153. Kierkegaard, *Seducer's Diary,* 63; 95.
154. Schlegel, "Dialogue on Poetry," 109.
155. Kierkegaard, *Concept of Irony*, 265.
156. Kierkegaard, *Concept of Irony*, 289.
157. Kierkegaard, *Concept of Irony*, 301.
158. Kierkegaard, *Concept of Irony*, 290.
159. Sylvia Walsh, *Living Poetically: Kierkegaard's Existential Aesthetics* (University Park, PA: Pennsylvania State University Press, 1994), 64.

160. Walsh, *Living Poetically,* 63.
161. Schlegel, "Dialogue on Poetry," 112; Smyth, *A Question of Eros,* 13.
162. Kierkegaard, *Concept of Irony,* 291.
163. Kierkegaard, *Seducer's Diary,* 153.
164. Kierkegaard, *Seducer's Diary,* 101–102.
165. Lukács, *Soul and Form,* 53.
166. Kierkegaard, *Seducer's Diary,* 27, 81; Gottfried Wilhelm Leibniz, *The Monadology and Other Philosophical Writings*, trans. Robert Latta (Oxford: Oxford University Press, 1965), 262–263.
167. Kierkegaard, *Seducer's Diary,* 126–127.
168. Kierkegaard, *Seducer's Diary,* 160.
169. Kierkegaard, *Either/Or,* I: 14.
170. Qtd. in Walsh, *Living Poetically,* 91.
171. Kierkegaard, *Either/Or* I: xii.
172. Kierkegaard, *Either/Or* I: xii.
173. Coincidentally, it happens to be just over a century before the birth of Lolita. If she is twelve years old when Humbert first meets her in 1947, then she would have to be born in 1935. This year and the preceding one were also when Nabokov began writing the earliest premise for the novel (Proffer, *Keys to Lolita*, 3–4).
174. Kierkegaard, *Seducer's Diary,* 124.
175. Pattison, "Bonfire of the Genres," 39.
176. Pattison, "Bonfire of the Genres," 39.
177. Pattison, "Bonfire of the Genres," 45–47.
178. Edward F. Mooney, "Kierkegaard's Disruptions of Literature and Philosophy: Freedom, Anxiety, and Existential Contributions," in *Kierkegaard, Literature, and the Arts,* ed. Eric Ziolkowski (Evanston, IL: Northwestern University Press, 2018), 56.
179. Mooney, "Kierkegaard's Disruptions of Literature and Philosophy," 60.
180. Joakim Garff, "Kierkegaard's Christian Bildungsroman," in *Kierkegaard, Literature, and the Arts,* ed. Eric Ziolkowski (Evanston, IL: Northwestern University Press, 2018), 89.
181. Pattison, "Bonfire of the Genres," 50.
182. Smyth, *A Question of Eros,* 13.
183. The review was published by J. L. Heiberg, who led an exclusive group of writers. Andersen had fallen out of favor with the Heiberg circle at the same time that Kierkegaard caught their attention, often gatecrashing their gatherings and sending unsolicited manuscripts to Heiberg (Ong, *Art of Being,* 50).
184. Kierkegaard, *Early Polemical Writings*, xxiv; Kierkegaard, *The Concept of Irony*, vii.
185. Kierkegaard, *Early Polemical Writings*, xxv.
186. Kierkegaard did seem to have warned Andersen after this exchange that the review would not be favorable. One week before the review's publication, Andersen "noted in his calendar that he felt an agony of mind over 'Kierkegaard's still unpublished review'" (Kierkegaard, *Early Polemical Writings,* xxv). When the review was finally published, Andersen reports, upon reading it, having to be given "cooling

powders. Walked as if in a coma" (qtd. in Ong, *Art of Being,* 49). A year later, though, Andersen gloated in a letter to a friend about how everyone liked his novel abroad and that there was only one sour local review that had a tone of "whimsicality" to it (qtd. in Kierkegaard, *Early Polemical Writings,* xxvi). Moreover, relations between Andersen and Kierkegaard seemed to have thawed a decade after that when Kierkegaard sent Andersen a copy of the second edition of *Either/Or,* to which Andersen responded warmly (Kierkegaard, *Either/Or,* I: xix).

187. Kierkegaard, *Early Polemical Writings,* 55.
188. Kierkegaard, *Early Polemical Writings,* 55.
189. Kierkegaard, *Early Polemical Writings,* 55.
190. Kierkegaard, *Early Polemical Writings,* 55. Howard V. Hong and Edna H. Hong read this line instead as an allusion to Aristotle, when he writes in *Magna Moralia,* "When we wish to describe a very great friend, we say 'my soul and his are one'" (qtd. in Kierkegaard, *Early Polemical Writings,* fn.5: 248). But the fact that Kierkegaard ends up saying the reverse of this statement, that his relationship is defined as two distinct souls in one body, could suggest a movement from Aristotle to Plato, especially in light of the prevalence of other references to Plato's erotic texts throughout his work.

191. Kierkegaard, *Early Polemical Writings,* 56.
192. Kierkegaard, *Early Polemical Writings,* xxvi–xxvii, 67.
193. Kierkegaard, *Early Polemical Writings,* xxix.
194. Schlegel, "Dialogue on Poetry," 103.
195. Kierkegaard, *Early Polemical Writings,* xxix.
196. Kierkegaard, *Early Polemical Writings,* 61.
197. Kierkegaard, *Early Polemical Writings,* 61.
198. Kierkegaard, *Early Polemical Writings,* 62.
199. Kierkegaard, *Early Polemical Writings,* 73.
200. Andersen, "Little Mermaid," 120.
201. Kierkegaard, *Early Polemical Writings,* 73.
202. Kierkegaard, *Early Polemical Writings,* 56.
203. Smyth, *A Question of Eros,* 112.
204. Kierkegaard, *Either/Or,* I: 30.
205. Kierkegaard, *Early Polemical Writings,* 76.
206. Kierkegaard, *Early Polemical Writings,* 76.
207. Kierkegaard, *Early Polemical Writings,* 81.
208. Ong, *Art of Being,* 19.
209. Ong argues that the section of his dissertation on Schlegel was most likely written around the same time he finished *From the Papers of One Still Living* (Ong, *Art of Being,* 60).
210. Kierkegaard, *A Literary Review,* ed. and trans. Alastair Hannay (London: Penguin Books, 2001), vii.
211. Bakhtin, *Problems of Dostoevsky's Poetics,* ed. and trans. Caryl Emerson (Minneapolis, MN: University of Minnesota Press, 1984), 47.

Chapter 13

In Search of Lost Being
Heidegger's Novelistic Quest

HEIDEGGER'S ANXIETY OF INFLUENCE

April 1964. It was the 150th anniversary of Kierkegaard's birth, and UNESCO had organized a conference in Paris called *"Kierkegaard vivant."*[1] In attendance were Jean-Paul Sartre, Karl Jaspers, Emmanuel Levinas, and other luminaries. But the star of the conference was Martin Heidegger, who had dramatically overcome metaphysics with his magnum opus *Being and Time* in 1927, which marked a definitive break from thousands of years of Western ontology, rethinking the human subject not in terms of subjectivity anymore, but as Dasein, a historical mode of existence that eluded static categories of theorization.[2] Despite his somewhat exaggerated claims to originality, Heidegger still acknowledged the way thinkers like Heraclitus, Kant, Hegel, and Nietzsche shaped his thought. Already in his seventies at this point, he had not yet given the same treatment to Kierkegaard. This conference would be the momentous occasion for such an acknowledgment, and the conference participants were eager to hear his own take on how Kierkegaard lived on in his work.

Even when *Being and Time* was first published in 1927, it "was initially considered a crucial supplement to and extension of general existentialist and specifically Kierkegaardian themes."[3] And still today, Claire Carlisle asks, "to what extent is a contemporary reader's interpretation of Kierkegaard already shaped by Heidegger's philosophy?—and, indeed, is one also reading Heidegger in the light of Kierkegaard?"[4] Symptoms of this crossover emerge when scholars like Edward F. Mooney say that Kierkegaard "creates *anxiety*, that forerunner of change of self or recovery of soul," something that could just as easily be said of Heidegger.[5] Mooney goes on to say, using Heideggerian language, that Kierkegaard makes an existential contribution that only *I* can complete. *His* contribution is to offer me an existential space distinct from social space. If I accept this offer, I accept the open space where existential possibilities are vividly acknowledged, and then I *close* that radical openness through decisive resolution and action.[6]

Heidegger's entire philosophy is predicated on offering an "existential space distinct from social space." This is what he calls "authenticity"—*Eigentlichkeit* in German, my "own-ness," which is why Mooney italicizes the "*I*." Authenticity, in Heidegger's jargon, is the "decisive resolution and action" that only *I* can take for my own existence. And yet we're not even talking about Heidegger here, but Kierkegaard. That Kierkegaard had an "undeniable influence" on Heidegger was never in dispute; some scholars even refer to his impact as "obvious."[7] The only thing that was missing was Heidegger coming out and saying so.

The only thing that was also missing from the Kierkegaard conference, it turned out, ended up being Heidegger himself, despite his much-anticipated role. He had sent a written lecture in his absence, called "*La fin de la philosophie et la tâche de la pensée*" ("The End of Philosophy and the Task of Thought"). There wasn't a single mention of Kierkegaard in the paper. In the discussion that followed, Jean Beaufret, who was tasked with the unfortunate role of presenting it at the conference, uncomfortably and somewhat apologetically addressed the elephant that wasn't even in the room, of how his mentor "had spoken without speaking of Kierkegaard."[8] Jean Wahl, also in attendance, sneered at how Heidegger still "kept Kierkegaard in the shadows."[9]

Before Heidegger was famous for reinventing philosophy, he didn't always go out of his way to hide his fascination with Kierkegaard. Between 1910 and 1914, he admitted to "enthusiastically reading Nietzsche, Dostoevsky, and Kierkegaard."[10] Kierkegaard had already been widely translated into German before the twentieth century, and new translations preceded the Kierkegaard renaissance of the 1920s. Theodor Haecker's translations with accompanying commentary appeared in *Der Brenner*, an Austrian journal of cultural and literary criticism, which Heidegger had subscribed to from 1911 until it went out of business in 1954.[11] In 1919, he reviewed Jaspers's book *The Psychology of Worldviews*, which discusses Kierkegaard's concept of the moment in *The Concept of Anxiety*, a concept that would become central to *Being and Time*.[12] In the courses he taught right before the publication of *Being and Time*, Heidegger quoted *Either/Or* and *Practice in Christianity* regularly.[13]

But an abrupt shift happened when *Being and Time* was published. Kierkegaard was buried in the footnotes, just as someone who "remained completely dominated by Hegel" and was not "correspondingly successful" in his ontology.[14] And by the time Heidegger taught his lecture course,

"What is Called Thinking?" in 1950-51, he was more brazen and flippant in his dismissal, going so far as to claim: "But about the decisive question—the essential nature of Being—Kierkegaard has nothing whatever to say."[15]

Kierkegaard, however, is not the only influential figure whom Heidegger dismissed, ignored, or relegated to footnotes in his work. Lukács and Tolstoy also suffer the same fate in Heidegger's thought. The purpose of this chapter is not to rehash all the ways in which Kierkegaard had influenced Heidegger, especially since they are so "obvious," but, in light of the larger project at hand, to demonstrate the extent to which reflections on the novel as a site of pessimism shaped *Being and Time*, and how Heidegger absorbed these specific reflections on the novel from Kierkegaard, Lukács, and Tolstoy. What is at stake for Heidegger in trying to hide the traces of the novel or novel theory in his work? And when these traces are brought to light, how do they shape our understanding of *Being and Time* as a work that, despite itself, is in conversation with the novel? Despite the fact that scholars have long acknowledged how similar these two thinkers are, Dienstag notes that they are "writers whose relationship to pessimism needs further exploration."[16] Maybe it is through their connection to the novel that we can explore how their pessimism is also connected.

For this, we have to pick up with Kierkegaard where we left him at the end of the previous chapter. *From the Papers of One Still Living* wasn't Kierkegaard's only novel review. After nearly a decade of writing under his pseudonyms, he published under his own name again, this time in a review of two Danish novels that were popular at the time, *A Story of Everyday Life* and *Two Ages*. This review was translated into German for *Der Brenner* in 1914, at the same time when Heidegger still professed to read Kierkegaard enthusiastically.[17] Kierkegaard used this review of these novels as a pretext to address the issue of average everydayness, taking up his pessimistic task to demonstrate its inadequacies, deficiencies, and disappointments, especially in how the individual relates to one's society. And although this review, unlike *From the Papers of One Still Living*, begins with praise, it ends up "preparing the way for a far more pessimistic account of the present age."[18]

Being and Time, like Kierkegaard's *A Literary Review*, is also a portrait of Being in its "average *everydayness*," negotiating between the idle chatter, curiosity, and ambiguity of fallen inauthenticity as one mode of existence, versus the silence, care, and anticipatory resoluteness of projected authenticity as another mode.[19] Authentic Dasein is, quite literally, when Dasein is its own self—as opposed to the inauthentic existence of "the 'they'" [*das Man*], which can also be thought of as "the public." Heidegger even identifies the use of public transportation and newspapers as features of "the dictatorship of the 'they'" in Dasein's average everydayness.[20]

To Heidegger, one does not so much "fall" into the inauthentic existence of "the 'they'" as much as one has always already fallen.[21] We are "thrown" into a world that we fall into; this is the facticity of existence.[22] "In falling," though, "Dasein turns away from itself."[23] To turn back toward itself—to essentially become itself—Dasein can provide a counter-movement against this movement of falling, of being thrown, twisting itself away from inauthenticity into authenticity. This is called Projection [*Entwurf*].[24]

Kierkegaard has a startlingly similar analysis of everyday life in *A Literary Review*. Instead of "falling," he uses the term "leveling," a process that subsumes the individual into a "monstrous abstraction," pressuring the individual to conform to the tastes and ideology of the "all-encompassing something that is nothing, a mirage—this phantom is *the public*."[25] Kierkegaard, like Heidegger, blames newspapers and journals for the leveling of modern culture, in which—as in "falling"—"everything impotently sinks down."[26] On the contrary, a single individual can be "the head of an uprising," but leveling rises above nothing; it just absorbs individuals as it sinks, as it falls.[27] "You might say that a person belongs to the public for a few hours a day," Kierkegaard writes, "that is, during the hours when he is nothing; because during the hours in which he is the definite person he is, he does not belong to the public."[28] The time that he does not belong to the public is the time that he is (what Heidegger would call) authentic.[29]

So already the supposedly groundbreaking work of Heidegger's understanding of Dasein as a historical entity, caught between the demands of the public and the call of its own distinct self, had been worked out by Kierkegaard in his review of novels. The parallels don't end there. One of the features of "the 'they'" for Heidegger is what he calls "idle talk" [*Gerede*]—the chatter, the rambling, the gossip, the logorrhea that superficially hides over the fact that this kind of language is a language that ultimately is about nothing but disguises this nothing with empty words as a distraction.[30] When it comes to idle talk, though, Kierkegaard asks:

> What is it to *chat*? It is to have repealed the passionate disjunction between being silent and speaking. Only the person who can remain essentially silent can essentially speak; only the person who can remain essentially silent can essentially act. Silence is inwardness. Talking forestalls essential speaking, and reflection's utterance weakens action by stealing a march on it.[31]

To Heidegger, idle chatter is also the opposite of true discourse [*Rede*], which emerges only in silence, in the Nothing that clears the space for one to hear the authentic call of conscience:[32]

> *What* does the conscience call to him to whom it appeals? Taken strictly, nothing. The call asserts nothing, gives no information about world-events, has

nothing to tell. . . . "Nothing" gets called *to* [*zu*-gerufen] this Self, but it has been *summoned* [*aufgerufen*] to itself—that is, to its ownmost potentiality-for-Being. . . . *Conscience discourses solely and constantly in the mode of keeping silent.*[33]

To Kierkegaard, "Talkativeness gains in extensity: it has everything to talk about and goes on incessantly. . . . But chat dreads the moment of silence that would make the emptiness plain."[34] That "moment of silence that would make the emptiness plain" is precisely the Nothing that gets called forth in authenticity, according to Heidegger.

Kierkegaard has an ambiguous stance toward idle talk in the novel. "In the novel," he writes, "one finds excellent examples of this kind of chatting, a matter of mere trifles but always about specific persons mentioned by name, whose trivial circumstances are interesting as much as anything for their names."[35] It is as though idle talk is only tolerable to Kierkegaard within the context of a novel, and for that context to be ironic—something that he found lacking in Andersen, the subject of his previous review. Except for a footnote, Heidegger never mentions the novel outright in *Being and Time*, even though he does disparage "scribbling [*das Geschreibe*]" as a form of idle talk.[36] It is unclear whether he would relegate the novel to this category of writing. "In 'poetical discourse,'" he concedes, however, that "the communication of the existential possibilities of one's state-of-mind can become an aim in itself, and this amounts to a disclosing of existence."[37] Would this "poetical" discourse include or exclude a prosaic or novelistic discourse? If Heidegger is trying to capture the experience of average everydayness, would prosaic discourse belong to idle talk?

Dasein seems poetic only to the extent that it hears and belongs (*hören* and *gehören*) to the *logos*. It is poetic in that it dwells in *poiesis*—in making, in doing. "Dasein understands itself in terms of that *which* it is customarily concerned. 'One *is*' what one does."[38] Existing in (or rather, as) ecstatic temporality, Dasein for Heidegger is *"das Eks-tatische."* The same hyphen that emphasizes the *Eks-*, the state of being outside of oneself, also draws attention to the *-tatische*. Dasein is the result of a *Tat*, a deed, a process of existential action instead of material substance.[39] Dasein is thus *tatisch*, "deedly." Dasein outdoes itself; that is, it outdoes its Self in being the *Eks-tatische*. But it is in this poetry, in this ecstasy, that Dasein paradoxically finds itself in a world of prose, and it is this prose of average everydayness that Heidegger analyzes. But, as Eugene Thacker notes, "The problem with the world is that one must always speak from within it."[40] Heidegger's answer to this problem is to come up with a jargon and syntax so far removed from the prose of average everydayness so that he can have the proper distance to carry out his analysis of it, and essentially narrate Dasein's heroic account of discovering its authenticity in silent Discourse as opposed to idle talk, removed from the publicness of "the 'they.'"

Bakhtin, on the other hand, sees the novel almost as the precise opposite of Heidegger's heroic account. It is the expression of the silence and loneliness in an age where people are no longer bound by any public unity.[41] This account of loneliness is similar to Walter Benjamin's. As opposed to the figure of the storyteller, the novelist to Benjamin "has isolated himself. The birthplace of the novel is the solitary individual who is no longer able to express himself by giving examples of his most important concerns, is himself uncounseled, and cannot counsel others."[42] Benjamin sees this as "the earliest symptom of a process whose end is the decline of storytelling [and] is the rise of the novel at the beginning of modern times."[43] This pessimistic account of the novel as the site of alienation also echoes Lukács's characterization of the novel as an expression of "transcendental homelessness."[44] But Bakhtin, despite his focus on loneliness, sees in the novel a Kierkegaardian opportunity to acquire a life-view, and to make one's world one's "own."[45]

Maybe Heidegger stuck to the idea of "poetical discourse" as opposed to prosaic discourse in communicating "the existential possibilities of one's state-of-mind," and ultimately "a disclosing of existence," because he saw that Kierkegaard, too, defines prose as "unconstrained speech . . . so prosiness is an unconcern that does not know a decorum."[46] Furthermore, "prosiness lacks a concept."[47] This must have struck a chord with Heidegger, who tries to come up with a language for Dasein in its authenticity, abiding by a structure of care—the very opposite of the inauthentic "unconcern" with which Kierkegaard diagnosed prose. This clumsy, awkward—albeit precise—language that Heidegger comes up with, though, is not to everyone's taste, least of all novelists.

"SHOULD NOT SUCH WRITING BE SUBJECT TO PUNISHMENT?"

"Heidegger—I could never stand this Nazi *par existence*. The challenge of reading his philosophical jargon of terror made it difficult to keep hold of the book. *One's own-ness!* Should not such writing be subject to punishment?" One can almost picture the derisive smirk on Thomas Mann's face as he penned these words to Paul Tillich in 1944 from his sun-drenched California home, a few houses away from his fellow expatriate Theodor Adorno, Tillich's former student, who would later take his own opportunity at slamming Heidegger with his *Jargon of Authenticity*.[48] Like Nietzsche, who also preferred hurling his insults at Wagner's boorish German nationalism from a sunnier climate, Mann cuts through Heidegger's Nazism with a

French barb. Heidegger is the Nazi *"par existence,"* not *par excellence*, as one would expect this phrase to read; this is a man whose entire existence is that of a Nazi. Here he is, this Nazi railing against "the dictatorship of the 'they'"—of newspapers and journals that, in part, are established to help foster an informed, critical public—while having enjoyed the ceremony of being sworn in as Nazi Rector of the University of Freiburg in 1933. Even though he stepped down as Rector a year later, he benefited from the fascist regime that he never ended up denouncing without any kind of equivocation. But it would be a mistake to read Mann's dismissal as one of political affiliation alone. Mann reserves his harshest words not for Heidegger's politics, but for his writing. It is Heidegger's philosophical writing that ought to be subject to the punishment of the novelist's ridicule.

The antipathy Mann expresses for Heidegger is emblematic of the larger rift between philosophers and novelists. One thinks of D. H. Lawrence writing to Bertrand Russell only a generation before, "Do stop working and writing altogether and become a creature instead of a mechanical instrument."[49] Kierkegaard, though—straddling both philosophical and novelistic writing—reflects on the novel as providing us with the tools to approach philosophy's most fundamental questions about what it means to exist in modernity—reflections that provide the blueprint for Heidegger's *Being and Time*.

And yet Heidegger chose to belong to the philosophical tradition of ignoring the novel—but at a time when no one else was anymore. *Being and Time* was published in the decade that witnessed the most exhilarating novelistic experiments, when the reputations of Proust, Mann, Kafka, Rilke, Joyce, and Woolf were firmly cemented in the public consciousness. Furthermore, scholars—taking Kierkegaard's cue—were now beginning to take the novel as an art form seriously, though many of these scholarly works would be published in the coming decades—decades in which Heidegger would stick ever more steadfastly to poetry as the beacon of literature, even going so far as to write a number of embarrassing poems himself.

Even so, Lukács—just as steeped in Kierkegaard as Heidegger was—published *The Theory of the Novel* in 1915, well before the publication of *Being and Time*. Bakhtin, influenced not only by Kierkegaard but also by Max Scheler and the Marburg School at the time Heidegger was teaching there, began writing his essays on the novel that would later be published as *The Dialogical Imagination*.[50] Benjamin wrote his influential essay on Goethe's *Elective Affinities*—rather than *Faust*, which philosophers like Nietzsche felt more comfortable quoting—in 1922. Auerbach had written his *Habilitationsschrift* on the Early Renaissance novella a year earlier, laying the groundwork for his monumental *Mimesis* in 1946, devoting half of his study of "Representation of Reality in Western Literature" exclusively to the rise of the novel. Heidegger, it seems, had to go out of his way to avoid writing about the novel, especially in a work that takes on the same project as the novel in its portrait of average everydayness.

ONTOLOGICAL GUILT IN THE NOVEL: TOLSTOY, DOSTOEVSKY, KAFKA

It seems that we can learn more about *Being and Time* from what Heidegger leaves out of it, or from what he hides in its footnotes, than what he says outright in the text. Although he doesn't acknowledge Kierkegaard's work on the novel as an influence, he does cite Tolstoy in a fleeting remark. The footnote appears in §51, in Heidegger's treatment of Being-toward-death and the everydayness of Dasein: "In his story 'The Death of Ivan Ilyitch' Leo Tolstoi has presented the phenomenon of the disruption and breakdown of having 'someone die.'"[51] That's certainly the bare minimum of an acknowledgment, and maybe there's more to this Tolstoy connection than Heidegger is willing to let on. While William Irwin maintains that as "a novelist and a philosopher, Tolstoy and Heidegger are doing very different things," just how "very different" these things are may be called into question upon closer reading.[52]

In *The Death of Ivan Ilyich*, the eponymous antihero epitomizes the character of "the 'they.'" His "life had been most simple and most ordinary and most terrible."[53] His being is the being of others, even as everyone else views his death as an irritating inconvenience:

> The awful, terrible act of his dying was, he could see, reduced by those around him to the level of a casual, unpleasant, almost indecorous incident (as if someone entered a drawing-room diffusing an unpleasant odor) and this was done by that very decorum which he had served his whole life long.[54]

Heidegger dissects this phenomenon when he writes, "Indeed the dying of Others is seen often enough as a social inconvenience, if not even a downright tactlessness, against which the public is to be guarded," echoing Kierkegaard's critique of the public "for not know[ing] a decorum."[55] He inserts the footnote at the end of this sentence, alluding to the experience of witnessing another's death. In Tolstoy's novella, Ivan Ilyich himself is the Other witnessing the death that hardly seems to be his own. The tragedy, though, is that it can only be his own. On the verge of death, he—like every Dasein—"had to live thus all alone on the brink of an abyss, with no one who understood him."[56]

Perhaps Heidegger's understanding of inauthenticity as an act of "falling" derives from Ivan Ilyich's final thoughts: "And the example of a stone falling downwards with increasing velocity entered his mind. Life, a series of increasing sufferings, flies further and further towards its end—the most terrible suffering."[57] He muses over the course of his life, thinking,

> It is as if I had been going downhill while I imagined I was going up. And that's really what it was. I was going up in public opinion, but to the same extent life was ebbing away from me. And now it's all over and there's only death.[58]

In this vertigo of experience, rising in the world of "the 'they'" corresponds to a state of falling away from authenticity, from owning one's Self. If Heidegger understands falling in this way, then it is hardly convincing when he tries stripping his discussion of inauthenticity from any normative or ethical denunciation, trying to insist that "the inauthenticity of Dasein does not signify any 'less' Being or any 'lower' degree of Being."[59] It is puzzling to imagine a world in which falling to inauthenticity does not signify a process of lowering oneself, but even if it were a lateral movement, Heidegger clearly seems to favor the authentic over the inauthentic.[60]

Ivan Ilyich's call of conscience, arresting the movement of falling, also abides by a structure that Heidegger would later work out in *Being and Time*: "Then he grew quiet and not only ceased weeping, but even held his breath and became all attention. It was as though he were listening not to an audible voice, but to the voice of his soul."[61] In response to the inaudible call, Ivan cries out, "But I'm not guilty!"[62] Dasein, despite any protestation, is always already guilty—not in a moral sense, but in an ontological sense of lack, of being *schuldig*.[63] This "primordial Being-guilty" makes possible the basis of Dasein's Being, which is essentially the basis of a nullity.

Perhaps this concept of guilt, which Heidegger takes great pains to distinguish from prior moralistic conceptions of it (even though Nietzsche had already articulated just as much in *On the Genealogy of Morals* §2), can be read back into the history of novels. Maybe Ivan Ilyich is also alluding to guilt ontologically, referring to the lack that has constituted his life, and the final lack, the final nothingness, toward which the remains of his life are rapidly hurtling. Maybe this is the ontological guilt that also pervades Dostoevsky's *The Brothers Karamazov*, a novel that explores every iteration of guilt, beginning with Dmitri's debt of three thousand roubles to Katerina Ivanovna.[64] He is found guilty of his father's murder by a court of law, even though Smerdyakov, who had just hanged himself, was the one who dealt the final deathblow to Fyodor Pavlovich.

Smerdyakov, in turn, is guilt personified. He is the nothingness that constitutes the lives of the Karamazovs. At once the unacknowledged brother and also just their lackey, he is born out of silence, out of illiteracy, out of suppressed language. His mother, Stinking Lizaveta, "could not even speak a word, and would only rarely move her tongue and mumble."[65] Even the narrator, after sparse description, relegates him back to silence by writing:

> I ought to say a little more about him in particular, but I am ashamed to distract my reader's attention for such a long time to such ordinary lackeys, and therefore I shall go back to my narrative, hoping that with regard to Smerdyakov things will somehow work themselves out in the future course of the story.[66]

The "future course of the story" is folded back into this anterior past before the novel's beginning, making possible the unfolding of events in a proto-Heideggerian display of "ecstatic temporality."

Smerdyakov's non-being pervades all the brothers Karamazov. He emerges as Ivan's own potentiality-for-Being, turning his own confession into an indictment of Ivan when he tells him, "still you are guilty of everything, sir."[67] Ivan, anticipating the following chapter with his dialogue with the Devil, tells Smerdyakov, "You know what; I'm afraid you're a dream, a ghost sitting there in front of me."[68] Perhaps it is this Devil, both Ivan's and Smerdyakov's double, who is the "black smear" that is enunciated in the name "Karamazov."[69] Everyone is a Karamazov to the extent that everyone is born with this "black smear," and so everyone is guilty of Fyodor Pavlovich's murder. Even Katerina Ivanovna, who brings Dmitri's letter as evidence to the court—although she knows that he is not the one who killed his father—says at the end, "I am the cause of it all, I alone am guilty!"[70] On the witness stand, Rakitin asks, "Who could say which of them was to blame or calculate who owed what to whom, with all that muddled Karamazovism, in which no one could either define or understand himself?"[71] In the words of Zosima, "each of us is guilty before everyone, for everyone and everything."[72] Dostoevsky's murder mystery, then, is just a cipher for a project of articulating a primordial guilt that cannot be explained away by law or theology, given the farce of Dmitri's trial and the persuasiveness of Ivan's atheism. This is a primordial, pre-ethical absence at the core of Being.

Dasein responds to this verdict of ontological guilt with anticipatory resoluteness [*vorlaufene Entschlossenheit*]. "Anticipatory resoluteness discloses the current Situation of the 'there' in such a way that existence, in taking action, is circumspectively concerned with what is factically ready-to-hand environmentally."[73] In Kafka, it is this mood of anticipatory resoluteness that characterizes K.'s factical resoluteness in insisting that he must fulfill the role of Land Surveyor in *The Castle* [*Der Schloss*], despite the bureaucratic machinery informing him that he is mistaken. K.'s *Entschlossenheit* is what discloses the *Schloss* of the title—the Situation, the place, the "there," the *Da* of his Dasein. The *Schloss* also represents the limits of his understanding, what Heidegger—and later Lacan—would call "the Real" as opposed to just "reality."[74] K. is there to take action, but he is impotent and inconsequential in the village, in the world of "the 'they.'" K.'s "anticipatory resoluteness understands Dasein in its own essential Being-guilty."[75] He is not persecuted for a crime he has not committed, like Josef K. in *The Trial*, but both of them understand their existence in relation to a lack. The question, then, is whether Josef K. even has Dasein, since he dies, "Like a dog!" and Dasein's death must be distinguished from "the going-out-of-the-world of that which merely has life."[76] If dogs do not have Dasein, their death is merely a perishing of a lower order. And yet Dostoevsky demonstrates, in *The Brothers Karamazov*, that when Smerdyakov teaches Ilyusha how to feed the dog Zhuchka a piece of bread with a needle in it, that the death of a dog marks as great an absence as the death of a human.

THE NOVEL AS FUNDAMENTAL ONTOLOGY

"For the first time in the history of Western philosophical inquiry," Ong says of *Being and Time*, "Heidegger gives ontological primacy to those facets of the world that are privileged in the realist novel more than any other philosophical text."[77] Heidegger "argues that any ontological consideration of Dasein must begin by showing it 'as it is *proximally and for the most part*—in its average everydayness,' within a world of tools, idle chatter, neighbors, newspapers, and mortality."[78] I brought Kafka into the discussion in order to challenge Ong's limitation of Heidegger's engagement with just "the realist novel," because I see Heidegger giving ontological primacy to the facets of the world that are privileged in the novel at large, as does Milan Kundera. In his *Art of the Novel*, Kundera writes that the novel had already spent four centuries working through "all the great existential themes Heidegger analyzes in *Being and Time*."[79] Guido Mazzoni also uses Heideggerian language to describe his project in his own *Theory of the Novel*: "only in mimesis and fiction do human beings become aware of themselves as individual, particular beings, thrown into time, located in a world, and placed among others."[80] Furthermore, he defines the "everyday" as what "represents the heart of the private condition. It is the life that barely juts out: it is particular existence in its pure being-there."[81]

It is difficult even to theorize about the novel without Heidegger or without the material that Heidegger was working with. The reverse should also be true. Heidegger believes that what he is doing in *Being and Time* is giving us a "fundamental ontology, from which alone all other ontologies can take their rise," and which "must be sought in the *existential analytic of Dasein*."[82] He is explicit about his understanding of other disciplines and other modes of inquiry into knowledge, including psychology, anthropology, and biology, as derivative of fundamental ontology.[83] But more fundamental than fundamental ontology, then, is the advent of the novel—which Heidegger himself demonstrates in his debt to Tolstoy.

In *The Death of Ivan Ilyich*, the entire ontic analytic is laid out, from falling to the call of conscience in the void, from the understanding of existence as Being-toward-death to a portrait of "the 'they.'" The novel is, then, what fundamental ontology is derived *from*. "I'm too fearful of the professors for whom art is only a derivative of philosophical trends," Kundera writes:

> The novel dealt with the unconscious before Freud, the class struggle before Marx, it practiced phenomenology (the investigation of the essence of human situations) before the phenomenologists. What superb 'phenomenological descriptions' in Proust, who never even knew a phenomenologist![84]

How different are these projects that Proust and Heidegger both take up in their quest for the forgotten meaning of Being, a quest that thematizes time and memory (aside from the fact that reading Proust is delicious, and reading Heidegger is painful)? The novel is not derived from modern philosophy but takes up similar questions adjacent to—and even prior to—it. For this reason, Heidegger, "a poetry lover, was wrong to disregard the history of the novel, for it contains the greatest treasury of existential wisdom."[85] Kundera defines a self as "determined by the essence of its existential problem," which is what a novelist works out through character—"not a simulation of a living being. It is an imaginary being. An experimental self."[86] If Being is Time, then a self is one of the myriad possibilities of an intersection between time and world unfolding into each other.

This is precisely how Bakhtin also characterizes the innovation of the novel: "For the first time in artistic-ideological consciousness, time and the world become historical; they unfold, albeit at first still unclearly and confusedly, as becoming."[87] However revolutionary Heidegger's concept of time may seem, Bakhtin sees this revolution taking place in the novel long before: "The novel, from the very beginning, developed as a genre that had at its core a new way of conceptualizing time."[88] To Bakhtin, the novel is the space in which "Time, as it were, thickens, takes on flesh."[89] Like Heidegger's concept of Dasein as Being-toward-death, Bakhtin identifies this as "a time maximally tensed toward the future."[90] It is in this sense, then, that the question of optimism and pessimism—two claims about the future, about whether things will turn out for the best or the worst—is a question that fundamentally coincides with the novel.

In tracing Heidegger's project of *Being and Time* back to the advent of the novel, Kundera supports "Hermann Broch's insistence in repeating: The sole *raison d'être* of a novel is to discover what only the novel can discover."[91] In this sense, Joyce is exemplary in using the novel as a "matter of a *discovery* that might be termed *ontological*: the discovery of the structure of the present moment; the discovery of the perpetual coexistence of the banal and the dramatic that underlies our lives."[92] Instead of reading Heidegger against the novel, then, perhaps it is possible—if not more challenging—to read *Being and Time* as a kind of novelistic experiment in its own right, if not a crucial corollary text that coincides with the contemporary innovation of the modernist novel and novel theory.

Both the novel and *Being and Time* overlap in their shared project of discovery as dis-covery [*Ent-deckung*], of un-covering the truth (*alethea* in Greek, which, to Heidegger, operates by a movement of covering and uncovering, concealment and unconcealment). This is the movement of Albertine in Proust's *Recherche*, less of an embodied being than she is a principle for Marcel of truth concealing and revealing itself by turns. "*Dasein*," Heidegger writes, as though it were not just a character in a novel but the character in every novel,

> *in its familiarity with significance, is the ontical condition for the possibility of discovering entities which are encountered in a world with involvement (readiness-to-hand) as their kind of Being, and which can thus make themselves known as they are in themselves [in seinem An-sich].*[93]

It is worth noting that Lukács ends his *Theory of the Novel* with an analysis of Tolstoy. Heidegger seems to pick up where Lukács left off, organizing *Being and Time* around his own interpretation of Tolstoy while trying to hide the traces. Lukács defines the novel as a kind of phenomenological exercise in which the "contingent world and the problematic individual are realities which mutually determine one another."[94] By "problematic," Lukács understands the individual as someone for whom the meaning of existence is an issue. This is exactly how Heidegger defines Dasein: "the Being of *Dasein*, for which, in its Being, that very Being is essentially an *issue*."[95] And when Heidegger speaks of "world" as "a characteristic of Dasein itself," this contingent world seems to abide by the Lukácsian model of the novel.[96] It is a world that derives meaning from a network of referentiality. As Heidegger explains, "*the 'wherein' of an act of understanding which assigns or refers itself, is that for which one lets entities be encountered in the kind of Being that belongs to involvements; and this 'wherein' is the phenomenon of the world.*"[97]

This logic of referentiality is precisely what is at work in the novel, in order to unconceal the phenomenon of the world. Bakhtin writes of "the language of the novel" also as a referential "*system* of languages that mutually and ideologically interanimate each other. It is impossible to describe and analyze it as a single unitary language."[98] And Ian Watt, too, maintains that, "the function of language is much more largely referential in the novel than in other literary works."[99] To this degree, John Brenkman concludes that, "Novels do not reproduce reality; they refer to it, with deep awareness of its elusiveness. [. . . The] novelist invents worlds to unmask the world."[100]

This referentiality of this Heideggerian "wherein" is also responsible for Heidegger's dissolution of the Kantian subject-object split into Being-in-the-world. In Heidegger's fundamental ontology, there are no subjects or objects per se, but Dasein and equipment.[101] Dasein is no longer a subject because it is always already involved in the world, in its ontic facticity; it is always running ahead of itself, so it is always "outside" of itself. But being "outside" of itself is always already part of "Being-in-the-world." As Ong explains it, "The 'in' of 'Being-in-the-world' is not the 'in' of location, in the sense of spatial coordinates, but rather the 'in' of involvement, implication, embeddedness."[102] Heidegger thereby deconstructs the binary of interiority and exteriority. This also corresponds to what Sartre, both a philosopher and a novelist (not to mention playwright), calls "Situation":

> The situation cannot be *subjective*, for it is neither the sum nor the unity of the *impressions* which things make on us. . . . But neither can the situation be *objective* in the sense that it would be a pure given which the subject would establish without being in any way engaged in the system thus constituted. . . . It is the total facticity, the absolute contingency of the world.[103]

It is this "absolute contingency of the world" that brings us back to Lukács, whom Heidegger ignores and dismisses just as much as he ignores Kierkegaard, perhaps because he took so much from them while trying to take the credit for originality. In *The Theory of the Novel*, Lukács writes, "In its experience of nature, the subject, which alone is real, dissolves the whole outside world in mood, and itself becomes mood by virtue of the inexorable identity of essence between the contemplative subject and its object."[104]

Heidegger translates Lukács's understanding of "mood" into "State-of-mind" [*Befindlichkeit*], which is one of the three equiprimordial terms of the existential (authentic) disclosure of Being, the other two being Understanding [*Verstehen*] and Discourse [*Rede*], as opposed to the corresponding categories in inauthentic facticity, which are curiosity, ambiguity, and idle talk.[105] Authenticity for Heidegger reveals the nothingness underlying all Being, which also parallels Lukács's observation that, "All the fragments live only by the grace of the mood in which they are experienced, but the totality reveals the nothingness of this mood in terms of reflexion [*sic*]."[106] Furthermore, Lukács's "inexorable identity of essence between the contemplative subject and object" also prefigures Heidegger's dissolution of the subject-object binary into Being-in-the-world.

Authenticity is the disclosure of Being in the mode of anxiety. Like Heidegger's concept of guilt, "anxiety" for him is not psychological, but ontological. It is "a kind of entranced calm," a silent confrontation with Being as Nothingness.[107] Anxiety for Heidegger is the authentic condition of Dasein in modernity; it is a purely modern experience. The Greeks did not have a concept of anxiety. There was fear, which Aristotle analyzes along with pity in his *Poetics* as part of our experience of catharsis. Fear must have an object; one is afraid of something. But anxiety is a confrontation with existential nothingness. The Greeks also had rage, for sure—the legendary rage of Achilles, for instance, which inaugurates all of Western literature.

But nothing quite illustrates the movement from this ancient rage to modern anxiety as the novel. Take, for instance, Albert Camus's *The Stranger*, which ends with Meursault coming to terms with his impending death:

> As if that blind rage had washed me clean, rid me of hope; for the first time, in that night alive with signs and stars, I opened myself to the gentle indifference of the world. Finding it so much like myself—so like a brother, really—I felt that I had been happy and that I was happy again. For everything to be consummated, for me to feel less alone, I had only to wish that there be a large crowd of spectators the day of my execution and that they greet me with cries of hate.[108]

This passage moves from the ancient affect of rage to the Heideggerian mode of anxiety, in which Dasein "opened" itself "to the gentle indifference of the world." In "blind rage" there are also echoes of Schopenhauer, washing him clean of hope. But there is almost a kind of subdued, unnerving cheerfulness in Meursault's tone. To Heidegger, the "anxiety of those who are daring" is actually "in secret alliance with the cheerfulness and gentleness of creative longing."[109]

Perhaps he wrote this in response to Nietzsche, who wanted to figure out why the Greeks were so cheerful. The answer is that they were *pessimists*; like Cassandra, they dared to look into the abyss and danced in joy as a result. We can read Meursault as a reincarnation of this kind of pessimist who cheerfully indulges in his absence of hope, who identifies a "brother" in the "indifference of the world" disclosed to him by the "signs and stars" that are just as indifferent to his fate as he is to theirs. These are signs that signify nothing. In tragedy, Lukács tells us, the soul that, in its loneliness, "has attained itself through its destiny can have brothers among the stars, but never an earthly companion."[110] In the novel, though, that genre which emerges in a world "beyond all hope," the lonely soul can't find brotherhood even in the stars, and the only brotherhood it can find in the world is one marked by indifference.[111]

If Meursault has any "brotherhood" with anyone, it would be with the likes of Ishmael from *Moby-Dick*, who demonstrates this Heideggerian anxiety as a form of joyful calm when he writes that,

> amid the tornadoed Atlantic of my being, do I myself still for ever centrally disport in mute calm; and while ponderous planets of unwaning woe revolve around me, deep down and deep inland there I still bathe me in eternal mildness and joy.[112]

Meursault also seems to share a brotherhood with Hamlet right before his death, which may not be actually as tragic as it is pessimistic. Both of them are strangers in the works that supposedly refer to them in their titles. Hamlet, by nature, is a comic genius who, as though by mistake, stumbles into a tragedy that he's not quite ready to be a part of. He speaks his first line as an aside, on the periphery of his own play, closer to us than anyone else on stage because he doesn't actually belong there, in this play that bears his name but largely carries on without him. He refuses to act because everyone else is doing enough acting and performing as it is, so he sits and thinks. And enough time goes by so that he does actually end up answering his question, *the* question.

In the choice of "To be or not to be," Hamlet chooses neither, but comes across a third option, right before his duel with Laertes: "Let be."[113] Hamlet and Meursault, both of them, "let be." Heidegger, in response to his own question of the meaning of Being, comes to the same answer: *Gelassenheit*, which is often translated as "letting-be," or "releasement," or—with some poetic license and inspiration from Kundera—may be rendered as "the unbearable lightness of being." *Gelassenheit* is the "openness to the mystery" of that "which shows itself and at the same time withdraws," following the dance of concealment and unconcealment inscribed in the Greek word for "Truth," *alethea*.[114] This letting-be is therefore the truth of the meaning of Being. It is in this space that happiness can be achieved—but just for a moment, for a Heideggerian *Augenblick*—before Meursault slips back into inauthenticity, in the mode of "the 'they,'" viewing his life from the perspective of the "large crowd of spectators," sinking back to their level, because spite is too delicious to give up for the pessimist, and their cries of hate will be his last taste of it.

In this single passage of the novel, Dasein dramatically fluctuates across history and across the temporal boundaries between authenticity and inauthenticity. Heidegger ultimately reveals that Being is the passage of Time; the point of *Being and Time* is that Being *is* Time.[115] Dienstag points out that this is an insight he owes to Schopenhauer.[116] To Cioran, this insight is what drives his pessimism:

Still to divine the timeless and to know nonetheless that we *are* time, that we produce time, to conceive the notion of eternity and to cherish our nothingness; an absurdity responsible for both our rebellions and the doubts we entertain about them.[117]

And to Lukács, "only the novel, the literary form of the transcendent homelessness of the idea, includes real time . . . among its constitutive principles."[118] Moreover, he continues, in an insight that Heidegger takes without any attribution: "Time is the fullness of life, although the fullness of time is the self-abolition of life and, with it, of time itself."[119]

If the novel marks the turn away from the world of extraordinary figures like Achilles, Odysseus, and Oedipus to the ordinariness of Tristram Shandy, Clarissa Dalloway, and Meursault, then *Being and Time* shares the same contemplation of the experience of average everydayness [*durchschnittlichen Alltäglichkeit*]. Lukács even uses this phrase to describe the novel when he sees it as a study of "the average, everyday nature of the real world."[120] Heidegger's own study of Dasein in its average everydayness is no less novelistic than George Eliot's in *Middlemarch*, which itself claims to be a "Study" in its subtitle, of provincial life (perhaps an ambitious German translator would render the title *Durchschrittlichkeit*).[121] As with the fictional character of Dasein in *Being and Time*, Eliot's characters are most vividly sketched in terms of what they grasp with their hands and ears. The same hand that Casaubon uses to write his failed manuscript, *The Key to all Mythologies*, becomes the hand that reaches from the grave in Book V, "The Dead Hand," dictating his wife Dorothea's future with the marriage codicil in his will.[122] At the root of ordinary experience, both for Eliot and for Heidegger, is what can and cannot be grasped, what can and cannot be heard:

> If we had a keen vision and feeling of all ordinary human life, it would be like hearing the grass grow and the squirrel's heart beat, and we should die of that roar which lies on the other side of silence. As it is, the quickest of us walk about well wadded with stupidity.[123]

Perhaps this roar on the other side of silence is the roar of the call of conscience, a call that shatters the stupidity of "the 'they.'" It is this same roar that Don DeLillo accesses in *White Noise*, when the world-weary professor Jack Gladney—Chair of Hitler Studies, no less—finds himself buying groceries in the supermarket:

> I realized the place was awash in noise. The toneless systems, the jangle and skid of carts, the loudspeaker and coffee-making machines, the cries of children.

And over it all, or under it all, a dull and unlocatable roar, as of some form of swarming life just outside the range of human apprehension.[124]

The paradox is that it is just as difficult to communicate the obviousness of everydayness as it is to communicate the roar on the other side of silence, and Heidegger—like Eliot before him and DeLillo after him—attempts to do both.

Like every other novelist of his time, Heidegger resorts to foregrounding the means of communication itself, radicalizing the expectations and possibilities for language to narrate the banality of quotidian life. "That which is *ontically* so familiar in the way Dasein has been factically interpreted that we never pay any heed to it, hides enigma after enigma existential-ontologically."[125] By adding yet another layer of enigmatic language, thereby defamiliarizing the familiar, Heidegger draws attention to the mystery of everydayness. It is as though he performs the process of authenticity on the level of style, taking the prose of "the 'they'" and modifying it into something else, something that cannot be called poetry, but a prose of a different order—a prose that, for lack of a better characterization, is entirely its own. It is *eigentlich*, distinctively Heideggerian in its disavowal of the cliché even as it aggressively interrogates and works its way through it. It is a prose that only tenuously relies on the scaffolding of prior philosophical discourse, climbing up the ladder of metaphysics only to kick it from under, once having reached a certain aerial perspective.

Karl Ove Knausgaard, in an interview with James Wood, spoke of the Russian formalists' treatment of Tolstoy: "As the Russian formalists showed, the reason Tolstoy is so good is that he makes the world strange, so you can see it."[126] Heidegger perhaps shared the same insight into Tolstoy as the Russian formalists, using *Being and Time* as a means of also making the phenomenon of the world strange, with his strange use of language, so we can see it. His project is very much about discovering or inventing the proper form and style for his content, a false binary that he deconstructs early on: "The right way of presenting it is so far from self-evident that to determine what form it shall take is itself an essential part of the ontological analytic of this entity."[127]

In this Lukácsian take on form as inseparable from content, the tension between the banality of the experience and the unusual means of expressing it is where the *durchschnittlich* and the *durchsichtig* become the *durchbrechend*, where the average and transparent become the groundbreaking and the opaque, and where the simple is rendered baroque.[128] Since ordinariness is always already a cliché, the task of the novel—and, ostensibly, of *Being and Time*—is to refashion this cliché with a new kind of language, a new kind of approach. At stake in *Being and Time* is the "task of *liberating* grammar from logic," which "requires *beforehand* a *positive* understanding of the basic *a priori* structure of discourse in general as an *existentiale*."[129] He is wrestling with what, to Kundera, "goes to the deepest conviction of every novelist: there is nothing so thoroughly disguised as the prose of life."[130] In order to unmask—to dis-cover—the disguise that conceals truth, he must also unmask the prose of life with a new kind of prose. And if we take Kundera's point that the novel's "discovery of prose is its *ontological mission*, which no art but the novel can take on entirely," then it is impossible to think of *Being and Time* as something removed from the project of the novel.[131]

Heidegger's reflection of his own prose may just as well apply to modernist fiction:

> With regard to the awkwardness and "inelegance" of expression in the analyses to come, we may remark that it is one thing to give a report in which we tell about *entities*, but another to grasp entities in their *Being*. For the latter task we lack not only most of the words but, above all, the "grammar."[132]

Modernist novels move away from representation and standardized grammar in an effort to "grasp entities in their *Being*," in a gesture of performing Being itself.

"Grasping" implies seizing and arresting. There is a remarkable velocity to Dasein, a turbulence, which is at odds with the painstakingly slow text that narrates its frenzied, ecstatic movements. The heavy plodding of the prose also enacts the process of authenticity, itself, by arresting the subject matter in its movement and taking multiple panoramic shots of its suspension in high resolution—or, as Heidegger would have it, in high resoluteness. It is a technique akin to the shifting structure of Woolf's *The Waves*, published four years after *Being and Time*. The kaleidoscopic perspective of the novel moves through the individual experiences of a group of friends across time, each one focusing their attention on the absent center, Percival, whose death early on in the novel marks a principle of nothingness that both organizes and dissolves their lives. Percival's non-being is inscribed into the being of everyone who contemplates him, including the reader.

And, of course, Woolf rehearsed this technique in *To the Lighthouse*, published in the same year as *Being and Time*, in which Mrs. Ramsay marks the absent center of the novel. And we see the development of Lily Briscoe coming into her own, discovering herself at the moment of completing her painting, when she "had had her vision"—what Heidegger would call her *Augenblick*, the moment of authenticity that emphasizes, in its etymology of the eyes (*Augen-*), vision itself.[133]

"AN IMPOSSIBLE FICTION"

Heidegger does not narrate the experience of just any Being, but *our* Being, just as the sinuous sentences of Proust, Woolf, Joyce, and Mann mimic the movement and pattern of the reader's own wandering mind even as it lapses over passages of lush detail. The hero of *Ulysses* is not so much Bloom as it is the reader of the novel, struggling to find their way back home to meaning after setting out on the epic journey through Joyce's language. In epic, the hero finds his way home, but Lukács defines the novel as an expression of "transcendental homelessness."[134] He quotes Novalis in the beginning of his study, who expressed that "Philosophy is really homesickness . . . it is the urge to be at home everywhere."[135] Both homesick and homeless, the philosopher and the novelist struggle and ultimately fail at making a stable home of meaning in a world of "falling," of inauthenticity, of ambiguity, idle talk, and curiosity.[136] To Lukács, the "artistic task" of the novelist "consists of revealing the point at which such a character's *being-there* and *being-thus* coincides with his inevitable failure."[137] Dasein—Lukács's italicized *"being-there"*—is a failed project, a project that Heidegger would later reformulate in *Being and Time* as Articulated Thrown Projection.

Like Don Quixote imposing his imagination on a world that remains indifferent and unchanged in response to his valiant efforts, the philosopher and the novelist embark on a similar quest, both employing the motif of the road to chart their journey through a Lukácsian transcendental homelessness, reformulated by Heidegger as "uncanniness," toward a tenuous sense of meaning.[138] "Can our analysis of Dasein up to this point give us any prescriptions for the ontological task we have now set ourselves," Heidegger asks, "so that what we have before us may be kept on a road of which we can be sure?"[139] Earlier, Heidegger implicitly refers to the road in his example of the motor car to illustrate his concept of signs announcing themselves as a ready-to-hand totality of referential signals.[140]

The novel, in a sense, moves philosophy out of the comfortable homes of attractive, hospitable young Greek men and into the unsheltered and often hostile expanse of the open road. Unlike the epic, in which the gods presided over the travels and travails of Odysseus and Aeneas, the novel "is the epic of a world abandoned by God."[141] From Cervantes to Kerouac to Cormac McCarthy, the road enables Being to reveal and conceal itself by turns, just as "the novel seeks, by giving form, to uncover and construct the concealed totality of life."[142] The highway, then, in Stendhal's definition of the novel as a "mirror moving along a highway," may be more significant to that definition than the mirror.[143] Even the metaphorical cliché of the twists and turns of a plot becomes literal in the image of a road, and Heidegger reimagines this metaphor, simulating its movement, its twisting and turning, in his structure of care as Articulated Thrown Projection. Dasein is thrown into a world marked by inauthenticity, but it is the twisting and turning and projecting away from inauthenticity that Dasein discovers—in an act of dis-covering, of uncovering—its authentic selfhood. Therein lies the plot, the heroic effort of Dasein wresting itself away from "the 'they'" by violently hurling itself into the void, and only for brief, discrete moments in time.

Being and Time can perhaps be read as a kind of road novel of Dasein, narrating its "running ahead" into its own realm of possibility, its *Vorlaufen in die Möglichkeit*.[144] Heidegger's fundamental ontology aims to document the concealment and unconcealment of Truth in its totality, and does so in the same terms of failure, of impotence, of "being-there" that Lukács uses in his *Theory of the Novel*.[145] In the introductory paragraph of the First Analytic, Heidegger writes that, "That entity which in its Being has this very Being as an issue, comports itself towards its Being as its ownmost possibility."[146] Dasein comports itself towards its Being in the optative mood, in the subjunctive mood, in the mood of possibility. What else are novels if not an exploration of possibilities for the self? "All novels, of every age, are concerned with the enigma of the self," says Kundera, echoing Heidegger's formulation of Dasein as an enigma.[147]

Being is an enigma, a riddle—a *Rätsel*—without a solution. What was once the answer to the Sphinx's riddle in forms of literature prior to the advent of the novel now becomes an uncanny repetition—a Heideggerian (and Kierkegaardian) *Wiederholung*—of the same term, but there is no stable unity of meaning every time the term is reiterated.[148] What was once the answer (and the answerer) to that original riddle, "Man," now also becomes the question and the questioner, and yet there is no identical meaning of this term every time it is uttered. Dasein is what Dasein itself calls into question, but it is a question called forth, and answered, in silence. The reticence of the Sphinx now becomes the reticence of Dasein in confrontation with itself through the call of conscience. What the call discloses is not any information; it is not anything at all. It is nothing, and this nothing reveals Dasein as nothing, as well. Between the *Niemand* [nobody] of *das Man* [the "they"] and the *Nichts* [the nothing] of anxiety, Dasein oscillates between varying modes of nothingness.

But nothingness opens a clearing for a multitude of possibilities, and the discourse most aptly suited to the exploration of possibilities is the discourse of the novel. Even Heidegger himself thinks of nothingness in relation to Dasein as a modification of "an impossible fiction" into "something positive": "A free-floating call from which 'nothing ensues' is an impossible fiction when seen existentially. With regard to Dasein, 'that *nothing* ensues' signifies something *positive*."[149] Heidegger's fundamental ontology is a way of grasping this positively transformed fiction without recourse to derivative modes of understanding, such as psychology, anthropology, and epistemology. Likewise, Kundera sees the novel in similar terms:

> What lies beyond the so-called psychological novel? Or, put another way: What is the nonpsychological means to apprehend the self? To apprehend the self in my novels means to grasp the essence of its existential problem. . . . A novel examines not reality but existence. And existence is not what has occurred, existence is the realm of human possibilities, everything that man can become, everything he's capable of. Novelists draw up the *map of existence* by discovering this or that human possibility. But . . . to exist means: 'being-in-the-world.' Thus *both* character *and* his world must be understood as *possibilities*.[150]

In *The Captive*, Marcel names this novelistic principle explicitly, saying, "by nature, I have always been more open to the world of possibilities than to that of real events. This helps us to understand the human heart, but we are apt to be taken in by individuals."[151] The "individuals" here can be understood as the individuals of *das Man*, of that mode of inauthentic existence that is held in tension with the clearing of possibilities from which a self (or, in Marcel's case, multiple selves) can emerge.

But more radical than Proust in exploring the realm of possibilities is Robert Musil, whose comical antihero Ulrich, in *The Man without Qualities*, takes a "vacation from life" in order to dwell in the possibilities that emerge from the "Baroque of the Void."[152] By perpetually postponing every moment in August 1913—conceivably so as not to enter the European nightmare beginning exactly a year later—Ulrich slips into "The Other Condition" in the second volume of the uncompleted work, where the conditional and the possible become the new reality. *Der Mann ohne Eigenschaften* becomes the man with all the possibilities of own-ness, of authenticity, of *Eigentlichkeit*, by approaching a kind of zero-state of Being.

The Man Without Qualities also illustrates Heidegger's account of inauthentic time,

> which is accessible to the ordinary understanding [as it consists], among other things, precisely in the fact that it is a pure sequence of "nows," without beginning and without end, in which the ecstatical character of primordial temporality has been leveled off.[153]

Using Kierkegaard's concept of "leveling," Heidegger contrasts this concept of inauthentic time with the authentic experience of non-linear time, of ecstatic temporality, in which past, present, and future all unfold out of each other, outside of the "pure sequence of 'nows.'"[154] Before both Heidegger and Musil, Joyce had already worked through this vision in *Ulysses*, when John Eglinton tells Stephen before his lecture on *Hamlet*, "Hold to the now, the here, through which all future plunges to the past."[155] Bloom echoes this statement, with more of a proto-Heideggerian verve, in the "Circe" chapter, when he says, "But tomorrow is a new day will be. Past was is today. What now is will then tomorrow as now was be past yester."[156]

In Musil's novel, Ulrich reflects on time in similar terms, and these reflections lead this novelistic character to insights into the nature of the novel as a genre:

> It struck him that when one is overburdened and dreams of simplifying one's life, the basic law of this life, the law one longs for, is nothing other than that of narrative order, the simple order that enables one to say: "First this happened and then that happened." . . . This is the trick the novel artificially turns to account . . . this tried and true "foreshortening of the mind's perspective" . . . It now came to Ulrich that he had lost this elementary, narrative mode of thought to which private life still clings, even though everything in public has already ceased to be narrative and no longer follows a thread, but instead spreads out as infinitely interwoven surface.[157]

The "law of this life" is then to live as if one were in a novel with its narrative sequence. But the paradox is that this particular novel undoes the "trick" that the novel "artificially turns to account." The novel reinvents itself to accommodate new experiences of temporality, and Musil's narrative—if it can even be called that—also "spreads out as infinitely interwoven surface," never-ending in its unfinished state of nearly 2,000 pages. This may seem to be a feature of "the public," of "the 'they,'" but this narrative technique allows Ulrich actually to escape from "the 'they'" and enter "The Other Condition" [*der andere Zustand*], a condition that "enables us to see what isn't there."[158]

To "see what isn't there" is the Pauline message of messianism embedded in Heidegger's understanding of the call of conscience, but it is also the injunction of every novel to every reader. If the novel is an epic in a world abandoned by God, according to Lukács's formulation, then it is a kind of secular messianism that calls on its reader to hold oneself out to the nothing of the novel's fictional universe and to see not only that which is not in the world, but to see the world itself as if it is not.[159] This is the kind of apocalyptic vision we see in *Lady Chatterley's Lover*, in *Lolita*, and even in the "Time Passes" section of *To the Lighthouse*. Both the novel and Heidegger's ontology reveal being as non-being—*to on* as *to me on*, in Greek. Or, as Beckett would have it, "On. Say on. Be said on. Somehow on. Till nohow on. Said nohow on."[160]

The reader approaches the novel as Dasein approaches the world: full of fascination and meaning, toward which Dasein "comports itself understandingly."[161] Both the reader and the characters are absorbed, entangled, in *Bewandtnis* (involvement), which is the existential meaning of Being-in-the-world. The characters' struggles derive from the tension between thrownness and projection, which we understand meaningfully. But behind the meaning is the anxiety that reveals the nothingness of the world and the contrived fictionality of the novel. This anxiety is the uncanniness of Don Quixote coming across a book called *Don Quixote* in Part II of the novel. It is Isabel Archer refusing her own novelist, Henry James, to narrate the events of her inheritance, her marriage proposal, and the death of her child, so that she stands as more of a cipher of nothingness, of fictionality, that in some ways may even reflect the nothingness of the reader. She does not belong in *The Portrait of a Lady* any more than we do. If anything, she is just a parody of that other archer, Gwendolen Harleth, from George Eliot's *Daniel Deronda*. Or, as the transgender beauty queen Brandy Alexander tells Shannon McFarland in Chuck Palahniuk's road novel *Invisible Monsters*, "There isn't any real *you* in you."[162] "Relax," she says, her boyfriend Manus tied up in the trunk of their car as they cross state lines—and as the narrative crosses boundaries in both genre and gender—"Nothing of you is all-the-way yours."[163]

IRONY AND VOMIT

Heidegger may take issue with the novel as a medium of expressing authentic Dasein because of its embrace of inauthenticity, of its demonstration that "Nothing of you is all-the-way yours." In its simulation of idle talk, the novel seems to stand as far away from the project of *Being and Time* as possible. One thinks of the stupid prattle of Lydia Bennet in *Pride and Prejudice* or the insipid garrulousness of Mme. Verdurin in Proust's *Recherche*. The novel is very much a product of the *Offentlichkeit*, the offending public, that Heidegger interprets as the "dictatorship of the 'they'" with its use of newspapers and public transportation.[164] The novel, which owes much of its history to the rise of the newspaper with its serialization, conceivably belongs to this category of inauthenticity, with its idle talk, its curiosity, its ambiguity, although Heidegger never specifies either way. As such, it represents a kind of cowardly fleeing from one's existence and wasting one's time in evasive immersion in fictional characters' lives and struggles as opposed to allowing the reader to confront, in anxiety, the state of their own nothingness.

But there is something to be said for the use of irony in the novel, for the ways in which Austen and Proust ironize themselves out of inauthenticity by the very language of inauthenticity itself, deftly tracing the oscillations of characters between modes of existentiality and facticity. Mazzoni sees the novel arising out of an age in which it has become clear that our life, the life that we have led ourselves to view as our own property, is always constitutively improper, *uneigentlich*, in the sense that Heidegger gives to this word. The ideas, habits, and behaviors that we have introjected precede us: they are products of the world that includes us; they do not really belong to us. If observed with an attitude of estrangement, they reveal that we are serial beings, like everyone else.[165]

But this "attitude of estrangement" can also propel us out of this inauthentic torpor to a realization of authenticity, in the same way that Mooney reads Kierkegaard as a writer who "creates *anxiety*, that forerunner of change of self or recovery of soul."[166] Recall that Kierkegaard, for Mooney,

> makes an existential contribution that only *I* can complete. *His* contribution is to offer me an existential space distinct from social space ... where existential possibilities are vividly acknowledged, and then I *close* that radical openness through decisive resolution and action.[167]

What Mooney is saying about Kierkegaard—in heavy-handed Heideggerian language—may just as well apply to the novel. Novels also provide an "existential space distinct from social space," in which one can observe social space from a distance and see the array of "existential possibilities" from which one may learn, in one's own life, how to "*close* that radical openness through decisive resolution and action." Or, as Gabriel Josipovici puts it, also in Heideggerian terms:

> Kierkegaard ... remind[s] us that we cannot begin to understand what novels are, what fiction is, until we recognize that how we think about fiction depends on how we think about ourselves. In other words, if the concept of fiction cannot be taken for granted, it is because story-telling is intimately bound up with what we are, not in any absolute sense but in our concrete social and historical reality.[168]

Kierkegaard, Heidegger, and the novel, then, all seem to converge at this point of irony. Irony constitutes both the organizing principle of Kierkegaard's thought and Kundera's Heideggerian definition of the novel: "the novel is, by definition, the ironic art: its 'truth' is concealed, undeclared, undeclarable.... Irony irritates. Not because it mocks or attacks but because it denies us our certainties by unmasking the world as an ambiguity."[169] As if the novel itself were a character like Humbert Humbert, it ironically masks itself in order "to unmask the world."[170] And in this seemingly Nabokovian universe of the novel, we get a "paradox that only seems one: the more calculated the construction machinery, the more real and natural the characters."[171]

In this ironic art, on the opposite side of the spectrum from the idle talk of Lydia Bennet and Mme. Verdurin, we have characters who dwell in the silence of authenticity, like Melville's Billy Budd and Bartleby, Faulkner's Benjy, Grass's Oskar Matzerath, and Palahniuk's Shannon McFarland, all of whom seem to exist outside of language, only to break into it in brief moments of devastating violence. It is this violence that Dasein performs on itself in order to attain authenticity: "Existential analysis . . . constantly has the character of *doing violence* [*Gewaltsamkeit*], whether to the claims of the everyday interpretation, or to its complacency and its tranquillized obviousness."[172]

Dasein performs violence on itself in order to risk "the mode of *evasion*" that "tranquillizes" us into inauthenticity.[173] Evasion keeps us from ourselves, relegating us to the inauthentic existence of idle talk, curiosity, and ambiguity. Heidegger seems to lift this concept straight out of *A Literary Review* again, where Kierkegaard writes, "One person is curious about another, all wait in indecision and versed in evasion for someone to come along who wills something."[174] However, Levinas, in response to Heidegger's take on Kierkegaard, offers a different account of evasion. In *De l'évasion* (translated as *On Escape*), he identifies evasion itself as the "experience of pure being."[175]

But for Levinas, evasion is experienced as nausea. In contrast to the abstract construct of Dasein, Levinas grounds Being in all its sordid physicality. This is not the metaphorical nausea of Sartre's Roquentin—it is the literal "state of nausea that precedes vomiting," a nausea that does not comply with any Heideggerian tendency of being-toward-death, but of being-toward-nakedness: "death is not the exit toward which escape thrusts us. Death can only appear to it if escape reflects upon itself. As such, nausea discovers only the nakedness of being in its plenitude and in its utterly binding presence."[176] Escape runs up against the limits of Being, in which one experiences one's own Being not in terms of Heideggerian possibility, but precisely in terms of its opposite, of impossibility: "In nausea—which amounts to an impossibility of being what one is—we are at the same time riveted to ourselves, enclosed in a tight circle that smothers. We are there, and there is nothing to be done."[177]

Nausea can be interpreted not only as a prevalent motif of the novel but as its structural principle. The novel is a genre that regurgitates prior genres, like the monster Error in Spenser's *Faerie Queene*, hurling a "vomit full of bookes and papers," her "cole black bloud" the same color as ink.[178] *Moby-Dick* can be read as an instructional manual for the whaling industry in the same way that *Fight Club* is a manual for how to make homemade bombs. *Like Water for Chocolate* is a recipe book. *Lolita* is a road map. *Carmen* was first marketed as a travelogue. The novel is new, is truly "novel," to the extent that it coughs up old forms in new guises. Beckett recognizes this in Proust when he writes, "habit is the ballast that chains a dog to his vomit."[179] Marcel's habits are indicative of the literary habits of other writers that Proust mimics, re-presents, and ultimately surpasses in his *Recherche*.

The novel is a vomitorium of barely digested modes of storytelling, as it is in the encyclopedic *Don Quixote*. Early on, Quixote and Sancho Panza violently puke on each other when they drink what they think is a holy balm, a balm that makes Quixote—after recovering from "the nausea and spasms of vomiting"—think "that he could engage in fights from then on without any fear of disasters, battles, or clashes, no matter how perilous they might be."[180] The "holy balm" is aligned with the imaginary world of chivalric romance, a world that Quixote literally and figuratively imbibes. But this ventriloquized imaginary world sharply collides with his material reality, drawing attention to the materiality of the novel, to the fact that the novel is the first form of literature in which the work of art could not be distinguished from its material commodity.[181] This is material language, as Roberto González Echevarría explains:

> Vomiting here and in the inn suggests the existence of a concretely repulsive language of pure meanings, language whose effect is repulsion, mutual repulsion, but that is nevertheless a form of communication. One vomit elicits the other, as in dialogue. It is in this sense that it is a pure language, an ironic fusion of words and things. If you think that words reflect reality, vomit is reality itself expressed as words through the mouth. Vomit contains objects, not signs.[182]

Don Quixote is not an isolated example. In fact, the history of the novel seems to frequently return to the motif not just of nausea, but of vomit. Emma Bovary, who consumes cheap romance novels in the same way that Quixote consumes chivalric romances, dies after chasing her own windmills of erotic desire. Her mind—and the novel—is just as saturated with clichéd narratives as her bloated corpse is saturated with the black bile that oozes out of her mouth. It is as though vomit functions as an ironizing principle, distancing the overall project of the novel from the hackneyed tropes it consumes but can hardly stomach.

This image appears again in *Sanctuary*, a novel Faulkner purportedly wrote in a cynical stab at lurid pulp fiction—by definition, a pastiche of a well-worn form, but which becomes something different and far more sinister in Faulkner's hands. Horace Benbow imagines seeing Temple with "something black and furious go roaring out of her pale body . . . the blackness streaming in rigid threads overhead."[183] Like the "black smear" inscribed in the name "Karamazov," the melancholic black bile in *Sanctuary* and *Madame Bovary* signals at once both an excess and a lack at the core of Dasein, which is simultaneously in excess of running ahead of itself as well as being founded on a null basis.

In *The Bell Jar*, vomit can be interpreted as an engagement with—and withdrawal from—"the 'they'" [*das Man*]. Early in the novel, Esther Greenwood feels as though everything her friend Doreen "said was like a secret voice speaking straight out of my own bones."[184] She tries to distance herself from Doreen, and manages to do so only after "a jet of brown vomit flew" from Doreen's mouth and "spread in a large puddle at my feet."[185] It is as though Esther can only manage this distance from "the 'they'" through vomit, but can't fully escape it. Esther thinks to herself how the "pool of vomit" is "like an ugly, concrete testimony to my own dirty nature," and it haunts her even when she tries getting closer to other friends, like Betsy.[186] At one point, she eats bad crabmeat with her, and starts throwing up, but here, she thinks that, "There's nothing like puking with somebody to make you into old friends."[187] Vomit is what simultaneously connects and distances her from *das Man*.

It is also no coincidence that Henry Miller dismisses *Ulysses* as "a vomit spilled by a delicate child whose stomach has been overloaded with sweetmeats."[188] Both the language of *Being and Time* and of *Ulysses* seem to become present-at-hand, with a jarring effect that jolts us into considering what rarely rises to the level of consideration.[189] The words themselves become material strewn out across the page—the "litter of literature" according to Simon Critchley and Tom McCarthy, in their reading of *Finnegans Wake*. They are objects of speculation, like debris from a language that can no longer be used.[190] "When its unusability is thus discovered," says Heidegger, "equipment becomes conspicuous."[191] And language, the primordial equipment of Dasein's Being, becomes no more conspicuous than in the "Circe" chapter of *Ulysses*, when "The End of the World," the gong, and the gramophone all perform lines as if they were characters in a play. A "Dummymummy" even inquires, "Bbbbblllbbblblodschbg?"[192]

Before this exploration of language as a material object, the novel begins with Stephen Dedalus overlooking the Dublin bay, where he "saw the sea hailed as a great sweet mother . . . [that] held a dull green mass of liquid," which makes him think of his own deceased mother and the "bowl of white china [that] had stood beside her deathbed holding the green sluggish bile which she had torn up from her rotting liver by fits of loud groaning vomiting."[193] Joyce's novel is "a vomit" indeed, a vomit that pukes out every established literary form, unifying these forms with the black liquid that could only come from Joyce's pen.

Does Dasein vomit? Heidegger never specifies, although it is tempting to think of care as *cura*, at once a cure and a poison, like Socrates's *pharmakon*, or the emetic that doubles as Don Quixote's holy balm. In light of Echevarría's analysis, one can almost visualize Articulated Thrown Projection as the thrown-up projectile of articulated words. But articulation, or discourse [*Rede*] for Heidegger does not necessarily have to rise to the level of language, or even orality.[194] Dasein is authentic in its reticence, in its withdrawal from the idle talk—the prose—that narrates "the 'they.'" It is as though Dasein favors the tragic space of Aeschylean tragedy with its staged silences rather than the vomit of words that characterizes novelistic irony.

Heidegger signals his own irony with the use of quotation marks, as though ejecting the quoted terms from his own text, or at least keeping them at arm's length. These terms are handy, as are all things in Heidegger's universe, but handy from a distance—as though handling the contents of a motion sickness bag in the turbulence, the *Wirbel*, of Dasein's falling.[195] But perhaps there are further layers of irony in *Being and Time*, even if unbeknownst to its author. Heidegger spends an awful lot of his own prose narrating the silence that he supposedly values so much. As if his insistent baroque refrain of previously established definitions were not rambling enough, he resorts to spaced-out lettering for emphasis, as well as italics, as well as italics-in-bold, as well as a combination of italicized and unitalicized words in bold. Despite his brilliant etymological constellations, his style is loud, loquacious, and awkward, even as he disparages the monotony and the noise of "the 'they.'"

Knausgaard satirizes Heidegger's verbosity in his novel *My Struggle*, the first volume of which begins with a graphic description of what happens to the body in death, and of the "black substance in the Mesencephalon" that accumulates.[196] In the fourth volume, the protagonist Karl Ove, who is as related to the actual author as the fictionalized Marcel is to Proust, sits down for supper with his extended family when his uncle Kjartan goes for a "ten-minute monologue" about Heidegger. "Not everyone here has heard about Heidegger," Yngve chimes in. "Surely there must be other topics we can discuss apart from some obscure German philosopher."[197] In one line, the most influential thinker of the twentieth century is demoted to the status of "some obscure German philosopher." Kjartan retorts:

> Yes, I suppose there are. . . . We can talk about the weather. But what shall we talk about then? The weather is what it always is. The weather is what existence reveals itself through. Just as we reveal ourselves through the mood we are in through what we feel at any given moment. It's not possible to imagine a world without weather or ourselves without feelings. But both elements automate *das Man* [the 'they']. *Das Man* talks about the weather as though there is nothing special about it, in other words he doesn't see it.[198]

Of course, the joke is that *das Man* may actually know nothing about the weather, but Heidegger—the veteran meteorologist—certainly did.

As much as Knausgaard sharply pokes fun at Heidegger, he may be embarking on a Heideggerian project of his own. His entire work is a process of articulating authenticity, of his ownness, of the struggle that is his. The irony is that the allusion in the title indicates someone else's struggle entirely, posing a rather awkward conundrum for his German translators (who settled on the anodyne *Sterben* [*To Die*], maintaining a kind of Heideggerian being-toward-death). Knausgaard's struggle, though, is one of renewing the world:

> I try to imagine a world without words, a world without language, and the world collapses. It's nothing. It's chaos. Language is the thing that makes the world, and it's the thing that makes the world disappear. Writing is a kind of ongoing struggle to renew the world.[199]

Here he sheds light on Heidegger's insight of the primordiality of discourse [*Rede*], and how *Rede* is inseparable from the world that it constitutes.

In this same interview, he laments the state of novels in the same way that Heidegger laments the state of philosophy for its forgetting of Being, for its covering up of the world: "Before I wrote *My Struggle*, I had a feeling that novels tend to obscure the world instead of showing it, because their form is so much alike from novel to novel."[200] Perhaps this lament is endemic to the chutzpah of every novelist who thinks that their novel will have killed and brought back to new life the novel form itself. The novel is a form that novelists love to claim having killed—like the painter Nikolai who rushes to confess to the murder he hadn't committed in *Crime and Punishment*—only to find themselves in a position where they magnanimously resurrect it on their own terms. In the same way Heidegger sought to overcome metaphysics, Joyce apparently wrote the novel to end all novels, and Knausgaard apparently came with his own unprecedented novel—that is, unprecedented in that every novel claims to have no precedent. The resilience of the Phoenix-like genre of the novel, with all its hybridity, lies in the very fact that it is always absorbing, appropriating, and vomiting prior forms.

The novel never seems to escape being a parody of itself, and of everything that had come before it. "Why must almost everything appear to me as its own parody?" asks Adrian Leverkühn in *Doctor Faustus*, the novel Mann was in the process of writing when he coolly dismissed Heidegger as the "Nazi *par existence*."[201] In Leverkühn, Mann sketched the ultimate heroic act of *Eigentlichkeit*, of seeking his own authenticity through an effort of achieving a musical art that parodies nothing. And yet this non-parody is what deprives Leverkühn of his humanity, and Mann restores the humanity back to the text by framing the story in a novel, a genre of parodies.

As much as Leverkühn aspires to a state of *Eigentlichkeit*, the narrator, Dr. Serenus Zeitblom, moves in the opposite direction, dispersing his identity and dissolving it into his text, which he repeatedly insists is "not . . . a novel," a protestation ultimately negated by Mann, himself.[202] Zeitblom's "own-ness," if it is possible to use a Heideggerian term that grated on Mann's nerves, is an own-ness that cannot possibly be his: "And what is closest and most intriguing, most truly *my own*," Zeitblom says of Leverkühn, "is not mere 'material,' it is the person himself."[203] Perhaps *Doctor Faustus* makes the case for an ethical inauthenticity against the very jargon that Mann saw as precipitating the events of the Second World War and the Holocaust, using the novel as a form to disrupt the philosophy he saw governing his nation, whom he had disparaged as an "all too docile people, a people all too happy to live by a theory!"[204]

"THE GREATEST SEDUCTION"

September 2014. The latest installments of Heidegger's *Black Notebooks* from 1931 to 1941 had just been published, sending shockwaves throughout the academic community. I was in the audience of an international conference organized at The Graduate Center (CUNY) to see scholars perform their outrage, disbelief, and apparent shock that yes, Heidegger—a Nazi who had never condemned the Holocaust—was also an antisemite. From an anthropological point of view, it was fascinating and a bit cringeworthy to see scholars who had had the evidence in their faces for decades just now wake up to the realization of what he always was. Were they really once this seduced by the most original of thinkers into assuming his politics weren't more despicable than what we had already known? Did they also not realize that he wasn't terribly original, either, and that he took more from Kierkegaard than he had ever admitted?

We can trace Heidegger's defensive attitude against Kierkegaard back to a letter he had sent to Karl Löwith in 1920, where he writes:

> What is of importance in Kierkegaard must be appropriated anew, but in a *strict* critique that grows out of *our own* situation. Blind appropriation is the greatest seduction. . . . Not everyone who talks of 'existence' has to be a Kierkegaardian. My approaches have already been misinterpreted in this way.[205]

The lady doth protest too much, methinks. He had spent his entire career trying to control his image, his reception, and his legacy. Maybe now is the time, given the new willingness to reconsider Heidegger overall in the aftermath of the *Black Notebooks*—if not to dismiss him altogether, to at least approach him "anew."

In light of the correspondence between *Being and Time* and the history of novels, I would like to make a modest interjection in the otherwise vicious spat that took place between Thomas Sheehan and Emmanuel Faye at this conference, as the rest of us squirmed in our seats. Faye calls for Heidegger's works to be thrown off the philosophy shelves and relocated to the "historical archives of Nazism and Hitlerism."[206] Sheehan, in turn, wants to do the same to Faye's work on Heidegger, but relocate that to HV6691 .F353, in the history of fraud section.[207]

Would Heidegger really want *Being and Time* on the philosophy shelves anyway, after having ostensibly overcome metaphysics? Wouldn't he bristle at the idea of being sandwiched between Hegel and Husserl, despite his passive aggressive dedication to his former colleague? The thought of being moved to the "historical archives of Nazism and Hitlerism" would be a rather fortuitous event if it were to occur in DeLillo's novelistic world of *White Noise*, where Jack Gladney is struggling to maintain his status as "the most prominent figure of Hitler studies in North America."[208] Would that make more people read it?

If *Being and Time* cannot be read as a novel, perhaps it can be read as a way of understanding novels, from Cervantes to DeLillo and beyond. Maybe in this light, there might be an empty spot on the shelves of Literary Theory to accept it (not far from de Man, Paul—that other Nazi). If there can be Freudian and Marxist theories of literary criticism, then why not a Heideggerian theory of the novel? Aristotle's *Poetics* falls under Literary Theory, not Philosophy, and perhaps that strange work is not so much a normative statement of aesthetics as it is an observation of the natural sciences, a kind of anatomy, its emphasis on the natural order of tragedy corresponding to the natural development of humans. Perhaps his concept of *mimesis praxeos* is just as much an account of how people learn to take action through imitation as it is a commentary on how a play is staged.[209] If Aristotle's *Poetics* is a kind of phenomenological treatise, then can *Being and Time*, Heidegger's phenomenological treatment of Aristotle, be read as a kind of *Prosaics*, a study of Being in its average everydayness instead of its imitation of a noble action, switching out the dramatic tragic form for the novel as its ideal expression?

Either way, maybe moving Heidegger around the library is not such a terrible idea, since it would dramatically call into question how we think of him in terms of all of the other books we have read and have yet to read. Maybe it would only be appropriate for *Being and Time*, in performing the ecstatic movements of Dasein, to float ecstatically across various sections without being tethered to one. Maybe the next section, after it has made its way from Philosophy to Nazi History to Fiction to Literary Theory, would be Music, so we could listen to it better—as, indeed, it instructs us to do. Wherever it is shelved, there is a tendency to keep falling back to *Being and Time*, and—in the shadow of Kierkegaard—to keep thinking of the way it generates novelty in ideas, if not ideas in and of the novel.

NOTES

1. Carlisle, "Kierkegaard and Heidegger," 422.
2. Patricia J. Huntington, "Heidegger's Reading of Kierkegaard Revisited: From Ontological Abstraction to Ethical Concretion," in *Kierkegaard in Post/Modernity*, ed. Martin J. Matuštík and Merold Westphal (Bloomington, IN: Indiana University Press, 1995), 46.
3. Huntington, "Heidegger's Reading of Kierkegaard Revisited," 43.
4. Carlisle, "Kierkegaard and Heidegger," 422.
5. Mooney, "Kierkegaard's Disruptions of Literature and Philosophy," 61.
6. Mooney, "Kierkegaard's Disruptions of Literature and Philosophy," 63.
7. Adam Buben, "Heidegger's Reception of Kierkegaard: The Existential Philosophy of Death," *British Journal for the History of Philosophy* 21, no. 5 (September 5, 2013): 967; Carlisle, "Kierkegaard and Heidegger," 422
8. Qtd. in Carlisle, "Kierkegaard and Heidegger," 422.
9. Qtd. in Carlisle, "Kierkegaard and Heidegger," 422.
10. Buben, "Heidegger's Reception of Kierkegaard," 969.
11. Buben, "Heidegger's Reception of Kierkegaard," 969.
12. Carlisle, "Kierkegaard and Heidegger," 429.
13. Buben, "Heidegger's Reception of Kierkegaard," 969.
14. Heidegger, *Being and Time*, fn.vi: 494, fn.iii: 497.
15. Heidegger, *What is Called Thinking?*, trans. J. Glenn Gray (New York: Harper & Row, 1968), 213.
16. Dienstag, *Pessimism*, 124.
17. Buben, "Heidegger's Reception of Kierkegaard," 970.
18. Alastair Hannay, introduction to *A Literary Review* by Kierkegaard, ed. and trans. Alastair Hannay (London: Penguin Books, 2001), xv.
19. Heidegger, *Being and Time*, 38.
20. Heidegger, *Being and Time*, 164.
21. Heidegger, *Being and Time*, 210, 219.
22. Heidegger, *Being and Time*, 223.
23. Heidegger, *Being and Time*, 230.
24. Heidegger, *Being and Time*, 219. A synonym for *Entwurf* is *Projekt*, hence the English translation of "Projection." It could be that Heidegger took this concept from Schlegel, along with Schlegel's challenge to the subject-object binary, in this quote from his *Athenaeum Fragments*: "A project [*Projekt*] is the subjective embryo of a developing object. A perfect project should be at once completely subjective and completely objective, should be an indivisible and living individual" (Schlegel, "Athenaeum Fragments," §64: 122).
25. Kierkegaard, *A Literary Review*, ed. and trans. Alastair Hannay (London: Penguin Books, 2001), 80.

26. Kierkegaard, *Literary Review*, 80–83; 75.
27. Kierkegaard, *Literary Review*, 75.
28. Kierkegaard, *Literary Review*, 83.
29. Carlisle, "Kierkegaard and Heidegger," 432. Heidegger also takes Kierkegaard's concept of anxiety from *The Concept of Anxiety*.
30. Heidegger, *Being and Time*, 211.
31. Kierkegaard, *Literary Review*, 87.
32. Heidegger, *Being and Time*, 56.
33. Heidegger, *Being and Time*, 318. Here is another corresponding passage from *A Literary Review* that illustrates this point Heidegger is making about silence:

> Anyone who experiences something originally also experiences, through ideality, the possibilities of the same and the possibility of the opposite. These possibilities are his literary legal property. But his own private, personal actuality is not. His speaking, his producing, are thus borne by silence. The ideal perfection of his speaking, his producing, will correspond to his silence, and the absolute expression of that silence will be that the ideality contains the qualitatively opposite possibility. (Kierkegaard, *Literary Review*, 87–88)

Where Kierkegaard uses the word "original," Heidegger uses the word "authentic."
34. Kierkegaard, *Literary Review*, 87.
35. Kierkegaard, *Literary Review*, 89.
36. Heidegger, *Being and Time*, 212.
37. Heidegger, *Being and Time*, 215.
38. Heidegger, *Being and Time*, 283.
39. Cf. Goethe, whose Faust abandons the biblical line, "In the beginning was the Word" and instead writes, "In the beginning was the Deed!" ["*Im Anfang war die Tat!*"] (Goethe, *Faust*, I.1224: 34, I.1237: 34).
40. Thacker, *Infinite Resignation*, 122.
41. Bakhtin, *Dialogic Imagination*, 135–136.
42. Benjamin, "The Storyteller," *Illuminations*, 87.
43. Benjamin, "The Storyteller," *Illuminations*, 87.
44. Lukács, *Theory of the Novel*, 92.
45. Bakhtin, *Dialogic Imagination*, 234.
46. Heidegger, *Being and Time*, 215; Kierkegaard, *Literary Review*, 56.
47. Kierkegaard, *Literary Review*, 56.
48. Qtd. in Leland de la Durantaye, *Giorgio Agamben: A Critical Introduction* (Stanford, CA: Stanford University Press, 2009), 395. Tillich was also the professor who had finally accepted Adorno's dissertation on Kierkegaard in 1936 after it had been rejected by Hans Cornelius three years earlier (Hullot-Kentor, introduction to *Kierkegaard* by Adorno, xii).
49. Lawrence, *Letters*, II: 547. Russell's misplaced optimism was no match for Lawrence's pessimism. In 1930, as the threat of fascism was looming overhead, Russell published *The Conquest of Happiness*, a naïve and tone-deaf work that chalked up the unhappiness of modern life to "mistaken views of the world, mistaken ethics, [and] mistaken habits of life," saying, furthermore, that our fears have "no obvious external cause" (Bertrand Russell, *The Conquest of Happiness* [New York: W. W. Norton, 2013], 24).

50. Holquist, introduction to *Dialogic Imagination*, xxiii. Heidegger cites Scheler five times in *Being and Time* (Heidegger, *Being and Time*, 73).

51. Heidegger, *Being and Time*, fn.xii: 495. Nabokov considers *The Death of Ivan Ilyich* second only to *Anna Karenina* as the greatest work of nineteenth-century literature (Nabokov, *Strong Opinions*, 147).

52. William Irwin, "Death of Inauthenticity: Heidegger's Debt to Ivan Il'ich's Fall," *Tolstoy Studies Journal* 25 (Annual 2013): 15, http://www.utoronto.ca/tolstoy/journal.html.

53. Tolstoy, "Death of Ivan Ilyich," 89.

54. Tolstoy, "Death of Ivan Ilyich," 115. Cf. An earlier passage:

> Besides considerations as to possible transfers and promotions likely to result from Ivan Ilyich's death, the mere fact of the death of a near acquaintance aroused, as usual, in all who heard of it the complacent feeling that, "it's he who is dead and not I." (Tolstoy, "Death of Ivan Ilyich," 84)

In "The Storyteller," where Benjamin defines the novel as the pessimistic site of the "solitary individual," he writes, "Dying was once a public process in the life of the individual and a most exemplary one. . . . In the course of modern times dying has been pushed further and further out of the perceptual world of the living" (Benjamin, *Illuminations*, 93–94).

55. Heidegger, *Being and Time*, 298; Kierkegaard, *Literary Review*, 56.

56. Tolstoy, "Death of Ivan Ilyich," 107. Maurice Blanchot revises Heidegger's claims about death, to make it much more pessimistic, and also in the context of analyzing Tolstoy's fiction:

> He dies alone because he dies as everyone; and this too makes for great solitude. From this we also see why death rarely seems to be achieved. To those who remain and surround the dying person, death comes as a death to be died still more. And it rests with them: they must preserve and prolong it until the moment when, time being at an end, everyone will die joyfully together. In this sense everyone is in agony till the end of the world. (Blanchot, *Space of Literature*, 165)

The work in question is Tolstoy's "Master and Man."

57. Tolstoy, "Death of Ivan Ilyich," 124.

58. Tolstoy, "Death of Ivan Ilyich," 122.

59. Heidegger, *Being and Time*, 68.

60. This unconvincing attempt at disguising an ethically normative claim as an ontologically descriptive one is also symptomatic of Heidegger's inability to distance himself enough from Kierkegaard, leaving scholars like Patricia J. Huntington in the awkward position of unsuccessfully vouching for Heidegger, claiming that,

> by ontologizing Kierkegaard's existential categories, Heidegger depletes the latter's thought of its ethical import, central to the focus on personal edification. For this reason, I believe *Being and Time* constitutes not a development and extension of Kierkegaard's thought but rather a significant transmutation. (Huntington, "Heidegger's Reading of Kierkegaard Revisited," 44)

Byung-Chul Han notes how, "Heidegger does not consistently describe the they or idle talk in phenomenologically neutral terms. Frequently his interpretation is colored by value judgments or representations with clearly religious roots. Idle talk retains

a 'disparaging sense'" (Han, *Good Entertainment: A Deconstruction of the Western Passion Narrative*, trans. Adrian Nathan West [Cambridge, MA: Massachusetts Institute of Technology Press, 2019], 72–73).
61. Tolstoy, "Death of Ivan Ilyich," 122.
62. Tolstoy, "Death of Ivan Ilyich," 123.
63. Heidegger, *Being and Time*, 325.
64. Dostoevsky, *Brothers Karamazov*, 618.
65. Dostoevsky, *Brothers Karamazov*, 98.
66. Dostoevsky, *Brothers Karamazov*, 100.
67. Dostoevsky, *Brothers Karamazov*, 627.
68. Dostoevsky, *Brothers Karamazov*, 623.
69. Dostoevsky, *Brothers Karamazov*, 201. Richard Pevear and Larissa Volokhonsky provide a footnote to Arina Petrovna's mispronunciation of "Karamazov" as "Chernomazov": "Arina Petrovna inadvertently brings out the implicit meaning of Alyosha's surname: *cherny* is Russian for 'black'; however, in the Turkish and Tartar languages, *kara* also means 'black' (the root, *maz*, in Russian conveys the idea of 'paint' or 'smear')" (Richard Pevear and Larissa Volokhonsky, in an explanatory note to Dostoevsky, *Brothers Karamazov*, n.2.4.6.2: 784).
70. Dostoevsky, *Brothers Karamazov*, 759.
71. Dostoevsky, *Brothers Karamazov*, 667.
72. Dostoevsky, *Brothers Karamazov*, 289.
73. Heidegger, *Being and Time*, 373.
74. Heidegger, *Being and Time*, 255.
75. Heidegger, *Being and Time*, 373.
76. Kafka, *Trial*, 229; Heidegger, *Being and Time*, 284.
77. Ong, *Art of Being*, 163.
78. Ong, *Art of Being*, 163; Heidegger, *Being and Time*, 37–38.
79. Kundera, *Art of the Novel*, 5.
80. Mazzoni, *Theory of the Novel*, 13.
81. Mazzoni, *Theory of the Novel*, 229.
82. Heidegger, *Being and Time*, 34.
83. Heidegger, *Being and Time*, 75.
84. Kundera, *Art of the Novel*, 32.
85. Kundera, *Testaments Betrayed*, 165. Curiously, though, Kundera traces the origin of the rapprochement between philosophy and the novel not to Heidegger, but to Nietzsche, who adamantly despised novels. However,

> Nietzsche's refusal of systematic thought has another consequence: an immense *broadening of theme*; barriers between the various philosophical disciplines, which have kept the real world from being seen in its full range, are fallen, and from then on everything human can become the object of a philosopher's thought. That too brings philosophy nearer to the novel: for the first time philosophy is pondering not epistemology, not aesthetics or ethics, the phenomenology of mind or the critique of reason, etc. but *everything human.* (Kundera, *Testaments Betrayed*, 175)

86. Kundera, *Art of the Novel*, 32–34.
87. Bakhtin, *Dialogic Imagination*, 30.

88. Bakhtin, *Dialogic Imagination*, 38.
89. Bakhtin, *Dialogic Imagination*, 84.
90. Bakhtin, *Dialogic Imagination*, 207.
91. Kundera, *Art of the Novel*, 5–6.
92. Kundera, *Testaments Betrayed*, 131.
93. Heidegger, *Being and Time*, 120.
94. Lukács, *Theory of the Novel*, 78.
95. Heidegger, *Being and Time*, 116–117.
96. Heidegger, *Being and Time*, 92. Bakhtin has a similar understanding of "world." In "Epic and Novel," he characterizes the shift from epic to novel in terms of its world-view: "The world has already opened up; one's own monolithic and closed world (the world of the epic) has been replaced by the great world of one's own plus 'the others'" (Bakhtin, *Dialogic Imagination*, 29). This would also correspond to Heidegger's account of "world" as "Being-in-the-world." The "great world of one's own plus 'the others'" would translate to a world composed just as much of one's own authenticity as "the 'they'" of the others. The world for Bakhtin, as for Lukács, is constitutive: "Through contact with the present, an object is attracted to the incomplete process of a world-in-the-making" (Bakhtin, *Dialogic Imagination*, 30).
97. Heidegger, *Being and Time*, 119 (emphasis in original).
98. Bakhtin, *Dialogic Imagination*, 47.
99. Watt, *Rise of the Novel*, 30.
100. John Brenkman, "Innovation: Notes on Nihilism and the Aesthetics of the Novel," in *The Novel* Vol. 2, ed. Franco Moretti (Princeton, NJ: Princeton University Press, 2007), 811.
101. One would be hard-pressed to locate a tradition of anatomy here, as one sees readily in the novel. And yet the term he uses for equipment (sometimes translated as "tool") in German, *Zeug*, is the translation of the Greek word for "organ."
102. Ong, *Art of Being*, 163.
103. Sartre, *Being and Nothingness*, 548. In Sartre's explanation of the "Situation," Ong sees "philosophy struggl[ing] to enter into the condition of the novel, in its desire to achieve the impossible—call it necessarily fictional—aim of reflecting existence upon itself" (Ong, *Art of Being*, 165).
104. Lukács, *Theory of the Novel*, 65.
105. Heidegger, *Being and Time*, 172.
106. Lukács, *Theory of the Novel*, 118–119.
107. Heidegger, "What is Metaphysics?," in *Pathmarks*, ed. William McNeill, trans. David Farrell Krell (Cambridge: Cambridge University Press, 1998), 90. Heidegger explains, "By such anxiety we do not mean the quite common anxiousness, ultimately reducible to fearfulness, which all too readily comes over us. Anxiety is fundamentally different from fear.... Much to the contrary, a peculiar calm pervades it" (88). Fear is always a specific fear "in the face of" something (Heidegger, "What is Metaphysics?", 88). Anxiety, by contrast, is "in the face" of "the nothing." Because Dasein itself is nothing ("Da-sein means: being held out into the nothing"), anxiety is the mode of authenticity, the mode by which Dasein finds itself, its "own-ness" (Heidegger, "What is Metaphysics?," 91).

108. Camus, *The Stranger*, trans. Matthew Ward (New York: Vintage Books, 1989), 122–123.

109. Heidegger, "What is Metaphysics?," 93.

110. Lukács, *Theory of the Novel*, 45.

111. Lukács, *Theory of the Novel*, 38.

112. Melville, *Moby-Dick*, 561.

113. Shakespeare, *Hamlet*, 5.2.238.

114. Heidegger, *Discourse on Thinking*, trans. John M. Anderson and E. Hans Freund (New York: Harper & Row, 1966), 55.

115. Heidegger, *Being and Time*, 488.

116. "In a perspective that foreshadows Heidegger's, Schopenhauer finds time to be 'not merely a form *a priori* of our knowing, but . . . the foundation or ground-bass thereof; it is the primary woof for the fabric of the whole world that manifests itself to us . . . it is the archetype of everything" (Dienstag, *Pessimism*, 88; Schopenhauer, *Parerga and Paralipomena*, trans. E. F. J. Payne [Oxford: Oxford University Press, 1974], II: 42–43).

117. Cioran, *Temptation to Exist*, 46.

118. Lukács, *Theory of the Novel*, 122.

119. Lukács, *Theory of the Novel*, 123. Lukács also writes, "time gives them the essential quality of their existence" (Lukács, *Theory of the Novel*, 125).

120. Lukács, *Theory of the Novel*, 99.

121. The portmanteau would combine *Schritt* (a step, a march) with *Durchschnittlichkeit* (averageness, a state of being in the middle).

122. Eliot, *Middlemarch*, 267.

123. Eliot, *Middlemarch*, 124.

124. Don DeLillo, *White Noise* (New York: Penguin Books, 2009), 36.

125. Heidegger, *Being and Time*, 423.

126. Karl Ove Knausgaard, interviewed by James Wood, "Writing *My Struggle*: An Exchange," *The Paris Review* 211 (Winter 2014), http://www.theparisreview.org/interviews/6345/writing-emmy-struggle-em-an-exchange-james-wood-karl-ove-knausgaard.

127. Heidegger, *Being and Time*, 69.

128. Bakhtin also writes that, "Form and content in discourse are one, once we understand that verbal discourse is a social phenomenon." (Bakhtin, *Dialogic Imagination*, 259).

129. Heidegger, *Being and Time*, 209.

130. Kundera, *Testaments Betrayed*, 132–133.

131. Kundera, *Testaments Betrayed*, 133.

132. Heidegger, *Being and Time*, 63.

133. Woolf, *To the Lighthouse*, 170; Heidegger, *Being and Time*, 387.

134. Lukács, *Theory of the Novel*, 41.

135. Lukács, *Theory of the Novel*, 29.

136. Heidegger, *Being and Time*, 210–219.

137. Lukács, *Theory of the Novel*, 116.

138. Heidegger, *Being and Time*, 233. "In anxiety one feels *uncanny*. . . . But here 'uncanniness' also means 'not-being-at-home' [das Nicht-zuhause-sein]" (Heidegger,

Being and Time, 233). The German word for "uncanny" is *unheimlich,* literally "un-home-like."

139. Heidegger, *Being and Time,* 304.
140. Heidegger, *Being and Time,* 108–109.
141. Lukács, *Theory of the Novel,* 88. Cf. In the famous *Der Spiegel* interview, Heidegger views the world in the same way that Lukács views the novel, lamenting that, "Only a god can save us" ("*Der Spiegel* Interview with Martin Heidegger" [1966], http://web.ics.purdue.edu/~other1/Heidegger%20Der%20Spiegel.pdf.).
142. Lukács, *Theory of the Novel,* 60.
143. Stendhal, *The Red and the Black,* 297.
144. Heidegger, *Being and Time,* fn.3: 306.
145. Heidegger, *Being and Time,* fn.1: 57. In "The Origin of the Work of Art," Heidegger writes, "Truth is un-truth, insofar as there belongs to it the reservoir of the not-yet-covered, the un-covered, in the sense of concealment" (Heidegger, "The Origin of the Work of Art," in *Poetry, Language, Thought,* trans. Albert Hofstadter [New York: Harper & Row, 1971], 58).
146. Heidegger, *Being and Time,* 68.
147. Kundera, *Art of the Novel,* 23; Heidegger, *Being and Time,* 188.
148. Heidegger, *Being and Time,* 394. Kierkegaard wrote an entire work on the subject in this manner called *Repetition,* published in 1843.
149. Heidegger, *Being and Time,* 324.
150. Kundera, *Art of the Novel,* 29.
151. Proust, *The Captive,* 19.
152. Robert Musil, *The Man without Qualities,* Vol. 1, trans. Sophie Wilkins (New York: Vintage Books, 1995), I: 286.
153. Heidegger, *Being and Time,* 377.
154. Heidegger, *Being and Time,* 474.
155. Joyce, *Ulysses,* 186.
156. Joyce, *Ulysses,* 515.
157. Musil, *Man without Qualities,* I.708–9. Faulkner also explores these two modes of experiencing time in *The Sound and the Fury,* when Quentin's father tells him, "time is dead as long as it is being clicked off by little wheels; only when the clock stops does time come to life" (Faulkner, *The Sound and the Fury,* 54). He visualizes this pessimistic account of time as a "gull on an invisible wire attached through space dragged. You carry the symbol of your frustration into eternity" (Faulkner, *The Sound and the Fury,* 66).
158. Musil, *Man without Qualities,* Vol. 2, trans. Sophie Wilkins (New York: Vintage Books, 1996), II: 1206.
159. The history of the novel, based on the epistolary tradition, is predicated on the call. That the rise of the novel coincides with the rise of the silent reading public demonstrates the link Heidegger makes between silence and the call. Fredric Jameson says that it

> would be better to translate the term *bildungsroman* as the novel of a calling or vocation, a *Beruf,* to use that word which Max Weber charged with its most intense Lutheran accents in order to make his point about the new innerworldliness of Protestant behavior and

virtue. (Fredric Jameson, "The Experiments of Time: Providence and Realism," in *The Novel*, Vol. 2, ed. Franco Moretti [Princeton, NJ: Princeton University Press, 2007], 102)

160. Beckett, "Worstward Ho," in *Nohow On* (New York: Grove, 1996), 89. I thank Charles Snyder for this connection.
161. Heidegger, *Being and Time*, 78.
162. Chuck Palahniuk, *Invisible Monsters* (New York: W. W. Norton, 1999), 217.
163. Palahniuk, *Invisible Monsters*, 218.
164. Heidegger, *Being and Time*, 164.
165. Mazzoni, *Theory of the Novel*, 372.
166. Mooney, "Kierkegaard's Disruptions of Literature and Philosophy," 61.
167. Mooney, "Kierkegaard's Disruptions of Literature and Philosophy," 63.
168. Josipovici, "Kierkegaard and the Novel," in *Kierkegaard: A Critical Reader*, ed. Jonathan Rée and Jane Chamberlain (Oxford: Blackwell, 1998), 114.
169. Kundera, *Art of the Novel*, 134.
170. Brenkman, "Innovation," 811.
171. Kundera, *Testaments Betrayed*, 19.
172. Heidegger, *Being and Time*, 359.
173. Heidegger, *Being and Time*, 298.
174. Kierkegaard, *Literary Review*, 94.
175. Emmanuel Levinas, *On Escape*, trans. Bettina Bergo (Standford, CA: Stanford University Press, 2003), 67.
176. Levinas, *On Escape*, 66–67.
177. Levinas, *On Escape*, 66–67.
178. Cascardi, "The Novel," 163; Edmund Spenser, *The Faerie Queene*, in *The Norton Anthology of English Literature*, ed. Stephen Greenblatt, Vol. 1, 10th ed. (New York: W. W. Norton, 2019), 421–422.
179. Beckett, *Proust*, 8.
180. Miguel de Cervantes, *Don Quixote*, trans. Tom Lathrop (New York: Signet, 2011), 133.
181. Brenkman, "Innovation," 829.
182. Roberto González Echevarría, *Cervantes' "Don Quixote"* (New Haven, CT: Yale University Press, 2015), 78.
183. William Faulkner, *Sanctuary* (New York: Vintage Books, 1993), 223.
184. Sylvia Plath, *The Bell Jar* (New York: Harper Perennial, 2006), 7.
185. Plath, *The Bell Jar*, 22.
186. Plath, *The Bell Jar*, 23.
187. Plath, *The Bell Jar*, 44.
188. Qtd. in Sam Bluefarb, "Henry Miller's James Joyce: A Painful Case of Envy," *New English Review* (April 2012), http://www.newenglishreview.org/custpage.cfm/frm/110561/sec_id/110561.
189. Heidegger himself does not see language as present-at-hand, even though his own language seems to gesture in that direction despite himself (Heidegger, *Being and Time*, 201).

190. Simon Critchley and Tom McCarthy, "Of Chrematology: Joyce and Money," *Hypermedia Joyce Studies*. hjs.ff.cuni.cz. This passage from Joyce's *Finnegans Wake* exemplifies this littered literary landscape:

> But by writing thithaways end to end and turning, turning and end to end hithaways writing and with lines of litters slittering up and louds of latters slettering down, the old semetomyplace and jupetbackagain from tham Let Rise till Hum Lit. Sleep, where in the waste is the wisdom? (James Joyce, *Finnegans Wake* [New York: Penguin Books, 1999], 114.16–20)

191. Heidegger, *Being and Time*, 102.
192. Joyce, *Ulysses* (New York: Vintage Books, 1990), 550.
193. Joyce, *Ulysses*, 5.
194. Heidegger, *Being and Time*, 342; 316.
195. Heidegger, *Being and Time*, 223.
196. Knausgaard, *My Struggle*, Vol. 1, trans. Don Bartlett (New York: Farrar, Straus & Giroux, 2012), I: 3.
197. Knausgaard, *My Struggle*, Vol. 4, trans. Don Bartlett (New York: Archipelago, 2015), IV: 226.
198. Knausgaard, *My Struggle*, IV: 226–227.
199. Knausgaard, "Writing *My Struggle*: An Exchange."
200. Knausgaard, "Writing *My Struggle*: An Exchange."
201. Mann, *Doctor Faustus*, 143.
202. Mann, *Doctor Faustus*, 348.
203. Mann, *Doctor Faustus*, 187 (emphasis added).
204. Mann, *Doctor Faustus*, 506.
205. Qtd. in Theodore Kisiel and Thomas Sheehan (eds.), *Becoming Heidegger: On the Trail of his Early Occasional Writings* (Evanston, IL: Northwestern University Press, 2007), 98.
206. Emmanuel Faye, *Heidegger: The Introduction of Nazism into Philosophy in Light of the Unpublished Seminars of 1933-1935* (New Haven, CT: Yale University Press, 2011), 319.
207. Thomas Sheehan, "Emmanuel Faye: The Introduction of Fraud into Philosophy?" *Philosophy Today* 59, no. 3 (Summer 2015): fn.7: 370.
208. DeLillo, *White Noise*, 31.
209. I owe this reading to Charles Snyder, who articulated this interpretation of Aristotle far more eloquently in person.

Chapter 14

Seduction Against Production

The Novel as a Tool of Pedagogy in a World Doomed to Neoliberal Optimism

THE EROS OF FAILURE

In *Being and Time*, the fraught history between philosophy and the novel, from its origins in Plato's *Symposium*, culminates in a reunion of sorts, despite whatever Heidegger's intentions may have been for the project. As seemingly different as these works are, and as odd as they may be to compare, what we get in *Symposium* is the narrative of a self divided in two, these halves of the self reaching out across the void to find each other. In *Being and Time*, we have a novelistic Dasein also reaching out into the void in order to find itself, but without a sense of fragmentation, or of physicality, or maybe even—on the surface, at least—of any kind of erotic activity. But what is it exactly that impels Dasein to twist itself out of inauthenticity for a moment? Where does this call of conscience come from? To say it comes from nothing is somewhat of a tautology; Dasein recognizes itself, in authenticity, as nothing, so that answer doesn't help. Could it actually be eros, after all—an eros for itself, an eros for the nothing that "is"?

This would certainly be an idiosyncratic interpretation to take. Heidegger thinks in terms of the One—of Dasein as a singularity caught up in "the 'they,'" before it comes into its own, its unique selfhood, in authenticity. This leaves much to be desired when it comes to ethics. What is Dasein's ethical commitment to someone else? Are ethical bonds, as mediations between the Self and the Other, strictly relegated to the mode of inauthenticity? Can there be an ethics of authenticity? Is it even possible to have an ontology without ethics? Heidegger doesn't address these points outside of his discussion of multiplying Dasein into *das Volk*—and we've already seen in history what kind of ethical catastrophe that has led to.

Where Heidegger thinks the One, Emmanuel Levinas thinks the Two. This is why Levinas is so concerned with the role of ethics in philosophy. Another post-Heideggerian thinker who thinks the Two is Alain Badiou, who, in response to Heidegger's distracting silence on the topic, asks,

> what kind of world does one see when one experiences it from the point of view of two and not one? What is the world like when it is experienced, developed and lived from the point of view of difference and not identity? That is what I believe love to be.[1]

Love is a "two scene" as opposed to the silent monologue of Dasein in the moment of its authenticity.[2] Challenging Heidegger's rhetoric of falling, and offering a new existential analytic in its place, Badiou specifies that, "Love doesn't take me 'above' or indeed 'below.' It is an existential project: to construct a world from a decentered point of view other than that of my mere impulse to survive or re-affirm my own identity."[3]

For all its falling, how come we never see Dasein fall in love? It is curious that in *Being and Time*, we get no direct account of eros. There are afflictions and addictions; Dasein is both stimulated and tranquilized; but eros is one of the many glaring omissions from this supposed study of existence in its average everydayness. There is no eros because there is no body. Aside from its handedness and its ability to hear, there is no concrete description of Dasein's physicality, which is perhaps why Levinas responds to his notion of evasion with the most visceral of bodily processes, to remind us that we are not abstract concepts (what exactly "is" Dasein, after all? who qualifies for this title? who doesn't?), but embodied beings whose physicality cannot be dismissed or ignored.

Heidegger's approach to physicality, like his approach to Kierkegaard and the novel, is to hide it, to undermine its importance in his thinking. There is an awkwardness in leaving this out of an account of Dasein that nevertheless includes other seemingly less important details about its existence, like reading newspapers or driving cars. Could physicality, could eros, really be this unimportant to Heidegger's understanding of average everydayness? It turns out that Heidegger's omission is disingenuous, as evidenced by a letter to his wife in 1950, when he writes about dedicating his work on Plato to her. With Plato then explicitly on his mind, he writes this:

> The other thing, inseparable in a different way from my love for you and from my thinking, is difficult to say. I call it Eros, the oldest of the gods according to Parmenides. . . .

The beat of that god's wings moves me every time I take a substantial step in my thinking and venture onto untrodden paths. It moves me perhaps more powerfully and uncannily [*starker und unheimlicher*] than others when something long intuited is to be led across into the realm of the sayable and when what has been said must after all be left in solitude for a long time to come. To live up to *this* purely and yet retain what is ours, to follow the flight and yet return home safely, to accomplish both things as equally essential and pertinent, this is where I fail too easily and then either stray into pure sensuality [*bloße Sinnlichkeit*] or try to force the unforceable through sheer work [*bloßes Arbeiten*].[4]

The struggle, the *agon*, to convert thought into the "sayable," is an *agon* rooted in eros. In *The Agony of Eros*, in which Byung-Chul Han laments the evacuation of eros from contemporary life—a life governed and controlled by Big Data, digital technology, and an ethics and ontology of neoliberal selfhood—Han reads this letter as evidence that, "Without seduction by the atopic Other, which sparks erotic desire, thinking withers into mere *work*, which always reproduces the *Same*. Calculative thought lacks the negativity of atopia."[5] What does Han mean when he refers to "the seduction by the atopic Other"? Behind this elusive figure in his analysis of Heidegger is the image of Socrates: "It is not by chance that Socrates the lover is called *atopos*. The Other, whom I desire and who fascinates me, is *placeless*."[6]

What Socrates represents in this placelessness, in this erotic negativity, is the root of our contemporary "crisis of love," which "does not derive from too many *others* so much as from the erosion of the *Other*. This erosion is occurring in all spheres of life; its corollary is the mounting narcissification of the Self."[7] In the absence of eros, the narcissistic Self engages in transactional pursuits of pleasure instead. Eros has been reduced and "positivized into sexuality, and by the same token, subjected to a commandment to perform."[8] In our neoliberal understanding of existence, sex becomes a function of what Heidegger would call "mere work." It "means achievement and performance," and sexiness is "capital to be increased." Neoliberalism reduces the body to a commodity so that "one cannot love—one can only consume."[9]

Eros is scarce, but there is plenty of porn—a flattening of sexuality into images that dictate our desires. Porn is the allegory of capitalism itself: people are reduced to bodies, which in turn are reduced to interchangeable, disposable commodities, each one competing for attention by being faster, harder, bigger, stronger, cheaper than the next. Porn is the substitution of erotics with economics. Love under neoliberalism is an industry that profits from images representing "profiles," which are arranged according to algorithms that convert identities into data, boiling down to the binary that governs computer science, a binary of zeroes and ones: swipe left or swipe right—the gradation of infinite ambiguity limited to a new Manichaeism. "Matches" lead to dialogues that either dwell in clichés or read as bad pastiches of Pinter or Beckett at their most terse. Often, they lead to no exchange of words whatsoever.

In *A Literary Review*, Kierkegaard anticipated the future of what would replace eros in modernity:

> And just as the public is a pure abstraction, so in the end will it be with human speech—there will no longer be someone speaking but an objective reflection will gradually impart an atmospheric something, an abstract sound that will render human speech redundant, just as machines make workers redundant. In Germany there are even manuals for lovers, so it will probably end with lovers sitting and speaking anonymously to each other.[10]

"Lovers sitting and speaking anonymously to each other"—nothing else better captures the essence of modern eros in its newest and most ubiquitous forms: online dating and pornography. The same mechanics at work in the machines that "make workers redundant" operate here, as well, in a tendency that will eventually "render human speech redundant."

The redundancy of human speech coincides with the redundancy of philosophy and the evacuation of eros. Han does not see this as a coincidence, arguing that eros is at the core of philosophy. Philosophy itself is where eros and logos intersect.[11] As evidence, he cites Plato's *Symposium*, where Alcibiades says that no other orator, not even Pericles, can say anything that moves him in the way Socrates can, because only Socrates knows how to use language erotically, as a form of seduction.[12] Philosophy, then—from Plato to Kierkegaard to Heidegger to Badiou—is nothing but seduction. By the means of eros, it "leads and seduces (*führt und verführt*) thinking down untrodden paths."[13]

This is a compelling argument to make; one may even call it seductive. Except that there is one mistake. Han gets a bit too carried away when he writes that, "Until now, attention has hardly been paid" to this "remarkable fact."[14] Attention has been paid, over and over again, to this connection between eros, logos, and thought—but that attention comes from the history of the novel. Kierkegaard comes to this conclusion in his reflections on the novel, and in *Death in Venice*, Aschenbach—in an erotic rapture that leads him to fantasize about being Socrates engaging in silent discourse with Phaedrus, a role played by Tadzio on the beach—says in his unspoken dialogue, "Eros is in the word."[15] *Lady Chatterley's Lover* is a work that wrestles with the crisis of language after the First World War, with the "hypocrisy of words" that covers over "the only reality," which is "a reality of nothingness."[16] Connie and Mellors seem to reinvent language as they have to reinvent eros out of the ashes of the War, approaching them as interchangeable. To Connie, "sex is just another form of talk, where you act the words instead of saying them"—but it is talk nonetheless, or something closer to what Heidegger meant by *Rede* [discourse], which dwells in silence, the same kind of silence that Aschenbach dwells in to ironically link the word with eros.[17]

And just as Heidegger wrote in the letter to his wife about his struggle to reach "across into the realm of the sayable" with philosophy, Woolf, in a letter to Vita Sackville-West, wrote that the novel is the space that allows one to access the "far side of a gulf, which words can't cross . . . a novel, as I saw, to be good should seem, before one writes, something unwriteable."[18] And in *To the Lighthouse*, her novel modeled on *Symposium*, she comes to the same conclusion about love and eros as Mann and Lawrence, even though she is more subdued in its articulation. As Mrs. Ramsay comes closer to her husband in bed, "she could feel his mind like a raised hand shadowing her mind; and he was beginning now that her thoughts took a turn he disliked— toward this 'pessimism' as he called it—to fidget, though he said nothing."[19] But even in this pessimism, "she began to smile, for though she had not said a word, he knew, of course he knew, that she loved him."[20] Eros resides in the word of their wordless, telepathic conversation. And Humbert, too, plays on the tension between the wordiness and wordlessness of eros, silencing Dolores as if she were the little mermaid, but then lamenting, "Oh, my Lolita, I have only words to play with!"[21]

In order to understand how we have arrived at this eros-deprived age, it is necessary to turn to the novel in articulating possibilities of lived experience across modern history. Jonathan Arac takes a Hegelian approach when he invokes arguments for the "death of the novel."[22] These arguments largely emerge from Lukács, who sees the history of the novel beginning with *Don Quixote* and ending with Dostoevsky. Arac points out that,

> Among Lukács's English-speaking contemporaries, Virginia Woolf too saw "the Russians" as ending the old novel of H.G. Wells, John Galsworthy, and Arnold Bennett, and D.H. Lawrence even more closely approximated Lukács's sense of crisis in the novel as part of the crisis of the Western soul at the moment of the Great War.[23]

Woolf and Lawrence are then more aligned than one might initially assume— not necessarily in terms of their aesthetic styles or literary techniques, but in their overall vision of the role of the novel in culture. The death of the novel, for Arac, is just a recognition that "the novel generally no longer does what it used to."[24] But he concedes that, "in the United States now, and for some decades past, perhaps only in those cases in which new groups gain a powerful relationship to print can the novel again seem fully consequential, as for instance with Toni Morrison's *Beloved*."[25]

This point is well taken and difficult to dispute, even with fascinating, important, and recent exceptions. Trump's presidency, for example, saw publishing houses reprinting George Orwell's *1984* and Sinclair Lewis's *It Can't Happen Here* to a point that even Amazon could not keep up with the demand.[26] Even so, it's not like either Orwell's or Lewis's novels surpass a sixth-grade level. And the Nobel Prize, once an illustrious recognition of world-historical literary writers, mainly novelists, who had their fingers on the pulse of our culture at the given moment and who were also voices of a moral conscience—giants like Thomas Mann, William Faulkner, Jean-Paul Sartre, and Toni Morrison—has recently recognized Bob Dylan and Peter Handke for their work. Dylan is more of a music legend than a literary icon, and Handke defended Milošević's war crimes.

It is difficult to imagine a society in which a demanding novel like *Middlemarch* or *Ulysses* could reach as much of a wide readership if they were published for the first time today as they did in 1871 and 1922, not to mention a work like *In Search of Lost Time*. Would anyone outside of academia bother? The novel is not what it once was, and neither is the novelist. The novelistic word has lost the grip it once had on the world. Maybe it has lost its eros. In a 2009 interview, Philip Roth stated that he didn't believe the novel would survive another twenty-five years due to shortened attention spans; the only readers of novels would belong to a "cultic" minority.[27] Han, who only ever really cites Handke when he veers into the territory of the novel at all—and not in a critical way, but in a way that seems to celebrate his parallels with Heidegger without recognizing just how problematic both figures are in comparison with each other—doesn't seem to recognize the novel as a site of exploring how our society today, stuck in "the inferno of the same," has turned its back on eros, the "atopic Other."[28] And yet he sounds remarkably like D. H. Lawrence when he writes, "In the inferno of the same, the arrival of the atopic Other can assume apocalyptic form. In other words: today, only an apocalypse can liberate—indeed, redeem—us from the inferno of the same, and lead us toward the Other."[29]

Here he presents a romanticized vision of apocalypse, a vision that only makes sense in the kind of universe that the Tristan lovers inhabit, and that Lawrence invokes in *Lady Chatterley's Lover*. In the tradition of apophatic medieval mysticism, Han writes, "Only the negativity of *withdrawal* brings forth the Other in its atopic otherness."[30] But maybe there is something even too optimistic in Han's apocalyptic vision, something too tethered to a Christian metaphysics with its claim to redemption. Even so, this is the only alternative he can imagine to the achievement-society of neoliberalism, the society that rewards every aspect of our being that can be monetized according to our achievement, performance, and ability.

Ours is a society that replaces prohibitions with injunctions of "I can," encouraging an "auto-compulsion" that ultimately leads to "exploitation without domination," and consequently burnout and depression.[31] The only resistance to this ontology is an embrace of apocalyptic eros—and with it, failure: "Eros is a relationship to the Other situated beyond achievement, performance, and ability. *Being able not to be able (Nicht-Können-Können)* represents its negative counterpart."[32] If neoliberal ideology fetishizes success and achievement so much, maybe failure is the only recourse available to us. Han explains that, "A successful relationship with the Other finds expression as a kind of *failure*. Only by way of *being able not to be able* does the Other appear."[33]

FAILURE AS AUTONOMY IN THE WORKPLACE: MELLORS, BARTLEBY, ZARATHUSTRA

What does the erotic potential of "being able not to be able" look like, especially in a world where Big Business has hijacked the rhetoric of eros, exploiting its terminology to sell the myth of happiness for profit? The slogan of WeWork, which could be a slogan of any capitalist corporation, is "Do What You Love." This company ended up laying off 20 percent of its staff, while the CEO Adam Neumann walked away with roughly $1 billion.[34] One must "love" working at an underpaid job that could let you go at a moment's notice. This is the pursuit of happiness.

It is against this hijacked rhetoric of passion, co-opted by the corporate workplace, that the novels of D. H. Lawrence acquire a new sense of urgency today. *Lady Chatterley's Lover* shows what a resuscitation of passion actually looks like and how it represents a force that shields the lovers from "that outside Thing that sparkled viciously in the electric lights," that monolith of industrial capitalism, reducing humans to machines.[35] In their pessimism, though, the lovers know that this shield will not last long. But there is the recognition of a private humanity governed by eros struggling against the forces of dehumanization. The corporate use of the word "passion" is fundamentally dehumanizing; reading Lawrence today wrests the word from the corporate and restores it to the corporeal, breathing new life into the word, but a new life that is also actually ancient and medieval, conjuring up the spirits of the Tristan lovers. As the narrator remarks, it is not just passion in this specific novel, but passion in the novel at large, which, "properly handled, can reveal the most secret places of life: for it is in the *passional* secret places of life, above all, that the tide of sensitive awareness needs to ebb and flow."[36]

In a world where social media and corporate interests like the Big Data firm Acxiom, which promises clients a "360-degree customer view" of nearly 300 million U.S. citizens—officially knowing more about our daily lives than the FBI, to which it sells its information—any sense of, or right to, our own individual interiority feels like an impossibility.[37] But Lawrence carves out this space for us. The novel is one of the last vestiges of interiority that we have left. In 1956, Erich Fromm noted how the "emphasis on team spirit, mutual tolerance and so forth," which are part of the propaganda of Big Business, "is a relatively recent development. It was preceded, in the years after the First World War, by a concept of love in which mutual sexual satisfaction was supposed to be the basis for satisfactory love relations."[38] Lawrence was a key proponent in this specific concept and context of love—a love that is intolerant of what Big Business stands for, a love that rejects "team spirit" for private passion.

While rediscovering passion, both of the body and of the novel, can be one form of resisting the neoliberal pillaging of this world, another response of resistance could be its exact opposite. If employers or other figures of authority demand passion, one way of defending one's sense of interiority is to express passionlessness. This is the stance of Bartleby, who belongs to a work that can be regarded as a failed novel, nowhere near the length of *Moby-Dick*, which Melville had just published, and which had received mild to terrible reviews. While there was so much to say about Captain Ahab, hundreds of pages documenting his passion that became an obsession, the narrator of *Bartleby* laments that "no materials exist for a full and satisfactory biography of this man. It is an irreparable loss to literature."[39] The pessimistic work itself is already announced as a loss, as something incomplete, as a biography or a novel that never was. And in this ghost of a novel, Bartleby is also described as a "ghost" and an "apparition."[40] As if he were all that remained of Melville's broken spirit after the poor reception of *Moby-Dick*, Bartleby is described as "alone, absolutely alone in the universe. A bit of wreck in the mid-Atlantic."[41]

In *Moby-Dick*, Ishmael marvels at the austerity of the whale, asking, "what has the whale to say? Seldom have I known any profound being that had anything to say to this world, unless forced to stammer out something by way of getting a living. Oh! happy that the world is such an excellent listener!"[42] The world of *Bartleby*, though, is not quite so happy, and is not an excellent listener. It doesn't even know how to listen to Bartleby, perhaps this reincarnation of the sublime, "profound being," whose reticence itself is a sign of his profundity. But he is someone "forced to stammer out something by way of getting a living." So he applies for a job as a scrivener, or law-copyist, spending all day transcribing dense, dull, legal prose that is not even his own. His employer, the narrator, makes an implicit comparison between Bartleby and the archetype of Romantic poetry and passion, writing, "I cannot credit that the mettlesome poet Byron would have contentedly sat down with Bartleby to examine a law document of, say, five hundred pages, closely written in a crimped hand."[43] Maybe Bartleby—like Melville himself—was thrown into a world that could not recognize his talents; maybe a Byron was lurking inside him, but could not be noticed by the Wall Street bureaucrats he has to work for. Walled in by Wall Street, Bartleby—all that remains of the profound vision of the White Whale—is rendered inert, staring at a white wall.

Melville attacks optimism and happiness for their cruel, dismissive stance toward suffering: "happiness courts the light, so we deem the world is gay; but misery hides aloof, so we deem that misery there is none."[44] Bartleby, always aloof, finally comes to the point where he says hardly anything else except for, "I would prefer not to."[45] This is the only autonomy he can win for himself, embodying Han's principle of *Nicht-Können-Können* ["Being able to not be able"].[46] By showing up to work and not doing it, but just staring straight at the wall in front of him, he exposes the uselessness and utter meaninglessness of this drudgery, this ritual business and busy-ness of capitalism, of what boils down to what Agamben would call "bare life," or what Heidegger wrote in his letter to his wife about eros, "mere work." Bartleby is the opposite of a D. H. Lawrence character. Whatever passion he may have never rises to the level of expression, but rather takes on the form of radical passivity.

Here we see Bartleby as an unlikely relative of Nietzsche's Zarathustra, emptied of all exuberance and sermonizing, but still abiding by Zarathustra's contempt for the life of hectic work that is somehow supposed to fill the gap of meaninglessness in existence:

> All of you who are in love with hectic work and whatever is fast, new, strange— you find it hard to bear yourselves, your diligence is escape and the will to forget yourself. If you believed more in life, you would hurl yourself less into the moment. But you do not have enough content in yourselves for waiting—not even for laziness![47]

All the self-help nonsense about "living in the moment" shatters to pieces in light of Zarathustra and Bartleby. But Bartleby's autonomy, in Melville's pessimistic vision, is hardly a consolation, and is ultimately stripped away when he is thrown into prison. The fact that he does not fit into the capitalist order of things, the fact that he does not value optimism or productivity or work for the sake of work, makes him a criminal. In the final, puzzling line, the narrator cries out, "Ah Bartleby! Ah humanity!"[48] Here is the pessimistic realization that humanity itself dies with Bartleby, and with people like him. There is no humanity to be found in the optimistic insistence on labor and drudgery, on profits and workplace dynamics. These dynamics are what kill humanity, which is why Leo Marx reads this as a parable not only of Wall Street, but of the walls that Wall Street represents, "the walls which hem in the meditative artist and for that matter every reflective [person]."[49] Life in a world run by Wall Street is reduced to a choice between "submission"—a word used like a leitmotif by Bartleby's co-workers, Nippers, Turkey, and Ginger-Nut (their nicknames also indicative of consumption under capitalism)—and a stance of "I would prefer not to," which eventually leads to prison.

THE PURSUIT OF HAPPINESS

Perhaps the bleakest aspect of Bartleby's stance is that it is a luxury few can afford. There is not only coercion to work but also to perform a masochistic gratitude for this coercion, rooted in the propaganda of the Protestant work ethic, an ontology that dictates how the meaning of one's life is tethered to work—a very useful ideology to benefit your boss at your expense. The performance of happiness is as much an expectation as it is a threat. In 2009, Barbara Ehrenreich noted how toxic positivity was "beginning to be an obligation imposed on all American adults."[50] But on May 16, 2018, *Newsweek* ran an article exposing the fact that optimism was an obligation imposed not only on all American adults, but American children as well:

> Northern Lebanon School District students in Pennsylvania must smile while walking the hallways at the institution or they will be punished, according to a report.
> Students who do not smile in the hallways between periods will be instructed to, and if they refuse, they will be sent to the guidance counselor's office to talk through their problems, reported *Lebanon Daily News*. Meanwhile, parents claim that reports of bullying in the district are mostly ignored by administrators.[51]

This is perhaps the most succinct, microcosmic portrait of how optimism functions. Coinciding with systems of power, it operates by punishment, by bullying, and by pathologizing any traces of dissidence or even just a simple lack of enthusiasm. Or, as William Davies puts it, "a culture which values only optimism will produce pathologies of pessimism."[52] If students fail to comply with the injunction to smile, then they are both blamed and pathologized by this institutional gaslighting, and are sent to the guidance counselor, which does more to inflict psychological harm in this case and interrupt their studies than anything else. Just the thought of seeing teenagers with manic smiles plastered on their faces instead of sulking in a pissed-off way—the affect that is, if not the most natural, at least the most conducive to developing a critical awareness of the world in adolescence—is alarming in itself. Long gone are the days when it actually smelled like teen spirit.

How did we get here? This widespread obsession with optimism, with happiness, with positivity, can be traced back to the foundation of this nation, a nation built on the rhetoric of optimism, a rhetoric weaponized by wealthy white men who could only feel so positive in their outlook on the backs of the enslaved, in land cleared by genocide. Happiness, in fact, was running so high among these men that it was even inscribed into the nation's Declaration of Independence, which gleefully distinguishes American citizens not just from British subjects, but from "merciless Indian savages."[53] This document adopted John Locke's idea that citizens should have rights to "life, liberty, and property," but with a slight modification. The "pursuit of happiness" certainly sounds prettier than "property," but it conceals an ugly motive. In a footnote to *In Defense of Lost Causes*, Slavoj Žižek writes that "the somewhat awkward 'pursuit of happiness'" replaces Locke's idea of a right to property "during negotiations of the drafting of the Declaration, *as a way to negate the black slaves' right to property.*"[54]

In *The Counter-Revolution of 1776: Slave Resistance and the Origins of the United States of America*, the historian Gerald Horne argues that the American Revolution was actually a conservative counter-revolution against the growing movement of abolition in Britain and the colonies, which would have disastrous consequences for the American economy. These white settlers wanted to cut ties with the British Empire so that they could regulate slavery on their own and establish their own separate economy, without having to pay taxes to the Empire. Less than a century later, the Civil War was fought along the same ideological lines, in which the Southern Confederates were defending the same economic system that the American Revolutionaries were defending against the British Empire.

It is no coincidence that, right after the Civil War, new American colleges were established with close ties to the business world, ties that would grow even closer as time wore on. The world's first business school, Wharton Pennsylvania, was established in 1881. "Management," the core principle of business, "originated as a technique for controlling slaves on plantations."[55] In the nominal eradication of slavery in this country, its principles and its strategies nevertheless transitioned perfectly well into the construction of corporate America. Friedrich Engels, who had covered the Civil War as a foreign correspondent for *Die Presse* in Vienna, saw this trend a few decades earlier in England, where he observed that

> the only difference as compared with the old, outspoken slavery is this, that the worker of today seems to be free because he is not sold once and for all, but piecemeal by the day, the week, the year, and because no one owner sells him to another, but he is forced to sell himself in this way instead, being the slave of no particular person, but of the whole property-holding class.[56]

The rage that socialists and communists expressed at this injustice was met with the infuriatingly condescending response of the capitalist class of executives and entrepreneurs. Instead of ameliorating the dismal socioeconomic conditions that have been giving rise to this rage, capitalists instead addressed only the rage itself, paternalistically trying to defuse it with the ideology of happiness as an individual pursuit, selling the mendacious narrative that hard work will be rewarded, and if we all just shut up, get back to work, and quit whining, we'll be happy.

This is the capitalist-to-fascist pipeline that is built on the lie that *Arbeit macht frei*. Adorno recognized

> a straight line of development between the gospel of happiness and the construction of camps of extermination so far off in Poland that each of our own countrymen can convince himself that he cannot hear the screams of pain. That is the model of an unhampered happiness.[57]

That model of unhampered happiness has its origins in American politics more than in German politics. That Hitler took much of his inspiration from American politics after the Civil War, from Manifest Destiny (which he applied to his concept of *Lebensraum*) to the Jim Crow South (which was the model for his racist Nuremberg Laws), is no surprise.[58]

Executives after the Civil War must have lamented that employees were not technically slaves—at least not legally—but the idea that labor would be tethered to one's sense of identity and one's own pursuit of happiness gradually became a job requirement, so that the word "passionate" became a buzzword in job descriptions of every kind, concealing the ideological motivation behind using such a word. If someone is passionate about something, they don't need to be properly compensated for it, since they love doing it anyway.[59] It is not enough simply to get the job done; one must do it with—yet another insidious buzzword of neoliberalism—"gratitude" for the opportunity to devote one's life, one's mind, and one's identity to labor.

Michel Foucault, in fact, cites gratitude as a modern form of acquiescing to punishment in prisons—a literal example of Stockholm Syndrome: "At each visit, a few benevolent words flow from this honest mouth [of the warder] and bring to the heart of the inmate gratitude, hope and consolation; he loves his warder; and he loves him because he is gentle and sympathetic."[60] By the early twentieth century, a businessman named Elton Mayo sought to extend this warder-prisoner relationship to the workplace. Mayo believed that both socialism and workplace dissatisfaction were psychiatric disorders that needed treatment.[61] A worker's happiness is only an issue for the employer if it affects productivity, so instead of making any changes to the unjust working conditions or offering the employees a substantial raise, Mayo suggested fostering a sense of belonging and collaboration to boost morale, which is the root of all the team-building bullshit that pervades corporate culture to this day.[62] On the basis of this idea, Mayo was hired by the Harvard Business School.[63]

This is the same pernicious logic of employers who won't pay a living wage, but offer free yoga sessions or "mindfulness" training to combat stress, or organize "team-building" events or work parties for "fun" at the expense of employees' already limited time outside of work, which is de facto swallowed up by the necessities of bare life: cooking, cleaning, running errands, attending to family obligations. And yet this time is still interrupted by work. We can still be reached and harassed by bosses and co-workers via email, text, phone, or now even the cruelly and ironically titled "Slack" app. Even employers who do offer higher salaries may throw in free gym membership and free counseling, not out of any sense of human benevolence, but only because it meets their bottom line of extracting more labor from their employees, since Gallup has estimated that the unhappiness of employees costs the U.S. economy $500 billion a year in "lost productivity, lost tax receipts, and health-care costs."[64]

At the same time that American universities in the wake of the Civil War began to aggressively operate in collusion with Big Business to promote capitalist interests rather than do what the university was established to do—namely, to provide spaces for people to become critical and informed citizens—education in England took a different turn. The English major was a brand new academic discipline that "was first institutionalized not in the Universities, but in the Mechanics' Institutes, working men's colleges and extension lecturing circuits."[65] English "was literally the poor man's Classics—a way of providing a cheapish 'liberal' education for those beyond the charmed circles of public school and Oxbridge."[66] The emphasis of this new discipline "was on solidarity between the social classes, the cultivation of 'larger sympathies,' the instillation of national pride and the transmission of 'moral' values."[67] What this curriculum included was not only Shakespeare and poetry, but, for the first time, the modern novel—written in a vernacular that was readily accessible to people of all backgrounds and prior levels of education.

The novel was now deemed an item worthy of academic study, and not just a form of cheap entertainment. It was this new form of education that made its way through the poorest mining towns of England, which is how D. H. Lawrence was given the opportunity to study the novel before writing his own. By the time he wrote *Lady Chatterley's Lover* in 1928, the study of English Language and Literature had not only made its way into Oxford and Cambridge, but had become "the most central subject of all," as students and professors increasingly saw in this subject the receptacle of culture and critique in a world that was eroding it with destructive forces.[68]

Just a year before the publication of *Lady Chatterley's Lover*, E. M. Forster gave his famous lectures on the novel at Cambridge, which were then published as *Aspects of the Novel*, to reach a wider audience, encompassing the historical range of the English novel from Richardson and Defoe to his friend Virginia Woolf, who had just published *To the Lighthouse*. To Forster, nothing was more immediate to understanding contemporary culture than the novel, which is why he rejected a chronological interpretation of the novel's development in favor of visualizing "English novelists not as floating down that stream which bears all its sons away unless they are careful, but as seated together in a room, a circular room, a sort of British Museum reading-room—all writing their novels simultaneously."[69] This vision seems not only to evoke the image of the gathering in Plato's *Symposium*, but to modify Schlegel's idea of the novel as that space where "things of the past would live in it in new forms," so that the novel—even in its engagement with the past—is committed, as its name demands, to make it new.[70] Perhaps it is no coincidence that Schlegel makes his way into Forster's *Howards End* as the surname of Margaret and Helen, as well.

Nabokov, who had emigrated from Russia as a result of the Revolution, graduated from Cambridge University with a BA in 1922, the year that was "the dividing line in literary history."[71] It was the year that saw the publication of *Ulysses*, *Jacob's Room*, *Aaron's Rod*, and *Siddhartha*. Proust had just died that year, too, having transformed the novel, and consciousness with it, into a seismograph of modernity. All eyes were on the novel at this time.

Three years later, Woolf published the first edition of *The Common Reader*, a selection of brief essays introducing readers, with an engaging tone and breezy style, to some of the masterpieces in European literature. Without any condescension or scholarly jargon, her essays cover Chaucer and Elizabethan drama, but they overwhelmingly come back to the novel, from Defoe and Austen to the Brontës and George Eliot, even going all the way up to Joseph Conrad, who had just died a year earlier. Woolf saw herself as actively participating in the public life of England as an informal educator, much like Socrates in Athens. And, like the Socrates of *Symposium*, she imagines *The Common Reader* itself as a kind of "tea-table training," inviting her common readers over to relax, eat, and drink, which is a more natural setting to discuss literature than in the formal classroom:

> I see myself handing plates of buns to shy young men and asking them, not directly and simply about their poems and their novels, but whether they like cream as well as sugar. . . . [This] surface manner allows one to say a great many things which would be inaudible if one marched straight up and spoke out.[72]

Woolf was writing *The Common Reader* while working on *To the Lighthouse*, which may explain why Plato's *Symposium* suffuses the entire work. In her essay "Notes on an Elizabethan Play," for example, she writes,

> For we are apt to forget . . . how great a power the body of literature possesses to impose itself: how it will not suffer itself to be read passively, but takes us and reads us; flouts our preconceptions; questions principles which we had got into the habit of taking for granted, and, in fact, splits us into two parts as we read, making us, even as we enjoy, yield our ground or stick to our guns.[73]

If we read correctly, we allow the body of literature to *read us*. And when this body reads us, it is as though this body "splits" our own "into two parts as we read." How do we learn to read correctly? In the casual company of a great mentor, of a Socrates or a Woolf, invited over either to nurse a hangover, like most of the interlocutors in the *Symposium*—or, more modestly, to drink tea. And through this training, we learn how to change our reading habits from the passive to the passionate. And in this passionate mode, we learn how to question "principles which we had got into the habit of taking for granted." Woolf, Lawrence, and Nabokov (not to mention the Brontës, Balzac, Kierkegaard, Proust, and Mann, if not every novelist) all approach the novel in this way: as a form of education, as a form of critique, and as a form of eros. For us common readers, Woolf ignites our eros for the novel just as much as Socrates ignites his common listeners' eros for philosophy.

The study of the novel, then, arises out of an emancipatory effort that recognizes the need for everyone, of all strata of society, to have a right to leisure. And in this leisure, freed from the constraints of the workplace, one could participate in the life of the mind, independent of capitalist forces. It is this sphere where one is most human. The academic collusion with Big Business, however, represents the opposite tendency: people must work as much as possible so that most of their time is swallowed up by labor, leaving them little time or space for thoughtful reflection, which could breed critique—and, by extension, retaliatory political action. A society governed by Big Business treats the subject of literature as a frivolous luxury rather than a central social principle to be explored in ludic freedom. This dismissive stance toward art and literature is by design.

The English and American academic traditions, then, represent opposite poles of what it means to be human. The modern English academic tradition confronts the classism that is built into its culture by centering the study of the novel as an emancipatory act, as a space to explore the meaning of Being outside of capitalist constraints. The modern American academic tradition is predicated on budget cuts to the humanities while increasingly centering the study of business management, that ossification of practices stemming from plantation slavery. Just the absurd notion that one must answer to Big

Business in order to justify the study of the humanities is itself the problem. For centuries, we have seen the case for poetry made by some of the greatest minds, like Sidney and Shelley, naming their tracts as an "Apology" or a "Defense." Maybe what's needed for the novel, instead, is the genre of the attack, the offense, the venomous insult aimed at anyone who dismisses it. This is the instinct that the Marquis de Sade acts on when he answers the utilitarian question, "Of what use are novels?" His exasperated, irate answer is worth quoting at length:

> Of what use, indeed! hypocritical and perverse men, for you alone ask this ridiculous question: they are useful in portraying you as you are, proud creatures who wish to elude the painter's brush, since you fear the results, for the novel is . . . the representation of secular customs, and is therefore, for the philosopher who wishes to understand man, as essential as is the knowledge of history. For the etching needle of history only depicts man when he reveals himself publicly, and then 'tis no longer he: ambition, pride cover his brow with a mask which portrays for us naught but these two passions, and not the man. The novelist's brush, on the contrary, portrays from within . . . seizes him when he drops this mask, and the description, which is far more interesting, is at the same time more faithful. This, then, is the usefulness of novels, O you cold censors who dislike the novel.[74]

In *Lolita*, Nabokov's own sadistic novel of masks, the scene at Beardsley—where headmistress Pratt explains the optimistic school philosophy as "turn[ing] our backs to the fog and squarely fac[ing] the sunshine"—must have struck its initial readers as obviously a moment of absurd humor. This is a school that has gotten rid of "irrelevant topics" like Shakespeare from its curriculum, for a "financially remunerative modern touch."[75] What is unsettling is that this is exactly the direction that education is heading in today.[76]

An optimistic rhetoric of progress, armed with the newest technology, joins the forces of Big Business and Big Data to eviscerate the humanities. The endlessly generating machine of idle chatter that Heidegger distinguished from authentic discourse has now spawned ChatGPT, an algorithmic enterprise that bypasses thought only to regurgitate so many mechanical parodies of what had already been said. A useful tool in business, no doubt—or any other perfunctory endeavor that makes little or no demands on the intellect. But anyone in academia who critiques this cynical and dangerous program is dismissed as a Luddite, or—worse still—is encouraged to use it as a tool in the classroom as a way of fostering what can only end up being the most tedious, hackneyed debates about the draws and limitations of new technology, which just take time away from actually discussing literature itself. I would prefer not to. Soon a degree in English Literature will have eroded into a degree in Data Analysis, and gone will be the days when you could just show up to class with a book and discuss it in depth, without any digital gadgets or distractions or log-ins to accounts of companies that sell your private information. The mandate of a liberal arts education is turning into everything it has tried to ward off, rewarding instant gratification instead of long stretches of time wrestling with difficult texts, sitting with ambiguity, and finding one's own voice. The autonomy that one learned to cultivate through the practice of taking literature seriously, and of reading novels especially, has already dissolved into automation. This is the result of having to answer to Big Business.

"NONSENSE UPON STILTS": BENTHAM'S IDEOLOGY OF HAPPINESS AND HIS ASSAULT ON NARRATIVE

Despite the Civil War, slavery hasn't gone away. During the transatlantic slave trade, 13 million people were captured and sold as slaves between the fifteenth and nineteenth centuries. Today, the UN International Labor Organization estimates that 40.3 million people are living under slavery, often euphemistically referred to as "human trafficking."[77] Slavery, if anything, has become more and more lucrative over the centuries and is central to the functioning of global capital. It is hardly a coincidence that the governments and private interests that perpetuate the rise of slavery are the same ones that are the most aggressive in their discourse of happiness as a matter of policy, like the United Arab Emirates.[78] Its Minister of Happiness, Ohood Al Roumi, told CNN that the role of the country was "to create an environment where people can flourish—can reach their potential—and choose to be happy."[79]

There's not much of a choice, though, when choice itself is stripped away, and when subversive expression is punished. The 2019 Human Rights Watch World Report has documented its "sustained assault on freedom of expression and association," in addition to its dismal labor laws, discrimination on the basis of sex and gender, sexual orientation, and permission by law of domestic violence, in addition to its widespread sex trafficking.[80] Those who can ostensibly "choose" to be happy are the ones wealthy and lucky enough to live outside of slavery or exploitation while benefiting from it.

This rhetoric of "choosing" to be happy, instead of seeing happiness as what its term originally meant—as something that just happens—is endemic to the global politics of conservatism as a way of deflecting from systemic injustices that benefit the wealthy.[81] This is why conservatives like David Cameron and Nicholas Sarkozy also "ordered their respective national statistics bureau to start gathering information on people's happiness. The idea was to introduce the concept of Gross Happiness Product (GHP) as an indicator that went beyond Gross National Product (GNP)."[82] These conservative practices are bolstered by so-called "research," such as a report published in a 2017 issue of *Social Science Research*, in which social scientists like Jonathan Kelley and M.D.R. Evans can actually get away with writing, "In developing countries, inequality if anything increases happiness. This suggests that current efforts by such agencies as the World Bank directed towards reducing income inequality are potentially harmful to the well-being of the citizens of poor countries."[83] The discourse of happiness, or the pursuit of happiness, allows governments to place the blame of its predatory policies on its own citizens (or subjects), insisting that individuals ought to turn critique inward to themselves in order to find happiness instead of critiquing the government for systemic failures that threaten their livelihoods, if not their lives.

This inversion, or perversion, of critique is what serves as the ideological basis of what William Davies calls "the happiness industry," a confluence of economic, medical, and political interventions that violate individual autonomy in the name of happiness, well-being, and positivity.[84] In *Eros and Civilization*, Marcuse notes how this industry "alters the contents of happiness" itself so that the

> individual does not really know what is going on; the overpowering machine of education and entertainment unites him with all the others in a state of anaesthesia from which all detrimental ideas tend to be excluded. And since knowledge of the whole truth is hardly conducive to happiness, such general anaesthesia makes individuals happy.[85]

Against the anesthetic is the aesthetic; against the political imperatives of happiness and optimism is the novel as a site of pessimism. Whereas the happiness industry operates by inspection, the novel provides a space for introspection. As the English translator of Foucault notes in *Discipline and Punish*, "Jeremy Bentham used the term 'inspect'—which Foucault translates as '*surveiller*' in the French title *Surveiller et punir*."[86] Introspection is done by the subject on itself; inspection is done by another as an act of subjection and subjugation. Foucault identifies Bentham's vision of the Panopticon as a key shift in our understanding of modern subjectivity. "Modernity," to Foucault, "is characterized by a shift in penal justice."[87] We cannot understand who we are as modern subjects without understanding the rise of modern technologies in surveillance and punishment.

To Nancy Armstrong, "the history of the novel and the history of the modern subject are, quite literally, one and the same."[88] Foucault's *Discipline and Punish*, then, can be read as a parallel history of the novel. In describing Bentham's Panopticon, he notes how a "real subjection is born mechanically from a fictitious relation," and how the Panopticon itself was a "way of defining power relations in terms of the everyday life of men."[89] It works in a "diffused, multiple, polyvalent way throughout the whole social body" as though performing a Bakhtinian kind of heteroglossia.[90] Modernity is characterized by the minute attention that surveillance gives to the lives of its subjects in average everydayness, which is why the novel best captures this experience. As psychiatry rose as a discipline to enforce punishment and docility, it also engaged a new form of writing: "For a long time ordinary individuality—the everyday individuality of everybody—remained below the threshold of description. To be looked at, observed, described in detail, followed from day to day by an uninterrupted writing was a privilege."[91] And finally, Foucault explicitly makes the connection between the history of modern punishment and the rise of the novel himself:

> the normal took over from the ancestral, and measurement from status, thus substituting for the individuality of the memorable man that of the calculable man, that moment when the sciences of man became possible is the moment when a new technology of power and a new political anatomy of the body were implemented. And if from the early Middle Ages to the present day the 'adventure' is an account of individuality, the passage from the epic to the novel, from the noble deed to the secret singularity, from long exiles to the internal search for childhood, from combats to phantasies, it is also inscribed in the formation of a disciplinary society.[92]

This is how the intersection of the genre of the anatomy with the criminal biography gives rise to the modern novel, a genre that both reflects and resists new forms of authority. Anatomy itself began to fork into two distinct directions—the largely pessimistic narrative that would become the novel on the one hand, and the scientific endeavor of optimism on the other. Bacon used the modern innovations of anatomy as a metaphor for his project in *The New Organon*, a project that optimistically aimed to encompass all knowledge and "remov[e] . . . despair" through scientific methods and machinery, inaugurating the tradition that Bentham would later inherit.[93]

The legibility of the body for signs of criminality is the impetus for modern practices of punishment, from Bentham's fantasy of the Panopticon to the photographic genre of mug shots. In *The Novel and the Police*, D. A. Miller sees the "novelistic techniques of 'panoptic narration' [as] normaliz[ing] a sophisticated process of surveillance with which the reader is made complicit," and Gérard Genette also speaks of "an omniscient narrator, capable like God himself of seeing beyond actions and of sounding body and soul."[94] Both of these views echo Ian Watt, who compares characters' minds to their domestic spaces, allowing the reader to survey the contents of both.[95] But Yi-Ping Ong cites other critics, like Jonathan Culler and Ann Banfield, who disagree with this thesis.[96] To Culler, this is just "a fantasy of omniscience, which ... oppresses at the same time that it obfuscates the narrative effects that lead us to posit it."[97]

By the time we get to *Lolita*, even the first-person narrator aspires but fails to achieve omniscient narration, laying bare the blind spots of so-called "panoptic narration." But even a century earlier, in Ivan Turgenev's *Fathers and Sons*, the narrator—who, for lack of a better word, is "omniscient"—hardly presumes to know what's going on in Bazarov's mind, writing, "God knows where his thoughts wandered," and instead just describes the "expression on his face," which "was intense and gloomy."[98] One could even argue that in novels like *The Portrait of a Lady*, Isabel Archer resists the novelist's narration of key moments in her life. James thematizes power itself on the level of the narrative, a power that even an omniscient narrator has no access to. *Bartleby*, too, is a work that fundamentally could not be told by any kind of omniscient narrator, which is why Melville narrates it from the first-person voice of Bartleby's former employer. The text revolves around Bartleby's inaccessible interiority, the one space he has left for himself in a world dictated by Wall Street.

If anything, we can read the novel as a site of resistance against panopticism. Bentham, the "Enlightenment optimist and modernizer" responsible for the panopticon, hated descriptive language just as much as he hated the idea of human rights.[99] "Natural rights is simple nonsense," he wrote, "natural and imprescriptable rights, rhetorical nonsense—nonsense upon stilts."[100] The problem of politics, in his mind, was that it was built on such stilts, and it dwelled too much in what he called "the tyranny of sounds"—description, abstraction, metaphysics, rhetoric.

He inherited this distrust of language from Bacon, who wrote in his *New Organon* that words have "rendered philosophy and the sciences sophistical and inactive."[101] Words for Bacon "stand in the way," and "even definitions cannot cure this evil in dealing with natural and material things, since the definitions consist of words, and those words beget others."[102] This is the problem with all prior philosophy to him, beginning with Aristotle, which has been a practice that can only ever "affirm something positive in words, than about the inner truth of things."[103] The problem with words, specifically, is that they have too much of an ambiguously wide semantic field of possible meaning, and "will not bear to be reduced to any constant meaning."[104] Language is fundamentally too ambiguous, too *zweideutig*, to be the proper conduit for either knowledge or happiness.

Bacon's project, ironically through language itself, is to liberate "human thought" from the "bondslave of words."[105] But Bentham goes further, wanting to establish a politics that would do away with all of that altogether, a politics that would replace language with science. He therefore is the "inventor of what has since come to be known as 'evidence-based policy-making,' the idea that government interventions can be cleansed of any moral or ideological principles, and be guided purely by facts and figures."[106] It is because of Bentham that a policy is either proposed or eliminated based on a cost-benefit analysis.[107]

Dickens, who used the novel as a way to leverage critique against the status quo, satirizes Bentham and his data-fetishist followers in his novel *Hard Times*, which begins with Superintendent Thomas Gradgrind insisting that,

> Now, what I want is, Facts. Teach these boys and girls nothing but Facts. Facts alone are wanted in life. Plant nothing else, and root out everything else. You can only form the minds of reasoning animals upon Facts: nothing else will ever be of any service to them. This is the principle on which I bring up my own children, and this is the principle on which I bring up these children. Stick to Facts, sir![108]

In response to this command, the

> speaker, and the schoolmaster, and the third grown person present, all backed up a little, and swept with their eyes the inclined plane of little vessels then and there arranged in order, ready to have imperial gallons of facts poured into them.[109]

What Dickens exposes about Bentham is that there is no room for the human in utilitarian philosophy. Humans are either "reasoning animals" or "vessels" who view "facts" as ideologically neutral: "What is called Taste, is only another name for Fact."[110] It makes sense for someone who espouses this philosophy to be such a disciplinarian. Even Gradgrind's face is described as "utilitarian, matter-of-fact."[111] Dickens often slips into sentimental territory, but he satirically nails the Benthamite spirit when Gradgrind only accepts, as a definition of a horse, the following answer from one of his pupils: "Quadruped. Graminivorous. Forty teeth, namely twenty-four grinders, four eye-teeth, and twelve incisive. Sheds coat in the spring; in marshy countries, sheds hoofs, too. Hoofs hard, but requiring to be shod with iron."[112]

In addition to Louisa and Thomas, Gradgrind has three other children, one of whom is hilariously named Adam Smith, and the other Malthus, named after the thinkers who, along with Bentham, privileged data and statistics over any other form of knowledge. He walks Louisa through the "statistics of marriage, so far as they have yet been obtained, in England and Wales" of age disparity between partners when suggesting that Louisa marry Bounderby.[113] As though writing in response to Gradgrind, Bentham, and his like, Nietzsche exclaims in frustration, "And way up at the top, where the great minds are, you no longer can make any calculations at all: when, for example, have great artists ever gotten married! You are hopeless, you who want to discover a law in this."[114]

It is from the viewpoint of the novel that Benthamite philosophy comes into relief, exposed for the ridiculous, reductive, and damaging tenets that it upholds. Iterations of Thomas Gradgrind get reincarnated through the history of the novel after Bentham, leading up to Woolf's gently mocking portrait of Mr. Ramsay as someone who sternly believes that everyone "should be aware from childhood that life is difficult; facts uncompromising."[115] We also see this figure in Dr. Sloper from Henry James's *Washington Square*, who "cares for nothing but facts; he must be met by facts!"[116] Dr. Sloper, armed with facts, prides himself on "dividing people into classes, into types."[117] Perhaps this is why his own daughter Catherine is the source of so much frustration, because he cannot quite classify her. He hardly even knows who she is, from his scientific perspective. He speaks of his convictions as "geometrical propositions," and says that "Catherine and her young man are my surfaces; I have taken their measure."[118] Just as Gradgrind stands for "the necessity of infinite grinding at the mill of knowledge," in Dr. Sloper's name we can discern his perspective as one that looks down the slope of his geometric scheme from his wealthy position to condescend to Morris Townsend and to keep his daughter under control.[119]

The issue is that Catherine resists this control with a passivity that aligns her with Bartleby. No one quite knows how to read her or how to access her interiority. Like Bartleby, she also appears as a "ghost," and maybe even the opposite of a ghost: "though you are still here in body, you are already absent in spirit."[120] Whether she is described as a spirit with no body or a body with no spirit, she is not fully realized or imagined; there is a vacuous space of character that all the surrounding characters struggle to fill in and control but are unable to. She is therefore a "disappointment" to her father, who thinks that she is "about as intelligent as the bundle of shawls," but her intelligence may reside precisely in the fact that she is able to elude his scientific scrutiny.[121] Who she is as a person cannot be measured, counted, and accounted for. It can only be recounted. When her suitor Morris Townsend tells Dr. Sloper that she "seems to me quite her own mistress," he responds, "Literally, she is."[122]

What Dickens, James, and Woolf demonstrate, in the wake of Benthamism, is what Melville and Lawrence also engage in their treatment of the novel. The novel is a space that turns Bentham on his head; humans—and the meaning we create—cannot be reduced to mere data and facts. Anyone who subscribes to utilitarianism in the novel is seen as woefully comical in their limited pursuit of a highly specified and inconsequential kind of knowledge. Even a sympathetically sketched character like Bazarov in *Fathers and Sons* cannot sustain the curious combination of nihilism and positivism throughout the entire novel. When visiting his friend Arkady's home, he arrogantly tells Arkady's father, Pavel Petrovich, "We act on the basis of what we recognize as useful."[123]

But all of his fetishism of utility and his scientific experiments do not bring him any closer to knowledge than his frustrated experience of eros, which destabilizes and dissolves his rigid ideological beliefs, as though eros itself were performing an anatomy of his soul, however much he wants to ignore it by performing his own anatomy of the body, carrying out an autopsy on a corpse without taking proper precaution, and contracting typhus as a result. This most nihilistic and utilitarian character dies with a "passionate, sinful, rebellious . . . heart."[124] This is the same passion that Lispector's G.H. eventually realizes in her disavowal of facts for something else:

> G.H. had lived a good bit, by which I mean, had lived many facts. Perhaps I was in some kind of rush to live everything there was to live all at once so I'd have time left over to . . . to live without facts? to live . . . and be free to go in search of my tragedy.[125]

The pessimism comes in, however, because the world largely adopted by Bentham's philosophy renders the novel inconsequential. As Adorno lamented, "Anything that is not reified, cannot be counted and measured, ceases to exist."[126] A figure whom Bentham influenced greatly was the mechanical engineer Frederick Winslow Taylor, the world's first management consultant. Born into wealth, he never had to work under toil, but he enjoyed watching and inspecting others who did, measuring their accuracy and efficiency of output.[127] He anatomized labor into an increasingly minute series of tasks, each one subject to scrutiny, turning micromanagement into a nightmarish science of precision, and viewing laborers as nothing more than machines.[128]

This becomes central not only to the history of labor and management (establishing the foundation for notoriously ruthless consulting firms like McKinsey & Co., Accenture, and Price Waterhouse Cooper, as well as the horrendously inhumane treatment of Amazon warehouse workers), but to the history of the novel. Yevgeny Zamyatin satirized Taylorism in the first dystopian novel of the twentieth century, *We*—which would later influence *Brave New World* and *1984*. Set in the distant future, the protagonist D-503 writes of a world governed entirely by the principles of Taylor, with the ultimate aim of achieving a "Taylorized happiness" through a reduction of human experience to mere data that is constantly being monitored.[129] Early in the novel, D-503 writes about Taylor as the founding thinker of his civilization:

> No doubt about it, that Taylor was *the* genius of antiquity. True, it never finally occurred to him to extend his method over the whole of life, over every step you take right around the clock. He wasn't able to integrate into his system the whole spread from hour 1:00 to hour 24:00. But still, how could they write whole libraries about someone like Kant and hardly even notice Taylor—that prophet who could see ten centuries ahead?[130]

It is no coincidence that this Taylorist society, also known as OneState, had consolidated its power by attempting to eradicate eros. D-503 explains that, "OneState mounted an attack on that other ruler of the world, Love. Finally, this element was also conquered, i.e. organized, mathematicised."[131] This is the de-eroticization of love that Han analyzes in *The Agony of Eros* as the current state of our own reality, not some dystopian fiction. Love itself is something that has been "organized, mathematicised" into algorithms that profit dating apps, symptomatic of the general way in which all life experiences are now re-organized into data-driven models under late capitalism. Both Zamyatin and Han demonstrate, in a novel and in a work of theory respectively, how eros is incompatible with a society that fetishizes data.

It logically follows that such a society is averse to narrative as well. The "greatest of all monuments of ancient literature that has come down to us," D-503 says, is "the *Railroad Timetable*."[132] He even exclaims, "Thank goodness . . . the antediluvian times of all those Shakespeares and Dostoevskys, or whatever you call them, are over."[133] We see this same dismissal of literature not only at Beardsley in *Lolita*, but in the current push for STEM education at the expense of the humanities. Education, in its push for a ubiquitous online presence, and now with the advent of ChatGPT, has turned into content creation and data points, prefigured by Zamyatin's imaginary classrooms where robots teach the students.[134] The absurdity of Zamyatin's novel is turning into a passively accepted reality. His novel has been traditionally read as a mere historical artifact of sorts in its critique of communism, but it reads today more as a nightmarish vision of what capitalism has become.

Even the imaginative space of Zamyatin's dystopia coincides with the architectural space of contemporary corporations with their sterile aesthetics. The auditorium that the protagonist D-503 attends is an "immense sunlit hemisphere composed of massive glass sections," and the "Benefactor" of this cultish society lives in "the Cube," a monolithic structure made of glass.[135] It is worth noting that the flagship Apple retail store on Fifth Avenue in New York, with its all-glass exterior, is also referred to as "the Cube."[136] The technology and devices it sells, dependent on sweatshop labor, are designed for use in all aspects of life, from work to leisure, so that it becomes increasingly difficult to escape its reach as it monitors us, converting the data we generate into corporate profits. The optics of transparency conceal a politics of opacity.

As in the novel, the Taylorist ideology behind this panoptic surveillance is masked with the rhetoric of empowerment, joy, and happiness.

Questioning this happiness, or even the attempt to hold corporate authorities accountable for the lies they perpetrate, is met with harsh retaliation, which is something that is true both of Zamyatin's fictional *We* and Adam Neumann's company WeWork, where he replaced the term "CEO" with the gimmicky "C-We-O." One member of WeWork, Justin Zhen, had published a blog post—using publicly available data—about the rate at which WeWork members were leaving the company. Within hours of publishing the blog post, he received an email from a WeWork community manager requesting that he take it down; after he ignored the email, the manager followed up with a notice that Zhen had "violated our membership happiness clause," and that he had half an hour to evacuate the WeWork premises.[137]

The problem is that there are few spaces left, if any, to evacuate from this Taylorist ideology, which is not limited to WeWork, but saturates all of corporate (and even much of non-corporate) culture. Happiness is wielded as a threat, as a punitive measure to keep its subjects in line, on pain of losing their livelihood. The threat has a panoptic reach, thanks to digital technology. And because of the threat of not obeying this perverse model of a Taylorist happiness, we are forced to live in a world where the dystopia of *We* becomes the reality of a WeWork, where eros becomes sublimated into the command "Do What You Love," where corporate culture is poised to wipe out culture itself, leaving in its wake only a massive cult—a blind devotion to efficiency and productivity instead of a life of meaning and critical reflection outside of the confines of labor. To Aldous Huxley, "The right to the pursuit of happiness is nothing else than the right to disillusionment phrased in another way."[138] But maybe even "disillusionment" is too mild to describe the actual effects of not conforming to this model of happiness, as it had descended from Taylor, Jefferson, Bentham, and Bacon.

One should not forget that the guiding principle of Bentham's political philosophy is happiness, which he had learned from Bacon's "new philosophy" of "the removing of despair and the raising of hope through the dismissal or rectification of the errors of past time." To Bacon, "Truth . . . and utility are . . . the very same things."[139] But he also took this utilitarian understanding of truth and happiness from the English religious reformer and founder of the Unitarian Church, Joseph Priestley. Priestley had written that, "The good and happiness of the members, that is, the majority of the members, of any state, is the great standard by which everything relating to that state must finally be determined."[140] This is the birth of utilitarianism, and in Bentham's mind, all happiness could be reduced to the economy of pleasure and pain. The free market would be responsible for pleasure, and his proposal of the Panopticon prison, a circular structure in which every subject would be viewable at all times by a central tower, would address the pain of society. Instead of the "tyranny of sounds," Bentham proposed an actual tyranny, something that Napoleon would fantasize about:

> [Napoleon] wished to arrange around him a mechanism of power that would enable him to see the smallest event that occurred in the state he governed; he intended, by means of the rigorous discipline that he imposed, "to embrace the whole of this vast machine without the slightest detail escaping his attention."[141]

This is the groundwork of totalitarianism, one that demands absolute docility, obedience, and happiness.

Everything in Bentham's totalitarian vision of happiness would be reduced to calculation and science; any nuance provided by description would be rendered superfluous. This is the fulfillment of Bacon's Renaissance dream to guide the mind "at every step" away from despair, "and the business be done as if by machinery."[142] William Davies traces a frightening genealogy of influence from Bentham through the history of economics, medicine, and politics, which all demonstrate a suspicion of language and narrative, favoring numerical figures instead. At the doctor's office, you are given a scale of 1 to 10 to indicate pain—as though this scale were any more accurate than an attempt at describing one's particular experience with language. Neuroscientists like Martin Lindstrom make careers out of the notion that "people lie, but brains don't."[143] Facial recognition software now detects smiles as an indicator of happiness.[144] (But how would it detect an axe-wielding Jack Nicholson smiling in *The Shining*?). "Happiness science" has now emerged on the premise that happiness can be located in the brain, and that the nucleus accumbens is what triggers decisions to buy a product.[145]

What parades as cutting-edge science on this front is no more of an advance than those Renaissance barber-surgeons who were poking around the human anatomy in search of the soul. It would be comical if it didn't have such sinister repercussions. "Why would anyone believe that, in our fundamental biological nature," Davies asks, "we operate like accounting machines? The answer is simple: to rescue the discipline of economics and, with it, the moral authority of money."[146] This moral authority of money is a view popularized by the "Chicago School" of economics, which, like Bentham, viewed all human behavior through statistics instead of description, and believed that there is nothing morally wrong with hoarding as much wealth as possible at the expense of other people's survival.[147] Money is equated with happiness, so more money would equal more happiness to whoever has it. Milton Friedman, who had advised Pinochet on economic matters, wrote in the *New York Times* that the single moral duty of a corporation is to make as much money as possible.[148]

Gary Becker, also of the Chicago School, came up with the term "human capital," a "concept that has helped shape and justify the privatization of higher education through demonstrating that individuals receive a monetary return from 'investment' in their skills."[149] The entire student loan crisis today can be traced back to this lie. For all their fetishization of "facts" and data, economists who are blinded by this ideology—the same economists influencing policy—ignore the overwhelming data that proves there is little monetary return from "investment" in skills today, but just the opposite. Our generation is worse off financially than the previous generation for the first time since the Great Depression precisely because of issues like student loans, but we are somehow the ones to blame for this policy we had no hand in shaping. But this was the plan all along for these Chicago School economists. American education was never about equality or opportunity, but rather about solidifying class lines and rewarding the already wealthy by punishing those who are already financially precarious.

This is not to mention the wider problem that money itself is a fictional entity, abiding by a made-up narrative authored every day on Wall Street and in government treasuries. The values that are arbitrarily and magically assigned to commodities, services, and any area of lived experience that could be exploited under neoliberalism is a fantasy that is rendered a reality only by the agreement of the wealthy in positions of power and enforceable by police and even military intervention. But there is nothing natural about this value. The paradox of this Benthamite tradition is that it rejects language and novels as fiction, while scripting a fiction of its own, forcing the rest of us to live by its artificial terms. The fictional "truth" expressed by money evokes Nietzsche's definition of truth, but in reverse: "Truths are illusions which we have forgotten are illusions; they are metaphors that have become worn out and have been drained of sensuous force, coins which have lost their embossing and are now considered as metal and no longer as coins."[150] The fiction of money is that we are expected to treat it as coins rather than metal—and not even that anymore, but some kind of immaterial, digital fantasy of finance.

A PEDAGOGY OF PESSIMISM

"'We invented happiness,' say the last men, and they blink"—thus spoke Zarathustra.[151] In Malcolm Gladwell's bestseller *Blink*, the nauseating subtitle of which is *The Power of Thinking Without Thinking*, he rehashes the positive psychology mantra of conditioning one's mind to make good choices on the spur of the moment. Or something like that. He even cites a psychologist, à la Thomas Gradgrind, who can supposedly tell whether a marriage will last within minutes of meeting a couple. This is the level of stupidity that our culture has sunk to. The inventors of happiness, as Nietzsche saw it, may very well be the "last men," the last inhabitants of this earth, blinking at the white light of nuclear annihilation or irreparable climate change. It seems almost silly to invoke the novel as a form of resistance to such catastrophic forces looming over the horizon. The fact that it may articulate a critique, or a rant, or an exposure of dire circumstances, may be a mild palliative in this dangerously optimistic culture that values happiness more than justice.

In a 2008 issue of *Wired*, Chris Anderson gleefully proclaimed, in a way that seemed to ventriloquize the specter of Bentham haunting the whole world, that "every theory of human behavior" has no meaning—the only thing that matters is data, because, "With enough data, the numbers speak for themselves."[152] The problem is that numbers do not, in fact, speak for themselves. They don't even speak at all. As Han reminds us, "There is no such thing as *data-driven* thinking. Only calculation is data-driven. The negativity of the incalculable is inscribed in thinking. As such, it is prior and superordinate to 'data.'"[153] Theory is the space of negativity that provides a clearing for thought.

Heidegger made this point in "What is Metaphysics?", a work that examines the role of the sciences in the academic institution. Tauntingly, and with some wry humor, he writes:

> The nothing—what else can it be for science but an outrage and a phantasm? If science is right, then only one thing is sure: science wishes to know nothing of the nothing. Ultimately this is the scientifically rigorous conception of the nothing. We know it, the nothing, in that we wish to know nothing about it.[154]

Dasein, of course, "is" nothing. So to take the scientific prejudice of not wanting to investigate the nothing is to say that you don't want to know anything about the meaning of Being—that is to say, anything about us, about who we are. Since we are the ones doing the investigating, aggressively avoiding this blind spot is anti-intellectual and counter to the role of the university. Science, then, ought to be a branch of the humanities, rather than what is happening today with the humanities being increasingly annexed to the sciences, filtered through the narrow lens of positivism and data analysis. In "What Calls for Thinking?" Heidegger is more blunt:

> Science does not think. This is a shocking statement. Let the statement be shocking, even though we immediately add the supplementary statement that nonetheless science always and in its own fashion has to do with thinking. That fashion, however, is genuine and consequently fruitful only after the gulf has become visible that lies between thinking and the sciences, lies there unbridgeably. There is no bridge here—only the leap.[155]

Heidegger counters the positivism of science with the negativity of theory. This is not a polemical position for him, but an ontological one.[156] He is not opposed to science, but to scientism, to the privileging of science and statistics as a way of accessing the most meaningful truths, a prejudice that has only become more and more ingrained with the data revolution. All inquiry must begin with the nothing: "We assert that the nothing is more originary than the 'not' and negation."[157] Since the nothing is the foundation of all knowledge, this is where all academic study, research, and instruction ought to proceed from:

> Only because the nothing is manifest in the ground of Dasein can the total strangeness of beings overwhelm us. Only when the strangeness of beings oppresses us does it arouse and evoke wonder. Only on the ground of wonder—the manifestness of the nothing—does the "why?" loom before us. Only because the "why" is possible as such can we in a definite way inquire into the grounds and ground things. Only because we can question and ground things is the destiny of our existence placed in the hands of the researcher.[158]

Positivism cannot address this "why," this inquiry into the way things are. Only a discipline paradoxically grounded in the nothing can. To Han, this negativity takes on the form of theory, which he specifies is a form of narration as opposed to data accumulation. "As highly selective *narration*, it cuts a clearing of differentiation through untrodden terrain."[159]

Fundamentally opposed to the positivism of science and Big Data, narration is what links the novel to theory. Even E. M. Forster explains the title of his own work on novel theory, *Aspects of the Novel*, by embracing the fact that the word "Aspects" is "unscientific and vague."[160] Here he seems to draw on Friedrich Schiller, who at the end of the eighteenth century was already lamenting in *On the Aesthetic Education of Man* how "the frontiers of Art are contracted as the boundaries of science are enlarged," in an age when "Necessity is master, and bends a degraded humanity beneath its tyrannous yoke."[161] Art is what breaks this yoke and offers us a vision of political freedom. Echoing both Schiller and Schlegel, Forster argues that this "unscientific and vague" approach to the novel is something to be championed, "because it leaves us the maximum of freedom, because it means both the different ways we can look at a novel and the different ways a novelist can look at his work."[162] The novel explores freedom through its innovation of form, just as much as Han sees theory as conferring "*form* on the world"—which, in itself, reiterates Lukács's point in *Theory of the Novel*.[163]

Data just represents an accumulation of information. But after "a certain point, information ceases to be informative. It becomes deformative. Likewise, communication stops being communicative; henceforth, it is only cumulative."[164] Where theory and narration confer form, information overload ultimately deforms. Michael Butor, "the representative of the *nouveau roman* in France," writes of a "literary crisis" in which the "tremendous noise" caused by the "new means of communication" and its emergent technologies is drowning out literature.[165] Since thinking for Han, as it is for Butor and Heidegger, is "an expedition into quietness," it is fundamentally opposed to the "tremendous noise" generated by the information overflow of digital technology.[166] "Clearly, digital communication is destroying quiet and calm."[167]

The aspiration of Big Data is "making it possible to predict human behavior. This means that the future is becoming calculable and controllable. . . . Big Data has announced the end of the *person* who possesses free will."[168] This is why it fuels a new kind of totalitarian politics that twentieth-century tyrants could only dream of. Does the end of the novel, as Arac defines it, coincide with Nancy Armstrong's observation that "the history of novel and the history of the modern subject are quite literally one and the same"?[169] Is that history over? Has it been subsumed by Big Data? If not, it is well on its way.

The neoliberal politics of Big Data "seduces the soul; it preempts it in lieu of opposing it. It carefully protocols desires, needs, and wishes instead of 'depatterning' them. By means of calculated prognoses, it anticipates actions—and acts ahead of them instead of cancelling them out."[170] The Greeks had a term for "seduction of the soul": *psychagogia*, which is also the literal definition of *education*, its Latin root *ducere* signifying that one's soul is being led. This is what Socrates lambasted the sophists for. They bewitched and seduced the souls of people who weren't critical enough to discern the truth. But the only way he could fight against this seduction was to provide a seduction of his own, an education of his own, to lure the young men of Athens into another kind of love, a love of wisdom, of philosophy against sophistry. This is the same strategy he uses in *The Republic*, to "chant this argument we are making to ourselves as a countercharm, taking care against falling back again into this love."[171]

Big Data seduces without eros, thereby eroding the logos as well.[172] Maybe we are not so much seduced by Big Data as numbed by it, or, as Heidegger would say, "tranquillized." That is what numbers do—they numb. One would think that academia would be one of the last bastions for us to take seriously thought itself—which, in Han's terms, amounts to theory as narration, and which would also set up barriers against Big Data. The study of the novel, then, would be crucial to education. Outside of academia, it is increasingly more difficult to hold on to this promise of education. If you are working several jobs to barely make ends meet, chances are that you don't have time to indulge in a novel, which is part of the design of this neoliberal machinery—to extract as much labor, as much profit, as possible from its subjects, even in their leisure time, or to exhaust them so much that they can't use their leisure for the kind of attention and stimulation demanded by the novel. The more we are numbed and dumbed down, or threatened on the pain of losing employment, the easier it is for our society to slip out of the practice of critical thought and fall instead for the kind of facile sloganeering that, in the past, gained traction in the universities and ended in atrocities.

Eagleton reminds us that the rise of studying literature at the university, beyond just the classics, emerged out of a deep-seated social mission at the end of the nineteenth century:

> George Gordon, early Professor of English Literature at Oxford, commented in his inaugural lecture that "England is sick, and . . . English literature must save it. The Churches (as I understand) having failed, and social remedies being slow, English literature has now a triple function: still, I suppose, to delight and instruct us, but also, and above all, to save our souls and heal the State."[173]

Gordon's message may come off as trite, as overly Romantic, but I believe that pessimists today—being failed Romantics, which explains our disappointment—would agree with the diagnosis, and agree even with the proposed cure, but wouldn't believe that this cure will actually work now. The fact that we continue to do our criminally underpaid work, showing up to our classes with this cure that has long since passed its expiration date, is just a testament to our embrace of the absurd, or, at best, a Gramscian pessimism of the intellect and optimism of the will—a phrase actually coined by the novelist Romain Rolland. This is a pessimism that cannot be confused with nihilism.

It was precisely Gordon's mission that, by the 1930s, made English "not just one discipline among many but the most central subject of all, immeasurably superior to law, science, politics, philosophy, or history."[174] There's not much hope of that happening again anytime soon. Our society today is also sick, sick with Big Data. And in the business model of the university, there is an increasing pressure to treat students as customers rather than global citizens, and to subordinate academic pursuits to matters of customer service, all under the guise of "student-centered" learning, which, like any other model of customer service, ultimately devolves into mollifying whoever is loudest, most petulant, and most aggressive.

What if the center was the work of art, rather than any neoliberal appeal to the narcissism of the reader? The novel has long been recognized as the rebellious champion of average everydayness against snobby elitism, written for ordinary readers. But the politics of this art form, while ostensibly democratic, can easily slip into fascism, appealing to a dangerous folksy populism. This is perhaps why Mann uses the novel to push it in the opposite direction, using Zeitblom as his mouthpiece in *Doctor Faustus* to write:

> Art is intellect, mind, and spirit, which has no need whatever to feel obligated to society, to the community—dare not do so, in my opinion, for the sake of its freedom, of its nobility. Art that "joins the *volk*," that makes the needs of the crowd, of the average man, of small minds, its own, will end in misery, and such needs will become a duty, for the sake of the state perhaps; to allow only the kind of art that the average man understands is the worst small-mindedness and the murder of mind and spirit. It is my conviction that the intellect can be certain that in doing what most disconcerts the crowd, in pursuing the most daring, unconventional advances and explorations, it will in some highly indirect fashion serve man—and in the long run, all men.[175]

The name "Zeitblom" can be translated as "the flower of the time," and Zeitblom here is very much that flower, but in the sense that Schiller instructs us all to be flowers of our time: "Live with your century, but do not be its creature; render to your contemporaries what they need, not what they praise."[176] Fascist, reactionary mobs will never praise what they need. The kind of pursuit of art that Schiller and Mann are engaged in is one that is always on the side of actual freedom, not what demagogues will claim is freedom, desecrating that word as indeed all anti-intellectuals have a deliberate way of desecrating language, hijacking words away from their meanings.

Schiller wrote *On the Aesthetic Education of Man* in 1793, at the height of the Reign of Terror. This treatise isn't an escapist, whimsical foray into trivialities but the result of seeing just how delicate political freedom is, and how tyranny is inextricably tied to the worship of utility, which is why art, encountered in the free play of the imagination, is a political category for him, and "is closely related to the better portion of our happiness."[177] He is disturbed how, "*Utility* is the great idol of the age, to which all powers must do service and all talents swear allegiance. In these clumsy scales the spiritual service of Art has no weight."[178] The kind of pessimism that emerges from this Romanticism is one that counters utility with futility.

It is the novel for Mann that becomes the receptacle not only of his pessimism but also of the limits of that pessimism. In the wake of the Second World War and the Holocaust, this was his message to the world: that we have a responsibility to art, that it is imperative to our humanity, that it demands our attention and our work, that we must cultivate an appreciation for it at the highest and most rigorous levels our intellects are capable of. Otherwise, we lose ourselves.

If there is a pessimism worth holding onto, it is a pessimism which rejects the aggressive anti-intellectualism that is always so eager to make a mockery of the humanities. It is a pessimism that can't even be bothered to dignify the charges of "uselessness" and "elitism" leveled at the study of literature by those who have no inner lives or meaningful connection with the world, and who can only imagine value as something tethered to capitalist principles. (Some "elite" we belong to, with all the exploitation and instability that our labor is subject to, with enough student loans that would take lifetimes to pay off. . . . Do people really think we did this just to feel "superior," to justify some kind of snobbery?).

The pessimism worth holding onto is the kind that Mann espoused. Even if we are all doomed, it's worth retreating to a magic mountain where we can reflect on the ideas that brought our world to this moment, even as we see those ideas—and the world—battle and ultimately annihilate each other. It is a pessimism that stands on the side of art against the "worst small-mindedness and the murder of mind and spirit," as he says in *Doctor Faustus*. It is a pessimism that calls into the silence of the classroom, to see if there is any willingness to transform the resentment into something that allows us to imagine the world anew—a world that begins, as it always does, with a gathering centered around the exchange of stories. It is a pessimism resigned to the fact that this call will often be met with cold silence, but it continues to make this call into the void nonetheless, for as long as literature continues to exist. But maybe even this is too hopeful, too optimistic.

NOTES

1. Alain Badiou, with Nicolas Truong, *In Praise of Love,* trans. Peter Bush (New York: The New Press, 2012), 22.
2. Badiou, *In Praise of Love,* 75.
3. Badiou, *In Praise of Love,* 25.
4. Qtd. in Han, *Agony of Eros,* trans. Erik Butler (Cambridge, MA: Massachusetts Institute of Technology Press, 2017), 47.
5. Han, *Agony of Eros,* 47–48.
6. Han, *Agony of Eros,* 1. Cf. Barthes writes in *A Lover's Discourse* that the

atopia of Socrates is linked to Eros. . . . The other whom I love and who fascinates me is *atopos*. I cannot classify the other, for the other is, precisely, Unique, the singular Image which has miraculously come to correspond to the specialty of my desire. The other is the figure of my truth, and cannot be imprisoned in any stereotype (which is the truth of others). (Barthes, *A Lover's Discourse,* 34)

7. Han, *Agony of Eros,* 1.
8. Han, *Agony of Eros,* 12.
9. Han, *Agony of Eros,* 12.
10. Kierkegaard, *Literary Review,* 93.
11. Han, *Agony of Eros,* 52.
12. Han, *Agony of Eros,* 52.
13. Han, *Agony of Eros,* 52.
14. Han, *Agony of Eros,* 51.

15. Mann, *Death in Venice*, 86.
16. Lawrence, *Lady Chatterley's Lover*, 50.
17. Lawrence, *Lady Chatterley's Lover*, 34.
18. Qtd. in Dalgarno, *Virginia Woolf and the Visible World*, 1.
19. Woolf, *To the Lighthouse*, 99.
20. Woolf, *To the Lighthouse*, 100.
21. Nabokov, *Lolita*, 32.
22. Arac, "What Kind of a History Does a Theory of the Novel Require?," 193.
23. Arac, "What Kind of a History Does a Theory of the Novel Require?," 191.
24. Arac, "What Kind of a History Does a Theory of the Novel Require?," 194.
25. Arac, "What Kind of a History Does a Theory of the Novel Require?," 194.
26. Jeva Lange, "Amazon has Sold Out of *1984*," *The Week*, January 27, 2017, https://theweek.com/speedreads/676249/amazon-sold-1984.
27. Alison Flood, "Philip Roth Predicts Novel Will Be Minority Cult Within 25 Years," *The Guardian*, October 26, 2009, https://www.theguardian.com/books/2009/oct/26/philip-roth-novel-minority-cult.
28. Han, *Agony of Eros*, 3.
29. Han, *Agony of Eros*, 3.
30. Han, *Agony of Eros*, 38.
31. Han, *Agony of Eros*, 9–11.
32. Han, *Agony of Eros*, 11.
33. Han, *Agony of Eros*, 11.
34. Peter Eavis, "WeWork Will Lay Off 2,400 Workers," *The New York Times*, November 21, 2019, https://www.nytimes.com/2019/11/21/business/wework-layoffs.html.
35. Lawrence, *Lady Chatterley's Lover*, 120.
36. Lawrence, *Lady Chatterley's Lover*, 101.
37. Han, *Psychopolitics*, 56, 65.
38. Erich Fromm, *The Art of Loving* (London: Thorsons, 1985), 69.
39. Melville, *Bartleby*, 4.
40. Melville, *Bartleby*, 15–16.
41. Melville, *Bartleby*, 22. In 1851, while still working on *Moby-Dick*, Melville wrote to Nathaniel Hawthorne, who was enjoying significantly greater success as a writer despite the fact that his work is far inferior to Melville's, "My dear Sir, a presentiment is on me,—I shall at last be worn and perish. . . . What I feel most moved to write, that is banned,—it will not pay. Yet, altogether, write the *other* way I cannot" (qtd. in Leo Marx, "Melville's Parable of Walls," in *Melville's Short Novels*, ed. Dan McCall [New York: W. W. Norton, 2002], 239).
42. Melville, *Moby-Dick*, 538.
43. Melville, *Bartleby*, 10.
44. Melville,*Bartleby*, 18.
45. Melville, *Bartleby*, 11.
46. Han, *Agony of Eros*, 11.
47. Nietzsche, *Thus Spoke Zarathustra*, trans. Thomas Common (Mineola, NY: Dover, 1999), 32.

48. Melville, *Bartleby*, 34.
49. Leo Marx, "Melville's Parable of Walls," in *Melville's Short Novels*, ed. Dan McCall (New York: W. W. Norton, 2002), 241.
50. Ehrenreich, *Bright-Sided*, 96.
51. Christina Zhao, "Students Not Smiling at School Will be Punished, Say Teachers," *Newsweek*, May 16, 2018, https://www.newsweek.com/students-not-smiling-school-will-be-punished-says-principle-928674.
52. Davies, *Happiness Industry*, 177.
53. Thomas Jefferson et al., "The Declaration of Independence," 1776, https://www.archives.gov/founding-docs/declaration-transcript.
54. Slavoj Žižek, *In Defense of Lost Causes* (London: Verso Books, 2009), fn.43: 492.
55. Davies, *Happiness Industry*, 124.
56. Friedrich Engels, *The Condition of the Working Class in England*, trans. Florence Wischnewetzky, ed. Victor Kiernan (London: Penguin Books, 1987), 114–115.
57. Theodor W. Adorno, *Minima Moralia: Reflections from Damaged Life*, trans. E. F. N. Jephcott (New York: Verso Books, 2005), 63.
58. James Q. Whitman, *Hitler's American Model: The United States and the Making of Nazi Race Law* (Princeton, NJ: Princeton University Press, 2017), 9.
59. Miya Tokumitsu, "In the Name of Love," *Jacobin*, January 12, 2014, https://www.jacobinmag.com/2014/01/in-the-name-of-love/.
60. Michel Foucault, *Discipline and Punish: The Birth of the Prison*, trans. Alan Sheridan (New York: Vintage Books, 1995), 239.
61. Davies, *Happiness Industry*, 121.
62. Davies, *Happiness Industry*, 123.
63. Davies, *Happiness Industry*, 122.
64. Davies, *Happiness Industry*, 135, 9.
65. Terry Eagleton, *Literary Theory: An Introduction*, 2nd ed. (Minneapolis, MN: University of Minnesota Press, 2003), 23.
66. Eagleton, *Literary Theory*, 23.
67. Eagleton, *Literary Theory*, 23.
68. Eagleton, *Literary Theory*, 28.
69. E. M. Forster, *Aspects of the Novel* (New York: Harcourt, Brace & Company, 1927), 9.
70. Schlegel, "Dialogue on Poetry," 109.
71. Bill Goldstein, *The World Broke in Two: Virginia Woolf, T. S. Eliot, D. H. Lawrence, E. M. Forster, and the Year that Changed Literature* (New York: Henry Holt, 2017), 1.
72. Woolf, *Common Reader*, I: xiii.
73. Woolf, *Common Reader*, I: 48.
74. Sade, "Reflections on the Novel," 109–110.
75. Nabokov, *Lolita*, 178.
76. Cabanas and Illouz cite a number of different "positive education" initiatives across North America and Europe that cut the humanities for the sake of business

skills and anything else that involves data rather than critical thinking (Cabanas and Ilouz, *Manufacturing Happy Citizens*, 74–80).

77. Kate Hodal, "One in 200 People is a Slave. Why?," *The Guardian*, February 25, 2019, https://www.theguardian.com/news/2019/feb/25/modern-slavery-trafficking-persons-one-in-200.

78. Cabanas and Illouz, *Manufacturing Happy Citizens*, 45.

79. Qtd. in Cabanas and Illouz, *Manufacturing Happy Citizens*, 45.

80. "World Report 2019," Human Rights Watch, https://www.hrw.org/world-report/2019/country-chapters/united-arab-emirates.

81. Cabanas and Illouz, *Manufacturing Happy Citizens*, 44.

82. Cabanas and Illouz, *Manufacturing Happy Citizens*, 35.

83. Qtd. in Cabanas and Illouz, *Manufacturing Happy Citizens*, 35.

84. Davies, *Happiness Industry*, 11.

85. Marcuse, *Eros and Civilization*, 103–104.

86. Alan Sheridan, translator's note to *Discipline and Punish* by Foucault, 1.

87. Foucault, *Discipline and Punish*, 7.

88. Armstrong, *How Novels Think*, 3.

89. Foucault, *Discipline and Punish*, 205.

90. Foucault, *Discipline and Punish*, 208–209.

91. Foucault, *Discipline and Punish*, 191.

92. Foucault, *Discipline and Punish*, 193.

93. Bacon, "The New Organon," CVIII: 100.

94. Ong, *Art of Being*, 31; D. A. Miller, *The Novel and the Police* (Berkeley, CA: University of California Press, 1988), 24; Gérard Genette, *Narrative Discourse: An Essay in Method*, trans. Jane Lewin (Ithaca, NY: Cornell University Press, 1980), 209.

95. Ong, *Art of Being*, 31; Watt, *Rise of the Novel*, 175.

96. Ong, *Art of Being*, 32.

97. Jonathan Culler, *The Literary in Theory* (Stanford, CA: Stanford University Press, 2007), 201.

98. Ivan Turgenev, *Fathers and Sons*, trans. Michael R. Katz (New York: W. W. Norton, 1996), 14.

99. Davies, *Happiness Industry*, 14.

100. Qtd. in Davies, *Happiness Industry*, 17.

101. Bacon, "The New Organon," LIX: 56.

102. Bacon, "The New Organon," LIX: 56–57.

103. Bacon, "The New Organon," LXIII: 60.

104. Bacon, "The New Organon," LX: 57.

105. Bacon, "The New Organon," LXIX 66–67.

106. Davies, *Happiness Industry*, 17.

107. Davies, *Happiness Industry*, 17.

108. Charles Dickens, *Hard Times* (Amersham: Transatlantic Press, 2012), 9.

109. Dickens, *Hard Times*, 10.

110. Dickens, *Hard Times*, 15.

111. Dickens, *Hard Times*, 120.

112. Dickens, *Hard Times*, 13.
113. Dickens, *Hard Times*, 119.
114. Nietzsche, *Unpublished Writings from the Period of Unfashionable Observations*, trans. Richard T. Gray (Stanford, CA: Stanford University Press, 1995), 208.
115. Woolf, *To the Lighthouse*, 8.
116. Henry James, *Washington Square* (New York: Penguin Books, 2007), 89.
117. James, *Washington Square*, 78.
118. James, *Washington Square*, 115.
119. Dickens, *Hard Times*, 71.
120. James, *Washington Square*, 99, 176.
121. James, *Washington Square*, 5, 131.
122. James, *Washington Square*, 65.
123. Turgenev, *Fathers and Sons*, 38.
124. Turgenev, *Fathers and Sons*, 157.
125. Lispector, *Passion According to G.H.*, 17.
126. Adorno, *Minima Moralia*, 47.
127. Davies, *Happiness Industry*, 117.
128. Davies, *Happiness Industry*, 118.
129. Yevgeny Zamyatin, *We*, trans. Clarence Brown (New York: Penguin Books, 1993), 44.
130. Zamyatin, *We*, 34.
131. Zamyatin, *We*, 22.
132. Zamyatin, *We*, 12.
133. Zamyatin, *We*, 43.
134. Zamyatin, *We*, 39.
135. Zamyatin, *We*, 16, 46.
136. Chris Welch, "Apple's Iconic Fifth Avenue Store is Back and Bigger Than Ever," *The Verge*, September 19, 2019, https://www.theverge.com/2019/9/19/20874180/apple-cube-store-new-york-city-fifth-avenue-reopening-date-tour.
137. Alissa Wilkinson, "American Believe in Work. WeWork Preyed on That Instinct," *Vox*, March 31, 2021, https://www.vox.com/22358597/wework-documentary-hulu-neumann.
138. Qtd. in Wootton, "The Impossible Dream," 14.
139. Bacon, "The New Organon," CXXIV: 114.
140. Qtd. in Davies, *Happiness Industry*, 13.
141. Foucault, *Discipline and Punish*, 141.
142. Bacon, "The New Organon," 33.
143. Qtd. in Davies, *Happiness Industry*, 32.
144. Davies, *Happiness Industry*, 36.
145. Davies, *Happiness Industry*, 67.
146. Davies, *Happiness Industry*, 67.
147. Davies, *Happiness Industry*, 154.
148. Davies, *Happiness Industry*, 159.
149. Davies, *Happiness Industry*, 151.
150. Nietzsche, *Philosophy and Truth*, 84.

151. Nietzsche, *Thus Spoke Zarathustra*, 7.
152. Qtd. in Han, *Agony of Eros,* 48.
153. Han, *Agony of Eros,* 49.
154. Heidegger, "What is Metaphysics?," 84.
155. Heidegger, *What is Called Thinking?*, trans. J. Glenn Gray (New York: Harper & Row, 1968), 373.
156. Heidegger, *What is Called Thinking?*, 378.
157. Heidegger, "What is Metaphysics?," 86.
158. Heidegger, "What is Metaphysics?," 95–96.
159. Han, *Agony of Eros,* 49.
160. Forster, *Aspects of the Novel*, 24.
161. Friedrich Schiller, *On the Aesthetic Education of Man in a Series of Letters*, trans. Reginald Snell (New York: Frederick Ungar Publishing Co., 1981), 26.
162. Forster, *Aspects of the Novel*, 24.
163. Lukács, *Theory of the Novel,* 50.
164. Han, *In the Swarm,* 61.
165. Han, *In the Swarm,* 50.
166. Han, *In the Swarm,* 50.
167. Han, *In the Swarm,* 19.
168. Han, *In the Swarm,* 12.
169. Armstrong, *How Novels Think,* 3.
170. Han, *Psychopolitics*, 36.
171. Plato, *Republic*, X.608A: 291.
172. Han, *Agony of Eros*, 43.
173. Eagleton, *Literary Theory,* 20.
174. Eagleton, *Literary Theory,* 28.
175. Mann, *Doctor Faustus*, 339–340.
176. Schiller, *Aesthetic Education of Man*, 54.
177. Schiller, *Aesthetic Education of Man*, 23.
178. Schiller, *Aesthetic Education of Man*, 26.

Concluding Unscientific Postscript

A LUDICROUS INTERPRETATION OF A
LUDICROUS INTERRUPTION:
MIMESIS FROM HOMER TO LUDACRIS

In the depressing new genre of "quit lit," in which academics with great promise and talent write about leaving academia because of the neoliberal circumstances that squeeze them out of the field—whether it is a poor salary that is incommensurate with both experience and with the student loans it took to get the degree in the first place, or the increasing bureaucratization of the job, or budget cuts, a toxic or dangerous work environment, or a number of other debilitating factors—Tim Parks contributed his own account to *The New York Review of Books*. The reason he was quitting academia was the rampant digital technology that "changed the cognitive skills required of individuals. Learning is more and more a matter of mastering various arbitrary software procedures than they allow information to be accessed."[1] As a result of this digital infiltration, the "idea of a relationship between teacher and class, professor and students, is consequently eroded." And with

> the erosion of that relationship goes the environment that nurtured it: the segregated space of the classroom where, for an hour or so, all attention was focused on a single person who brought all of his or her experience to the service of the group:
>
> There was an element of seduction in this; it required a certain performance, the ability to impose what in the best circumstances you might call a collective enchantment. One thinks of the lesson that D.H. Lawrence, himself a schoolteacher, describes in *Women in Love*: Lawrence has his teacher, Ursula, "absorbed in the passion of instruction," while her students are so hypnotized by

her lesson that the arrival of an unexpected visitor is experienced as a shocking intrusion.[2]

In Lawrence's image of Ursula interrupted by the arrival of an unexpected visitor while "absorbed in the passion of instruction," we see the history not only of education itself but of mimesis and its seductive power.

There is a genealogy of this image that can be traced back to *The Iliad* when Achilles is playing on his lyre to the Myrmidons, with his lover Patroclus in the front row, and is interrupted by Odysseus, Ajax, and Phoenix, sent by Agamemnon in an attempt to assuage Achilles' rage and win him over so that they can fight the Trojans as a united front:

So these two walked along the strand of the sea deep-thundering
with many prayers to the holder and shaker of the earth, that they
might readily persuade the great heart of Aiakides.
Now they came beside the shelters and ships of the Myrmidons
and they found Achilleus delighting his heart in a lyre, clear-sounding,
splendid and carefully wrought, with a bridge of silver upon it,
which he won out of the spoils when he ruined Eëtion's city.
With this he was pleasuring his heart, and singing of men's fame,
as Patroklos was sitting over against him, alone, in silence,
watching Aiakides and the time he would leave off singing.
Now these two came forward, as brilliant Odysseus led them,
and stood in his presence. Achilleus rose to his feet in amazement
holding the lyre as it was, leaving the place where he was sitting.
In the same way Patroklos, when he saw the men come, stood up.
And in greeting Achilleus the swift of foot spoke to them:
"Welcome. You are my friends who have come, and greatly I need you,
Who even to this my anger are dearest of all the Achaians."[3]

Mazzoni points to this passage as the "most ancient Western representation of storytelling, the practice that Plato would later identify using the inclusive term of *mimesis*."[4] What we see here is the "function of the epic song" itself, which "is hedonistic, commemorative, celebratory, and pedagogic."[5] I'd like to look at this passage a bit more closely, though, to see what else emerges here about the elements of storytelling, narrative, and pedagogy that would eventually find their way into the novel.

For one thing, the notion of the world's instability, its penchant for fragmentation rather than wholeness, is somehow passed off as distinctly modern, but it undergirds the entire Greek understanding of their relationship to earth and world, emblemized by the moody Poseidon, the "holder and shaker of the earth" in the second quoted line, who in an instant can disrupt human relations in catastrophic, devastating ways with no notice whatsoever. Existence itself is predicated on interruption, on intrusion, and it's often violent. Homer focuses on this aspect of existence more clearly in the sequel, *The Odyssey*—just a series of interruptions that keep Odysseus away from home for an additional ten years after fighting the Trojan War because Poseidon disrupts his journey.

Homer here also interrupts the image of Achilles as the archetype of rage personified, the interpretation that has been hammered into us by bad high school teachers and less astute readers who just latch on to the first line of the epic and refuse to see him in any other light. Achilles here is "delighting his heart" and "pleasuring his heart" in artistry that is "splendid and carefully wrought." Maybe rage really never was what twenty-first-century readers might call his dominant affect. Maybe, more than just a highly skilled warrior, he's even more of a highly skilled artist who can't do what he's meant to do except for in this brief episode. He had done everything he could to avoid being drafted into the war because, in his heart of hearts, he never felt like he was a warrior. He had even tried that artistic trick used centuries later by the first Greek actors—themselves war veterans, from the Persian War to the Peloponnesian War—when they invented tragedy: he dressed up as a woman. But even this travesty couldn't help him avoid his fate.

So yes, he was in a bad mood, like any pessimist who sees the promising trajectory of their life suddenly give out from under them, and he let anyone and everyone in his vicinity know that he was pissed off. (Odysseus went to far greater lengths to avoid conscription, feigning madness.) Things obviously didn't get much better when Agamemnon took Briseis away from him. And it's just at that moment when Homer begins to tell his story. But in Book IX we see him in his element—yet even in this all-too-brief glimpse into Achilles' identity, otherwise shielded under so many layers of pain and aggression, he's interrupted, he can't finish his damn song. If he's really that cliché of rage and wrath, he would have thrown a fit at this interruption, but instead he welcomes his new guests politely, even warmly right here, and later hears them out, but sees through their nonsense. He asks Odysseus not to patronize him with the promise of gifts and rewards for reconciling with Agamemnon. He may be characterized as enraged, but he gives—with the eloquence of an artist—a lucid, coherent insight into why this war is stupid, absurd, and why he shouldn't be fighting in it:

... Yet why must the Argives fight with the Trojans?
And why was it the son of Atreus assembled and led here
these people? Was it not for the sake of lovely-haired Helen?
And the sons of Atreus alone among mortal men the ones
who love their wives? Since any who is a good man, and careful,
loves her who is his own and cares for her, even as I now
loved this one from my heart, though it was my spear that won her.[6]

Who is the hothead now? Helen left Menelaus, so now his brother Agamemnon is fighting this war for him and dragging Achilles into it—while having the gall to take Briseis from him, the same kind of action that started the Trojan War in the first place. Achilles' response, unlike the unhinged Menelaus, who is the true figure of unbridled wrath in this story, is the opposite: he wants to withdraw from war altogether and be an artist instead, to be in this sacred space where he can sing to his listeners in a work of art that simultaneously instructs them about their own history. But he can't. He's interrupted. And it's not even Odysseus or Ajax or Phoenix who end up being able to persuade him, despite their talents. He ends up persuading himself, knowing that works of art are composed of valiant heroes. If he can't sing his story, he may as well be sung about. In art, he then lets himself be the creator and the created, Homer singing his rage through the Muse. He is split apart, anatomized across these different aesthetic categories of artist and artwork.

What Mazzoni leaves out from his analysis of this first moment of mimesis in Western literature is who exactly is doing the mimesis. This may seem like a pedantic point: obviously, it's Achilles, the artist, singing on his lyre. But this is a musical moment of creation rather than mimesis per se; Schopenhauer argues that, "music does not, like all the other arts, exhibit the *Ideas* or grades of the will's objectification, but directly the *will itself*."[7] It's an art that belongs to will, not representation. He may be "singing of men's fame," but that's not quite the same thing as singing the fame itself, the way that Homer invokes the Muse to "Sing, goddess, the anger of Peleus' son Achilleus"—to sing the anger itself, to channel it in its immediate form, rather than sing *about* the anger.[8] So there's actually not much mimesis coming from him. If anything, what he's doing is closer in genre to what Thucydides would later include in his *History of the Peloponnesian War*, Pericles's "Funeral Oration," accompanied by a lyre. The only imitation we actually see belongs to the audience, namely to Patroclus himself, who, when Agamemnon's ambassadors arrive, imitates the actions of the artist—he "stood up" only after his lover "rose to his feet in amazement." Patroclus, in the presence of Achilles, always "obeyed his beloved companion."[9]

So much of literary theory focuses on mimesis as a one-sided phenomenon, originating from the artist. But what about those of us on the other side of that aesthetic threshold, on the other side of the stage, of the page, or of the lectern? Socrates speaks of tragedy's audience as passive vessels of these mimetic products, who may be corrupted as a result of seeing such a spectacle and may behave in questionable or even dangerous ways after leaving the theater. But is it possible to think of the recipient of art taking a more active role—not in the way that reader-response theory has tried to propose—but in the constitutive act of mimesis in the process of its own creation? That there is a certain performativity at work in us when we see a work of art we love, and that it's love itself that binds creator to the creation, as well as to the beholder?

This, of course, is how Socrates illustrates Eros in *Phaedrus*. The pursued beloved is seduced by his own image conjured up in the words of the lover. Socrates calls this "backlove."[10] Is this not mimesis at work? Is the lover, who is pursuing the beloved with language, with rhetoric, with persuasion, not an artist? A transformation happens; the passive beloved awakens to what is stirred in them, which has been awoken by the lover. Now they're both active, participating in a backlove that goes back and forth and back again, corresponding with each other in dialogue rather than monologue. The artist seduces us to ourselves, but a self at this moment is something that both creates and allows itself to be created—it opens up to the art and to the artist. The self is not an entity apart; it is being-in-the-world, but a world that is mutually created and triangulated between the artist, the artwork, and the audience, each of these terms constituting their own kind of equiprimordiality. Every work of art, then, is a work of love, and every work of love is split between the artist and the beholder, both of whom animate each other through the work.

Socrates reminds us that when we see beauty, we recollect our former lives when we would travel cosmic distances with wings. As these wings fell in our descent to earth, the limbs we had to rely on in order to move are now our legs. But in beauty, in love, in art, we do not so much move as let ourselves be moved. Stationary and silent, and in the shadows like Patroclus, we give up motion for emotion—whether we're in the theater or reading a novel that happens to seduce us into its world. The memory of our wings comes back, encouraging us to stand up and see what it's like to be transported by these wings, restored to us in love, rather than our legs. Sitting in the shadows, something in us also shadows the movement of the work of art before us so that when Achilles stands up, Patroclus stands up too.

Artists from Homer to Ludacris have intuitively understood this. Ludacris's number one hip-hop single from 2003, "Stand Up," features the call of his own lyrics ("When I move, you move") with the response of Shawnna ("Just like that?") before they switch lines.[11] In the music video, the dancers, representing Ludacris's audience, are separated into couples during this sequence, each one erotically leaning into each other, back and forth, mirroring each other's moves, with every repetition of the chorus. This is the movement, distilled in its purest form, of mimesis throughout its entire history.

This kind of mimetic shadowing is also demonstrated in J. M. Barrie's *Peter Pan*, which is fundamentally a work about the role of the audience shadowing the movements in a work of art. The novel, based on the play, opens with the Darling children listening to a bedtime story, but when Peter Pan loses his shadow among this audience, they actively participate in the story they had been passively listening to. Wendy successfully manages to sew his shadow back on to him, but in the process seems to shadow this shadow. What ends up happening is that she and her siblings become further iterations of his own shadow themselves, taking flight and imitating his movements, following him to Neverland. The experience is, for Wendy at least, tinged with eros, and ultimately a sense of loss when she realizes that the utopian space of Neverland is a land she can never fully belong to. It is a space like the realm of Plato's eternal forms that can only be seen in flight. A place without time, these forms never change, never grow old, and never grow up. So Wendy becomes an Ariadne figure, using her thread to lead Peter Pan to his prize, that darker side of himself, and she falls in love with this adventurous Theseus figure only to be abandoned.

And then, of course, there is the story of Paolo and Francesca in Dante's *Inferno*, two lovers doomed to the realm of shades for their transgressive love, who learn to love through the act of reading, an erotic, Girardian triangulation that also exists with the Tristan lovers, with Romeo who kisses Juliet "by the book," with Werther and Lotte, Tatiana and Onegin, Cathy and Hareton, Emma Bovary and Léon and Rodolphe, Anna Karenina and Vronsky, Johannes and Cordelia, Humbert and Dolores, Robbie and Cecilia. In *The Art of Courtly Love*, Capellanus writes that, "Love is a thing that copies Nature herself," which is perhaps why these lovers gravitate to each other through mimesis.[12] And maybe the originary mimetic act was that of imitating our severed half in the myth from Plato's *Symposium*, reaching out to embrace each other, gesturing toward each other as in a mirror. The act of reading is an erotic act and a neurotic act, as we explore the different "experimental selves" that lie within us, learning about love and its futility, reaching out to ourselves in a way that also explores meaning in the world.[13] This is how Proust opens *Swann's Way*, with Marcel in bed after putting down a book, noting the "peculiar turn" his thoughts take when "it seemed to me that I myself was what the book was talking about."[14] By the end of *In Search of Lost Time*, the reader may say the same thing.

Eve Kosofsky Sedgwick ends her landmark study in queer theory, *Epistemology of the Closet*, with a meditation on the reader's experience of Proust, writing,

> I wonder if other novel-critics who set out to write about Proust feel that if the task is more irresistible than others it is also, not more difficult in degree, but almost prohibitively distinctive in kind: the problem being, not that [*In Search of Lost Time*] is so hard and so good, but that "it's all true."[15]

The "truth-effect of Proust" cannot be reduced to the kernels of wisdom that Alain de Botton transforms into a self-help manual, but rather in the way it activates something in us to undergo similar kinds of self-reflection, mirroring Marcel to this degree, even if, in the case of Sedgwick, she found herself on the side of "the most buoyant temperamental, cognitive, all but theoretical erotic optimism" after the odyssey that Proust took her through in his "unswerving erotic pessimism."[16]

Proust ends the entire *Recherche* with a tension between rising, standing, and falling. On his way to the Guermantes's party, he accidentally stumbles and regains his balance, which inexplicably gives him

> that same happiness which at various epochs of my life had been given to me by the sight of trees which I had thought that I recognized in the course of a drive near Balbec, by the sight of the twin steeples of Martinville, by the flavor of a madeleine dipped in tea.[17]

It is a happiness that finally and inexplicably gives him the resolution to follow his vocation and write. All of his doubts about his literary talents "were removed as if by magic," and so too does he seem to untether the stumbling from the etymology of "pessimism" as if by magic, as well. He literally stumbles into happiness. He even tries re-creating the stumble, which he is unable to do, but "again the dazzling and indistinct vision fluttered near me, as if to say: 'Seize me as I pass if you can, and try to solve the riddle of happiness which I set you.'"[18]

The extent to which he does end up solving this riddle is ambiguous, and, as Han notes, the end of the *Recherche* "is anything but triumphant."[19] Marcel almost falls three more times after that initial stumble into happiness, which leaves him with the opposite effect, feeling as though he "no longer possessed either memory or the power of thought or strength or existence of any kind."[20] It doesn't seem to get any better, since he says that,

> Since the day of the staircase, nothing in the world, no happiness, whether it came from friendship or the progress of my book or the hope of fame, reached me except as a sunshine unclouded but so pale that it no longer had the virtue to warm me, to make me live, to instill in me any desire.[21]

The final image of the entire novel returns to the shakiness of our feet as we age, as though walking on stilts that elongate with the passage of time. These stilts are long enough to "touch the distant epochs through which they have lived."[22] And as he contemplates this distance, so too does the reader in reflecting on their own life. And as Proust stands on these stilts, reaching magisterial heights, he invites the reader to meet him there, inspiring in us an eros for the text we are reading—a text which also reads us.

This mimesis is staged in the reader's own mind, own desire, for the text itself. To Aristotle, mimesis is what picks us out as human beings:

It can be seen that poetry was broadly engendered by a pair of causes, both natural. For it is an instinct of human beings, from childhood, to engage in mimesis (indeed, this distinguishes them from other animals: man is the most mimetic of all, and it is through mimesis that he develops his earliest understanding); and equally natural that everyone enjoys mimetic objects. A common occurrence indicates this: we enjoy contemplating the most precise images of things whose actual sight is painful to us, such as the forms of the vilest animals and of corpses. The explanation of this too is that understanding gives great pleasure not only to philosophers but likewise to others too, though the latter have a smaller share in it. This is why people enjoy looking at images, because through contemplating them it comes about that they understand and infer what each element means, for instance that "this person is so-and-so."[23]

Mimesis here is linked to pain and understanding, to a fundamental pessimism at the core of life in portraying images of the worst. This is the "sadness at the back of life" that Woolf identified in the Greeks, the imitation of which paradoxically makes life more livable.[24] She turned to the novel to put a silent language to this sadness, as did Lawrence and Nabokov, as well as the novelists who paved the way for them to achieve their literary innovations. Dienstag identifies this mimesis at the core of *Don Quixote*, arguing that

> Quixote's art of living simply consists in imitating, that is *living out,* the narrative art that describes previous lives he finds admirable. And what is admirable about such lives are not the fixed values of their subjects but their *activity*, their attempts to change the world.[25]

As futile as these attempts may be, what this observation illuminates is that the study of mimesis, as it has evolved through the ages in the form of the novel, is central to who we are, to the meaning of being, to the understanding of how we relate to a world that is indifferent to our pain. An appreciation of this art is one of the last hopes available to us in a world on its way out, even though it is a hope that is quickly vanishing.

NOTES

1. Tim Parks, "The Dying Art of Instruction in the Digital Classroom," *The New York Review of Books*, July 31, 2019, https://www.nybooks.com/daily/2019/07/31/the-dying-art-of-instruction-in-the-digital-classroom/.
2. Parks, "Dying Art of Instruction in the Digital Classroom."
3. Homer, *Iliad,* IX.185–98: 203.
4. Mazzoni, *Theory of the Novel,* 20.
5. Mazzoni, *Theory of the Novel,* 21.
6. Homer, *Iliad,* IX.337–43: 207.

7. Schopenhauer, *World as Will and Representation*, II: 448.
8. Homer, *Iliad,* I.1: 59.
9. Homer, *Iliad,* IX: 205.
10. Plato, *Phaedrus,* 255D-E: 46.
11. Ludacris feat. Shawnna, "Stand Up," Island Def Jam Music Group, 2003, https://www.youtube.com/watch?v=pZG7IK99OvI.
12. Andreas Capellanus, *Art of Courtly Love*, trans. John Jay Parry (New York: Columbia University Press, 1960), 45.
13. Kundera, *Art of the Novel,* 34.
14. Proust, *Swann's Way*, 3.
15. Eve Kosofsky Sedgwick, *Epistemology of the Closet* (Berkeley, CA: University of California Press, 2008), 240.
16. Sedgwick, *Epistemology of the Closet*, 241.
17. Proust, *Time Regained*, 255.
18. Proust, *Time Regained*, 255.
19. Han, *The Crisis of Narration* (Cambridge: Polity, 2024), 17.
20. Proust, *Time Regained*, 518.
21. Proust, *Time Regained*, 522.
22. Proust, *Time Regained*, 532.
23. Aristotle, *Poetics,* ed. and trans. Stephen Halliwell (Chapel Hill, NC: University of North Carolina Press, 1987), 37–39.
24. Woolf, *Common Reader,* I: 58–59.
25. Dienstag, *Pessimism,* 212.

Bibliography

Adorno, Theodor W. *Kierkegaard: Construction of the Aesthetic*. Translated and edited by Robert Hullot-Kentor. Minneapolis, MN: University of Minnesota Press, 1989.

Adorno, Theodor W. *Minima Moralia: Reflections from Damaged Life*. Translated by E. F. N. Jephcott. New York: Verso Books, 2005.

Alain of Lille. *The Complaint of Nature*. Translated by Douglas M. Moffat. New York: Henry Holt & Company, 1908.

Alighieri, Dante. *The Divine Comedy*. Translated by John Ciardi. New York: New American Library, 2003.

American Library Association. "Top 100 Most Banned and Challenged Books: 2010-2019." https://www.ala.org/advocacy/bbooks/frequentlychallengedbooks/decade2019.

Améry, Jean. *Charles Bovary, Country Doctor*. Translated by Adrian Nathan West. New York: New York Review Books, 2018.

Andersen, Hans Christian. "The Little Mermaid." In *The Annotated Hans Christian Andersen,* translated by Maria Tatar and edited by Maria Tatar and Julie K. Allen, 119–55. New York: W. W. Norton, 2008.

Andersen, Hans Christian. "The Red Shoes." In *The Annotated Hans Christian Andersen*, translated by Maria Tatar and edited by Maria Tatar and Julie K. Allen, 251–62. New York: W. W. Norton, 2008.

Apter, T. E. *Virginia Woolf: A Study of her Novels*. New York: New York University Press, 1979.

Apuleius. *The Golden Ass*. Translated by P. G. Walsh. Oxford: Oxford University Press, 1999.

Arac, Jonathan. "What Kind of a History Does a Theory of the Novel Require?" *NOVEL: A Forum on Fiction* 42, no. 2, "Theories of the Novel Now, Part I" (Summer 2009): 190–195.

Aristotle. "Metaphysics." In *The Basic Works of Aristotle,* translated by W. D. Ross, edited by Richard McKeon. New York: Modern Library, 2001.

Aristotle. *Poetics*. Edited and Translated by Stephen Halliwell. Chapel Hill, NC: University of North Carolina Press, 1987.
Armstrong, Nancy. *How Novels Think: The Limits of British Individualism from 1719-1900*. New York: Columbia University Press, 2006.
Arnaud, Claude. *Chamfort: A Biography*. Translated by Deke Dusinberre. Chicago, IL: University of Chicago Press, 1992.
Auerbach, Erich. *Mimesis: The Representation of Reality in Western Literature*. Translated by Willard R. Trask. Princeton, NJ: Princeton University Press, 2003.
Austen, Jane. *Sense and Sensibility*. New York: Modern Library, 1995.
Bacon, Francis. *The New Organon and Related Writings*. Edited by Fulton H. Anderson. New York: Macmillan, 1960.
Bader, Julia. *Crystal Land: Artifice in Nabokov's English Novels*. Berkeley, CA: University of California Press, 1972.
Badiou, Alain, with Nicolas Truong. *In Praise of Love*. Translated by Peter Bush. New York: The New Press, 2012.
Bakhtin, M. M. *The Dialogic Imagination: Four Essays*. Translated by Caryl Emerson and Michael Holquist. Edited Michael Holquist. Austin, TX: University of Texas Press, 1981.
Bakhtin, M. M. *Problems of Dostoevsky's Poetics*. Translated and edited by Caryl Emerson. Minneapolis, MN: University of Minnesota Press, 1984.
Balzac, Honoré de. *Lost Illusions*. Translated by Raymond N. MacKenzie. Minneapolis, MN: University of Minnesota Press, 2020.
Balzac, Honoré de. *Lost Souls*. Translated by Raymond N. MacKenzie. Minneapolis, MN: University of Minnesota Press, 2020.
Balzac, Honoré de. *Père Goriot*. Translated by Burton Raffel and edited by Peter Brooks. New York: W. W. Norton, 1994.
Banfield, Ann. "'Proust's Pessimism' as Beckett's Counter-Poison." *The Romantic Review* 100, no. 1–2 (January 2009): 187–202. doi:10.1215/26885220-100.1-2.187.
Barney, Rachel. "*Eros* and Necessity in the Ascent from the Cave." *Ancient Philosophy* 28 (2008): 1–16. http://individual.utoronto.ca/rbarney/Eros.pdf.
Barrie, J. M. *Peter Pan*. Chicago, IL: Suzeteo Enterprises, 2019.
Barthes, Roland. *A Lover's Discourse: Fragments*. Translated by Richard Howard. New York: Hill and Wang, 1979.
Barthes, Roland. *The Pleasure of the Text*. Translated by Richard Miller. New York: Hill and Wang, 1975.
Bataille, Georges. *Erotism: Death and Sensuality*. Translated by Mary Dalwood. San Francisco, CA: City Lights Books, 1986.
Baudelaire, Charles. *Les Fleurs du Mal*. Translated by Richard Howard. Boston, MA: David R. Godine, 1983.
Baudelaire, Charles. "Let us Flay the Poor." In *Baudelaire: His Prose and Poetry*, translated by T. R. Smith. New York: Boni and Liveright, 1919.
Beauvoir, Simone de. "My Experience as a Writer." In *"The Useless Mouths" and Other Literary Writings,* edited by Margaret A. Simons and Marybeth Timmerman. Translated by Marybeth Timmerman. Champaign, IL: University of Illinois Press, 2011.

Beckett, Samuel. *Endgame*. New York: Grove Press, 2009.
Beckett, Samuel. *Proust*. New York: Grove Press, 1961.
Beckett, Samuel. "Worstward Ho." In *Nohow On,* 87–116. New York: Grove Press, 1996.
Bell, Michael. "*Lolita* and Pure Art." In *Vladimir Nabokov's* Lolita: *Modern Critical Interpretations,* edited by Harold Bloom. New York: Chelsea House, 1987.
Benjamin, Walter. "The Image of Proust." In *Illuminations*. Translated by Harry Zohn and edited by Hannah Arendt. New York: Schocken, 1968.
Benjamin, Walter. "On Some Motifs in Baudelaire." In *Illuminations*. Translated by Harry Zohn and edited by Hannah Arendt. New York: Schocken, 1968.
Benjamin, Walter. "The Storyteller." In *Illuminations*. Translated by Harry Zohn. New York: Schocken, 1968.
Benjamin, Walter. "Theses on the Philosophy of History." In *Illuminations*. Translated by Harry Zohn. New York: Schocken, 1968.
Benjamin, Walter. *Selected Writings, Volume 1: 1913-1926*. Edited by Marcus Bullock and Michael W. Jennings. Cambridge, MA: Harvard University Press, 1996.
Bettelheim, Bruno. *The Uses of Enchantment: The Meaning and Importance of Fairy Tales*. New York: Alfred A. Knopf, 1976.
The Bible: Authorized King James Version. Edited by Robert Carroll and Stephen Prickett. Oxford: Oxford University Press, 2008.
Bingen, Hildegard of. *Holistic Healing*. Translated by Manfred Pawlik, Patrick Madigan, and John Kulas. Edited by Mary Palmquist and John Kulas. Collegeville, PA: Liturgical Press, 1994.
Blanchot, Maurice. *The Space of Literature*. Translated by Ann Smock. Lincoln, NE: University of Nebraska Press, 1989.
Blanchot, Maurice. *The Writing of the Disaster*. Translated by Ann Smock. Lincoln, NE: University of Nebraska Press, 1995.
Bloom, Allan. "The Ladder of Love." In *Plato's Symposium*. Translated by Seth Benardete. Chicago, IL: University of Chicago Press, 2001.
Bluefarb, Sam. "Henry Miller's James Joyce: A Painful Case of Envy." *New English Review,* April 2012. http://www.newenglishreview.org/custpage.cfm/frm/110561/sec_id/110561.
Blum, Beth. "Modernism's Anti-Advice." *Modernism/Modernity* 24, no. 1 (2017): 117–139. doi:10.1353/mod.2017.0005.
Boccaccio, Giovanni. *The Decameron*. Translated by Wayne A. Rebhorn. New York: W. W. Norton, 2013.
Boethius. *The Consolation of Philosophy*. Translated by David R. Slavitt (Cambridge, MA: Harvard University Press, 2008).
Bologna, Caroline. "Why the Phrase 'Pull Yourself up by Your Bootstraps' is Nonsense." *The Huffington Post,* September 8, 2018. https://www.huffpost.com/entry/pull-yourself-up-by-your-bootstraps-nonsense_n_5b1ed024e4b0bbb7a0e037d4?guccounter=1.
Bond, Candis. "Embodied Love: D. H. Lawrence, Modernity, and Pregnancy." *DHLR* 41, no. 1 (2016): 21–44.

Bowlby, Rachel. "*Lolita* and the Poetry of Advertising." In *Vladimir Nabokov's Lolita: A Casebook*, edited by Ellen Pifer, 155–180. Oxford: Oxford University Press, 2003.
Boyd, Brian. "Even Homais Nods." In *Vladimir Nabokov's* Lolita: *A Casebook*, edited by Ellen Pifer, 57–82. Oxford: Oxford University Press, 2003.
Boyd, Brian. *Vladimir Nabokov: The American Years*. Princeton, NJ: Princeton University Press, 1991.
Bradatan, Costica. "The Philosopher of Failure: Emil Cioran's Heights of Despair." *Los Angeles Review of Books,* November 28, 2016. https://lareviewofbooks.org/article/philosopher-failure-emil-ciorans-heights-despair/.
Brenkman, John. "Innovation: Notes on Nihilism and the Aesthetics of the Novel." In *The Novel*. Vol. 2. Edited by Franco Moretti. Princeton, NJ: Princeton University Press, 2007.
Brenkman, John. *Mood and Trope: The Rhetoric and Poetics of Affect*. Chicago, IL: University of Chicago Press, 2020.
Britton, Derek. *Lady Chatterley: The Making of the Novel*. Sydney: Unwin Hyman, 1988.
Brontë, Emily. *Wuthering Heights*. Edited by Alexandra Lewis. New York: W. W. Norton, 2019.
Browne, Sir Thomas. *Religio Medici* and *Urne-Buriall*. Edited by Stephen Greenblatt and Ramie Targoff. New York: New York Review of Books, 2012.
Buben, Adam. "Heidegger's Reception of Kierkegaard: The Existential Philosophy of Death." *British Journal for the History of Philosophy* 21, no. 5 (September 5, 2013): 967–988.
Burack, Charles Michael. *D.H. Lawrence's Language of Sacred Experience: The Transfiguration of the Reader*. New York: Palgrave Macmillan, 2005.
Burke, Peter. *The Fortunes of the Courtier: The European Reception of Castiglione's Cortegiano*. University Park, PA: Penn State University Press, 1995.
Cabanas, Edgar and Eva Illouz. *Manufacturing Happy Citizens: How the Science and Industry of Happiness Control our Lives*. Cambridge: Polity Press, 2019.
Caldwell, Janis McLarren. "*Wuthering Heights* and Domestic Medicine: The Child's Body and the Book." In *Wuthering Heights,* edited by Alexandra Lewis, 423-44. New York: W. W. Norton, 2019.
Camus, Albert. *The Myth of Sisyphus and Other Essays*. Translated by Justin O'Brien. New York: Vintage Books, 1983.
Camus, Albert. *The Rebel: An Essay on Man in Revolt*. Translated by Anthony Bower. New York: Alfred A. Knopf, 1960.
Camus, Albert. *The Stranger*. Translated by Matthew Ward. New York: Vintage Books, 1989.
Capellanus, Andreas. *The Art of Courtly Love*. Translated by John Jay Parry. New York: Columbia University Press, 1960.
Carlisle, Claire. "Kierkegaard and Heidegger." In *The Oxford Handbook of Kierkegaard,* edited by John Lippitt and George Pattison. Oxford: Oxford University Press, 2013.
Carson, Anne. *Eros the Bittersweet*. Princeton, NJ: Princeton University Press, 2015.

Carter, William C. *Marcel Proust: A Life*. New Haven, CT: Yale University Press, 2000.
Carter, William C. *The Proustian Quest*. New York: New York University Press, 1992.
Cartwright, David E. *Schopenhauer: A Biography*. Cambridge: Cambridge University Press, 2013.
Cascardi, Anthony J. "The Novel." In *The Oxford Handbook of Philosophy and Literature*, edited by Richard Eldrige, 162–79. Oxford: Oxford University Press, 2013.
Cashdan, Sheldon. *The Witch Must Die: The Hidden Meaning of Fairy Tales*. New York: Perseus, 1999.
Castiglione, Baldesar. *The Book of the Courtier*. Translated by George Bull. London: Penguin Books, 2003.
Cervantes, Miguel de. *Don Quixote*. Translated by Tom Lathrop. New York: Signet, 2011.
Chateaubriand, François-René de. "René." In *Atala / René*. Translated by Irving Putter. Berkeley, CA: University of California Press, 1980.
Chesterton, G. K. "The Fallacy of Success." *All Things Considered*. New York: John Lane, 1909.
Cioran, E. M. *All Gall is Divided*. Translated by Richard Howard. New York: Arcade Publishing, 2019.
Cioran, E. M. *On the Heights of Despair*. Translated by Ilinca Zarifopol-Johnston. Chicago, IL: University of Chicago Press, 1992.
Cioran, E. M. *A Short History of Decay*. Translated by Richard Howard. New York: Arcade Publishing, 2012.
Cioran, E. M. *The Temptation to Exist*. Translated by Richard Howard. New York: Arcade Publishing, 2012.
Cioran, E. M. *The Trouble with Being Born*. Translated by Richard Howard. New York: Arcade Publishing, 2013.
Cixous, Hélène. "Ay yay! The Cry of Literature." In *Ways of Re-Thinking Literature*, edited by Tom Bishop and Donatien Grau, 199–217. London: Routledge, 2018.
Cixous, Hélène. "Ay Yay: The Shout of Literature." Keynote Address at the New York University Re-Thinking Literature Conference, New York, September 20, 2013.
Coleridge, Samuel Taylor. *Collected Letters of Samuel Taylor Coleridge*. Vol. I: 1785-1800. Edited by Earl Leslie Griggs. Oxford: Clarendon Press, 1966.
Collins, Emily. "Nabokov's *Lolita* and Andersen's 'The Little Mermaid.'" *Nabokov Studies* 9 (2005): 77–100.
Conrad, Joseph. *Heart of Darkness*. Edited by Robert Kimbrough. New York: W. W. Norton, 1988.
Critchley, Simon and Tom McCarthy. "Of Chrematology: Joyce and Money." *Hypermedia Joyce Studies* 4 (2003): hjs.ff.cuni.cz.
Critchley, Simon. *Very Little... Almost Nothing: Death, Philosophy, Literature*. 2nd ed. London: Routledge, 2004.
Culler, Jonathan. *The Literary in Theory*. Stanford, CA: Stanford University Press, 2007.

"Cynosure." Oxford English Dictionary Online. https://www.lexico.com/en/definition/cynosure.

Dalgarno, Emily. "Reality and Perception: Philosophical Approaches to *To the Lighthouse*." In *The Cambridge Companion to* To the Lighthouse, edited by Allison Pease. Cambridge: Cambridge University Press, 2015.

Dalgarno, Emily. *Virginia Woolf and the Visible World*. Cambridge: Cambridge University Press, 2001.

Davies, William. *The Happiness Industry: How the Government and Big Business Sold us Well-Being*. London: Verso Books, 2016.

DeLillo, Don. *White Noise*. New York: Penguin Books, 2009.

De Lorris, Guillaume and Jean De Meun. *The Romance of the Rose*. Translated by Frances Horgan. Oxford: Oxford University Press, 2008.

de Man, Paul. "Anthropomorphism in the Lyric." In *The Rhetoric of Romanticism,* by Paul de Man, 239–262. New York: Columbia University Press, 1984.

de Man, Paul. "Hypogram and Inscription: Michael Riffaterre's Poetics of Reading," *Diacritics* 11, no. 4 (Winter 1981): 17–35.

de Man, Paul. "Reading (Proust)." In *Modern Critical Interpretations: Marcel Proust's* Remembrance of Things Past, edited by Harold Bloom, 117–134. New York: Chelsea House Publishers, 1987.

"*Der Spiegel* Interview with Martin Heidegger." (1966). http://web.ics.purdue.edu/~other1/Heidegger%20Der%20Spiegel.pdf.

Derrida, Jacques. "Plato's Pharmacy." In *Dissemination*. Translated by Barbara Johnson, 61–171. Chicago, IL: University of Chicago Press, 1981.

Dickens, Charles. *Great Expectations*. London: Penguin Books, 1996.

Dickens, Charles. *Hard Times*. Amersham: Transatlantic Press, 2012.

Dienstag, Jonathan Foa. *Pessimism: Philosophy, Ethic, Spirit*. Princeton, NJ: Princeton University Press, 2006.

Dostoevsky, Fyodor. *The Brothers Karamazov*. Translated by Richard Pevear and Larissa Volokhonsky. New York: Farrar, Straus and Giroux, 2002.

Dostoevsky, Fyodor. *Crime and Punishment*. Translated by Jessie Coulson. Oxford: Oxford University Press, 1981.

Dostoevsky, Fyodor. *Notes from Underground*. Translated by Richard Pevear and Larissa Volokhonsky. New York: Vintage Books, 1993.

Dovere, Edward-Isaac. "Joe Biden's Endless Search for the Middle on Race." *The Atlantic,* June 21, 2019. https://www.theatlantic.com/politics/archive/2019/06/bidens-anachronistic-comments-race-and-civil-rights/592252/.

Dowling, Linda. *Hellenism and Homosexuality in Victorian Oxford*. Ithaca, NY: Cornell University Press, 1994.

Durantaye, Leland de la. *Giorgio Agamben: A Critical Introduction*. Stanford, CA: Stanford University Press, 2009.

Eagleton, Terry. *Hope Without Optimism*. New Haven, CT: Yale University Press, 2017.

Eagleton, Terry. *Literary Theory: An Introduction*. 2nd ed. Minneapolis, MN: University of Minnesota Press, 2003.

Eavis, Peter. "WeWork Will Lay Off 2,400 Workers." *The New York Times*, November 21, 2019. https://www.nytimes.com/2019/11/21/business/wework-lay-offs.html.

Echevarría, Roberto González. *Cervantes' "Don Quixote."* New Haven, CT: Yale University Press, 2015.

Ehrenreich, Barbara. *Bright-Sided: How Positive Thinking is Undermining America*. New York: Picador, 2009.

Eliot, George. *Middlemarch*. New York: W. W. Norton, 2000.

Eliot, T. S. "*Ulysses,* Order, and Myth." In *Modernism: An Anthology,* edited by Lawrence Rainey. Oxford: Blackwell, 2005.

Eliot, T. S. *The Waste Land*. Edited by Michael North. New York: W. W. Norton, 2001.

Ellis, David. *Love and Sex in D. H. Lawrence*. Clemson, SC: Clemson University Press, 2015.

"E. M. Cioran on Beckett." Translated by Thomas Cousineau. *The Beckett Circle: The Newsletter of the Samuel Beckett Society* 28, no. 1 (Spring 2005): 5. http://citeseerx.ist.psu.edu/viewdoc/download?doi=10.1.1.732.4610&rep=rep1&type=pdf.

Engels, Friedrich. *The Condition of the Working Class in England*. Translated by Florence Wischnewetzky. Edited by Victor Kiernan. London: Penguin Books, 1987.

Engelstein, Stefani. *Anxious Anatomy: The Conception of the Human Form in Literary and Naturalist Discourse*. Albany, NY: State University of New York, 2008.

Epstein, Joseph. *The Novel, Who Needs It?* New York: Encounter Books, 2023.

Euripides. "Medea." In *The Norton Anthology of World Literature*. Vol. A, 3rd ed. Translated by Diane Arnson Svarlien, 723–823. New York: W. W. Norton, 2012.

Faye, Emmanuel. *Heidegger: The Introduction of Nazism into Philosophy in Light of the Unpublished Seminars of 1933-1935*. New Haven, CT: Yale University Press, 2011.

Faulkner, William. *As I Lay Dying*. New York: Vintage Books, 1985.

Faulkner, William. *Sanctuary*. New York: Vintage Books, 1993.

Faulkner, William. *The Sound and the Fury*. Edited by David Minter. 2nd ed. New York: W. W. Norton, 1994.

Ferrante, Elena. *My Brilliant Friend*. Translated by Ann Goldstein. New York: Europa, 2011.

Feuerlicht, Ignace. *Thomas Mann*. Boston, MA: Twayne Publishers, 1968.

Flaubert, Gustave. *Madame Bovary*. Translated by Lydia Davis. New York: Penguin Books, 2010.

Flaubert, Gustave. *Memoirs of a Madman and November*. Translated by Andrew Brown. London: Alma, 2005.

Flock, Elizabeth. "James Frey Returning to Oprah Five Years Later." *The Washington Post,* May 17, 2011. https://www.washingtonpost.com/blogs/blogpost/post/james-frey-returning-to-oprah-five-years-later/2011/05/17/AF9A3j5G_blog.html.

Flood, Alison. "Philip Roth Predicts Novel Will Be Minority Cult Within 25 Years." *The Guardian,* October 26, 2009. https://www.theguardian.com/books/2009/oct/26/philip-roth-novel-minority-cult.

Folkenberg, Judith, Benjamin A. Rifkin, and Michael J. Ackerman. *Human Anatomy: A Visual History From the Renaissance to the Digital Age.* New York: Abrams, 2006.

Forster, E. M. *Aspects of the Novel.* New York: London: Harcourt, Brace & Company, 1927.

Foucault, Michel. *Discipline and Punish: The Birth of the Prison.* Translated by Alan Sheridan. New York: Vintage Books, 1995.

Fowler, Douglas. *Reading Nabokov.* Ithaca, NY: Cornell University Press, 1974.

Freud, Sigmund. *Beyond the Pleasure Principle.* Translated by James Strachey. New York: W. W. Norton, 1989.

Freud, Sigmund. *Civilization and its Discontents.* Translated and edited by James Strachey. New York: W. W. Norton, 2000.

Freud, Sigmund. "A Difficulty in the Path of Psycho-Analysis." In *The Standard Edition of the Complete Psychological Works of Sigmund Freud.* Vol. XVIII. Translated and edited by James Strachey, 135–144. London: Hogarth Press, 1955.

Freud, Sigmund. "Mourning and Melancholia." In *The Standard Edition of the Complete Psychological Works of Sigmund Freud.* Vol XIV. Translated by James Strachey, 237–258. New York: Vintage Books, 1999.

Freud, Sigmund. *The Psychology of Love.* Translated by Shaun Whiteside. New York: Penguin Books, 2007.

Freud, Sigmund. "The Uncanny." https://web.mit.edu/allanmc/www/freud1.pdf.

Friedman, Alan W. "D. H. Lawrence: Pleasure and Death." *Studies in the Novel* 32, no. 2 (Summer 2000): 207–228.

Fromm, Erich. *The Art of Loving.* London: Thorsons, 1985.

Frosch, Thomas R. "Parody and Authenticity in *Lolita*." In *Vladimir Nabokov's Lolita: A Casebook*, edited by Ellen Pifer, 39–56. Oxford: Oxford University Press, 2003.

Frost, Laura. *The Problem with Pleasure: Modernism and Its Discontents.* New York: Columbia University Press, 2013.

Frye, Northrop. *Anatomy of Criticism: Four Essays.* Princeton, NJ: Princeton University Press, 1957.

Garff, Joakim. "Kierkegaard's Christian Bildungsroman." In *Kierkegaard, Literature, and the Arts,* edited by Eric Ziolkowski, 85–98. Evanston, IL: Northwestern University Press, 2018.

Genette, Gérard. *Narrative Discourse: An Essay in Method.* Translated by Jane Lewin. Ithaca, NY: Cornell University Press, 1980.

Gilbert, Sandra M. and Susan Gubar. "Looking Oppositely: Emily Brontë's Bible of Hell." In *Wuthering Heights,* edited by Alexandra Lewis, 355-69. New York: W. W. Norton, 2019.

Girard, René. *Deceit, Desire, and the Novel: Self and Other in Literary Structure.* Translated by Yvonne Freccero. Baltimore, MD: Johns Hopkins University Press, 1961.

Gladwell, Malcolm. *Blink: The Power of Thinking Without Thinking.* Boston, MA: Back Bay, 2007.

Goethe, Johann Wolfgang von. *Faust.* The Original German and a Translation by Walter Kaufmann. New York: Anchor Books, 1963.

Goethe, Johann Wolfgang von. *Faust: A Tragedy.* Translated by Walter Arndt. Edited by Cyrus Hamlin. New York: W. W. Norton, 2001.

Goethe, Johann Wolfgang von. *The Sorrows of Young Werther / Die Leiden des jungen Werther.* Translated by Stanley Appelbaum. Mineola, NY: Dover Publications, 2004.

Goethe, Johann Wolfgang von. *The Sorrows of Young Werther* and *Selected Writings.* Translated by Catherine Hutter. New York: Signet Classics, 1962.

Gold, Herbert. "Interview with Vladimir Nabokov." In *Vladimir Nabokov's Lolita: A Casebook*, edited by Ellen Pifer, 195–206. Oxford: Oxford University Press, 2003.

Goldman, Jane. "*To the Lighthouse*'s Use of Language and Form." In *The Cambridge Companion to To the Lighthouse*, edited by Allison Pease. Cambridge: Cambridge University Press, 2015.

Goldstein, Bill. *The World Broke in Two: Virginia Woolf, T. S. Eliot, D. H. Lawrence, E. M. Forster, and the Year that Changed Literature.* New York: Henry Holt, 2017.

Gorgani, Fakhraddin. *Vis and Ramin.* Translated and edited by Dick Davis. London: Penguin Books, 2008.

Gorgias. "On Non-Being." In *The Greek Sophists*, Translated and edited by John Dillon and Tania Gergel. London: Penguin Books, 2003.

Grabes, H. *Fictitious Biographies: Vladimir Nabokov's English Novels.* Berlin: Mouton, 1977.

Grass, Günter. *The Tin Drum.* Translated by Breon Mitchell. Boston, MA: Mariner Books, 2009.

Grayson, Jane. "*Rusalka* and the Person from Porlock." In *Symbolism and After: Essays on Russian Poetry in Honour of Georgette Donchin*, edited by Arnold McMillin, 162–185. Bristol: Bristol Classical Press, 1992.

Gregorio, Laurence A. "The Gaze of History." In *The Princess of Clèves*, edited by Madame de Lafayette. New York: W. W. Norton, 1994.

Grimm, The Brothers. "Cinderella." In *The Annotated Brothers Grimm,* translated and edited by Maria Tatar, 113-27. New York: W. W. Norton, 2004.

Grimm, The Brothers. "Rumpelstiltskin." In *The Annotated Brothers Grimm,* translated and edited by Maria Tatar, 256-63. New York: W. W. Norton, 2004.

Grimm, The Brothers. "Snow White." In *The Annotated Brothers Grimm,* translated and edited by Maria Tatar, 240-55. New York: W. W. Norton, 2004.

Gross, Terry. "Reporter: White House Knew of Coronavirus' 'Major Threat,' But Response Fell Short. Fresh Air." *National Public Radio,* March 12, 2020. https://www.npr.org/2020/03/12/814881355/white-house-knew-coronavirus-would-be-a-major-threat-but-response-fell-short.

Halberstam, Jack. *The Queer Art of Failure.* Durham, NC: Duke University Press, 2011.

Halperin, David M. "Love's Irony: Six Remarks on Platonic Eros." In *Erotikon: Essays on Eros, Ancient and Modern,* edited by Shadi Bartsch and Thomas Bartscherer, 48–58. Chicago: University of Chicago Press, 2005.

Han, Byung-Chul. *The Agony of Eros*. Foreword by Alain Badiou. Translated by Erik Butler. Cambridge, MA: Massachusetts Institute of Technology Press, 2017.

Han, Byung-Chul. *The Crisis of Narration*. Cambridge: Polity, 2024.

Han, Byung-Chul. *Good Entertainment: A Deconstruction of the Western Passion Narrative*. Translated by Adrian Nathan West. Cambridge, MA: Massachusetts Institute of Technology Press, 2019.

Han, Byung-Chul. *In the Swarm: Digital Prospects*. Translated by Erik Butler. Cambridge, MA: Massachusetts Institute of Technology Press, 2017.

Han, Byung-Chul. *Psychopolitics: Neoliberalism and New Technologies of Power*. Translated by Erik Butler. London: Verso Books, 2017.

Hardt, Michael and Antonio Negri. *Empire*. Cambridge, MA: Harvard University Press, 2000.

Hardy, Thomas. *Tess of the D'Urbervilles*. New York: W. W. Norton, 1991.

Harrison, Andrew. *The Life of D. H. Lawrence: A Critical Biography*. Oxford: Wiley-Blackwell, 2016.

Hegel, G. W. F. *Hegel's Aesthetics: Lectures on Fine Art*. Vols. I–II. Translated by T. M. Knox. Oxford: Clarendon Press, 1988.

Hegel, G. W. F. "Love." Translated by T. M. Knox, 1970. https://www.marxists.org/reference/archive/hegel/works/love/index.htm.

Hegel, G. W. F. *Phenomenology of Spirit*. Translated by A. V. Miller. Oxford: Oxford University Press, 1977.

Heidegger, Martin. *Being and Time*. Translated by John Macquarrie and Edward Robinson. New York: HarperPerennial, 2008.

Heidegger, Martin. *Discourse on Thinking*. Translated by John M. Anderson and E. Hans Freund. New York: Harper & Row, 1966.

Heidegger, Martin. "Letter on Humanism." In *Basic Writings*, edited by David Farrell Krell. London: HarperPerennial, 2008.

Heidegger, Martin. "The Origin of the Work of Art." In *Poetry, Language, Thought*, translated by Albert Hofstadter. New York: Harper & Row, 1971.

Heidegger, Martin. *Parmenides*. Translated by André Schuwer and Richard Rojcewicz. Bloomington, IN: Indiana University Press, 1998.

Heidegger, Martin. *What is Called Thinking?* Translated by J. Glenn Gray. New York: Harper & Row, 1968.

Heidegger, Martin. "What is Metaphysics?," In *Pathmarks*, translated by David Farrell Krell, edited by William McNeill. Cambridge: Cambridge University Press, 1998.

Heilbut, Anthony. *Thomas Mann: Eros and Literature*. Berkeley: University of California Press, 1997.

Heliodorus. *Aethiopica: An Ethiopian Romance*. Translated by Moses Hadas. University Park, PA: University of Pennsylvania Press, 1957.

Heller, Erich. *Thomas Mann: The Ironic German*. Cleveland, OH: Meridian, 1961.

Historia and Tale of Doctor Johannes Faustus. http://lettersfromthedustbowl.com/fbk1.html.

Hodal, Kate. "One in 200 People is a Slave. Why?" *The Guardian*, February 25, 2019. https://www.theguardian.com/news/2019/feb/25/modern-slavery-trafficking-persons-one-in-200.

Homer. *The Iliad.* Translated by Richmond Lattimore. Chicago, IL: University of Chicago Press, 1961.

Homer. *The Odyssey.* Translated by Robert Fitzgerald. New York: Farrar, Straus, & Giroux, 1998.

Horkheimer, Max and Theodor W. Adorno. *Dialectic of Enlightenment.* Translated by John Cumming. London: Continuum, 2000.

Horne, Gerald. *The Counter-Revolution of 1776: Slave Resistance and the Origins of the United States of America.* New York: New York University Press, 2014.

Human Rights Watch. "World Report 2019." https://www.hrw.org/world-report/2019/country-chapters/united-arab-emirates.

Huntington, Patricia J. "Heidegger's Reading of Kierkegaard Revisited: From Ontological Abstraction to Ethical Concretion." In *Kierkegaard in Post/Modernity*, edited by Martin J. Matuštík and Merold Westphal. Bloomington, IN: Indiana University Press, 1995.

Huxley, Aldous. "The Censor." In *The Critical Response to D.H. Lawrence*, edited by Jan Pilditch. Westport, CT: Greenwood Press, 2001.

Ignatieff, Michael. *On Consolation: Finding Solace in Dark Times.* New York: Metropolitan Books, 2021.

Irwin, William. "Death of Inauthenticity: Heidegger's Debt to Ivan Il'ich's Fall." *Tolstoy Studies Journal* 25 (Annual 2013): 15. http://www.utoronto.ca/tolstoy/journal.html.

James, Henry. *The Art of the Novel.* New York: Charles Scribner's Sons, 1962.

James, Henry. "The Portrait of a Lady." In *Novels, 1881-1886*, edited by William T. Stafford. Vol. 2. New York: Library of America, 1985.

James, Henry. *Washington Square.* New York: Penguin Books, 2007.

Jameson, Fredric. "The Experiments of Time: Providence and Realism." In *The Novel*, edited by Franco Moretti. Vol. II. Princeton, NJ: Princeton University Press, 2007.

Jaucourt, Louis. "The Novel." In *The Encyclopedia of Diderot & D'Alembert: Collaborative Translation Project.* University of Michigan. http://hdl.handle.net/2027/spo.did2222.0000.108.

Jefferson, Thomas et al. "The Declaration of Independence." 1776. https://www.archives.gov/founding-docs/declaration-transcript.

Jones, Sarah. "Why Tyrants Dehumanize the Powerless." *The New Republic,* June 20, 2018. https://newrepublic.com/article/149232/tyrants-dehumanize-powerless.

Josipovici, Gabriel. "Kierkegaard and the Novel." In *Kierkegaard: A Critical Reader*, edited by Jonathan Rée and Jane Chamberlain. Oxford: Blackwell, 1998.

Josipovici, Gabriel. *On Trust: Art and the Temptations of Suspicion.* New Haven, CT: Yale University Press, 1999.

Joyce, James. *Finnegans Wake.* New York: Penguin Books, 1999.

Joyce, James. *Ulysses.* New York: Vintage Books, 1990.

Kafka, Franz. *The Blue Octavo Notebooks.* Edited by Max Brod, translated by Ernst Kaiser and Eithne Wilkins. Cambridge: Exact Change, 1991.

Kafka, Franz. *The Castle.* Translated by Mark Harman. New York: Schocken, 1998.

Kafka, Franz. "A Country Doctor." In *The Complete Stories*, translated by Willa and Edwin Muir, edited by Nahum N. Glatzer. New York: Schocken, 1983.

Kafka, Franz. *Letters to Friends, Family, and Editors*. Translated by Richard Winston and Clare Winston. New York: John Calder, 1978.

Kafka, Franz. "The Metamorphosis." In *The Complete Stories*, translated by Willa and Edwin Muir, edited by Nahum N. Glatzer. New York: Schocken, 1983.

Kafka, Franz. "Poseidon." In *The Complete Stories*, translated by Willa and Edwin Muir, edited by Nahum N. Glatzer. New York: Schocken, 1983.

Kafka, Franz. "The Silence of the Sirens." In *The Complete Stories*. translated by Willa and Edwin Muir, edited by Nahum N. Glatzer. New York: Schocken, 1983.

Kafka, Franz. *The Trial*. Translated by Willa and Edwin Muir. New York: Schocken, 1992.

Kant, Immanuel. "An Answer to the Question: What is Enlightenment?" In *"Toward Perpetual Peace" and Other Writings on Politics, Peace, and History*, edited by Pauline Kleingold and translated by David L. Colclasure. New Haven, CT: Yale University Press, 2006.

Kant, Immanuel. *Critique of Judgment*. Translated by Werner S. Pluhar. Indianapolis, IN: Hackett, 1987.

Kant, Immanuel. *Grounding for the Metaphysics of Morals*. Translated by James W. Ellington. Indianapolis, IN: Hackett, 1981.

Kierkegaard, Søren. *Early Polemical Writings*. Edited and translated by Howard V. Hong and Edna V. Hong. Princeton, NJ: Princeton University Press, 1990.

Kierkegaard, Søren. *Either/Or*. Vols. I–II. Edited and translated by Howard V. Hong and Edna V. Hong. Princeton, NJ: Princeton University Press, 1987.

Kierkegaard, Søren. *The Concept of Irony, with Continual Reference to Socrates*. Edited and translated by Howard V. Hong and Edna H. Hong. Princeton, NJ: Princeton University Press, 1989.

Kierkegaard, Søren. *Fear and Trembling*. Translated by Alastair Hannay. London: Penguin Books, 2003.

Kierkegaard, Søren. *A Literary Review*. Edited and translated by Alastair Hannay. London: Penguin Books, 2001.

Kierkegaard, Søren. *The Seducer's Diary*. Foreword by John Updike. Edited and translated by Howard V. Hong and Edna H. Hong. Princeton, NJ: Princeton University Press, 1989.

Kierkegaard, Søren. "Supplement." In *Fear and Trembling / Repetition*, edited and translated by Howard V. Hong and Edna V. Hong. Princeton, NJ: Princeton University Press, 1983.

Kisiel, Theodore and Thomas Sheehan, Editors. *Becoming Heidegger: On the Trail of his Early Occasional Writings*. Evanston, IL: Northwestern University Press, 2007.

Kinkead-Weekes, Mark. "D.H. Lawrence: 'A Passionately Religious Man.'" *The Sewanee Review* 109, no. 3 (Summer 2001): 379–397.

Kleist, Heinrich von. "On the Theater of Marionettes." Translated by Peter Wortsman. New York: Archipelago, 2010.

Knausgaard, Karl Ove. *My Struggle*. Vol. 1. Translated by Don Bartlett. New York: Farrar, Straus & Giroux, 2012.

Knausgaard, Karl Ove. *My Struggle*. Vol. 4. Translated by Don Bartlett. New York: Archipelago, 2015.

Koulouris, Theodore. *Hellenism and Loss in the Work of Virginia Woolf*. London: Routledge, 2011.

Koulouris, Theodore. "Virginia Woolf's 'Greek Notebook' (VS Greek and Latin Studies): An Annotated Transcription." *Woolf Studies Annual* 25, no. 1 (2019): 1–72.

Kreilkamp, Ivan. "Petted Things: Cruelty and Sympathy in the Brontës." In *Wuthering Heights*, edited by Alexandra Lewis, 386–406. New York: W. W. Norton, 2019.

Kristeva, Julia. *Desire in Language: A Semiotic Approach to Literature and Art*. Edited by Leon S. Roudiez and translated by Thomas Gora, Alice Jardine, and Leon S. Roudiez. New York: Columbia University Press, 1980.

Kundera, Milan. *The Art of the Novel*. Translated by Linda Asher, New York: Harper & Row, 1988.

Kundera, Milan. *Testaments Betrayed: An Essay in Nine Parts*. Translated by Linda Asher. New York: HarperCollins, 1993.

Landler, Mark and Somini Sengupta. "Trump and the Teenager: A Climate Showdown at Davos." *The New York Times,* January 21, 2020. https://www.nytimes.com/2020/01/21/climate/greta-thunberg-trump-davos.html.

Landy, Joshua. "'*Les Moi en Moi*': The Proustian Self in Philosophical Perspective." *New Literary Review* 32, no. 1 (Winter 2001): 91–132.

Lange, Jeva. "Amazon has Sold out of 1984." *The Week,* January 27, 2017. https://theweek.com/speedreads/676249/amazon-sold-1984.

Lawrence, D. H. *Lady Chatterley's Lover and "À Propos of Lady Chatterley's Lover."* Edited by Michael Squires. Cambridge: Cambridge University Press, 1993.

Lawrence, D. H. *The Letters of D.H. Lawrence*. Vol. II: 1913-1916. Edited by George J. Zytaruk and James T. Boulton. Cambridge: Cambridge University Press, 2002.

Lawrence, D. H. "The Future of the Novel." In *Study of Thomas Hardy and Other Essays,* edited by Bruce Steele, 151–155. Cambridge: Cambridge University Press, 1985.

Lawrence, D. H. "Morality and the Novel." In *Study of Thomas Hardy and Other Essays*, edited by Bruce Steele, 171–176. Cambridge: Cambridge University Press, 1985.

Lawrence, D. H. "From *Study of Thomas Hardy*." In *Selected Literary Criticism*, edited by Anthony Beal. New York: Viking Press, 1966.

Lawrence, D. H. "Why the Novel Matters." In *Study of Thomas Hardy and Other Essays*, edited by Bruce Steele, 193–198. Cambridge: Cambridge University Press, 1985.

Lee, Hermione. *Virginia Woolf*. New York: Vintage Books, 1999.

Leibniz, Gottfried Wilhelm. *The Monadology and Other Philosophical Writings*. Translated by Robert Latta. Oxford: Oxford University Press, 1965.

Leopardi, Giacomo. *The Moral Essays*. Translated by Patrick Creagh. New York: Columbia University Press, 1983.

The Letters of Abelard and Heloise. Translated by Betty Radice and revised by M. T. Clanchy. London: Penguin Books, 2003.

Levinas, Emmanuel. *On Escape.* Translated by Bettina Bergo. Stanford, CA: Stanford University Press, 2003.

Levinas, Emmanuel. "The Other in Proust." In *Proper Names.* Translated by Michael B. Smith. Stanford, CA: Stanford University Press, 1996.

Levine, George. *Lady Chatterley's Lover.* In *D.H. Lawrence*, edited by Harold Bloom. New York: Chelsea House Publishers, 1986.

Lewis, C. S. *The Allegory of Love.* Cambridge: Cambridge University Press, 2013.

Lichtenberg Georg Christoph. *Aphorisms.* Translated by R. J. Hollingdale. London: Penguin Press, 1990.

Ligotti, Thomas. *The Conspiracy Against the Human Race: A Contrivance of Horror.* New York: Penguin Press, 2018.

Lispector, Clarice. *The Passion According to G. H.* Translated by Idra Novey. New York: New Directions, 2012.

Locke, John. *An Essay Concerning Human Understanding.* Edited by Roger Woolhouse. London: Penguin Press, 1997.

Love, Jean O. *Worlds in Consciousness: Mythopoetic Thought in the Novels of Virginia Woolf.* Berkeley, CA: University of California Press, 1970.

Ludacris feat. Shawnna. "Stand Up." Island Def Jam Music Group, 2003. https://www.youtube.com/watch?v=pZG7IK99OvI.

Lukács, Georg. *Essays on Thomas Mann.* Translated by Stanley Mitchell. London: Merlin Press, 1979.

Lukács, Georg. *Realism in Our Time: Literature and the Class Struggle.* Translated by John and Necke Mander. New York: Harper & Row, 1971.

Lukács, Georg. *Soul and Form.* Edited by John T. Sanders and Katie Terezakis, introduction by Judith Butler. New York: Columbia University Press, 2010.

Lukács, Georg. *Studies in European Realism.* New York: Grosset & Dunlap, 1964.

Lukács, Georg. *The Theory of the Novel.* Translated by Anna Bostock. Cambridge, MA: Massachusetts Institute of Technology Press, 1971.

Machiavelli, Niccolò. *The Prince.* In *The Prince and The Discourses*, translated by Luigi Ricci. Modern Library College Edition. New York: Random House, 1950.

Mackey, Louis. *Kierkegaard: A Kind of Poet.* Philadelphia, PA: University of Pennsylvania Press, 1972.

Magee, Bryan. *The Philosophy of Schopenhauer.* Oxford: Oxford University Press, 1983.

Mann, Thomas. *Buddenbrooks.* Translated by John E. Woods. New York: Vintage Books, 1993.

Mann, Thomas. *Death in Venice.* Translated by Michael Henry Heim. New York: Ecco, 2004.

Mann, Thomas. *Der Tod in Venedig und andere Erzählungen.* Frankfurt: Fischer Taschenbuch Verlag, 1986.

Mann, Thomas. *Doctor Faustus: The Life of the German Composer Adrian Leverkühn as Told by a Friend.* Translated by John E. Woods. New York: Vintage Books, 1999.

Mann, Thomas. *Essays of Three Decades*. Translated by H. T. Lowe-Porter. New York: Alfred A. Knopf, 1947.

Mann, Thomas. *The Magic Mountain*. Translated by John E. Woods. New York: Vintage Books, 1996.

Marasco, Robyn. *The Highway of Despair: Critical Theory after Hegel*. New York: Columbia University Press, 2015.

Marcuse, Herbert. *Eros and Civilization: A Philosophical Inquiry into Freud*. Boston, MA: Beacon Press, 1974.

Martin, Timothy. *Joyce and Wagner: A Study of Influence*. Cambridge: Cambridge University Press, 1991.

Marx, Karl. *Capital: Volume One*. In *The Marx-Engels Reader*, edited by Robert C. Tucker. 2nd ed. New York: W. W. Norton, 1978.

Marx, Karl. "Theses on Feuerbach." In *The Marx-Engels Reader*, edited by Robert C. Tucker. 2nd ed. New York: W. W. Norton, 1978.

Marx, Leo. "Melville's Parable of Walls." In *Melville's Short Novels*, edited by Dan McCall. New York: W. W. Norton, 2002.

Maupassant, Guy de. *Pierre et Jean*. Translated by Julie Mead. Oxford: Oxford University Press, 2001.

Mauriac, François. *Mémoires Interieurs*. Translated by Gerard Hopkins. London: Eyre & Spottiswoode, 1960.

Mazzoni, Guido. *Theory of the Novel*. Translated by Zakiya Hanafi. Cambridge, MA: Harvard University Press, 2017.

McEwan, Ian. *Atonement*. New York: Anchor Books, 2003.

McKay, Melanie. "Spatial Form and Simultaneity in Nabokov's Fiction." PhD Dissertation, Tulane University, New Orleans, LA, 1983.

McKeon, Michael. *The Origins of the English Novel: 1600-1740*. 15th Anniversary Edition. Baltimore: Johns Hopkins University Press, 2002.

Melville, Herman. *Bartleby, The Scrivener: A Story of Wall-Street*. In *Melville's Short Novels*, edited by Dan McCall, 3–34. New York: W. W. Norton, 2002.

Melville, Herman. *Moby-Dick, or, the Whale*. New York: Modern Library, 2000.

Merimée, Prosper. *Carmen and Other Stories*. Translated by Nicholas Jotcham. Oxford: Oxford University Press, 1998.

Meyer, Priscilla and Jeff Hoffmann. "Infinite Reflections in Pale Fire: The Danish Connection (Hans Andersen and Isak Dinesen)." *Russian Literature* 41 (1997): 197–221.

Meyer, Priscilla and Rachel Trousdale. "Vladimir Nabokov and Virginia Woolf." *Comparative Literature Studies* 50, no. 3 (2013): 490–522.

Meyers, Jeffrey. "Kafka's Dark Laughter." *The Antioch Review* 70, no. 4 (Fall 2012): 760–768. https://www.jstor.org/stable/10.7723/antiochreview.70.4.0760.

Michael, Michael Love. "Meet Neff Davis, Anna Delvey's Only Friend in New York." *Paper Magazine,* June 13, 2018. https://www.papermag.com/neff-davis-2577568832.html.

Michaud, Derek. "Ludwig Feuerbach (1804-1872)." In *Boston Collaborative Encyclopedia of Western Theology,* http://people.bu.edu/wwildman/bce/feuerbach.htm.

Michelucci, Stefania. *Space and Place in the Works of D.H. Lawrence.* Translated by Jill Franks. London: McFarland, 2002.

Miller, D. A. *The Novel and the Police.* Berkeley, CA: University of California Press, 1988.

Mooney, Edward F. "Kierkegaard's Disruptions of Literature and Philosophy: Freedom, Anxiety, and Existential Contributions." In *Kierkegaard, Literature, and the Arts,* edited by Eric Ziolkowski, 55–70. Evanston, IL: Northwestern University Press, 2018.

Moretti, Franco. "A Capital *Dracula.*" In Bram Stoker, *Dracula,* edited by Nina Auerbach and David J. Skal. New York: W. W. Norton, 1997.

Moretti, Franco. *Modern Epic: The World-System from Goethe to García-Márquez.* Translated by Quintin Hoare. London: Verso Books, 1996.

"Movie Day at the Supreme Court or 'I Know it When I See it': A History of the Definition of Obscenity." https://corporate.findlaw.com/litigation-disputes/movie-day-at-the-supreme-court-or-i-know-it-when-i-see-it-a.html.

Moynahan, Julian. *The Deed of Life: The Novels and Tales of D.H. Lawrence.* Princeton, NJ: Princeton University Press, 1963.

Muhlstein, Anka. *Monsieur Proust's Library.* New York: Other Press, 2012.

Musil, Robert. *The Man without Qualities.* Vol. 1. Translated by Sophie Wilkins. New York: Vintage Books, 1995.

Musil, Robert. *The Man without Qualities.* Vol. 2. Translated by Sophie Wilkins. New York: Vintage Books, 1996.

Nabokov, Vladimir. "An Affair of Honor." In *The Stories of Vladimir Nabokov,* edited by Dmitri Nabokov, 199–221. New York: Vintage Books, 2008.

Nabokov, Vladimir. *The Enchanter.* Translated by Dmitri Nabokov. New York: Vintage Books, 1991.

Nabokov, Vladimir. *The Gift.* Translated by Michael Scammell with the collaboration of the author. New York: Vintage Books, 1991.

Nabokov, Vladimir. *Lolita.* Annotated and edited by Alfred Appel, Jr. New York: Vintage Books, 1991.

Nabokov, Vladimir. *Pale Fire.* New York: Vintage Books, 1989.

Nabokov, Vladimir. *Speak, Memory: An Autobiography Revisited.* New York: Vintage Books, 1989.

Nabokov, Vladimir. *Strong Opinions.* New York: Vintage Books, 1990.

Nabokov, Vladimir Dmitrievich. "1904 Library Catalogue." *The Nabokovian.* https://thenabokovian.org/sites/default/files/2018-06/VDNabokov%20Library%20Catalog%201904.pdf.

Nabokov, Vladimir Dmitrievich. "1911 Library Catalogue." *The Nabokovian.* https://thenabokovian.org/sites/default/files/2018-06/VDNabokov%20Library%20Catalog%201904.pdf.

Naiman, Eric. *Nabokov, Perversely.* Ithaca, NY: Cornell University Press, 2010.

"NASA Readies Perseverance Mars Rover's Earthly Twin." September 4, 2020. https://www.jpl.nasa.gov/news/nasa-readies-perseverance-mars-rovers-earthly-twin.

Ndahiro, Kennedy. "In Rwanda, We Know all About Dehumanizing Language." *The Atlantic,* April 13, 2019. https://www.theatlantic.com/ideas/archive/2019/04/rwanda-shows-how-hateful-speech-leads-violence/587041/.

Nietzsche, Friedrich. *Beyond Good and Evil: Prelude to a Philosophy of the Future.* Translated by Walter Kaufmann. New York: Vintage Books, 1966.

Nietzsche, Friedrich. *The Birth of Tragedy / The Case of Wagner.* Translated by Walter Kaufmann. New York: Vintage Books, 1967.

Nietzsche, Friedrich. *Daybreak.* Edited by Maudemarie Clark and Brian Leiter. Translated by R. J. Hollingdale. Cambridge: Cambridge University Press, 2005.

Nietzsche, Friedrich. *The Gay Science.* Translated by Walter Kaufmann. New York: Vintage Books, 1974.

Nietzsche, Friedrich. *Human, All Too Human.* Translated by R. J. Hollingdale. Cambridge: Cambridge University Press, 2009.

Nietzsche, Friedrich. *On the Genealogy of Morals / Ecce Homo.* Translated by Walter Kaufmann and R. J. Hollingdale. New York: Vintage Books, 1989.

Nietzsche, Friedrich. *Philosophy and Truth: Selections from Nietzsche's Notebooks of the Early 1870s.* Edited and translated by Daniel Breazeale. Amherst, NY: Humanity Books, 1999.

Nietzsche, Friedrich. *Thus Spake Zarathustra.* Translated by Thomas Common. Mineola, NY: Dover Publications, 1999.

Nietzsche, Friedrich. *Twilight of the Idols / The Anti-Christ.* Translated by R. J. Hollingdale. London: Penguin Books, 1990.

Nietzsche, Friedrich. *Unpublished Writings from the Period of Unfashionable Observations.* Translated by Richard T. Gray. Stanford, CA: Stanford University Press, 1995.

Nussbaum, Martha. "Fictions of the Soul." *Philosophy and Literature* 7, no. 2 (October 1983): 145–161. doi:10.1353/phl.1983.0040.

Nussbaum, Martha. "The Romantic Ascent: Emily Brontë." In *Wuthering Heights*, edited by Alexandra Lewis, 369-86. New York: W. W. Norton, 2019.

Nussbaum, Martha. "The Speech of Alcibiades: A Reading of Plato's *Symposium*." *Philosophy and Literature* 3, no. 2 (Fall 1979): 131–172. doi:10.1353/phl.1979.0024.

Ong, Yi-Ping. *The Art of Being: Poetics of the Novel and Existentialist Philosophy.* Cambridge, MA: Harvard University Press, 2018.

Packman, David. *Vladimir Nabokov: The Structure of Literary Desire.* Columbia, MO: University of Missouri Press, 1982.

Palahniuk, Chuck. *Invisible Monsters.* New York: W. W. Norton, 1999.

Palmer, Emily. "A Fake Heiress Called Anna Delvey Conned the City's Wealthy. 'I'm Not Sorry,' She Says." *The New York Times,* May 10, 2019. https://www.nytimes.com/2019/05/10/nyregion/anna-delvey-sorokin.html?auth=login-email&login=email.

Papaioannou, Sophia. "Charite's Rape, Psyche on the Rock and the Parallel Function of Marriage in Apuleuius' 'Metamorphoses.'" *Mnemosyne* 51, no. 3 (June 1998): 302–324. https://www.jstor.org/stable/4432843.

Parker, Stephen Jay. "Library." In *The Garland Companion to Vladimir Nabokov,* edited by Vladimir E. Alexandrov, 283–290. New York: Garland Publishing, 1995.

Parks, Tim. "The Dying Art of Instruction in the Digital Classroom." *The New York Review of Books,* July 31, 2019. https://www.nybooks.com/daily/2019/07/31/the-dying-art-of-instruction-in-the-digital-classroom/.

Pascal, Blaise. *Pensées.* Translated by A. J. Krailsheimer. New York: Penguin Books, 1995.

Pattison, George. "The Bonfire of the Genres: Kierkegaard's Literary Kaleidoscope." In *Kierkegaard, Literature, and the Arts,* edited by Eric Ziolkowski, 39–54. Evanston, IL: Northwestern University Press, 2018.

Penda, Petar. *Aesthetics and Ideology of D.H. Lawrence, Virginia Woolf, and T.S. Eliot.* Lanham, MD: Lexington Books, 2018.

"Pessimism." https://www.etymonline.com/word/pessimism.

Pifer, Ellen. "Nabokov's Novel Offspring: Lolita and her Kin." In *Vladimir Nabokov's Lolita: A Casebook*, edited by Ellen Pifer, 83–110. Oxford: Oxford University Press, 2003.

Pinkard, Terry. *German Philosophy 1760-1860: The Legacy of Idealism.* Cambridge: Cambridge University Press, 2010.

Platen, August von. "Tristan." In *Great German Poems of the Romantic Era / Berühmte Gedichte der deutschen Romantik,* edited and translated by Stanley Appelbaum. Mineola, NY: Dover Publishing, 1995.

Plath, Sylvia, *The Bell Jar.* New York: HarperPerennial, 2006.

Plato. *Apology.* In *Five Dialogues,* translated by G. M. A. Grube, revised by John M. Cooper. Indianapolis, IN: Hackett, 2002.

Plato. *Phaedrus.* Translated by Alexander Nehamas and Paul Woodruff. Indianapolis, IN: Hackett, 1995.

Plato. *Plato's Symposium.* Translated by Seth Benardete. Chicago, IL: University of Chicago Press, 2001.

Plato. *The Republic of Plato.* Translated by Allan Bloom. New York: Basic Books, 2016.

Price, Brian. *A Theory of Regret.* Durham: Duke University Press, 2017.

Proffer, Carl R. *The Keys to Lolita.* Bloomington, IN: Indiana University Press, 1968.

Proust, Marcel. *The Captive.* In *The Captive and the Fugitive,* edited by William C. Carter and translated by C. K. Scott Moncrieff. New Haven, CT: Yale University Press, 2023.

Proust, Marcel. *The Fugitive.* In *The Captive and the Fugitive,* edited by William C. Carter and translated by C. K. Scott Moncrieff. New Haven, CT: Yale University Press, 2023.

Proust, Marcel. *The Guermantes Way.* Edited by William C. Carter. Translated by C. K. Scott Moncrieff. New Haven, CT: Yale University Press, 2018.

Proust, Marcel. *In the Shadow of Young Girls in Flower.* Edited by William C. Carter. Translated by C. K. Scott Moncrieff. New Haven, CT: Yale University Press, 2015.

Proust, Marcel. *Letters of Marcel Proust.* Translated by Mina Curtiss. New York: Turtle Point Press, 2006.

Proust, Marcel. *Remembrance of Things Past.* Vols. 1–3. Translated by C. K. Scott Moncrieff and Terence Kilmartin. New York: Vintage Books, 1982.

Proust, Marcel. *Sodom and Gomorrah*. Edited by William C. Carter. Translated by C. K. Scott Moncrieff. New Haven, CT: Yale University Press, 2021.

Proust, Marcel. *Swann's Way*. Translated by Lydia Davis. New York: Viking Press, 2002.

Proust, Marce. *Time Regained*. Translated by Andreas Mayor and Terence Kilmartin. Revised by D. J. Enright. New York: Modern Library, 2003.

Pushkin, Aleksandr. *Eugene Onegin: A Novel in Verse*. Translated by Vladimir Nabokov. Princeton, NJ: Princeton University Press, 2018.

Pynchon, Thomas. *Gravity's Rainbow*. New York: Penguin Books, 2006.

Quintana, Anna. "Fake NYC Heiress Anna Delvey's Scams Landed her a Netflix Show." *Distractify,* May 2019. https://www.distractify.com/p/what-did-anna-delvey-do.

Rabelais, François. *The Histories of Gargantua and Pantagruel*. Translated by J. M. Cohen. New York: Penguin Books, 1985.

Revel, Jean-François. *On Proust*. Translated by Martin Turnell. New York: The Library Press, 1972.

Richardson, Samuel. *Pamela: or, Virtue Rewarded*. Oxford: Oxford University Press, 2001.

Robert, Marthe. "From *Origins of the Novel*." In *Theory of the Novel: A Historical Approach*, edited by Michael McKeon. Baltimore, MD: Johns Hopkins University Press, 2000.

Ronell, Avital, in conversation with Anne Dufourmantelle. *Fighting Theory*. Translated by Catherine Porter. Champaign, IL: University of Illinois Press, 2010.

Ronell, Avital. "The Turn of the Screwed." Re-Thinking Literature Conference, New York University, New York, September 21, 2013.

Roper, Robert. *Nabokov in America: On the Road to* Lolita. London: Bloomsbury, 2015.

Rougement, Denis de. *Love in the Western World*. Translated by Montgomery Belgion. New York: Doubleday, 1956.

Rougement, Denis de. *The Myths of Love*. Translated by Richard Howard. London: Faber & Faber, 1964.

Russell, Bertrand. *The Conquest of Happiness*. New York: W. W. Norton, 2013.

Rutsala, Kirsten. "A Garden and a Twilight and a Palace Gate: Lolita Outside Humbert's Control." In *Critical Insights:* Lolita, edited by Rachel Stauffer. Amenia, NY: Grey House, 2016.

Sade, Marquis de. "Reflections on the Novel." In *The 120 Days of Sodom and Other Writings*, translated by Austryn Wainhouse and Richard Seaver. New York: Grove Press, 1966.

Sæverot, Herner. *Indirect Pedagogy: Some Lessons in Existential Education*. Edited by Michael A. Peters. Rotterdam: Sense, 2012..

Sanders, Scott R. "Lady Chatterley's Loving and the Annihilation Impulse." In *D.H. Lawrence's 'Lady': A New Look at Lady Chatterley's Lover*, edited by Michael Squires and Dennis Jackson, 1–16. Athens, GA: University of Georgia Press: 1985.

Sartre, Jean-Paul. *Being and Nothingness*. Translated by Hazel E. Barnes. New York: Philosophical Library, 1956.

Sartre, Jean-Paul. *Nausea*. Translated by Lloyd Alexander, introduction by Hayden Carruth. New York: New Directions, 1964.
Sartre, Jean-Paul. "On *The Sound and the Fury*: Time in the Work of Faulkner." In *The Sound and the Fury*, by William Faulkner, edited by David Minter. 2nd ed. New York: W. W. Norton, 1994.
Schaffer, Talia. "The Homoerotic History of *Dracula*." In Bram Stoker, *Dracula*, edited by Nina Auerbach and David J. Skal. New York: W. W. Norton, 1997.
Schiller, Friedrich. *On the Aesthetic Education of Man in a Series of Letters*. Translated by Reginald Snell. New York: Frederick Ungar Publishing Co., 1981.
Schlegel, Friedrich von. "Aphorisms from the Lyceum." In *Friedrich Schlegel's* Lucinde *and the Fragments*, translated by Peter Firchow. Minneapolis, MN: University of Minnesota Press, 1971.
Schlegel, Friedrich von. "Athenaeum Fragments." In *Friedrich Schlegel's* Lucinde *and the Fragments*, translated by Peter Firchow. Minneapolis, MN: University of Minnesota Press, 1971.
Schlegel, Friedrich von. "Brief über den Roman." http://www.zeno.org/Literatur/M/Schlegel,+Friedrich/Ästhetische+und+politische+Schriften/Gespräch+über+die+Poesie/Brief+über+den+Roman.
Schlegel, Friedrich von. "Dialogue on Poetry." In *German Romantic Criticism*, edited by A. Leslie Willson and translated by Ernst Behler and Roman Struc. London: Continuum, 1982.
Schopenhauer, Arthur. *Essays and Aphorisms*. Translated by R. J. Hollingdale. London: Penguin Books, 1970.
Schopenhauer, Arthur. "The Metaphysics of Love." In *Essays of Schopenhauer*, translated by Mrs. Rudolf Dircks. London: Scott Library Ltd., 1897.
Schopenhauer, Arthur. "On the Fourfold Root of the Principle of Sufficient Reason." In *Two Essays*, by Arthur Schopenhauer, translated by Mme. Karl Hillebrand. Revised Edition. Oxford: Benediction Classics, 2010.
Schopenhauer, Arthur. "On the Sufferings of the World." In *Suffering, Suicide, and Immortality*, translated by T. Bailey Saunders. 1–17. Mineola, NY: Dover Publications, 2006.
Schopenhauer, Arthur. *The Wisdom of Life and Counsels and Maxims*. Translated by T. Bailey Saunders. Mineola, NY: Dover, 2004..
Schopenhauer, Arthur. *The World as Will and Representation*. Vols. I–II. Translated by E. F. J. Payne. Mineola, NY: Dover Publications, 1969.
Schwartz, Daniel R. *Reading the Modern British and Irish Novel 1890-1930*. Oxford: Blackwell, 2005.
Sedgwick, Eve Kosofsky. *Epistemology of the Closet*. Berkeley, CA: University of California Press, 2008.
Senf, Carol A. "*Dracula*: The Unseen Face in the Mirror." In Bram Stoker, *Dracula*, edited by Nina Auerbach and David J. Skal. New York: W. W. Norton, 1997.
Shakespeare, William. *Hamlet*. New York: Folger, 1992.
Shakespeare, William. *King Lear*. New York: Penguin Books, 1998.
Shakespeare, William. *Macbeth*. New York: Folger, 2013.
Shakespeare, William. *Othello*. New York: Folger, 2004.

Shakespeare, William. *Richard III*. New York: Folger, 1996.
Shakespeare, William. *Romeo and Juliet*. New York: Bantam Books, 1988.
Shakespeare, William. "Sonnet 98." In *Shakespeare's Sonnets and Poems*, edited by Barbara A. Mowat and Paul Werstine. New York: Folger, 2006.
Sheehan, Thomas. "Emmanuel Faye: The Introduction of Fraud into Philosophy?" *Philosophy Today* 59, no. 3 (Summer 2015): 367–400.
Shelley, Mary. *Frankenstein*. New York: W. W. Norton, 1996.
Smyth, John Vignaux. *A Question of Eros: Irony in Sterne, Kierkegaard, and Barthes*. Gainesville, FL: Florida State University Press, 1986.
Sommers, Elena. "Nabokov's Mermaid: 'Spring in Fialta.'" *Nabokov Studies* 12 (2009/2011): 31–48.
Son, Youngjoo. *Here and Now: The Politics of Social Space in D.H. Lawrence and Virginia Woolf*. London: Routledge, 2006.
Sophocles. *Oedipus the King*. Translated by David Grene, edited by David Grene and Richard Lattimore. Chicago, IL: University of Chicago Press, 2013.
Spenser, Edmund. *The Faerie Queene*. In *The Norton Anthology of English Literature*, edited by Stephen Greenblatt, Vol. 1, 10th ed., 413–486. New York: W. W. Norton, 2019.
Spilka, Mark. "Lawrence's Quarrel with Tenderness." In *The Critical Response to D.H. Lawrence*, edited by Jan Pilditch. Westport, CT: Greenwood Press, 2001.
Stendhal. *Love*. Translated by Gilbert and Suzanne Sale. London: Penguin Books, 1975.
Stendhal. *The Red and the Black*. Translated by Robert M. Adams. New York: W. W. Norton, 2008.
Sterne, Laurence. *The Life and Opinions of Tristram Shandy, Gentleman*. London: Penguin Books, 1978.
Stoker, Bram. *Dracula*. Edited by Nina Auerbach and David J. Skal. New York: W. W. Norton, 1997.
Strassburg, Gottfried von. *Tristan*. Translated by A. T. Hatto. London: Penguin Books, 1976.
Sugg, Richard. *Murder After Death*. Ithaca, NY: Cornell University Press, 2007.
Swinburne, Charles Algernon. *Tristram of Lyonesse*. London: Chatto and Windus, 1882..
Tamir-Ghez, Nomi. "The Art of Persuasion in Nabokov's *Lolita*." In *Vladimir Nabokov's* Lolita: *A Casebook*, edited by Ellen Pifer. 17–38. Oxford: Oxford University Press, 2003.
Tanner, Michael. *Wagner*. Princeton, NJ: Princeton University Press, 1995.
Tennyson, Alfred Lord. *Idylls of the King*. London: Penguin Books, 1989.
Thacker, Eugene. *Cosmic Pessimism*. Minneapolis, MN: Univocal, 2015.
Thacker, Eugene. *In the Dust of this Planet: Horror of Philosophy*. Volume 1. Alresford: Zero Books, 2011.
Thacker, Eugene. *Infinite Resignation*. London: Repeater, 2018.
Tokomitsu, Miya. "In the Name of Love." *Jacobin*, January 2014. https://www.jacobinmag.com/2014/01/in-the-name-of-love/.
Tolstoy, Leo. *Anna Karenina*. Translated by Richard Pevear and Larissa Volokhonsky. London: Penguin Books, 2002.

Tolstoy, Leo. *The Death of Ivan Ilyich*. In *Tolstoy's Short Fiction*, translated by Louise and Aylmer Maude, edited by Michael R. Katz. New York: W. W. Norton, 2008.

Turgenev, Ivan. *Fathers and Sons*. Translated by Michael R. Katz. New York: W. W. Norton, 1996.

Tweedle, James. "Nabokov and the Boundless Novel." *Twentieth Century Literature* 46, no. 2 (Summer 2000): 150–170.

Unamuno, Miguel de. *Tragic Sense of Life*. Translated by J. E. Crawford Flitch. Mineola, NY: Dover Publications, 1954.

Vaget, Hans Rudolf. "Werther, the Undead." In *The Sufferings of Young Werther*. Edited and translated by Stanley Corngold. New York: W. W. Norton, 2013.

Vicks, Meghan. *Narratives of Nothing in Twentieth-Century Literature*. London: Bloomsbury, 2015.

Volney, Constantin François. *A New Translation of Volney's Ruins; or Meditations on the Revolution of Empires*. Translated by Robert D. Richardson, Jr. under inspection of author. 1802. New York: Garland Publishing, 1979.

Voltaire. *Candide*. In *Candide and Other Stories*, translated and with an introduction by Roger Pearson. Oxford: Oxford University Press, 1998.

Voltaire. *Micromegas*. In *Candide and Other Stories*, translated and with an introduction by Roger Pearson. Oxford: Oxford University Press, 1998.

Wagner, Richard. *My Life*. Translated by Andrew Gray. Edited by Mary Whittall. Cambridge: Cambridge University Press, 1983.

Walsh, Sylvia. *Living Poetically: Kierkegaard's Existential Aesthetics*. University Park, PA: Pennsylvania State University Press, 1994.

Watt, Ian. *The Rise of the Novel: Studies in Defoe, Richardson, and Fielding*. Berkeley, CA: University of California Press, 1957.

Weinman, Sarah. *The Real Lolita: A Lost Girl, an Unthinkable Crime, and a Scandalous Masterpiece*. New York: Ecco, 2018.

Whitman, James Q. *Hitler's American Model: The United States and the Making of Nazi Race Law*. Princeton, NJ: Princeton University Press, 2017.

Wilde, Oscar. *The Picture of Dorian Gray*. New York: W. W. Norton, 1988.

Wittgenstein, Ludwig. *Philosophical Investigations*. Translated by G. E. M. Anscombe, P. M. S. Hacker, and Joachim Schulte. London: Wiley-Blackwell, 2009.

Wood, James and Karl Ove Knausgaard. "Writing Welch, Chris. "Apple's Iconic Fifth Avenue Store is Back and Bigger Than Ever." *The Verge*, September 19, 2019. https://www.theverge.com/2019/9/19/20874180/apple-cube-store-new-york-city-fifth-avenue-reopening-date-tour.

Wharton, Edith. *Ethan Frome*. Mineola, NY: Dover Publications, 1991.

White, Edmund. *Marcel Proust*. New York: Viking Press, 1999.

Whitman, James Q. *Hitler's American Model: The United States and the Making of Nazi Race Law*. Princeton, NJ: Princeton University Press, 2017.

Wood, Michael. *The Magician's Doubts: Nabokov and the Risks of Fiction*. Princeton, NJ: Princeton University Press, 1994.

Wood, Michael and Karl Ove Knausgaard. "*My Struggle*: An Exchange." *The Paris Review* no. 211 (Winter 2014). http://www.theparisreview.org/interviews/6345/writing-emmy-struggle-em-an-exchange-james-wood-karl-ove-knausgaard.

Woolf, Virginia. *The Common Reader I*. Annotated Ed. Edited by Andrew McNeillie. San Diego, CA: Harcourt Brace Jovanovich, 1984.

Woolf, Virginia. *The Diary of Virginia Woolf*. Volume II: 1920-1924. Edited by Anne Olivier Bell, assisted by Andrew McNeillie. San Diego, CA: Harcourt Brace Jovanovich, 1978.

Woolf, Virginia. *The Diary of Virginia Woolf*. Volume III: 1925-1930. Edited by Anne Olivier Bell, assisted by Andrew McNeillie. San Diego, CA: Harcourt Brace Jovanovich, 1981.

Woolf, Virginia. *The Diary of Virginia Woolf*. Volume IV: 1931-1935. Edited by Anne Olivier Bell, assisted by Andrew McNeillie. San Diego, CA: Harcourt Brace Jovanovich, 1983.

Woolf, Virginia. *The Essays of Virginia Woolf*. Volume II: 1912-1918. Edited by Andrew McNeillie. London: Hogarth Press, 1987.

Woolf, Virginia. *The Letters of Virginia Woolf*. Volume II: 1912-1922. Edited by Nigel Nicolson. San Diego, CA: Harcourt Brace Jovanovich, 1976.

Woolf, Virginia. *Moments of Being: A Collection of Autobiographical Writing*. 2nd ed. Edited by Jeanne Schulkind. San Diego, CA: Harcourt Brace Jovanovich, 1985.

Woolf, Virginia. *Mrs. Dalloway*. Edited by David Bradshaw. Oxford: Oxford University Press, 2000.

Woolf, Virginia. *To the Lighthouse*. Edited by David Bradshaw. Oxford: Oxford University Press, 2006.

Woolf, Virginia. *The Waves*. London: Penguin Books, 2000.

Wootton, David. "The Impossible Dream." *Lapham's Quarterly* XII, no. 3 (Summer 2019): 13–21.

Worthen, John. *D.H. Lawrence: The Life of an Outsider*. New York: Penguin Books, 2005.

Wright, Daniel. "Thomas Hardy's Groundwork." *PMLA* 134, no. 5 (October 2019): 1028–1041.

Wyatt, Edward. "Author is Kicked out of Oprah Winfrey's Book Club." *The New York Times,* January 27, 2006. https://www.nytimes.com/2006/01/27/books/27oprah.html.

Yates, Richard. *Revolutionary Road*. New York: Vintage Books, 2008.

Zamyatin, Yevgeny. *We*. Translated by Clarence Brown. London: Penguin Books, 1993.

Zhao, Christina. "Students Not Smiling at School Will be Punished, Say Teachers." *Newsweek,* May 16, 2018. https://www.newsweek.com/students-not-smiling-school-will-be-punished-says-principle-928674.

Žižek, Slavoj. *In Defense of Lost Causes*. London: Verso Books, 2009.

Zweig, Stefan. *Balzac, Dickens, Dostoevsky: Master Builders of the Spirit*. Vol. I. Edited by Laurence Mintz. New Brunswick, NJ: Transaction Publishers, 2010.

Index

Abelard, Peter, 105–8, 110, 116; *Historia Calamitum*, 105–6
academia, 1–5, 10, 37, 38, 48, 66, 87, 103, 105, 159, 206, 235, 247, 395, 412, 419, 421, 422, 434–37, 445. *See also* education
Accenture, 429
Ackerman, Michael J.: *Human Anatomy: A Visual History From the Renaissance to the Digital Age*, 240n68
Adorno, Theodor W., 4, 9, 24, 29–31, 190, 191, 203, 208n23, 211n114, 361n134, 370, 398n48, 418, 429, 441n57, 443n226; *Dialectic of Enlightenment*, 190, 208nn23–24, 208nn29–31, 211n114; *Jargon of Authenticity*, 370; *Minima Moralia*, 441n57, 443n126
Agnete and the Merman, 329–32, 352
Agostinelli, Alfred, 77
Alain of Lille: *The Complaint of Nature*, 186nn177–78
Alighieri, Dante, 63, 106, 110, 128, 138, 214, 216, 228, 229, 238n6, 276, 307, 346, 450; *Divine Comedy*, 63, 238n6; *Inferno*, 106, 128, 138, 214, 228, 238n6, 307, 346, 449
allegory, 14, 62, 74, 83, 84, 86, 100, 103, 105, 108, 109, 119nn26–27, 120n45, 113, 130, 279, 307, 329, 337, 409, 438
Al Roumi, Ohood, 423
alternative facts, 153
Amazon, 412, 429, 440n26
ambiguity, 30, 31, 54n78, 62, 64, 79, 87, 92, 110, 111, 148, 151–52, 168, 219, 348, 367, 369, 378, 384, 388–90, 409, 423, 426, 451
American Library Association, 147, 181n2
Améry, Jean, 198; *Charles Bovary, Country Doctor: Portrait of a Simple Man*, 198, 210nn76–79
Amyot, Jacques, 223
anatomy: of novel, 223–33; novelty of, 218–23
Andersen, Hans Christian, 4, 35, 47, 168, 302, 304–6, 308–10, 312–16, 318, 320, 322nn27–31, 324nn53–56, 324n65, 324n68, 325n84, 326n103, 326n109, 330, 331, 335, 353–56, 362n183, 362n186, 363, 363n200, 369; "The Little Mermaid," 35, 47, 57n179, 168, 238, 301–21, 322n31, 324nn53–56, 324n65, 324n66, 324n68, 325n84, 326n103, 326n109, 330, 340, 353, 355, 363n200; *Only a Fiddler*, 353, 354; "The Red Shoes," 35, 168

Index

Anderson, Chris, 434
androgyne, 47, 74, 161; Charlus as, 62–63, 175–77; Dracula as, 160–63, 172, 180. *See also* Plato, *Symposium*; Proust, Marcel; Stoker, Bram
antifoundationalism, 36
anxiety, 7, 11, 46, 49, 63, 64, 80–82, 84, 112, 190, 204, 217–18, 234, 261, 262, 337, 351, 355, 362n178, 379, 380, 385, 388, 389, 398n29, 401n107, 402n138; Heideggerian *Angst*, 80–82, 365–70, 379, 380; psychological, 81, 379
apocalypse, 24, 29, 162, 166, 276, 281, 292, 311, 412; in Lawrence, D. H., 275, 276, 285, 301, 412–13; in Nabokov, Vladimir, 29, 301, 311, 325n79; in Proust, Marcel, 275, 285, 325n79; in the Tristan legend, 44, 275, 276, 278, 279, 281, 292, 301, 311, 412
Apollo, 30, 31. *See also* myth
Apter, T. E., 254; *Virginia Woolf: A Study of her Novels*, 269n80
Apuleius: *The Golden Ass*, 73–74, 78, 94n81, 94n82, 94n85, 95n88, 95n93, 95n96, 109, 110, 203, 211n117, 226
Arac, Jonathan, 411, 436; "What Kind of a History Does a Theory of the Novel Require?," 142n30, 440nn22–25
Arendt, Hannah: *amor mundi*, 124
Ariosto, Ludovico, 219; *Orlando Furioso*, 219, 222
Aristophanes, 11, 17, 21, 71, 91, 132, 179, 203, 217, 245, 254, 258, 264, 265, 268n22, 342
Aristotle, 14, 32, 54n89, 100, 105, 133, 140, 148, 205, 232, 363n190, 379, 396, 405n209, 426, 451, 453n23; *Metaphysics*, 32, 54n89; *Poetics*, 148, 205, 232, 379, 396, 453n23
Armstrong, Nancy, 424, 436; *How Novels Think*, 442n88, 444n169

Arnaud, Claude: *Chamfort: A Biography*, 211nn99–101
The Athenäum, 136
Auerbach, Erich, 164, 222, 250, 265; *Mimesis: The Representation of Reality in Western Literature*, 164, 184nn97–98, 265, 269n50, 272n152, 371
Austen, Jane, 49, 58n196, 332, 388, 420; *Pride and Prejudice*, 388; *Sense and Sensibility*, 49, 58n196
authenticity *[Eigentlichkeit]*, 55n94, 366, 386, 394, 395. *See also* Heidegger, Martin
autonomy, 29, 225, 318, 340, 348, 356, 413–16, 423, 424. *See also* freedom

Bacon, Francis, 190, 191, 208n22, 231, 242nn140–43, 242n150, 425, 426, 431, 432, 442n93, 442nn101–5, 443n139, 443n142; *New Organon*, 208n22, 231, 242nn140–42, 425, 426, 442n93, 442nn101–5, 443n139, 443n142
Bader, Julia, 318, 321n9; *Crystal Land*, 327n128
Badiou, Alain, 408, 410; *In Praise of Love*, 439nn1–3
Bakhtin, Mikhail, 4, 12, 18nn18–20, 20n61, 133, 134, 138–40, 143n64, 144n91, 144n96, 145nn103–6, 145n108, 203–6, 212nn127–30, 212n132, 212n136, 212n138, 217, 233, 239n36, 239n37, 344, 352, 356, 357, 363n211, 370, 371, 376, 377, 398n41, 398n45, 400n87, 401nn88–90, 401n96, 401n98, 402n128; *The Dialogical Imagination*, 371; "Discourse on the Novel," 140; "Epic and Novel," 12, 139, 401n96; heteroglossia, 140, 217, 425; *Problems of Dostoevsky's Poetics*, 363n211
Balzac, Honoré de, 27, 34, 50, 53nn44–49, 58n198, 63, 149, 157–66,

173–77, 180, 181n6, 183nn55–65, 184n95, 185nn140–56, 192, 242n156; *Human Comedy*, 63; *Lost Illusions*, 27, 53nn46–47, 53n49, 149, 157, 158, 162, 164, 165, 168, 183n55, 184n95, 233, 242n156; *Lost Souls* [*Splendeurs et misères des courtisanes*], 50, 53n45, 58n198, 157, 158, 164, 183n56, 183nn61–64; *Père Goriot*, 53n44, 158–59, 164, 173–75, 177, 183nn57–60, 183n65, 185nn140–56; pessimistic fairy tale, 173–75

Banfield, Ann, 92n12, 425; "'Proust's Pessimism' as Beckett's Counter-Poison," 92n12

barber-surgeon, 218, 226, 432

Barney, Rachel, 14; "Eros and Necessity in the Ascent from the Cave," 20n66

Barrie, J. M.: *Peter Pan*, 448–49

Barthes, Roland, 30, 47, 53n73, 57n181, 109, 120n50, 210n80, 222, 240n74, 333, 360n113, 439n6; *A Lover's Discourse*, 47, 53n73, 57n181, 439n6; *The Pleasure of the Text*, 109, 120n50, 240n74

Bataille, Georges, 14; *Erotism: Death and Sensuality*, 20n65

Baudelaire, Charles, 64–68, 77, 81, 82, 89, 93n40, 245, 274; definition of modernity, 245; influence on Proust, Marcel, 64; *Les fleurs du mal*/The Flowers of Evil, 64–66 ("*Alchimie de la douleur*"/"Alchemy of Suffering," 77; "*À une passante*"/"In Passing," 81; "*Correspondances*"/"Correspondences," 59–71, 89; "*Le goût de néant*"/"Craving for Oblivion," 76; "Let Us Flay the Poor," 295n10; "*L'Idéal*"/"The Ideal," 75; "*Obsession*"/"Obsession," 22, 24, 43, 59–71, 76–82, 89, 172, 279, 319, 340, 414, 416; *Spleen et Idéal*, 68)

beauty, 10, 27, 34, 38, 72–75, 82, 103, 129, 168, 170, 174, 203, 204, 216, 225, 234, 237, 244–45, 247, 256, 260, 263, 267, 268n22, 280, 388, 449; in Plato, 74, 75

Beauvoir, Simone de, 348, 361n147

Becker, Gary, 433

Beckett, Samuel, 2, 23, 35, 60–61, 67, 89, 177, 226, 387, 391, 409; *Endgame*, 37, 56n120; on failure, 2; "Worstward Ho," 387, 404n160; *Proust*, 52n18, 92nn10–11, 94n45, 96n166, 185n169, 241n103, 404n179

Bell, Michael, 320; *Lolita and Pure Art*, 328nn143–45

Benjamin, Walter, 4, 8, 26, 59, 64, 68, 82, 89, 138, 204, 370, 371; *Arcades Project*, 4; "The Image of Proust," 52n41, 92nn1–2, 92n4, 94nn48–50, 96n163, 212nn122–23; "*The Origin of German Tragic Drama*," 4–5; "On Some Motifs in Baudelaire," 93n31, 96n130, 165; "The Storyteller," 144nn92–93, 398nn42–43, 399n54; "Theses on the Philosophy of History," 18n21

Bentham, Jeremy: *Hard Times*, 427; ideology of happiness, 423–33

Bersani, Leo, 45–46

Bettelheim, Bruno, 168, 306; *The Uses of Enchantment: The Meaning and Importance of Fairy Tales*, 168–69, 184nn111–12

Biden, Joe, 7, 19n36

Big Business, 413, 414, 419, 421–23

Big Data, 409, 413, 422, 435–37

Bildungsroman, 125, 129, 306, 312, 352, 358n43, 362n180, 403n159

Bingen, Hildegard von, 22; Holistic Healing, 51n7

Blanchot, Maurice, 54n85, 81, 199, 399n56; *The Space of Literature*, 96n128, 199, 210n88, 211n89

blindness, 25, 79–80, 82, 101, 110, 205, 224, 273, 275, 281, 379, 395, 426, 431, 433, 434
Bloom, Allan, 11–12, 19n56, 82, 178, 227, 384, 387; "Ladder of Love," 20n57, 268n20
Bluefarb, Sam, 404n188
Blum, Beth, 274, 276, 277, 288; "Modernism's Anti-Advice," 295n7–9, 295n13, 296n28, 297n60
Blum, René, 59
Boccaccio, Giovanni, 127–29, 135, 148, 154; *The Decameron*, 127, 129, 130, 135, 142nn24–26, 142nn28–29, 142n32, 143n72, 346, 367n137
Boehme, Jakob, 36
Boethius, 15, 99–109, 116, 130, 181, 214, 233, 258; *The Consolation of Philosophy*, 15, 100, 102, 118n2, 119n3, 119nn5–6, 119nn8–9, 119nn13–14, 165–66, 238n9
Bologna, Caroline, 56n121
Bonaparte, Napoleon, 112, 432
Bond, Candis, 286; "Embodied Love: D. H. Lawrence, Modernity, and Pregnancy," 298n79
Bowlby, Rachel: *Lolita and the Poetry of Advertising*, 321n2
Boyd, Brian, 324n59; "Even Homais Nods," 323n42; *Vladimir Nabokov: The American Years*, 324n59
Bradatan, Costica: "The Philosopher of Failure: Emil Cioran's Heights of Despair," 17n6
Brathwaite, Richard, 153–54
Brenkman, John, 80, 81, 378; "Innovation: Notes on Nihilism and the Aesthetics of the Novel," 401n100, 404n170, 404n181; *Mood and Trope: The Rhetoric and Poetics of Affect*, 95n122, 95nn125–27, 96n131
Britton, Derek: *Lady Chatterley: The Making of the Novel*, 298n76
Broch, Hermann, 376
Brod, Max, 9, 203, 331

Brontë, Emily, 37, 39, 41, 44, 47, 51, 56nn122–24, 56n127, 56nn129–36, 56nn138–45, 56nn148–51, 57nn152–54, 57nn156–60, 57nn169–72, 131, 134, 169, 183nn75–85, 186n185, 239nn56–59, 360nn118–19, 420; "The Butterfly," 37–39, 41, 56nn123–24, 56n127; *Wuthering Heights*, 37–46, 51, 115–18, 131, 160–62, 168, 169, 174, 181, 187, 219–20, 237, 343, 345
Browne, Sir Thomas, 190, 219; *Religio Medici*, 239n54; *Urne-Buriall*, 219, 239n54
Buben, Adam: "Heidegger's Reception of Kierkegaard: The Existential Philosophy of Death," 397n7, 397n10, 397n11, 397n13, 397n17
Bunyan, John: *The Pilgrim's Progress*, 148
Burack, Charles Michael: *D. H. Lawrence's Language of Sacred Experience: The Transfiguration of the Reader*, 296n27
Burke, Peter, 155; *The Fortunes of the Courtier: The European Reception of Castiglione's Cortegiano*, 182nn46–47
Burton, Robert, 222, 232, 233; *Anatomy of Melancholy*, 222, 232
Bush, George W., 6, 7
business, 27, 76, 112, 231, 289, 294, 346, 366, 413, 414, 415, 417–19, 421, 422, 423, 432, 437, 441n76. See Big Business; Big Data
Butor, Michael, 436

Cabanas, Edgar, 441n76; *Manufacturing Happy Citizens*, 442nn78–79, 442nn81–83
Caldwell, Janis McLarren, 38
Camus, Albert, 58n200, 150, 201, 202; *The Myth of Sisyphus*, 211nn103–4, 211n106; *The Rebel*, 181n15; *The Stranger*, 379, 402n108

Capellanus, Andreas, 9, 60, 105, 107, 116–17, 154, 155, 180; *The Art of Courtly Love*, 5, 104–5, 111, 119nn31–32, 154, 180, 182n45, 186n184, 344, 450, 453n12
capitalism, 6, 50, 112, 157, 161, 163, 190, 409, 413, 415, 416–19, 421, 430, 439; industrial, 413; late, 430. *See also* Big Business; neoliberalism
Carleton, Mary, 151, 153
Carlisle, Claire, 337, 359nn66–70, 365, 397n1, 397n4, 397n12, 398n29
Carroll, Lewis, 179
Carson, Anne, 333, 338, 340, 341, 343, 344, 346–48; *Eros the Bittersweet*, 358nn36–38, 359n79, 360nn103–6, 360n117, 360n125, 361n132, 360nn135–36, 361n149
Carter, William C., 24, 78, 90; *Marcel Proust: A Life*, 93n19, 93n30; *The Proustian Quest*, 52n23, 95n106, 97n171
Cartwright, David E.: *Schopenhauer*, 17n9
Cascardi, Anthony J., 148–50; "The Novel," 181n5, 404n178
Case, Janet, 245, 246, 251, 264
Cashdan, Sheldon, 306; *The Witch Must Die: The Hidden Meaning of Fairy Tales*, 322n35
Castiglione, Baldesar, 154–56, 158; *The Book of the Courtier*, 154–56, 182nn40–44, 182nn48–50, 344, 360nn123–24; *sprezzatura*, 154
Cervantes, Miguel de, 32, 138, 148, 155, 177, 197, 384, 396; *Don Quixote*, 9, 76, 102, 111, 136–38, 151, 155, 164, 177, 197, 237, 323n44, 384, 388, 391, 393, 404n180, 411, 452
Chamfort, Nicolas, 201
Chateaubriand, François-René de, 66, 89; *René*, 89, 96n162
ChatGPT, 422, 430
Chaucer, Geoffrey, 9, 232, 420; *Canterbury Tales*, 9

Chesterton, G. K., 274; "The Fallacy of Success," 295n12
"Chicago School" of economics, 432, 433
Cioran, E. M., 2, 35, 36, 47, 194, 195, 199, 200, 201n80, 215, 218, 341, 380–81; *All Gall is Divided*, 57n180, 210n87; "Beyond the Novel," 194–95; *On the Heights of Despair*, 199–200, 211n91; *A Short History of Decay*, 2, 35, 55n109, 55n118, 195, 209nn53–54, 238n19, 239n43, 360n110, 380; *The Temptation to Exist*, 2, 209nn47–52, 209n55, 402n117; *The Trouble with Being Born*, 2, 199, 210n86, 211n90, 211n97
Civil War, American, 417–19, 423
Cixous, Hélène, 22, 23, 46; "Ay yay! The Cry of Literature," 51n13; "Ay Yay: The Shout of Literature," 22, 51n6
Cocteau, Jean, 26
Cognitive Behavioral Therapy, 100
Coleridge, Samuel Taylor, 47, 48; *Collected Letters of Samuel Taylor Coleridge*, 57nn183–84
Collins, Emily, 304–5, 314; "Nabokov's *Lolita* and Andersen's 'The Little Mermaid,'" 322n27, 322n31, 326n103
Conceptualism, 105, 376. *See also* Abelard, Peter
Conrad, Joseph, 169–72, 188–90, 194, 420; *Heart of Darkness*, 23, 36, 52n15, 52n16, 55nn111–13, 56n119, 170–72, 184nn125–30, 185n131, 185n139, 188–90, 192, 208nn8–19, 213–14, 238n1, 262; *Youth: A Narrative and Two Other Stories*, 172
consolation, 11, 15, 33, 40, 41, 50, 67, 71, 79, 80, 90–92, 97n175, 99–118, 130, 132, 166, 179, 197, 200, 229, 237, 245, 256, 258, 265, 272n158,

319, 356, 415, 418; in Boethius, 15, 100–102, 104, 105, 116, 130, 258; during COVID-19, 99; failure of, 92, 99, 104, 108, 130; in Goethe, Johann Wolfgang von, 109, 115; in Proust, Marcel, 90, 92, 200, 229; self-consolation, 67; in Woolf, Virginia, 200, 229, 258, 265, 272n158
constellations, 24, 213–38, 393
contingency, 15, 24, 50, 58n199, 67, 83, 86, 378
Copernicus, Nicolaus, 214
cosmos, 207, 258, 277, 288; cosmic pessimism, 273–94; planets, 214, 217, 335; scale, 276–79; stars, 10–11, 24, 101, 128, 207, 213–20, 277, 379. *See also* Copernicus; Ptolemaic system
courtly love, 290, 291
COVID-19 pandemic, 7, 99, 190
criminality, 7, 34, 62, 100, 107, 147–81, 218, 220, 221, 230, 238, 320, 415, 425, 437
Critchley, Simon, 392; "Of Chrematology: Joyce and Money," 405n190; *Very Little... Almost Nothing: Death, Philosophy, Literature*, 141n1
Culler, Jonathan, 425–26; *The Literary in Theory*, 442n97
Cupid, 73–75, 78, 80, 84, 203, 226. *See also* Eros; myth

Dalgarno, Emily, 245, 251, 256, 268n22; "Reality and Perception: Philosophical Approaches to *To the Lighthouse*," 267n3, 269n58; *Virginia Woolf and the Visible World*, 268nn15–17, 270n92, 270n98, 270n99
Dante. *See* Alighieri, Dante
Dasein, 32, 131, 225, 334, 352, 355, 365, 367–70, 372–85, 387, 388, 390–93, 396, 401n107, 407, 408, 434, 435. *See also* Heidegger, Martin

data, 313, 409, 413, 422, 427, 428–31, 433, 434–37, 442n76. *See also* Big Data
Daudet, Lucien, 26, 204
Davies, William, 416, 424, 432; *The Happiness Industry*, 441n52, 441n55, 441nn61–64, 442n84, 442n99, 442n106, 442n107, 443nn127–28, 443nn144–49
death, 22, 26, 27, 34, 36, 38–40, 45, 46, 57n175, 60, 68, 73, 74, 76–79, 81, 84, 88, 90, 104, 107, 112, 113, 114, 116, 127, 128, 131, 132, 148, 157, 164, 170, 174, 178, 188, 190, 198, 199, 200, 202, 203, 206, 215, 221, 222, 224, 225, 227, 228, 230, 235, 237, 246, 249, 250, 252, 255, 257, 279, 283, 285, 287, 288, 291, 293, 294, 296n27, 299n130, 300n156, 302, 306, 307, 320, 342, 343, 372, 373, 375, 376, 379, 380, 383, 388, 390, 392, 393, 394, 397, 399n54, 399n56, 411. *See also* grief
de Botton, Alain, 87, 450; *How Proust Can Change Your Life*, 86–87, 96nn152–54
Defoe, Daniel, 148, 155, 420
de La Fayette, Madame, 173; *La Princesse de Clèves*, 155, 166, 167; *Zayde*, 134
de La Rochefoucauld, François, 61
Deleuze, Gilles, 25–26; *Proust and Signs*, 52nn36–40
de Lille, Alain, 180; *Complaint of Nature*, 179–80, 192
DeLillo, Don, 381, 382, 396; *White Noise*, 396, 402n124, 405n208
de Lorris, Guillaume, 103, 104, 108, 111; *Romance of the Rose*, 75–76, 102–5, 107, 109, 110, 113, 115, 117, 165, 179, 180
Delvey, Anna, 150–57
de Man, Paul, 17, 20n82, 64, 65, 67, 81, 82, 89, 396; "Anthropomorphism in the Lyric," 93nn34–36, 94n47;

Index

"Hypogram and Inscription: Michael Riffaterre's Poetics of Reading," 20n82; "Reading (Proust)," 64, 93n29
de Maupassant, Guy: *Pierre and Jean*, 139, 144n101
de Meun, Jean: *Romance of the Rose*, 75, 102–5, 107, 109, 110, 113, 115, 117, 119nn15–25, 120n46, 120n49, 120n59, 165, 179, 180, 186nn182–83
Derrida, Jacques, 316; "Plato's Pharmacy," 20n58
de Rougemont, Denis, 5, 276, 282, 301, 311; *Love in the Western World*, 18n22, 276, 295n19
de Sade, Marquis, 135, 137, 144n77, 148, 422
despair, 9, 17n6, 23, 24, 31, 33, 34, 40, 63, 64, 76, 100, 102, 157, 165, 167, 196, 197, 199, 200, 202, 214, 228, 231, 243, 256, 257, 280, 302, 305, 315, 329, 352, 425, 431, 432; nihilistic, 76; suicidal, 157, 165, 200; *Verzweiflung* ("despair"), 31
de Staël, Mme., 134
de Troyes, Chrétien, 107
de Unamuno, Miguel: *The Tragic Sense of Life*, 197, 200, 210nn69–71, 210nn73–74, 239n42
Deus absconditus, 148
dialectic, 9, 60, 69, 89, 123, 124, 137, 233, 343, 354; Hegel, Georg Wilhelm Friedrich, 9, 123–24; Plato, 124, 233
Diamond, Dan, 7
Dickens, Charles, 169, 192, 311, 427, 428; *Great Expectations*, 29, 168, 184nn113–20; *Hard Times*, 261, 427, 442nn108–11, 443nn112–13
Diderot, Denis, 48, 49; *Encyclopedia*, 48, 135
Dienstag, Jonathan Foa, 48, 50, 137, 193, 197, 202, 367, 380, 452, 453n25; *Pessimism: Philosophy, Ethic, Spirit*, 58n190, 58n200, 144n86, 209nn37–38, 210n72, 211nn109–10, 397n16

Dies irae, 35
di Medici, Lorenzo, 156
dis-individuation, 115, 131
dissimulation, 154–55, 158, 167, 318
Dostoevsky, Fyodor, 140, 145n106, 148, 152, 157–63, 166, 195, 203, 352, 356, 357, 366, 372–75, 411, 430; *The Brothers Karamazov*, 23, 29, 32, 53n65, 53n66, 54n87, 152, 182nn26–30, 203–4, 211n116, 212nn120–21, 373–75, 400nn64–72; *Crime and Punishment*, 28, 53nn57–59, 159, 165, 183nn66–69, 203, 211n115, 394; *Notes from Underground*, 53n53, 55n110, 195; Underground Man, 36
Dovere, Edward-Isaac: "Joe Biden's Endless Search for the Middle on Race," 19n36
Dowling, Linda: *Hellenism and Homosexuality in Victorian Oxford*, 270n105
dream, 24, 25, 35, 40, 46, 68, 74, 75, 89, 91, 100, 110–13, 117, 148, 159, 166, 169, 202, 256, 261, 289, 305, 306, 338, 345, 374, 387, 432, 436. See also; Apuleius/*The Golden Ass*; Proust, Marcel/*The Captive*; *The Romance of the Rose*; sleep
Durantaye, Leland de la: *Giorgio Agamben: A Critical Introduction*, 398n48
Dürer, Albrecht: *Melencolia I*, 214
Dylan, Bob, 412

Eagleton, Terry, 6, 8, 9, 90, 437; *Hope Without Optimism*, 6, 18nn29–30, 18n32, 19nn38–40, 19nn42–43; *Literary Theory: An Introduction*, 97n172, 441nn65–68, 444nn173–74
Eavis, Peter, 440n34
Echevarría, Roberto González, 391, 393, 404n182
Eckhart, Meister, 36

Eco, Umberto: *The Name of the Rose*, 205
education, 313, 332, 419, 421–24, 430, 433, 436, 438, 441, 446. *See also* academia; pedagogy; STEM
Ehrenreich, Barbara, 6, 8, 416; *Bright-Sided: How Positive Thinking Is Undermining America*, 6, 18n31, 18n33, 19n37, 19n40, 441n96; on pessimism, 8
Eikhenbaum, Boris, 138
Eleanor of Aquitaine, 105
Eliot, George, 126, 188, 229, 381, 382, 420; *Daniel Deronda*, 388; *Middlemarch*, 129–30, 188, 229–31, 241nn131–39, 381, 402nn122–23, 412
Eliot, T. S., 48, 126, 132, 133, 244, 376; "*Ulysses*, Order, and Myth," 143n53; *The Waste Land*, 48, 57n187, 276, 295n18
Ellis, David, 273, 295n1, 295n4
Engels, Friedrich, 417; *The Condition of the Working Class in England*, 441n56
Engelstein, Stefani, 116; *Anxious Anatomy: The Conception of the Human Form in Literary and Naturalist Discourse*, 121n90, 240n61
Enlightenment, 5, 16, 108, 111, 118, 134, 137, 138, 191, 194, 295n6, 426
entomology, 21–51, 59. *See also* insects
epic, 45, 85, 90, 125, 133, 158, 174, 188, 191, 214, 216, 217, 222, 278, 279, 384, 387, 401n96, 425, 446, 447
epistemology, 25, 26, 71, 84, 151, 152, 166, 178, 197, 247, 386, 400n85
Epstein, Joseph: *The Novel, Who Needs It?*, 20n73
eros, 10–17, 21, 23, 25, 26, 29, 30, 41, 50, 60–62, 67, 69, 71, 72, 77, 82, 84–86, 88, 90–92, 103, 104, 106, 107, 117, 118, 123, 124, 127, 129, 132, 133, 135, 136, 155, 161, 179, 223, 226, 234–38, 245–47, 265, 301, 333, 337, 338, 340–44, 348, 407–13, 415, 421, 429–31, 436, 439n6, 448, 450, 451; as consolation in Plato, 14, 17, 50, 90, 179, 245; of failure, 407–13; as a mythical god, 238, 408. *See also* Cupid; as psychological drive, 16, 409
Esquivel, Laura: *Like Water for Chocolate*, 390
ethics, 9, 84, 112, 148, 197, 317–21, 334, 349, 350, 373, 374, 395, 397n2, 398n49, 399n60, 400n85, 407–9, 416
etymology, 21–51, 54n85, 214, 306, 383, 393, 451
Evans, M. D. R., 424
evasion, 6, 390, 408. *See also* Levinas, Emmanuel
existentialism, 201, 202, 365, 388. *See also* Camus, Albert; Heidegger, Martin; Sartre, Jean-Paul

failure: as autonomy in workplace, 413–16, 424; as *Aufgabe* (Task), 2; Beckett on, 2; eros of, 104, 407–13; genre of, 1–17, 99, 104, 130, 232; of realism, 163–72, 286; utopia of, 127, 281–82, 307
fairy tale: disenchantment of, 163–72, 306; failed, 44, 46, 163–72, 305–9, 330; pessimistic, 35, 168, 171–75, 301–5
fake news, 7, 153
fascism, 371, 398n49, 437, 438. *See also* Nazism
Faulkner, William: *As I Lay Dying*, 22, 51nn8–11, 196, 391, 403n157, 412; *Sanctuary*, 404n183; *The Sound and the Fury*, 23, 36, 114n55, 196
Faye, Emmanuel, 396; *Heidegger: The Introduction of Nazism into Philosophy in Light of the Unpublished Seminars of 1933-1935*, 405n206

Faust legend, 23, 157, 159, 164, 175, 352; Mephisthophelean characteristics, 157, 159, 164, 175, 352. *See also* Balzac, Honoré de; Conrad, Joseph; Goethe, Johann Wolfgang von; Mann, Thomas; Marlowe, Christopher

feet/legs, 5, 23, 30–32, 34–37, 171, 174, 181, 189, 206, 221, 223, 224, 263, 264, 289, 302, 309, 310, 318, 325n93, 392, 446, 448, 449, 451

Ferrante, Elena, 35; *My Brilliant Friend*, 35

Feuerbach, Ludwig: *Thoughts on Death and Immortality*, 3

Feuerlicht, Ignace: *Thomas Mann*, 185nn133–34

Flaubert, Gustave, 148, 198, 202, 214, 253, 274, 352; *Madame Bovary*, 167, 210n75, 211n108, 223–26, 237, 238n5, 240nn80–97, 269n71; *Memoirs of a Madman and November*, 274, 295n11

Flock, Elizabeth: "James Frey Returning to Oprah Five Years Later," 145n114

Flood, Alison: "Philip Roth Predicts Novel Will Be Minority Cult Within 25 Years," 440n27

Folkenberg, Judith, 221; *Human Anatomy: A Visual History From the Renaissance to the Digital Age*, 240n68

formal realism, 151–52

Forster, E. M., 420, 435; *Aspects of the Novel*, 420, 441n60, 444n160, 444n162; *Howards End*, 420

fort-da, 90, 91, 99. *See also* Freud, Sigmund

Foucault, Michel, 333, 418, 424, 425; *Discipline and Punish*, 424, 441n60, 442n87, 442nn89–92, 443n141

Fowler, Douglas, 319, 322n34, 327n133; *Reading Nabokov*, 328n139

fragmentation, 5, 14, 42, 69, 70, 83, 84, 123, 126, 136, 144n82, 152, 177, 178, 195, 196, 222, 225–29, 233, 234, 245, 246, 248, 250, 254–56, 260, 266, 378, 397n24, 407, 446

freedom, 8, 24, 136, 137, 139, 163, 258, 311–13, 333, 338–40, 349, 362n178, 421, 423, 435, 438; artistic, 78; political, 435, 438. *See also* autonomy

French Academy, 48

Freud, Sigmund, 199, 219, 226, 277, 333, 341, 342, 376; *Beyond the Pleasure Principle*, 90, 91, 97n170, 97nn173–74, 190, 208n21; *Civilization and Its Discontents*, 190, 208n25, 298n105; "A Difficulty in the Path of Psycho-Analysis," 240n98; "Mourning and Melancholia," 296n29; *The Psychology of Love*, 360n109; "The Uncanny," 219, 239n52

Frey, James, 147; *A Million Little Pieces*, 141

Friedman, Alan W., 294; "D. H. Lawrence: Pleasure and Death," 300n156

Friedman, Milton, 432

Fromm, Erich, 414; *The Art of Loving*, 440n38

Frost, Laura, 283, 297n65; *The Problem with Pleasure: Modernism and its Discontents*, 297n61

Fry, Roger, 234; *Vision and Design*, 248

Frye, Northrop, 45, 205, 213, 217, 229, 231–33; *Anatomy of Criticism*, 57n166, 212nn133–35, 231–32, 238n2, 239n38, 241n130, 242nn144–52

futility, 3, 28, 46, 62, 139, 191, 198, 213, 308, 438, 450

Garff, Joakim, 352–53; "Kierkegaard's Christian Bildungsroman," 362n180

Genette, Gérard, 425

German Idealism, 123, 166; Hegel, Georg Wilhelm Friedrich, 9, 123–24;

Kant, Immanuel, 5, 15, 118, 123–25, 202, 216, 365, 430; rejection of: (Heidegger, Martin, 13–14, 36, 48, 165, 196, 209n41, 346, 357, 434–35; Nietzsche, Friedrich, 4, 9, 113–14, 200, 203, 275; Schopenhauer, Arthur, 2–3, 31, 33, 50, 54n85, 58n200, 17n9, 79, 88, 125, 170, 189, 190, 194, 198, 199, 202, 205, 206, 215, 255, 273–75, 307, 379, 380, 402n116, 448); Schelling, Friedrich Wilhelm Joseph von, 219; Schlegel, Friedrich von, 12, 20n60, 123, 126, 127, 132–36, 138, 139, 142nn18–22, 143nn51, 143n60, 143n67, 143n69, 144nn80–82, 144n90, 144n95, 144n99, 150, 192, 202, 215, 238n22, 349, 350, 353, 354, 361n154, 362n161, 363n194, 363n209, 397n24, 420, 435, 441n70
German Idealist, 126
GHP. *See* Gross Happiness Product (GHP)
Gilbert, Sandra M., 40–41, 45, 56n137; "Looking Oppositely: Emily Brontë's Bible of Hell," 56n137, 57nn162–63, 57nn167–68
Girard, René, 225; *Deceit, Desire, and the Novel: Self and Other in Literary Structure*, 240n92, 346, 361n138
Gladwell, Malcolm: *Blink*, 433–34
GNP. *See* Gross National Product
God: narrator as, 225, 229, 425, 426; rejection of, 39, 104; world without, 160
God of Love, 103, 104, 108, 109, 180. *See also* Cupid; eros
Goethe, Johann Wolfgang von: *Faust*, 55n106, 138, 371, 398n39; *The Sorrows of Young Werther*, 50, 109–18, 120nn52–58, 120nn60–64, 120nn66–68, 120nn71–74, 123–25, 131, 192, 196, 334, 335, 351; Spinozism, 114
Goldman, Jane, 266; "*To the Lighthouse*'s Use of Language and Form," 268n19, 268nn35–37, 269nn54–55, 272n160, 272nn163–64
Goldstein, Bill: *The World Broke in Two*, 441n71
Goncourt Brothers, 126
Gordon, George, 437
Gorgani, Fakhraddin, 9, 279–81; *Vis and Ramin*, 9, 279–81, 296n40, 296nn42–45, 296n48, 297n53
Gorgias, 200; "On Non-Being," 211n98
Grabes, H., 319, 320; *Fictitious Biographies: Vladimir Nabokov's English Novels*, 328n136
Grass, Günter, 390; *The Tin Drum*, 23
Grayson, Jane, 302, 305; "*Rusalka and the Person from Porlock*," 322n14, 322n30, 322n32
Great Depression, 433
Gregorio, Laurence A., 166–67; "The Gaze of History," 184nn104–7
grief, 11, 63, 66, 71, 78–83, 88, 91, 99, 106, 176, 253, 257–58, 264, 278. *See also* death
Grimm, The Brothers, 171, 172; "Cinderella," 34, 35, 55n104; "Hans in Luck," 171; "Rumpelstiltskin," 31, 54n79, 173; "Snow White," 35, 55n107, 179
Gross, Terry, 7
Gross Happiness Product (GHP), 423
Gross National Product (GNP), 423
Gubar, Susan, 40–41, 45; "Looking Oppositely: Emily Brontë's Bible of Hell," 56n137, 57nn162–63, 57nn167–68

Halberstam, Jack: *Queer Art of Failure*, 6, 18n28
Halloran, Robert, 234
Halperin, David M., 133, 143nn57–59; "Love's Irony: Six Remarks on Platonic Eros," 143n56
Hamsun, Knut: *Hunger*, 196
Han, Byung-Chul, 33, 399n60, 409, 410, 412, 413, 430, 434–36, 439n6,

451; *The Agony of Eros*, 409, 430, 439nn4–9, 439nn11–14, 440nn28–33, 440n46, 444n152, 444n153, 444n159, 444n172; *The Crisis of Narration*, 453; *Good Entertainment: A Deconstruction of the Western Passion Narrative*, 400n60; *In the Swarm: Digital Prospects*, 54n91, 444nn64–68; *Psychopolitics: Neoliberalism and New Technologies of Power*, 440n37, 444n170
Handke, Peter, 412
happiness, 14, 27, 31, 38, 43, 49, 50, 54–55n94, 59–61, 63, 66–68, 72, 79, 83–92, 100, 104, 108, 130, 154–56, 167–70, 173, 174, 176, 201, 207, 214–16, 220, 223, 224, 228–31, 261, 263, 264, 271n143, 274, 281, 284, 294, 303–4, 312, 320, 325n79, 326n94, 345, 346, 351, 352, 379, 380, 395, 413–34, 438, 451
Hardy, Thomas, 36, 51, 102, 170, 189, 194, 268n18; *Tess of the D'Urbervilles*, 47, 57n182, 119n12, 169, 184nn122–24, 187–89, 192, 208nn1–4, 208n6, 216–17, 239nn30–35
Harrison, Andrew, 285; *The Life of D. H. Lawrence: A Critical Biography*, 297n65, 297n75
Hegel, Georg Wilhelm Friedrich, 3, 17n8, 123, 141n3, 141n10, 193, 349, 354, 365, 366, 396; *Hegel's Aesthetics: Lectures on Fine Art*, 125, 141n0, 142nn11–15; on perpetual becoming, 25; *The Phenomenology of Spirit*, 31, 54n81, 124, 125, 352
Héger, Constantin, 37
Heidegger, Martin, 13–14, 36, 48, 165, 196, 209n41, 346, 357, 434–35; anticipatory resoluteness, 90, 366, 367, 374, 375, 436; anxiety *[Angst]*, 80–82, 84, 337, 365–70, 379, 380, 385, 398n29, 401n107, 402n138; Articulated Thrown Projection, 384, 385, 393; authenticity *[Eigentlichkeit]*, 54–55n94, 334, 348, 366, 367, 369, 370, 378–80, 382, 383, 386, 394, 395, 401n96, 401n107, 408; average everydayness, 13, 131, 367, 369, 372, 375, 381, 396, 408; *Basic Writings*, 55n116; *Being and Time*, 80, 124–25, 358n40, 358n42, 365–67, 369, 371–73, 375–77, 380–85, 388, 392, 393, 396, 397n14, 397nn19–24, 398n30, 398n32, 398n33, 398nn36–38, 398n46, 399n50, 399n51, 399n55, 399n59, 399n60, 400n63, 400nn73–76, 400n78, 400n82, 400n83, 401n93, 401nn95–97, 401n105, 402n115, 402n125, 402n127, 402n129, 402n132, 402n133, 402n136, 402nn138–40, 403n140, 403nn144–49, 403n153, 403n154, 404n161, 404n164, 404n172, 404n173, 405n191, 405n194, 405n195, 407, 408; Being-in-the-world, 32, 124, 343, 378, 386, 388, 401n96; discourse *[Rede]*, 48, 368–70, 378, 382, 385, 393, 394, 410, 422; *Discourse on Thinking*, 402n114; ecstatic temporality, 369, 374, 386, 396; *Ent-fernung*, 204; equiprimordiality, 378, 449; facticity, 368, 378, 382, 388; falling, 165, 368, 372, 373, 376, 384, 393, 396, 408; fundamental ontology, 124, 375–83, 385; guilt, 372–75, 379; idle talk *[Gerede]*, 368–70, 378, 384, 388, 390, 393, 399n60; inauthenticity, 165, 334, 348, 367, 368, 372, 373, 380, 384, 385, 388, 390, 395, 407; letting-be *[Gelassenheit]*, 380; *Parmenides*, 32–33, 54n90, 408; *Pathmarks*, 95n123, 209n41, 401n107; *Poetry, Language, Thought*, 403n145; on problem of forgetting of Being, 354, 394; projection *[Entwurf]*, 354,

368, 388, 397n24; "scribbling" *[das Geschreibe]*, 369; state-of-mind *[Befindlichkeit]*, 369, 370, 378; "they, the" *[das Man]*, 54–55n94, 225, 343, 355, 367, 368, 371, 373, 382, 385–88, 392–94, 401n96; Understanding *[Verstehen]*, 378; *What is Called Thinking?*, 397n15, 444n155, 444n156; "What is Metaphysics?," 81, 95n123, 95n124, 209n41, 401n107, 402n109, 434, 444n154, 444nn157–58
Heilbut, Anthony: *Thomas Mann: Eros and Literature*, 143n45
Heliodorus, 188, 189, 222; *Aethiopica*, 180, 208n7, 222, 223
Heller, Erich, 15, 133, 194; *Thomas Mann: The Ironic German*, 20n74, 20n75, 143n52, 143n54, 143n55, 209n43, 241n121
Heloïse, 105–8, 116, 224
Henry VIII, 218, 219
Hephaestus, 14, 342, 343, 345, 354
Hodal, Kate: *The Guardian*, 442n77
Hoffman, Jeff, 331
Holquist, Michael, 140
Homer, 13, 112, 164, 191, 207, 216, 445, 447–49, 452n3, 452n6, 452n8, 452n9; *The Iliad*, 446, 452n6, 453n8, 453n9; *The Odyssey*, 447
homosexuality, 62, 93n20, 175, 180. *See also* Balzac, Honoré de; Lille, Alain de; Mann, Thomas; Proust, Marcel; Stoker, Bram; Wilde, Oscar
hope, 1, 9, 14, 23, 29, 30, 36, 38, 39, 43, 71–73, 76, 86, 88, 99, 103, 110, 116, 118, 130, 164, 168, 170, 179, 194, 196, 197, 199, 219, 231, 232, 258, 262, 263, 266, 283, 285, 288, 294, 308, 309, 313, 320, 337, 343, 351, 379, 418, 431, 437, 451, 452
hopelessness, 29, 99, 155, 196, 238, 301, 310–12, 321, 324n52, 337

Horkheimer, Max, 191, 203; *Dialectic of Enlightenment*, 190, 208n23, 208n24, 208nn29–31, 211n114
Horne, Gerald: *Counter-Revolution of 1776: Slave Resistance and the Origins of the United States of America*, 417
Hrabal, Bohumil: *Too Loud a Solitude*, 196
Huet, Pierre-Daniel, 155
Hugo, Victor, 126
Human Rights Watch World Report (2019), 423
human trafficking, 423
humor, 9, 38, 62, 136, 178, 202, 204, 206, 214, 236, 251, 264, 313, 342, 422, 434. *See also* laughter
Huntington, Patricia J., 397n3, 399; "Heidegger's Reading of Kierkegaard Revisited: From Ontological Abstraction to Ethical Concretion," 397n2
Huxley, Aldous, 431; "The Censor," 297n72
hypocrisy, 2, 110, 282, 284, 285, 410, 422. *See also* Kant, Immanuel
hypogram, 17
hysteria, 162, 180, 204

Ignatieff, Michael: *On Consolation: Finding Solace in Dark Times*, 97n175, 99, 118n1, 119n4
illegitimacy, 147–81, 193
Illouz, Eva, 441n76; *Manufacturing Happy Citizens*, 442nn78–79, 442nn81–83
immaturity, 5, 204, 321n9. *See also* Kant, Immanuel
impossible spaces, 279–81
Index Librorum Prohibitorum (Catholic Church), 148
infantile messianism, 99
insects: bee, 25; beetle, 21, 27, 29, 225; butterfly, 29, 37–39, 41, 237, 266, 302, 308; cicada, 21–24; cockroach,

22, 29; gadfly, 1, 21, 340; mosquito, 27, 31; spider, 22, 26, 28, 29, 338; wasp, 24, 26. *See also* entomology; metamorphosis
interruption, 42, 73, 126, 155, 189, 190, 203, 222, 223, 226–29, 233, 250, 254, 255, 280, 308, 309, 316, 345, 416, 419, 445–52
irony, 5, 10–12, 18n12, 33, 104, 131–33, 151, 197, 198, 202, 205, 231, 232, 236, 265, 338–40, 349–51, 353, 355, 356, 388–95; as defining feature of the novel, 140. *See also* Bakhtin, Mikhail; Kundera, Milan; Lukács, Georg; Kierkegaard, Søren; Mann, Thomas; Plato
Irwin, William, 372

James, Henry, 139, 323n44, 388; *The Art of the Novel*, 144n100; *The Portrait of a Lady*, 347, 361n143, 388, 426; *Washington Square*, 428, 443nn116–18, 443nn120–22
Jameson, Fredric, 403n159
Jaspers, Karl, 365; *The Psychology of Worldviews*, 366
Jaucourt, Louis, 135; *The Encyclopedia of Diderot & D'Alembert: Collaborative Translation Project*, 144n74
jealousy, 24, 42, 60, 61, 71–73, 86, 117, 224, 226, 236
Jefferson, Thomas, 441n53
Josipovici, Gabriel, 333, 389; *Kierkegaard: A Critical Reader*, 404n168; *On Trust: Art and the Temptations of Suspicion*, 358nn32–35
Joyce, James, 227, 234, 323n44, 371, 377, 394; *Exiles*, 275; *Finnegans Wake*, 392, 405n190; *Ulysses*, 132, 133, 138, 140, 148, 178, 185n172, 185n173, 186n174, 186n175, 213, 214, 238n4, 241n107, 298n76, 317, 384, 386, 392, 403n155, 413n156, 405n192, 405n193, 412, 420

Kafka, Franz, 112, 331, 345, 371, 374, 375; *The Blue Octavo Notebooks*, 200, 211n93; *The Castle*, 195, 345, 361n133, 374–75; *The Complete Stories*, 57n185, 120n69, 208n26; "The Country Doctor," 48, 57n185, 57n186; *Letters to Friends, Family, and Editors*, 211n94, 357n16; *The Metamorphosis*, 28, 34, 323n44; "The Silence of the Sirens," 191, 208nn26–28; *The Trial*, 152, 203, 375
Kant, Immanuel, 5, 15, 118, 123–25, 202, 216, 365, 430; *Critique of Judgment*, 141n9; *Grounding for the Metaphysics of Morals*, 36–37; *"Toward Perpetual Peace" and Other Writings on Politics, Peace, and History*, 18n27
Kelley, Jonathan, 424
Kierkegaard, Søren, 3–4, 9, 124, 203, 329–57; *The Concept of Anxiety*, 366; *The Concept of Irony, with Continual Reference to Socrates*, 18n12, 18n13, 353, 361nn155–58, 393n162, 362; *Contribution to a Theory of the Kiss, A*, 340–46; *Early Polemical Writings*, 18n16, 362nn184–86, 363nn187–93, 363n196, 363n201, 363n202, 363nn205–7; *Either/Or*, 4, 34, 55n103, 143n68, 198, 210n83, 211n111, 330–34, 344, 349–52, 355, 358n41, 358n43, 361n150, 361n151, 362n169, 362n171, 362n172, 363n186, 363n204, 366; falling, 368; *Fear and Trembling*, 329, 330, 337, 357nn1–6, 357n10, 357n11; *Fear and Trembling/Repetition*, 357n6; leveling, 368, 386; life-view, 356, 370; *Literary Review, A*, 363n210, 367, 368, 390, 397n25, 398n33, 410; as novel theorist, 351–57; *From the Papers of One Still Living, Published Against His Will*, 353, 367; *Point of*

View for my Activity as an Author, 356; *Practice in Christianity,* 366; prosiness, 349, 370; the public, 367, 387; *The Seducer's Diary,* 2, 4, 10, 17n3, 18n15, 124, 194, 331, 332, 334–37, 340, 347–54, 357nn12–14, 358nn25–31, 358n39, 358nn44–51, 359n53, 359nn55–58, 359n61, 359n65, 359nn71–78, 359nn80–92, 360n93, 360n94, 360nn96–99, 360n101, 360n102, 360n107, 360n108, 360n112, 360n116, 361n146, 361n148, 361n152, 361n153, 362n163, 362n164, 362nn166–68, 362n174; *Story of Everyday Life, A,* 367; *Two Ages,* 367

Kinkead-Weekes, Mark, 278, 295n5, 296n37

Kirkman, Francis, 151, 153

Kisiel, Theodore: *Becoming Heidegger: On the Trail of his Early Occasional Writings,* 405n205

kissing, 63, 73, 74, 103, 106, 131, 180, 213, 282, 309, 329, 340–46, 350, 351, 450

Kleist, Heinrich von: "On the Theater of Marionettes," 99

Knausgaard, Karl Ove, 196, 382, 402n126; *My Struggle,* 393–94, 405nn195–99

Koulouris, Theodore, 246; *Hellenism and Loss in the Work of Virginia Woolf,* 268nn21–23, 269n79, 270n105; "Virginia Woolf's 'Greek Notebook' (VS Greek and Latin Studies): An Annotated Transcription," 270n87

Kreilkamp, Ivan, 220

Kristeva, Julia, 12–13, 138, 233; *Desire in Language: A Semiotic Approach to Literature and Art,* 20n62, 242nn153–55

Kundera, Milan, 32, 124, 130, 133, 134, 137, 138, 140, 217, 375–77, 380, 383, 385, 386; *The Art of the Novel,* 54n86, 137, 141n4, 143n61, 143n65, 143n66, 144n85, 144n100, 145n109, 239n40, 239n41, 240n78, 240n79, 375, 400n79, 400n84, 400n86, 401n91, 403n147, 403n150, 404n169, 453n13; *Testaments Betrayed: An Essay in Nine Parts,* 142n42, 144n94, 400n85, 401n92, 402n130, 402n131, 404n171

Lagerkvist, Pär: *The Dwarf,* 196

Landler, Mark, 19n34

landscapes, 10, 23, 37, 39, 40, 44, 47, 54n78, 63, 110, 114, 130, 170, 187–92, 204, 213, 216, 220, 250, 255, 258–60, 262, 264, 265, 281, 312, 404n190

Landy, Joshua, 69, 70; "'Les Moi en Moi'; The Proustian Self in Philosophical Perspective," 60, 94n58

Lange, Jeva, 440n26

laughter, 179, 187, 190, 202–7, 213, 232, 233, 264

Lawrence, D. H., 14–15, 51, 126, 128, 234–35, 371, 411, 412, 415; *Aaron's Rod,* 420; "The Future of the Novel," 276, 295n23, 296n24; *Lady Chatterley's Lover,* 126, 135, 140, 142n20, 142n27, 144n75, 144n76, 148, 235–38, 242nn165–67, 252, 253, 258, 274, 276–77, 279, 284, 286, 288, 293, 295n20, 296n25, 296nn30–34, 296n39, 296n41, 296n46, 296n47, 297n54, 297nn57–59, 297n65, 297n67, 297n68, 297nn70–72, 297n73, 298n76, 298n77, 298n78, 298nn85–90, 298nn92–99, 298nn104–9, 299nn111–28, 299n129, 299n131, 300n133, 300n134, 300nn137–41, 300n143, 300nn145–52, 300n154, 300n155, 301, 302, 387, 410, 412, 413, 419, 420, 440n16, 400n17, 400n35, 400n36; *The Letters of*

D. H. Lawrence, 296n26; "Morality and the Novel," 276, 284, 289, 295n21, 295n22, 298n103; "À Propos of *Lady Chatterley's Lover*," 282; *Sons and Lovers*, 273; Tristan legend, 9, 15, 66, 104, 105, 107, 111, 238, 273–94, 300n153, 301, 311, 312; "Why the Novel Matters," 283, 288, 297n63, 297n64, 298n102; *Women in Love*, 445–46

Lazarillo de Tormes, 220–21

Lebensraum, 418. See also Nazism

Lee, Hermione, 247; *Virginia Woolf*, 268n32, 269nn61–64

Leibniz, Gottfried Wilhelm, 8, 189, 198, 206, 223, 351; *The Monadology and Other Philosophical Writings*, 362n166; *Theodicy*, 48

Leopardi, Giacomo, 177, 193; *The Moral Essays*, 209n39

The Letters of Abelard and Heloise (Radice), 119nn33–40, 120nn41–44

Levinas, Emmanuel, 84, 365, 390, 408; *On Escape*, 390, 404nn175–77; "The Other in Proust," 96nn143–45

Levine, George, 286; "Lady Chatterley's Lover," 298n81, 298n82

Lewis, C. S., 104, 108; *The Allegory of Love*, 119n26, 119n27, 120n45

Lewis, Sinclair: *It Can't Happen Here*, 412

Lichtenberg, Georg Christoph, 316; *Aphorisms*, 327n114

lightning/thunder, 41, 44, 70, 78, 81, 83, 117–18, 131, 132, 171, 247, 255–57, 259, 265, 276, 292, 325n93, 446; in Baudelaire, Charles/"À une passante," 81; in Brontë, Emily/*Wuthering Heights*, 39, 41, 44–46, 51, 56nn122–23, 115–18, 125–26, 129–60, 164, 169–72, 174, 181, 183nn75–85, 186n185, 187, 219, 237, 239nn56–59, 343, 345, 360nn118–19; in Goethe, Johann Wolfgang von/*The Sorrows of Young Werther*, 50, 109, 110, 115, 117, 120nn52–58, 120nn60–64, 120nn66–68, 120nn71–73, 120n75, 121nn79–80, 121n82, 121n85, 121nn91–94; in Mann, Thomas/*The Magic Mountain*, 28, 53n55, 128, 131–33, 142nn33–41, 142nn43–50, 171, 181, 185nn132, 185nn135–37, 186n187, 202, 226, 228, 233, 241nn99–100, 241nn105–6, 241n120, 241n122, 344, 345, 360nn126–27; in Plato/*Symposium*, 11–17, 19n55, 19n56, 20n69, 21, 23, 25–27, 29, 30, 41, 42, 44, 47, 51n3, 53n72, 53n74, 61, 62, 69–72, 74, 81, 83–85, 88, 90–92, 103, 106, 108, 117, 123, 126–29, 131, 133–36, 154, 179, 203, 209n33, 218, 225, 238, 245, 246, 251, 254–56, 258, 260, 264, 265, 267, 268n22, 342–45, 354, 360nn114–15, 407, 410, 411, 420, 421, 450; in Proust, Marcel/*The Captive*; *Time Regained*, 24, 52nn19–22, 52nn24–28, 52n31, 52n38, 60, 66, 68, 69, 71, 88–90, 92n14, 93n21, 93nn40–42, 93n44, 94nn51–53, 93n57, 93n59, 93n64, 93n72, 93nn75–79, 95n92, 95n107, 96nn139, 96nn141–42, 96nn146–49, 96nn155–60, 96n164, 97nn179–80, 123, 141n2, 175, 185nn161, 185n163, 200, 211n95, 226, 237, 241n102, 241n104, 242n172, 344, 386, 403n151, 453nn17–18, 453nn20–22; in Shelley, Mary/*Frankenstein*, 53n54, 115–18, 121nn86–89, 220; in Woolf, Virginia/*To the Lighthouse*, 149, 200, 227, 229, 233, 234, 237, 238, 241nn108–9, 241n111, 241nn125–29, 242nn157–59, 242n174, 243, 245, 246, 251, 254, 256–58, 264, 265, 267nn1–4, 268n19, 268n22, 268nn24–26, 268nn28–31, 268nn33–38, 269nn39–45, 269nn47–49,

269nn51–57, 269n59, 269nn65–70, 269n72, 269nn74–77, 270nn81–86, 270nn88–91, 270n97, 270n107, 270nn109–12, 271nn113–16, 271nn118–42, 271nn144–48, 272nn149–50, 272nn153–56, 272nn158–65, 272n167
Ligotti, Thomas, 31; *The Conspiracy Against the Human Race: A Contrivance of Horror*, 54n83, 210n81, 210n82
Lispector, Clarice: *The Passion According to G.H.*, 22, 29, 51n12, 53nn68–71, 193, 209n42, 443n125
Locke, John, 417
love, 3, 5, 10, 11, 13–16, 21, 22, 25–27, 29, 30, 41, 42, 44–47, 50, 51, 59–62, 67, 69, 71–75, 77, 79–87, 91, 100, 102–15, 117, 118, 123, 124, 126, 129, 131–36, 141n3, 149, 150, 154, 155, 170, 171, 173, 174, 176, 179, 180, 191, 200, 214, 215, 219, 220, 223, 225, 226, 233, 235–37, 244–55, 260, 261, 265–67, 271n143, 273–84, 287–94, 296n35, 299nn129–30, 301–3, 306–9, 311, 312, 314, 315, 319, 327n133, 329, 332–55, 376, 394, 408–15, 418, 430, 431, 436, 439n6, 446–50; courtly, 290, 291; definition of, 69; erotic, 105, 348; religious, 105
Love, Jean O., 254; *Worlds in Consciousness: Mythopoetic Thought in the Novels of Virginia Woolf*, 269n78
Love, Michael: "Meet Neff Davis, Anna Delvey's Only Friend in New York," 182n34
Löwith, Karl, 395
Lucie de Lammermoor, 225
Ludacris, 445, 449, 453n11
Lukács, Georg, 9, 45, 48, 50, 51, 127–30, 133–34, 136–38, 140, 148, 150, 158, 164, 191, 195, 205, 215–17, 219, 331, 340, 356, 357, 367, 370, 371, 377–79, 381, 384, 385, 387, 411; on *Don Quixote*, 136–37; *Essays on Thomas Mann*, 185n138; *Soul and Form*, 360n100, 361n134, 362n165; *Studies in European Realism*, 183n54, 184n96, 184n99; *Theory of the Novel: A Historico-Philosophical Essay on the Forms of Great Epic Literature*, 9, 19nn44–48, 51, 57n165, 128, 129, 137, 140, 141n10, 142n23, 143n62, 143n63, 144n83, 144n84, 144n94, 145n106, 145n107, 215–16, 239nn24–29, 239n53, 352, 357n15, 371, 377, 378, 385, 398n44, 401n94, 401n104, 401n106, 402n110, 401n111, 402n118, 402n119, 402n120, 402nn134–35, 402n137, 403n141, 403n142, 435, 444n163; transcendental homelessness, 133, 134, 137, 219, 370, 381, 384
Lyly, John: *Anatomy of Wit*, 222

Machiavelli, Niccolò, 150–58, 160, 197; Machiavellianism, 156–60, 162; *The Prince*, 109, 156, 160, 182nn51–53
Mackey, Louis: *Kierkegaard: A Kind of Poet*, 358n43
Magee, Bryan, 194; *The Philosophy of Schopenhauer*, 209n45, 209n46
Mainländer, Philip: *Philosophy of Redemption*, 198
Malory, Thomas: *Le Morte Darthur*, 32
Manichaeism, 409
Manifest Destiny, 418
Mann, Thomas, 15, 23, 33, 128–30, 132–34, 171, 181, 194, 227, 229, 274–75, 331, 370, 371, 384, 394, 395, 438; *Buddenbrooks*, 15, 33, 54nn92–94; *Death in Venice*, 33–34, 55nn98–101, 143n45, 275, 323n44, 410, 440n15; *Der Tod in Venedig und andere Erzählungen*, 55n102; *Doctor Faustus: The Life of the German Composer Adrian Leverkühn as Told by a Friend*, 23,

29, 33, 52n14, 53n64, 55nn95–97, 205, 352, 395, 405nn201–4, 437–39, 444n175; *Essays of Three Decades*, 209n44; on Heidegger, 131, 371, 394; *The Magic Mountain*, 28, 53n55, 128, 131–33, 142nn33–41, 142n43, 143nn44–50, 171–72, 181, 185n132, 185nn135–37, 186n187, 202, 226, 228–29, 233, 241n99, 241n100, 241n105, 241n106, 241n120, 241n122, 344, 345, 360n126, 360n127

Marasco, Robyn: *The Highway of Despair: Critical Theory after Hegel*, 54n80

Marcuse, Herbert: *Eros and Civilization*, 50, 58nn201–3, 424, 442n85

Marlowe, Christopher, 23

Martin, Timothy: *Joyce and Wagner: A Study of Influence*, 295n17

Marx, Karl, 160, 172, 192, 333, 376; *Capital: Volume One*, 183n71; *Das Kapital*, 192; Marxism, 164, 396; "Theses on Feuerbach," 209n34

Marx, Leo, 415; "Melville's Parable of Walls," 440n41, 444n49

Maupassant, Guy de, 139; *Pierre et Jean*, 144n101

Mauriac, François, 252; *Mémoires Interieurs*, 269n63, 269n64

Mazzoni, Guido, 54n94, 58n191, 58n192, 58n195, 125, 137–38, 147, 222–23, 239n39, 240nn75–77, 375, 388–89, 446, 448; *Theory of the Novel*, 58n191, 58n192, 58n195, 143n70, 143n71, 144n88, 144n89, 181n1, 239n39, 240nn75–77, 375, 400n80, 400n81, 404n165, 452n4, 452n5

McCarthy, Tom, 392

McEwan, Ian: *Atonement*, 149, 150, 181nn7–14, 237

McKay, Melanie, 316; "Spatial Form and Simultaneity in Nabokov's Fiction," 327n115

McKeon, Michael, 137, 151; *The Origins of the English Novel: 1600-1740*, 58n193, 58n194, 137, 144n78, 144n79, 181n4, 181nn17–20, 182nn21–23, 182nn35–38, 242n143

McKinsey & Co., 429

Medicare for All, 7

medicine, 218, 230, 432. *See also* anatomy, Medicare for All

medieval/Middle Ages, 5, 15, 22, 32, 44, 45, 51, 74, 75, 80, 82, 99–111, 127, 137, 153, 156, 180, 197, 218, 221, 222, 235, 237, 274, 275, 308, 412, 413, 425

melancholia, 8, 68, 78, 214, 224, 232, 260, 265, 276–79, 281, 282, 331, 347, 391

melodrama, 111, 131, 178, 217, 262, 334

Melville, Herman, 415, 426, 428; *Moby-Dick, or, the Whale*, 30–31, 53n75, 53n76, 54n77, 380, 390, 402n112, 414, 440n41, 440n42; *Bartleby*, 1, 17n2, 112, 120n70, 390, 413–16, 426, 428, 440nn39–41, 440nn43–45, 441n48

memory, 10, 11, 14, 24, 72, 77, 80, 81, 83, 90–92, 115, 131, 133, 141, 153, 170, 171, 175, 204, 225, 226, 237, 247, 254, 259, 303, 306, 308, 340, 346, 376, 425, 449, 451; involuntary, 24, 68, 69, 79, 89; traumatic, 22. *See also* oblivion

Menippean satire, 100, 232, 233

Merimée, Prosper: *Carmen and Other Stories*, 140, 145n113, 390; *La Guzla*, 140

metamorphosis, 23–25, 27, 29, 70, 237, 302, 303, 311, 316. *See also* insects

metaphor, 23, 25, 26, 30, 33, 41, 47, 65, 67–72, 74, 76, 83, 86, 89, 139, 158, 165, 187, 217, 222, 225, 227, 250, 253, 262, 268n18, 274, 276, 287,

289, 306, 314, 316, 337, 341, 384, 390, 425, 433; as method, 67, 70. *See also* Proust, Marcel
Meyer, Priscilla, 331; "Infinite Reflections in Pale Fire: The Danish Connection (Hans Andersen and Isak Dinesen)," 322n30, 357n19; "Vladimir Nabokov and Virginia Woolf," 357n18
Meyers, Jeffrey: "Kafka's Dark Laughter," 211n18, 211n119
Michaud, Derek: "Ludwig Feuerbach (1804–1872)," 18n18
Michelstaedter, Carlo, 198; *Persuasion and Rhetoric*, 198
Michelucci, Stefania, 276; *Space and Place in the Works of D.H. Lawrence*, 288, 298n100, 298n101
Miller, D. A.: *The Novel and the Police*, 425, 442n94
Miller, Henry: *The Tropic of Cancer*, 148
mimesis/imitation, 12, 75, 151, 156, 162, 164, 177, 195, 225, 247, 316, 344, 375, 396, 422, 445–52
mindfulness, 419
mirror, 11, 14, 35, 42, 43, 63, 65, 75, 101, 102, 108–10, 116, 129, 137, 140, 151, 163–72, 177–81, 188, 195, 229, 243, 249, 255–57, 267, 282, 289, 302, 312, 318, 323, 335, 337, 353, 384, 449–51
misogyny, 195, 319
modernism/modernity, 9, 85, 110, 113, 118, 132, 154, 155, 174, 178, 179, 197, 233, 245, 274–76, 283, 285, 286, 311, 371, 377, 379, 383, 410, 420, 424–26; Beckett, Samuel, 2, 23, 35, 52n18, 56n120, 60, 61, 67, 89, 177, 226, 387, 391, 409; Benjamin, Walter, 4, 8, 18n21, 26, 53n41, 59, 64, 68, 82, 89, 92nn1–2, 92n4, 93n31, 94nn48–50, 96n136, 96n163, 96n165, 138, 144n92, 144n93, 204, 212nn122–23, 370, 398nn42–43, 399n54; Camus, Albert, 58n200, 150, 181n15, 202, 211nn103–4, 211n106, 323, 402n108; Eliot, T. S., 48, 58n187, 276, 295n18; Faulkner, William, 22, 23, 36, 51nn8–11, 52–53n13, 55n114, 145n106, 196, 209–10nn62–65, 403n157; Grass, Günter, 23; Joyce, James, 132, 133, 138, 140, 143n53, 148, 178, 185–86nn172–75, 213, 214, 238n4, 241n107, 298n76, 317, 384, 386, 392, 403nn155–56, 404–5n190, 404n192, 404n193, 412, 420; Kafka, Franz, 28, 34, 152, 195, 203, 345, 361n133, 374; Lawrence, D. H., 126, 128, 135, 140, 142n20, 142n27, 144n75, 144n76, 148, 235–38, 242nn165–67, 252, 253, 258, 273, 274, 276, 277, 279, 282, 284, 286, 288, 293, 295n20, 296n25, 296nn30–34, 296n39, 296n41, 296nn46–47, 297n54, 297nn57–59, 297n65, 297nn67–68, 297nn70–73, 298nn76–78, 298n81, 298n82, 298nn85–90, 298nn92–99, 298nn104–6, 299nn107–9, 299nn111–31, 300nn133–34, 300nn137–41, 300n143, 300nn145–52, 300nn154–55, 301, 302, 387, 410, 412, 413, 419, 420, 440nn16–17, 440nn35–36, 445; Mann, Thomas, 23, 28, 29, 33, 52n14, 53nn55, 64, 55nn95–101, 128, 131–33, 142n33, 143n45, 171, 181, 202, 205, 226, 228, 233, 275, 323, 344, 345, 352, 394, 395, 405nn201–4, 410, 437, 439, 440n15, 444n175; Musil, Robert, 386, 403n152; Proust, Marcel, 24, 52n17, 52nn19–22, 52nn24–29, 52nn31–35, 52n38, 53nn42–43, 53nn59–61, 53n63, 66, 68–71, 74, 77, 80, 84, 88–90, 92nn5–7, 92n9, 92nn13–16, 92n18, 93nn20–23, 93nn25–28, 93nn40–42, 93n44,

94nn51–57, 94n59, 94nn61–64, 94nn66–79, 94n83, 94n84, 95n86, 95n87, 95n89, 95n92, 95n95, 95n99, 95n102, 95n104, 95n105, 95n107, 95n108, 95nn111–12, 95nn114–20, 96nn132–42, 96nn146–49, 96nn155–61, 96n164, 96n167, 97n168, 97n169, 97nn176–80, 123, 141n2, 166, 175, 176, 184n103, 185nn157–61, 185nn163–67, 200, 211n95, 226, 235, 237, 241n102, 241n104, 242n169, 242n172, 275, 295n15, 325n79, 341, 344, 359n91, 360n128, 361nn129–31, 386, 403n151, 450, 453n14, 453nn17–18, 453nn20–22; Woolf, Virginia, 149, 200, 227, 229, 233, 234, 237, 238, 241nn108–19, 241nn123–29, 242nn157–59, 242n174, 243, 245, 246, 251, 254, 256–58, 264, 265, 267nn1–4, 268nn19, 268n22, 268nn24–26, 268nn28–31, 268nn33–38, 269nn39–45, 269nn47–49, 269nn51–57, 269nn59, 269nn65–70, 269n72, 269nn74–77, 270nn81–86, 270nn88–91, 270n97, 270n107, 270nn109–12, 271nn113–16, 271nn118–42, 271nn144–48, 272nn149–50, 272nn153–56, 272nn158–65, 272n167; Zamyatin, Yevgeny, 429, 431, 443nn129–35
monstrosity, 4, 23, 34, 109, 114–16, 118, 168, 171, 172, 180, 220, 221, 304, 318, 320, 368
Monty Python, 87
Mooney, Edward F., 352, 365–66, 389; "Kierkegaard's Disruptions of Literature and Philosophy: Freedom, Anxiety, and Existential Contributions," 362nn178–79, 397nn5–6, 404nn166–67
Morell, Ottoline, 277
Moretti, Franco, 140, 160; "A Capital Dracula," 183nn73–74, 183n91; *Modern Epic: The World-System from Goethe to García-Márquez*, 145n110
Morrison, Toni, 412; *Beloved*, 411
mosaic technique, 246–55, 259, 261, 265, 266
Moynahan, Julian, 286; *The Deed of Life: The Novels and Tales of D.H. Lawrence*, 298n83, 298n84
mud/dirt, 101, 102, 174, 175, 177–81, 187
Muhlstein, Anka: *Monsieur Proust's Library*, 185n162
Musil, Robert, 353, 386, 387; *The Man Without Qualities*, 386, 403n152, 403n157, 403n158
mutability, 77, 113, 141n10
mysticism, 22, 29, 30, 36, 109, 172, 227, 251, 258, 282, 285, 288, 412. *See also* Porete, Marguerite; Tristan legend
myth, 11–15, 17, 21, 30, 50, 71, 73, 83, 91, 103, 136, 163, 168, 191, 247, 258, 265, 342, 413, 450. *See also* Apuleius/*The Golden Ass*; Eros; Plato/*Symposium*

Nabokov, Vladimir, 9, 14, 19n49, 19n54, 20nn70–72, 29, 47, 53n63, 124, 139, 141n6, 141n7, 144n98, 152, 167, 168, 178n57, 182nn31–2, 184mn108–11, 196, 209n62, 236, 237, 238, 242n175, 242n176, 301–21, 321nn1–13, 322nn15–34, 322nn36–39, 323n40, 323n42, 323n44, 323n46, 323n47, 323n49, 323n50, 324n51, 324n52, 324n57, 324n58, 324nn60–68, 325nn69–79, 325nn82–92, 326nn94–108, 326n110, 326n113, 327nn115–17, 327nn119–30, 328nn134–39, 328n142, 328n143, 328n146, 328n147, 331–33, 335, 336, 339, 342, 347, 357, 357nn17–18, 358n24, 358n30, 359n52, 359n54, 359n59, 359n60, 360n95, 360n111, 361n144, 362n173, 399n51, 420–22, 440n21,

441n75, 452; "An Affair of Honor," 323n46; *The Enchanter*, 303, 304, 322n13, 322nn16–17, 322nn19–20, 324n51, 328n142, 336, 359n59; *The Gift*, 304, 322n23; *Lolita*, 29, 19n54, 47, 53n63, 57n178, 125, 133, 152, 168, 182nn31–32, 184n108, 184n110, 196, 236–38, 242n176, 301–21, 321nn2–3, 321nn5–12, 322nn21–22, 322nn25–29, 322nn36–39, 323nn40–45, 323nn49–50, 324n51, 324n57, 324nn60–68, 324nn69–79, 325nn82–92, 326nn94–108, 327nn117–33, 328nn134–48, 335, 339, 347, 358n30, 359n52, 359n54, 359n61, 360n95, 360n111, 387, 390, 411, 422, 426, 430, 440n21; *Pale Fire*, 238, 322n30, 331, 359n19, 424n175; *Speak, Memory*, 307–8, 316, 321n13, 323n47, 324n52, 326n113, 327n113, 327n117; *Strong Opinions*, 19n49, 20nn70–72, 141nn6–7, 144n98, 184n109, 209n62, 321n1, 322n24, 323n44, 328n138, 357n17
Naiman, Eric, 317–18; *Nabokov, Perversely*, 327n126, 328n133
Narcissism, 7, 220, 409, 437
Narcissus, 34, 75, 84, 103, 108, 110, 111, 113, 116, 180, 220
nature, 11, 14, 21, 22, 27, 30–32, 38, 39, 41, 44, 49, 60, 62, 75, 87, 89, 112, 114–18, 131, 133, 134, 136, 149, 162, 165, 167, 170, 176–80, 190–92, 194, 216, 221, 228, 242n150, 245, 248, 252, 256–58, 273, 287, 348, 350, 367, 378, 380, 381, 386, 387, 392, 432, 450; landscapes, 10, 23, 37, 39, 40, 44, 47, 54n78, 63, 110, 114, 130, 170, 187–92, 204, 213, 216, 220, 250, 255, 258–60, 262, 264, 265, 281, 312, 404n190; trees, 10, 63–67, 69, 73, 78, 192, 217, 228, 238, 245, 246, 249, 250, 268n18, 280, 289, 290, 451; wastelands, 279, 281, 282

Nazism, 147, 370, 371, 394–96. See also fascism
Nehamas, Alexander, 10, 19n50
neoliberalism, 231, 407, 409, 412–14, 418, 433–37, 445; productivity, 294, 415, 418, 419, 431; rhetoric of gratitude, 2, 413. See also Biden, Joe; capitalism
New Testament, 215
New Woman, 161, 162
New World, 189, 190, 276, 289, 292, 293
Nicht-Können-Können ["Being able to not be able"], 415
Nietzsche, Friedrich, 4, 9, 113–14, 200, 203, 275; *amor fati*, 124; *The Anti-Christ*, 108, 120n48, 142n16; *Beyond Good and Evil*, 114, 119n28, 121n81, 211n92; *The Birth of Tragedy*, 3, 18n11, 120nn76–78, 142n31, 211n112, 272n158, 128; *The Case of Wagner*, 3, 18n11, 120n76; *Daybreak*, 126, 142n17; *The Gay Science*, 239n45; *On the Genealogy of Morals*, 373; *Human, All Too Human*, 17n4; *Thus Spoke Zarathustra*, 126, 433, 440n47, 444n151; *Philosophy and Truth*, 184nn100–101, 443n150; *Twilight of the Idols/The Anti-Christ*, 120n48, 142n16, 143n52; on transvaluation of values, 113, 130, 156, 292; on truth, 165–66; *Übermensch* (Overman), 27; *Unpublished Writings from the Period of Unfashionable Observations*, 443n114
nominalism, 8, 105, 417
nothingness, 36, 47, 64, 66, 76, 77, 84, 219, 252, 266, 284, 315–17, 321, 373, 378, 379, 381, 383, 385, 388, 410
novel: anatomy of, 116, 205, 218–34, 238, 396, 401n101, 425, 429; definition of, 17, 45, 50, 63, 101, 134–41, 148, 162, 177, 180, 192–93, 217, 219, 348, 377, 384, 389, 399n54;

as fundamental ontology, 375–83, 385; as seducer, 86, 163, 346–49, 449
Nussbaum, Martha, 11, 15, 17, 23, 32, 85, 87; "Fictions of the Soul," 15, 20n76, 20nn78–81, 51n1, 96nn150–51, 241n101; "The Speech of Alcibiades," 16, 19n55, 20n77, 94n65, 360n120; "The Romantic Ascent: Emily Brontë," 56n126

oblivion, 66, 76, 78–83, 188, 219. *See also* memory
obsession, 22, 24, 25, 43, 59–74, 76, 78–80, 82, 89, 112, 172, 198, 244, 258, 262, 279, 281, 302, 319, 325n79, 329, 340, 414, 416. *See also* Abelard, Peter; Andersen, Hans Christian/"The Little Mermaid"; Heloise; Tristan legend; Baudelaire, Charles/"*Obsession*"; Brontë, Emily/*Wuthering Heights*; Goethe, Johann Wolfgang von/*The Sorrows of Young Werther*; Nabokov, Vladimir/*Lolita*; Kierkegaard, Søren, *The Seducer's Diary*; Mann, Thomas/*Death in Venice*/*Doctor Faustus*; Proust, Marcel; romance, medieval
Office of Dead Letters, 1. *See also* Melville, Herman; *Bartleby*
Ong, Yi-Ping, 150, 347, 425; *The Art of Being*, 181n16, 182n25, 361n139, 361nn142–43, 363n183, 363n186, 363nn208–9, 400nn77–78, 401nn102–3, 442nn94–96
ontology, 25, 26, 41, 45, 61, 69, 71, 79, 84, 85, 124, 138, 180, 214, 247, 251, 338, 365, 366, 372, 375–85, 387, 399n60, 407, 409, 413, 416, 435; ontological slipperiness, 45. *See also* Heidegger, Martin, fundamental ontology
optimalism, 8
optimism, 2, 5–9, 16, 17n8, 29, 31, 37, 38, 41, 46, 48, 49, 60, 68, 87–89, 101, 102, 136, 150, 168, 190, 191, 198–200, 206, 218, 223, 231, 256, 257, 263, 274, 276, 277, 294, 312–14, 319, 320, 351, 360n109, 376, 398n49, 407, 412, 415, 416, 422, 424–26, 434, 437, 439, 451
OPTIMISM (Operational Perseverance Twin for Integration of Mechanism and Instruments Sent to Mars), 190
ordinariness, 12, 224, 381, 382. *See also* Heidegger, Martin; average everydayness
Orpheus, 80, 81, 84, 205. *See also* myth
Orwell, George: *1984*, 412
Ovid, 104, 105
Oxford English Dictionary, 213, 222

Packman, David, 318; *Vladimir Nabokov: The Structure of Literary Desire*, 327n127
Palahniuk, Chuck: *Fight Club*, 390; *Invisible Monsters*, 388, 404nn162–63
Palmer, Emily: "A Fake Heiress Called Anna Delvey Conned the City's Wealthy. 'I'm Not Sorry,' She Says," 182n33
Papaioannou, Sophia, 73; "Charite's Rape, Psyche on the Rock and the Parallel Function of Marriage in Apuleuius' 'Metamorphoses,'" 94n80
Parker, Stephen Jay, 358nn21–23
panopticism, 425, 426, 431. *See also* Bentham, Jeremy; Foucault, Michel
paradox, 32, 39, 46, 48, 67, 72, 75, 79, 92, 101, 114, 131, 134, 136, 152, 165, 166, 177, 179, 180, 199, 206, 209n41, 226, 228, 243–67, 278, 279, 281–83, 288, 312, 369, 382, 387, 389, 433, 435, 452
Parks, Tim, 445; "The Dying Art of Instruction in the Digital Classroom," 452nn1–2
Pascal, Blaise: *Pensées*, 323n48

parody, 33, 116, 131, 133, 134, 151, 202, 205, 221, 224, 236, 237, 261, 323n40, 323n43, 323n45, 324n68, 327n119, 332, 334, 335, 347, 350, 351, 388, 394, 422

passion, 28, 46, 54n85, 61, 67, 75, 79, 104, 106, 111–13, 117, 132, 134, 158, 161, 171, 188, 199, 226, 273, 275, 278, 287, 288, 290, 292, 293, 312, 314, 335, 337, 350, 351, 368, 413–15, 418, 421, 422, 429, 445, 446; corporate appropriation of, 413; erotic, 199, 278, 287; fatal, 312; religious, 199; as suffering, 287

Pattison, George, 352, 359n66; "The Bonfire of the Genres: Kierkegaard's Literary Kaleidoscope," 18n14, 362nn175–77, 362nn118

pedagogy, 106, 284, 332, 358n20, 407–39, 446. *See also* academic; education

Penda, Petar, 284, 286; *Aesthetics and Ideology of D.H. Lawrence, Virginia Woolf, and T.S. Eliot*, 297n66

Pifer, Ellen, 311, 321, 323n40, 323n42, 323n44, 325n82, 328n135; "Nabokov's Novel Offspring: Lolita and her Kin," 325n82

perpetual becoming, 25, 265, 354, 377, 386. *See also* metamorphosis

pessimism, 1–9, 11, 12, 15, 17, 21–24, 27–38, 40, 41, 43, 46–48, 50, 51, 54nn78, 85, 60–62, 67, 68, 71, 75, 79, 84, 85, 87–89, 91, 92, 100–104, 110, 112, 116, 118, 123, 129, 130–35, 137, 138, 141n10, 147, 150, 152, 155–57, 164, 166–69, 171–77, 179, 187, 190, 193–207, 214–18, 220, 223, 224, 230, 231, 233, 234, 238, 243, 253, 255, 257, 259, 261–67, 273–78, 281, 283, 292, 301–3, 305, 307, 315, 317–19, 329, 330, 337, 341, 345, 346, 349, 354, 360n109, 367, 370, 376, 380, 398n49, 399nn54–56, 403n157, 411, 413–16, 424, 425, 429, 433, 437, 438, 439, 447, 451, 452; anti-democratic, 130; definition of, 137, 194, 205, 341; ethical, 9, 317–21; etymology of, 31, 451; fatalistic basis of, 167; pedagogy of, 433–39; podiatry of, 30–37

physical violence, 206

picaresque, 151, 152. *See also Lazarillo de Tormes*

Pickard, P. M., 308

Pinkard, Terry, 111–12, 124; *German Philosophy 1760–1860: The Legacy of Idealism*, 120n51, 120n65, 141n5

Platen, August von: "Tristan," 282

plague, 7, 8, 11, 127, 198, 222, 244, 260, 290, 317

Plath, Sylvia: *The Bell Jar*, 31, 54n84, 392, 404nn184–87

Plato, 10–17, 104, 408–9; *Apology*, 14, 19n56, 20n68; backlove, 11, 340, 449; Ladder of Love, 14, 19n56, 82, 154, 268n20; *Phaedo*, 26; *Phaedrus*, 10, 12–14, 19nn50–53, 21–22, 25, 51nn4–5, 66, 67, 72, 74, 76, 77, 79, 95nn97–98, 105, 129, 138, 238, 245, 340, 449, 453n10; Platonic equanimity, 46, 262; *The Republic*, 12–14, 20n59, 26, 32, 179, 191, 245; *Symposium*, 11–17, 19nn55–56, 20n69, 21, 23, 25–27, 29, 30, 41, 42, 44, 47, 61, 62, 69–72, 74, 83–85, 88, 90, 91, 103, 106, 108, 117, 123, 126–29, 131, 135, 136, 154, 203, 217–18, 225, 238, 245–46, 251, 254–56, 258–66, 268n22, 342, 343, 345, 407, 410, 411, 420, 421, 450

Poe, Edgar Allan, 309

poetry, 13, 15, 27, 29, 47, 67, 90, 100, 102, 118, 125, 136, 155, 158, 202, 217, 250, 281, 283, 330, 333, 344, 345, 348, 369, 371, 376, 382, 414, 419, 422, 452. *See also* Baudelaire, Charles; Eliot, T. S.

Pontano, Giovanni, 27, 53n50
Porete, Marguerite, 109
pornography, 140, 410
positivism, 5, 6, 8, 87, 103, 117, 305, 353, 360n109, 383, 385, 409, 416, 417, 424, 426, 428, 433–35. *See also* Big Data; scientism
Price, Brian: *A Theory of Regret*, 58n199
Proffer, Carl R.: *The Keys to Lolita*, 323n41
Price Waterhouse Cooper, 429
Priestley, Joseph, 431
Proust, Marcel, 15, 16, 59, 66; *À la recherche du temps perdu/Recherche* (*In Search of Lost Time*), 24–26, 59, 61, 66, 68–70, 72, 74, 77, 80, 81, 86, 87, 90, 117, 131, 155, 167, 176, 226, 234, 235, 345, 377, 388, 391, 412, 450, 451 (*The Captive*, 52nn19, 52n21–22, 52n38, 69, 71, 92n14, 94nn51–53, 94n57, 94n64, 94nn75–79, 95n92, 95n107, 97n180, 97n123, 141n2, 241n104, 386, 403n151; *The Fugitive*, 52n19, 52n21, 66, 70, 71, 80, 92n8, 92n16, 93n20, 94nn61–62, 94nn67–69, 94n71, 94nn73–74, 94n83, 95n86, 95n99, 95n102, 95n104, 95nn111–12, 95nn114–15, 95nn119–20, 96n132, 96nn135–38, 97nn176–78, 235, 242n169, 341, 360n105; *The Guermantes Way*, 92n5, 94n70, 95n89, 95n95, 185n160, 325n79, 344, 361nn129–31; *In the Shadow of Young Girls in Flower*, 52n29, 52n33, 63, 66, 71, 92nn6–7, 92n9, 93nn25–28, 94n66, 95nn116–18, 96n134, 96n161, 185n166, 185n168, 360n128; *Sodom and Gomorrah*, 52n30, 52n32, 71, 77, 93n20, 93n22, 94n63, 95n87, 95n105, 95n108, 97n169, 97nn175–76, 185nn157–59, 185n164, 185n167; *Swann's Way*, 52nn34–35, 53nn42–43, 59, 61, 63, 68, 74, 84, 90, 92n15, 92n18, 93n23, 94nn54–56, 84, 96n133, 96n140, 96n167, 97n168, 166, 176, 184n103, 185n165, 226, 275, 295n15, 344, 359n91, 450, 453n14; *Time Regained*, 24, 52n20, 52nn24–28, 52n31, 60, 66, 68, 69, 88–90, 92, 93nn21, 93nn40–42, 93n44, 94n59, 94n72, 96n139, 96nn141–42, 96nn46–49, 96nn155–60, 96nn164, 97n179, 97n175, 185nn161, 185n163, 200, 211n95, 226, 237, 241n102, 242n172, 343, 453nn17–18, 453nn20–22); imagery of insects, 23–30; influence on modern writers, 234–38; *Letters of Marcel Proust*, 92n3; Questionnaire, 76, 318; *Remembrance of Things Past*, 93n29, 241n139; transvertebration, 26
protestant work ethic, 112, 416. *See also* capitalism
psychagogia, 191, 436
Psyche (in myth). *See* Cupid
psyche/psychology, 6, 16, 42, 60, 63, 65, 70, 73–76, 78, 80–82, 84, 89, 99, 113, 149, 152, 166, 226, 235, 342, 375, 379, 386, 416, 433
psychological realism, 149, 166
Ptolemaic system, 214, 217, 231
Pushkin, Alexander: *Eugene Onegin*, 347, 361nn144–45
Pynchon, Thomas: *Gravity's Rainbow*, 23, 52n13

quit lit, 445
Quixotism, 9, 32, 76, 102, 111, 137, 194, 197
Quintana, Anna: "Fake NYC Heiress Anna Delvey's Scams Landed her a Netflix Show," 182n33

Rabelais, François, 148, 158, 159, 204, 205, 207; *Gargantua and Pantagruel*, 148, 204–6, 212n128, 212n137, 212n139
Raphael: *The School of Athens*, 32

rationalism, 46, 76, 89, 117, 118, 197, 235, 360n109

realism, 8, 9, 105, 149, 151, 154, 160, 173, 175, 177, 178, 235, 286, 403n159; failure of, 163–72; formal, 151–52; psychological, 149, 166. *See also* Balzac, Honoré de; Dostoevsky, Fyodor; Eliot, George; Flaubert, Gustave; Hardy, Thomas; James, Henry; Maupassant, Guy de; Stendhal; Tolstoy, Leo; Turgenev, Ivan

reality, 6, 8, 32, 39, 49, 50, 59, 62, 67–69, 71, 75, 80, 82, 89, 91, 102, 105, 107, 108, 110, 111, 113, 116, 127, 148, 150, 151, 157, 159, 163–67, 171–73, 176, 177, 179, 196, 200, 215, 236, 245, 251–54, 257, 275, 284–86, 306, 310, 314, 321, 341, 347, 356, 371, 375, 378, 386, 389, 391, 410, 430, 431, 433

Rebhorn, Wayne A., 128, 142, 361n137

reconfiguration of space, 287–89

Rembrandt: *The Anatomy Lesson*, 227

Renaissance, 27, 100, 137, 189, 213, 218, 226, 227, 366, 371, 432. *See also* Alighieri, Dante; Bacon, Francis; barber-surgeon; Boccaccio, Giovanni; Castiglione, Baldesar; Cervantes, Miguel de; Copernicus, Nicolaus; Henry VIII; Machiavelli, Niccolò; Marlowe, Christopher; Rabelais, François; Shakespeare, William; Spenser, Edmund

representation, 124

Revel, Jean-François, 61, 67; *On Proust*, 92n17, 94n46, 95n113, 242n168

Rice, Condoleezza, 6

Richardson, Samuel, 49, 101, 110, 148; *Clarissa*, 149; *Pamela: Or, Virtue Rewarded*, 49, 135, 143n73

Richter, Friedrich, 126

Riffaterre, Michael, 17, 20n82

Rifkin, Benjamin A.: *Human Anatomy: A Visual History From the Renaissance to the Digital Age*, 240n68

Robert, Marthe, 139, 162, 193; "From *Origins of the Novel*," 144n97, 183n89, 209n36

role reversal, 314–17

romance (genre), 26, 40, 44–46, 51, 74, 75, 80, 90, 99, 103, 105, 110, 111–13, 116, 117, 125, 129, 134, 135, 137, 147, 148, 151, 153, 169, 179, 225, 229, 235–37, 276, 290, 293, 306, 307, 312, 346, 391; Arthurian Romance, 26

romance, medieval, 44, 45, 51, 74, 75, 80, 99–109, 235, 237; allegory, 14, 74, 83, 84, 108, 109, 113, 307, 337, 409; Arthurian Romance, 26; Provençal troubadours, 104, 111; *The Romance of the Rose*, 75, 102, 104, 105, 107, 109, 110, 113, 115, 117, 119nn15–25, 165, 179, 180. *See also* courtly love; Tristan legend; Troyes, Chrétien de

romanticism, 8, 13, 44, 68, 80, 103, 112, 113, 123, 125, 126, 134, 136, 178, 225, 256, 293, 296n35, 306, 311, 319, 320, 346, 350, 412, 414, 437, 438; Andersen, Hans Christian, 4, 35, 57n179, 168, 308, 309, 314, 320, 322n30, 324nn53–56, 324n65, 324n66, 324n68, 325n84, 325n93, 326n109, 330, 331, 353–56, 357n19, 362n183, 362n186, 363n200, 369; Baudelaire, Charles, 64–68, 77, 81, 82, 89, 93n40, 245, 274; Brontë, Emily/*Wuthering Heights*, 39, 41, 44–46, 51, 56nn122–23, 56nn125–26, 56nn129–36, 56nn138–51, 57nn152–60, 164, 169–72, 115–18, 131, 160, 168, 169, 174, 181, 183nn75–85, 186nn185–87, 219, 237, 239nn56–59, 343, 345, 360nn118–19; Byron, Lord (George Gordon), 112, 414; Chateaubriand, François-René de, 89, 96n162; Coleridge, Samuel Taylor, 47, 48, 57nn183–84; Goethe, Johann Wolfgang von Goethe/*The Sorrows of*

Young Werther; *Faust*, 50, 109, 110, 115, 117, 120nn52–58, 120nn60–64, 120nn66–68, 120nn71–73, 120n75, 121n85, 121nn91–94, 124, 125, 192, 196, 334, 335, 351; Grimm, The Brothers, 54n79, 55nn104–5, 55n107, 171; Keats, John, 10; Kleist, Heinrich von, 99; Melville, Herman/*Bartleby*; *Moby-Dick*, 1, 17n2, 112, 120n70, 390, 413–15, 426, 428, 440nn39–41, 440nn43–45, 441n48; Schiller, Friedrich, 319, 435, 438, 444nn161, 444nn176–78; Schlegel, Friedrich von, 12, 20n60, 123, 126, 127, 132–36, 138, 139, 142nn18–22, 143nn51, 143n60, 143n67, 143n69, 144nn80–82, 144n90, 144n95, 144n99, 150, 192, 202, 215, 238n22, 349, 350, 353, 354, 361n154, 362n161, 363n194, 363n209, 397n24, 420, 435, 441n70; Shelley, Mary/*Frankenstein*, 53n54, 115–18, 121nn86–89, 220. *See also* fairy tale

Ronell, Avital, 113, 118; *Fighting Theory*, 120n74, 121n95

Roper, Robert: *Nabokov in America: On the Road to Lolita*, 19n49

Roth, Philip, 412, 440n27

Rougement, Denis de: *Love in the Western World*, 18n22, 276, 295n19, 297n55, 298n91; *The Myths of Love*, 321n4, 325n80

Royal Danish Theater, 330

Rutsala, Kirsten, 319, 327n133; "A Garden and a Twilight and a Palace Gate," 327n113, 328n134

Russell, Bertrand, 371; *The Conquest of Happiness*, 398n49

Sade, Marquis de, 135, 137, 148, 222, 422; "Reflections on the Novel," 144n77, 144n87, 441n74

sadism/masochism, 1, 26, 40–43, 63, 72, 78, 91, 312, 416, 422

Sand, George, 126

Sanders, Scott R., 292; "Lady Chatterley's Loving and the Annihilation Impulse," 299n129, 300nn135–36

Sartre, Jean-Paul, 196, 311, 325n81, 365, 378, 390, 401n103, 412; *Being and Nothingness*, 325n81, 401n103; *Nausea*, 360n109; "On *The Sound and the Fury*: Time in the Work of Faulkner," 145n106, 210nn63–65

satire, 100, 202, 205, 232, 233

Sæverot, Herner, 331–32; *Indirect Pedagogy: Some Lessons in Existential Education*, 332, 358n20

Schaffer, Talia, 180; "The Homoerotic History of *Dracula*," 186n181

Schlegel, Friedrich, 12, 127, 136, 138, 139, 202, 232–33, 283; "Aphorisms from the Lyceum," 20n60, 143n60; Athenaeum Fragments, 144n82, 397n24;"Dialogue on Poetry," 126, 142nn18–22, 143n51, 143n69, 144n80, 144n90, 144n95, 144n99, 238n22, 361n154, 362n161, 363n194, 441n70; "Letter About the Novel"/*Brief über den Roman*, 16–17, 126, 134–35, 143n67; *Lucinde*, 349–51, 356

Schelling, Friedrich Wilhelm Joseph von, 219

Schiller, Friedrich, 29, 319; *On the Aesthetic Education of Man*, 435, 438, 444nn161, 444nn176–78

school desegregation, 7

Schopenhauer, Arthur, 2–3, 31, 33, 50, 54n85, 58n200, 17n9, 79, 88, 125, 170, 189, 190, 194, 198, 199, 202, 205, 206, 215, 255, 273–75, 307, 379, 380, 402n116, 448; *Essays and Aphorisms*, 58n200; "On the Fourfold Root of the Principle of Sufficient Reason," 17n8; "The Metaphysics of Love," 273, 275, 295nn2–3; "On the Sufferings of the World," 17n7; *The Wisdom of Life and Counsels and Maxims*, 323n48; *The World as Will and Representation*, 17n7, 54n85, 124, 195, 211n105, 212n131, 212n142, 238n18, 295n11, 453n7

Schwartz, Daniel R., 285; *Reading the Modern British and Irish Novel 1890–1930*, 296n36, 297n74

science, 27, 91, 118, 207, 223, 227, 231, 232, 330, 333, 396, 409, 425, 426, 429, 432, 434, 435, 437

scientism, 435. *See also* Big Data; positivism

Sedgwick, Eve Kosofsky, 451; *Epistemology of the Closet*, 450, 453nn15–16

seduction, 11, 86, 103, 116, 127, 129–30, 163, 173, 191, 192, 236, 330, 335, 336, 339, 340, 344, 346–49, 351, 395–97, 446; against production, 407–39

self-help, 86, 88, 273–77, 283, 284, 286, 415, 450

Senf, Carol A., 162–63; "*Dracula*: The Unseen Face in the Mirror," 183n90, 183n92, 184n93

sexual desire, 152, 282, 306

sexuality, 63, 91, 93n20, 106, 135, 152, 162, 163, 175, 176, 180, 234, 273–75, 282, 292, 294, 305, 306, 308, 314, 315, 327n133, 341, 409, 414, 423

Shakespeare, William, 138; *Hamlet*, 27–28, 53n51, 95n94, 119n7, 125, 178, 179, 185nn170–71, 200, 201, 214–15, 239n11, 239nn13–14, 239nn20–21, 239n23, 308, 386, 402n113; *King Lear*, 25, 27, 44, 45, 47, 53n52, 57n161, 57n176, 58n188, 174–76, 214, 238n10, 238n12, 336, 337, 359nn62–64; *Othello*, 306; *Macbeth*, 215, 238n13; *Midsummer Night's Dream*, 76; *Richard III*, 28, 53n60, 188, 208n5; *Romeo and Juliet*, 125, 186n180, 235, 238nn15– 17, 343, 360n122; "Sonnet 98," 215, 260, 271n117, 271n120, 344; *Twelfth Night*, 42–43

Sheehan, Thomas, 396; "Emmanuel Faye: The Introduction of Fraud into Philosophy," 396, 405nn206–7

Shelley, Mary, 422; *Frankenstein*, 53n54, 115–18, 121nn86–89, 220

sigh, 44–51, 59, 311, 329

silence, 1, 47, 48, 58n200, 66, 99, 171, 188–92, 208nn26–28, 215, 224, 251–53, 281, 284–86, 307, 316, 320, 323, 337, 348, 367–70, 373, 374, 381, 382, 385, 390, 393, 398n33, 403n159, 408, 410, 411, 439, 446

Slack app, 419

slang, 158–59, 164

sleep, 73, 74, 76, 89, 90, 168, 170, 171, 237, 256, 286, 309, 310, 315, 347, 405; Apuleius/*The Golden Ass*, 73; Proust, Marcel/*The Captive*, 76. *See also* dream

Smiles, Samuel: *Self-Help*, 274

Smith, Adam, 427

Smyth, John Vignaux, 342, 353, 355; *A Question of Eros: Irony in Sterne, Kierkegaard, and Barthes*, 360n113, 362n161, 362n182, 363n203

Socrates, 10–14, 16, 19n56, 21, 32, 33, 42, 66, 79, 100, 101, 104, 106, 117, 118, 148, 191–94, 203, 233, 236, 238, 245, 260, 332, 340, 353, 409, 410, 420, 421, 436, 439n6, 448, 449; dialogue, 10–13, 102, 127, 129, 138, 192, 233, 350, 410; Socratic method, 15, 106. *See also* Plato

Sommers, Elena, 317; "Nabokov's Mermaid: 'Spring in Fialta,'" 327n123

Solzhenitsyn, Aleksandr, 148; *The Gulag Archipelago*, 148

sophistry, 90, 191, 199, 200, 211n98, 235, 236, 279, 285, 288, 425, 426, 436. *See also* Gorgias

Southey, Robert, 47

sparagmos, 205, 217
Spenser, Edmund, 324; *The Faerie Queene*, 390, 404n178
sprezzatura, 154. *See also* Castiglione, Baldesar; dissimulation
Spilka, Mark, 293, 300n142, 300n144; "Lawrence's Quarrel with Tenderness," 300n142, 300n144
STEM, 313, 430
Stendhal, 9, 47, 60, 63, 101, 108, 140, 157, 177, 180, 192, 202, 222, 276, 323n44, 333, 384; *The Charterhouse of Parma*, 157; *Love*, 5, 18nn23–26, 47, 57n177, 120n47, 222, 240n73; *The Red and the Black*, 93n24, 119n10, 145n111, 202, 211n107, 403n143
Sterne, Laurence, 223; *The Life and Opinions of Tristram Shandy*, 201, 206, 207, 212n147, 381
Stockholm Syndrome, 418
Stoker, Bram, 157–64, 166, 180, 192; *Dracula*, 28, 29, 53nn61–62, 160–64, 167, 172, 180, 183n73, 183nn86–88, 183n90, 186n181
stoicism, 104
suffering, 4, 8, 15, 16, 17n7, 21, 27, 34, 37–38, 50, 60–62, 72, 74, 77, 79, 83, 85, 87, 88, 91, 92, 100, 104, 105, 107, 110, 112, 115, 121n83, 129–30, 135, 150, 169, 174, 190, 193, 232, 236, 257, 263, 287, 289, 308, 336, 337, 344, 367, 373, 415, 421
Sugg, Richard: *Murder After Death*, 239nn46–51, 240n67, 240nn69–72
suicide, 17n7, 31, 34, 35, 114, 115, 130, 157, 165, 187–207, 210n80, 215, 227, 228, 234, 260, 302, 308, 334, 346
Swinburne, Algernon Charles: *Tristram of Lyonesse*, 274, 289, 297n54
symbol, 24, 29, 38, 64, 65, 75, 117, 128, 159, 171, 178, 188, 202, 205, 247, 276, 307, 312, 322n14, 324, 403n157; *symbollein*, 342–43; *symbolon*, 343

Tamir-Ghez, Nomi, 319; "The Art of Persuasion in Nabokov's *Lolita*," 328n135
Tanner, Michael: *Wagner*, 296n35
Taylor, Frederick Winslow, 431; Taylorism, 429–30
technology, 19n44, 54n91, 153, 162, 166, 190, 400n60, 409, 422, 424, 425, 430, 431, 436, 439n4, 445
Tennyson, Alfred, 252; *Idylls of the King*, 253, 269n73
Thacker, Eugene, 1, 101–2, 193; *Cosmic Pessimism*, 257, 270nn100–101, 283, 297n62; *Infinite Resignation*, 17n1, 17n5, 57nn173–74, 58n189, 119n11, 197, 209n35, 209n40, 209nn56–61, 210nn66–68, 210, 211n97, 211n102, 239n44, 398n40; *In the Dust of this Planet: Horror of Philosophy*, 212
Thucydides: *History of the Peloponnesian War*, 448
time, 2, 3, 5–8, 10–12, 16, 22–24, 27, 29, 31, 38, 41, 44, 47, 50–51, 54n78, 59–62, 66–72, 75–78, 80, 84, 86–90, 92, 103–7, 109–13, 123–25, 127, 129–32, 134–38, 141, 141n8, 148–52, 155, 157, 158, 160, 161, 164, 166–68, 172, 175, 179, 189, 191, 193, 195–98, 200, 204, 213, 215–16, 218, 221, 222, 226, 228, 229, 231, 234, 236, 237, 245, 247, 250, 251, 253–57, 261, 263–65, 267, 268n22, 271n143, 273, 274, 279, 287, 290, 292, 294, 298n105, 303, 308, 312, 316, 317, 320, 323n50, 324n52, 324n57, 329, 331, 336, 339, 341, 344, 346–48, 350, 352, 354, 357n15, 362n183, 363n209, 366–68, 370, 371, 374–76, 380–88, 390, 392–93, 395–96, 399n54, 399n56, 400n85, 402n116, 402n119, 403n157, 408, 409, 417, 419–23, 425, 426, 429–33, 437, 438, 446, 450, 451. *See also* Heidegger, Martin; Mann, Thomas; Proust, Marcel; Woolf, Virginia

Tolstoy, Leo, 47, 346, 367, 372–77, 382, 399n56; *Anna Karenina*, 49–50, 58n197, 60, 194, 346, 361nn139–41; *The Death of Ivan Ilyich*, 23, 57n175, 372, 376, 399n51, 399nn53–54, 399nn56–58, 400nn61–62; *War and Peace*, 194
tragedy, 3, 12, 13, 22, 23, 49, 51, 60–62, 124, 148, 178, 187, 188, 201, 216, 217, 224, 236, 265, 304, 312, 314, 319, 372, 379, 380, 393, 396, 429, 447, 448
transvaluation of values, 113, 130, 156, 292. *See also* Nietzsche, Friedrich
Travers, P. L.: *Mary Poppins*, 308–9
Tristan legend. *See* Goethe, Johann Wolfgang von; Gorgani, Fakhraddin Lawrence, D. H.; medieval/Middle Ages; mysticism; Platen, August Graf von; romance; Strassburg, Gottfried von; Rougemont, Denis de; Wagner, Richard
troubadour, Provençal, 104, 111. *See also* courtly love
Trump, Donald, 7, 19n34, 411
truth, 12, 13, 15, 16, 33, 34, 47, 50, 67, 69–72, 82, 84–88, 90, 91, 101, 102, 106, 123, 124, 149, 151–53, 164–66, 170, 178, 193, 200, 202, 221, 222, 227, 231, 235, 245, 246, 299n128, 304, 323, 333, 337, 340, 341, 377, 380, 383, 389, 424, 426, 431, 433, 435, 436, 439n6; definition of, 165
Turgenev, Ivan: *Fathers and Sons*, 426, 428–29, 442n98, 443nn123–24
Tweedle, James: "Nabokov and the Boundless Novel," 326n110

Unamuno, Miguel de, 211n120, 218; *Tragic Sense of Life*, 197, 200, 210nn69–71, 210nn73–74, 239n42
the uncanny, 219, 239n52. *See also* Unheimlich

unhappiness, 48–50, 59–61, 85, 88, 89, 92, 169, 190, 330, 398n49, 419
"Unhappy Consciousness," 31, 230, 352. *See also* Hegel, Georg Wilhelm Friedrich
Unheimlich ("uncanny"), 219, 403, 409. *See also* Freud, Sigmund; Schelling, Friedrich Wilhelm Joseph von
UNESCO, 365
UN International Labor Organization, 423
Urteil (judgment), 123. *See also* Kant, Immanuel
utility, 50, 313, 422, 427–29, 431, 438
utopia, 16, 123, 127, 130, 132, 133, 137, 281–82, 307, 450

Vaget, Hans Rudolf, 115; "Werther, the Undead," 121nn83–84
vagina dentata, 161
vampires/vampirism, 29, 39, 160–63, 192
Venus, 73, 75, 78, 104, 149. *See also* myth
verisimilitude, 164, 177, 179, 253
Verzweiflung ("despair"), 31
Vesalius, Andreas, 230; *De Humani Corporis Fabrica*, 221–22
Vicks, Meghan, 315; *Narratives of Nothing in Twentieth-Century Literature*, 326nn111–12
Volney, Constantin François: *Ruins of Empires*, 220; *A New Translation of Volney's Ruins; or Meditations on the Revolution of Empires*, 239n60
Voltaire: *Candide*, 8, 31, 48, 199, 206–7, 210n85, 212nn140–41, 212n143; *Micromegas*, 207, 212nn143–46, 219, 239n55
vomit, 224, 388–94
von Bingen, Hildegard, 22
von Kleist, Heinrich: "On the Theater of Marionettes," 99
von Platen, August Graf, 282

von Strassburg, Gottfried, 104, 278, 284; *Tristan*, 119n29, 148, 179n186, 181n3, 186n179, 236, 275, 276, 280–81, 283, 296n38, 296nn49–52, 29n56, 29n69, 299n110, 345

Wagner, Richard, 3, 278, 282, 370; *Gesamtkunstwerk*, 286; *Tristan und Isolde*, 274, 276, 286, 296n35; *My Life*, 295n14
Walsh, Sylvia, 350; *Living Poetically: Kierkegaard's Existential Aesthetics*, 361n159, 362n160, 362n170
Watt, Ian, 137, 151, 377–78, 425; *The Rise of the Novel: Studies in Defoe, Richardson, and Fielding*, 182n24, 401n99, 422n95
Wattle, Wallace: *The Science of Getting Rich*, 274
Weinman, Sarah, 319–20; *The Real Lolita*, 324n51, 326n94, 327nn131–32, 328nn140–41, 357n17, 359n61
Weston, Jessie L., 276
WeWork, 413, 431, 440n34, 443n137. *See also* Big Business; capitalism; neoliberalism
Whitman, James Q.: *Hitler's American Model: The United States and the Making of Nazi Race Law*, 441n58
Wilde, Oscar, 163, 164, 166, 258; *The Picture of Dorian Gray*, 163, 167, 178–80, 184n94, 186n176
Wharton, Edith: *Ethan Frome*, 34, 149
Will, 1, 3, 7, 8, 13, 17n7, 27–30, 33, 35, 38–39, 41, 44, 45, 47, 48, 52, 54n85, 61, 63, 64, 70–72, 79, 85, 86, 89, 90, 99, 100, 101, 103, 109, 110, 111–13, 123, 124, 129–32, 134–36, 139, 148, 151, 153, 163, 170, 174, 175, 193, 194, 195, 197–99, 203, 204, 211n105, 212n131, 212n142, 218, 234–37, 238n18, 244, 247, 253, 256, 257, 261, 262, 264, 265, 266, 273, 275, 276, 278, 280, 281, 286, 294, 301, 312, 315, 319, 320, 323, 330, 338, 339, 345, 350, 351, 353, 355, 374, 376, 380, 381, 387, 394, 398n33, 399n56, 410, 413, 415, 416, 418, 421, 422, 426, 427, 433, 436–39, 440n27, 440n34, 440n41, 441n51, 448, 453n7. *See also* Schopenhauer, Arthur
William of Aquitaine, 104–5
Wilson, Edmund, 323n44
window, 39, 40, 43, 62, 82, 175, 176, 226, 227, 245, 256, 259–61, 263
Winfrey, Oprah, 141, 145n113
Wittgenstein, Ludwig, 21; *Philosophical Investigations*, 51n2
Woodward, Bob, 6
Welch, Chris: "Apple's Iconic Fifth Avenue Store is Back and Bigger Than Ever," 443n136
Wood, Michael, 316, 327n116, 327n118. *See also* Knausgaard, *My Struggle*
Woolf, Virginia, 39, 251, 275–76, 411, 420, 427, 451; *On Being Ill*, 244; *The Common Reader*, 56n128, 245, 270n104, 420–21, 441nn72–73, 453n24; *Jacob's Room*, 244, 276, 420; *To the Lighthouse*, 149, 200, 227, 229, 233, 234, 237, 238, 241nn108–9, 241n111, 241nn125–29, 242nn157–59, 242n174, 243–67, 267nn1–4, 268n19, 268n22, 268nn24–26, 268nn28–31, 268nn33–38, 269nn39–49, 269nn51–57, 269n59, 269nn65–70, 269n72, 269nn74–77, 270nn81–86, 270nn88–91, 270n97, 270n107, 270nn109–10, 383, 387, 411, 420, 421; *Moments of Being*, 244, 258, 267n5, 270n102, 270nn110–11, 270n112, 271nn113–16, 271nn118–43, 271nn144–48, 272nn149–50, 272nn153–67, 383, 387, 402n133, 411, 420–21, 440nn19–20, 443n115; *Mrs. Dalloway*, 227, 241n110,

241nn112–19, 241nn123–24; mythical consciousness, 254; "Sketch of the Past," 259; *The Waves*, 149, 258, 263, 333, 383; *The Diary of Virginia Woolf*, Volume III, 211n96; *The Essays of Virginia Woolf*, Volume II, 208n13

Wootton, David: "The Impossible Dream," 443

Wright, Daniel: "Thomas Hardy's Groundwork," 55n115

Wyatt, Edward: "Author is Kicked out of Oprah Winfrey's Book Club," 145n114

World Bank, 424

X-ray, 132, 226, 227, 238

Yates, Richard: *Revolutionary Road*, 28, 53n56

Zamyatin, Yevgeny, 429–31; *We*, 429, 431, 443nn129–35

Zeus, 11, 30, 31, 41, 131, 247, 265. *See also* lightning/thunder; myth

Zhen, Justin, 431

Zola, Émile, 126

Zhao, Christina: "Students Not Smiling at School Will be Punished, Say Teachers," 441n51

Žižek, Slavoj, 417; *In Defense of Lost Causes*, 417, 441n54

Zweig, Stefan: *Balzac, Dickens, Dostoevsky: Master Builders of the Spirit*, 145n106

About the Author

Tom Ribitzky has a PhD in comparative literature from The Graduate Center (CUNY). He has taught literature and humanities courses at Baruch College, Hunter College, The City College of New York, and Macaulay Honors College.